THE YALE EDITION

OF

HORACE WALPOLE'S

CORRESPONDENCE

EDITED BY W. S. LEWIS

VOLUME ELEVEN

HORACE WALPOLE'S
CORRESPONDENCE

WITH

MARY AND AGNES BERRY

AND

BARBARA CECILIA SETON

I

EDITED BY W. S. LEWIS

AND

A. DAYLE WALLACE

WITH THE ASSISTANCE OF

CHARLES H. BENNETT

AND

EDWINE M. MARTZ

NEW HAVEN

YALE UNIVERSITY PRESS

LONDON : HUMPHREY MILFORD : OXFORD UNIVERSITY PRESS

1944

ADVISORY COMMITTEE

LIST OF SUBSCRIBERS

H. M. KING GEORGE VI

Alameda Free Library, Alameda, California
Albertus Magnus College Library, New Haven, Connecticut
Allegheny College, The Reis Library, Meadville, Pennsylvania
All Souls College Library, Oxford
Joseph W. Alsop, Jr, Esq., Avon, Connecticut
American University Library, Washington, D. C.
Amherst College, Converse Memorial Library, Amherst,
    Massachusetts
Atlanta University Library, Atlanta, Georgia
C. C. Auchincloss, Esq., New York, N. Y.
Hugh D. Auchincloss, Esq., McLean, Virginia
Avon Old Farms, Avon, Connecticut
F. W. Bain, Esq., London
James Bain, Ltd, London
Richard B. Baker, Esq., Providence, Rhode Island
R. E. Balfour, Esq., Cambridge
Sir T. D. Barlow, k.b.e., London
Bath Municipal Library, Bath
Bavarian State Library, Munich
C. F. Bell, Esq., Kensington
Berkeley College Library, Yale University, New Haven,
    Connecticut
Theodore Besterman, Esq., London
Biblioteca Nacional de Perú, Lima, Peru
Mrs Norman H. Biltz, Reno, Nevada
Birmingham Public Library, Birmingham
Charles L. Black, Esq., Austin, Texas
Miss Anna G. Blair, Edinburgh
Boston Athenæum, Boston, Massachusetts
Boston College Library, Chestnut Hill, Massachusetts
Boston Public Library, Boston, Massachusetts
Boston University Graduate School, Boston, Massachusetts
Bowdoin College Library, Brunswick, Maine

vii

JULIAN BOYD, Esq., Princeton, New Jersey
Miss EMMA JEANNETTE BRAZIER, New York, N. Y.
BRISTOL PUBLIC LIBRARY, Bristol
WALLACE BROCKWAY, Esq., New York, N. Y.
BROOKLYN COLLEGE LIBRARY, Brooklyn, New York
BROWN UNIVERSITY, JOHN HAY MEMORIAL LIBRARY, Providence, Rhode Island
BRYN MAWR COLLEGE LIBRARY, Bryn Mawr, Pennsylvania
JOHN N. BRYSON, Esq., Oxford
BUCKNELL UNIVERSITY LIBRARY, Lewisburg, Pennsylvania
CHARLES EATON BURCH, Esq., Washington, D. C.
BUTLER UNIVERSITY LIBRARY, Indianapolis, Indiana
CALHOUN COLLEGE LIBRARY, YALE UNIVERSITY, New Haven, Connecticut
CALIFORNIA STATE LIBRARY, Sacramento, California
CARDIFF PUBLIC LIBRARY, Cardiff
The Right Honourable, the Countess of CARLISLE, London
CARNEGIE LIBRARY OF PITTSBURGH, Pittsburgh, Pennsylvania
LAURENCE R. CARTON, Esq., Towson, Maryland
CATHOLIC UNIVERSITY LIBRARY, Washington, D. C.
The Honourable Sir EVAN CHARTERIS, K.C., London
CICERO PUBLIC LIBRARY, Cicero, Illinois
CLAREMONT COLLEGES LIBRARY, Claremont, California
CLARK UNIVERSITY LIBRARY, Worcester, Massachusetts
CLEVELAND PUBLIC LIBRARY, Cleveland, Ohio
COE COLLEGE LIBRARY, Cedar Rapids, Iowa
COLBY COLLEGE LIBRARY, Waterville, Maine
COLGATE UNIVERSITY LIBRARY, Hamilton, New York
COLLEGE OF ST. TERESA LIBRARY, Winona, Minnesota
COLLEGE OF WOOSTER LIBRARY, Wooster, Ohio
COLORADO COLLEGE, COBURN LIBRARY, Colorado Springs, Colorado
COLUMBIA UNIVERSITY LIBRARY, New York, N. Y.
G. MAURICE CONGDON, Esq., Providence, Rhode Island
CONNECTICUT COLLEGE, PALMER LIBRARY, New London, Connecticut
CONNECTICUT STATE LIBRARY, Hartford, Connecticut
REGINALD G. COOMBE, Esq., Greenwich, Connecticut
CORNELL UNIVERSITY LIBRARY, Ithaca, New York
THOMAS R. COWARD, Esq., New York, N. Y.
DARTMOUTH COLLEGE, BAKER MEMORIAL LIBRARY, Hanover, New Hampshire

DAVENPORT COLLEGE LIBRARY, YALE UNIVERSITY, New Haven,
  Connecticut
DENVER PUBLIC LIBRARY, Denver, Colorado
DES MOINES PUBLIC LIBRARY, Des Moines, Iowa
DETROIT PUBLIC LIBRARY, Detroit, Michigan
Mrs ROBERT CLOUTMAN DEXTER, Belmont, Massachusetts
CHARLES D. DICKEY, Esq., Chestnut Hill, Philadelphia, Pennsylvania
DICKINSON COLLEGE LIBRARY, Carlisle, Pennsylvania
Mrs FRANK F. DODGE, New York, N. Y.
DRAKE UNIVERSITY LIBRARY, Des Moines, Iowa
DREW UNIVERSITY LIBRARY, Madison, New Jersey
DUKE UNIVERSITY LIBRARY, Durham, North Carolina
EDINBURGH PUBLIC LIBRARY, Edinburgh
EDINBURGH UNIVERSITY LIBRARY, Edinburgh
RODNEY R. ELLIS, Esq., Poultney, Vermont
ALBERT H. ELY, Esq., Coldspring Harbor, Long Island, New York
EMORY UNIVERSITY LIBRARY, Emory University, Georgia
ENOCH PRATT FREE LIBRARY, Baltimore, Maryland
FARMINGTON VILLAGE LIBRARY, Farmington, Connecticut
HENRY FIELD, Esq., Chicago, Illinois
MAURICE FIRUSKI, Esq., Salisbury, Connecticut
HARRY HARKNESS FLAGLER, Esq., Millbrook, New York
Mrs MARGARET MITCHELL FLINT, Westport, Connecticut
FLORIDA STATE COLLEGE FOR WOMEN LIBRARY, Tallahassee, Florida
FORBES LIBRARY, Northampton, Massachusetts
FORDHAM UNIVERSITY LIBRARY, New York, N. Y.
FRANKLIN AND MARSHALL COLLEGE LIBRARY, Lancaster, Pennsylvania
FREE LIBRARY OF PHILADELPHIA, Philadelphia, Pennsylvania
DONALD T. GAMMONS, Esq., Boston, Massachusetts
GEORGETOWN UNIVERSITY, RIGGS MEMORIAL LIBRARY,
  Washington, D. C.
GLASGOW ART GALLERIES, Glasgow
GLASGOW UNIVERSITY LIBRARY, Glasgow
HOWARD L. GOODHART, Esq., New York, N. Y.
PHILIP L. GOODWIN, Esq., New York, N. Y.
Mrs WILLIAM GREENOUGH, Newport, Rhode Island
LAUDER GREENWAY, Esq., Greenwich, Connecticut
Mrs OCTAVIA GREGORY, Parkstone, Dorset
WILLIAM V. GRIFFIN, Esq., New York, N. Y.
FARNHAM P. GRIFFITHS, Esq., San Francisco, California

SAN BERNARDINO VALLEY JUNIOR COLLEGE LIBRARY, San Bernardino, California
SAN FRANCISCO PUBLIC LIBRARY, San Francisco, California
PAUL S. SCHOEDINGER, Esq., Durham, New Hampshire
SEATTLE PUBLIC LIBRARY, Seattle, Washington
GEORGE SHERBURN, Esq., Cambridge, Massachusetts
RICHARD SMART, Esq., London
SMITH COLLEGE LIBRARY, Northampton, Massachusetts
Mrs THEODORE J. SMITH, Geneva, New York
WILLARD SMITH, Esq., Oakland, California
P. H. B. OTWAY SMITHERS, Esq., London
SOUTH AFRICAN PUBLIC LIBRARY, Capetown
SOUTHERN METHODIST UNIVERSITY LIBRARY, Dallas, Texas
SOUTHWESTERN COLLEGE LIBRARY, Memphis, Tennessee
T. M. SPELMAN, Esq., Harrison, New York
STANFORD UNIVERSITY LIBRARIES, Palo Alto, California
STATE UNIVERSITY OF IOWA LIBRARIES, Iowa City, Iowa
JAMES STRACHEY, Esq., London
STRATFORD LIBRARY ASSOCIATION, Stratford, Connecticut
SWARTHMORE COLLEGE LIBRARY, Swarthmore, Pennsylvania
HENRY C. TAYLOR, Esq., Coldspring Harbor, Long Island, New York
TEMPLE UNIVERSITY, SULLIVAN MEMORIAL LIBRARY, Philadelphia, Pennsylvania
TEXAS STATE COLLEGE FOR WOMEN LIBRARY, Denton, Texas
THACHER SCHOOL LIBRARY, Ojai, California
TOLEDO PUBLIC LIBRARY, Toledo, Ohio
TRANSYLVANIA COLLEGE LIBRARY, Lexington, Kentucky
TRUSLOVE AND HANSON, London
TULANE UNIVERSITY LIBRARY, New Orleans, Louisiana
UNION COLLEGE LIBRARY, Schenectady, New York
UNIVERSITY CLUB LIBRARY, New York, N. Y.
UNIVERSITY COLLEGE LIBRARY, Hull
UNIVERSITY COLLEGE LIBRARY, London
UNIVERSITY COLLEGE, Southampton
UNIVERSITY OF ALABAMA LIBRARY, University, Alabama
UNIVERSITY OF ARIZONA LIBRARY, Tucson, Arizona
UNIVERSITY OF BIRMINGHAM LIBRARY, Birmingham
UNIVERSITY OF BUFFALO, LOCKWOOD MEMORIAL LIBRARY, Buffalo, New York

UNIVERSITY OF CALIFORNIA AT LOS ANGELES LIBRARY,
   West Los Angeles, California
UNIVERSITY OF CALIFORNIA LIBRARY, Berkeley, California
UNIVERSITY OF CHICAGO LIBRARIES, Chicago, Illinois
UNIVERSITY OF CINCINNATI LIBRARY, Cincinnati, Ohio
UNIVERSITY OF COLORADO LIBRARY, Boulder, Colorado
UNIVERSITY OF CONNECTICUT LIBRARY, Storrs, Connecticut
UNIVERSITY OF DELAWARE LIBRARY, Newark, Delaware
UNIVERSITY OF DURHAM LIBRARY, Durham
UNIVERSITY OF FLORIDA LIBRARY, Gainesville, Florida
UNIVERSITY OF GEORGIA LIBRARIES, Athens, Georgia
UNIVERSITY OF ILLINOIS LIBRARY, Urbana, Illinois
UNIVERSITY OF KANSAS LIBRARY, Lawrence, Kansas
UNIVERSITY OF KENTUCKY LIBRARY, Lexington, Kentucky
UNIVERSITY OF LIVERPOOL LIBRARY, Liverpool
UNIVERSITY OF LONDON LIBRARY, London
UNIVERSITY OF MANCHESTER LIBRARY, Manchester
UNIVERSITY OF MARYLAND LIBRARY, College Park, Maryland
UNIVERSITY OF MICHIGAN LIBRARY, Ann Arbor, Michigan
UNIVERSITY OF MINNESOTA LIBRARY, Minneapolis, Minnesota
UNIVERSITY OF MISSOURI LIBRARY, Columbia, Missouri
UNIVERSITY OF NEBRASKA LIBRARY, Lincoln, Nebraska
UNIVERSITY OF NEW HAMPSHIRE, HAMILTON SMITH LIBRARY, Durham,
   New Hampshire
UNIVERSITY OF NEW MEXICO LIBRARY, Albuquerque, New Mexico
UNIVERSITY OF NORTH CAROLINA LIBRARY, Chapel Hill,
   North Carolina
UNIVERSITY OF NORTH DAKOTA LIBRARY, Grand Forks, North Dakota
UNIVERSITY OF NOTRE DAME LIBRARY, Notre Dame, Indiana
UNIVERSITY OF OKLAHOMA LIBRARY, Norman, Oklahoma
UNIVERSITY OF OMAHA LIBRARY, Omaha, Nebraska
UNIVERSITY OF OREGON LIBRARY, Eugene, Oregon
UNIVERSITY OF PENNSYLVANIA LIBRARY, Philadelphia, Pennsylvania
UNIVERSITY OF PITTSBURGH LIBRARY, Pittsburgh, Pennsylvania
UNIVERSITY OF RICHMOND LIBRARY, University of Richmond, Virginia
UNIVERSITY OF ROCHESTER LIBRARY, Rochester, New York
UNIVERSITY OF SOUTHERN CALIFORNIA LIBRARY, Los Angeles,
   California
UNIVERSITY OF TENNESSEE LIBRARY, Knoxville, Tennessee
UNIVERSITY OF TEXAS LIBRARY, Austin, Texas

TABLE OF CONTENTS

VOLUME I

LIST OF ILLUSTRATIONS

VOLUMES I AND II

hand, with a note by Richard Bull, 'only 60 proofs were taken off,' is now WSL.

Grateful acknowledgment is made to H. M. King George VI, the Henry E. Huntington Library and Art Gallery, and the Yale Art Gallery for permission to reproduce illustrations listed here.

INTRODUCTION

WALPOLE'S last ten years have been likened to the Fifth Act of a comedy: they were dominated, it has been said, by the society of the Berrys with whom he was hopelessly in love; thus was Mme du Deffand avenged, and the last curtain came down upon the old man conquered by the grand passion which he had too successfully resisted earlier.

The trouble with this is that, like so much that has been written on Horace Walpole, it oversimplifies and exaggerates. He was 'in love' with the Berrys much as he was in love with the Duchess of Richmond and Margaret Young, his housekeeper, with Rosette and Tory, Salvator Rosa and Domenichino, Shakespeare, and Strawberry Hill. The Berrys brought to him in his old age nearly all that he liked most in life: wit, good-breeding, common sense, wide reading, good looks, eager attention to everything he said, and the touch of sentimentality provided by the circumstance of their father's having, through romantic high-mindedness, been disinherited by a rich and soulless uncle. Above all, he was in love with their youth and the promise which it gave that their intelligence and their interest would represent him favourably to the posterity which was never far from his awareness. He made Mary Berry his literary executrix, a happy election, for she lived into the second half of the nineteenth century.

These last ten years were pleasant ones, largely because of the Berrys. What greater felicity could there have been for him than to be able to tell, with all the verve still at his command, the stories of his life to two fascinated young women who asked for no livelier pleasure? They set him to writing his *Reminiscences* and to digging up out of his teeming memory the great scenes in which he had been an actor. They brought to his dinner table the news of the neighbourhood in an amusing and initiated way, and so contributed to the history of his time which he wrote to the end.

Walpole 'first saw' the Berrys in the winter of 1787–8, according to his letter to Lady Ossory of 11 October 1788. They had 'accidentally' taken a house at Twickenham with their father for the season. 'Their story is singular enough to entertain you. The grandfather [really Mr Berry's maternal uncle, Robert Ferguson, a merchant who had bought Raith in Fifeshire], a Scot, had a large estate in his own country, £5000 a year it is said; and a circumstance I shall tell you makes it probable. The eldest son married, for love, a woman with no fortune. The old man was enraged and would not see him. The wife died and left these two young ladies. Their grandfather wished for an heir male, and pressed the widower to remarry, but could not prevail; the son declaring he would consecrate himself to his daughters and their education. The old man did not break with him again, but much worse, totally disinherited him, and left all to his second son, who very handsomely gave up £800 a year[1] to his elder brother. Mr Berry has since carried his daughters for two or three years to France and Italy, and they are returned the best-informed and the most perfect creatures I ever saw at their age. They are exceedingly sensible, entirely natural and unaffected, frank, and, being qualified to talk on any subject, nothing is so easy and agreeable as their conversation—not more apposite than their answers and observations. The eldest, I discovered by chance, understands Latin and is a perfect Frenchwoman in her language. The younger draws charmingly, and has copied admirably Lady Di's gipsies, which I lent, though for the first time of her attempting colours. They are of pleasing figures; Mary, the eldest, sweet, with fine dark eyes, that are very lively when she speaks, with a symmetry of face that is the more interesting from being pale; Agnes, the younger, has an agreeable sensible countenance, hardly to be called handsome, but almost. She is less animated than Mary, but seems, out of deference to her sister, to speak seldomer, for they dote on each other, and Mary is always praising her sister's talents. I must even tell you they dress within the bounds of fashion, though fashionably; but without the excrescences and balconies with which modern hoydens overwhelm and barricade their persons. In short, good sense, information, simplicity, and ease characterize the

1. £1000, according to Miss Berry (MBJ i. 10).

Berrys; and this is not particularly mine, who am apt to be preju-
diced, but the universal voice of all who know them. The first
night I met them I would not be acquainted with them, having
heard so much in their praise that I concluded they would be all
pretension. The second time, in a very small company, I sat next
to Mary, and found her an angel both inside and out. Now I do not
know which I like best, except Mary's face, which is formed for a
sentimental novel, but is ten times fitter for a fifty times better
thing, genteel comedy. This delightful family comes to me almost
every Sunday evening, as our region is too *proclamatory* to play
at cards on the seventh day. . . . I forgot to tell you that Mr Berry
is a little merry man with a round face, and you would not suspect
him of so much feeling and attachment. I make no excuse for such
minute details; for, if your Ladyship insists on hearing the hu-
mours of my district, you must for once indulge me with sending
you two pearls that I found in my path.' Walpole's first letter to
Miss Berry was written three days after the above letter to Lady
Ossory, but his list of visitors to Strawberry Hill shows that they
had been there three months earlier and that he had shown them
around himself.

The Berrys were aged twenty-four and twenty-three when they
met Walpole. He was seventy, two years older than their maternal
grandmother, Mrs Seton, whose grand-daughter, Cecilia, figures
in this correspondence. The ridicule which Walpole dreaded all
his life flickered over the attachment, but did not come near to
breaking it. Walpole was much too devoted to the Berrys to permit that, and it must be acknowledged that only in his excessive
anxieties while they were abroad does he appear ridiculous. Pinkerton reports a rumour, which Macaulay, Thackeray, and Cunningham later spread, that before his death Walpole offered marriage to both Berrys in succession; but what actually took place is
made quite clear by Charles Greville. He called on Miss Berry one
day in 1843 'and found her in great indignation at Croker's recent
article in the "Quarterly" upon the series just published of Lord
Orford's letters to Mann, angry on his account and on her own.
Croker says, what has been often reported, that Lord Orford of-

fered to marry Mary Berry, and on her refusal, to marry Agnes. She says it is altogether false. He never thought of marrying Agnes, and what passed with regard to herself was this: The Duchess of Gloucester was very jealous of his intimacy with the Berrys, though she treated them with civility. At last her natural impetuosity broke out, and she said to him, "Do you mean to marry Miss Berry or do you not?" To which he replied, "That is as Miss Berry herself pleases"; and that, as I understood her, is all that passed about it.'[1a] 'Let me repeat to both,' Walpole writes 26 February 1791, 'that distance of place and time can make no alteration in my friendship: It grew from esteem for your characters and understandings and tempers, and became affection from your good-natured attentions to me, where there is so vast a disproportion in our ages.' It was a thoroughly common-sensical relationship on both sides. They delighted in each other's company, and that was that.

> An estate and an earldom at seventy-four!
> Had I sought them or wish'd them, 'twould add one fear more,
> That of making a countess when almost fourscore.
> But Fortune, who scatters her gifts out of season,
> Though unkind to my limbs, has still left me my reason;
> And whether she lowers or lifts me, I'll try
> In the plain simple style I have liv'd in, to die;
> For ambition too humble, for meanness too high.

So Walpole put it in his 'Epitaphium vivi auctoris, 1792.'

'I write to you two just as I should talk, the only comfortable kind of letters' (*post* ii. 76). This is proved by those letters where, unable to write further because of the gout, he called in Kirgate and dictated the remainder. The dictation continues as easily as the writing, a facility remarked by his contemporaries. The materials of the correspondence are much the same as those of his other intimate correspondences—reports on great names and events, and entertaining trivialities—but here we have more neighbourhood gossip and more of his own hopes and fears. The reports of

1a. Charles C. F. Greville, *A Journal of the Reign of Queen Victoria from 1837 to 1852,* 1885, ii. 202.

world events come less and less from the actors themselves, and
more and more from the newspapers, which Walpole abused but
which he sedulously copied in his letters and memoirs. We do, occasionally, have glimpses of the actors, as on the night when he met
Mme du Barry at Queensberry House just before she returned to
France and the guillotine, and he discussed with her, in a kind of
postscript, her overthrow of his friends the Choiseuls twenty years
earlier. But there is more of Twickenham and Richmond and
Hampton Court. The Pepyses' little boy Harry, who is one day to
become the Bishop of Sodor and Man, falls from a chaise and
breaks his arm. Partridges have arrived from Houghton and will
be given to Lady Cecilia Johnston. Tonton has been clipped and
the shearing has revealed a nose an ell long. Later, however, it
seems that 'Tonton's nose is not, I believe, grown longer, but only
come to light by being clipped. When his beard is recovered, I
dare to say he will be as comely as my Jupiter Serapis. In his taste
he is much improved, for he eats strawberries, and is fond of them,
and yet they never were so insipid from want of sun and constant
rain. One may eat roses and smell to cherries and not perceive the
difference from scent or flavour. If tulips were in season, I would
make a rainbow of them to give other flowers hopes of not being
drowned again' (*post* i. 29).

'As delightful as ever,' the reader says many times in this correspondence, although the agonies over the Berrys' Channel cross-
ing and Mary's bumping her nose in Pisa become tiresome. Mrs
Damer speaks of 'his grand fusses.' These he had all his life, but
they naturally grew in frequency and violence as he got older, and
they were readily inspired by anything which concerned the
Berrys. In one respect we are reminded strongly of Mme du Deffand: he promises to stop fretting and scolding about their absence
and he breaks his promise before he has finished his letter.

Although, following the Berrys' return from abroad, Walpole
continues almost to the end in, for him, serenity, one becomes in-
creasingly aware of disturbing and even unpleasant influences in
the background. The Berrys were not free from a certain restless-
ness, and Mary had to conduct her distressing love-affair with

General O'Hara in fear of Walpole's finding it out. Mrs Damer emerges as a distinctly unattractive character. That she was in love with Mary Berry is proved by her journals, and a weakness for her own sex was noticed in 'A Sapphic Epistle' directed to her by an anonymous author of the 1770's. On Walpole's recovering from an indisposition she writes to Miss Berry, 'I am sure when I think of *what* his dinners are, and *how* he eats them, I wonder he and his cat are not sick together every day for their dessert' (*post* ii. 171). Walpole made her his executrix, left her £4000, the life use of Strawberry Hill with £2000 to maintain it, and in the end the residue of the estate, some £40,000.[1b] Her final return for all the affection he gave her from the moment she was born to his cousin and closest friend, Conway, was to have the letters he wrote to her for upwards of forty years destroyed after her death. Then there is the shadowy figure of Lady Mary Churchill, 'sa chère sœur,' the daughter of Sir Robert by his mistress, Maria Skerrett. Walpole had stood godfather to her children and grandchildren, had written her hundreds of letters now lost, and loved her best of all his brothers and sisters. She regarded the young women with a jealous eye while she hovered about her brother, and they silently banded against her. Finally there is the Duchess of Gloucester, the illegitimate daughter of his brother Edward, whose first husband had been Lord Waldegrave, and whose second was the King's brother. All her life she had turned to Walpole for the counsel and support she did not get from her father. She had lost more than she had gained by becoming a royalty, and had she followed her uncle's advice she would have been a happier woman. She came to see him out of duty and affection, but her jealousy of the Berrys did not escape his eye.

He was crippled with gout, rich, old, and a bachelor, and none of them knew what was in that long will which he quite frequently tinkered with. But until the very end, when his mind went and he thought himself abandoned by those he loved best, he made out very well. Perhaps he elected to be carried to the sofa in the Blue

---

1b. Owing to the decline in value of Walpole's stocks the residue of the estate proved to be virtually nothing.

Bedchamber and be left with a catalogue of books and prints. If he wanted anything he fumbled with the whistle which hung about his neck until he got it to his lips, and then he blew away until James or Philip rushed in to him. 'The pots of tuberose or of canary heliotropes, the papers of orange flowers that perfumed his chamber, were luxuries rather feminine,'[2] but he had long since ceased to worry about what people might think of such æsthetics. The frail little boy who had come too early into the world and had not been expected to remain in it had now completed nearly eight decades on his own terms. One by one his old Eton friends disappeared—Hertford and Conway were the last to go—but he was not unduly preoccupied with thoughts of death, although he was the first to call himself 'a Methusalem.' Life continued to furnish him with interests and news: there was the 'infinity' of his nephews and nieces who came to visit him as the oldest Walpole alive; there was his new correspondence with William Roscoe, the young historian who wrote so brilliantly about Lorenzo di Medici; there was the new edition of *The Castle of Otranto,* and the goings-on of the Prince of Wales. The horrors in France which had swept away his 'republicanism' had abated, and had not yet been succeeded by Buonaparte. Life gradually came to a stop.

He was never alone except when he wished to be. Those he most wanted to see would drop in to be with him, and there was always Strawberry, now grown to almost feudal proportions, lovely in rain or sun. He does not seem to have remarked the circumstance that the gardens were not as trim as they once were, or that from Kirgate down his staff had become more concerned with their own welfare than with his. Strawberry was to go eventually, when Mrs Damer left it, to the Waldegraves, that branch of his family which gave the fairest promise of maintaining it and all its treasures to the end of time. And across the fields was Little Strawberry, his gift to his latest and in some respects his dearest friends, the Berrys.

In addition to Little Strawberry Hill, Walpole left the Berrys

2. *Walpoliana* i. p. xlix.

£4000 each and 'a square wooden box marked with an O on the outside' which contained 'all such of my own literary works as have been heretofore published or have been printed or still remain in manuscript.' These were to be delivered to Mr Berry and he was to publish them, the three Berrys dividing 'all the profits and advantages arising from such publication.' It was never expected, of course, that cheerful little Mr Berry would assume the task of editing; he was merely the front behind which Mary Berry would do the work and so respect the conventions of the time which still were against ladies' writing for gain.

In the following year appeared Lord Orford's *Works* in five bulky volumes with a preface written for her father by Miss Berry. Lord Orford himself, she pointed out, had commenced to print his *Works* as early as 1768. The present work had been carefully discussed with him before his death and he had indicated what unpublished material he wished incorporated in it. Part of the fourth and all of the fifth volume contained letters from him, the first collection of them to appear in print.

The remainder of Miss Berry's long life may be best followed in *Extracts from the Journals and Correspondence of Miss Berry from the year 1783 to 1852*, edited in three volumes by Lady Theresa Lewis in 1865. In 1802 there appeared at Drury Lane her *Fashionable Friends*, a play in which Lady Theresa Lewis was shocked to find 'easy licence.' It had been acted to great applause at the private theatricals Mrs Damer had introduced at Strawberry Hill. In London the first actors of the day were engaged for it, but it was withdrawn after three nights. Later in the year it was printed with an Advertisement which stated that it had been 'found among the papers of the late Earl of Orford, and remaining unclaimed in the hands of his executors for five years, was brought forward at the request of Mr Kemble on [sic] the Theatre Royal, Drury Lane. After the extraordinary abuse that has been lavished upon it, the executors considered it as a duty to the unknown author to publish it.' Miss Berry's journals and letters are silent on this remarkable statement which, since it occurs in her complete works, we can assume she wrote herself.

In 1810 appeared her four-volume edition of Mme du Deffand's letters to Walpole; in 1819, *Some Account of the Life of Rachael Wriothesley, Lady Russell;* in 1828, *A Comparative View of the Social Life of England and France from the Restoration of Charles the Second to the French Revolution;* and in 1831, *Social Life in England and France from the French Revolution in 1789 to that of July 1830.*

Mr Berry died in 1817 while the Berrys were at Genoa. The £1000 per annum which came to him from his younger brother ceased, and the Berrys were left with only a few hundred pounds a year to live on. They rarely went to Little Strawberry, its charms had fled, and in 1810 they were able to get it off their hands. They were not so straitened in their circumstances that they could not make frequent and long trips to the Continent where they 'met every one' (including Napoleon) 'and went everywhere.' In London they established themselves in Curzon Street and received not only Samuel Rogers, Sydney Smith, and bright young men like Macaulay, Kinglake and Thackeray, but the smart world as well. 'With the lives of the sisters closed a society which will be ever remembered by all who frequented those pleasant little gatherings in Curzon Street,' writes Lady Theresa Lewis (MBJ iii. 516). 'Sometimes a note, sometimes a word, and more often the lamp being lighted over the door, was taken as notice to attend, and, on entering, it might be to find only a few *habitués,* or a larger and more brilliant assembly. All that was uncertain; but it was certain to find the cordial welcome of the two genial, lively, well-dressed, distinguished-looking hostesses—the comfortable tea-table, over which their friend Miss Anne Turner presided for years, and Lady Charlotte Lindsay, the third partner in the firm, clever and agreeable to the last.'

Not but what there were dissident voices. Lady Louisa Stuart found Miss Berry pushing, tactless, shallow, and loud, although 'such a pair of eyes never were in another head. But the manner I cannot like. It was involuntarily characterized by her friend the late Mrs Chomely, half provoked and half vexed,—"Oh dear! I wish she would not put on that air of—of—*Damme Jack!* she does so often." '³ A more tolerant judgment was passed by Lady Granville: 'We are fond of Berry. Since I have reflected upon her age, which is not often present, *vu* the gaudy colours, noise and constant aboutishness, I think she deserves much excuse for what is disagreeable, much esteem and approbation for what is pleasant. Sociable by habit, *exigeante* by situation and intimate by force. There is something goes against one in the process, but the result is great delight when she obtains what she must naturally consider her due in society, and an enjoyment of it, that neither the young nor the happy can come up to.'⁴

Both the Berrys died in 1852, Agnes going in January and Mary in November. Miss Kate Perry in her *Reminiscences of a London Drawing-Room* says that 'after a time [following Agnes's death] the light was again placed in the window. . . . Yet now that the kind sister was gone, we all knew that it was the union of the two sisters which formed the peculiar charm of these evenings in Curzon Street' (p. 12). In this her ninetieth and last year Mary Berry had the honour of being sent for by the Queen, whom she found 'pleasing' and 'unaffected.' Less than six months afterwards she was laid beside Agnes at Petersham, with an inscription to them both by Lord Carlisle.

For us the chief interest in Miss Berry's later life was what she did for Walpole's reputation. That she had been the closest friend of his declining years and, allegedly, might have been his wife, was never lost sight of. A considerable controversy has always raged about Walpole. It began when his will was read—he had left too much to the Duchess of Gloucester, too little to Kirgate, and nothing at all, Pinkerton objected, to Pinkerton; he was blamed for the death of Chatterton, a canard which is repeated even today; he had been hateful to Mme du Deffand; J. W. Croker and Lord Liverpool agreed that he was 'as bad a man as ever lived' because he had, they said, poisoned history at its source.⁵ Byron came to his rescue with equal extravagance in the preface to *Marino Faliero* (1821) :

3. *Letters of Lady Louisa Stuart to Miss Louisa Clinton*, ed. Hon. James A. Home, Edinburgh, 1901, i. 339–40.

4. *Letters of Harriet Countess Granville,*

1810–1845, ed. Hon. F. Leveson Gower, 1894, ii. 171.

5. *The Croker Papers*, 1884, i. 270–2.

'It is the fashion to underrate Horace Walpole; firstly, because he was a nobleman, and secondly, because he was a gentleman; but to say nothing of the composition of his incomparable letters, and of the *Castle of Otranto,* he is the "Ultimus Romanorum," the author . . . of the first romance and of the last tragedy in our language, and surely worthy of a higher place than any living writer, be he who he may.'

But by all odds the most formidable attack on Walpole was made in the *Edinburgh Review* by Macaulay, then on the eve of his thirty-third birthday. 'I have laid it on Walpole so unsparingly that I shall not be surprised if Miss Berry should cut me,' he wrote to his sister, 14 October 1833.[6] Two or three weeks later, however, he is off to Miss Berry's *soirée.* 'I do not know whether I told you that she resented my article on Horace Walpole so much that Sir Stratford Canning advised me not to go near her. . . . You know that in *Vivian Grey* she is called Miss Otranto. I always expected that my article would put her into a passion, and I was not mistaken; but she has come round again, and sent me a most pressing and kind invitation the other day.'[7]

The article is one of the most brilliant Macaulay ever wrote. It has been read by generations of schoolboys and it has had more influence on Walpole's reputation than all other writing on him combined. It is a caricature, but like all good caricatures the victim is recognizable. Every page, nearly every sentence, contains statements which are untrue, but there does emerge a likeness, distorted though it is.

Miss Berry's anger did not last long, as we have seen, but seven years later she answered Macaulay and with spirit in an Advertisement to Bentley's edition of Walpole's *Letters.* Macaulay's picture, she said, of Walpole's character was 'entirely and offensively unlike the original.' She replied to Macaulay's untrue charges one by one and had the final word on the most serious charge of all: Walpole's alleged coldness of heart. She had decided to publish his letters to her and her sister to give proof 'that the warmth of his

6. G. O. Trevelyan, *The Life and Letters*   7. Ibid. 339.
of Lord Macaulay, 1876, i. 330.

feelings, and his capacity for sincere affection, continued unenfeebled by age.'[8]

There is no record of Macaulay and Miss Berry dining together pleasantly after her defence, but there is at Farmington a statement not without interest, although it is two removes from the principals. It was written by George Bentley, the son of Miss Berry's publisher, and was given me by the present Mrs Richard Bentley. 'Miss Berry had inoculated him [the first Richard Bentley] with a feeling of affection for Walpole's character, and he could never bear to hear him ill spoken of. . . . It was his great wish that his letters should be collected and chronologically arranged.

'Macaulay was consulted on the subject. His character of Walpole is well known, but Macaulay's opinion had modified in his later days as he confessed to Miss Berry, and as Miss Berry told my father.'

W. S. L.

8. Walpole's *Letters*, 1840, vi. p. xi.

BIBLIOGRAPHY AND METHOD

WALPOLE'S correspondence with the Berrys now consists of 176 letters, of which 164 were written by Walpole to Mary and Agnes Berry, one by Walpole to Robert Berry, and eleven by Mary Berry to Walpole. One of Walpole's letters—that of 7 Sept. 1796—is now printed for the first time.[1]

Lady Theresa Lewis states that 'Miss Berry had bequeathed all her papers to the late Sir Frankland Lewis. Not long before the close of her life, she informed Lady Theresa Lewis that she had done so, adding that, in case of his death, and of his not having had time to deal with these MSS, she wished her to promise to take charge of them, and not let them pass into any other hands. After the death of her father-in-law, the contents of two large trunks were put into Lady Theresa Lewis's hands' (MBJ i. p. ix). On her death they went to Sir Thomas Villiers Lister, a son by her first marriage, and on his death Walpole's letters to the Berrys, two manuscript drafts of the *Reminiscences,* and various other Walpolian manuscripts were acquired from Lady Lister by the first J. Pierpont Morgan. Miss Berry's other manuscripts passed to the British Museum.

There is no record of what the trunks contained at any time, but it is clear that Miss Berry repaired to them on occasion and sold some of their contents. In the edition of Walpole's *Supplement to the Historic Doubts* which E. C. Hawtrey published in the Philobiblon Society volume for 1860 he states: 'I procured the MS from which the following pages are printed, several years since, from White, a well-known bookseller, then residing in Pall Mall. He had bought it of Miss Berry, into whose possession it had come with many other MSS and printed books of Horace, Earl of Orford' (p. 3). Furthermore, I secured in 1937 from the Trustees of the late Mr Richard Bentley of Slough, a large quantity of Wal-

---

1. The original is among the Berry papers in the British Museum, Add. MSS 37728, ff. 23–4.

pole's manuscripts which Miss Berry had sold to the first Richard Bentley, her publisher. These contained about one hundred unpublished letters to and from Walpole, his 'Short Notes of My Life,' the *Hieroglyphic Tales,* the essays which appeared in *The World,* verses, and the unpublished memoirs from 1783 to 1791. (These last have been edited and have been referred to in this correspondence, but the exigencies of the war have delayed their publication.)

During the Berrys' lifetime 58 of Walpole's letters to them were printed, more or less incompletely, in the sixth volume of Richard Bentley's *Letters of Horace Walpole, Earl of Orford,* edited by John Wright and published in 1840. To this volume is prefixed Mary Berry's defence of Walpole, headed 'Advertisement to the letters addressed to the Miss Berrys' and signed 'MB.'

The manuscripts give extensive evidence of Miss Berry's labours for this edition. As an editor she leaves something to be desired. In 1830 she wrote to Lord Dover to congratulate him on becoming the editor of Walpole's letters to Mann. She and Mrs Damer had dreaded their falling into unworthy hands, 'for never was the pruning knife so necessary, nor so necessary to be exercised by a hand experienced in the world and all its tales for the last half century' (MBJ iii. 385). Such a hand, of course, was her own, and she exercised the knife freely, marking out with ink whole paragraphs, encircling names which she wished omitted, and scribbling her notes on blank portions of the manuscripts. On some of those formerly in the Bentley collection she has written 'Unimportant. Destroy,' and it is clear that she exercised this final editorial decision in occasional holocausts. That she did not spare her own letters is proved by the regrettably few which have survived.

Peter Cunningham, who did not have access to the manuscripts, printed Wright's selection in his *Letters of Horace Walpole,* 1857–9 (see List of Letters).

Lady Theresa Lewis published her *Extracts from the Journals and Correspondence of Miss Berry* in 1865. Her transcript was frequently inaccurate: e.g., in the passage about Tonton quoted earlier, the sentence 'one may eat roses and smell to cherries and not perceive the difference from scent or flavour' was transformed into 'One may eat roses and small cherries, and not perceive the difference from want of flavour.' Lady Theresa printed, wholly or in part, all but four of the remainder of Walpole's letters to the Berrys, and made restorations in those already published, with the following explanation: 'Many passages in the letters already printed having been suppressed—some probably for the sake of brevity, and some perhaps from a wish on the part of the Miss Berrys to avoid a too frequent repetition of their own praises—may now without scruple be published' (MBJ i. 163). This is not altogether candid; many of the restored passages had been omitted because of their supposed indelicacy or abusiveness.

Mrs Paget Toynbee, in her *Letters of Horace Walpole,* 1903–5, printed the letters to the Berrys from the original manuscripts, and for the first time completely and accurately. Three which she printed were new, those of ?11 April 1789, 25 June 1796 (*bis*), and 14 Dec. 1796.

The present edition has been printed from photostats of the original manuscripts in the Morgan Library and the British Museum.

Mary Berry's letters to Walpole were returned to her and it is clear that she later destroyed most of them, probably at the time of her revision of Walpole's letters for the 1840 edition (see the preliminary note to her letter of 9 Dec. 1791, *post* i. 374). Lady Theresa Lewis, however, had access to at least four more than are at present known to exist. These four (28 Sept. 1794, 1 and 5 Oct. 1794, and 19 May 1796) are here printed from her texts; the remaining seven are printed from photostats of the originals in the Morgan Library.

Walpole's letters to Cecilia Seton were first published in the third volume of Paget Toynbee's *Supplement to the Letters of Horace Walpole,* 1918–25. They had been in the possession of Mrs Graves of Naphill, High Wycombe, Bucks, but were sold by her at Sotheby's 6 Dec. 1921, as a pendant to the Waller sale. They are now WSL.

Biographical notes without reference are from the *Dictionary of National Biography* or the *Complete Peerage* or *Complete Baronetage*. Other sources quoted in the biographical footnotes are assumed to be supplemented by these works.

All English books, unless otherwise stated, are assumed to be published in London.

In all the letters, the hyphenization and capitalization have been modernized here. The spelling has also been modernized (for lists of Walpole's obsolete spellings see COLE i. p. xliii and MONTAGU i. p. xxxiii), except that of proper names, which are spelled as in the manuscripts. As before, Walpole's punctuation has been retained, but Miss Berry's, which is somewhat erratic, has been revised.

W. S. L.

C. H. B.

ACKNOWLEDGMENTS

OUR first acknowledgment is to the Trustees of the Pierpont Morgan Library for permission to reproduce Walpole's letters to the Berrys, and to their librarian, Miss Belle da Costa Greene, for her generous help in answering many queries.

We are also greatly indebted to the Harvard University Library for permission to print for the first time Walpole's 'Book of Visitors.' Permission to edit this was first granted me by the late Mr and Mrs Percival Merritt who then owned the manuscript and who thus again made an invaluable contribution to this edition.

Permission to reproduce the drawing of the Misses Berry by Paul Sandby in the Royal Library at Windsor Castle has been graciously accorded by H.M. King George VI.

Sir Wathen A. Waller, Bt, has once more permitted us to publish manuscript material in his possession. A brief description of his manuscripts used in this Correspondence will be found in the following section, 'Cue-Titles and Abbreviations,' under 'Berry-Damer.' We are also grateful to Dr J. Q. Adams for allowing us to make generous extracts from Walpole's 'Books of Materials' in the possession of the Folger Shakespeare Library.

The Trustees of the Henry E. Huntington Library and Art Gallery have kindly allowed us to reproduce for the first time John Carter's delightful sketches of Walpole at Strawberry Hill. We are indebted to the Yale Art Gallery for permission to reproduce the lithograph of Sylvester Douglas in the Edward B. Greene Collection.

Messrs Ketton-Cremer, Morshead, and Pottle have spent hours on the proofs and have again not only saved us from ourselves, but have called our attention to points which we had missed. In addition, Mr Morshead has supplied us with many unpublished extracts from Farington's Diary under his custody at Windsor. Dr Chapman, Mr Leonard Bacon, and Professor Benjamin Boyce of the University of Omaha have also read the proofs and have contributed valuable help which is most gratefully received.

Dr Dayle Wallace commenced work on this correspondence at New Haven in the summer of 1939, continued on it until September 1940 (being on leave from the University of Omaha and an Honorary Sterling Fellow at Yale for 1939–40), and returned for further work on it the following two summers. During the intervening winters he added what time a busy teaching life at Omaha permitted. My absence in government work in Washington prevented me from doing much more than reading proof, and for the past year the work in New Haven has been in the hands of Dr Charles H. Bennett and Mrs Louis L. Martz. They have edited the 'Book of Visitors,' made the Index, dealt with the usual last minute confusions, and seen the work through the press.

Our additional thanks are due to the following persons: Mr Vincent Adley; Mr A. W. Aspital of the British Museum; Prof. A. R. Bellinger of Yale University; Dr Lewis P. Curtis of Yale University; Dr Philip B. Daghlian of the University of Rochester; Mrs Frank Durand; Mr Robert C. Gooch of the Library of Congress; Dr Allen T. Hazen of Hunter College; Miss Mary A. Hopkins of Washington, D.C.; Mr William A. Jackson of the Harvard Library; Mr Gerrit P. Judd; Dr John P. Kirby of Mary Washington College; Dr George L. Lam; Mr Robert F. Lane, formerly librarian of the University of Omaha, now of the U.S. Navy; Dr James V. Logan of Ohio State University; Miss Ellen Lord, acting librarian of the University of Omaha; Miss Julia T. McCarthy; Mr Ben Miller; Miss Anna M. Monrad of the Yale Library; Mr Leon Nemoy of the Yale Library; the Rev. W. Paton of Brentford, Middlesex; Prof. Carl F. Schreiber of Yale University; Dr Warren H. Smith; Sir Wathen A. Waller, Bt; Dr Joseph L. Walsh of New Haven; and Mr A. J. Watson of the British Museum.

The first breaks in the Advisory Council have occurred since the appearance of the Montagu correspondence.

Leonard Whibley brought to the study of Gray a mind trained in the classics and a life-long devotion to Pembroke. Gray was our constant companion in our walks along the lanes and across the fields of Frensham with the dogs coursing ahead of us. At first Whibley did not at all approve of this edition's appearing by correspondences rather than chronologically, but he almost at once generously acknowledged that the course decided upon was the wiser one. He never did change his views on our normalizing the text, but he was too warm-hearted ever to mention his objection once the decision had gone against him. The earlier volumes have already borne witness to his constant help; the forthcoming Gray correspondence will bear even more.

Although Karl Young was not a specialist in eighteenth-century studies, his interest in scholarship was so wide and deep that he was the ardent friend of it, no matter what its subject. His particular aid to this edition was with the mediæval Latin passages. This aid, which was eagerly given, was less, however, than the almost parental interest which he had in the undertaking as a whole, and which he was entitled to take since he played a decisive rôle in its initiation. The first stage of our long journey was made easier by his unfailing support and devotion.

W. S. L.

CUE-TITLES AND ABBREVIATIONS

Add. MS . . . Additional Manuscript, British Museum.

Ædes Walpolianæ, Works Horace Walpole, *Ædes Walpolianæ: or, A De-*
ii . . . . *scription of the Collection of Pictures at Hough-*
ton Hall in Norfolk, the Seat of . . . Sir Robert
Walpole, in *The Works of Horatio Walpole,*
Earl of Orford, 1798, vol. ii.

Alumni Oxon. . . Joseph Foster, *Alumni Oxonienses: The Mem-*
bers of the University of Oxford, 1500–1714,
Oxford, 1891–2, 4 vols; *1715–1886,* London,
1887–8, 4 vols.

Anecdotes, Works iii . Horace Walpole, *Anecdotes of Painting in*
England, in *The Works of Horatio Walpole,*
Earl of Orford, 1798, vol. iii.

Army Lists . . . [Great Britain, War Office], *A List of the Offi-*
cers of the Army and of the Corps of Royal Ma-
rines.

B . . . . Mary Berry.

'Berry-Damer' . . Four notebooks containing extracts made by
Mrs Damer from Mary Berry's letters to her,
1789–1804. The originals are not known to exist, and the extracts have never been published.
In vol. i, p. 2, is the note, 'These 4 vols found
among Mrs Damer's papers and in her own
handwriting.' They are now in the possession
of Sir Wathen Waller, Bt, who has kindly given
permission for their use in this edition.

Berry Papers . . *The Berry Papers: Being the Correspondence*
Hitherto Unpublished of Mary and Agnes
Berry (1763–1852), ed. Lewis Melville, 1914.

Bibl. Nat. Cat. . . Catalogue de la Bibliothèque nationale, Paris,
1897—.

BM Cat. . . . British Museum Catalogue.

BM, *Satiric Prints* . . British Museum, Department of Prints and
Drawings, *Catalogue of Prints and Drawings*
. . . Political and Personal Satires, 1870–1938,
6 vols.

'Book of Materials' . Three manuscript volumes, the first two entitled by Walpole 'Book of Materials,' the third

	entitled 'Miscellany'; begun in 1759, 1771, and 1786 respectively. The originals are in the Folger Shakespeare Library; photostatic copies in the possession of WSL.
Boswell, *Johnson* . .	*Boswell's Life of Johnson,* ed. George Birkbeck Hill, revised by L. F. Powell, Oxford, 1934—, 6 vols.
Boswell Papers . .	*Private Papers of James Boswell,* ed. Geoffrey Scott and Frederick A. Pottle, privately printed, 1928–34, 18 vols.
Burke, *Commoners* .	John Burke, *A Genealogical and Heraldic History of the Commoners of Great Britain and Ireland,* 1833–8, 4 vols.
Burke, *Landed Gentry* .	Sir John Bernard Burke, *A Genealogical and Heraldic History of the Landed Gentry of Great Britain.*
Burke, *Peerage* . .	Sir John Bernard Burke and Ashworth P. Burke, *A Genealogical and Heraldic History of the Peerage and Baronetage.*
COLE	*The Yale Edition of Horace Walpole's Correspondence: The Correspondence with the Rev. William Cole,* New Haven, 1937, 2 vols.
Collins, *Peerage* . .	Arthur Collins, *The Peerage of England,* 1768, 1779, 1812 (ed. Sir Samuel Egerton Brydges).
Country Seats . .	*Horace Walpole's Journals of Visits to Country Seats, &c.,* ed. Paget Toynbee, in *The Walpole Society,* Oxford, vol. xvi, 1928.
Cunningham . .	*The Letters of Horace Walpole, Earl of Orford,* ed. Peter Cunningham, 1857–9, 9 vols.
Delany Corr. . .	*The Autobiography and Correspondence of Mary Granville, Mrs Delany,* ed. the Right Hon. Lady Llanover, 1861, 3 vols; 2d series, 1862, 3 vols.
'Des. of SH,' *Works* ii .	Horace Walpole, 'A Description of the Villa of Mr Horace Walpole at Strawberry Hill near Twickenham,' in *The Works of Horatio Walpole, Earl of Orford,* 1798, vol. ii.
Directory to the Nobility, Gentry . . . for 1793	*Directory to the Nobility, Gentry, and Families of Distinction, in London, Westminster, &c. Being a Supplement to the British Directory of Trade, Commerce, and Manufacture, for 1793.*

DNB . . . . *Dictionary of National Biography,* ed. Leslie Stephen and Sidney Lee.

du Deffand . . . *The Yale Edition of Horace Walpole's Correspondence: The Correspondence with Mme du Deffand,* New Haven, 1939, 6 vols.

GEC . . . . George Edward Cokayne, *The Complete Peerage,* revised by Vicary Gibbs *et al.,* 1910—; *The Complete Baronetage,* Exeter, 1900–9, 6 vols.

'Genesis of SH' . . W. S. Lewis, 'The Genesis of Strawberry Hill,' *Metropolitan Museum Studies,* vol. v, pt i, June 1934.

GM . . . . *The Gentleman's Magazine.*

Gray's Corr. . . . *The Correspondence of Thomas Gray,* ed. Paget Toynbee and Leonard Whibley, Oxford, 1935, 3 vols.

Harcourt Papers . . *The Harcourt Papers,* ed. Edward William Harcourt, Oxford, n.d., 13 vols.

Hazen, *SH Bibliography* A. T. Hazen, *A Bibliography of the Strawberry Hill Press,* New Haven, 1942.

HW . . . . Horace Walpole.

Johnson, *Lives of the Poets* . . . Samuel Johnson, *Lives of the English Poets,* ed. George Birkbeck Hill, Oxford, 1905, 3 vols.

Journal of the Printing-Office . . . Horace Walpole, *Journal of the Printing-Office at Strawberry Hill,* ed. Paget Toynbee, 1923.

La Grande encyclopédie *La Grande encyclopédie,* Paris, [1886–1902,] 31 vols.

Last Journals . . Horace Walpole, *The Last Journals of Horace Walpole during the Reign of George III from 1771–1783,* ed. Archibald Francis Steuart, 1910, 2 vols.

Lond. (London), sold . *See* Sold London.

MBJ . . . . *Extracts from the Journals and Correspondence of Miss Berry from the Year 1783 to 1852,* ed. Lady Theresa Lewis, 2d edn, 1866, 3 vols.

'Mem. 1783–91' . . Horace Walpole's manuscript journal 1783–1791, in the possession of wsl.

Mem. Geo. II . . Horace Walpole, *Memoirs of the Reign of King George the Second,* ed. Henry R. V. Fox, Lord Holland, 1847, 3 vols.

Mem. Geo. III . . Horace Walpole, *Memoirs of the Reign of King George the Third,* ed. G. F. Russell Barker, 1894, 4 vols.

Moniteur . . .	*Gazette nationale, ou le Moniteur universel.*
MONTAGU . . .	*The Yale Edition of Horace Walpole's Correspondence: The Correspondence with George Montagu,* New Haven, 1941.
MS Cat. . .	Horace Walpole, 'Catalogue of the Library of Mr Horace Walpole at Strawberry Hill, 1763,' unpublished manuscript in the possession of Lord Walpole, Wolterton Park, Norwich.
Musgrave, *Obituary* .	*Obituary Prior to 1800 . . . Compiled by Sir William Musgrave,* ed. Sir George J. Armytage, Harleian Society Publications, 1899–1901, 6 vols.
N&Q	*Notes and Queries.*
NBG	*Nouvelle biographie générale,* ed. Jean-Chrétien-Ferdinand Hoefer, Paris, 1852–66, 46 vols.
OED	*New English Dictionary on Historical Principles,* ed. Sir James A. H. Murray *et al.,* Oxford, 1888–1933.
Old Westminsters . .	*The Record of Old Westminsters,* ed. G. F. Russell Barker and Alan H. Stenning, 1928, 2 vols. *A Supplementary Volume,* ed. J. B. Whitmore and G. R. Y. Radcliffe [1938?].
'Paris Journals' . .	Horace Walpole, *Paris Journals,* in *The Yale Edition of Horace Walpole's Correspondence: The Correspondence with Madame du Deffand,* New Haven, 1939, v. 255–417.
Royal and Noble Authors, Works i . .	Horace Walpole, *A Catalogue of the Royal and Noble Authors,* in *The Works of Horatio Walpole, Earl of Orford,* 1798, vol. i.
Scots Peerage . .	*The Scots Peerage,* ed. Sir James Balfour Paul, Edinburgh, 1904–14, 9 vols.
SH . . .	Strawberry Hill.
SH, sold . . .	*See* Sold SH.
SH Accounts . .	*Strawberry Hill Accounts . . . Kept by Mr Horace Walpole from 1747 to 1795,* ed. Paget Toynbee, Oxford, 1927.
'Short Notes' . .	Horace Walpole, 'Short Notes of the Life of Horatio Walpole, youngest son of Sir Robert Walpole Earl of Orford and of Catherine Shorter, his first wife,' first printed in Walpole's *Letters to Mann,* 1843, iv. 335–58, reprinted by Mrs Paget Toynbee, *Letters of Horace Wal-*

pole, Oxford, 1903–5, i. pp. xxxiv–lvi. Now WSL.

Sold London . . *A Catalogue of the Collection of Scarce Prints, Removed from Strawberry Hill, 13–23* June 1842. The number following each entry is the lot number in the sale.

Sold SH . . . *A Catalogue of the Classic Contents of Strawberry Hill Collected by Horace Walpole, 25* April—21 May 1842. The roman and arabic numerals which follow each entry indicate the day and lot number in the sale.

T . . . . *The Letters of Horace Walpole,* ed. Mrs Paget Toynbee, Oxford, 1903–5, 16 vols.

Toynbee Supp. . . *Supplement to the Letters of Horace Walpole,* ed. Paget Toynbee, Oxford, 1918–25, 3 vols.

Tracts of Geo. 3 . . 'A collection of tracts and pamphlets, historical and political, published during the reign of King George III,' 1760–90, 59 vols (2 vols numbered 47), collected by HW; sold SH iii. 110; now WSL.

Venn, *Alumni Cantab.* . *Alumni Cantabrigienses,* Part I, to 1751, ed. John Venn and J. A. Venn, Cambridge, 1922–7, 4 vols.

'Visitors' . . . Horace Walpole's manuscript list of visitors to Strawberry Hill, in the Percival Merritt Collection, Harvard University. Printed *post* ii. 221–74.

Voltaire, *Œuvres* . . *Œuvres complètes de Voltaire,* ed. Louis-Émile-Dieudonné Moland, Paris, 1877–85, 52 vols.

Walpoliana . . . John Pinkerton, *Walpoliana* [1799], 2 vols.

Woelmont de Brumagne Henri de Woelmont, Baron de Brumagne, *Notices généalogiques,* Paris, 1923–35, 8 vols.

Works . . . . Horace Walpole, *The Works of Horatio Walpole, Earl of Orford,* 1798, 5 vols.

Wright . . . *The Letters of Horace Walpole,* ed. John Wright, 1840, 6 vols.

WSL (NOW WSL) . . In the possession of W. S. Lewis.

LIST OF LETTERS IN
BERRY CORRESPONDENCE

The missing letters are marked by an asterisk after the date.

		YALE	TOYNBEE	CUNNINGHAM
1788	14 Oct.	i. 1	xiv. 90	
	1 Nov.			
	from Mary Berry	i. 1		
1789	2 Feb.	i. 3	xiv. 104	ix. 163
	4 Feb.			
	from Mary Berry	i. 4		
	20 March	i. 4	xiv. 121	ix. 176
	25 March	i. 6	xiv. 122	
	?11 April	i. 7	xv. 439	
	12 April			
	from Mary Berry	i. 7		
	14 April	i. 8	xiv. 122	
	18 April			
	from Mary Berry	i. 9		
	28 April	i. 10	xiv. 125	ix. 178
	29 April			
	from Mary Berry	i. 12		
	23 June	i. 13	xiv. 131	ix. 180
	30 June	i. 18	xiv. 139	ix. 184
	3 July*	i. 24		
	4 July*			
	to Agnes Berry	i. 24		
	9 July	i. 24	xiv. 148	ix. 189
	10 July	i. 30	xiv. 153	
	19 July	i. 38	xiv. 161	
	29 July	i. 41	xiv. 170	ix. 200
	6 Aug.	i. 47	xiv. 181	
	13 Aug.			
	to Agnes Berry	i. 51	xiv. 186	
	20 Aug.	i. 55	xiv. 193	
	27 Aug.	i. 58	xiv. 198	ix. 213

		YALE	TOYNBEE	CUNNINGHAM
	4 Sept.	i. 62	xiv. 201	ix. 214
	18 Sept.	i. 69	xiv. 214	
	30 Sept.	i. 72	xiv. 221	
1790	ca 28 June*	i. 74		
	2 July	i. 74	xiv. 256	
	3 July	i. 77	xiv. 258	ix. 247
	ca 7 July*			
	to Agnes Berry	i. 83		
	10 July	i. 83	xiv. 261	
	17 July	i. 90	xiv. 266	
	23 July	i. 97	xiv. 270	
	29 July	i. 103	xiv. 276	
	2 Aug.	i. 107	xiv. 279	
	10 Oct.	i. 110	xiv. 293	ix. 256
	12 Oct.	i. 113	xiv. 296	
	16 Oct.	i. 117	xiv. 299	
	22 Oct.	i. 122	xiv. 303	
	31 Oct.	i. 125	xiv. 305	ix. 258
	8 Nov.	i. 130	xiv. 312	ix. 259
	13 Nov.			
	to Barbara Cecilia			
	Seton	i. 137	*Supp.* iii. 63	
	13 Nov.	i. 138	xiv. 317	
	18 Nov.	i. 142	xiv. 320	ix. 262
	26 Nov.	i. 147	xiv. 324	ix. 265
			misdated	misdated
	10 Dec.	i. 155	xiv. 335	
	11 Dec.			
	to Barbara Cecilia			
	Seton	i. 157	*Supp.* iii. 65	
	16 Dec.	i. 159	xiv. 337	
	17 Dec.	i. 161	xiv. 339	
	17 Dec.			
	to Barbara Cecilia			
	Seton	i. 166	*Supp.* iii. 68	
	20 Dec.	i. 167	xiv. 343	ix. 273
	21 Dec.			
	to Barbara Cecilia			

		YALE	TOYNBEE	CUNNINGHAM
	Seton	i. 170	*Supp.* iii. 69	
	22 Dec.		xiv. 347	
	to Robert Berry	i. 171	misdated	
1791	2 Jan.	i. 173	xiv. 349	
	9 Jan.	i. 177	xiv. 353	
	15 Jan.	i. 178	xiv. 355	
	22 Jan.	i. 180	xiv. 357	ix. 275
	29 Jan.	i. 183	xiv. 360	ix. 277
	4 Feb.	i. 188	xiv. 363	ix. 280
	12 Feb.	i. 192	xiv. 367	ix. 282
	13 Feb.			
	to Agnes Berry	i. 196	xiv. 370	ix. 284
	18 Feb.	i. 200	xiv. 376	ix. 288
	26 Feb.	i. 205	xiv. 379	ix. 291
	5 March	i. 212	xiv. 384	ix. 294
	11 March	i. 216	xiv. 387	
	19 March	i. 222	xiv. 391	ix. 296
	27 March	i. 226	xiv. 395	ix. 298
	31 March	i. 231	xiv. 399	
	3 April	i. 234	xiv. 401	ix. 301
	10 April	i. 240	xiv. 409	
	15 April	i. 246	xiv. 413	ix. 303
	23 April	i. 251	xiv. 417	ix. 306
	4 May	i. 257	xiv. 426	
	12 May	i. 261	xiv. 428	ix. 312
	19 May	i. 266	xiv. 432	ix. 315
	26 May	i. 272	xiv. 436	ix. 317
	2 June	i. 279	xiv. 441	ix. 321
	8 June	i. 283	xiv. 444	ix. 322
	14 June	i. 289	xv. 1	ix. 325
	23 June	i. 294	xv. 4	ix. 327
	28 June	i. 297	xv. 9	
	4 July	i. 303	xv. 13	
	12 July	i. 309	xv. 17	ix. 331
	17 July	i. 312	xv. 20	
	20 July	i. 316	xv. 22	
	26 July	i. 318	xv. 24	ix. 332
	3 Aug.	i. 324	xv. 28	

	YALE	TOYNBEE	CUNNINGHAM
8 Aug.	i. 327	xv. 34	
10 Aug.	i. 330	xv. 36	
15 Aug. to Barbara Cecilia Seton	i. 333	*Supp.* iii. 70	
17 Aug.	i. 335	xv. 38	ix. 336
23 Aug.	i. 339	xv. 46	ix. 340
ca 1 Sept.*	i. 343		
5 Sept.	i. 343	xv. 48	
11 Sept.	i. 348	xv. 56	ix. 344
16 Sept.	i. 351	xv. 58	ix. 346
25 Sept.	i. 356	xv. 63	ix. 348
3 Oct.	i. 359	xv. 74	
9 Oct.	i. 361	xv. 76	ix. 356
16 Oct.	i. 367	xv. 80	
20 Oct.	i. 368	xv. 81	
27 Oct.	i. 371	xv. 86	
11 Nov. to Barbara Cecilia Seton	i. 373	*Supp.* iii. 72	
12 Nov. to Barbara Cecilia Seton	i. 374	*Supp.* iii. 72	
?9 Dec. from Mary Berry	i. 374		
?11 Dec.	i. 376	xv. 93	
13 Dec.	i. 376	xv. 94	
Dec.	i. 377	xv. 95	
1793 6 April	ii. 1	xv. 185	
17 Sept.	ii. 4	xv. 194	ix. 411
24 Sept.	ii. 6	xv. 195	
25 Sept.	ii. 10	xv. 198	ix. 412
26 Sept.	ii. 13	xv. 201	
29 Sept.	ii. 17	xv. 205	
2 Oct.	ii. 20	xv. 208	
6 Oct.	ii. 23	xv. 214	ix. 413
10 Oct.	ii. 26	xv. 219	
15 Oct.	ii. 30	xv. 222	ix. 417

		YALE	TOYNBEE	CUNNINGHAM
	17 Oct.			
	to Agnes Berry	ii. 35	xv. 225	
	19 Oct.	ii. 37	xv. 228	
	22 Oct.	ii. 39	xv. 230	
	24 Oct.	ii. 42	xv. 233	
	25 Oct.	ii. 45	xv. 234	
	29 Oct.	ii. 47	xv. 238	
	5 Nov.	ii. 50	xv. 242	
	7 Nov.	ii. 53	xv. 244	ix. 419
	14 Nov.	ii. 60	xv. 251	
	19 Nov.	ii. 64	xv. 255	
	23 Nov.	ii. 68	xv. 258	
	30 Nov.	ii. 75	xv. 263	
	4 Dec.	ii. 78	xv. 266	ix. 423
	6 Dec.	ii. 82	xv. 269	
	13 Dec.	ii. 85	xv. 273	ix. 426
1794	17 April	ii. 91	xv. 283	ix. 433
			misdated	misdated
	21 April	ii. 95	xv. 286	
	1 May	ii. 97	xv. 289	
	31 July			
	to Agnes Berry	ii. 99	xv. 297	
	21 Sept.	ii. 101	xv. 301	
	24 Sept.	ii. 104	xv. 303	
	27 Sept.	ii. 106	xv. 304	ix. 440
	28 Sept.			
	from Mary Berry	ii. 112		
	29 Sept.	ii. 114	xv. 310	
	1 Oct.	ii. 119	xv. 312	
	1 Oct.			
	from Mary Berry	ii. 122		
	4 Oct.	ii. 125	xv. 316	
	5 Oct.			
	from Mary Berry	ii. 126		
	6 Oct.			
	from Mary Berry	ii. 127		
	7 Oct.	ii. 129	xv. 319	ix. 444
	14 Oct.	ii. 133	xv. 324	

		YALE	TOYNBEE	CUNNINGHAM
	15 Oct.	ii. 135	xv. 326	
	17 Oct.	ii. 136	xv. 327	ix. 447
1795	7 April	ii. 138	xv. 344	
	18 Aug.	ii. 139	xv. 350 misdated	
	22 Aug.	ii. 143	xv. 352	
	23 Aug.	ii. 144	xv. 354	
	25 Aug.	ii. 146	xv. 356	
	26 Aug.	ii. 149	xv. 358	
	1 Sept.	ii. 155	xv. 362	
	6 Sept.	ii. 159	xv. 365	
	8 Sept.	ii. 162	xv. 368	
	10 Sept.	ii. 163	xv. 369	
	15 Sept.	ii. 166	xv. 374	
	18 Sept.	ii. 168	xv. 376	
	4 Nov.	ii. 173	xv. 381	
	6 Nov.	ii. 174	xv. 379 misdated	
	22 Nov.	ii. 177	xv. 383	
	24 Nov.	ii. 178	xv. 385	
	25 Nov.	ii. 181	xv. 384 misdated	
	26 Nov.		xv. 387	
	to Agnes Berry	ii. 182	misdated	
	1 Dec.	ii. 182	xv. 387	
	3 Dec.	ii. 183	xv. 388	
	6 Dec.	ii. 183	xv. 389	
1796	19 May from Mary Berry	ii. 184		
	30 May	ii. 184	xv. 400	
	2 June	ii. 186	xv. 401	
	25 June	ii. 189	xv. 402	
	25 June, *bis*	ii. 190	xv. 403	
	25 July	ii. 194	xv. 406	
	26 July	ii. 195	xv. 408	
	29 July	ii. 197	xv. 409	
	5 Aug.	ii. 199	xv. 411	
	9 Aug.	ii. 199	xv. 412	

'THE Berrys were to come and see my printing-press. I recollected my gallantry of former days, and they found these stanzas ready set:

> *"To Mary's lips has ancient Rome*
> *Her purest language taught,*
> *And from the modern city home*
> *Agnes its pencil brought.*
>
> *"Rome's ancient Horace sweetly chants*
> *Such maids with lyric fire;*
> *Albion's old Horace sings nor paints—*
> *He only can admire.*
>
> *"Still would his press their fame record,*
> *So amiable the pair is!*
> *But, ah! how vain to think his word*
> *Can add a straw to Berrys!"*

'The next morning the Latian nymph sent me these lines:

> *"Had Rome's famed Horace thus addrest*
> *His Lydia or his Lyce,*
> *He had ne'er so oft complain'd their breast*
> *To him was cold and icy.*
>
> *"But had they sought their joy to explain,*
> *Or praise their generous bard,*
> *Perhaps, like me, they had tried in vain,*
> *And felt the task too hard."* '

(HW to Lady OSSORY, 19 Oct. 1788.)

To Mary Berry, Tuesday 14 October 1788

Dated by HW's statement that Mary Berry's verses were sent to him the morning after her visit of 13 Oct. to the SH press (*Journal of the Printing Office* 20–1, 72–4; HW to Lady Ossory 19 Oct. 1788). Presumably HW replied the same day.

[Strawberry Hill, Tuesday, Oct. 14, 1788.]

To Miss Mary Berry
on her stanzas in answer
to his from the press at Strawberry Hill.

I WILL certainly not contend when I am so glad to be *foiled,* as I am in every sense of the word; for you perceive my great ambition is to *set you off;* and since *clinquant*[1] is of no other use, and as Strawberry *Hill* is the lowest in all the parish of Parnassus, I hope you will allow me the honour of being your *Phébus en titre d'office;* though I shall be the reverse of all deputies, for my charge will be a sinecure, as my principal, the true inspirer, will, I am persuaded, always execute his office himself, and leave on the superannuated list

Your devoted servant
Hor. Walpole

From Mary Berry, Saturday 1 November 1788

Address: To the Honourable Horace Walpole, Strawberry Hill.

Twickenham Common,[1] Saturday morning, [Nov. 1, 1788.][2]

AS an apology for the enclosed, I must tell you that your verses to us have occasioned half a dozen others (some of them by people whom we never saw), in which our *name* and praises have been played upon a thousand different ways.[3] Our sentiments upon them I have

1. Translate *foil* (tinsel), to parallel HW's use of *foiled* in the opening line. Cf. HW to Lady Ossory 4 Jan. 1781.

1. The Berrys occupied at this time a house owned by Henry Collingwood Selby: 'a very small but neat box with a pretty garden, in the middle of which is an elegant little octagon room, thatched at top, which has a pretty appearance from the road' (Edward Ironside, *History and Antiquities of Twickenham*, 1797, p. 108). See also *post* 23 June, 27 Aug. 1789.

2. Added by HW.
3. Of the 'half a dozen' verses mentioned, only one has been found. Richard Owen Cambridge wrote:
'To sound your praises I dare not try,
My pen so prone to err is;
I tremble whilst I write, lest I
Should add a goose to Berries.'
(MBJ i. 154. See also R. D. Altick, 'Mr Cambridge serenades the Berry sisters,' in N&Q 12 Sept. 1942, clxxxiii. 158–61.)

ventured to express to you in the following lines. Rhyming seems to be catching, but I fear I have got the disorder of a bad sort.

I have the honour to be much yours,

M. BERRY.

PS. If we are to have the pleasure of meeting you at Mrs Grenville's[4] this evening, will it be inconvenient to you to bring us home at night?

To the Honourable Horace Walpole

Far in a wood not much exposed to view,
With other forest fruit, two berries grew;
Unheeded in their native shade they lay,
Nor courting much, nor too much shunning day.
A wand'ring sage, whose footsteps oft had roam'd
Out of the beaten track that fashion own'd,
Observ'd these berries half concealed from sight,
And or from chance, or whim, or his delight
Of bringing unregarded worth to light,
Tasted the fruit, and in a lucky hour
Finding it neither vapid yet, nor sour,
A sort of lively, rather pleasant taste,
A flavour, which he thought he lik'd at last,
Something perhaps upon the strawberry cast;
The new-found fruit with partial care he prais'd,
And so the berries' reputation raised.
Others their taste cried up, their goodness sung,
In various verse their name and virtues rung;
Some call'd them food for gods and heroes fit,
While some forgot their theme, to show their wit.
The berries, conscious all this sudden name
Prov'd not their value, but their patron's fame,
Conscious they only could aspire to please
Some simple palates, satisfied with ease,
But if with nobler, finer fruit compar'd,
They many faults and few perfections shar'd,
Wisely determin'd still to court the shade,

4. Margaret Eleanor ('Peggy') Banks (d. 1793), dau. of Joseph Banks of Revesby Abbey, Lincs; m. (1757) Hon. Henry Grenville (1717–84), Governor of Barbados 1746–56, brother of Richard, 2d E. Temple (Burke, *Peerage*, 1928, p. 2242). A 'celebrated beauty' (HW to Mann 28 March 1746), she 'was one of the favourite toasts of George II's reign, of all the superior gaieties of which she had her share, as well as of the best society to be found in later periods' (GM 1793, lxiii pt i. 581). She died 'in an advanced age' at Hampton Court Green (ibid.), where she probably was living in 1788.

To those that *sought* them, only pleasing made;
No greater honours anxious to obtain,
But still, *your* fav'rite berries to remain.

To MARY BERRY, Monday 2 February 1789

Address: To Miss Berry, Somerset Street.[1]

[Berkeley Square,] Feb. 2, 17—and *71*.[1a]

I AM *sorry,* in the sense of that word before it meant, like a Hebrew
word, *glad* or *sorry,*[2] that I am engaged this evening;[3] and I am at
your command on Tuesday, as it is always my inclination to be. It is a
misfortune that words are become so much the current coin of society,
that like King William's shillings they have no impression left; they
are so smooth, that they mark no more to whom they first belonged
than to whom they do belong, and are not worth even the twelve pence
into which they may be changed[4]—but if they mean too little, they may
seem to mean too much too, especially when an old man (who is often
synonymous for a miser) parts with them: I am afraid of protesting how
much I delight in your society, lest I should seem to affect being *galant*
—but if two negatives make an affirmative, why may not two ridicules
compose one piece of sense? And therefore, as I am in love with you
both, I trust it is a proof of the good sense of

Your devoted

H. WALPOLE

1. The Berrys had taken a house there in
1786 (MBJ i. 150).

1a. 'The date is thus put alluding to his
age which in 1789 was 71' (B). Mary Berry
also numbered the letter: 'No. 1.'

2. HW is alluding to biblical exegesis
such as is typified by John Gill's *Exposition
of the Book of Solomon's Song* (first published 1728, 4th edn 1805). Dr Gill comments as follows on the phrase 'rafters of
fir' in i. 17: 'The Hebrew word, here translated "rafters," is in Gen. xxx. 38–41 and
Exod. ii. 16 rendered "gutters". . . . R.
Aben Ezra observes that [the phrase should]
be read thus, "Our canals are of marble
stone." ' See *post* 27 March 1791.

3. Probably to General Conway and Lady
Ailesbury, who were much affected by the
death (12 Jan.) of Lady Ailesbury's niece,
Miss Caroline Campbell (see HW to Lady
Ossory 6 Feb. 1789).

4. 'On the accession of George III . . .

shillings were estimated to have lost a sixth'
of their weight (George C. Brooke, *English
Coins from the Seventh Century to the Present Day* [1932], p. 223). Except for £100 of
shillings which were struck for distribution
by the Duke of Northumberland when he
went to Dublin as Lord Lieutenant in 1763,
no more were coined until 1787, when shillings and sixpence to the amount of £55,459
were struck. At that time the average shil-
ling in circulation was estimated to have
lost one fourth of its original weight. Much
of the coinage of 1787 was melted down by
forgers and reissued in lighter weight (Edward Hawkins, *The Silver Coins of England,* 3d edn, 1887, pp. 410–11). Cf. *The
World* 26 Aug. 1789: 'So much base silver
. . . is circulating that, without the utmost
scrupulosity, hourly imposition may happen.' See also *The London Chronicle* 1–3
Oct. 1789, lxvi. 323.

From Mary Berry, Wednesday 4 February 1789

The date is conjectural. In the preceding letter HW mentions his engagement with the Berrys of Tuesday, 3 Feb., and in this letter Mary Berry refers to 'your company last night.'

Address: The Honourable Horace Walpole, Berkeley Square.

Somersett St, Wednesday night, [Feb. 4, 1789.]

YOU will oblige us by honouring this portrait of Cardinal de Bernis[1] with a place among your prints. We happen to have two or three impressions of it. Could I borrow for a moment the lively language, elegant expression, and polished wit, which in conversation animates these vulgar, heavy features, I would thank you in such terms as the subject deserves for your company last night, and the many pleasant hours we have passed in your society; but as there is no borrowing abilities, even upon usury, I must content myself with reminding you that as, in this portrait, a most heavy unpromising countenance conceals an active, intelligent mind, so the homeliest expression of thanks often accompanies the truest sense of obligation.   M. Berry

To Mary and Agnes Berry, Friday 20 March 1789

Berkeley Square, March 20, 1789.[1]

MRS DAMER[2] had lent her Madame de la Motte,[3] and I have but this moment recovered it—so, you see, I had not forgotten it

1. François-Joachim de Pierre de Bernis (1715–94), cardinal, 1758; poet, author, statesman; friend and correspondent of Voltaire; known for his kindness and hospitality. An opponent of the French Revolution, he received the daughters of Louis XV, Mesdames Adélaïde and Victoire, when they came to Rome in 1791, and they lived in his house until his death. The Berrys were presented to Cardinal de Bernis at Rome 23 Dec. 1783, and during the five months following were his guests on several occasions (see MBJ i. 57, 62, 70, 94, 98, 109, 114). For another account of the Cardinal about 1780, see Cornelia Knight, *Autobiography*, 1861, i. 50 ff.

1. 'No. 2' (B).
2. Anne Seymour Conway (1748–1828), only child of HW's cousin, Hon. Henry Seymour Conway, by Lady Ailesbury; m.

(1767) Hon. John Damer, eld. son of Bn Milton later E. of Dorchester; after her husband's suicide in 1776, she devoted much time to sculpture; intimate friend of Mary Berry (see their correspondence in the *Berry Papers*); HW's executrix and residuary legatee (DNB; *Scots Peerage* i. 386). Mrs Damer's unpublished journal, in the possession of Sir Wathen A. Waller, Bt, at Woodcote, Warwickshire, contains many ardent references to Miss Berry.

3. 'The memoirs of Madame de la Motte relative to her conduct in the famous *procès* of the Cardinal de Rohan' (B). Jeanne de Saint-Remy de Valois (1756–91), orphan and beggar befriended by a nobleman, m. (1780) Marc-Antoine-Nicolas Lamotte, a young policeman. They assumed the titles of Count and Countess de La Motte. Her adventurous career led to imprisonment in 1786 for her part in the affair of the Dia-

any more than my engagements to you—nay, were it not ridiculous at
my age to use a term so almost run out as *never,* I would add that you
will find I *never* can forget you.

I hope you are not engaged this day sevennight, but will allow me
to wait on you to Lady Ailesbury,[4] which I will settle with her when I
have your answer. I did mention it to her in general, but have no day
free before Friday next, except Thursday, when, if there is another illumination,[5] as is threatened, we should neither get thither nor thence;
especially not the latter, if the former is impracticable—

Quicquid delirant reges, plectuntur Achivi.[6]

Your devoted remembrancer[7]

Hor. Walpole

PS. I have got a few hairs of Edward IV's *head,* not *beard;*[8] they are
of a darkish brown, not auburn.

mond Necklace, but she escaped, joined her
husband (4 Aug. 1787) in England, and
died in London as the result of injuries received when she jumped from a two-story
window to avoid arrest for debt. Her sensa-
tional *Mémoires justificatifs* were published in London, 1788, and in the following year several editions in French appeared
(see Bibl. Nat. Cat.). An English version,
*Memoirs of the Countess de Valois de La
Motte,* was published in February (advertised 'This day are published' in *The
World* 18 Feb.), and a second edition, 'with
alterations and additions,' appeared in the
same year. Her authorship (with the assistance of a journalist, Serres de Latour,
and the ex-minister Calonne) has been
questioned (cf. Frantz Funck-Brentano, *La
Mort de la reine,* 1902, p. 111 ff.; L. de la
Sicotière in Joseph-Marie Quérard, *Les Su-
percheries littéraires dévoilées,* 1869–70, ii.
col. 647–9). A *Second mémoire justificatif*
appeared also in 1789.

4. Caroline Campbell (1721–1803), dau.
of Gen. John Campbell; m. (1) (1739) as 3d
wife, Charles Bruce (1682–1747), Bn Bruce
of Whorlton, afterwards (1741) 3d E. of
Ailesbury; m. (2) (1747) Hon. Henry Seymour Conway, HW's cousin. Lady Ailesbury lived in Little Warwick Street, near
Charing Cross. Among Mary Berry's memoranda for 1789 is the entry: 'Introduced by
Mr W. to Lady Ailesbury and Mrs D[amer]'
(MBJ i. 159).

5. London was illuminated on March 10

in honour of George III's recovery from his
second attack of insanity, a recovery 'hailed
as a national blessing' (Mary Berry, *Comparative View of Social Life in England and
France,* 1844, i. 340). According to HW, it
was 'the most universal illumination in
every house in London and Westminster
that ever had been seen, and without the
least mobbing or disorder' ('Mem. 1783–
91,' *sub* 10 March 1789; see also GM 1789,
lix pt i. 270–1). The illumination 'threatened' for 26 March did not materialize until 24 April, when HW recorded 'great illuminations, but not so general as before'
('Mem. 1783–91,' *sub* that date; see also GM
1789, lix pt i. 370). In a letter dated 23 Aug.
1821, Lady Louisa Stuart said that the
Duchess of Kingston's trial in 1776 and the
illuminations in 1789 were 'the only fine
public sights it was ever my good luck to
see' (*Letters of Lady Louisa Stuart to Miss
Louisa Clinton, First Series,* ed. Hon. James
A. Home, Edinburgh, 1901, p. 176).

6. 'Alluding to the public rejoicings on
the recovery of George III from his first illness in 1788' (B). The passage is from Horace, *Epist.* I. ii. 14.

7. A reference to his *Reminiscences written . . . in 1788 for the Amusement of Miss
Mary and Miss Agnes Berry,* the final draft
of which he had completed 13 Jan. 1789
(see ibid., ed. Paget Toynbee, Oxford, 1924,
pp. 1, 97).

8. In the rosewood cabinet (designed by
HW) in the Tribune was 'Hair of King Ed-

To MARY BERRY, Wednesday 25 March 1789

[Berkeley Square,] March 25, 1789.[1]

YOU have not half the quickness that I thought you had—or, which is much more probable, I suspect that I am a little in love, and you are not, for I think I should have understood *you* in two syllables, which has not been your case. I had sealed my note[2] and was going to send it when yours[3] arrived with the invitation for Saturday. I was to dine abroad[4] and had not time to break open my note or write it again, and so lifted up a corner and squeezed in *I will*[5]—what could those syllables mean, but that I will do whatever you please? Yes, you may keep them as a note of hand always payable at sight of your commands—or your sister's, for I am not less in love with my wife Rachel, than with my wife Leah;[6] and though I had a little forgotten my matrimonial vows at the beginning of this note, and was awkward and haggled a little about owning my passion; now I recollect that I have taken a double dose, I am mighty proud of it; and being more in the right than ever lover was, and twice as much in the right too, I avow my sentiments *hardiment,* and am,

Hymen, O Hymenæe!

ward IV, cut from his corpse when discovered in St George's Chapel at Windsor, 1789; given by Sir Joseph Banks' ('Des. of SH,' *Works* ii. 477). The relic was sold SH xv. 57. On 13 March, while repairs were being made in St George's Chapel, 'two of the canons and the surveyor' entered the vault of Edward IV (GM 1789, lix pt i. 271–2). How the hair came into the possession of Sir Joseph Banks is not known, but it may have been through George III, with whom he was intimate, or through Sir William Chambers, Surveyor-General of the Board of Works, with whom he was acquainted (Banks MSS in the Yale University Library).

———

1. 'No. 3' (B).
2. Presumably the preceding letter.
3. Missing.
4. Date and place not known.
5. This does not appear on the MS of HW's letter of 20 March, the cover of which is missing.
6. HW has reversed the degree of affection: Jacob 'loved . . . Rachel more than Leah' (Genesis xxix. 30).

To Mary and Agnes Berry, Saturday ?11 April 1789

The date is conjectural.
Address: To Misses Berrys.

[Berkeley Square,] Saturday, [?April 11, 1789.]

Mes très chères Fraises,

AS the honeymoon[1] is not over, I hope you will come to me again to-morrow evening, and that our papa[2] will not be sleepy so very early.

Your most affectionate
and *doubly* constant husband

H. W.

From Mary Berry, Sunday 12 April 1789

Dated by HW's reply of 14 April 1789.
Address: Honourable Horace Walpole.

[Somerset Street,] Sunday evening, [April 12, 1789.]

A THOUSAND thanks, my good Sir, for your *earnestness* last night and your kind attention this morning about a house for us. My father goes to Twickenham tomorrow or next day and carries with him our best wishes to find a place in that neighbourhood. He will inquire after the house you mention,[1] the situation of which I do not immediately recollect, but be assured a short distance from Strawberry Hill will be one of the first recommendations to us.

To our many obligations to you we must add that of the *very* agreeable evening we spent last night. I fear we shall not meet often this week; except you are to be at Lady J. Penn's[2] on Wednesday; perhaps

1. Cf. *post* 23 June 1789, paragraph 3.
2. In this letter and in those of 14 April and 30 June 1789 occur HW's only references to Robert Berry as 'our papa.'

1. Not identified.
2. Lady Juliana Fermor (1729–1801), 4th dau. of 1st E. of Pomfret, m. (1751) Thomas Penn (1702–75), then one of the proprietors of Pennsylvania, and of Braywick, in Berkshire (Collins, *Peerage*, 1812, iv. 207; How-

ard M. Jenkins, *The Family of William Penn*, Philadelphia, 1899, p. 150 ff.; DNB); a lifelong friend of HW's. HW to Lady Ossory 16 Aug. 1788 refers to Lady Juliana as 'the late Queen of Pennsylvania,' 'once mistress of a revenue of £36,000 a year, [who] is now lodging modestly, humbly, and tranquilly at Petersham on £600 a year; and her mind is so reconciled to her fortune, that she is still very handsome. She is to breakfast here soon.'

not at all, for we go on Thursday to the Duke of Argyll's[3] and shall probably stay till Saturday. Allow us, therefore, to lay a plan already for next week, and to beg the favour of seeing you tomorrow sennight, which will be the 21st.[4] Without a little arrangement and considera-tion beforehand, I find one's time passes away in London *nec recte nec suaviter*,[5] while we insure both when we are lucky enough to spend the evening with you.

M. BERRY

PS. Do tell me where Mrs Damer lives.[6] Though we are not to have the pleasure of being admitted till next week, we wish no longer to delay leaving our name at her door.

To MARY BERRY, Tuesday 14 April 1789

Address: To Miss Berry, Somerset Street.

[Berkeley Square,] April 14, 1789.[1]

Suavissima Maria,

I COULD not answer your note yesterday, for I was at dinner, as I do not wait till the Great Mogul, Fashion, gives me leave to sit down to table[2]—besides I was to go [to] the play[3] and [I] like to see the begin-ning as well as the end.

---

3. Ealing Grove, a small estate six miles from London, purchased about 1780 by John Campbell (1723–1806), 5th D. of Ar-gyll, from the Duke of Marlborough, who had purchased it about 1775 from Joseph Gulston, the print-collector (Horace Bleack-ley, *The Story of a Beautiful Duchess*, 1908, p. 296, and the references there cited; COLE i. 357 and n. 5). After the death of the Duchess in 1790, the Duke of Argyll sold the estate to 'Mr Baillie of Bedford Square for 6000 guineas' (*Times* 19 Sept. 1791).
4. The dates are slightly confused: the 21st was Tuesday (not Monday) sevennight. Cf. following letter.
5. Horace, *Epist.* I. viii. 4.
6. Apparently HW did not reply in writ-ing to this request. Mrs Damer lived from 1778 until about 1795 in a small house in Sackville Street (see *Berry Papers* 21; Henry B. Wheatley, *Round About Piccadilly and Pall Mall*, 1870, p. 180; *Directory to the No-*

bility, Gentry . . . for 1793, p. 15, where she is erroneously called Hon. Mrs G. Da-mer; *post* 27 Sept. 1794).

---

1. 'No. 4' (B).
2. HW usually dined about four o'clock (DU DEFFAND iv. 178 n. 12; Joseph Farington, *Diary*, ed. James Greig, 1922–8, i. 1), al-though Farington records (ibid. i. 3) that dinner at SH 21 July 1793 was at five. An undated note from Lady Ailesbury to Jer-ningham invited him for dinner at four, to go to the play afterward (*Edward Jerning-ham and His Friends*, ed. Lewis Bettany, 1919, p. 189). In 1790 the dinner hour at the fashionable clubs in the West End was 'at half after six, dinner on table at seven' (*London Chronicle* 16–18 Nov. 1790, lxviii. 483).
3. *Love for Love*, by Congreve, and *Rich-ard Cœur de Lion*, by Michel-Jean Sedaine (1719–97), were performed at Drury Lane

I pray that our papa may find a house at Twickenham—Hampton Court[4] is half way to Swisserland.

I am not asked to Lady Juliana's—and therefore must give you up for this week as vagrants; but when you are passed back to your parish, I will certainly see you, especially on this day sennight.

In the middle of the last act last night there was an interlude of a boxing match, but it was in the front boxes. The folks in the pit, who could not see behind them better than they generally can before them through domes and pyramids of muslin,[5] hinted to the combatants to retire, which they did into the lobby, where a circle was made, and there the champions pulled one another's hair, and a great deluge of—powder ensued; but being well greased like Grecian pugilists, not many curls were shed. Adieu!

From MARY BERRY, Saturday 18 April 1789

Dated by the tone of the letter and by the phrase, 'tickets to the trial,' presumably a reference to the trial of Warren Hastings which lasted for 148 sittings of the High Court of Parliament between 13 Feb. 1788 and 23 April 1795. As HW did not become intimate with the Berrys until late in 1788, when the Court was not in session, this letter probably belongs to 1789 or 1790. In 1789 there were nineteen sittings of the Court 21 April–8 July; the Berrys, who left London for Yorkshire 17 June (post 23 June 1789), presumably could have attended any of the sessions except the last six. In 1790 the trial continued 16 Feb.–9 June for fourteen sittings, any one of which the Berrys might have attended. See The History of the Trial of Warren Hastings, 1796, pts ii, iii. The tone of the letter, however, suggests an early stage of friendship; accordingly the date assigned is the Saturday preceding the first sitting of 1789.

Address: The Honourable Horace Walpole.

The letter has not been through the post.

13 April (World, that date). In Love for Love, Elizabeth Farren ('Angelica'), William Parsons ('Foresight'), and John Philip Kemble ('Valentine') produced 'some of the best comic acting extant. And with St Monday [the theatres were closed during Holy Week] they had a house accordingly' (ibid. 14 April 1789).

4. Three miles from Twickenham.

5. In The Evening Mail 17–20 April 1789 a correspondent who signed himself 'Anti-Bonnet-Curtain' attacked the fashion for 'flowing drapery that hangs in such deep festoons over the ladies' faces at present.' Cf. the print, 'Fashionable Full Dress of Paris,' in The Lady's Magazine, Feb. 1789, xx. opp. p. 59, and the prints in The Town and Country Magazine for 1789–90. 'New Fashions from Paris,' a description of five new hats and bonnets, is in The London Chronicle 5–7 March 1789.

[Somerset Street,] Saturday afternoon, [April 18, 1789.]

WAS I to begin thanking you, when should I have done? And what is three tickets or three dozen of tickets for any show upon earth in comparison of my other obligations to you, in comparison of that flattering regard, that lively interest, that real friendship with which upon every occasion you act towards us? Believe me, and it is all I feel able to say, it is not lost upon us. We feel it all, and the impossibility of ever thanking you for such obligations. For tickets to the trial,[1] to anybody else I could write a fine note; to you it is impossible.

M. B.

To MARY and AGNES BERRY, Tuesday 28 April 1789

[Berkeley Square,] April 28, at night, 1789.[1]

BY my not saying *no* to Thursday, you I trust understood that I meant *yes,* and so I do. In the meantime I send you the most delicious poem upon earth.[2] If you don't know what it is all about, or why, at least you will find glorious similes about everything in the world, and I defy you to discover three bad verses in the whole stack.[3] Dryden was but the prototype of *The Botanic Garden* in his charming 'Flower and Leaf';[4] and if he had less meaning, it is true he had more plan, and I must own that his white velvets and green velvets and

1. For reproductions of a ticket (Fanny Burney's), see Constance Hill, *Fanny Burney at the Court of Queen Charlotte*, 1912, facing p. 158, and Muriel Masefield, *Story of Fanny Burney*, Cambridge, 1927, p. 102.

1. 'No. 5' (B).
2. *The Botanic Garden, Part II, Containing The Loves of the Plants, A Poem. With Philosophical Notes. Volume the Second,* Lichfield and London, 1789, by Erasmus Darwin (1731–1802), physician, botanist, poet, and evolutionist; grandfather of Charles Darwin (James Venable Logan, *The Poetry and Aesthetics of Erasmus Darwin*, Princeton, 1936, p. 149 *et passim*). It was published about the last of March or first of April (advertised 'In a few days will be published,' *London Chronicle* 19–21, 26–8 March 1789). The citations that follow refer to the 2d edn, 1790. HW's copy was in the London sale, lot 1066.

3. HW wrote Hannah More 22 April 1789 that he found only 'a single bad verse: in the last canto one line ends *e'er long.*' He refers to l. 415, in which the linnet 'Chirps in the gaping shell, bursts forth erelong.' A more recent critic has estimated that ninety-nine per cent of Darwin's rhymes are 'blameless' (Logan, op. cit. 142, and the reference there cited).
4. Dryden's modernization of the poem formerly attributed to Chaucer, but now accepted as the work of an anonymous lady, ca 1450. The original has been called 'the most exquisite product of the fifteenth century' (Émile Legouis and Louis Cazamian, *A History of English Literature*, New York, 1929, p. 163), and Skeat considered Dryden's 'free' version 'finer than the original' (*Chaucerian and Other Pieces*, ed. W. W. Skeat, 1897, p. lxviii).

rubies and emeralds[5] were much more virtuous gentlefolks, than most of the flowers of the creation, who seem to have no fear of Doctors' Commons before their eyes. This is only the second part, for like my king's eldest daughter in the *Hieroglyphic Tales,* the first part is not born yet[6]—no matter; I can read this over and over again forever, for though it is so excellent, it is impossible to remember anything so disjointed, except you consider it as a collection of short enchanting poems,[7] as the Circæa and her tremendous devilries in a church;[8] the intrigue of the dear nightingale and rose;[9] and the description of Medea;[10] the episode of Mr Howard[11] which ends with the most sublime of lines[12]—in short all, all; all is the most lovely poetry—and then one sighs, that such profusion of poetry, magnificent and tender, should be thrown away on what neither interests nor instructs, and with all the pains the notes take to explain, is scarce intelligible.

How strange it is that a man should have been inspired with such enthusiasm of poetry by poring through a microscope,[13] and peeping through the keyholes of all the seraglios of all the flowers in the universe!—I hope his discoveries may leave any impression but of the universal polygamy going on in the vegetable world, where however it is more *galant* than amongst human race, for you will find that they are the botanic *ladies* who keep harems and not the *gentlemen*—Still, I

5. See especially ll. 160–6, 245–53, 266, 341–55 of Dryden's poem.

6. The second of HW's *Hieroglyphic Tales,* 'The King and His Three Daughters,' begins: 'There was formerly a king, who had three daughters—that is, he would have had three, if he had had one more—but somehow or other the eldest never was born' (*Works* iv. 330). Six copies and the revised copy of *Hieroglyphic Tales* were printed at SH in 1785 (*Journal of the Printing Office* 20, 69–71); the MS is now WSL. The first part of Darwin's poem did not appear until 1791.

7. Cf. Darwin's 'proem,' in which he tells the reader he may contemplate the poem 'as diverse little pictures suspended over the chimney of a lady's dressing room, connected only by a slight festoon of ribbons.'

8. See iii. 7–38, where Circæa (Enchanter's Night-Shade) and 'two imps obscene' enter a church.

'O'er the still choir with hideous laugh they move,
(Fiends yell below, and angels weep above!)

Their impious march to God's high altar bend,
With feet impure the sacred steps ascend;
With wine unbless'd the holy chalice stain,
Assume the mitre, and the cope profane;
To heaven their eyes in mock devotion throw,
And to the cross with horrid mummery bow;
Adjure by mimic rites the powers above,
And plight alternate their Satanic love.'

(ll. 29–38.)

9. iv. 305–20.

10. iii. 135–78. Medea and Jason appear also in i. 383–92.

11. John Howard (ca 1726–90), prison reformer and philanthropist.

12. The section on Howard (ii. 439–72) ends with ' "And murmuring Demons hate him, and admire." ' But HW may be thinking of the line that closes the first part of the episode: 'Thy Howard journeying seeks the house of woe' (l. 446).

13. MS reads 'miscrope.'

will maintain that it is much better that we should have *two* wives, than your sex two husbands—so pray don't mind Linnæus and Dr Darwin: Dr Madan[14] had ten times more sense. Adieu!

Your doubly constant

Telypthorus[15]

From Mary Berry, Wednesday 29 April 1789

Dated from the foregoing letter, to which this is a reply.
Address: Honourable Horace Walpole.

Somerset St, Wednesday morning, [April 29, 1789.]

A THOUSAND thanks for *The Botanic Garden.* The first thirty lines, which I have just read, are delicious, and make me quite anxious to go on, for I must at last own with blushes what I have hitherto concealed, perhaps improperly, from my husband: but as I *am* married it must at last come out that I was early initiated into all the amours and loose manners of the plants by that very guilty character, Dr Solander,[1] and passed too much time in the society and observance of some of the most abandoned vegetable coquettes. I hope my having long entirely forsaken all such odd company and lived a very regular life will in some degree apologize to you for my having been early led astray.

We rejoice in the hopes of seeing you tomorrow evening.

M. Berry

14. The Rev. (but not Dr) Martin Madan (1726–90), follower and correspondent of John Wesley, and friend of Lady Huntingdon; author of *Thelyphthora,* 1780, in favour of polygamy.

15. Mary Berry altered the signature to 'Thelypthorus.'

———

1. Daniel Charles Solander (1736–82), Swedish botanist; pupil of Linnæus; came to England, 1760; catalogued natural history collection at British Museum; accompanied Joseph Banks on Cook's voyage, 1768–71, and to Iceland, 1772; D.C.L. Oxford, 1771; keeper of the Natural History department of the British Museum, 1773. As he published nothing independently, Mary Berry may refer to his edition of Linnæus's *Elementa Botanica,* Upsala, 1756, or to the collection at the British Museum. It has not been found that Solander gave public lectures, or that the Berrys were acquainted with him.

The Misses Berry

MARY AND AGNES BERRY, BY PAUL SANDBY

To Mary and Agnes Berry, Tuesday 23 June 1789

Address: Missing, but probably the same as that for *post* 30 June 1789. Cf. the last section of this letter, under *Saturday.*

Strawberry Hill, Tuesday, June 23, 1789.[1]

I AM not a little disappointed and mortified at the post bringing me no letter from you today; you promised to write on the road.[2] I reckon you arrived at your station[3] on Sunday evening: if you do not write till next day, I shall have no letter till Thursday![4]

I am not at all consoled for my double loss: my only comfort is, that I flatter myself the journey and air will be of service to you both—the latter has been of use to me, though the part of the element of air has been chiefly acted by the element of water, as my poor haycocks feel![5] Tonton[6] does not miss you so much as I do, not having so good a taste, for he is grown very fond of *me*, and I return it for your sakes, though he deserves it too, for he is perfectly good-natured and tractable—but he is not beautiful like his *god-dog*, as Mr Selwyn, who dined here on Saturday,[7] called my poor late favourite;[8] especially as I have had him clipped; the shearing has brought to light a nose an ell long; and as he has now *nasum rhinocerotis*, I do not doubt but he will be a better critic in poetry than Dr Johnson, who judged of harmony by the principles of an author, and fancied, or wished to make others believe, that no Jacobite could write bad verses, nor a Whig good.[9]

1. 'No. 6' (B).
2. To Yorkshire, where the Berrys were to visit friends and relatives (see *post*). They left London Wednesday 17 June (HW to Lady Ossory, ca 15 June 1789).
3. Presumably the seat of Thomas Cayley at Middleton near Pickering (see address to *post* 30 June 1789).
4. A letter posted at York before 10:30 P.M. on Monday would leave at midnight and would reach London about 4:00 A.M. Wednesday (distance, 197 miles; average speed of mail coaches, seven miles per hour), too late to be included in the Wednesday post to Twickenham (*Universal British Directory*, 1791–8, iv. 969; Herbert Joyce, *History of the Post Office*, 1893, p. 290; *post* 19 July, 6 Aug. 1789, 2 Oct. 1793).
5. Storms and heavy rains were general in England during the last half of June and

the first half of July (see GM 1789, lix pt ii. 665, 754). Cf. *post* 10 July 1789.
6. 'A dog of the Miss Berrys, left in Mr Walpole's care during their absence in Yorkshire' (B, MBJ i. 164).
7. Lady Ossory and her 'two lady daughters,' Lady Anne and Lady Gertrude Fitzpatrick, planned to accompany Selwyn, but, according to 'Visitors,' Lady Ossory was accompanied by Lord Ossory's niece, Hon. Caroline Fox (HW to Lady Ossory, ca 15 June, 22 June 1789).
8. 'The dog which had been bequeathed to Mr Walpole by Madame du Deffand at her death, and which was likewise called Tonton' (B, Wright vi. 315). For Tonton (1773–17 Feb. 1789), a black spaniel, see DU DEFFAND, *passim;* HW to Lady Ossory 24 Feb. 1789; Toynbee, *Supp.* ii. 179.
9. Cf. Johnson's *Lives of the Poets, passim.* For HW's considered estimate of John-

I passed so many evenings of the last fortnight with you,[10] that I almost preferred it to our two honeymoons,[11] and consequently am the more sensible to the deprivation—and how dismal was *Sunday* evening compared to those of last autumn![12] If you both felt as I do, we might surpass any event in the annals of Dunmow:[13] Oh! what a prodigy it would be if a husband and *two wives* should present themselves and demand the flitch of bacon on swearing that not one of the three in a year and a day had wished to be unmarried! For my part I know that my affection has done nothing but increase; though, were there but one of you, I should be ashamed of being so strongly attached at my age. Being in love with both, I glory in my passion, and think it a proof of my sense. Why should not two affirmatives make a negative, as well as the reverse? and then a double love will be wisdom—for what is wisdom in reality but a negative? It exists but by correcting folly; and when it has peevishly prevailed on us to abstain from something we have a mind to, it gives itself airs, and inaction pretends to be a personage, a nonentity sets up for a figure of importance. It is the case of most of those phantoms called virtues, which by smothering poor vices, claim a reward as thief-takers do. You know I have a partiality for drunkenness, though I never practised it: it is a reality—but what is sobriety, only the absence of drunkenness!—however, *mes chères femmes,* I make a difference between women and men, and do not extend my doctrine to your sex. Everything is excusable in us, and nothing in you—and pray remember, that I will not lose my flitch of bacon —*though.*[14]

Have you shed a tear over the Opera House?[15] or do you agree with

son, see his 'General Criticism on Dr Johnson's Writings,' *Works* iv. 361–2.

10. In London, where HW, after recovering from a fit of the gout which confined him throughout May, remained until the Berrys left for Yorkshire (see HW to Gough 28 May; to Sir John Fenn 1 June; to Mrs Carter 13 June; to Lady Ossory, ca 15 June 1789).

11. Cf. *ante* 11 April 1789.

12. 'This delightful family [the Berrys] comes to me almost every Sunday evening' (HW to Lady Ossory 11 Oct. 1788).

13. According to a custom said to have been instituted *ante* 1234 and still occasionally observed at Dunmow, Essex, any couple who had been married for a year and a day, and could swear to perfect harmony and

fidelity for that period, were given a flitch of bacon. During the eighteenth century three couples, two in 1701 and one in 1751, were rewarded, and in 1772 another couple who claimed the flitch were turned away by the lord of the manor. In 1778 a ballad opera by Henry Bates, *The Flitch of Bacon* (published 1779), was acted at the Haymarket Theatre. See William Andrews, *History of the Dunmow Flitch of Bacon Custom,* 1877, *passim.*

14. An imitation of Mrs Piozzi's use of the word (see following letter).

15. The Opera House, or King's Theatre in the Haymarket, designed by Sir John Vanbrugh, burnt down on the night of 18 June (GM 1789, lix pt ii. 755–6). The first stone of its successor was laid 3 April 1790

me, that there is no occasion to rebuild it? The nation has long been tired of operas, and has now a good opportunity of dropping them. Dancing protracted their existence for some time—but *the room-after* was the real support of both, and was like what has been said of your sex, that they never speak their true meaning but in the postscript of their letters. Would not it be sufficient to build an *after-room* on the whole emplacement, to which people might resort from all assemblies! It should be a codicil to all the diversions of London; and the greater the concourse, the more excuse there would be for staying all night, from the impossibility of ladies getting their coaches to drive up. To be crowded to death in a waiting room at the end of an entertainment is the whole joy; for who goes to any diversion till the last minute of it? I am persuaded that instead of retrenching St Athanasius's[16] Creed, as the Duke of Grafton[17] proposed, in order to draw *good company* to church,[18] it would be more efficacious, if the congregation were to be indulged with an after-room in the vestry; and instead of *two or three being gathered together*, there would be *all the world*, before prayers would be quite over.

by the Earl of Buckinghamshire (GM 1790, lx pt i. 563). In June 1789 Mrs Damer wrote to Sir Charles Hotham: 'You know by this time that the poor Opera House is no more; people say that 'tis lucky, and I know not what, and that there will be a better, but I regret it: it was an old acquaintance, and to it I owe many pleasant hours. I have one *comfort*, however, which is that I saw it burned, and so fine a sight! it is far beyond description—from the top of Cosway's house in Pall Mall did I see it, perched between the Golden Sun and the statue of Minerva. I hope you recollect them' (A. M. W. Stirling, *The Hothams*, 1918, ii. 244).

16. MS reads 'Athanius's.'

17. Augustus Henry Fitzroy (1735–1811), 3d D. of Grafton, who late in life was attracted to Unitarianism and wrote pamphlets promulgating its doctrines.

18. HW refers to a passage in an anonymous pamphlet by the Duke of Grafton, *Hints, &c. Submitted to the Serious Attention of the Clergy, Nobility and Gentry, Newly Associated*, by a Layman, 1788 (see *Monthly Review*, Feb. 1789, lxxx. 186); 2d edn, 'revised, with additions,' 1789. Because of the illness of George III, the first edition was called in after very few copies

had been sold. The following passages occur in the 2d edn (HW's copy, now WSL, is bound in vol. 52 of *Tracts of Geo. 3;* on the title-page HW wrote: 'by A. Henry Duke of Grafton'): '. . . the Creed, under the name of Athanasius, has given more offence, and for a longer time, than any other part of our service; not because it appears there under a feigned name, but as it holds forth doctrines derogatory to the honour of God, a merciful and all-powerful Creator' (p. 31). HW's phrase, 'to draw *good company* to church,' states the author's purpose more baldly than his words in the pamphlet, but the sense is identical: To show that 'the mass of the people can never be brought to have a proper sense of their duty to God and their neighbour, until they shall see in their superiors more attention paid to religion in general, and particularly, by a more constant and zealous attendance on *public* divine worship' (p. 3). Revision of the liturgy, 'retrenching' St Athanasius's Creed, etc., he believes will attract the 'fine world' (p. 10) to more regular church attendance. As the author foresaw (ibid.), his views subjected him to the 'derision of many,' and he was attacked and ridiculed in anonymous pamphlets (see DNB).

Wednesday.

I calculated too rightly; no letter today!—yet I am not proud of my computation; I had rather have heard of you today; it would have looked like keeping your promise—it has a bad air, your forgetting me so early! Nay, and after your scoffing me for supposing you would not write till your arrival I don't know where! You see I think of *you* and write every day, though I cannot dispatch my letter, till you have sent me a direction. Much the better I am indeed for your not going to Swisserland! Yorkshire is in the glaciers for me! and you are as cold as Mr Palmer.[19] Miss *Agnes* was coy, and was not so flippant of promising me letters—well, but I do trust *she will* write, and then, Madam, she and I will go to Dunmow without you. Apropos, as Mrs Cambridge's[20] beauty has kept so unfaded, and Mr Cambridge's passion is so undiminished,[21] and as they are good economists, I am astonished they have laid in no stock of bacon, when they could have it for asking!

Thursday night.

Despairing beside a clear stream
A shepherd forsaken was laid—[22]

not very close to the stream, but within doors in sight of it, for in this damp weather a lame old Colin cannot lie and despair with any comfort on a wet bank—but I smile against the grain, and am seriously alarmed at Thursday being come and no letter! I dread one of you being ill, and then shall detest the D. of Northumberland's[23] rapacious

---

19. Possibly '——— Palmer, Esq.,' HW's neighbour in Berkeley Square (*Directory to the Nobility, Gentry . . . for 1793*).

20. Mary Trenchard (ca 1717–1806), dau. of George Trenchard of Woolveton, Dorset; m. (1740) Richard Owen Cambridge (1717–1802), son of Nathaniel Cambridge of Whitminster, Glos. Their son, George Owen Cambridge, refers to Mrs Cambridge's 'beauty of . . . person . . . cheerful temper, and pleasing manners . . . a peculiar delicacy of form . . . [combined] with an uncommon strength of constitution' (*The Works of Richard Owen Cambridge*, 1803, p. x). Cambridge was HW's contemporary at Eton. In 1751 he bought a house in Twickenham Meadows, near Richmond and across the Thames from Rich-

mond Hill, where he lived for the remainder of his life (R. S. Cobbett, *Memorials of Twickenham*, 1872, pp. 95, 236–40; Richard D. Altick, *Richard Owen Cambridge*, Philadelphia, 1941).

21. Cambridge told Fanny Burney in 1783 that 'to and at this moment there is no sight so pleasing to me as seeing Mrs Cambridge enter a room; and that after having been married to her for forty years' (*Diary and Letters of Madame D'Arblay*, ed. Charlotte Barrett and Austin Dobson, 1904–5, ii. 220, quoted in Altick, op. cit. 12).

22. Nicholas Rowe, 'Colin's Complaint,' ll. 1–2.

23. Hugh Percy (Smithson before 1750) (1742–1817), 2d D. of Northumberland (n.c.), 1786.

steward[24] more than ever. Mr Batt[25] and the Abbé Nichols[26] dined with me today, and I could talk of you *en pays de connaissance*. They tried to persuade me that I have no cause to be in a fright about you; but I have such perfect faith in the kindness of both of you, as I have in your possessing every other virtue, that I cannot believe but some sinister accident must have prevented my hearing from you. I wish Friday was come! I cannot write about anything else till I have a letter.

Friday 26.

My anxiety increases daily, for still I have no letter. You cannot all three be ill, and if any one is, I should flatter myself, another would have written, or if any accident has happened. Next to your having met with some ill luck, I should be mortified at being forgotten so suddenly. Of any other vexation I have no fear. So much goodness and good sense as you both possess, would make me perfectly easy, if I were really your husband. I must then suspect some accident, and shall have no tranquillity till a letter puts me out of pain. Jealous I am not, for two young ladies cannot have run away with their father to Gretna

24. Henry Collingwood Selby (ca 1748–1839) of Swansfield, near Alnwick, Northumberland; of Gray's Inn (admitted 1770; called to the bar 1777; twice treasurer); clerk of the peace for Middlesex 1777–1838; sometime alderman of Alnwick (GM 1839, n.s. xi. 662; George Tate, *History of . . . Alnwick*, 1866–9, ii. 65, 324). He is mentioned as early as 1777 as steward to the 1st Duke of Northumberland (ibid. ii. 296), and in 1817, in the account of the funeral of the 2d Duke, as 'the Duke's secretary' (GM 1817, lxxxvii pt ii. 84). The Berrys had rented his house on Twickenham Common in 1788 (*ante* 1 Nov. 1788), and evidently he had charged an exorbitant price, or wished to rent it in 1789 at a higher price, which the Berrys were unwilling to pay (*post* 6, 20 Aug. 1789). HW's charge of rapacity and avarice (*post* 20 Aug. 1789) is supported by Selby's conduct in a legal battle at Alnwick 1777–87 (Tate, ii. 295–301), but a more agreeable side of his character is shown by his entertainment of the apprentices at Alnwick (ibid. ii. 324) and his benefaction to the town (ibid. ii. 152).

25. John Thomas Batt (1746–1831), son of John Thomas Batt, M.D., of Westminster; Westminster School and Christ Church, Oxford (B.A. 1766); admitted to Lincoln's Inn, 1763; called to the bar, 1770; a commissioner of bankrupts ca 1775–85; through friendship with the younger Pitt, appointed a commissioner for auditing the public accounts 1785–1807; clerk of the Crown for the County Palatine of Lancaster ca 1794–1831; F.S.A., 1795; friend and executor of Gibbon and Archbishop Markham; among Fanny Burney's 'high favourites'; considered a good classical scholar and conversationalist; inherited property from his uncle in 1792, and lived thereafter at New Hall, near Salisbury, Wilts, and in London (*Old Westminsters* and *Supp.;* GM 1831, ci pt i. 274; *Diary and Letters of Madame D'Arblay*, ed. Charlotte Barrett and Austin Dobson, 1904–5, v. 85; *Royal Kalendar* 1775–1831; *post* 26 July 1791).

26. Rev. Norton Nicholls (ca 1742–1809), friend and correspondent of Gray from 1762, Nicholls then being an undergraduate at Cambridge. He became rector of Lound and Bradwell in Suffolk, 1767, and accompanied Gray on a tour through the midland counties, 1770 (*Gray's Corr.*, *passim*). On first acquaintance with Nicholls, HW thought highly of him, but gradually tired of his gossip.

Green. Hymen, O Hymenæe, bring me good news tomorrow, and a direction too, or you do nothing!

Saturday.

Io pæan! Io Tonton!—at last I have got a letter, and you are all well! and I am so pleased, that I forget the four uneasy days I have passed—at present I have neither time or paper to say more, for our post turns on its heel and goes out the instant it is come in. I am in some distress still, for, thoughtless creature, you have sent me no direction—Luckily Lady Cecilia[27] told me yesterday you had bidden her direct to you to be left at the post-house at York, which was more than you told me; but I will venture. If you do receive this, I beseech you never forget, as you move about, to send me new directions.

Do not be frightened at the enormity of this—I do not mean to continue so four-paginous in every letter. Mr C.[28] is this instant come in—and would damp me, if I were going to scribble more. Adieu, adieu! adieu! all three.

Your dutiful son-in-law and most affectionate husband,

H. W.

PS. I beg pardon, I see on the last page of your letter there is a direction.

To Mary Berry, Tuesday 30 June 1789

Address: To Miss Mary Berry, to be left at the Post House, York. [Redirected in unknown hand: 'at Thos Cayley's Esq., at Middleton near Pickering.'][1] *Postmark:* 30 JU 89.

27. Lady Henrietta Cecilia West (1727–1817), dau. of John, 7th Bn, cr. (1761) E. De La Warr; m. (1762) Col. (afterwards Gen.) James Johnston. Her beauty, wit, vanity, absurdity, and pride in her husband are mentioned by her contemporaries (see Montagu i. 269; *Murray's Magazine*, 1887, i. 488; *Letters of Lady Louisa Stuart to Miss Louisa Clinton*, ed. Hon. James A. Home, 1st Ser., Edinburgh, 1901, p. 180). In the 1780's and 1790's she was frequently satirized as an elderly leader of fashion (see BM, *Satiric Prints*).

28. Richard Owen Cambridge.

1. Thomas Cayley (1732–92), who succeeded his father in 1791 as 5th Baronet, of High Hall, Brompton, married (1763) the eldest maternal aunt of the Misses Berry, Isabella Seton (d. 1828). Mrs Seton, mother of Mrs Cayley, and grandmother of the Misses Berry, lived with the Cayleys (see below). Pickering is 32½ miles NE of York; Middleton is 1¼ miles NW of Pickering.

Strawberry Hill, June 30, 1789.[2]

I AM more an old Fondlewife[3] than I suspected, when I could put
myself into such a fright on not hearing from you exactly on the day
I had settled I should—but you had[4] promised to write on the road;
and though you did, your letter was not sent to the post at the first
stage, as Almighty Love had concluded it would be, and as Almighty
Love would have done; and so he imagined some dreadful calamity
must have happened to you—but you are safe under grand-maternal
wings,[5] and I will say no more on what has not happened. Pray, present
my duty to Grandmama, and let her know what a promising young
grandson she has got.

Were there any such thing as sympathy at the distance of two hundred miles, you would have been in a mightier panic than I was, for on
Saturday sennight[6] going to open the glass case in the Tribune,[7] my
foot caught in the carpet and I fell with my whole weight (*si* weight
y a) against the corner of the marble altar, on my side, and bruised the
muscles so badly, that for two days I could not move without scream-
ing. I am convinced I should have broken a rib, but that I fell on the
cavity whence two of my ribs were removed, that are gone to Yorkshire.[8] I am much better both of my bruise and my lameness, and shall
be ready to dance at my own wedding, when my wives return. Philip,[9]
who has been prowling about by my order, has found a clever house,
but it is on Ham Common,[10] and that is too far off; and I think Papa
Berry does not like that side of the water, and he is in the right. Philip

2. 'No. 7' (B).

3. The uxorious old husband in Congreve's *The Old Bachelor*.

4. HW wrote 'had you.'

5. Cf. n. 1 above. Elizabeth Seton (1719–
97), dau. of James Seton of Belsies (Belshes
or Belsislands), Haddingtonshire or East
Lothian; m. her cousin, the representative
of the Parbroath line of the family, John
Seton (1712–d. before 1760), of Camberwell,
Surrey, and of London; buried in the Cayley vault at Brompton, Yorks. For her portrait in 1785, and for extracts from her letters to her son William, founder of the
New York branch of the family, see Robert
Seton, *An Old Family*, New York, 1899, pp.
240–3, 255–64.

6. 20 June, the night Selwyn, Lady Ossory and her family dined at SH.

7. There was a glass case on each side of
the marble altar in the Tribune. Both cases
contained rings, seals, jewels, snuff-boxes,
and many other curiosities (see 'Des. of SH,'
Works ii. 470–1, 478–86, and the print facing p. 470; 'Genesis of SH' fig. 25).

8. 'As I did not break a rib, I have only
lost the two that are gone to Yorkshire'
(HW to Lady Ossory 22 June 1789).

9. Philip Colomb (d. 1799), HW's Swiss
valet, to whom he left in his will an annuity
of £25, £1500 outright, 'all my wearing apparel as well linen as silken and woollen'
and 'my copyhold messuage or tenement
. . . called the Walnut Tree House' in
Twickenham (DU DEFFAND iii. 89–90).

10. Across the Thames, and about a mile
from SH.

shall hunt again and again, till he puts up better game—now to answer
your letter.

If you grow tired of the *Arabian Nights*,[11] you have no more taste
than Bishop Atterbury,[12] who huffed Pope for sending him them or the
Persian Tales,[13] and fancied he liked Virgil better,[14] who had no more
imagination than Dr Akenside.[15] Read Sinbad the Sailor's voyages, and
you will be sick of Aeneas's: what woeful invention were the nasty
poultry that dunged on his dinner,[16] and ships on fire turned into
Nereids[17]—a barn metamorphosed into a cascade in a pantomime is
full as sublime an effort of genius.[18] I do not know whether the *Arabian
Nights* are of Oriental origin or not:[19] I should think not, because I
never saw any other Oriental composition that was not bombast with-

11. Perhaps she was reading HW's copy
(6 vols, 1736, sold SH iii. 15).

12. Francis Atterbury (1662–1732), Bishop
of Rochester 1713–23; deprived of his offices and banished for his loyalty to the
House of Stuart; correspondent of Pope and
Swift.

13. In his letter of 23 Sept. 1720 Pope
mentioned that he was sending some 'tales,'
and in his reply, undated, Atterbury says:
'And now, Sir, for your *Arabian Tales*. . . .
I have read as much of them as ever I shall
read while I live. Indeed they do not please
my taste; they are writ with so romantic an
air, and, allowing for the difference of eastern manners, are yet, upon any supposition
that can be made, of so wild and absurd a
contrivance, (at least to my northern understanding,) that I have not only no pleasure,
but no patience, in perusing them. They
are to me like the odd paintings on Indian
screens, which at first glance may surprise
and please a little; when you fix your eye
intently upon them, they appear so extravagant, disproportioned, and monstrous,
that they give a judicious eye pain, and
make him seek for relief from some other
object. . . . To read those two volumes
through . . . would be a terrible penance.
. . . Who that *Petit de la Croise* is, the pretended author of them, I cannot tell.' HW
read this in *The Epistolary Correspondence . . . of the Right Reverend Francis
Atterbury, D.D., Lord Bishop of Rochester*,
1783, i. 68–70. His copy is now wsl, and although he read this passage with enough
attention to appropriate the figure of the
Indian screen (see below), he thought so

little of the book that he left it in its original boards. Atterbury's letter is reprinted
in Pope, *Works,* ed. Elwin and Courthope,
ix. 22–3. Since in 1720 there was apparently
no edition of the *Arabian Nights* in two
volumes (Victor Chauvin, *Bibliographie des
ouvrages arabes,* Liége et Leipzig, 1892–
1922, iv. 70–4), Atterbury presumably refers to the English translation of *The Persian and the Turkish Tales,* 2 vols, 1714 (or
a later edition). This translation was made
from *Les Mille et un jours. Contes persans,*
a translation by François Pétis de la Croix
(1653–1713) and others from the original.

14. Atterbury did not say so. HW was
probably thinking of Pope's remark in his
letter to Atterbury 23 Sept. 1720: 'Your
Lordship may criticize from Virgil to these
tales; as Solomon wrote of everything, from
the cedar to the hyssop' (*Works,* ed. Elwin
and Courthope, ix. 19–20). In his correspondence with Pope, Atterbury frequently
quotes or refers to Virgil, and he translated Virgil's First Eclogue (see his *Epistolary Correspondence,* 1783–98, iii. 503–7).

15. Mark Akenside (1721–70), poet and
physician, author of *The Pleasures of Imagination,* 1744, rewritten and published as
The Pleasures of the Imagination, 1757.

16. *Æneid* iii. 219–28.

17. Ibid. ix. 1–122, especially ll. 80–122.

18. HW is thinking of some of the meta-
morphoses of Rich; see *post* 27 Sept. 1794.

19. Although the framework is Persian,
most of the tales are Arabian, and were
probably collected by a professional story-
teller in Egypt sometime between the fourteenth and sixteenth centuries.

out genius, and figurative without nature, like an Indian screen, where you see little men on the foreground, and larger men hunting tigers above in the air, which they take for perspective. I do not think the Sultaness's[20] narratives very natural or very probable, but there is a wildness in them that captivates. However, if you could wade through two octavos of Dame Piozzi's[21] *though's* and *so's,* and *I trow's,*[22] and cannot listen to seven volumes[23] of Scheherezade's narrations, I will sue for a divorce *in foro Parnassi,* and Boccalini[24] shall be my proctor. The cause will be a counterpart to the sentence of the Lacedæmonian, who was condemned for breach of the peace by saying in three words what he might have said in two.[25]

You are not the first Eurydice that has sent her husband to the devil, as you have kindly proposed to me;[26] but I will not undertake the

20. Scheherazade's, in the *Arabian Nights.*

21. Hester Lynch Salusbury (1741–1821), only child of John Salusbury of Bachycraig, Flintshire; m. (1) (1763) Henry Thrale; m. (2) (1784) Gabriel Piozzi, an Italian musician; published *Anecdotes of the Late Samuel Johnson,* 1786, and correspondence with him, 1788. HW refers to her *Observations and Reflections Made in the Course of a Journey through France, Italy, and Germany,* 2 vols, published 4 June (see *The World* 18 May, 2, 4 June 1789). See also HW to Mrs Carter 13 June 1789. HW's copy was sold SH v. 186.

22. Of Mrs Piozzi's use of 'though,' 'so,' and 'I trow,' that of 'so' is by far the most noticeable. In the two volumes totalling 831 pages, including the preface, she uses 'so' more than 750 times, as many as five (i. 149, 183, 362; ii. 100, 327, 375), six (i. 87), seven (i. 173; ii. 115), and even eight (ii. 74) times to a page. HW probably objected most to its use as an intensive: cloth that 'would make one *so* happy in London' (i. 257); 'the other is *so* discriminated, *so* tasteful, *so* classical!' (i. 414); a statue '*so* beautiful!' (ii. 142) and Antwerp '*so* melancholy' (ii. 380); 'she liked England *so,* and the King and Queen were *so* kind to her, and she was *so* happy, she said' (ii. 313). (Mary Berry was guilty of the same fault, as appears from a passage in her *Comparative View of Social Life in England and France,* 1844, i. 233, where she mentions Pope's abuse of Lady

Mary Wortley Montagu, 'whom he had professed *so* to admire.') A passage in the preceding letter indicates that HW particularly disliked 'though' as used in passages such as: 'It is time to have done with all this though' (ii. 208); 'no people in the town almost except soldiers though' (ii. 353); 'a beautiful building though after all' (i. 342); 'a very slight one though' (i. 422). Only one example of Mrs Piozzi's use of 'I trow' has been found: 'That such enchantresses should inhabit such regions could have been scarce a wonder in Homer's time I trow' (ii. 92–3). Mrs Elizabeth Carter found the style 'sometimes elegant, sometimes colloquial and vulgar, and strangely careless in the grammatical part' (*Letters . . . to Mrs Montagu,* ed. Montagu Pennington, 1817, iii. 314).

23. Six volumes, if she was reading HW's set (*ante* n. 11). No edition in seven volumes has been found.

24. Traiano Boccalini (1556–1613), Italian satirist, author of *De' Ragguagli di Parnaso,* Venice, 1612–13, 'in which Apollo is represented as receiving the complaints of all who present themselves, and distributing justice according to the merits of each particular case' (*Encyclopædia Britannica,* 14th edn). HW's copy was in two volumes, Amsterdam, 1669; sold SH iii. 179.

25. See *De' Ragguagli di Parnaso, Centuria prima, Ragguaglio VI.*

26. Unexplained, in the absence of Mary Berry's letter.

jaunt, for if old Nicholas Pluto should enjoin me not to look back to you, I should certainly forget the prohibition like my predecessor. Besides I am a little too old to take a voyage twice, which I am so soon to repeat; and should be laughed at by the good folks on the other side of the water, if I proposed coming back for a twinkling only. No, I choose as long as I can

> Still with my fav'rite Berries to remain.[27]

So you was not quite satisfied, though you ought to have been transported with King's College Chapel because it has no aisles, like every common cathedral[28]—I suppose you would object to a bird of paradise, because it has no legs, but shoots to heaven in a *trait,* and does not rest on earth.[29] Criticism and comparison spoil many tastes. You should admire all bold and unique essays that resemble nothing else—*The Botanic Garden,* the *Arabian Nights* and King's Chapel are above all rules, and how preferable is what no one can imitate to all that is imitated even from the best models! Your partiality to the pageantry of Popery I do approve, and I doubt whether the world will not be a loser (in its visionary enjoyments) by the extinction of that religion, as it was by the decay of chivalry and the proscription of the heathen deities.[30] Reason has no invention; and as plain sense will never be the legislator of human affairs, it is fortunate when taste happens to be regent.—But now I must talk of family affairs. I am delighted that my next letter is to come from Wife the Second.[31] I love her as much as you —nay, and I am sure you like that I should. I should not love either so much, if your affection for each other were not so mutual. I observe

27. 'A line from some verses that he had received' (B, Wright vi. 320). See *ante* 1 Nov. 1788.

28. Mary Berry wrote in her journal 18 Oct. 1809: 'Walked to King's College Chapel. The small towers on the outside very light and beautiful. The inside struck me much more than it did in the year 1786 [?1789], when I first saw it. I did not feel so much the want of the intersecting arches of aisles as I remember I did then. It is disfigured by an organ-loft of the worst style of Henry VIII; sort of sprigged pilasters. The painted glass windows very fine. The east window, though very large, not remarkable for the beauty of its tracery' (MBJ ii. 397).

29. MS reads 'does not to rest on earth.'

Cf. John Latham's account of birds of paradise in his *General Synopsis of Birds,* 3 vols, 1781-5, quoted in the *Encyclopædia Britannica,* 3d edn, Edinburgh, 1797, xiii, *sub* Paradisea: 'The whole of this genus have, till lately, been very imperfectly known . . . nor has any set of birds given rise to more fables . . . such as, their never touching the ground from their birth to death; living wholly on the dew; being produced without legs. . . . This last error is scarcely at this moment wholly eradicated.' See also Alfred Newton, *Dictionary of Birds,* 1893-6, *sub* Bird of Paradise.

30. Cf. Cole ii. 100.

31. Agnes Berry's letter and HW's reply (4 July) are missing.

and watch all your ways and doings, and the more I observe you, the more virtues I discover in both—nay, depend upon it, if I discern a fault, you shall hear of it. You came too perfect into my hands, to let you be spoiled by indulgence. All the world admires you, yet you have contracted no vanity, advertise no pretensions; are simple and good as nature made you, in spite of all your improvements—mind, *you* and *yours* are always, from *my* lips and pen, of what grammarians call *the common of two,* and signify *both:* so I shall repeat that memorandum no more.

Your friends Lady Harriot Conyers[32] and Lady Juliana Penn have again settled in our environs, the former within a few paces of Lady Cecilia,[33] the latter in the parsonage of Hanworth,[34] where she must be content, in an evening, with the House of St Albans,[35] who are not quite in her style; for the Heath[36] at night will terrify all the lozenges[37] in the neighbourhood. Your friends are charming, but will not comfort me for what I have lost!

Mrs Anderson,[38] who you know arrived too late, described the ad-

---

32. Lady Henrietta Fermor (1727–93), older sister of Lady Juliana Penn; m. (1747) John Conyers (ca 1718–75) of Copt Hall in Essex (Collins, *Peerage*, 1812, iv. 207).

33. Lady Cecilia Johnston lived at Hampton (see *post* 8 June 1791).

34. About two miles SW of Twickenham, across Hounslow Heath. The rector from 1778 to 1804 was Robert Burd Gabriel (ca 1750–1804) of Worcester College, Oxford (B.A. 1770, B.D. 1781, D.D. 1784), who at this time was 'proprietor and preacher at the Octagon Chapel, Bath.' He was the author of a pamphlet, *Facts Relating to the Reverend Dr White's Bampton Lectures,* published 31 Oct. 1789 (Joseph Foster, *Alumni Oxonienses . . . 1715–1886,* 1887–8; GM 1804, lxxiv pt ii. 1250; *Facts . . . Lectures,* pp. 10, 13, 84; *Oracle. Bell's New World* 27, 31 Oct., 2 Nov. 1789).

35. The Duke and Duchess of St Albans: Aubrey Beauclerk (1740–1802), 2d Bn Vere of Hanworth, 1781, and 5th D. of St Albans, 1787; m. (1763) Catharine Ponsonby (1742–89), 1st dau. of 2d E. of Bessborough. The Duchess died 4 Sept. 1789 and was buried at Hanworth (cf. *post* 27 Aug. 1789). Their house, Hanworth House, was burned down 26 March 1797 (GM 1797, lxvii pt i. 247–8).

36. Hounslow Heath.

37. I.e., the carriages of dowagers, on which their arms were emblazoned in 'lozenges.' See OED.

38. Caroline Georgina Johnston (ca 1764–1823), only surviving dau. of Gen. James and Lady Cecilia Johnston; m. (1780) after eloping with him, Francis Evelyn Anderson (1752–1821), 2d son of Francis Anderson of Manby, Lincs, and brother of Charles Anderson (-Pelham from 1763), cr. (1794) Bn Yarborough. Anderson entered the army, 1770, attained the rank of lieutenant-colonel, 1794, and from 1783 until his death was major (on half-pay) of the 85th Regiment of Foot. He was M.P. for Great Grimsby 1773–80, and for Beverley 1780–4 (Collins, *Peerage,* 1812, viii. 397; *The Marriage, Baptismal, and Burial Registers of the Collegiate Church or Abbey of St Peter, Westminster,* ed. Joseph Lemuel Chester, 1876, p. 460 n.; Burke, *Peerage,* 1928, p. 2469; GM 1821, xci pt ii. 286; *Annual Register,* 1823, lxv pt ii. 199; *Army Lists*). The mother of James Harris, afterwards Lord Malmesbury, described the Andersons at the time of their elopement, 27 March 1780: 'Miss J. is very pretty, tall and genteel, but a most thorough chip of the old block—I mean her mother; and I wish Anderson much good of her. She is but sixteen years old. . . . For the General I am really sorry, but Miss

venture of Major Dixon[39] to the Duchess of Gloucester,[40] and diverted her with it exceedingly; but I immediately found out that she had related it as if he had talked French the whole time, though not a word had passed in that language. This showed her parts and invention.[41]

What a confusion of seasons! The haymakers are turning my soaked hay, which is fitter for a water-souchy, and I sit by the fire every night when I come home—Adieu! I dare not tap a fourth page, for when talking to you, I know not how to stop.

To Mary Berry, Friday 3 July 1789

Missing. See *post* 6 Aug. 1789.

To Agnes Berry, Saturday 4 July 1789

Missing. See *post* 6 Aug. 1789.

To Mary Berry, Thursday 9 July 1789

Address: To Miss Mary Berry to be left at the Post House at York. [Redirected in unknown hand: 'Thos Cayley's, Esq., Middleton near Pickering.']
Postmark: 9 JY 89.

and Mamma never seemed content with each other. General Johnstone is a good sort of man in many respects, and was fond of this girl to a degree. Lady Cecilia you know well: a most entertaining woman she is at times' (*A Series of Letters of the First Earl of Malmesbury . . . from 1745 to 1820,* ed. by his grandson, the Earl of Malmesbury, 1870, i. 456–7). Cf. *Delany Corr.* v. 516–18. HW's phrase, 'arrived too late,' is evidently to emphasize Mrs Anderson's lack of punctuality.

39. A character assumed by Edward Jerningham, the poet, friend and correspondent of HW (see *post* 4 Sept. 1789 and n. 39). The nature of his 'adventures' has not been found. Ten of Mrs Anderson's letters to Jerningham are printed in *Edward Jerningham and His Friends,* ed. Lewis Bettany, 1919, pp. 141–5.

40. HW's niece, Maria Walpole (1736–1807), illegitimate dau. of Sir Edward Walpole by Dorothy Clements; m. (1) (1759) James, 2d E. Waldegrave; m. (2) (1766) Wil-

liam Henry, D. of Gloucester, brother of George III.

41. William Johnston Temple dined 25 Sept. 1795 at Yarmouth with General Johnston and Mrs Anderson. He was delighted with Mrs Anderson's 'wit and parts; a person of very uncommon talents. An admirable painter of character and an excellent mimic, nothing escapes her penetrating eye and discernment: what an entertaining detail she gave of her own life and with what a mixture of candour, pleasantry and sensibility! and how admirably did she portray the General's family! The defects and weaknesses she seizes and ridicules in others, prove the correctness of her own taste and the generosity and nobleness of her own mind and heart' (*Diaries,* ed. Lewis Bettany, Oxford, 1929, p. 143). Apparently his first impression of her was not so favourable (ibid. 142–3). For HW's further reference to her talent for mimicry, see *post* 3 April 1791.

Strawberry Hill, July 9, 1789.[1]

Y OU are so good and punctual, that I will complain no more of
your silence—unless you are silent. You must not relax, especially
till you can give me better accounts of your health and spirits. I was
peevish before with the weather, but now it prevents your riding, I
forget hay and roses and all the comforts that are washed away, and
shall only watch the weathercock for an east wind in Yorkshire. What
a shame that *I* should recover from the gout and from bruises,[2] as I assure you I am entirely, and that *you* should have a complaint left! One
would think that it was *I* was grown young again, for just now, as I
was reading your letter in my bedchamber, while some of my *customers*[3] are seeing the house, I heard a gentleman in the Armoury ask
the housekeeper[4] as he looked at the bows and arrows,[5] 'Pray does Mr
Walpole shoot?'—No, nor with pistols neither. I leave all weapons to
Lady Salisbury[6] and Mr Lenox,[7] and since my double marriage have

1. 'No. 8' (B).
2. See *ante* 30 June 1789.
3. 'The name given by Mr Walpole to
parties coming to view his house' (B,
Wright vi. 323). His 'customers' for 9 July
were '4 from Mr Roffey' ('Visitors').
4. Ann Bransom, to whom HW left £100
in his will.
5. Among the curiosities in the Armoury
were 'two Indian quivers, full of arrows,'
'several other . . . Indian bows,' and 'an
Indian bow, painted' ('Des. of SH,' *Works*
ii. 440–1).
6. Emily Mary Hill (1751–1835), 3d dau.
of 1st M. of Downshire; m. (1773) James
Cecil, styled Vct Cranborne until 1780, 7th
E. of Salisbury, 1780, cr. (1789) M. of Salisbury. HW's reference to 'weapons' is explained by her fondness for archery. A few
days before the date of his letter, a newspaper reported: 'The rage for this noble art
is astonishing; there are already near sixty
societies in this kingdom. Lord and Lady
Salisbury have lately instituted and patronized a society which meets in their Park at
Hatfield every Saturday' (*English Chronicle; or, Universal Evening Post* 30 June–
2 July 1789). An account of the first meeting of the society, the 'Hertfordshire Arch-
ers,' at which Lady Salisbury presented a
gold medal to the winner of the contest,
appears in ibid. 7–9 July 1789. Continued
popularity of the sport is mentioned in *The
Sun* 13 Aug. 1794.

7. Charles Lennox (1764–1819), 4th D. of
Richmond, 1806; nephew of the 3d D. of
Richmond; entered army, 1785; General,
1813; died of hydrophobia. HW refers to
two duels Lt-Col. Lennox had recently
fought with pistols. The first (26 May 1789)
was with the Duke of York, his superior
officer (Colonel) in the Coldstream Foot
Guards, who remarked that words had been
used to Lennox to which no gentleman
ought to submit. Unable to find from the
Duke of York or from anyone else what
words were meant, Lennox challenged his
superior to a duel. Neither was injured;
Lennox missed, and the Duke refused to
fire. Lennox's associates concluded he had
acted with more courage than judgment. As
a result of the affair, Lennox exchanged
(13 June; see *The World* 16 June) his post
in the Coldstream Foot Guards for the same
rank in the 35th Foot. The second duel,
with Theophilus Swift (1746–1815), author
of a pamphlet reflecting on Lennox's conduct in the first affair, was fought 2 July
1789. Swift was injured. (The date of the
second duel is usually given as 1 or 3 July,
but contemporary newspaper reports place
it on Thursday, 2 July: *World*, 4 July,
where 'Thursday' is mentioned; *St James's
Chronicle* 2–4 July; *English Chronicle; or,
Universal Evening Post* 2–4 July.) For further particulars, see DNB; GM 1789, lix pt i.
463–4, 565, and pt ii. 668; and the several
pamphlets dealing with the two affairs. HW

suspended my quiver in the Temple of Hymen. Hygeia shall be my goddess, if she will send you back blooming to this region. Lady Cecilia[8] thinks the house at Bushy Park Gate will be untenanted by the time of your return.[9]

I wish I had preserved any correspondence in France,[10] as you are curious about their present history, which I believe very momentous indeed. What little I have accidentally heard, I will relate, and will learn what more I can. On the King's being advised to put out his talons,[11] Necker[12] desired leave to resign, as not having been consulted, and as the measure violated his plan.[13] The people hearing his intention thronged to Versailles, and he was forced to assure them from a balcony that he was not to retire.[14]—I am not accurate in dates,[15] nor warrant my intelligence, and therefore pretend only to send you detached scraps. Force being still in request, the Duc du Châtelet[16] acquainted the King, that he could not answer for the French Guards— Châtelet, who from his hot arrogant temper I should have thought would have been one of the proudest opposers of the people, is sus-

wrote an account of the first duel (see 'Mem. 1783–91,' *sub* May 1789), but it has not been traced.

8. Johnston.

9. HW had probably mentioned this house in one of his missing letters, 3 or 4 July. Cf. *post* 6 Aug. 1789. The road from London to Hampton entered Bushy Park about two miles south of Twickenham and came out at Hampton Court (John Cary, *Cary's New Itinerary*, 1798, col. 47). The house was near the South Gate, 't'other side of Bushy Park' from SH (*post* 13 Aug. 1789).

10. Cf. HW to Hon. Thomas Walpole 8 Oct. 1780: 'I have great regard for some persons at Paris, but I have done with France. It was for my dearest friend [Mme du Deffand] alone that I kept up any connection there.'

11. Following the advice of a majority of his ministers, Louis XVI opposed the Third Estate and 'put out his talons' in his address and declarations to the States-General 23 June (Saul K. Padover, *The Life and Death of Louis XVI*, 1939, pp. 165–9).

12. Jacques Necker (1732–1804), Swiss banker; Louis XVI's Director-General of Finance 1777–81, 1788–90 (except for a few days; dismissed 11 July, recalled 15 July 1789). See du Deffand, *passim*.

13. Of appeasement and moderation; see his *De la révolution française*, 1797, i. 225–77; Louis Blanc, *Histoire de la révolution française*, 1848, ii. ch. 2.

14. Cf. *The London Chronicle* 27–30 June 1789, lxv. 623; GM 1789, lix pt ii. 655–6.

15. As he proves in 'Short Notes.'

16. Louis-Marie-Florent (1727–93), Duc du Châtelet, 1777; resigned colonelcy of the French Guards 16 July 1789; formerly ambassador to England; son of Voltaire's mistress, Mme du Châtelet; 'warm, captious, and personally brave' (*Mem. Geo. III*, iii. 245). In *The World* 5 Aug. 1789 he was reported at Brussels, but he returned to Paris, and was guillotined in Dec. 1793, after attempting to escape by bribing his prison guards and to commit suicide by taking opium. At his trial he was found guilty of having wished to repress the insubordination of his regiment at Nancy in June and July 1789 (*La Grande encyclopédie; Journal de Paris* 21 juillet 1789; GM 1793, lxiii pt ii. 1216; Henri-Alexandre Wallon, *Histoire du tribunal révolutionnaire*, 1880–2, ii. 246; Voltaire, *Œuvres* xxiii. 521 n.; du Deffand i. 237 *et passim*; Sir John Carr, *Stranger in France*, 2d edn, 1807, pp. 125–6).

pected[17] to lean to them. In short, Marshal Broglio[18] is appointed Commander-in-Chief, and is said to have sworn on his sword that he will not sheathe it till he has plunged it into the heart of *ce gros banquier genevois*[19]—I cannot reconcile this with Necker's stay at Versailles. That he is playing a deep game is certain—It is reported that Madame Necker[20] tastes previously everything he swallows.[21] A vast camp is forming round Paris—but if the army is mutinous, the tragedy may begin on the other side. They do talk of an engagement at Metz, where the French troops espousing the popular cause, were attacked by two German regiments, whom the former cut to pieces.[22]

The Duke and Duchess of Devonshire,[23] who were at Paris, have thought it prudent to leave it—and my cousin Mr Th. Walpole[24] who

17. Apparently without foundation.

18. Victor-François (1718–1804), Duc de Broglie, 1745; Maréchal de France 1759–89 (see du Deffand, *passim*); 'Broglie the War-God' (Carlyle, *French Revolution*, I. bk v. ch. 3). 'The Marshal de Broglio is appointed *Generalissimo* of the army in and about Paris, which consists at present of near 30,000 men' (*Oracle. Bell's New World* 7 July 1789, from an account dated 'Paris, July 2'). After the dismissal of Necker on 11 July, he served for a few days as Minister of War, but was soon forced to leave France (cf. *post* 19 July 1789). He led an unsuccessful troop of émigrés in 1792. The Duke of Dorset, in his dispatch of 9 July 1789, describes Broglio as 'a man of a very determined character, and . . . what the French call *un bon serviteur du Roi*' (*Despatches from Paris 1784–1790*, ed. Oscar Browning [Camden Third Series, vols 16, 19], 1909–10, ii. 233).

19. Necker.

20. Suzanne Curchod (1739–94), dau. of a pastor near Lausanne; engaged at one time to Gibbon the historian, but m. (1764) Jacques Necker (du Deffand, *passim*).

21. Attempts to poison Necker were reported in *The World* 1, 8 July 1789.

22. In *The World*, 8 July 1789, the affair at Metz is reported: 'The first blow of a civil war is already struck. In consequence of the lately acquired spirit of the people, two German regiments then on duty were called in and ordered to fire on the populace; they obeyed their orders and some

lives were lost. On which two French regiments immediately joined the citizens, and cut the two German regiments to pieces.' For a more circumstantial account, as reported to Lord Elgin before he left Paris 5 July, see *The Oracle. Bell's New World* 9, 10 July 1789; and cf. *Letters from Mrs Elizabeth Carter to Mrs Montagu*, ed. Montagu Pennington, 1817, iii. 312.

23. William Cavendish (1748–1811), 5th D. of Devonshire, 1764; m. (1774) Georgiana Spencer (1757–1806), 1st dau. of 1st E. Spencer. She was the famous leader of fashion and politics. Their movements, but particularly those of the Duchess, can be followed in the newspapers. They were expected in Paris 24 June (*World* 30 June). On 8 July the Duchess was reported 'chiefly with Madame de Polignac,' and five days later 'the Duchess of Devonshire, if Madame de Polignac's advice be followed, is to leave Paris —and for fear of the popular tumults, which every day look more and more alarming.' In the same issue she is said to have written to a friend that 'Paris now gives her a *faint idea* of the late Westminster election.' Both arrived safely 17 July at Spa (ibid. 20 July; *Oracle. Bell's New World* 28 July 1789), where she remained several months (Louis Dutens, *Memoirs of a Traveller*, 1806, iv. 208–13).

24. Hon. Thomas Walpole (1727–1803), son of Horatio, 1st Bn Walpole of Wolterton; banker of London and Paris; HW's correspondent; frequently mentioned in du Deffand.

is near it,[25] has just written to his daughters,[26] that he is glad to be out of the town that he may make his retreat easily.

Thus, you see, the crisis is advanced far beyond orations, and wears all the aspect of civil war. For can one imagine that the whole nation is converted at once, and in some measure without provocation from the King, who far from enforcing the prerogative like Charles I, cancelled the despotism obtained for his grandfather[27] by the Chancellor Maupeou,[28] has exercised no tyranny, and has shown a disposition to let the constitution be amended. It did want it indeed—but I fear, the present want of temper grasps at so much that they may defeat their own purposes; and where loyalty has for ages been the predominant characteristic of a nation, it cannot be eradicated at once. Pity will soften the tone of the moment, and the nobility and clergy have more interest in wearing a royal than a popular yoke, for great lords and high priests think the rights of mankind a defalcation of their privileges. No man living is more devoted to liberty than I am—yet blood is a terrible price to pay for it! A martyr to liberty is the noblest of characters; but to sacrifice the lives of others, though for the benefit of all, is a strain of heroism that I could never ambition.

I have just been reading Voltaire's correspondence[29]—one of those heroes, who liked better to excite martyrs than to be one.[30] How vain would he be, if alive now! I was struck with one of his letters to La Chalotais,[31] who was a true upright patriot and martyr too! In the 221st letter of the sixth volume,[32] Voltaire says to him, 'Vous avez jeté des germes qui produiront un jour plus qu'on ne pense.'

25. 'He had a house at Clichy' (Toynbee xiv. 149 n).

26. Catherine Mary Walpole (1756–1816) and Elizabeth Walpole (1759–1842), both of whom died unmarried, the elder in Chesterfield Street, London, and the younger at Petersham (Collins, *Peerage*, 1812, v. 673; GM 1816, lxxxvi pt i. 635; *Annual Register*, 1842, lxxxiv pt ii. 275).

27. Louis XV.

28. René-Nicolas-Charles-Augustin de Maupeou (1714–92), Chancellor, 1768, who attempted to gain absolute power for Louis XV, especially by suppression of the parliaments, 1771. See DU DEFFAND, *passim*, but particularly the prophetic passage, iii. 67. Mary Berry refers to him as 'this man, whose plans were as bold and bad as his means were base and servile' (*Comparative View of Social Life in England and France*,

1844, i. 300), 'whose violent measures . . . brought into contempt even the institutions which had hitherto been considered as the least contaminated' (ibid. ii. 60).

29. In the Kehl edition, *Œuvres complètes de Voltaire*, 70 vols, 1785–9, sold SH v. 164.

30. Cf. Voltaire to d'Alembert 8 Feb. 1776, 'J'aime fort la vérité, mais je n'aime point du tout le martyre' (ibid. lxix. 257).

31. Louis-René de Caradeuc de la Chalotais (1701–85), legislator and economist. See *post* 29 July 1789; DU DEFFAND, *passim*.

32. That is, vol. 6, p. 440, of the *Correspondance générale*, which is vol. 57 of the Kehl edition. Voltaire's remark is in the letter of 21 July [1762] and is apropos of La Chalotais's recently published *Second Compte rendu sur l'appel comme d'abus des Constitutions de Jésuites.*

JUPITER SERAPIS

It was lucky for me that you inquired about France; I had not a half-penny-worth more of news in my wallet.

Tonton's nose is not I believe grown longer, but only come to light by being clipped: when his beard is recovered, I dare to say he will be as comely as my Jupiter Serapis.[33] In his taste he is much improved, for he eats strawberries, and is fond of them—and yet they never were so insipid, from want of sun and constant rain. One may eat roses and smell to cherries and not perceive the difference from scent or flavour. If tulips were in season, I would make a rainbow of them to give other flowers hopes of not being drowned again.

A person[34] who was very apt to call on you every morning for a minute and stay three hours, was with me the other day, and his grievance from the rain was the swarms of gnats: I said I supposed I have very bad blood, for gnats never bite me. He replied 'I believe I have bad blood too, for dull people, who would tire me to death, never come near me.'—Shall I beg a palletful of that repellant for you, to set in your window, as barbers do?

I believe you will make me grow a little of a newsmonger, though you are none; but I know that at a distance in the country letters of news are a regale. I am not wont to listen to the batteries on each side of me at Hampton Court and Richmond; but in your absence I shall turn a less deaf ear to them in hopes of gleaning something that may amuse you; though I shall leave their manufactures of scandal for their own home-consumption: you happily do not deal in such wares. Adieu! I used to think the month of September the dullest of the whole set, now I shall be impatient for it.

PS. I am glad you are to go [to] Mrs Cholmondeley:[35] she is extremely sensible and agreeable—but I think all your particular friends that I have seen are so.

---

33. In the Beauclerk Closet at SH was 'the head of Jupiter Serapis, in basaltes. The divine majesty and beauty of this precious fragment prove the great ideas and consummate taste of the ancient sculptors. This bust was purchased, with the celebrated vase, from the Barberini collection at Rome, by Sir William Hamilton; and was sold with the vase to the Duchess of Portland, and on her Grace's death was bought by Mr Walpole' ('Des. of SH,' *Works* ii. 505). It was sold SH xiii. 82 to William Beckford, at whose death it passed into the Hamilton Palace Collection and was sold 26 June 1882, 5th day, lot 469. 'All but the head itself was restored by the Hon. Mrs Damer, 1787' (*The Hamilton Palace Collection. Illustrated Priced Catalogue*, 1882, p. 63). See also HW to Conway 18 June 1786; Toynbee *Supp.* ii. 174.

34. Perhaps Richard Owen Cambridge.

35. Teresa Ann Englefield (d. 1810), only surviving sister of HW's acquaintance, Sir Henry Charles Englefield, 7th Bt; m. (1782) Francis Cholmeley (1750–1808) of Brandsby Hall, Yorks (Joseph Foster, *Pedigrees of the*

To Mary Berry, Friday 10 July 1789

The address and postmark are missing, but the letter was posted 16 July (see *post* 6 Aug. 1789; cf. second half of this letter).

Strawberry Hill, July 10, 1789.[1]

HOW angry you will be with me! and how insincere you will think all my professions! Why, here is Lady Dudley's house[2] let under my nose, let in my own lane,[3] and for a song!—*Patienza! mie care*—I am as white as snow. It had no bill upon it, though it was advertised,[4] but not in my newspaper,[5] and who knows truth or falsehood but from their own paper? And who of all the birds in the air do you think has got it?—only the Pepyses.[6] It is true too that had I had any inkling of the matter, I should not have inquired about it, for the rent asked was two hundred a year[7]—but a Master in Chancery, having a nose longer

County Families of Yorkshire, 1874, iii. pedigree of Cholmeley; Burke, *Landed Gentry*, 1937, p. 404). She is frequently mentioned in Mary Berry's *Journals and Correspondence* and in the *Berry Papers*. In 1810 Mary Berry wrote among some reflections for the year: 'Mrs Cholmeley's death recalls to me in a melancholy manner many passages in my own past life. . . . I became acquainted with her in the year 1785, when I was twenty-two, and was just returned from having been plunged for two years into the great world of Europe, from the most perfect retirement in England' (MBJ ii. 447). Maria Josepha Stanley, later Bns Stanley of Alderley, considered her 'a charming woman' (*Early Married Life of Maria Josepha Lady Stanley*, ed. Jane H. Adeane, 1899, p. 317). Brandsby Hall is about twelve miles SW of Middleton, where the Berrys were visiting relatives.

1. 'No. 9' (B).

2. Mary Fair (d. 1810), dau. of Gamaliel Fair of Norfolk; m. (2) (1788) John Ward (1725–88), 2d Vct Dudley and Ward of Dudley; m. (3) (1790) Benjamin Jennings (d. 1791); m. (4) (1791) John Smith, Capt. R. N. (*Times* 12 Dec. 1791; *Oracle* 19 Dec. 1791). Her house on the Thames was the manor-house of Teddington, said to have been built by Lord Buckhurst about 1602 (Daniel Lysons, *Environs of London*, 1792–6, iii. 504–5). After letting her house, Lady Dudley returned to London (*World* 21 July, 19 Aug. 1789). The house which the Berrys

occupied at Teddington later in the year was 'within a few yards' of hers (*A Later Pepys*, ed. Alice C. C. Gaussen, 1904, ii. 279; see also *post* 20 Aug. 1789).

3. That is, on the road leading from SH to Hampton Court.

4. The advertisement has not been found.

5. Perhaps *The Times* (see HW to Lady Ossory 12 Dec. 1789; *post* 10 July 1790). HW appears to have taken in several daily newspapers as well as *The London Chronicle*. Newspapers of this period from which HW made cuttings (now WSL) are *The Times, Morning Herald, The Morning Chronicle, The Public Advertiser*—these two last for 1783. See 'Mem. 1783–91.' Later he depended a great deal upon *The True Briton*.

6. 'William Weller Pepys, Esq., afterwards made a baronet, father to the present Lord Chancellor Cottenham' (B). Pepys (1741–1825), a Master in Chancery 1775–1807, member of the Bluestocking coterie, cr. (1801) Bt; m. (1777) Elizabeth Dowdeswell (d. 1830), dau. of William Dowdeswell, Chancellor of the Exchequer (Burke, *Peerage*, 1937, p. 633; Richard A. Austen-Leigh, *Eton College Register 1753–1790*, Eton, 1921). For much of his correspondence, which displays some of the scholarship and taste grudgingly acknowledged by Dr Johnson (*Johnsonian Miscellanies*, ed. George Birkbeck Hill, 1897, i. 244–5), see *A Later Pepys*, ed. Alice C. C. Gaussen, 1904.

7. 'Houses, particularly those situate to

than himself,[8] went to the executors[9] and struck a bargain of £70 for four months—The land would pay the rent—but then you must have got your hay in before the rains—and you must have been wiser than I, to have done that, and in hay concerns I don't know that the heads of two wives are better than that of one husband; and after all, had not you been shrewder than a Master in Chancery, it would have cost you three hundred pounds extraordinary before you could have shown your faces, as I am sure at least *I* should choose to have *my* wives appear —Why there is poor Mrs Pepys with not a rag of linen but the shift on her back. They sent their whole history[10] by water:[11] It was a most tempestuous night; the boatman dreading a shipwreck, cast anchor in Chelsea Reach, intending to put to sea next morning—but before daybreak pirates had carried off the whole cargo to the value, Mr Cambridge[12] says, of said three hundred pounds.[13] Now, am I as false or negligent as I thought I was? You both and Papa Berry together could not be so mad, as I was at myself at first, when I suspected that I had missed Palazzo Dudley for you.

As I keep a letter constantly on the anvil going on for you, I shall, before this gets its complement, tell you what I know more. The House of Edgcumbe[14] set out in perilous haste to prepare the Mount[15] for the

the Thames, are high rented, and when sold bear a high price, and in these delightful and desirable situations are very seldom empty' (Edward Ironside, *History and Antiquities of Twickenham*, 1797, p. 72).

8. 'Both he and his brother, Sir Lucas, were very small men, and Horace Walpole —whether in malice or pleasantry . . .— describes Sir William Pepys' nose as being "as long as himself [*sic*]" ' (*A Later Pepys* i. 7; cf. the frontispiece to ibid. vol. 1, a reproduction of Henry Thomson's portrait, painted in 1808).

9. Of the late Lord Dudley's will.

10. Not noticed by OED in this sense.

11. Which was cheaper than by land: 'The price of goods by land carriage is 1s. 8d. per hundred weight, or £1. 10s. per ton, and by water at 1s. 4d. per hundred weight, or £1. per ton' (Ironside, op. cit. p. 73).

12. 'Richard Owen Cambridge, Esq., then living in the house on the Twickenham side of Richmond Bridge now inhabited by Mr Bevan' (B).

13. In a letter to Hannah More 17 Sept. 1789 Pepys mentions the 'robbery by which we lost all our household linen, children's clothes, my desk . . . [and, wishing to invite a guest for the night] I . . . for very want of sheets was obliged to be silent' (*A Later Pepys* ii. 277–8).

14. George Edgcumbe (1721–95), 3d Bn Edgcumbe of Mount Edgcumbe, 1761, cr. (1781) Vct Mount Edgcumbe and Valletort and (31 Aug. 1789) E. of Mount Edgcumbe; Admiral of the White, 1782; D.C.L. Oxford, 1773; F.S.A., 1775; F.R.S., 1784; m. (1761) Emma Gilbert (1729–1807), only child of John Gilbert, Archbishop of York. They were probably accompanied by their only son Richard (afterwards 2d Earl) and his wife (for whom see *post* 10, 17 July 1790), who assisted in entertaining the royal visitors 21 Aug. (*World* 25 Aug. 1789; GM 1789, lix pt ii. 1144; following note). Lady Mount Edgcumbe was an accomplished musician and at her death was the 'oldest and most partial musical friend' of Dr Burney, for whose account of her see Frances Burney d'Arblay, *Memoirs of Doctor Burney*, 1832, iii. 375–6. For an account of her family and some of her letters, see *Edward Jerningham and His Friends*, ed. Lewis Bettany, 1919, pp. 193–225; *Harcourt Papers* viii. 274–87.

15. Lord Mount Edgcumbe's seat, Mount

reception of their Majesties if they are so inclined,[16] but were stopped at Pool[17] for want of post-horses, all being retained for the service of the Court. The royal personages arrived, and Lady Mount ———[18] was in the midst of the reiteration of her curtsies, when the mob gathering and pressing on her, she was seized with a panic, clung to her Lord, and screamed piteously, till a country fellow said to her, 'What dost thee make such a hell of a noise for? Why nobody will touch thee.'[19]

Passons à Paris: all I have yet learnt farther is, that the populace were going to burn the house of Monsieur d'Esprémesnil,[20] a Royalist. A cobbler getting on a stand begged their low-mightiness to hear four reasons against wilful fire-raising: the first was, *L'hôtel n'était point à M. d'Esprémesnil;* second, *les livres n'étaient pas à lui;* third, *les enfants[21] n'étaient pas à lui;* fourth and last, *sa femme[22] était au public.* The pathetic justice of those arguments, saved the hotel, and Monsieur d'E. keeps all those goods that do *not* belong to him.

I am sorry we have refused to supply their wants;[23] I am for heaping

Edgcumbe, in Devon (now Cornwall) on a peninsula opposite Plymouth.

16. 'King George III and his Queen were then on a progress to Plymouth [Weymouth]' (B). Accompanied by their three eldest daughters and members of the court, they left Windsor 25 June, reached Weymouth 30 June, remained in and near Weymouth until 14 Sept. (except for an excursion to Plymouth and its vicinity 15–28 Aug.), and returned to Windsor 18 Sept. (GM 1789, lix pt ii. 856, 951–2, 1046–7, 1142–4, 1202–4). They visited Mount Edgcumbe 21 Aug., on which day a long description of the estate appeared in *The World* (cf. *The Evening Mail* 17–20 July); the visit itself is described in superlatives in *The World* 25 Aug., and less extravagantly in GM 1789, lix pt ii. 1144. For Lady Mount Edgcumbe's account, see the *Harcourt Papers* viii. 281–7. Ten days after the visit Lord Mount Edgcumbe was made an Earl.

17. Poole, Dorset, through which the King and Queen passed 30 June on the way from Lyndhurst, Hants, to Weymouth (*World* 30 June, 1 July 1789).

18. '———, Countess of Mount Edgcumbe, mother to the present Earl' (B).

19. Lady Mount Edgcumbe's letter to Lady Harcourt 4 July 1789 indicates that the incident took place at Blandford: 'The King and Queen looked perfectly well and perfectly happy; the Princesses I did not

see, for, being nearly thrown down by the multitude who were passing behind me, I grew very much frightened, and was with difficulty dragged out of the crowd' (*Harcourt Papers* viii. 280). HW scolds Lady Mount Edgcumbe for her panics and 'transports both of grief and joy,' in his letter to her 29 Nov. 1794.

20. Jean-Jacques Duval d'Esprémesnil (1745–94), politician and lawyer; counsellor to the Parliament of Paris, 1775; opposed Marie Antoinette and supported the States-General, but later became an ardent royalist; guillotined (NBG; *La Grande encyclopédie*).

21. No record of his children has been found.

22. Françoise-Augustine Santuaré (ca 1754–94), m., as 2d wife, Jean-Jacques Duval d'Esprémesnil; guillotined about two months after her husband (Henri-Alexandre Wallon, *Histoire du tribunal révolutionnaire,* 1880–2, iv. 257; *La Grande encyclopédie*).

23. France's application for a supply of 20,000 sacks of flour was denied on the ground that government 'could not with prudence permit the exportation . . . without injury to the country at large, and particularly to the farther burden of the poorer part of the community' (GM 1789, lix pt ii. 668).

coals of corn on the heads of our enemies—but truth is, it looks as if it would not be quite prudent to be so generous: the incessant and heavy rains are alarming;[24] the corn begins to be laid, and fair weather is now wanted as much for use as for pleasure: It costs me a pint of wine a day to make my servants amends for being wet to the skin every time I go abroad.[25] Lord and Lady Waldegrave[26] have been with me for two days, and could not set their foot out of doors. I drank tea at Mrs Garrick's[27] with the Bishop of London and Mrs Porteous,[28] Mr Batt and Dr Cadogan and his daughter,[29] and they were all in the same predicament.

Apropos to the Bishop, I enclose a most beautiful copy of verses[30] which Miss H. More wrote very lately when she was with him at Fulham on his opening a walk to a bench called Bonner's.[31] Mrs Bosca-

---

24. See *ante* 23 June 1789, n. 5.

25. No record of HW's coachman has been found. His footman was presumably 'John' who committed suicide in October 1791 (*post* 16, 20 Oct. 1791).

26. 'Laura Countess of Waldegrave was great-niece to Lord Orford, being one of the granddaughters of his brother Sir Edward Walpole' (B). George Waldegrave (1751–17 Oct. 1789), styled Vct Chewton 1763–84, 4th E. Waldegrave, 1784, m. (1782) his first cousin, Elizabeth Laura Waldegrave (1760–1816), dau. of James, 2d. E. Waldegrave, by Maria Walpole, afterwards Ds of Gloucester.

27. 'The widow of David Garrick, then inhabiting the house he had built [bought in 1754] at Hampton' (B). Eva Maria Veigel (1725–1822), dancer, dau. of Johann Veigel of Vienna; assumed name of Violette; m. (1749) David Garrick (DNB, *sub* Garrick, David; GM 1822, xcii pt ii. 468–70). 'I like her exceedingly; her behaviour is all sense, and all sweetness too' (HW to Richard Bentley 15 Aug. 1755). Garrick's summer villa, altered, may still be seen.

28. Beilby Porteus (1731–1809), Bishop of Chester, 1776, and of London, 1787; energetic in attempts to ameliorate conditions in the slave trade and to obtain widespread observance of fast days; m. (1765) Margaret Hodgson (1741–1815) of Parliament Street, London, eldest dau. of Bryan Hodgson, landlord of the George Inn, St Martin's, Stamford, afterwards of Ashbourne in Derbyshire. She died 20 March 1815 in Queen Street, Mayfair (DNB; Venn, *Alumni Cantab.*; GM 1765, xxxv. 247; GM

1809, lxxix pt i. 485–6; GM 1815, lxxxv pt i. 285; N&Q 1888, 7th Ser. v. 330, 494).

29. William Cadogan (1711–97), M.D. (Leyden 1737, Oxford 1755), sometime physician to the army and to the Foundling Hospital, and author of *A Dissertation on the Gout*, 1771. His summer residence was Hurlingham House, Fulham, which he built about 1760 on ground leased from the Bishop of London; it now 'forms the central part of the existing premises' of the Hurlingham Club (Charles James Fèret, *Fulham Old and New*, 1900, iii. 242–4; DNB). His only dau., Frances Cadogan (1747–1819), m. (1788) William Nicholl (1751–1828), barrister of the Middle Temple, afterwards mayor of Cowbridge, Glamorganshire, and recorder of Cardiff (Fèret, op. cit. iii. 244; GM 1828, xcviii pt i. 190; Burke, *Landed Gentry*, 1879, p. 1166, *sub* Nicholl of the Ham; Lemuel John Hopkin-James, *Old Cowbridge*, Cardiff, 1922, p. 160).

30. *Bishop Bonner's Ghost*, SH, 1789; see Hazen, *SH Bibliography*.

31. Edmund Bonner (ca 1500–69), Bishop of London 1539–49, 1553–9; a strong supporter of Roman Catholicism after the death of Henry VIII; died in Marshalsea Prison. 'According to tradition the Monk's Walk [at Fulham Palace, a winding path in shrubbery now cleared away], at one end of which was an old chair, was haunted by the ghost of Bishop Bonner. . . . In this chair it was the custom of the persecuting Bishop to sit when he passed sentence on heretics' (Fèret, op. cit. iii. 139).

wen[32] showed them to me, and I insisted on printing them.[33] Only 200 copies are taken off, half for her and half for the printer[34]—and you have one of the first—How unlike are these lines to the chemical preparations of our modern poetasters, cock and hen! who leave one with no images but of garlands of flowers and necklaces of coloured stones. Every stanza of *Bonner's Ghost* furnishes you with a theme of ideas. I have read them twenty times, and every time they improve on me. How easy, how well kept up the irony! how sensible the satire! how delicate and genteel the compliments! I hold *Jekyll*[35] and *Bonner's*

32. Frances Glanville (1719–1805), only dau. by his first marriage of William Evelyn Glanville of St Clere, Ightham, Kent; m. (1742) Hon. Edward Boscawen, later an admiral. Her summer home was Rosedale, at the entrance of Richmond from Kew, formerly the home of Thomson, author of *The Seasons*, and now occupied by the site of the Royal Hospital (DNB, *sub* Boscawen, Edward; Helen Evelyn, *History of the Evelyn Family*, 1915, pp. 562–6; GM 1805, lxxv pt i. 289; Collins, *Peerage*, 1812, vi. 75–7; *London and Its Environs*, ed. Findlay Muirhead, 1927, p. 483). 'Her manners are the most agreeable, and her conversation the best, of any lady with whom I ever had the happiness to be acquainted' (Boswell, *Johnson* iii. 331). See Gen. Cecil Aspinall-Oglander, *Admiral's Wife, Being the Life and Letters of the Hon. Mrs Edward Boscawen from 1719–1761*, 1940, and *Admiral's Widow . . . 1761–1805*, 1943.

33. See HW to Hannah More 23 June, 2 July 1789, and her replies; Hazen, *SH Bibliography*.

34. HW. The last entry in HW's *Journal of the Printing Office* (p. 21) relates to *Bishop Bonner's Ghost*, which was printed without the author's name (ibid. pp. 74–5; HW to Hannah More 2 July 1789). In the *Journal*, HW states that Hannah More had 70 copies, Bishop Porteus, 30, and HW himself, 100.

35. *Jekyll: a Political Eclogue*, 1788, a satire in heroic couplets (175 lines), written to ridicule Joseph Jekyll (ca 1752–1837), 'the wag of law, the scribbler's pride,' according to the opening lines (see also GM 1837, n.s. viii. 208). DNB attributes the verses to Joseph Richardson (1755–1803), but they were by Lord John Townshend (1757–

1833), son of George, 4th Vct and 1st M. Townshend, as appears from HW's copy of the verses (now Harvard; they are bound in vol. 22 of HW's 'Collection of the most remarkable Poems Published in the Reign of King George the Third,' 4to). HW noted on the title 'By Lord John Townshend' and 'February' and made numerous MS notes throughout the poem. Townshend's authorship of it is supported by a copy (now WSL) of *The Rolliad*, 22d edn, 1812, printed for James Ridgway, in which 'Jekyll' is reprinted. This copy formerly belonged to Thomas Hill (1760–1840, see DNB) who has noted on the title, 'with their names [of the authors] taken from a MS copy in the possession of the late Mr Alderman Combe [Harvey Christian Combe, d. 1818], presented to him by R. B. Sheridan, Esq.' From Hill the copy passed to B. Holme of 10 New Inn, who wrote below Hill's note on the title, 'Also compared with the names inserted in a copy belonging to Mr Ridgway the publisher with which it agrees.' 'Lord John Townsend' is written opposite 'Jekyll.' Richard Tickell is said to have added lines 73–100 and to have 'altered and enlarged' lines 156–75 (N&Q 1850, 1st Ser. ii. 373). See also ibid. 43, 114, and *Review of English Studies*, 1927, iii. 220, for further confirmation of Lord John's authorship. HW tended to reserve ecstatic praise for the literary and artistic effusions of his personal friends, of whom Townshend was one. Anthony Morris Storer referred to it 8 Feb. 1788 as having 'run like wildfire. It is the cleverest thing ever written. Everybody has it by heart' (*Journal and Correspondence of William Lord Auckland*, ed. Robert John Eden, 3d Bn Auckland, 1861–2, i. 467).

Ghost perfect compositions in their different kinds—a great deal to say, when poetry has been so much exhausted.

Wednesday 15th.

The first part of my letter is superannuated before the second was ready. I had nothing from either of you to answer; I had no new news to send you, and Kirgate[36] is not *brought to bed* of *Bonner's Ghost* so soon as I had *reckoned;*[37] so you must wait for it; and should it *appear* to you while you are at Mrs Cholmondeley's,[38] that is, *in partibus infidelium,*[39] it will be decent not to scream out. Commonly it is not prudent to announce a poem with high panegyric beforehand; yet I think *Bonner* will answer all I have predicated of him—at least I shall be much disappointed, if you are at all.

My motive for sending this away with abortive notice, is, not to delay giving you an account of the news I heard this morning. Mr Mackinsy and Lady Betty[40] were with me this morning, and he showed me a letter he had just received from Monsieur Dutens:[41] a courier arrived yesterday with prodigious expedition from the Duke of Dor-

---

36. Thomas Kirgate (1734–1810), HW's printer and secretary for nearly thirty years.

37. Cf. HW to Lady Ossory 18 July 1789: 'I have been disappointed of the completion of *Bonner's Ghost*, by my rolling press being out of order, and was forced to send the whole impression to town to have the copperplate [on the title-page] taken off. . . . *At Night.* Kirgate has brought the whole impression, and I shall have the pleasure of sending your Ladyship this with a *Bonner's Ghost* tomorrow morning.'

38. Brandsby Hall, Yorks.

39. Mrs Cholmeley was a Roman Catholic, and might not relish Hannah More's light treatment of Bishop Bonner.

40. 'James Stuart-Mackenzie, only [surviving] brother to the minister [third] Earl of Bute. He was married to the Lady Eliz. Campbell, second [fourth] daughter of John the first [second] Duke of Argyll' (B). Hon. James Stuart (ca 1719–1800), according to the provision of the will of his great-grandfather, Sir George Mackenzie, assumed the surname and arms of Mackenzie and succeeded to the Rosehaugh estate;

M.P. 1742–84; Keeper of the Privy Seal of Scotland 1763–5, 1766–1800; m. (1749), his cousin, Lady Elizabeth Campbell (ca 1722–99) (*Scots Peerage* i. 377, ii. 300; GEC, *sub* Bute, 3d E. of; Collins, *Peerage,* 1812, ii. 574–5). They had a summer villa at Petersham (Daniel Lysons, *Environs of London,* 2d edn, 1811, i pt i. 293). For their appearance and character, see Lady Mary Coke, *Letters and Journals,* Edinburgh, 1889–96, i. pp. l–lvi *et passim.*

41. 'A French protestant clergyman who was chaplain in the family of the Duke of Northumberland, and had been secretary to Mr Mackenzie in his mission to the Court of Turin. He wrote an itinerary of Europe (the first book of that kind), *Les Mémoires d'un voyageur qui se repose,* etc., etc.' (B). Louis Dutens (1730–1812) was a close friend of Stuart-Mackenzie, who made him one of his executors and residuary legatees. See Dutens, *Memoirs,* 1806, *passim,* but especially iv. 176, 213–16, 227–9. HW's copy of his *Histoire de ce qui s'est passé pour l'établissement d'une régence en Angleterre,* 1789, was sold SH v. 191.

set[42]—Necker had been dismissed[43] and was thought set out for Geneva; an offer of his post was gone to Breteuil,[44] who is in the country. Everything at Paris was in the utmost confusion, and firing of cannon for four hours there had been heard on the road.[45] All this is confirmed by a courier from the D. and Duchess of Devonshire who were setting out precipitately:[46] that messenger had been stopped three times on his route, being taken for a courier from that court, but was released on pretending to be dispatched by the *Tiers État*. Madame de Calonne[47] told Dutens yesterday that the newly encamped troops desert by hundreds—but if the firing of cannon was from the Bastile, and whence else it should proceed I know not, it looks as if the King were not quite abandoned—Oh! but what a scene! how many lives of quiet innocent persons may have been sacrificed, if the artillery of the Bastile raked that multitudinous city!—I check myself, for what million of reflections present themselves![48]

I shall wish to send you accounts fresh and fresh,[49] but I only catch them by accident and by rebound. Miss Penn[50] has a correspondent at

42. John Frederick Sackville (1745–99), 3d D. of Dorset; ambassador to France 1784–9; Lord Steward of the Household 1789–99; better known for his profligacy than for his statesmanship. He left Paris on leave 8 Aug. (and reached London 13 Aug.; see *The World* 14 Aug. 1789), but did not return to Paris, although he was not officially recalled until 20 June 1790 (*British Diplomatic Representatives, 1789–1852*, ed. S. T. Bindoff *et al.*, 1934, p. 47). For HW's low opinion of him, see 'Mem. 1783–91,' *sub* 24 Dec. 1783.

43. 11 July. He went first to Brussels (not to Geneva), and then to Basle (Necker, *De la Révolution française*, 1797, ii. 17).

44. Louis-Charles-Auguste Le Tonnelier (1733–1807), Baron de Breteuil, succeeded Necker as Director-General of Finance, but was soon forced to resign and emigrate to Brussels (*World* 5 Aug. 1789) and later to Soleure, Switzerland, and to London (*Times* 18 Dec. 1794). In 1790 Louis XVI appointed him his 'secret agent and informal ambassador to the courts of Europe' (NBG; Saul K. Padover, *The Life and Death of Louis XVI*, 1939, pp. 207–8; DU DEFFAND, *passim*).

45. Evidently this report came from a messenger to Calonne (*London Chronicle* 14–16 July 1789, lxvi. 56).

46. For Spa (see preceding letter, n. 23).

47. Anne-Rose-Josèphe de Nettine (ca 1740–1813), dau. of a banker of an ancient family of Brussels; m. (1) (1761) Joseph Micault d'Harvelay, 'Counsellor of State'; m. (2) (1788) at Bath, as 2d wife, Charles-Alexandre de Calonne, ex-minister of France, but separated from him a few years later. At the time of her marriage she is said to have had a fortune of nearly £12,000 a year. They had a house at Hyde Park Corner (*Oracle. Bell's New World* 29 Oct. 1789), but were probably at this time at their Wimbledon villa (*Les Papiers de Calonne*, ed. Christian de Parrel, Cavaillon, 1932, pp. xiii–xiv, 15 n; *idem*, 'Les Papiers de Calonne,' *The French Quarterly*, 1925, vii, 1, 11–13; Daniel Lysons, *Environs of London*, 2d edn, 1811, i. 404).

48. This paragraph closely parallels HW to Conway 15 July 1789.

49. See MONTAGU i. 158.

50. Sophia Margaret (or Margaretta) Penn (1764–1847), youngest child and only surviving dau. of Lady Juliana Penn; m. (3 May 1796) William Stuart, 5th and youngest son of 3d E. of Bute; later Archbishop of Armagh (Howard M. Jenkins, *The Family of William Penn*, Philadelphia, 1899, pp. 152, 170–3). 'From her two family branches are in existence,—that of the Stu-

Paris and showed me part of a letter thence yesterday, but I suppose few English will remain there.

We have no open enemy but St Swithin;[51] but if he persists in his *quarantaine,* he will be a very serious one. The Pepysian robbery was exaggerated; it is difficult to get at truth, even at a stone's throw off.

I have scarce left myself any room for conjugal *douceurs*—but as you see how very constantly you are in my thoughts, I am at least not fickle —On the contrary I am rather disposed to jealousy; you have written to Mr Pepys, and he will have anticipated my history of his being established in Palazzo Dudley; and that will make this letter more and more wrinkled—Well! he cannot send you *Bonner's Ghost,* and I shall have the satisfaction of tantalizing you four or five days longer—If this is not love, the deuce is in it: does one grudge that the beloved object should be pleased by anyone but oneself, unless beloved object there be? Do not be terrified however; jealousy most impartially divided between two can never come to great violence. Wife Agnes has indeed given me no cause, but my affection for both is so compounded into one love, that I can think of neither separately. Frenchmen often call their mistress *mes amours,* which would be no Irish in me. Apropos, Lady Lucan[52] told me t'other day of two young Irish couple who ran away from Dublin, and landed in Wales, and were much surprised to find that Holyhead was not Gretna Green—Adieu! *mes amours!*

PS. Well, are not you charmed with *Bonner's Ghost?*—Oh! I forget; you have not seen it yet—how tantalizing!

arts, present representatives of the Penn inheritance in Pennsylvania, under the entail, and that of the Earl of Ranfurly' (ibid. 170–1).

51. St Swithin or Swithun (d. 862), Bishop of Winchester 852–62, commemorated 15 July. According to legend, if it rains on that day, there will be rain for the next forty days. 'The saying about St Swithin is a proof of how often they ['long rains'] recur; for proverbial sentences are the children of experience, not of prophecy' (HW to Conway 15 July 1789).

52. Margaret Smith (d. 1814), dau. and coheiress of James Smith, M.P., of Canons Leigh, Devon, and of St Audries, Somerset; m. (1760) at Bath, Sir Charles Bingham (1735–99), 7th Bt, cr. (1776) Bn Lucan of Castlebar and (1795) E. of Lucan. Her 'father is stated in *The Female Jockey Club* (1794) to have been "a stocking-weaver at Nottingham," and scathing comments are made on her affectations and aristocratic airs' (GEC). HW had a high opinion of her water-colours and miniatures.

To Mary Berry, Sunday 19 July 1789

Address and postmark missing, but doubtless posted 20 July (see last paragraph but one and *post* 6 Aug. 1789).

Ex Officinâ Arbutianâ, July 19, 1789.

SUCH unwriting wives I never knew! and a shame it is for an author and what is more, for a printer, to have a couple so unletteral. I can find time amidst all the hurry of my shop to write small quartos to them continually. In France, where nuptiality is not the virtue the most in request, a wife will write to her consort, though the *doux billet* should contain but two sentences, of which I will give you a precedent; a lady sent the following to her spouse; '*Je vous écris, parce que je n'ai rien à faire; et je finis, parce que je n'ai rien à vous dire.*'[1] I do not wish for quite so laconic a *poulet*—besides, your Ladyships *can* write. Mrs Damer dined here yesterday, and had just heard from you—Brevity, Mesdames, may be catching—don't pretend not to care, for you are dying for news from France, but not a spoonful shall you have from me today; and if I was not a man of honour, though a printer, and had not promised you *Bonner's Ghost,* I would be as silent as if I were in Yorkshire. Remember too that Miss Hannah More, though not so proper for the French Embassador's *fête*[2] as Miss Gunning,[3] can teach Greek and Latin as well as any young lady in the north of England, and might make as suitable a companion for a typographer—I will say no more, for this *shall* be a short note.

Sunday night late.

I break my word to myself, though you do not deserve it, for I have had no letter today from either of you, and now can have none till

---

1. Quoted also in *Walpoliana* i. 4. Mme du Deffand, to whom HW was apparently indebted for this bon mot, words it slightly differently and attributes it to 'une petite fille qui écrivait à son frère' (du Deffand v. 118–19). HW paraphrases it *post* 11 March 1791.

2. Anne-César de la Luzerne (1741–91), cr. (1788) Marquis de la Luzerne; minister to the United States 1779–84; ambassador to London 1788–91 (William Emmett O'Donnell, *The Chevalier de la Luzerne,* Bruges and Louvain, 1938, *passim*). On 29 May 1789 he entertained about 900 guests

at his house in Portman Square at a fête which 'for a private house, has had no equal in magnificence.' Queen Charlotte was so pleased with the entertainment that she stayed until half past four in the morning (*World* 1 June 1789). For HW's account of it, see 'Mem. 1783–91,' *sub* May 1789; he does not mention 'Miss Gunning.' See also the *Harcourt Papers* iv pt i. 265–7.

3. Elizabeth (1769–1823), only child of Maj.-Gen. John Gunning (brother of the famous Gunning sisters), by Susannah Minifie. After becoming involved with her mother in the 'Gunning affair' of 1790–1

Tuesday;[4] but I am just come from Richmond where I have seen an authentic account of the horrible scene at Paris[5]—There had been dismal accounts for three days, but I hoped they had been exaggerated— They are too true! The Duc de Luxembourg and his family are arrived in London,[6] having escaped with difficulty, 300,000 *livres* being set on his head, as the same sum is on Marshal Broglie's,[7] and 500,000, on the Comte d'Artois's.[8] The people rose on this day sennight,[9] seized all the arms they could find, searched convents, found stores of corn[10] and obliged the monks to deal it out at reasonable prices. They have

(see *post* 29 July 1790 ff.), she turned to the writing and translation of novels, and m. (1803) Maj. James Plunkett of Kinnaird, co. Roscommon.

4. Because the York-London post, which left York at midnight six days a week, was omitted on Friday (*Universal British Directory*, 1791–8, iv. 969; cf. *ante* 23 June 1789).

5. HW's account which follows anticipates the information given in the daily newspapers (*The Times, The World, The Oracle. Bell's New World*) for 20 and 21 July 1789. The source of his information is not known; a number of French émigrés, however, lived at Richmond, and they probably had fresh accounts.

6. Anne-Charles-Sigismund de Montmorency-Luxembourg (1737–1803), Duc de Luxembourg, president of the nobles in the States-General, 1789; m. (1771) Madeleine-Suzanne-Adélaïde de Voyer d'Argenson de Paulmy (1752–1813), later a lady-in-waiting to Marie-Antoinette. Their family consisted of four children: 1) Anne-Henri-Renier-Sigismund de Montmorency-Luxembourg (b. 1772, d. ca 1793–1803), Duc de Châtillon; 2) Charles-Emmanuel-Sigismund de Montmorency-Luxembourg (1774–1861), later (1814) Duc de Luxembourg, the last of his line; 3) Bonne-Charlotte-Renée-Adélaïde de Montmorency-Luxembourg (born 1773), m. (1788) Anne-Pierre-Adrien de Montmorency-Laval, Duc de Laval; 4) Marie-Madeleine-Charlotte-Henriette-Émilie de Montmorency-Luxembourg (born 1778), m. (1790 or 1791) at Lisbon, Miguel Cayetano Alvares Pereira de Mello, Duque de Cadaval of the House of Braganza (*Morning Chronicle* 6 Dec. 1791). According to some reports (GM 1789, lix pt ii. 660; *London Chronicle* 18–21 July 1789, lxvi. 71) only the two daughters were with them, and

only the younger daughter is included in the caricature mentioned *post* 13 Aug. 1789. On their arrival in London Saturday night, 18 July, the family went to Grenier's Hotel, Jermyn Street (GM 1789, lix pt ii. 658; *The Oracle. Bell's New World* 20 July 1789), and later to a 'large house,' 'ready furnished,' in Soho Square (*Times* 30 July 1789). In July 1790 the family went to Lisbon, 'from whence they go to Madrid. They sailed in the last packet boat from Falmouth' (*Times* 24 July 1790). See also Jean-Baptiste-Pierre Jullien de Courcelles, *Histoire généalogique . . . des pairs de France*, 1822–33, viii, 'Pairs de France,' 36–7; *Enciclopedia universal ilustrada*, Barcelona [1905–30], x. 292, xxxvi. 715, 721.

7. 'In the course of a few days, Marshal Broglio . . . the Luxemburghs, with all who were suspected of having accepted, or even intending to accept, places under the late short-lived administration [formed after the dismissal of Necker], disappeared one after another' (*Annual Register*, 1789, xxi pt i. 255*). Marshal Broglie fled to Metz, then to Luxembourg (*London Chronicle* 6–8 Aug. 1789, lxvi. 134).

8. Charles-Philippe (1757–1836), Comte d'Artois, youngest brother of Louis XVI; King of France (Charles X) 1824–30. He fled from Versailles on the night of 16–17 July 1789, went to Namur, then to an estate near Berne, and late in August to Turin (*Correspondance intime du Comte de Vaudreuil et du Comte d'Artois*, ed. Léonce Pingaud, 1889, i. p. xxviii). The price on his head is reported elsewhere as 300,000 livres (GM 1789, lix pt ii. 659).

9. 12 July, when Necker's dismissal of the preceding day became generally known.

10. 13 July.

beheaded the *lieutenant de police*,[11] or the *prévôt des marchands*[12] or both, and attacked the Bastile, which the governor[13] refused to surrender, and on the populace rushing in, he fired on them with four great guns loaded with nails, and killed 300 or 400[14]—but they mastered him, and dragged him and his major[15] to the *Place de Grève*, and chopped off their hands and heads. The *bourgeoisie* however have disarmed the mob, but have seized the arsenal, and the Hôtel de Ville and the treasure there, which they destine to pay the sums for the heads of the proscribed.

On Wednesday the King with only his two brothers[16] went to the *Assemblée Nationale* and offered to concur with them in any measures for restoring order. They returned him an answer by eighty deputies, but the result is not known.[17] The Duke of Dorset's courier is not arrived, nobody it is supposed being suffered to go out of the city.[18]

11. A false report (see *post* 13 Aug. 1789). Louis Thiroux de Crosne (1736–93), the last *lieutenant général de police* 1785–9, resigned 16 July 1789 and came to England. In Paris during the Reign of Terror, he was arrested and guillotined (*Moniteur* 13 Sept. 1793; Henri-Alexandre Wallon, *Histoire du tribunal révolutionnaire*, 1880–2, iii. 350, 354–5). Possibly HW met him in 1767 and 1769 in Paris (DU DEFFAND v. 321, 328–9). Henry Swinburne considered him a 'blockhead' (*The Courts of Europe*, 1895, ii. 41–2).

12. Jacques de Flesselles (1721–89), last *prévôt des marchands* (first magistrate of Paris) 1788–9, suspected of deceiving the populace, was being escorted (14 July 1789) by the mob to the Palais-Royal for trial when an unknown young man shot him in the head. His head was paraded on a pike to the Palais-Royal and through the principal streets.

13. Bernard-René Jourdan (1740–89), styled Marquis de Launey, governor of the Bastille 1776–89. 'The fate of the Governor M. de Launay, is generally lamented, for he was an officer of great merit, and always treated the prisoners committed to his charge with every degree of lenity and humanity of which the nature of their situations would admit' (Duke of Dorset to the Duke of Leeds, Paris, 30 July 1789, *Despatches from Paris 1784–1790*, ed. Oscar Browning, 1909–10, ii. 255).

14. An exaggerated report current in England (see GM 1789, lix pt ii. 658), but

contradicted a few days later by the Duke of Dorset who, in his dispatch to the Duke of Leeds 16 July 1789, set the number of dead above 40 (*Times* 21 July 1789; *Despatches from Paris 1784–1790* ii. 239), and in his dispatch of 30 July reduced it to 'not more than 7 or 8' (ibid. ii. 254–5). In the absence of an official document, the number remains questionable, but a contemporary report sets the number of dead at 98 (including the wounded who died of their wounds) and the wounded at 60 (Fernand-Auguste-Marie Bournon, *La Bastille*, 1893, p. 201).

15. Antoine-Jérôme de Losme-Salbray (d. 1789), deputy of staff 1782–7, and major of the Bastille, 1787 (ibid. 101–2, 198 *et passim*). Extracts from his journal have been printed in Alfred Bégis, 'Le Registre d'écrou de la Bastille de 1782 à 1789,' *La Nouvelle revue*, Nov.–Dec. 1880, vii. 522–47.

16. The Comte d'Artois and Louis-Stanislas-Xavier (1755–1824), Comte de Provence, afterwards (1814–24) Louis XVIII, King of France.

17. The deputies warned Louis XVI that 'none of his present ministers will ever obtain the confidence of the people,' and the cabinet resigned (Saul K. Padover, *The Life and Death of Louis XVI*, 1939, p. 181).

18. The Duke of Dorset's courier, Lanyun, was delayed, but, leaving as soon as possible after 11 P.M., 16 July, he reached London 20 July, in time for part of the in-

Marshal Broglie is encamped before Versailles with 25,000 men, who are said ready to support the King.

You will want to ask a thousand questions, which I could not answer —nor will I when I can, if neither of you will write to me.

I dined today at Mrs Walsingham's[19] with the Pen-hood,[20] and to-morrow I am to carry thirty *Ghosts* to the Bishop of London, so I am finishing this at past midnight, and shall send it[21] before I go to Mr Ellis[22] to be franked.

These two days have been very fine, and I trust have restored riding in Yorkshire—if I ever do receive another letter, I hope it will give me an account of restored health, for my anger is but a grain of mustard in comparison of my solicitude. Good night! good night!

To Mary Berry, Wednesday 29 July 1789

Address: To Miss Mary Berry to be left at the Post House at York. [Redirected in unknown hand: 'Weldrake.'] *Postmark:* 1 AU 89.
Wheldrake is seven miles SE of York.

Strawberry Hill, July 29, 1789.[1]

I HAVE received two dear letters from you of the 18th and 25th, and though you do not accuse me, but say a thousand kind things to me in the most agreeable manner, I allow my ancientry, and that I am an old fond, jealous and peevish husband, and quarrel with you, if I do not receive a letter exactly at the moment I please to expect one. You talk of mine, but if you knew how I like yours, you would not wonder that I am impatient, and even unreasonable in my demands. However though I own my faults, I do not mean to correct them. I have such pleasure in *your* letters (I am sorry I am here forced to speak in the

formation contained in the dispatch to be printed in *The Times* 21 July 1789. See *Despatches from Paris*, cited in n. 13, ii. 238–44.

19. Charlotte Williams (d. 1790), 2d dau. of Sir Charles Hanbury Williams, K.B., m. (1759) Hon. Robert Boyle-Walsingham, 5th son of 1st E. of Shannon (Burke, *Peerage*, 1928, p. 2085). She lived at Boyle Farm, Thames Ditton.

20. Lady Juliana Penn and her daughter, Sophia Margaret.

21. MS reads 'shall it send it . . .'

22. Welbore Ellis (1713–1802), cr. (13

Aug. 1794) Bn Mendip; M.P. Weymouth 1774–90; m. (1) (1747) Elizabeth Stanhope (d. 1761), only dau. and heir of Sir William Stanhope, K.B., by his first wife, Margaret Rudge; m. (2) (1765) Anne Stanley (ca 1725–1803), sister and heir of Hans Stanley, and 1st dau. of George Stanley of Paulton Park in the New Forest, Hants. He lived at Twickenham in Pope's villa, which he inherited through his first wife, her father having purchased it in 1744.

1. 'No. 10' (B). Renumbered in another hand, 'No. 9.'

singular number, which by the way is an Iricism) that I *will* be cross if you do not write to me perpetually. The quintessence of your last but one was in telling me you are better—how fervently do I wish to receive such accounts every post—but who can mend, but old I, in such detestable weather?—Not one hot day; and if a morning shines, the evening closes with a heavy shower.

The first object in my thoughts being a house for you, which I cannot find yet, I will only say that Lady Cecilia tells me that she has acquainted you that that at Bushy Gate may be had most reasonably—pho! but when?—at the end of September! I told her she was horridly mistaken, and that it is by the end of August you will want one. She would not have been in such an error, if she had calculated by a certain almanac in my heart. Mr Conway[2] and Lady Ailesbury are to be with her today, and Mrs Damer[3] tomorrow, but by General Conway's indecision, and not knowing when they should come this-waywards, I shall not see them on either of these days, having invited my sister, Mr Churchill,[4] and their daughter Sophia and Mr Walpole[5] to come to me precisely for these two days; nay, and on Friday I am to dine with the Bishop of London.[6]

Of French news I can give you no fresher or more authentic account than you can collect in general from the newspapers; but my present[7] visitants and everybody else confirm the veracity of Paris being in that anarchy that speaks the populace domineering in the most cruel and savage manner, and which a servile multitude broken loose calls liberty, and which in all probability will end, when their Massaniello-like[8] reign is over, in their being more abject slaves than ever—and

---

2. Hon. Henry Seymour Conway (1719–95), HW's cousin and correspondent; general, later marshal, in the army. He was the husband of Lady Ailesbury and the father of Mrs Damer.

3. Who returned to London, Sunday, 19 July, from a visit to her parents at Park Place (*World* 21 July 1789).

4. HW's half-sister, Lady Maria (or Mary) Walpole (ca 1725–1801), legitimated daughter of Sir Robert Walpole by Maria Skerrett, m. (1746) Charles Churchill (ca 1720–1812), son of Lt-Gen. Charles Churchill by Anne Oldfield the actress. Lady Mary was housekeeper at Kensington Palace 1762–4; and from 1764 until her death she was housekeeper at Windsor Castle (GM 1764, xxxiv. 499; GM 1801, lxxi pt ii. 861;

GM 1812, lxxxii pt i. 398; *Old Westminsters* i. 186 and *Supplement* p. 33; *Royal Kalendar* 1765–1801; Daniel Lysons, *Environs of London,* 2d edn, 1811, i pt ii. 567; information from Mr O. F. Morshead).

5. Sophia Churchill (d. 1797), their younger daughter, while still a minor, m. (1781) as his 1st wife her cousin Hon. Horatio Walpole (1752–1822), styled Bn Walpole 1806–9, succeeded his father as 2nd E. of Orford of the 3d creation, 1809.

6. The friendship between HW and Bishop Porteus was brought about by Hannah More's 'double treachery' (HW to Hannah More 20 July 1789).

7. MS reads 'presents.'

8. Tommaso Aniello (1623–47), contracted to Masaniello, was a Neapolitan

chiefly by the crime of their *États*,[9] who, had they acted with temper and prudence might have obtained from their poor undesigning King a good and permanent constitution. Who may prove their tyrant, if reviving loyalty does not in a new frenzy force him to be so, it is impossible to foresee—but much may happen first. The rage seems to gain the provinces,[10] and threatens to exhibit the horrors of those times when the peasants massacred the gentlemen.[11] Thus you see I can only conjecture, which is not sending you news; and my intelligence reaches me by so many rebounds, that you must not depend on anything I can tell you. I repeat, because I hear, but draw on you for no credit. Having experienced last winter, in superaddition to a long life of experience, that in Berkeley Square I could not trust to a single report from Kew,[12] can I swallow implicitly at Twickenham the distorted information that comes from Paris through the medium of London!

You asked me in one of your letters who La Chalotais was. I answer, *premier président* or *avocat général*,[13] I forget which, of the Parliament of Bretagne, a great, able, honest and most virtuous man, who opposed the Jesuits and the tyranny of the Duc d'Aiguillon[14]—but he was as indiscreet as he was good. Calonne[15] was his friend and confidant, to whom the imprudent patriot trusted by letter his farther plan of opposition and designs. The wretch pretended to have business with, or to be sent for by the Duc de la Vrillière,[16] Secretary of State, a courtier-wretch, whose mistress used to sell *lettres de cachet* for a louis.[17] Calonne was left to wait in the antechamber, but being, as he

fisherman who led in 1647 a successful revolt of the Neapolitans against Spanish misrule, but soon was assassinated by agents of the Spanish viceroy (Montagu i. 263).

9. In opposing the King.

10. Disturbances at Lyon, Rouen, Dijon, and Rennes were reported in GM 1789, lix pt ii. 660–1, 751. Cf. Philip-Joseph-Benjamin Buchez and Prosper-Charles Roux, *Histoire parlementaire de la révolution française,* 1834–8, ii. 139–44.

11. Perhaps he is thinking of the Jacquerie in France (1358), during the Hundred Years' War.

12. Where George III was during his attack of insanity (1788–9).

13. He was *procureur général.*

14. Emmanuel-Armand Vignerot du Plessis-Richelieu (1720–88), Duc d'Aiguillon, governor of Brittany 1753–70 (DU DEFFAND i. 65, n. 11 *et passim*).

15. Charles-Alexandre de Calonne (1734–1802), *avocat général* to the Council of Artois, *procureur général* to the parliament of Douai, later (1763) *maître des requêtes.* As Louis XVI's *contrôleur général des finances* 1783–7, he was responsible for an enormous deficit, and was exiled to Lorraine. He came to England in 1787 and lived there intermittently until a month before his death, when he was allowed to return to France.

16. Louis Phélypeaux (1705–77), Comte de Saint-Florentin; Duc de la Vrillière, 1770; secretary of state 1725–75 (DU DEFFAND i. 262, n. 7, *et passim*).

17. 'Under the late Duc de la Vrillière, his mistress, Madame Sabatin, had a bureau of printed *lettres de cachet* with blanks, which she sold for twenty-five louis apiece' (HW to Mason 25 Oct. 1775; see also HW to Mann 22 Oct. 1771). Marie-Madeleine-

said, suddenly called in to the minister, as he was reading (a most natural soil for such a lecture) the letter of his friend, he by a second *natural* inadvertence left the fatal letter on the chimney-piece. The consequence, much more *natural,* was that La Chalotais was committed to the Château du Taureau,[18] a horrible dungeon on a rock in the sea, with his son,[19] whose legs mortified there, and the father was doomed to the scaffold; but the Duc de Choiseul[20] sent a counter-reprieve by an express and a crossroad and saved him. At the beginning of this reign[21] he was restored. Paris however was so indignant at the treachery, that this Calonne was hissed out of the theatre, when I was in that capital.[22] When I heard some years after that a Calonne was made *contrôleur général,* I concluded it must be a son, not conceiving that so reprobated a character could emerge to such a height—but asking my sister who has been in France since I was,[23] she assured me it was not only the identic being, but that when she was at Metz, where I think he was *intendant,*[24] the officers in garrison would not dine with him. When he fled hither for an asylum,[25] I did not talk of his story, till I saw it in one of the pamphlets that were written against him in France and that came over hither.[26]

Joséphine de Cusack (styled Aglaé de Cusack) (1725–78), dau. of Richard-Edmond de Cusack (of Irish origin, maréchal-de-camp) by his first wife, Isabelle-Brigitte Fitzgerald; m. (1) —— Sabatin; m. (2) (1756) Étienne-Joseph de Lespinasse, Marquis de Langeac. By her second marriage, although she apparently never lived with her husband, she legitimated her seven children by the Duc de la Vrillière (Woelmont de Brumagne vi. 762–5).

18. Built in 1542 for defense against the English, and converted into a state prison by Louis XIV: it still stands on a rock at the mouth of the Morlaix. La Chalotais was imprisoned there in 1765.

19. Aimé-Jean-Raoul de Caradeuc de la Chalotais (1733–94), also *procureur général* to the parliament of Brittany; guillotined (NBG).

20. Étienne-François de Choiseul-Stainville (1719–85), Duc de Choiseul, minister of foreign affairs 1758–61 and 1766–70, in which post he was succeeded by his enemy, the Duc d'Aiguillon (DU DEFFAND i. 1, n. 1 *et passim*).

21. 1774.

22. In 1775, but HW does not mention the incident in his 'Paris Journals.'

23. HW's last visit to France was in 1775. Since Mme du Deffand does not mention the Churchills' being in Paris 1775–80, Lady Mary was probably in France sometime between 1783 and 1787, when Calonne was in power.

24. Calonne was intendant of Metz 1768–83 (*La Grande encyclopédie*).

25. Calonne, dismissed 8 April 1787, came to England before 14 May 1787 (Christian de Parrel, 'Les Papiers de Calonne,' *The French Quarterly*, 1925, vii. 1).

26. Presumably HW refers to La Chalotais' *Sixième développement de la requête qu'a fait imprimer M. de Calonne . . . ou . . . Calonne dénoncé à la nation française . . . Réédition de détails . . . sur la conduite de M. de Calonne à Versailles, à Rennes et à Saint Malo, en 1765 et 1766,* London, 1787 (BM Cat.). The same work with a different title appeared in London in 1788 (BM Cat.; Bibl. Nat. Cat.). The only French pamphlet of this period in HW's 'Tracts of Geo. 3' (now WSL) is *Réponse critique à la lettre adressée au roi, par M. de Calonne, le 9 février, 1789. Par M. de Soyres, Londres, 1789.* It does not contain the story.

Friday night 31st.

My company prevented my finishing this. Part left me at noon, the residue are to come tomorrow. Today I have dined at Fulham[27] along with Mrs Boscawen, but St Swithin played the devil so, that we could not stir out of doors, and had fires to chase the watery spirits. Quin[28] being once asked, if he had ever seen so bad a winter, replied, 'Yes, just such an one last summer.'[29]—And here is its youngest brother!

Mrs Boscawen saw a letter from Paris to Miss Sayer[30] this morning, which says Necker's son-in-law[31] was arrived, and had announced his father-in-law's promise of return from Basle.[32] I do not know whether his honour or ambition prompt this compliance—surely not his discretion. I am much acquainted with him,[33] and do not hold him great and profound enough to quell the present anarchy. If he attempts to moderate for the King, I shall not be surprised if he falls another victim to tumultuary jealousy and outrage. All accounts agree in the violences of the mob against the inoffensive as well as against the objects of their resentment, and in the provinces, where even women are not safe in their houses. The hotel of the Duc du Châtelet, lately built and

27. With Bishop and Mrs Porteus.
28. James Quin (1693–1766), the actor and wit.
29. 'One summer, when the month of July happened to be extremely cold, some person asked Quin if he ever remembered such a summer. "Oh yes," replied the wag, "last winter" ' (*The Life of Mr James Quin*, 1887, p. 100).
30. Frances Julia Sayer (1757–1850), who had been in Paris in 1788 (HW to Lord Strafford 2 Aug. 1788), was the only dau. of James Sayer of the Manor House, Marsh Gate, Richmond, by Mrs Boscawen's first cousin, Julia Margaret Evelyn. She m. (1805) in Holland, Marie-Charles-Joseph de Pougens (whom she had known since 1786), natural son of Louis-François de Bourbon, Prince de Conti (Helen Evelyn, *History of the Evelyn Family*, 1915, pp. 510–11; *Old Westminsters*, sub Sayer, Edward; NBG; *Mémoires de la société des antiquaires de France* xi [1835] p. xxxvii). After the death of her mother in 1777, she was a frequent guest of Mrs Boscawen, who in her correspondence with Mrs Delany refers to Miss Sayer as 'my young friend' and 'your favourite' (*Delany Corr.* v. 328–9; vi. *passim*).

For an affectionate letter from Mrs Boscawen to her 28 Oct. 1793 see Evelyn, op. cit. 564–5. She was also a friend of the Burneys (Frances Burney d'Arblay, *Memoirs of Doctor Burney*, 1832, iii. 352).
31. Eric-Magnus (d. 1802), Baron de Staël-Holstein, Swedish ambassador to France, m. (1786) Anne-Louise-Germaine Necker. 'The Baron de Stael . . . is arrived at Versailles charged with a letter from M. Necker to declare his consent to resume his situation at the head of the Finances . . .' (*Despatches from Paris 1784–1790*, ed. Oscar Browning, 1909–10, ii. 251).
32. Receiving his recall (dated 16 July) at Basle, Necker replied 23 July, returned to Paris 28 July, and made his appearance in the National Assembly on the following day (Necker, *De la Révolution française*, 1797, ii. 17–21; *Journal de Paris* 31 July 1789; *London Chronicle* 6–8 Aug. 1789, lxvi. 132; *Oracle. Bell's New World* 5 Aug. 1789).
33. HW had met the Neckers in Paris and had entertained them at Strawberry Hill (DU DEFFAND vi. 213); he never held a high opinion of Necker's ability (ibid. iv. 318, 327; HW to Lady Ossory 3 Dec. 1788; HW to Conway 15 July 1789).

superb,[34] has been assaulted and the furniture sold by auction[35]—but a most shocking act of a royalist in Burgundy,[36] who is said to have blown up a committee of forty persons, will probably spread the flames of civil rage much wider. When I read the account, I did not believe it; but the Bishop[37] says he hears the *États* have required the King to write to every foreign power not to harbour the execrable author, who is fled.[38] I fear this conflagration will not end as rapidly as that in Holland![39]

I have left myself no room but for a codicil of scraps. Mrs Damer will be with me tomorrow. With the Pepyses I have had small dealings yet, from his Chancery and the House of Lords.[40] Lady Juliana Penn had a very bad fall down stairs about a week ago at Windsor and was much bruised, but with no other bad consequences. Though wife Agnes's pen lies fallow, I hope her pencil does not. I will write but to

34. HW saw it in 1775, apparently soon after its completion (DU DEFFAND v. 348).

35. 'By letters received yesterday [?27 July] from Paris we learn that the mob proceeded to pull down the house of the Duc de Châtelet, and that the Marquis de Lafayette endeavoured to prevent it, but in vain' (*London Chronicle* 25–28 July 1789, lxvi. 96). The Duke of Dorset's dispatch from Paris 23 July 1789 gives a different account: 'The Duc de Châtelet's goods, which his servants were attempting to remove from Paris, were seized a few days ago in the street, and conducted to the Hôtel de Ville: the carriages in which the goods were packed and the horses were immediately sold in the Place Dauphine, and the money arising from the sale is to be as I understand divided amongst some of the French Guards, who had claims upon the Duc de Châtelet on the score of some transactions between them when he commanded the regiment' (*Despatches from Paris 1784–90* ii. 249).

36. Jean-Antoine-Marie de Mesmay (b. 1751), *conseiller* of the parliament of Franche-Comté 1780–9, Seigneur de Quincey, near Vesoul (Vicomte Alberic de Truchis de Varennes, *Le Rétablissement du Parlement de Franche-Comté*, Besançon, 1922, p. 64; GM 1789, lix pt ii. 750). For comments of English travellers who were in Burgundy during this part of the Revolution, see M. Peyre, 'Les Voyageurs anglais en Bourgogne au XVIIIᵉ siècle,' *Annales de Bourgogne*, Dijon, 1932, iv. 130–54, especially pp. 151–4.

37. Of London, Bishop Porteus.

38. A circumstantial account of this affair was read in the National Assembly 25 July 1789 (Buchez and Roux, op. cit. ii. 161–2), and was much publicized in France and England (see *The Oracle. Bell's New World* 31 July 1789; *London Chronicle* 30 July–1 Aug., 4–6 Aug. 1789, lxvi. 111–12, 127). It was repeated in GM 1789, lix pt ii. 750–1, with the closing sentence: 'On examination, report says, the whole was found to be a villainous fabrication.' Cf. *post* 13 Aug. 1789. Apparently de Mesmay, who had invited the soldiers and citizens of Vesoul for a fête, 'was going to give some fireworks, when some of the pieces and some of the gunpowder exploded: he fled in alarm' (Thomas Carlyle, *The French Revolution*, ed. J. Holland Rose, 1913, i. 270, n. 2). For a different version, see Maurice Cousin, *L'Esprit public dans le bailliage d'Amont*, Dijon, 1922, pp. 103–5. See also de Mesmay's own account, *Mémoire justificatif*, Besançon, 1789 (Bibl. Nat. Cat.). His innocence was not established in the courts until 4 June 1791 (Hippolyte-Adolphe Taine, *Les Origines de la France contemporaine: la révolution*, i [1878]. 98), although general belief in his innocence was reported in *The London Chronicle* 20–22 Aug., 12–15 Sept. 1789, lxvi. 182–3, 259.

39. Where a popular revolt, at its height in 1787, had been suppressed. See *Annual Register*, 1787, xxix pt i. 1–64.

40. One of the duties of Masters in Chancery was to assist the Lord Chancellor in the House of Lords.

one if but one will write to me, and I will not keep a new name I have just assumed, that of

HORACE FONDLEWIVES.

PS. Mrs Greville is dead.[41]

To Mary Berry, Thursday 6 August 1789

Address: To Miss Mary Berry to be left at the Post House at York. [Redirected in unknown hand: 'Weldrake.'] *Postmark:* 7 AU 89.

Strawberry, Thursday night, Aug. 6, 1789.

BY your letter of 1st and 3rd which I received this morning, you surprise me by complaining of my silence, when I thought I had talked your *eyes* to death. If I did pause, it was to give you time to answer. Here is a list of talks since you left London: June 27,[1] 30, July 3,[2] 4 to Miss A.,[3] 9, 16,[4] 19, 31.[5] If eight letters, and those, no scraps, in less than forty days, are not the deeds of something more than a correspondent, I wish I may never be in love again. If you have not received all these, the devil take the post house at York! By your answers I should not think above one had miscarried, which was about Mrs Shakerley's house,[6] to which I do not remember you replied. I did not think it would suit you.

---

41. Frances Macartney, dau. of James Macartney, M.P., m. (1748) Fulke Greville, grandson of 5th Bn Brooke. She wrote the much admired 'Ode to Indifference' and other poems, was the 'Fanny' of HW's poem, 'The Beauties' (*Works* i. 23), and was godmother of Fanny Burney, later Mme d'Arblay (DU DEFFAND i. 124 *et passim;* John Lodge and Mervyn Archdall, *Peerage of Ireland,* 1789, vii. 91; *Diary and Letters of Madame d'Arblay,* ed. Charlotte Barrett and Austin Dobson, 1904–5, ii. 137–8, iv. 329; D'Arblay, *Memoirs of Doctor Burney,* 1832, i. 55–61; *Register Book of Marriages . . . of St George, Hanover Square, Vol. I —1725 to 1787,* ed. John H. Chapman, 1886, p. 39).

1. *Ante* 23 June 1789.
2. Missing.
3. Missing.
4. *Ante* 10 July 1789.

5. *Ante* 29 July 1789.
6. Margaret Morris (1734–1803), dau. of Roger Morris of Netherby, Yorks; m. (1766) as 2d wife, Peter Shakerley (1709–81) of Somerford Park, Cheshire (*Old Westminsters, sub* Shakerley, Peter; GM 1803, lxxiii pt i. 197; Burke, *Landed Gentry,* 1851, i. 889). In the 'Plan of Twickenham . . . 1784' (frontispiece to Edward Ironside, *History and Antiquities of Twickenham,* 1797) the house of 'Mr Shackerly' joins Twickenham churchyard on the west. Apparently the Shakerleys occupied at one time a house later known as Cross Deep (ibid. 143; R. S. Cobbett, *Memorials of Twickenham,* 1872, p. 261), and after his death Mrs Shakerley rented Dial House for a time (Ironside, p. 144; Cobbett, loc. cit.). She died at Twickenham (GM, loc. cit.). In the absence of HW's letter, it is not clear to which house he refers.

I am not going to complain again, but to lament. I now find I shall not see you before the end of September—a month later than I expected would be nothing to an old husband, but it is a century to a husband that is old. Mrs Damer, who passed Saturday and Sunday here with her parents, and I settled it with them that Mr Berry and you two should meet us at Park Place[7] the beginning of September.[8] Now you will make me hate that month more than ever. Long evenings without a fire are tiresome, and without two wives insupportable!

Major Dixon[9] was here too, and on Sunday the Johnstones[10] and Mrs Grenville dined and passed the whole day with us. On Monday the Conways went to Ealing: the Duke is gone to Inverary,[11] but returns the beginning of ugly September to carry the Duchess[12] to Italy; and she, who, poor woman, loves a train, carries Lady Augusta and Mr Clavering[13] with them—She is very ill indeed.

I have not a penful of news for you—no, though Mr Cambridge was here this morning.[14] The arrival of Necker,[15] I suppose, has suspended the horrors of Paris for a moment, till the mob find that he does not propose to crown them all in the room of their late King. I shall go to London tomorrow for one night, yet I am not likely to see anybody that knows much authentic.

General Fitzwilliam[16] is dead at Richmond extremely rich. He has

7. Conway's seat in Berkshire, near Henley on Thames. See *post* 2 July 1790.

8. HW's visit to Park Place was delayed, and apparently the Berrys did not go there (*post* 27 Aug., 18, 30 Sept. 1789).

9. Edward Jerningham.

10. Lady Cecilia and her husband, Gen. James Johnston (ca 1721–97); see MONTAGU i. 28 *et passim.*

11. 'The Duke of Argyle passed through Edinburgh on Thursday last [13 Aug.], for Inverary' (*Oracle. Bell's New World* 18 Aug.; *Times* 19 Aug. 1789). Inveraray Castle, Argyllshire, the Duke's seat, was built 1744–61.

12. Elizabeth Gunning (1733–90), the famous beauty, m. (1) (1752) James Hamilton (1724–58), 6th D. of Hamilton, 1743; m. (2) (1759) Col. John Campbell (1723–1806), 5th D. of Argyll, 1770. For an account of the journey to Italy, see Horace Bleackley, *The Story of a Beautiful Duchess*, 1908, pp. 307–11.

13. Lady Augusta Campbell (1760–1831), elder dau. of the D. of Argyll, had attracted

considerable attention in 1788 by her elopement and marriage to Lt Henry Mordaunt Clavering (1766–1850), 2d son of Sir John Clavering, K.B., by Lady Diana West, later (1802) colonel and (1807; local rank in South America) brigadier-general (*Scots Peerage* i. 387; *Old Westminsters;* Bleackley, op. cit. 303–5; N&Q 1912, 11th ser. v. 98). Lady Augusta and her two children did not return until after her parents reached London (*post* 29 July 1790; *Times* 28 July 1790).

14. One of HW's numerous comments on Cambridge's love of gossip.

15. 28 July (see preceding letter).

16. Hon. John Fitzwilliam (1714–31 July 1789), 3d son of Richard, 5th Vct Fitzwilliam, entered the army ca 1732, served with the Duke of Cumberland (and was one of his grooms of the Bedchamber ca 1745–65), and attained the rank of general, 1778 (*Old Westminsters; Court and City Register,* 1748–65). His will, dated 18 Aug. 1786, with a codicil 30 June 1788, was proved in London 31 July 1789.

not I believe extremely disappointed his nephew the Viscount,[17] who did not depend on hopes that had been thrown out to him, nor is much surprised that the General's upper servant[18] and his late wife's[19] woman,[20] are the principal heirs, as the Abbé Nichols and others long foresaw. Lord Fitzwilliam has only an estate of £550 a year.[21] The man-servant, whom he originally took a shoeless boy in Wales playing on the harp, will have above forty thousand pounds;[22] the woman 300 a year[23] in long annuities. A will however pleases one, you know, if it pleases one anyhow. To General Conway (an old fellow-servant in the late Duke of Cumberland's[24] family, as were Lord Dover[25] and Lord

---

17. Richard Fitzwilliam (1745–1816), 7th Vct Fitzwilliam. 'I give to my nephew Richard Lord Viscount Fitzwilliam my large rosewood table, as also my marble statue of Hercules Reposing, with the plinth and mahogany frame on which it lays, and I give and devise the undivided fourth part or share which I have or am entitled to of and in all and every the manors, messuages, cottages . . . lands, rectory, advowsons . . . whatsoever in the county of Salop . . . heretofore the estate . . . of Sir Humphrey Briggs formerly of Haughton otherwise Houghton in the same county . . . mentioned and remprised in certain indentures of lease and release bearing date respectively the twenty-sixth and twenty-seventh days of June . . . one thousand seven hundred and thirty-four, both executed by the said Sir Humphrey Briggs, with the appurtenances unto my said nephew Richard Lord Viscount Fitzwilliam his heirs and assigns forever.'

18. Thomas Jones: 'I give and devise all the rest and residue of my estates real and personal whatsoever and wheresoever to my good and faithful and most excellent servant Thomas Jones whom I took from his parents in Wales when he was young and whom I have educated and brought up as my own child and to whom my dear and late wife and I have been much obliged, his heirs, executors, administrators and assigns for ever, and God bless him with it.'

19. Barbara Chandler (d. 1786), dau. of Edward Chandler, Bp of Durham, m. (1) (1731) William Cavendish (d. 1751), son of Lord James Cavendish; m. (2) (1751) Hon. John Fitzwilliam (GM 1731, i. 130; Collins, Peerage, 1812, i. 354; John Lodge and Mervyn Archdall, Peerage of Ireland, 1789, iv. 320; GM 1786, lvi pt i. 269).

20. 'I give to Mrs Mary Rocke, my present housekeeper, whose unremitted tenderness and care of my dear late wife well entitled her to my love and protection, the sum of five hundred pounds . . . and I give to the aforesaid Mrs Mary Rocke four hundred and thirty pounds a year long annuities transferable and payable at the Bank of England, and I give to the aforesaid Mary Rocke twelve hundred and ninety-six pounds Bank stock, and I also give to the said Mary Rocke my gold inlaid snuff box in the lid of which is an enamelled picture of my late dear wife Barbara Fitzwilliam, and I give to the said Mary Rocke my dumb repeating gold watch and also all my shirts, stocks, handkerchiefs, lace ruffles, with my two night gowns.'

21. See n. 17. HW elsewhere (to Lady Ossory 4 Aug. 1789) values the estate at £500 a year, as does Richard Owen Cambridge in a letter to Mary Berry (MBJ i. 182).

22. 'On Friday, August 21, the executors transferred into the name of . . . Mr Jones the sum of £40,000 3 per cent. consols and £1000 per annum, long annuities. The General's late residence at Richmond [Green] including the furniture, etc., are estimated at £20,000 more. When to these is added a considerable landed property, Mr J. may justly boast the possession of a more than commonly ample fortune' (GM 1789, lix pt ii. 766).

23. But see above, n. 20.

24. William Augustus (1721–65), 3d son of George II; D. of Cumberland, 1726; the famous military commander. Conway served in Germany and Scotland under him 1745–7, part of the time as his aide-decamp.

25. Joseph Yorke (1724–92), 3d son of 1st E. of Hardwicke; cr. (1788) Bn Dover; aide-

Frederic Cavendish,[26] similar legatees) he has given £500. This is so much to my mind, that I shall not haggle about the rest of the will.[27]

I am rejoiced that you do not go to York races.[28] Whatever I do myself, I should not like to have the P[rince] of Wales[29] have two or *three* wives.[30] Believe me, who have some cause for knowing, there is nothing so transitory as the happiness of red liveries![31]

It is not to fill up the page that I now advert to the weather, which at last is become fine and tolerably warm; but I enjoy it, as it will favour your riding, and both I trust will give you full health and spirits by the ugly month's end. Your old rapacious landlord[32] I flatter myself will be reasonable, when it is in vain to be otherwise—I should not like the house by Bushy Park for you, though better than none. The personage that will gain most by your delay will be Tonton, whose long nose begins to recover its curled rotundity. It is the best-tempered quiet animal alive, which is candid in me to own, as he, as long as it is

de-camp to the Duke of Cumberland 1745–9.

26. Lord Frederick Cavendish (1729–1803), 3d son of 3d D. of Devonshire, was the Duke of Cumberland's aide-de-camp in Germany, 1757, and one of his lords of the Bedchamber ca 1757–65 (*Court and City Register*). He was also M.P. for Derbyshire, 1751, and for Derby 1754–80, and field-marshal, 1796. In 1766, on inheriting the estate of Twickenham Park, he became HW's neighbour.

27. Richard Owen Cambridge comments on Gen. Fitzwilliam's will: 'General Fitzwilliam's will is a disgrace to misanthropy. Some large and useless legacies to people who neither want nor will be thankful, consume such a portion of his large wealth as would have made some others . . . comfortable. . . . To Lord Fitz—— £500 a year in Northamptonshire. His servant, Harper Tom Jones, residuary legatee, above £40,000. He came to Lord Fitz——; said he was overpowered; wished he had had only a suitable provision; did not know what to do with his fortune; had no friend; begged his Lordship's protection; offered all the books and pictures, and anything else his Lordship would accept. Lord F—— said to me: If the General had known he would have behaved so, he would not have left it him. I dare say if he looks upon Richmond from his present situation,

he is mortified to find his purpose is but half executed if misbehaviour is not added to privation' (MBJ i. 182–3).

28. 22–29 August 1789 (James Weatherby, *Racing Calendar . . . 1789*, 1790, xvii. 94–8).

29. George Augustus Frederick (1762–1830), P. of Wales, later (1820) George IV, attended the races at York 24–29 Aug. (*Oracle. Bell's New World* 26 Aug.–1 Sept. 1789), and raced several horses.

30. The 'two' wives would be Mary and Agnes Berry, and 'three' would include Mrs Fitzherbert, with whom the Prince went through a marriage ceremony in 1785; see 'Mem. 1783–91,' *sub* 17, 22 Feb. 1786; 26, 30 April 1787.

31. HW's niece was unhappily married to the Duke of Gloucester, whose servants (and those of the Prince of Wales) wore red, the royal livery. Lady Almeria Carpenter (1752–1809), Lady of the Bedchamber to the Duchess of Gloucester, was mistress to the Duke, by whom she had a daughter, born in 1781 (HW to Mann 28 March 1786; Violet Biddulph, *The Three Ladies Waldegrave* [1938], pp. 181–5; John Lodge and Mervyn Archdall, *Peerage of Ireland*, 1789, iii. 94; *Journal and Correspondence of William Lord Auckland*, ed. 3d Bn Auckland, 1861–2, i. 463).

32. Henry Collingwood Selby.

light, prefers my footboy,[33] or a bone on the lawn, to my company. In the evening as I allow him to lie on every couch and chair, he thinks me agreeable enough. I must celebrate the sense of Fidelle, Mrs Damer's terrier. Without making the slightest gesture, her mistress only said to her, 'Now, Fidelle, you may here jump on any chair you please'; she instantly jumped on the settee; and so she did in every room for the whole two days she stayed. This is another demonstration to me that dogs understand even language as far as it relates to their own affairs.

Now I have cleared my character, and that harmony is quite re-established, I will not attempt to eke out my letter, only to say that I am sorry there is but one pen in your family—I hinted in my last, that I would compound for a pencil. Of all your visits, that cost me a month, I grudge the least that to your grandmother and aunt, as I can judge how happy you make them—It is a good symptom too for your husband: duty and gratitude to parents are seldom, I believe, ingredients in bad wives. Adieu!

Yours most cordially and constantly,

H. W.

To Agnes Berry, Thursday 13 August 1789

Address: To Miss Agnes Berry to be left at the Post House at York.
Postmark: 14 AU 89.
This letter was printed as to Mary Berry in Mrs Toynbee's edition.

Strawberry Hill, Aug. 13, 1789.[1]

I HAVE received at once most kind letters from you both—too kind, for you both talk of gratitude—Mercy on me! Which is the obliged? and which is the gainer? Two charming beings, whom everybody likes and approves;[2] and who yet can be pleased with the company and conversation and old stories of a Methusalem? or I, who at the end of my days have fallen into a more agreeable society than ever I knew at any period of my life? I will say nothing of your persons, sense or accom-

---

33. Presumably 'John,' who committed suicide October 1791 (*post* 16, 20 Oct. 1791).

1. 'No. 11' (B). Renumbered in another hand, 'No. 10.'
2. Referring to the Berrys, William

Weller Pepys wrote to Hannah More 17 Sept. 1789: 'I believe you think with Mr Walpole and Mr Cambridge, who agree in declaring that in their long lives they have never seen their equals' (*A Later Pepys*, ed. Alice C. C. Gaussen, 1904, ii. 279).

plishments; but where, united with all those, could I find so much simplicity, void of pretensions and affectation? This from any other man would sound like compliment and flattery; but in me, who have appointed myself your guardian, it is a duty to tell you of your merits, that you may preserve and persevere in them. If I ever descry any faults, I will tell you as freely of them. Be just what you are, and you may dare my reproofs.

I will restrain even reproaches, though in jest, if it puts my sweet Agnes to the trouble of writing when she does not care for it. It is the extreme equality of my affection for both, that makes me jealous if I do not receive equal tokens of friendship from both—and though nothing is more just than the observation of two sisters repeating the same ideas, yet never was that remark so ill applied. Though your minds are so congenial, I have long observed how originally each of you expresses her thoughts. I could repeat to you expressions of both, which I remember as distinctly, as if I had only known either of you. For the future there shall be perfect liberty amongst us: either of you shall write when she pleases; while my letters are inseparably meant to both, though the direction may contain but one name, lest the postman should not comprehend a double address.

I can tell you nothing new from France, that is authentic, only that the explosion at Besançon,[3] I am assured, was a fable grounded on an accident that happened to a man who [was] going to see a train laid for blowing up a hill, and having a pipe in his mouth, some sparks fell, and setting fire, blew up him, his wife and child. The death of the Abbess of Monmartre[4] was false too, though written by Mrs Swinburn to her husband![5] What then can one believe?—nothing—nay, I can prove

3. See *ante* 29 July 1789. The explosion was near Vesoul, which is about 27 miles north of Besançon.

4. Marie-Louise de Montmorency-Laval (1723–94), dau. of the Comte de Laval, Maréchal de France. She was the Abbess of Montmartre from 1760 until its dissolution in 1792; guillotined 24 July 1794 (*Recueil des chartes de l'abbaye royale de Montmartre*, ed. Édouard de Barthélemy, 1883, pp. 34, 42, 309; Jean-Baptiste-Pierre Jullien de Courcelles, *Histoire généalogique . . . des pairs de France*, 1822–33, ii. 35; *Moniteur* 6 Aug. 1794). 'The Abbess of Montmartre has been brought to the Hôtel de Ville and accused of having concealed cannon and other warlike stores in her convent' (*World* 28 July 1789).

5. Martha Baker (1747–1809), dau. of John Baker of Chichester, Sussex, solicitor-general of the Leeward Islands; m. (1767) Henry Swinburne (1743–1803), the traveller. An excellent account of her life is given in her father's *Diary*, ed. Philip C. Yorke [1931], pp. 24–46 *et passim*. Because of business in connection with an estate, and her unwillingness to leave her son Henry, a page at the French court, she remained in Paris until late in November 1789. Seven of her letters written to her husband between 10 May and 9 Oct. 1789 are in Henry Swinburne, *The Courts of Europe*, 1895, ii. 68–79, but they contain no reference to the Abbess of Montmartre. 'Political Extracts from Mrs Swinburne's Letters from Paris 1788–1789' (BM, Add. MS 33,121, ff. 5–17)

that there is a man living who believes his ears against his own eyes. Listen! The minister of our parish[6] told me t'other day that Lord Camelford[7] is *not* the author of a pamphlet[8] of which there has been much talk lately—I said, 'Sir, I doubt you are mistaken.' He replied, 'Sir, I assure you Mr Cambridge told me an hour ago that he had just seen the D. of Queensberry[9] who had affirmed to him that the pamphlet is not Lord C's.' I lifted up my eyes to the third heaven! 'Mr C. told you so!'—'Yes, Sir, Mr C.'—'Bless my soul, Sir,' said I, 'why, but four days ago, Mr C. in this room told me Mr G. Hardinge[10] had shown him the pamphlet, and told him he had received it from Lord C. the author: Mr C. had read it, and gave me a minute account of the six letters it contained.'[11]

contains no notice of death, but there is the following entry for 22 July 1789: 'Mme de Montmorency, Abbess of Montmartre, was taken to the Hôtel de Ville yesterday because cannon was found in the Abbey and all implements for attacking Paris. The Intendant of Paris, Berthier, is also taken. Nobody yet knows what will be the fate of those two unfortunate royalists' (f. 14v.). The originals of Mrs Swinburne's letters have not been located.

6. Robert Burt (ca 1756–17 Oct. 1791), son of Burt of St Christopher's, West Indies; Trinity College, Cambridge (LL.B. 1781); chaplain to the Prince of Wales, ca 1785, at whose marriage to Mrs Fitzherbert he officiated in December of that year; rector of St Mary's, Hoo in Kent, 1786; vicar of Twickenham, 1788 (Edward Ironside, *History and Antiquities of Twickenham*, 1797, pp. 68, 136; Edward Hasted, *History of Kent*, Canterbury, 1797–1801, iv. 26–7; *Royal Kalendar*, 1785–91; *Admissions to Trinity College, Cambridge . . . 1701 to 1800*, ed. W. W. Rouse Ball and J. A. Venn, 1911, p. 234). He had been at SH 3 Aug. ('Visitors'), but HW apparently refers to a later meeting.

7. Thomas Pitt (1737–93), 1st Bn Camelford. HW's friendship for him cooled when they disagreed about politics (see HW to Mann, 17 Sept. 1778). For HW's unfavourable opinion of him, see 'Mem. 1783–91,' *sub* 24 Dec. 1783. He was in Paris from about the end of May to the end of August 1789 (John Nichols, *Literary Illustrations of the Eighteenth Century*, 1817–58, vi. 111–17).

8. *Lettres de la Comtesse de —— au*

Chevalier de —— [?Paris], 1789; both BM Cat. and Bibl. Nat. Cat. assign it to Jean Devaines. In *The Oracle* 5 Aug. 1789 and *The World* 6 Aug. 1789 it is attributed to Lord Camelford, who denied he was the author (MBJ i. 183; John Nichols, op. cit. vi. 117–18).

9. William Douglas (1725–1810), 4th D. of Queensberry, the notorious 'Old Q.'

10. George Hardinge (1743–1816), HW's friend and correspondent, whose account of HW is in John Nichols, *Literary Anecdotes of the Eighteenth Century*, 1812–15, viii. 525–7. He lived at Ragman's Castle, near Cambridge's house. For Lord Camelford's letters to Hardinge, see John Nichols, *Illustrations of the Literary History of the Eighteenth Century*, 1817–58, vi. 74–139.

11. According to *Correspondance littéraire . . . par Grimm*, etc., 1877–82, xv. 479–80, where extracts from the pamphlet are given, 'Ces Lettres . . . peignent avec autant de malice que de légèreté la nouvelle espèce de ridicules que l'effervescence actuelle des esprits vient de mettre à la mode.' 'A pamphlet had been published, supposed to have been the work of an English peer, but this has since been denied, to prove that the claims of the [French] people were in many instances unreasonable, and that France could not long have a monarchy, even limited, if the Three Orders were to unite, and vote in one body' (GM 1789, lix pt ii. 848). Apropos of this passage, a recent biographer of Cambridge observes: 'As a matter of fact, the case against Cambridge was not so black as Walpole painted it. A letter to Mary Berry, dated two days later, shows that at the

Was ever so strange a story! Lo! what a thirst of news can do! It can efface one's memory in four days! and leave no more impression, than if one's memory could not contain a tittle but what it has received last.

I do not vouch for my next story—but true or coined, the answer was good. The King of Spain[12] consulted his minister[13] whether he should march 40,000 men into France at the requisition of Louis Seize. 'I can send them if your Majesty commands me,' replied the minister—'but if I do, your Majesty will soon want them at home.'

The flame does seem spreading, and no doubt will rage in Austrian Flanders,[14] where a more real tyrant[15] than poor Louis has justly provoked them.

I have not seen Mrs A.[16] very lately, but should, like you, much disapprove jesting on such dreadful calamities. I am shocked at a brutality that disgraces us: in London a caricatura print has been published against M. de Luxembourg and some of the unhappy fugitives and the Queen of France.[17]

I approve of your suspending a new offer to your late landlord[18] till quite necessary—nay, I have heard of a house at Teddington likely to be vacant by your time, and have ordered an indirect inquiry to be made. It is much nearer to Twickenham than t'other side of Bushy Park.

Of the Pepyses I have seen very little yet: I called on them t'other

time Cambridge had spoken to Walpole he had been misled, not only by his ears, but also by his eyes—certain "false insinuations of the *Morning Post*" having made him believe in Camelford's authorship of the pamphlet. And when he shared his opposite opinion with the minister, it was after having seen a letter from Camelford, printed in another paper, which expressly denied the authorship' (Richard D. Altick, *Richard Owen Cambridge*, Philadelphia, 1941, p. 51). Cf. MBJ i. 183–4.

12. Charles IV (1748–1819), K. of Spain 1788; forced to abdicate, 1808.

13. José Moñino (1728–1808), Count of Florida Blanca; prime minister under Charles III 1777–88, and under Charles IV 1788–92 (*Enciclopedia universal ilustrada*, Barcelona, etc. [1905–30], xxxvi. 837–8).

14. HW's forecast was supported by a report of unrest and rebellion in Austrian Flanders, in *The Oracle. Bell's New World* 2 Nov. 1789.

15. Joseph II (1741–90), Holy Roman Emperor 1765–90.

16. Mrs Anderson. Cf. last paragraph of this letter.

17. The print satirizing the flight of the émigrés from France to England and Spain is entitled 'Salus in fugâ; La France se purge petit à petit.' Published anonymously 29 July 1789, it is now attributed to Isaac Cruikshank. Among the fourteen people satirized, some indecently, are the Duc and Duchesse de Luxembourg and their unmarried daughter, Calonne, Duc de Broglie, Baron de Breteuil, and the Duc and Duchesse de Polignac, the last of whom cries out, 'Mais où est donc Antoinette?' For a full description of the print, see BM, *Satiric Prints* vi. 687–8 (No. 7663) and Bibliothèque nationale, Département des estampes, *Un Siècle d'histoire de France par l'estampe, 1770–1871, Collection de Vinck*, 1909–, ii. 610–11; for a reproduction, see ibid., plate xv, p. 587. In both catalogues it is incorrectly assigned to 1790.

18. Henry Collingwood Selby.

day to ask them to dine here, but one of their little boys has broken his arm,[19] and the mother will not leave him, nor the husband her.

I have been at Lady Cecilia's this evening since I wrote the first part of my letter. Mr Wheler[20] is there and Mrs Anderson, who has seen, as she told you, swarms of refugees at the French Embassador's,[21] especially the *lieutenant de police,* Monsieur de Crosne, who had the rope about his neck, but made his escape while a new tumult arose.[22] They are savages, who have known so little of liberty, that they take murder for it. Goodnight!

To MARY BERRY, Thursday 20 August 1789

Address: To Miss Mary Berry to be left at the Post House, York.
Postmark: 22 AU 89.

Strawberry Hill, Thursday night, Aug. 20, 1789.

IF the worst comes to the worst, I think, I can secure you a house at Teddington, a very comfortable one, very reasonably, and a more agreeable one than the Cecilian destination[1] at Bushy Gate—at least *more agreeable to my Lord Castlecomer,* for it is nearer to me by half. That Strawberry proverb I must explain to you for your future use. There was an old Lady Castlecomer,[2] who had an only son,[3] and he had

19. The Pepyses' 'little boy Harry had the misfortune to break his arm by a fall out of a child's chaise, and his poor mother, who was all the time nursing her infant, and very ill herself, never lost sight of him for an hour during the course of a long five weeks, which has nearly been too much for her' (Pepys to Hannah More 17 Sept. 1789, *A Later Pepys,* ed. Alice C. C. Gaussen, 1904, ii. 277). Harry was their third son, Henry (1783–1860), Bp of Sodor and Man 1840–1, of Worcester 1841–60. Richard Owen Cambridge, in a letter to Mary Berry (undated, but written in August 1789) refers to him as a 'sweet patient boy' (MBJ i. 183).

20. Perhaps the Rev. Charles Wheler (1730–1821), who succeeded his brother as 7th Bt, of Leamington Hastings, Warwickshire, in 1799; Clare College, Cambridge; vicar of Leamington Hastings 1757–1821; prebendary of York 1779–1821.

21. The Marquis de la Luzerne's in Portman Square.

22. 'Monsieur de Crosne . . . *hanged* and *beheaded* in many papers on the first bursting forth of the disturbances, yesterday [29 July] arrived unhurt at the French ambassador's' (*World* 30 July 1789). It was reported that he escaped with 'a large sum' of money (*London Chronicle* 6–8 Aug. 1789, lxvi. 133).

———

1. The house suggested by Lady Cecilia Johnston.

2. Frances Pelham (d. 1756), sister of Thomas Pelham-Holles, 1st D. of Newcastle, n.c.; m. (1715 or 1717) Christopher Wandesford (1684–1719), 2d Vct Castlecomer (GEC; Collins, *Peerage,* 1768, ii. 129). She died at Twickenham, and HW bought some of her furniture for SH (*SH Accounts,* 7, 89–90).

3. Christopher Wandesford (1717–36), 3d Vct Castlecomer, 1719; matriculated at Christ Church, Oxford, 23 May 1733; created M.A. 17 March 1736; died of smallpox

a tutor called Roberts,[4] who happened to break his leg. A visitant lamented the accident to her Ladyship: the old rock replied, 'Yes, indeed, it is very inconvenient to my Lord Castlecomer!' This saying was adopted forty years ago into the phraseology of Strawberry, and is very expressive of that selfish apathy towards others, which refers everything to its own centre, and never feels any shock that does not vibrate to its own interest.[5]

The house in question is at the entrance of Teddington; you may shake hands with Mr Pepys out of the window. A Mrs Armstrong[6] took it for one year at fourscore pounds, but is tired of making hay and minded to leave it at Michaelmas; but says that her landlord[7] has behaved so well towards her, that though she will pay the whole, she will give it up to him at quitting it. I sent to him to inquire what he would ask for October and November—he replied, I should name my own price, and I am to have the refusal. I think he cannot expect above £20 at most. All I now dread is Madame Armstrong's loitering into October. Tell me your pleasure on this. Lady Anne Conolly[8] who visits Mrs Armstrong, says the house is perfectly neat and convenient. Let the Duke of Northumberland's steward[9] rust with his avarice!

I know nothing, nothing at all. Indeed I am too much engrossed by a sad misfortune too likely to fall on my family and me! Dear Lady Dysart[10] is in the utmost danger: her case is pronounced to be water on her breast, and every day may be her last. She suffers considerably, but with her unalterable patience!—But I will not afflict your tender hearts with dwelling on so melancholy a subject.

Lady Juliana Penn is still lying on a couch; what she thought a bruise on her leg has by neglect proved a wound. Her sister Lady Har-

in London 8 May 1736 (Joseph Foster, *Alumni Oxonienses . . . 1715–1886*, 1887–8).

4. Perhaps Thomas Roberts (d. 1740) of Christ Church, Oxford (B.A. 1711, M.A. 1714), rector of Frodsham, Cheshire 1725–40 (*Old Westminsters*; Joseph Foster, *Alumni Oxonienses . . . 1500–1714*, Oxford, 1891–2).

5. Apparently HW's earliest use of the expression in his correspondence is to Montagu 1 July 1770 (Montagu ii. 311).

6. Possibly the Mrs Armstrong who died 22 Jan. 1790 in Hill Street, Berkeley Square (GM 1790, lx pt i. 181).

7. —— Wickes (see following letter). Not further identified.

8. Lady Anne Wentworth (1713–97), 1st dau. of 1st E. of Strafford, n.c., and sister and heir of HW's friend and correspondent, 2d E. of Strafford; Queen Anne's goddaughter; m. (1733) William Conolly of Castletown, Kildare, sometime M.P. (Collins, *Peerage*, 1768, iv. 298; GM 1797, lxvii pt i. 253; *The Wentworth Papers 1705–1739*, ed. James J. Cartwright, 1883, pp. 322, 325).

9. Henry Collingwood Selby.

10. Charlotte Walpole (1738–89), illegitimate dau. of Sir Edward Walpole by Dorothy Clements; m. (1760) Lionel Tollemache (1734–99), 5th E. of Dysart. She died 5 Sept. 1789.

riot[11] was here the other morning[12] with her daughters,[13] and I showed them the whole house myself, as they are excellent people and the daughters have taste: the youngest especially struck me by her knowledge of good pictures which she immediately showed she understood. This of my house being shown is a dangerous subject for me to tap, such a grievance is it become—I have actually tickets given out till the middle of the week after next[14]—I write two or three every day, or as many excuses—Pray come, and make my evenings at least pleasant.

Summer is arrived at last, though as much after the due time, as if it was one of the *ton*.[15] It is more bounteous however, and will bless the poor by lowering bread. The whole face of the country is spread with luxurious harvests and gilt by shining suns.

The Johnstones are gone to Park Place where Lady Dysart's situation prevented my meeting them. Mr and Mrs Anderson are cooing tête-à-tête at Hampton,[16] as if they were Venus's own turtles left at home in her stable. They told me that on Tuesday night the Duchess of Argyle walked into old Brutus's[17] assembly at Hampton Court, but did look too like an apparition![18]

11. Lady Henrietta Conyers.

12. 19 Aug. ('Visitors').

13. Three daughters accompanied her ('Visitors'), but according to GM 1794, lxiv pt i. 275, she had five daughters living in 1794: 1) Matilda Conyers (1752–1803) (GM 1793, lxiii pt ii. 1151; GM 1803, lxxiii pt i. 391; Publications of the Harleian Society, vol. 14, *Visitations of Essex*, pt ii. 1879, p. 650); 2) —— Conyers; 3) Sophia Conyers (ca 1759–1847) for whom Mrs Elizabeth Carter had 'a particular regard and esteem' (*Letters from Mrs Elizabeth Carter to Mrs Montagu*, ed. Montagu Pennington, 1817, iii. 269), m. (1775) as 2d wife, William Baker of Bayfordbury, Herts, M.P., by whom she had fifteen children (Burke, *Landed Gentry*, 1851, i. 48, 253; ibid., 1900, p. 62; GM 1848, n.s. xxix, 107); 4) Charlotte Conyers (ca 1758–1839) (Burke, *Landed Gentry*, 1851, i. 253; *Proceedings of the Suffolk Institute of Archaeology and Natural History*, 1894, viii. 231); 5) Caroline Conyers (ca 1768–1848), m. (1799) John Barker, paymaster of the Chatham Barracks, later (1803) of Clare Priory, Suffolk (ibid. 231–2; GM 1799, lxix pt i. 525).

14. See 'Visitors.' As HW wrote on Thursday night, he probably had tickets given out until about Tuesday, 1 Sept.

15. 'The word *ton* is quite abolished. Everything that is fashionable is now called the *Nick*' (Lord Robert Seymour, 'Diary' for Jan. 1788, *Murray's Magazine*, 1887, i. 472).

16. Presumably at her parents' house.

17. Mrs French's, as is shown by HW's note in 'Visitors': 'Brutus [is] Latin for French—and Mrs French.' Katherine Lloyd (d. 1791), dau. of Richard Lloyd, Lord Chief Justice of Jamaica; m. (several years before 1743) Jeffrey French, sometime M.P. (Burke, *Commoners* iv. 91; MONTAGU i. 113). She had a house in New Street, Hanover Square, and a villa at Hampton Court. HW, who had known her for about fifty years (see HW to Mann 6 Jan. 1743), ridicules her taste (to Lord Strafford 28 July 1787), and depreciates her art collection (*post* 29 Jan., 11 March 1791). See also Vittoria Colonna Caetani, Duchessa di Sermoneta, *The Locks of Norbury* [1940], p. 33; Boswell, *Johnson* iv. 48, 480–1.

18. Lady Augusta Clavering, daughter of the Duchess of Argyll, wrote to Lady Stafford from Ealing, 1789: 'Such is the rage for cards in assemblies even at this season that Mrs French and several other people have parties frequently. Mrs F. had the other night I daresay 40 people assembled in a

I have exhausted all my nothings, and if I have no letter from you, shall send this away, meager as it is, because I want to know your will about the Teddingtonian villa.

Friday afternoon.

Monsieur de Teddington[19] has been with me and is all-accommodating—if Mrs Armstrong will not stay till after the first week in October. I asked his price—he said, should I think ten guineas a month too much—if I did, he would lower—therefore no doubt you may have it for eighteen for the two months, and you may tell me to offer sixteen. Pray let me have your answer soon, for I will convey to Mrs A.[20] that she will hurt her landlord, if she lingers beyond St Michaelmas.

I think, if my account should suit you, the best way will be, as soon as you arrive in town, for Mr Berry and you two to come and lodge with me for a day or two, and then you can go and view your future nest at your leisure, and *that* you may insert, with a little cavil at the price, in your answer to me, which will make your assent conditional.

Saturday.

I have no letter, so this departs; but pray answer it directly.

To Mary Berry, Thursday 27 August 1789

Address: To Miss Mary Berry to be left at the Post House at York. [Redirected in unknown hand: 'Thos Caley's, Esq., Middleton near Pickering.']
Postmark: 31 AU 89.

Strawberry Hill, Thursday evening, Aug. 27, 1789.[1]

I JUMPED for joy, that is, my heart did, which is all the remain of me, that is *in statu jumpante,* at the receipt of your letter this morning which tells me you approve of the house at Teddington. How kind you was to answer so incontinently! I believe you borrowed the best steed from the races. I have sent to the landlord[2] to come to me tomor-

---

very hot room. Mama says, however, that as they are chiefly composed of the old, the lame, and the blind, it is the best thing they could do' (*Intimate Society Letters of the Eighteenth Century*, ed. John, 9th Duke of Argyll [1910], i. 217).
19. Mr Wickes.

20. Probably through Lady Anne Conolly.

1. 'No. 12' (B). Renumbered in another hand, 'No. 10.'
2. Mr Wickes.

row; but I could not resist beginning my letter tonight, as I am at home alone with a little pain in my left wrist; but the right one has no brotherly feeling for it, and would not be put off so.

You ask how you have deserved such attentions—why, by deserving them; by every kind of merit, and by that superlative one to me, your submitting to throw away so much time on a forlorn antique, you two, who without specifying particulars (and you must at least be conscious that you are not two frights) might expect any fortune and distinctions, and do delight all companies. On which side lies the wonder? Ask me no more such questions, or I will cram you with reasons.

My poor dear niece[3] grows worse and worse; the medical people do not pretend to give us any hopes—they only say she may last some weeks, which I do not expect, nor do absent myself. I had promised Mr Barrett[4] to make a visit to my Gothic child his house[5] on Sunday, but I have written today[6] to excuse myself: so I have to the Duchess of Richmond[7] who wanted me to meet her mother, sister[8] and General Conway at Goodwood next week.[9]

I wish Lady Fitzwilliam[10] may not hear the same bad news as I expect, in the midst of her royal visitors:[11] her sister the Duchess of St

3. Lady Dysart.

4. Thomas Barrett (1744–1803), of Lee, near Canterbury; HW's correspondent (Cole ii. 237, n. 4).

5. For HW's description of Lee as it was in 1780, see *Country Seats* 76–7. Inspired by HW, and directed by James Wyatt, the Gothicizing of the house was begun about 1782 and was completed by 1790. A print 'from the designs of Mr James Wyatt' is in Edward Hasted, *Kent*, 1st edn, Canterbury, iii (1790). 664, Plate 36; and two views and a description are in J. P. Neale, *Views of the Seats of Noblemen and Gentlemen*, 2d ser., 1824–9, vol. ii. In Neale it is said, on what authority does not appear, that HW sent a description of Lee (quoted in Neale, and *post* 27 Sept. 1794, n. 31) to Hasted; if so, the description apparently was inserted without acknowledgment in Hasted's history (2d edn, Canterbury, 1797–1801, ix. 174). See also HW to George Hardinge [Sept. 1785]; *post* 23 July 1790.

6. Letter missing.

7. 'Lady Mary Bruce, daughter of the Earl of Ailesbury by Caroline Campbell, daughter of Gen. John Campbell, after-wards Duke of Argyll' (B). HW's letter to her is missing.

8. 'Anne Seymour Conway [Mrs Damer], only child of the Dowager Countess of Ailesbury by Marshal Henry Seymour Conway, her second husband; she was thus half-sister to the Duchess of Richmond' (B).

9. 'This day [8 Sept.] General Conway and his Lady accompanied by Miss [*sic*] Damer, set off from their house in Warwick Street, Pall Mall, on a visit to the Duke and Duchess of Richmond, at their seat at Goodwood near Chichester, Sussex' (*World* 8 Sept. 1789). Mrs Damer was reported at Park Place 14 Sept. (*World*, that date).

10. '——— Ponsonby, daughter of Earl of Bessborough, wife of Earl Fitzwilliam. George IV when Prince of Wales and his brother the Duke of York who this year attended York races were going to receive a great entertainment at Wentworth House, the seat of Earl Fitzwilliam in Yorkshire' (B). Charlotte Ponsonby (1747–1822), 2d dau. of 2d E. of Bessborough, m. (1770) William Fitzwilliam, 4th E. Fitzwilliam (Irish, 2d E., English).

11. For a description of the fête (2 Sept.)

Albans is dying in the same way as Lady Dysart and for some days has not been in her senses.[12]

How charming you are to leave those festivities for your good parents[13] who I do not wonder are impatient for you. I who am old enough to be your great-grandmother,[14] know one needs not be your near relation to long for your return. Of all your tour, next to your duteous visits, I most approve the jaunt to the sea; I believe in its salutary air more than in the whole College[15] and all its works.

Mrs Armstrong's secession is doubly fortunate. Your last year's mansion is actually taken by Lord Cathcart,[16] and what is incredible, his wife is to lie in there[17]—It must be in the round summer-house;[18] and though its person may have tempted her as an *étui* at present, I should think, as it is three parts of glass, it could not have allured any pregnant woman, unless she expected to be delivered of a melon.

You must not expect any news from me, French or homebred; I am not in the way of hearing any; your morning gazetteer[19] rarely calls on me, as I am not likely to pay him in kind. About royal progresses paternal or filial,[20] I never inquire, nor do you, I believe, care more than I

at which 40,000 persons were entertained and fifty-five hogsheads of ale were consumed, see *The Oracle. Bell's New World* 8 Sept. 1789. Two hundred guests were in the house party.

12. 'The Duchess of St Albans lies at the point of death at her seat at Hanworth. Her Grace's disorder proceeded from a cancer in her breast, which has turned to a mortification. Magnetism, and every medical assistance, has been called in without effect' (*Oracle. Bell's New World* 28 Aug. 1789). The Duchess died 4 Sept., Lady Dysart a day later.

13. That is, relatives, a meaning now obsolete or alien; the latest use of the word (in this sense) recorded in OED is 1771. The Berrys had declined an invitation to Wentworth House in order to prolong their visit with Mrs Seton (their grandmother) and Mrs Cayley (their aunt). See following letter.

14. HW was in fact two years older than the Berrys' grandmother.

15. Of Physicians. HW had a consistently low opinion of the medical profession.

16. William Schaw Cathcart (1755–1843), 10th Bn Cathcart, 1776; cr. (1807) Vct

and (1814) E.; m. (1779) at New York, Elizabeth Elliot (d. 1847), dau. and coheiress of Andrew Elliot, Lt-Gov. of New York, by Elizabeth Plumstead, an American (*Scots Peerage* ii. 524–7).

17. Their fourth (but third surviving) son, Hon. Frederick Cathcart (1789–1865) was born at Twickenham 28 Oct. 1789; entered the army, 1805; colonel, 1837; Knight of the Russian Order of St Anne; m. (1827) Jane McAdam, dau. of Quentin McAdam of Craigengillan, Ayrshire, and assumed the surname of McAdam (ibid. ii. 526; *Army Lists; Oracle. Bell's New World* 2 Nov. 1789).

18. It was octagonal, according to Ironside (see *ante* 1 Nov. 1788, n. 1), but was converted to 'round' by HW for the purposes of this paragraph.

19. Doubtless Richard Owen Cambridge.

20. George III was spending the summer in and near Weymouth and Plymouth, and the Prince of Wales and the Duke of York were at York races prior to their visit to Wentworth House. The Duke of York: Frederick Augustus (1763–1827), George III's 2d son; Bp of Osnaburgh 1764–1803, by which title he was known until 1784; cr.

do. The small wares in which the societies at Richmond and Hampton Court deal, are still less to our taste. My poor niece and her sisters[21] take up most of my time and thoughts. But I will not attrist[22] you to indulge myself—but will break off here, and finish my letter when I have seen your new landlord. Good night!

Friday.

Well! I have seen him, and nobody was ever so accommodating! He is as courteous as a candidate for a county. You may stay in his house till Christmas if you please, and shall pay but twenty pounds: and if more furniture is wanting, it shall be supplied. Mrs Armstrong talks of not quitting but the first week in October; but as she is prodigiously timorous about her health, he thinks the first round showers will send her to London. In any case you know you may come and stay in your conjugal castle, till the house of your separate maintenance is vacant for you. I was curious to learn whence Mr Wickes contracted all this *honnêteté:* I do not believe I have discovered, for all I can trace of his history, is, that he married a dowager mistress[23] of General Harvey,[24] whom the General called Monimia, though not the meekest of her calling, and with whom (Wickes) she did not at all agree. I am sure she was the aggressor, as he has captivated Mrs Armstrong and me by his flowing benignity. Besides I have no notion how one can use one's wife ill, even if one has two.

Berkeley Square, Aug. 29.

You will laugh at me, for I am just come to town, though it is the first real summer day we have had; but I had a little business and return tomorrow. As this very fine weather is arrived so late, I suppose it is some fugitive heat that has escaped from the troubles on the Continent, which are spreading along the Rhine. I hope it has left its sting behind it, and will not infect us, who have every reason to be happy! Adieu!

(1784) E. of Ulster and D. of York and Albany; Commander-in-Chief of the forces in Great Britain 1798–1809 and 1811–1827.

21. The Duchess of Gloucester and Mrs Keppel: Laura Walpole (ca 1734–1813) m. (1758) Hon. Frederick Keppel, Bp of Exeter.

22. Sadden; HW's use of the word *post* 28 June 1791 is the last cited in OED.

23. Not identified.

24. Edward Harvey (1718–78), 3d son of William Harvey of Chigwell, Essex; Lt-Gen., 1772; M.P. Gatton 1761–8 and Harwich 1768–78; Governor of Portsmouth 1773–7 (*Old Westminsters* and *Supplement*).

To Mary Berry, Friday 4 September 1789

Address: To Miss Mary Berry to be left at the Post House at York. [Redirected in unknown hand: 'Thos Caley's, Esq., Middleton near Pickering.']
Postmark: ISLEWORTH 7 SE 89.

Strawberry Hill, Sept. 4, 1789.[1]

I AM charmed that Mr Berry ratifies my negotiation for the house at Teddington; and I do not doubt *now* but Mrs Armstrong[2] will quit it even before Michaelmas; for though Saturday last was so glorious, it was the setting, not rising sun of summer. It rained a torrent all Sunday evening; so it has done almost every day since, and did last night and does at this instant. I grieve for the incomplete harvest; but as it is an ill rain that brings nobody good, I must rejoice if it washes away Dame Armstrong. Mr Wickes[3] I am sure will give me the earliest notice of her departure, for, as Spenser[4] says,

> A semely man our hoste is withal
> To ben a marshal in a lordis hall.

You ask whether I will call you wise or stupid for leaving York races in the middle—neither: had you chosen to stay, you would have done rightly: the more young persons see, where there is nothing blameable, the better, as increasing the stock of ideas early will be a resource for age. To resign pleasure to please tender relations is amiable, and superior to wisdom; for wisdom, however laudable, is but a selfish virtue. But I do decide peremptorily that it was very prudent to decline the invitation to Wentworth House, which was obligingly given; but as I am very proud for you, I should have disliked your being included in a mobbish kind of *cohue. You two* are not to go where any other two misses would have been equally *priées;* and where people would have been thinking of the princes[5] more than of the Berrys—Besides, princes are so rife now, that besides my *sweet* nephew in the Park,[6] we have

---

1. 'No. 13' (B). Renumbered in another hand, 'No. 11.'
2. 'The name of the person inhabiting the house at Teddington which Mr Berry had taken' (B).
3. 'The proprietor of the house' (B).
4. Chaucer, in the Prologue to *The Canterbury Tales,* ll. 751–2:

'A semely man oure Hooste was withalle
For to han been a marchal in an halle.'

Later passages in this letter (see notes 10,

46) show that HW had recently been reading Thomas Warton's *Observations on the Fairy Queen of Spenser,* 2d edn, 1762; his copy (MS Cat. K.4.8–9) was sold SH iii. 163. The passage from Chaucer is there quoted (ii. 210) exactly as HW has it, except that *is* reads *was,* and *marshal* reads *marshall.*

5. The Prince of Wales and the Duke of York.

6. 'William Henry, Duke of Gloucester, brother to George III and father to the last

another at Richmond: the Duke of Clarence[7] has taken Mr Henry Hobart's house,[8] point-blank over against Mr Cambridge's,[9] which will make the good woman of that mansion cross herself piteously, and stretch the throats of *the blatant beast* at Sudbrook,[10] and of all the other pious matrons *à la ronde,* for his R. H. to divert lonesomeness, has brought with him a Miss Polly Finch,[11] who being still more averse to solitude, declares that any tempter would make even paradise more agreeable than a constant tête-à-tête.[12]

Duke. He had married the Dowager Countess of Waldegrave, niece to Lord Orford' (B). William Henry (1743–1805), D. of Gloucester, m. (1765) Maria Walpole, Dowager Countess Waldegrave. He was Ranger of Hampton Court Park. HW was not on good terms with the Duke. See *post* 11 Mar. 1791 and 25 Oct. 1793.

7. William Henry (1765–1837), 3d son of George III; D. of Clarence, 1789; William IV, K. of England 1830–7.

8. Or, according to the newspapers (*Oracle. Bell's New World* 29 Aug. 1789; *World* 31 Aug. 1789), his late wife's house. Hon. Henry Hobart (1738–99), 4th son of 1st E. of Buckinghamshire; M.P. Norwich 1786–99; chairman of the Committee of Ways and Means; m. (1761) Anne Margaret Bristow, who died at Richmond 12 July 1788 (Burke, *Peerage*, 1928, p. 385, *sub* Buckinghamshire; *Old Westminsters*; GM 1788, lviii pt ii. 659). The Duke of Clarence was said to have taken the house until March 1790 (*London Chronicle* 29 Aug.–1 Sept. 1789), but he apparently did not occupy it after 11 Nov. 1789 (see following letter, n. 7).

9. The Hobart house was on Richmond Hill, directly across the Thames from Cambridge's. See *The Oracle. Bell's New World* 29 Aug. 1789.

10. 'Caroline Campbell, Baroness Greenwich' (Wright). Caroline Campbell (1717–94), 1st dau. of 2d D. of Argyll; m. (1) (1742) Francis Scott (ca 1721–50), styled E. of Dalkeith; m. (2) (1755) Hon. Charles Townshend (1725–67). In 1767 she was created Baroness of Greenwich. She was known as a gossip and newsmonger, 'that shrill Morning Post' (HW to Conway 16 Oct. 1774). HW's 'blatant beast' was doubtless suggested by his recent reading of Warton's

Observations on the Fairy Queen (see notes 4, 46), in which 'the blatant beast' is treated, i. 22–3, 221–2. Sudbrook, about two miles east of SH, was her chief seat.

11. 'His Highness has with him a sweet little *Finch,* to whom he seems much attached. The bird took its flight from a well known house in Berkley [*sic*] Street, and has lately been frequently seen hovering about a royal apartment at St James's, from three until twelve, or later' (*Oracle. Bell's New World* 29 Aug. 1789). Another newspaper notes the Duke's preference for 'the notes of a *Finch* on Richmond Hill to the animating thunders of the British navy, or the degrading pleasures of the turf' (*World* 3 Sept. 1789), and further explains that this is 'a Finch, who, from the price, may properly be denominated a *gold Finch*' (ibid. 11 Sept. 1789). The liaison is reported at an end in *The World* 14 Nov. 1789. See also *The World* 16 Nov. 1789. The couple appeared as 'The Royal Sailor and Polly Finch' in the 'Tête-à-Tête' series, *Town and Country Magazine,* Jan. 1790, xxii. 9–10. According to Sylvester Douglas, later (1800) Lord Glenbervie, 'It is said . . . Polly Finch quitted him because she could not persevere in hearing him read the *Lives of the Admirals.* She had borne this through one half of the work, but, finding that as much more remained, her patience sank under it, and a quarrel and separation ensued' (*Diaries,* ed. Francis Bickley, 1928, i. 63).

12. It was not constant, for the day after HW wrote this letter the Duke of Clarence gave 'a grand entertainment to several nobility, etc., at Richmond' (*World* 5 Sept.). The next day he gave 'a grand dinner to his two royal brothers, with several nobility, etc.' (ibid. 7 Sept.).

I agree with you in not thinking Beatrice one of Miss Farren's capital parts:[13] Mrs Pritchard[14] played it with more spirit, and was superior to Garrick's Benedict:[15] so is Kemble[16] too, as he is to Quin in Maskwell.[17] Kemble and Lysons the clergyman[18] passed all Wednesday here with me: the former is melting the three parts of *Henry VI* into one piece[19]—I doubt it will be difficult to make a tolerable play out of them.

I have talked scandal from Richmond like its gossips, and now by your queries after Lady L.[20] you are drawing me into more, which I do

13. Elizabeth Farren or Farran (b. 1759 *or* 1763, d. 1829) considered by HW 'the first of all actresses' (to Lady Ossory 12 Dec. 1786); m. (1797), as 2d wife, Edward Smith-Stanley, 12th E. of Derby. After a visit of two weeks to friends (the Hothams and Lady Milner) in Yorkshire, she was at York for four of the eight theatrical performances given there 24 Aug.–1 Sept. On Monday evening, 24 Aug., the Prince of Wales present, she played Beatrice in *Much Ado about Nothing,* in which role she 'experienced much approbation' (*Oracle. Bell's New World* 27 Aug. 1789; cf. *The World* 20 Aug. 1789). HW knew her well, and presented to her some of the SH editions.

14. Hannah Vaughan (1711–68) m. (before 1733) —— Pritchard, later treasurer of Drury Lane Theatre (Montagu i. 73). She acted in various London theatres 1733–68, but chiefly at Drury Lane.

15. Garrick first played Benedick 14 Nov. 1748, when 'the excellent acting of Mrs Pritchard in Beatrice was not inferior . . . every scene between them was a continued struggle for superiority; nor could the spectators determine to which of them the preference was due—(*Davies*)' ([John Genest,] *Some Account of the English Stage,* Bath, 1832, iv. 261).

16. John Philip Kemble (1757–1823), brother of Mrs Siddons. In 'the autumn of 1788 . . . he was made acting manager' at Drury Lane, and 'a year later . . . he was . . . made stage-manager' (Harold Child, *The Shakespearian Productions of John Philip Kemble,* 1935, p. 3). He first played Benedick to Miss Farren's Beatrice 30 April 1788 (Genest, op. cit. vi. 479).

17. The title rôle of Congreve's *The Double Dealer.*

18. Daniel Lysons (1762–1834), author of *The Environs of London,* 1792–6 (2d edn, 1811), dedicated to HW, his occasional correspondent. Probably he was assistant curate of Mortlake ca 1784–9 and of Putney, Surrey, 1789–1800, but DNB apparently is incorrect in saying he was curate of either place (*Parish Register of Putney* [*1735–1812*], ed. W. Bruce Bannerman, Croydon, 1915, pp. 434, 477; Owen Manning and William Bray, *History and Antiquities of . . . Surrey,* 1804–14, iii. 300, 310); he was also rector (1804–33) of Rodmarton, Glos, a living of which he became patron through the death of his father Rev. Samuel Lysons, in 1804. When HW became Earl of Orford, he appointed Lysons his chaplain, in accordance with noble practice (see Charles J. Abbey and John H. Overton, *English Church in the Eighteenth Century,* 1878, ii. 19; J. Wickham Legg, *English Church Life,* 1914, p. 155; Boswell, *Johnson* ii. 96). Lysons is the 'Stumpity' of this correspondence.

19. If Kemble had such a plan, he did not execute it: 'in his twenty-nine years of management, he staged' all of Shakespeare's histories 'except *King Richard II* and *King Henry VI*' (Child, op. cit. 4). Kemble's adaptation of *King Henry V* was first produced, with Kemble in the title role, at Drury Lane before 'a thin house' 1 Oct. 1789 (*Oracle. Bell's New World* 1, 2 Oct. 1789; cf. James Boaden, *John Philip Kemble,* 1825, ii. 2–3), and was published in the same year.

20. Mary Berry, emending many years later, erroneously expands to 'Lexington'; the context shows clearly it should be 'Luxborough.' See following note and HW to Lady Ossory 3 Aug. 1775, 20 Dec. 1775.

not love; but she is dead and forgotten, but on the shelves of an old library or on those of my old memory which you will be routing into. The lady you wot of then, was the first wife of Lord Catherlogh,[21] before he was an earl, and who was son of Knight the South Sea cashier,[22] and whose second wife lives here at Twickenham.[23] Lady Loughborough,[24] a high-coloured lusty black woman, was parted from her husband upon a gallantry she had with Dalton the reviver of *Comus*, and a divine.[25] She retired into the country,[26] corresponded, as you see by her letters,[27] with the small poets of that time,[28] but having no The-

21. Robert Knight (1702–72), cr. (1745) Bn Luxborough and (1763) E. of Catherlough; m. (1) (1727) Henrietta St John (1699–1756), half-sister to 1st Vct Bolingbroke. For an account of her, her portrait, and a discussion of their separation in 1736, see Walter Sichel, *Bolingbroke and His Times*, 1901–2, ii. 463–76, where (p. 469) exception is taken to HW's 'venomous' gossip, but no proof is given that it is false. See also Helen S. Hughes, *The Gentle Hertford*, N.Y., 1940.

22. Robert Knight (d. 1744), who absconded to Paris when an investigation of the South Sea Company was ordered, and died there (GEC, *sub* Catherlough).

23. Mary Knight (d. 1795) 'of Hampton,' m. (1) (1738) Sir John Lequesne, Kt and Alderman of London; m. (2) (1756) Robert Knight, Bn Luxborough, later E. of Catherlough (GM 1738, viii. 220; GEC). She is listed among the principal inhabitants of Twickenham in 1789 (Edward Ironside, *History and Antiquities of Twickenham*, 1797, p. 144).

24. Struck out by Mary Berry, who erroneously substituted 'Lexington'; read 'Luxborough.'

25. John Dalton (1709–63), D.D. 1750, whose adaptation of Milton's *Comus*, with music by Thomas Augustine Arne, was first produced in 1738 and 'kept its place on the stage for many years' (DNB). In Sichel, op. cit. ii. 469 (followed in William Shenstone, *Letters*, ed. Duncan Mallam, Minneapolis, 1939, p. 227, n. 4), he is confused with William Dalton (ca 1726–51), killed in a duel (MONTAGU i. 113).

26. To one of her husband's estates, Barrells, in Warwickshire, near Henley-in-Arden, and about fifteen miles from The Leasowes, Shenstone's seat.

27. *Letters written by the late Right Honourable Lady Luxborough, to William Shenstone, Esq.*, 1775, written, according to Shenstone, 'with abundant ease, politeness, and vivacity; in which she was scarce equalled by any woman of her time. They commenced in the year 1739, and were continued to the year of her death (1756), with some few intermissions' (p. iv). HW's copy of the book, sold SH vii. 37 (London 1055), was sold at the Parke-Bernet Galleries, 5 May 1939, lot 1108, to the Rosenbach Co. for an unrevealed buyer. In the sale catalogue is quoted a MS note by HW in the book: 'Henrietta St John, daughter of Henry Viscount St John by his second wife (a Frenchwoman) and half-sister of the famous Lord Bolingbroke, was wife of Robert Knight (son of the cashier of the South Sea Company), by whom she had a son, who died, without issue, before his father, and a daughter, Henrietta, mentioned in these letters. Robert Knight was created Lord Luxborough, and after his wife's death, Earl of Catherlogh. They had been parted many years, on her having an intrigue with Parson Dalton, the reviver of Comus, and tutor of Lord Beauchamp, only son of the Duchess of Somerset, mentioned in these letters.' For Shenstone's letters to her, see his letters ed. Mallam, *passim*. HW first mentions Lady Luxborough in *Royal and Noble Authors*, *Works* i. 551, the fourth edition to appear under HW's editorship, but he does not mention her *Letters*, which appeared five years after the third edition. He refers to them slightingly to Mason 27 Nov. 1775.

28. In addition to Shenstone, she was on friendly terms with Richard Jago and William Somerville, and erected at Barrells a monument in memory of the latter (see her *Letters*, *passim*).

seus amongst them, consoled herself, as it is said, like Ariadne, with Bacchus.[29] This might be a fable, like that of her Cretan Highness—no matter; the fry of little anecdotes are so numerous now, that throwing one more into the shoal is of no consequence if it entertains you for a moment, nor need you believe what I don't warrant.

Gramercy for your intention of seeing Wentworth Castle;[30] it is my favourite of all great seats; such a variety of ground, of wood and water;[31] and almost all executed and disposed with so much taste by the present Earl![32] Mr Gilpin[33] sillily could see nothing but faults there![34] The new front is in my opinion one of the lightest and most beautiful buildings on earth[35]—and pray like the little Gothic edifice and its position in the menagerie; your husband recommended it and had it

29. See *post* ii. 269 and n. 78.

30. Near Barnsley, Yorks; the seat of HW's friend and frequent correspondent, Lord Strafford.

31. Cf. HW to Richard Bentley August 1756: 'This place is one of the very few that I really like; the situation, woods, views, and the improvements, are perfect in their kinds; nobody has a truer taste than Lord Strafford.' For views of the house and grounds, see J. P. Neale, *Views of the Seats of Noblemen and Gentlemen*, iv, 1821.

32. William Wentworth (1722–91), 2d E. of Strafford, n.c., 1739.

33. Rev. William Gilpin (1724–1804), vicar of Boldre, Hants, 1777; 'Master of the Picturesque'; occasional correspondent of HW, to whom he dedicated the third edition of *An Essay on Prints*, 1781. (HW's copy is now WSL.)

34. 'From Bank-top we had a good descending view of Wentworth Castle—of the grounds which environ it—and the country which surrounds it. The whole together is grand. The eminence on which we stood is adorned with a great profusion of some-

thing in the way of an artificial ruin. It is possible it may have an effect from the castle below: but *on the spot* it is certainly no ornament. We found some difficulty in passing through Lord Strafford's park; and proceeded therefore to Wentworth House' (*Observations, Relative Chiefly to Picturesque Beauty, Made in the Year 1772*, 2d edn, 1788, ii. 207–8). HW may have been thinking of Gilpin's closing remark on Wentworth House, not Wentworth Castle: 'On the whole, I was not much pleased with anything I saw here' (ibid. 209).

35. HW visited Lord Strafford at Wentworth Castle in 1768: 'I had been there before [in 1756 and 1760; see HW to Bentley August 1756, and *Country Seats* 27–8], but had not seen the new front, entirely designed by the present Earl himself. Nothing ever came up to the beauty of it. The grace, proportion, lightness and magnificence of it are exquisite' (ibid. 65). Later HW referred to the Castle as 'the perfectest specimen of architecture I know' (to Lord Strafford 31 Aug. 1781).

drawn by Mr Bentley[36] from Chichester Cross.[37] Don't bring me a pair of scissors from Sheffield; I am determined nothing shall cut our loves,[38] though I should live out the rest of Methusalem's term as you kindly wish, and as I can believe, though you are my wives, for I am persuaded my Agnes wishes so too, don't you?

At night.

I am just come from Cambridge's, where I have not been in an evening time out of mind. Major Dixon, alias the Charming Man,[39] is there, but I heard nothing of the Emperor's rickets[40]—a great deal and many horrid stories of the violences in France, for his brother the Chevalier Jerningham[41] is just arrived from Paris. You have heard of the destruction of thirty-two chateaux in Burgundy[42] at the instigation of a demon, who has since been broken on the rack.[43] There is now assembled near Paris a body of 16,000 deserters, daily increasing, who they fear will encamp and dictate to the capital, in spite of their militia of 20,000 bourgeois. It will soon, I suppose, ripen to several armies and a civil war; a fine *acheminement* to liberty!

My poor niece[44] is still alive, though weaker every day, and pro-

36. Richard Bentley (1708–82), youngest son of the classical scholar and critic; HW's correspondent.

37. HW wrote to Bentley in August 1756: 'I shall bring you a ground-plot for a Gothic building, which I have proposed that you should draw for a little wood, but in the manner of an ancient market-cross.' For an account of the building, see Montagu i. 295.

38. The earliest (English) allusion to this superstition, cited in V. S. Lean's *Collectanea* (Bristol, 1902–4, ii. 160), is in Richard Barnfield's *Affectionate Shepherd*, 1594, pt ii, st. 17.

39. 'Edward Jerningham, Esq., of Cossey in Norfolk, uncle to the present Lord [8th Bn] Stafford. He was distinguished in his day by the name of *Jerningham the Poet*—but it was an unpoetical day. The stars of Byron, of Baillie, and of Scott had not risen on the horizon. The more merited distinction of Jerningham was the friendship, affection, and intimacy which his amiable character had inspired to the author and all of his society mentioned in these letters' (B). For a reference to him as 'Major Dixon,' see *ante* 30 June 1789.

40. 'This alluded to something said in a character which Jerningham had assumed for the amusement of a society some time before at Marshal Conway's' (B).

41. Charles Jerningham (1742–1814), younger brother of the poet, entered the French army, became colonel and eventually (1784) maréchal de camp; Knight of Malta, and of St Louis; lost his French property by confiscation during the Revolution. 'He was remarkable for the extent and elegance of his acquirements and literary accomplishments, the singular obligingness and courtesy of his manners, and the generous and noble qualities of his heart' (John Kirk, *Biographies of English Catholics in the Eighteenth Century*, ed. John Hungerford Pollen and Edwin Burton, 1909, p. 139; GM 1814, lxxxiv pt ii. 607–8).

42. 'Forty-four noblemen's seats have been destroyed in this province alone' (*London Chronicle* 1–3 Sept. 1789, lxvi. 223).

43. Not identified.

44. She died the following day, 5 Sept.

nounced irrecoverable; yet it is possible she may live some weeks, which however is neither to be expected nor wished, for she eats little and sleeps less. Still she is calm, and behaves with the patience of a martyr.

You may perceive by the former part of my letter that I have been dipping into Spenser again, though he is no passion of mine: there I lighted upon two lines that at first sight reminded me of Mlle d'Éon,[45]

> Now when Marfisa had put off her beaver,
> To be a woman everyone perceive her—[46]

but I do not think that is so perceptible in the *Chevalière*. She looked more feminine as I remember her in regimentals, than she does now.[47] She is at best a hen-dragoon, or an herculean hostess.[48] I wonder she does not make a campaign in her own country, and offer her sword to the almost-dethroned monarch, as a second Joan of Arc[49]—Adieu!—for three weeks I shall say, *Sancte Michael, ora pro nobis*.[50]—You seem to have relinquished your plan of sea-coasting—I shall be sorry for that: it would do you good.

45. Charles - Geneviève - Louis - Auguste - André-Timothée de Beaumont (1728–1810), Chevalier d'Éon, rumoured to be a woman, was proved by a *post mortem* to be a man (DU DEFFAND ii. 494 *et passim*). He lived in England 1762–77 and 1785–1810; during the second period he dressed as a woman.

46. This passage is not in Spenser, but in Sir John Harington's translation of Ariosto's *Orlando Furioso*, 1591, XXVI. xxiii. 7–8. HW found it in Warton's *Observations on the Fairy Queen of Spenser* (i. 210), which is the 'Spenser' he had been 'dipping into'; hence his confusion of Ariosto and Spenser. Cf. notes 4, 10.

47. Eighteen prints, some representing him as a man and others as a woman, are listed in Freeman O'Donoghue and Henry M. Hake, *Catalogue of Engraved British Portraits . . . in the British Museum*, 1908–25. Easily accessible are the four illustrations (one of which, the frontispiece, is labeled 'false' in op. cit.) to M. Coryn, *The Chevalier d'Éon*, New York [1932]. See also *The European Magazine*, 1791, xix. 163. During his first stay in England, d'Éon, who held the rank of a captain of dragoons in the French army and with slight justification considered himself primarily a soldier, sometimes dressed in the uniform of his regiment, and he may have been so attired when HW entertained him at SH (MONTAGU ii. 70–1). In HW's copy (now WSL) of d'Éon's *Lettres*, 1764, HW has inserted prints of d'Éon as a man and as a woman, in which he looks feminine when dressed as a man and masculine when dressed as a woman.

48. I.e., an innkeeper, such as Shakespeare's 'hostess' in *Henry IV*.

49. 'Why does not Mademoiselle d'Éon return and put herself at the head of the *poissardes?* and carry over a code from that Maccabee, Lord George Gordon?' (HW to Lady Ossory 9 Oct. 1789).

50. So that by Michaelmas Mrs Armstrong would vacate Mr Wickes's house at Teddington, which the Berrys were to have on her leaving.

To Mary Berry, Friday 18 September 1789

Address: To Miss Mary Berry to be left at the Post House at York.
Postmark: IS[LEWORTH].

Strawberry Hill, Sept. 18, 1789.[1]

I DON'T wonder that your grandmother is unwilling to part with you, when you sacrifice the amendment of your health to her, and give up bathing for her satisfaction—but between ourselves I do not admire her for accepting the sacrifice. You bid me be very kind to make up for your parting with her and your friends—I am like poor Cordelia,

> —I am sure my love's
> More pond'rous than my tongue—[2]

She reserved half her affection from her father for her husband—I will keep none of mine from my wives for my grandmother—but I promise nothing; come and try.

I will see Mr Wickes, and know more particularly about Mrs Armstrong's motions: I shall be a little fearful of haggling with him, lest I should sour his complaisance which hitherto has been all sugar. Still I will not be grandmaternal, and prefer myself to your interest.

I have had a most melancholy scene with the loss of dear Lady Dysart, and the affliction of the family, though her release was to be wished, and for which she wished earnestly herself. We have the comfort of finding that she is full as much regretted as she was known—indeed a more faultless being exists not within my knowledge. I will transcribe some lines that I have written on her, which have not the merit of poetry, but a much more uncommon one,—that of being an epitaph in which there is no exaggeration—however, I beg you will not give a copy of it—

> Adieu! sweet shade! complete was thy career,
> Though lost too soon, and premature thy bier;
> For each fair character adorn'd thy life

1. 'No. 14' (B).   2. *King Lear,* I. i. 79–80, with 'richer' altered to 'pond'rous.'

Of daughter, sister, friend, relation, wife.
Yet lest unalter'd fortune should have seem'd
The source, whence virtues so benignly beam'd,
Long-mining illness prov'd thy equal soul,
And patience, like a martyr's crown'd the whole.
Pain could not sour, whom blessings had not spoil'd;
Nor death affright, whom not a vice had soil'd.

You shall hear no more on this sad subject, though I have nothing else that will much amuse you, for besides confinement with my relations, I have been a prisoner in my own house for some days in consequence of a violent fall I had last week, in which it is wonderful that I lost nor life, nor limb, nor even a bone. I went to sit with my cousins the three Philippses[3] on Hampton Court Green; it was dusk, there was a very low step at the door, I did not see it, it tripped me up, I fell headlong on the stones, and against the frame of a table at the door, and battered myself so much, that my whole hip is as black as my shoe for above half a yard[4] long, and a quarter wide, besides bruising one hand, both knees and my left elbow,[5] into which it brought the gout next day. Now pray admire my lightness; if I had weighed a straw, what mischief might not have happened to me? Nay, I have had very little pain; and the gout, not to be out of the fashion, is gone too,[6] and I should have been abroad this morning, if I had not preferred writing to you.

Mrs Cambridge's prayers have been heard: the Duke of Clarence has already taken another villa at Rohampton;[7] and besides being so soon

3. HW's second cousins, only surviving daughters of Sir John Philipps, 6th Bt, of Picton Castle, Pembrokeshire, and sisters of Sir Richard Philipps, 7th Bt, cr. (1776) Bn Milford. All three died unmarried at Hampton Court: 1) Mary (ca 1734–1820) (GM 1820, xc pt i. 378; John Debrett, Peerage, 1822, ii. 1207); 2) Catharine (ca 1736–1801) (GM 1801, lxxi pt i. 379, where she is erroneously said to be the eldest); 3) Joyce (ca 1737–1820) (Debrett, loc. cit.; GM 1820, loc. cit.). See also John Lodge and Mervyn Archdall, Peerage of Ireland, 1789, vii. 100.

4. MS reads 'year.'

5. Cf. William Weller Pepys to Hannah More 17 Sept. 1789: 'You will be sorry to hear that Mr Walpole has had a fall, and is very much bruised' (A Later Pepys, ed. Alice C. C. Gaussen, 1904, ii. 278).

6. But HW later attributed to this fall a severe fit of the gout which lasted into November (HW to Lady Ossory 26 Nov. 1789); consequently (and because the Berrys were at Teddington) he remained at SH until 15 Dec. (HW to Pinkerton, that date).

7. The Duke of Clarence 'has taken a house at Roehampton for fourteen years' (World, 11 Sept. 1789). He did not leave Richmond, however, until 11 Nov., when he returned to his apartments in St James's Palace (World 12 Nov. 1789; cf. HW to Lady Ossory 9 Oct. 1789). According to HW, he was to go to Roehampton at Christmas (HW to Lady Ossory 26 Sept. 1789).

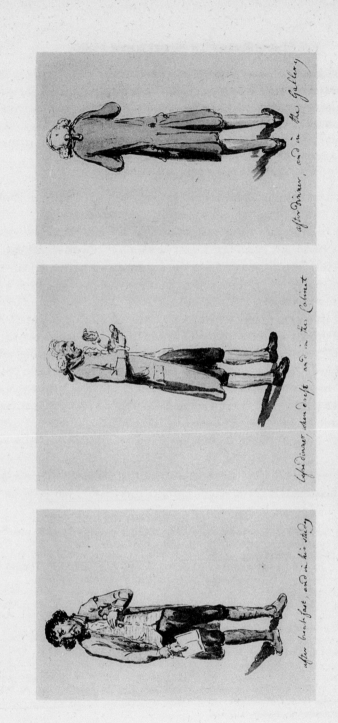

HORACE WALPOLE, BY JOHN CARTER, 1788

tired, I suppose he will new-furnish that in a week more.[8] Apropos a little, Mr Cambridge has given me the following very striking quotation from Michael Drayton's *Heroic Epistles*, but it was Lady Rothes[9] who found it out—it does *not* apply to Miss Polly—you must look a little higher in the family;[10]

> Twice as a bride to church I have been led;
> Twice have two lords enjoy'd my bridal bed,
> How can that beauty yet be undestroyed,
> That years have wasted and two men enjoy'd?
> Or should be thought fit for a prince's store,
> Of which two subjects were possess'd before?[11]

I shall go to Park Place on Monday for two or three days, and then come back to be ready to receive you—but you have not been very gracious, nor said a word of accepting my invitation till the house at Teddington is ready for you. Pray let me know when I may expect you, that I may not enter into any engagement even for an evening.

As the hour of my seeing you again approaches, and as I have nothing of the least import to tell, I shall not try to lengthen this to its usual complement, though the verses have saved some of my paper. Essays, that act the part of letters are mighty insipid things,[12] and when one has nothing occasional to say, it is better to say nothing.

The weather has been so cold since Monday, that for these two days I have had a carpenter[13] stopping chinks in window frames and listing the door of the blue room which I destine to wife Agnes: winds will

8. As he had new-furnished the Hobart house on Richmond Hill; see preceding letter.

9. Jane Elizabeth Leslie (1750–1810), *suo jure* Cts of Rothes, 1773; m. (2) (1772) Lucas Pepys (ca 1741–1830), physician to George III, cr. (1784) Bt; 'one of the best, as well as one of the most agreeable women I know' (Mrs Piozzi to Samuel Lysons 14 June 1785, *Autobiography . . . of Mrs Piozzi*, ed. A. Hayward, 2d edn, 1861, ii. 221). Cambridge probably received the quotation through his neighbour and Lady Rothes's brother-in-law, William Weller Pepys; cf. *A Later Pepys*, ii. 303–4.

10. To the Prince of Wales and Mrs Fitzherbert.

11. 'Alice Countesse of Salisburie to the Blacke Prince,' ll. 79–84, in Drayton's *Englands Heroicall Epistles*, first published in 1597, but evidently here quoted from Drayton's *Works*, 1748, p. 97, or from the revised edition, 4 vols, 1753 (of which HW's copy, MS Cat. K.5.50, was sold SH iii. 157). Drayton's note on the passage reads: 'The two Husbands of which she makes mention, objecting Bigamie against her selfe, as being therefore not meet to be married with a Batcheler-Prince, were Sir Thomas Holland, Knight, and Sir William Mountague, afterward made Earle of Salisburie' (*Works*, ed. J. William Hebel, Oxford, 1931–3, ii. 186).

12. Cf. *post* 31 March 1791 *ad fin.*

13. Not identified. There is no record in *SH Accounts* of payment for this work.

get into these old castles. Sultana Maria is to sleep in the red room, where the Sultan himself resides when he has the gout, and which his Haughtiness always keeps very comfortable. Adieu!

To Mary Berry, Wednesday 30 September 1789

Address: To Miss Mary Berry in Somerset Street, London.
Postmark: ISLEWOR[TH] 3 OC 89.

Strawberry Hill, Wednesday night, Sept. 30, 1789.[1]

WHEN an ancient gentleman marries it is his best excuse, that he wants a nurse; which I suppose was the motive of Solomon, who was the wisest of mortals, and a most puissant and opulent monarch, for marrying a thousand wives in his old age, when I conclude he was very gouty. I in humble imitation of that sapient king, and no mines of Ophir flowing into my exchequer, espoused a couple of helpmates; but being less provident than the son of David, suffered both to ramble into the land of Goshen, when I most want their attendance—I tell a great story—I do not want you—on the contrary, I am delighted that you did not accept my invitation. I should have been mortified to the death to have had you in my house, when I am lying helpless on my couch, or going to bed early from pain. In short, I came from Park Place last Thursday with an inflammation in my foot from a chalk-stone, which I was obliged to have lanced the next morning, and it is not well yet. Nay, it has brought the gout into the knee of the same side, and I suffered a good deal yesterday evening, and blessed myself you were not here—did you think it would ever come to that? I am truly a great deal better today; but I fear it will scarce be possible for me to be in town by Saturday, though I have ordered my house to be aired and ready for me then. In the meantime here is the state of your affairs: Mr Wickes goes into Norfolk tomorrow for three weeks to shoot. I told him you was much displeased at his asking new terms, and that till you should come to town, I could say nothing positive to him, and he must not depend on anything till then. He was all penitence and complaisance. I told him I must have a lease signed: he said there was no necessity for it. Oh yes, I said, but there is. He answered, if I

1. 'No. 15' (B).

would send one down to him signed by Mr Berry, he would sign it too —but what I shall do, when I know your determination, is to send to Mr Wickes a copy of the few lines which Mr Pepys, whom I have consulted twice, had from Lady Dudley, and which shall specify that you are to pay but £20 in full of all demands from the time you shall take possession of the house to December 25th,[2] and when Wickes returns that agreement signed, Mr Berry will sign it too. Thus you see I have acted with the utmost caution, nor have been to the house, nor sent anybody to see it that Wickes might not say we had taken possession.

Now hold a council incontinently, and let me know its decree or why should not Mr Berry come to me immediately, if I cannot come, as I fear. You know here is a dinner and a bed always at his service, which will save a great deal of time.

I am not quite for having your house in town new painted at this time of year when it cannot dry fast. There is nothing so very unwholesome as the smell of new paint. Cannot you make shift as it is for another year? I never perceived its wanting it—and you do not propose to give assemblies and concerts.

I shall write again by Friday's post,[3] and let you know more how I shall find myself—so, if I do not come, you will have time to answer by Saturday's post, that is, if you arrive on Friday, or in time on Saturday. If I hear nothing on Sunday morning, I shall conclude you arrived too late.

Thus I think I have foreseen and said all that can be necessary—and perhaps more like a nurse than a person that wants one.

Be sure that I find you both looking remarkably well—not that I have any reason for desiring it, but as I am not able to nurse you. Adieu!

2. They stayed until ca 15 Dec. HW wrote to Lady Ossory 6 Dec. 1789: 'The Berrys are at Teddington, and it is on their account that I have stayed here later than I ever did. They go to town next week, and so shall I.' As HW returned to London 15 Dec. (to Lady Ossory 12 Dec.; to Pinkerton 15 Dec. 1789), the Berrys probably returned at the same time.

3. That is, 2 Oct.; but if HW wrote a letter on Friday, 2 Oct., it has not been found. This letter was not posted until 3 Oct.

To Mary Berry, ca Monday 28 June 1790

Missing. Written at SH. It dealt with the Berrys' projected tour to Italy (see following letter).

To Mary Berry, Friday 2 July 1790

Address: To Miss Berry to be left at the Post Office at Lymington.
Postmark: 2 JY 90.

Strawberry Hill, July 2, 1790.

I WROTE a bit of a letter[1] to you t'other day in such a hurry, that I don't know what I said—though I fear more than I intended[2]—but no more of that—

My neighbourhood, though Richmond is brimful both of French[3] and English, furnishes no more entertainment than usual, for which I am much more sorry on your account than on my own, for my letters will not be amusing. My personal history is short and dull. I have made my chief visits;[4] my offices[5] advance, and I have got in most of my hay, and such a quantity, that I believe, I believe it will pay for half a yard of my building. All news have centered in elections; I care about none, nor have listened to any.[6] They, and the press-gangs[7] have swept the roads of footpads and highwaymen, who hide themselves, or are gone to vote. Whether they who used to come to see my house are of either complexion, I don't know, but I have had less demand for tickets than usual[8]—what else can I tell you?

I am glad you stayed long enough at Park Place to see all its beauties.[9]

1. Missing; ca 28 June 1790.
2. On the subject of their journey to Italy, to which HW was strongly opposed.
3. Richmond was a favourite resort of French émigrés.
4. To neighbours at Twickenham and the vicinity; see *post* 23 July 1790: 'I . . . have not been farther than Park Place these four years.'
5. The Offices, the last important addition to SH, were built under the direction of James Wyatt in 1790 at a cost of £1,855, from plans drawn by James Essex in 1776 (*SH Accounts* 16, 18, 175–6; 'Genesis of SH' 82–3 and fig. 29).
6. 'The general topic of elections is the

last subject to which I could listen: there is not one about which I care a straw; and I believe your Lordship quite as indifferent' (HW to Lord Strafford 26 June 1790). Nevertheless HW mentions to Conway 25 June 1790 an anecdote concerning Charles James Fox and the Westminster election.
7. Since the alarm in May of a possible war with Spain (see n. 14) the press-gangs had been very active. See 'Mem. 1783–91,' *sub* 5 May 1790.
8. Cf. 'Visitors.'
9. 'This is the finest place upon the Thames. Nature has given it a scale of feature not commonly found in the neighbourhood of London, and Art has well seconded

The cottage and all its purlieus are delicious;[10] so is the bridge and Isis;[11] and the Druids' temple[12] seems to have been born and bred on the spot where it stands. I wish you had seen Nuneham[13] too, which is another of my first favourites.

Mr Berry will want news of the Spanish war,[14] but I can send him none, nor do I at all believe that it will come to a head.[15] France seems

the designs of Nature. The hill rises in a beautiful swell; on the top of it stands the house; at the bottom flows the river. . . . The house is but indifferent' (*Times* 7 Aug. 1789). The house was torn down ca 1870 and another was built on the site (*Victoria History of Berkshire*, 1906–24, iii. 160). See also Percy Noble, *Park Place*, 1905. HW wrote to Conway 25 June 1790: 'I hope my wives were not at Park Place in your absence: the loss of them is irreparable to me, and I tremble to think how much more I shall feel it in three months, when I am to part with them for—who can tell how long?'

10. 'The cottage, which is on the river's margin, possesses much beautiful scenery. On one side, Henley Church; on a second, the meanders of the river; and in front, the river again in a confined form, but coloured with all the variety which intermediate foliage can give it' (*Times* 7 Aug. 1789).

11. 'The bridge at Henley offers an object of no common beauty or interest, as the two faces on the centre arch, representing the Thame and Isis, are the sculpture of Mrs Damer' (*Times* 7 Aug. 1789). 'The bridge is as perfect as if bridges were natural productions . . . and the masks as if the Romans had left them there' (HW to Lord Strafford 29 Aug. 1786). Built ca 1785–7 at a cost of £10,000, the bridge, designed partly by Conway, 'consists of five elliptical arches with balustrades of stone' (Percy Noble, *Anne Seymour Damer*, 1908, p. 80; HW to Lady Ossory 10 Aug. 1785). For illustrations of the masks of Thame and Isis, see Noble, op. cit. 79. HW describes Isis as 'a most beautiful nymph's face, simple as the antique, but quite a new beauty. The idea was taken from Mrs Freeman, of Fawley Court, a neighbour of General Conway' (HW to Mann 7 May 1785). The model of Isis, in terra cotta, was sold SH xix. 84. See also *Walpoliana* ii. 87.

12. 'On the hill, a little beyond the pleasure grounds [at Park Place], is placed a small Druidical temple, found near the town of St Helier, in the island of Jersey, in the year 1785, presented by the inhabitants to Marshal Conway, then their governor, and by him removed to its present situation' (Daniel and Samuel Lysons, *Magna Britannia*, 1806–22, i. 352). Cf. G. A. Cooke, *Topographical and Statistical Description of the County of Berks* [1830], p. 134. HW describes fully the temple and its situation in his letters to Lady Ossory 6 Sept. 1788 and to Lord Strafford 12 Sept. 1788. A model of the temple was in the Small Closet at SH ('Des. of SH,' *Works* ii. 494).

13. The seat of HW's friends and correspondents, Lord and Lady Harcourt, in Oxfordshire, about sixteen miles from Park Place. Mary Berry saw it in 1794; see *post* 31 July 1794.

14. Under the protection of the East India Company, English traders had established friendly relations with the natives on the northwest coast of North America, chiefly at Prince William Sound and Nootka Sound, and were carrying on a profitable trade in furs. In May 1789 a Spanish captain anchored his battleship in Nootka Sound and, exceeding his orders, took possession of English vessels and cargoes, and imprisoned English sailors (GM 1790, lx pt i. 487–90). After considerable negotiation the affair, on Spain's promise of full restitution and indemnity, was amicably settled by a convention signed at the Escurial 28 Oct. 1790 (*post* 8 Nov. 1790; GM 1790, lx pt ii. 760, 1046–7). For HW's account of the preparations for war and negotiations for peace, see 'Mem. 1783–91,' *sub* May–November 1790.

15. HW was not alone in his belief: 'In England and in Spain ministers never seemed more intent upon war than upon the present occasion. There are, however, some who (with us) think all this fire and fury will evaporate in smoke' (GM, May 1790, lx pt i. 461).

more likely to ripen to confusion; they go on levelling so madly, that I shall wonder if everybody does not think himself loosened from all restraints and bound to conform to none—a pretty experiment to throw society with all its improved vices and desires into a state of nature, which in its outset had many of them to discover, and no worse instrument than the jawbone of an ass to execute mischief with. That serene prince the Duke of Orleans[16] has bowed to the abolition of titles,[17] and calls himself *Monsieur Capet,* from whom he may be descended, if he is not from the Bourbons; but as he has failed in being such another usurper,[18] I wonder he did not avoid the allusion.

Since I began my letter, I have called on Madame de Boufflers,[19] and heard but too much news. Monsieur d'Olan,[20] a worthy man, and nephew of my dear friend Madame du Deffand, has been taken out of his bed, to which he was confined by the gout, at Avignon, and hanged by the mob! I have said for this year that I am happy she is dead; and now how much that reflection is fortified! The Prime Minister of Spain has been stabbed by a Frenchman, but is not dead[21]—the wretch

16. Louis-Philippe-Joseph de Bourbon (1747–93), Duc d'Orléans, 1785; 'Philippe-Égalité.' He had been in England since 21 Oct. 1789 (GM 1789, lix pt ii. 951).

17. French titles of nobility were abolished by decree of the National Assembly 19 June 1790. For debates in connection with the decree, see the *Moniteur* 21 juin 1790; *London Chronicle* 24–26 June 1790, lxvii. 606. For Mary Berry's comments, see her *Comparative View of Social Life in England and France,* 1844, i. 319, 350.

18. As Hugh Capet (ca 946–96), the first of the Capetian dynasty to whom the name Capet was applied. In 987, on the death of Louis V, last of the Carolingian Kings, he was elected King of the Franks. HW considered him a usurper because the Franks passed over Louis V's brother Charles, Louis's lawful heir, and crowned Hugh Capet in his stead. The Bourbons were the last of the Capetian families.

19. Marie-Charlotte-Hippolyte de Camps de Saujon (1725–1800), m. (1746) Édouard, Comte (later Marquis) de Boufflers-Rouverel; HW's correspondent (DU DEFFAND i. 12 *et passim*). She had been in England before, but 'made a second visit to England at the beginning of the French Revolution in 1789, and was resident here some time with her daughter-in-law the Comtesse

Amélie de Boufflers, celebrated for her skill on the harp' (B, quoted ibid. i. 15). Accompanied by her daughter-in-law and grandson (see *post* 10 July 1790), she fled from Paris on the night of 13 July 1789, stayed for a time at Valenciennes and Spa, reached England in September 1789, and lived at Richmond in a house lent her by Vorontsov, the Russian Minister (HW to Lady Ossory 26 Sept. 1789, 8 Nov. 1789; P.-E. Schazmann, *La Comtesse de Boufflers,* 1933, pp. 209–18).

20. Denis-François-Marie-Jean de Suarez (1729–90), Marquis d'Aulan; son of Mme du Deffand's sister, Anne de Vichy, by Jean-François de Suarez, Marquis d'Aulan (DU DEFFAND i. 400 *et passim*).

21. 'June 29. One of the King's messengers arrived from Madrid . . . with an account of a desperate attempt that had been made on the life of the Count de Florida Blanca, the Prime Minister of Spain, by an assassin, who, being rendered furious by an unsuccessful application to him, drew a stiletto from his bosom, and made three plunges at him, by which he was dangerously wounded, but providentially not mortally' (GM 1790, lx pt ii. 660). 'Madrid, Aug. 12. Yesterday the man who attempted to assassinate Count Florida Blanca was publicly executed, by having his

is taken—I hope Mr Berry will cease to reckon me a royalist, because I do not think that liberty is cheaply purchased by murders and every kind of violence and injustice.

You must tack this half-letter to that of t'other day, and call it a whole one. You are sure I must want matter, not inclination when I do not send you what pedants call *a just volume*. Pray return from Lymington[22] with blooming countenances; you must sit for your pictures before your long journey.[23] I have not mentioned that article lately, because you have both looked so pale—nor indeed has the subject been so agreeable, as when I first proposed it—portraits are but melancholy pleasures in long absences! With what a different emphasis does one say adieu! for a month, and for a year!—I scarce guess how one can say the latter—alas! I must learn!

To Mary Berry, Saturday 3 July 1790

Address: To Miss Berry to be left at the Post Office at Lymington, Hants.
Postmark: ISLEW[ORTH] 5 JY 90.

Strawberry Hill, Saturday night, July 3,1790.[1]

HOW kind to write the very moment you arrived![2] but pray do not think that, welcome as your letters are, I would purchase them at the price of any fatigue to you—a proviso I put in already against moments when you may be more weary than by a journey to Lymington. You make me happy by the good accounts of Miss Agnes; and I should be completely so, if the air of the sea could be so beneficial to you both, as to make your farther journey unnecessary to your healths, at least for some time; for—and I protest solemnly that not a personal thought enters into the consideration, I shall be excessively alarmed at your going to the Continent, when such a frenzy has seized it. You see by the papers that the flame has burst out at Florence[3]—

right hand cut off, and then hanged' (ibid. 852).

The would-be assassin was Juan Pablo Pairet, a French quack (*curandero*), who stabbed Florida Blanca in his left breast 18 June 1790 (*Enciclopedia universal ilustrada,* Barcelona, etc., 1905–30, xxxvi. 837, *sub* Moñino, José, where the date is erroneously given as 18 July 1790).

22. HW first wrote 'Weymouth.'

23. Before their Italian journey in Octo-ber, they sat to Miss Anne Foldsone (later Mrs Joseph Mee) for their miniature portraits; see *post* 8 Nov. 1790.

———

1. 'No. 16' (B).

2. At Lymington, after visiting Park Place (see preceding letter).

3. 'The levelling principles of *democracy* [have] pervaded the principal part of the Italian States.' At Florence 7–14 June 'various seditious and treasonable libels were

can Pisa[4] then be secure? Flanders can be no safe road[5]—and is any part of France so? I told you in my last of the horrors at Avignon. At Madrid the people are riotous *against* the war with us[6]—and prosecuted I am persuaded it will not be—but the demon of Gaul is busy everywhere—nay, its imps are here! Horne Tooke[7] declared on the hustings t'other day that he would exterminate those *locusts* the nobility.[8] Lord Lansdown[9] whose family name I suspect to have been *Petit* (a French one) not Petty, is suspected to have set Tooke at work,[10] and like Monsieur Capet would waive his marquisate to compass a revolution. Capet is gone to the new St Barthelemi or jubilee on the 14th.[11] The banquet tables, it is said, are to extend a *ligue*,[12] for *league* is not French enough; the King is to be declared Emperor of the Franks, but the dignity not to be *hereditary,* that Polish massacres may be so.[13] The *États,* who are as foolish as atro-

read' and posted; 'a tumultuous multitude' pillaged, destroyed, plundered, and demanded bread. A detachment of dragoons from Pisa arrived to assist in restoring order (*London Chronicle* 29 June–1 July 1790, lxviii. 7). Later it was reported that the disturbances were beginning to subside (ibid. 15–17 July 1790, lxviii. 58; *post* 17 July 1790), but in August the 'most alarming commotion' was reported (ibid. 19–21 Aug. 1790, lxviii. 184).

4. Where the Berrys planned to stay; see *post* 10 July 1790.

5. 'The states of Flanders have published an *ordonnance,* in date of the 12th inst. [June] forbidding the entry of all sorts of arms from foreign parts: the reason is that they apprehend another internal commotion' (*London Chronicle* 1–3 July 1790, lxviii. 10, in a letter from Brussels 28 June).

6. 'The latest letters from all parts of Spain unanimously hold out the same kind of language—that Spain is by no means prepared to make any stand against Great Britain' (*Times* 30 June 1790).

7. John Horne Tooke (1736–1812), politician and philologist.

8. 'Horne Tooke stood for Westminster against the coalition of Lord Hood and Mr Fox, but lost it by a great majority, especially for Fox. Horne declared he would destroy the *locusts,* the nobility' ('Mem.

1783–91,' *sub* June 1790). For an account of the hustings, Wednesday 16 June 1790, see *The London Chronicle* 15–17 June 1790, lxvii. 576. The word 'locusts' appears neither in Tooke's letter to the electors of Westminster (*Times* 17 June 1790) nor in any of the available newspaper accounts.

9. William Petty (formerly Fitzmaurice) (1737–1805), 2d E. of Shelburne, 1753; cr. (1784) M. of Lansdowne; Prime Minister 1782–3; a *bête noir* of HW's.

10. No evidence for the connection between Tooke and Lord Lansdowne has been found.

11. 'The Duke of Orleans leaves this country immediately, and returns to Paris to be present at the General Association, which is to take place there on the 14th inst.' (*London Chronicle* 1–3 July 1790, lxviii. 15). He did not leave England, however, until 9 July (see two following letters). HW's 'new Barthelemi' shows that he considered the taking of the Bastille another Massacre of St Bartholomew.

12. Not found in available newspaper accounts.

13. HW suggests that with the abolishing of hereditary rule in France, bloody political uprisings would occur, as in Poland, where the kingship was elective rather than hereditary.

cious, have printed lists of the surnames which the late noblesse are to assume or resume,[14] as if people did not know their own names. I like a speech I have heard of the Queen. She went with the King to see the manufacture of glass, and as they passed the Halles, the *poissardes* huzzaed them; 'Upon my word,' said the Queen, 'these folks are civiller when you visit them, than when they visit you.'—This marked both spirit and good humour—For my part, I am so shocked at French barbarity that I begin to think that our hatred of them is not national prejudice, but natural instinct; as tame animals are born with an antipathy to beasts of prey.

Mrs Damer tells me in a letter today,[15] that Lady Ailesbury was charmed with you both (which did not surprise either of us) and says she never saw two persons have so much taste for the country, who have no place of their own—it may be so; but begging her Ladyship's pardon and yours, I think that people who have a place of their own, are mighty apt not to like any other.

I feel all the kindness of your determination of coming to Twickenham in August,[16] and shall certainly say no more against it, though I am certain that I shall count every day that passes, and when *they are passed,* they will leave a melancholy impression on Strawberry, that I had rather have affixed to London. The two last summers[17] were infinitely the pleasantest I ever passed here, for I never before had an agreeable neighbourhood.[18] Still I loved the place, and had no comparisons to draw. Now, the neighbourhood will remain, and

14. *Liste des noms des ci-devant nobles . . . avec des notes sur leurs familles,* published in numbers by Louis Brossard, and attributed partly to Jacques-Antoine Dulaure (1755–1835), was not an official publication. The first number appeared before the end of June, as appears from the opening sentence: 'Le décret de l'assemblée nationale du 19 du mois, ayant obligé les ci-devant nobles à reprendre leurs noms de famille. . . .' Extracts from the second and third numbers appear in *The London Chronicle* 8–10 July 1790, lxviii. 39, and 15–17 July 1790, lxviii. 63. The Duc d'Orléans heads the second number as 'Philippe

Capet.' Dulaure in this work 'prépara, sans le savoir peut-être, les horribles exécutions destinées à épuiser sur l'échafaud tout le sang noble qui restait en France' (N. Batjin, *Histoire complète de la noblesse de France,* 1862, p. 45).

15. Missing.

16. 'Summer for three weeks in Montpelier Row,' Twickenham (Mary Berry's entry in her journal, 1790, quoted MBJ i. 194).

17. When the Berrys were HW's neighbours.

18. Not to be taken literally; see the Lady Browne correspondence.

will appear ten times worse, with the aggravation of remembering *two months*[19] that may have some transient roses, but I am sure, lasting thorns.

You tell me I do not write with my usual spirits—at least I will suppress, as much as I can, the want of them—though I am a bad dissembler. Miss Cambridge[20] told me you had charged her to search for a house for you—I did bid Philip, but I believe not with the eagerness of last year, and I am persuaded she will execute your commission punctually.

You do not mention the cathedral at Winchester, which I have twice seen and admired.[21] Nor do you say anything of Bevis-mount[22] and Netley, charming Netley.[23] At Lyndhurst[24] you passed the palatial hovel of my royal nephew,[25] who I have reason to wish had never been so, and did all I could to prevent his being.[26]

The home chapter will be dull as usual. The Boydels[27] and Nich-

---

19. HW evidently expected the Berrys to be at Twickenham during August and September, before their departure for Italy in October, but see n. 16.

20. Charlotte (1746–1823), only surviving dau. of Richard Owen Cambridge, died unmarried (R. S. Cobbett, *Memorials of Twickenham*, 1872, p. 95). She was one of Fanny Burney's 'four invaluable friends,' 'that noble-minded creature,' 'very good, and very affectionate, and very sincere' (*Diary and Letters of Madame d'Arblay*, ed. Charlotte Barrett and Austin Dobson, 1904–5, ii. 259, 293, 362, *et passim*).

21. After his first visit to Winchester Cathedral with Chute in 1755, HW wrote to Bentley, 18 Sept. 1755: 'I like the smugness of the cathedral, and the profusion of the most beautiful Gothic tombs.' No account of his second visit has been found.

22. Bevois Mount, Hants, a seat about a mile north of Southampton, east of the Winchester-Southampton road. Charles Mordaunt, 3d E. of Peterborough, bought it and 'converted it into a kind of wilderness, through which are various winding gravel walks' (Richard Warner, *Collections for . . . Hampshire*, 1795, i pt ii. 81; GM 1808, lxxviii pt i. 90; E. Monro Purkis, *Wil-*

liam Shenstone, Wolverhampton [1931], p. 135).

23. Netley Abbey, a Cistercian foundation ca 1239, long in ruins when HW saw it in 1755 (HW to Bentley 18 Sept. 1755), and still open to sightseers (*England*, ed. Findlay Muirhead, 1924, p. 88). For three views (1760–72) and an account of it, see Francis Grose, *Antiquities of England and Wales* [1783–97], ii. 211–14; also the title-page of George Keate, *Netley Abbey, An Elegy*, 1769.

24. The 'capital of the New Forest,' in Hampshire, halfway between Southampton and Lymington.

25. The Duke of Gloucester had been Lord Warden of the New Forest since 1771. As Warden, his residence was the King's House, built in the reign of Charles II; it was in poor repair (hence HW's 'hovel') in 1789 when George III and the royal party were entertained there 25–30 June (William Gilpin, *Remarks on Forest Scenery*, 3d edn, 1808, ii. 216–19).

26. For HW's account of his conduct at the time of his niece's marriage to the Duke of Gloucester, see *Mem. Geo. III* iii. 267–71. See also *ante* 6 Aug. 1789, n. 31.

27. John Boydell (1719–1804), engraver

olses[28] breakfasted here yesterday, in return for their civilities at the Shakespeare Gallery.[29] On Tuesday[30] is to come Lady Herries[31] and her clan.[32] The week before last I met the Marlboroughs[33] at Lady

and print-publisher, alderman (1782–1804), sheriff (1785), and Lord Mayor (1790–1) of London; and his nephew, Josiah Boydell (1752–1817), painter and engraver, alderman of London 1804–9. They were partners in the printselling business and in the Shakespeare Gallery, built by them in Pall Mall to house the originals of the illustrations of their *Shakespeare,* completed in 1802. See *A Catalogue of the Pictures, &c. in the Shakespeare Gallery,* 1789–1802.

28. MS reads 'Nichols's,' but 'Visitors' reads 'Nichols': George Nichol or Nicol (ca 1741–1828), bookseller to George III, was associated with the Boydells in the Shakespeare Gallery, and in charge of the typography of their *Shakespeare.* After this visit to SH, he became HW's occasional correspondent. Possibly he was accompanied by his wife, —— Boydell, niece of John Boydell, whom he had married 8 Sept. 1787 (H. R. Plomer, *Dictionary of the Printers and Booksellers . . . 1726–1775,* Oxford, 1932; GM 1787, lvii pt ii. 836).

29. The date and circumstances of HW's visit have not been discovered. The Shakespeare Gallery opened its 1790 season on 15 March with several additions: twenty-three new paintings illustrating Shakespeare, three pieces of sculpture by Mrs Damer, a number of miscellaneous paintings and drawings (*London Chronicle* 13–16 March 1790, lxvii. 256), and finally, 'drawings after the most capital pictures formerly in the possession of the Earl of Orford; at Houghton in Norfolk. Lately purchased by the Empress of Russia' (*Catalogue of the Pictures, &c. in the Shakespeare Gallery,* 1790, pp. 127–31). The Boydells had published *A Set of Prints* of the Houghton pictures in 1788, in two atlas folio volumes. For HW's comments on some of the pictures in the Shakespeare Gallery, see his letter to Sir David Dalrymple, Lord Hailes, 21 Sept. 1790.

30. 6 July, when HW, already suffering from gout in his heel, 'increased it . . . by limping about the house with a party I had to breakfast' (to Conway 7 July 1790).

31. Catherine Foote (ca 1758–1808), 2d dau. of Rev. Francis Hender Foote of Charlton Place, near Canterbury, rector of Boughton Malherb and vicar of Linton, Kent, by Catherine Mann, sister of HW's friend, Sir Horace Mann; m. (1) (1774) when a minor (with the consent of her widowed mother) John Ross; m. (2) (1777) as 2d wife, Sir Robert Herries (d. 1815), Kt (1774), founder of Herries' Bank (now amalgamated with Lloyd's Bank), M.P. Dumfries Burghs 1780–4 (Toynbee, *Supp.* ii. 183, from information supplied by Mr David C. Herries; Burke, *Landed Gentry,* 1937, p. 1101; Burke, *Commoners,* i. 372; *Register Book of Marriages . . . of St George, Hanover Square . . . 1725–1787,* ed. John H. Chapman, 1886, p. 240).

32. In 'Visitors' for 6 July HW recorded: 'Lady Herries and Footes, *myself.*' Lady Herries had two married brothers living at this time: 1) John Foote (1755–1800) of Charlton Place, Kent, m. Mary Cocket; 2) Rev. Robert Foote (1757–1804), rector of Boughton Malherb, 1782; prebendary of Lichfield 1795–8, and of Rochester 1798–1804; m. (1782) Ann Yate. Her youngest brother, Edward James Foote (1767–1833), Lt. R.N., 1785, afterwards (1821) vice-admiral and (1831) K.C.B., m. (1793) Nina Herries, Lady Herries' stepdaughter; it is unlikely, however, that he was in England at this time (Burke, *Commoners* i. 372; GM 1782, lii. 405; GM 1793, lxiii pt i. 184; GM 1833, ciii pt ii. 180–1; GM 1800, lxx pt ii. 909; John Le Neve and T. Duffus Hardy, *Fasti Ecclesiæ Anglicanæ,* Oxford, 1854).

33. George Spencer (1739–1817), 3d D. of Marlborough, m. (1762) Caroline Russell (1743–1811), dau. of 4th D. of Bedford. 'Queen Charlotte pronounced her to be the proudest woman in England' (GEC).

Di's.[34] The Duchess desired to come and see Strawberry again, as it had rained the whole time she was here last.[35] I proposed the next morning: no, she could not, she expected company to dinner, she believed their brother Lord Robert[36] would dine with them—I thought that a little odd, as they have just turned him out for Oxfordshire;[37] and I thought a dinner no cause at the distance of four miles.[38] In her Grace's dawdling way she could fix no time; and so on Friday[39] at half an hour after seven, as I was going to Lady North's,[40] they arrived; and the sun being setting and the moon not risen, you may judge how much they could see through all the painted glass by twilight.

It has rained all day and I have not been out of my house: in the morning I had three or four visitors, particularly my nephew George

34. The Duke of Marlborough's sister, Lady Diana Spencer (1734–1808), m. (1) (1757) Frederick St John, 2d Vct Bolingbroke, from whom she was divorced; m. (2) (1768) Topham Beauclerk. HW's occasional correspondent, she also drew for HW's *Mysterious Mother* seven illustrations which hung in the 'Beauclerk Closet' at SH. Four days after HW's death she wrote to her daughter: 'I have lost a real friend in him' (Mrs Steuart Erskine, *Lady Diana Beauclerk*, 1903, p. 264). She lived at this time at Little Marble Hill, Twickenham, on the Thames (see also *post* 17 Oct. 1793), a house sometimes known also as the 'White Bow-Window Villa' (*World* 19 Aug. 1789). For prints of Lady Diana and of Little Marble Hill, see Erskine, op. cit., *passim*. Two water-colour drawings of it by J. Barrow, 1789, were formerly HW's and are now WSL.

35. 28 June 1784 ('Visitors'). HW wrote to Conway 30 June 1784: 'The Duke and Duchess of Marlborough breakfasted here on Monday, and seemed much pleased, though it rained the whole time with an Egyptian darkness.'

36. Lord Robert Spencer (1747–1831), the younger of the Duke of Marlborough's brothers.

37. After representing New Woodstock 1768–71, Lord Robert was M.P. for Oxford (not Oxfordshire) 1771–90. Defeated in the election for Oxford 16 June 1790 (*London Chronicle* 17–19 June 1790, lxvii. 584), he was returned for Wareham 21 June 1790 and served until 1799. He subsequently represented Tavistock 1802–7, 1817–18, and New Woodstock 1818–20.

38. The Marlboroughs were at their seat at Syon Hill, Isleworth, which was torn down before 1840 (George James Aungier, *History and Antiquities of Syon Monastery*, 1840, p. 228; Daniel Lysons, *Environs of London*, 1792–6, iii. 98).

39. 2 July. The visit is not mentioned in 'Visitors,' because HW had not issued tickets.

40. Anne Speke (ca 1740–97), dau. and heiress of George Speke of White Lackington, Somerset; m. (1756) Frederick North (1732–92), styled Lord North 1752–90, 2d E. of Guilford, 4 Aug. 1790. Ranger of Bushy Park 1771–97, she lived at Bushy House, now part of the National Physical Laboratory.

Cholmondeley[41] with an account of his marriage settlements and the toothache. Tonight I am writing to you comfortably by the fireside, for we are forced to raise an English July in a hot-house like grapes. Pray tell me as much of your personal history and what company you have. I care much more about Lymington, than all the elections in the kingdom—and I seem to think that you interest yourself as much about *les amusements des eaux de Straberri*. Good night.

To Agnes Berry, ca Wednesday 7 July 1790

Missing. Written at Strawberry Hill. It probably dealt with the Berrys' proposed journey to Italy, and the disturbed conditions in Europe (see *post* 10 July 1790, paragraph following the quotation; 17 July 1790, second paragraph).

To Mary Berry, Saturday 10 July 1790

Dated by HW's heading, 'July 10,' which was Saturday, not Friday night; and by his reference to *The Times* of 'the day before yesterday,' 8 July.

Address: To Miss Mary Berry to be left at the Post House at Lymington, Hants. *Postmark:* 13 JY 90.

Strawberry Hill, Friday [Saturday] night, July 10, 1790.

I BEGIN my letter tonight, but shall not send it away till I hear again from you, that our letters may not jostle without answering one another—but how can I pass my solitary evenings so well as by talking to you? I laid on my couch for three days, but as never was so tractable a gout as mine, I have walked all over the house today without assistance.

41. HW's grandnephew, George James Cholmondeley (1752–1830), son of Hon. Robert Cholmondeley; commissioner of stamp duties 1781–2; commissioner (1782–1801) and sometime chairman of the Board of Excise. Seven years earlier HW referred to him as 'a young man of sense and honourable principles, and among the best of my nepotism . . . he has some humour, and some voice, and is musical; but he has not good health, nor always good spirits' (HW to Mann 8 July 1783). He m. (7 Aug. 1790) at Kingston House, near Dorchester, Marcia Pitt (1759–1808), dau. of John Pitt of Encombe, Dorset, and sister of William Morton Pitt, M.P., of Kingston House (Burke, *Peerage,* 1928, *sub* Cholmondeley, p. 521; GM 1790, lx pt ii. 764; John Hutchins, *Dorset,* 3d edn, Westminster, 1861–70, ii. 567, iv. 92; *Royal Kalendar* 1781–1801). In 1792 Sarah Francis, whose sister later became Cholmondeley's second wife, wrote that Cholmondeley 'was as absurd and as delightful as ever, and his wife strange to say quite animated and agreeable, well dressed and looking in great beauty' (*Francis Letters,* ed. Beata Francis and Eliza Keary [1901], ii. 400; see also *passim*). For his portrait, see ibid. ii. 688.

I did long to peep at my building, but as it has been a cold *dog-day,* I would not risk a relapse, and about dinner we had a smart shower—well, you cry, and was it worth while to write only to tell me it is cold? We know that at Weymouth![1]—Oh! yes, it was to tell you otherguess news than of heat or cold overhead. In short, as whatever may directly or indirectly affect you and your sister, is my principal occupation at present, I must transcribe two paragraphs from *The Times* of the day before yesterday:[2]

The subjects of Leopold[3] have assumed the cockade in *Leghorn,* and delivered to the Regency a *Bill of Rights.*

On the 31st of May the people in a tumultuous manner broke open two churches at *Leghorn.* They then advanced to the quarter of the Jews, threatening entirely to extirpate them. Some soldiers were hastily assembled and ordered to fire on the mutineers. Six were killed and a great number wounded. Still however the disturbances continued. They have opened other churches, and converted them into magazines, and have assumed the red and white cockade. The senate and governor have endeavoured to persuade them to adopt peaceable measures. They have answered by a memorial, stating their civil and religious grievances and demanding redress.

Thus Pisa, you see, is no sojourning place for you! Indeed, as I told Miss Agnes in my last,[4] till some of the ferment in Europe subsides, it would be very unadvised to change this country for any other. Mrs Boscawen, who came to visit my gout this morning, told me that Mr Prescot,[5] coming from Avignon, where poor Monsieur Dolan and four other persons have been hanged for refusing to disavow the Pope,[6] was thrown into prison in France and detained there

---

1. Read 'Lymington'; so altered in MS, probably by Lady Theresa Lewis, and so printed in MBJ i. 198. In his letter of 2 July 1790 HW wrote 'Weymouth,' but corrected his error.

2. HW's transcription varies only in minor details of punctuation from the account in *The Times* 8 July 1790.

3. Leopold II (1747–92), Grand Duke of Tuscany from 1765–21 July 1790, when he was succeeded by his second son, Ferdinand III; succeeded Joseph II as Holy Roman Emperor 20 Feb. 1790 (Alfred von Reumont, *Geschichte Toscanas seit dem Ende des Florentinischen Freistaates,* Gotha 1876–77, ii. 221).

4. Ca 7 July 1790 (missing); in his last letter to Mary Berry 3 July 1790, HW had written: 'I shall be excessively alarmed at your going to the Continent, when such a frenzy has seized it.'

5. Not identified.

6. Evidently only four persons, including the Marquis d'Aulan, were hanged by the mob 10 June 1790. The other three were: Marquis de Rochegude, 'ancien officier supérieur au service de la France, qui s'était mis quelques jours avant à la disposition du vice-légat pour rétablir l'ordre dans les rues'; Abbé Offray; and —— Aubert, 'tafetassier.' The last two, and possibly all four, were accused of lack of respect for the newly established municipal government. 'Les victimes . . . furent deux aristocrates,

all night before suffered to prosecute his journey through France. The Duchess of Gloucester, who called on me afterwards, says the like troubles are broken out in Swisserland—Surely this is not a season for expeditions to the Continent!

Monsieur Capet has been twice at Brighthelmstone,[7] and had sent Madame Buffon[8] before to feel his way.[9] She and others have warned him not to embark[10]—he has given it up, has sent for his pictures for sale[11]—and perhaps with them may buy an Irish peerage. Lord Carlisle[12] and Lord William Gordon[13] were going to Paris for the 14th—

un prêtre, et un homme du peuple. C'était tout l'ancien régime en une seule exécution' (Léopold de Gaillard, *Autres temps*, 1893, pp. 273–4). Two of the patriots were shot, but further bloodshed was prevented by the arrival of the national guard from Orange, eighteen miles away (ibid.; *Précis de l'Histoire d'Avignon*, Avignon, 1852, ii. 136–7).

7. Brighton, from which place he planned to embark, and eventually (9 July) did embark, for France (see following letter).

8. His mistress, Marguerite-Françoise Bouvier de Lamotte de Cépoy (1767–1808), dau. of Guillaume-François Bouvier de Lamotte, Marquis de Cépoy; m. (1) (1784) Georges-Louis-Marie Leclerc, Comte de Buffon, son of the famous naturalist; they were divorced 14 Jan. 1793 and she m. (2) (1799) Julien-Raphael Renouard de Bussierre, émigré living at Rome (Woelmont de Brumagne i. 63; Jean-Nicolas, Comte Dufort de Cheverny, *Mémoires*, 1909, i. 384–5, ii. 327).

9. 'Madame Buffon set out [for Paris] on Friday [2 July], and Mr Capet accompanied her a few miles from town, which gave rise to the report of his departure, inserted in some of the papers' (*London Chronicle* 3–6 July 1790, lxviii. 18).

10. After taking leave of George III on 29 June, the Duc d'Orléans made plans to leave for France 3 July. On the morning of that day, however, 'the French ambassador waited on me, accompanied by a Mr Boinville . . . one of M. LaFayette's aides-du-camp. The latter gentleman conjured me, in the name of M. LaFayette, to defer my journey to Paris [because of] . . . the danger that evil-disposed persons might abuse

my name to excite tumults.' Thereupon the Duc d'Orléans wrote to the National Assembly, asking for advice. His letter, from which the passage above is quoted, was read in the National Assembly and commented on 6–7 July, when LaFayette admitted that for public tranquillity he had requested the Duc's original absence and its continuance. No decision was reached, however, and no advice given, as one member of the Assembly called for the order of the day (*London Chronicle* 10–13, 13–15 July 1790, lxviii. 47, 53).

11. According to a letter from Paris, 15 July, 'It has long been under consideration to make a sale of the valuable collection of pictures in the Orléans gallery, and an eminent auctioneer of London is come over for the purpose of settling measures for the same. A stop is, however, put to it by the high powers of this kingdom, under the idea that the pictures belong to the nation, having been originally purchased by the Regent of the kingdom with the public money' (*St James's Chronicle* 17–20 July 1790). In 1792 the Duc d'Orléans sold his Italian and French pictures to a banker at Brussels, who in turn sold them to a Frenchman who was guillotined. The pictures were bought about 1798 by the Duke of Bridgwater, Earl Gower, and the Earl of Carlisle, who kept some of the pictures for themselves and sold the others 1798–1800. See Maurice W. Brockwell, *The 'Adoration of the Magi,'* 1911, p. 25, Appendix B, pp. 15–16; Frits Lugt, *Répertoire des catalogues de ventes publiques*, La Haye, 1938.

12. Frederick Howard (1748–1825), 5th E. of Carlisle; HW's occasional correspondent.

13. (1744–1823), brother of Alexander,

but hear it would be too perilous a service—*il n'y ferait pas bon pour tout aristocrate!*

General Conway in his last letter[14] asked me if it was not a theme to moralize on, this earthquake that has swallowed up all Montmorencis, Guises, Birons, and great names? I reply, it makes me *immoralize;* I am outrageous at the destruction of all the visions that make history delectable—without some romance it is but a register of crimes and calamities, and the French seem preparing to make their country one universal St Bartelemi; they are instructing the populace to lay everything waste! What is to restrain them? Will they obey those masters who tell them, preach to them, that all are equal—but who, good men! pay themselves twelve livres a day[15] for propagating that doctrine—I shall wonder if *their equals* do not recollect having an equal right to twelve livres a day!—Oh! go not into that conflagration, nor whither its sparks extend! Come to the banks of the gentle placid Thames—nor strow its shores with alarm and anxiety by leaving them. How I wished for you today—yes, don't you believe me, and particularly at three o'clock. Mrs Boscawen was sitting with me here in the blue bow-window:[16] in a moment the river was covered with little yachts[17] and boats, the road and the opposite meadow with coaches, chaises, horsemen, women and children. Mr George Hardinge had given three guineas to be rowed for by four two-oared boats from his Ragman's Castle[18] to Lady Dudley's and back, so we saw the confluence go and return. I had not heard of it, but all Richmond had, and was descended from its heights. Mrs Boscawen says you have at Weymouth[18a] the Dowager Duchess Plantaginet,[19] or as I translate

4th D. of Gordon, and of Lord George, the agitator; M.P. Elginshire 1779–84, Inverness-shire 1784–90, and Horsham 1790–96; vice-admiral for Scotland 1782–95 (*Scots Peerage* iv. 554).

14. Missing; HW's letter of 7 July is evidently a reply to it. See particularly the paragraph beginning, 'I am tired of railing at French barbarity and folly.'

15. In August 1789 the payment of deputies was fixed at eighteen livres (francs) per day (Gaston Dodu, *Le Parlementarisme . . . sous la révolution*, 1911, p. 91; Thomas Carlyle, *French Revolution*, ed. J. Holland Rose, 1913, i. 283). While the amount was generally considered fair, not extravagant, compensation, satirical attacks on the deputies were not lacking. See Dodu, op. cit. 91–2; HW to Lord Strafford 12 Aug.

1790; HW to Sir David Dalrymple, Lord Hailes, 21 Sept. 1790; *post* 26 May 1791.

16. In the bow-window of the Blue Bedchamber.

17. MS reads 'yatchs.'

18. Occupied by Hardinge ca 1783–1816, and previously (1755–68) by Mrs Pritchard the actress. Torn down ca 1850, it formerly was near the site of Orleans House, north of Eel Pie Island. See R. S. Cobbett, *Memorials of Twickenham*, 1872, pp. 215, 246–8. The distance from Ragman's Castle to Lady Dudley's and back was about three miles.

18a. I.e., Lymington. See *ante* p. 84, n. 1.

19. Elizabeth Berkeley (ca 1719–99), sister of the 4th Bn Botetourt; m. (1740) Lord Charles Noel Somerset, 4th D. of Beaufort, 1745. HW's 'Broomstick,' 'beaucoup d'honneur,' and later references to her stiffness,

her, Broomstick. *Beaucoup d'honneur,* but I don't believe she enlivens you like a boat race—adieu, *jusqu'au résumer!*

12th.

It is but Monday evening and I expect no letter till tomorrow, but I must go on; I have new horrors and dangers to relate. Monsieur Cordon,[20] who was Sardinian minister here, and now at Paris, fell under the displeasure of the new despots the mob: they met a man[21] whom they took for Cordon; and *sans dire gare!* hanged him.[22] Madame de St Alban,[23] who you know is a pinchbeck-niece of mine, was returning to Lord Cholmondeley[24] from Paris, but was arrested at the

uprightness, and inflexibility are supported by her supposed epitaph in Sir Herbert Croft, *The Abbey of Kilkhampton,* revised edn, 1788, p. 109: 'She had in her Veins the Blood of B—k—ley and of Bot—t, in her *Démarche* the Greatness of the Queen of Sheba, in the Fire of her Eye, the Pout of her Lip, and the Bend of her Neck, the Majesty of Cleopatra, the Spirit of Margaret of Anjou, and the I[nnocen]ce of Joan of Arc. She was pregnant with Nobility from the Crown of the Skull to the Point of the Toe.'

20. Francesco Giuseppe Sallier della Tour (1726–1800), Marchese di Cordon; general; minister to Holland; envoy to England 1774–84; ambassador to France 1788–91; fought against France 1792–4 (Domenico Carutti, *Storia della Corte di Savoia durante la rivoluzione e l'impero francese,* Torino-Roma, 1892, ii. 395). After his return from England, he wrote *La Relation du Marquis de Cordon, envoyé du roi de Sardaigne en Angleterre (1774–1784),* ed. Charles Miller, Florence, 1932.

21. Abbé Comte Cordon (see following note).

22. In his dispatch from Paris 5 July 1790, Lord Gower (later 1st D. of Sutherland), the English ambassador, gives a different account: 'The Abbé Comte de Cordon, a relation of the Sardinian Ambassador at this Court, in going from hence to Savoy, was attacked by the populace at a small village near and on this side of Pont-Beauvoisin; being, on account of his name, mistaken for the Ambassador, he was stript naked to discover if he had any letters about him; none however were found. I must here mention that he had had one,

written by the Ambassador upon private business, but not knowing the contents of it, he had contrived to eat it up before he was seized. The populace were long in suspense whether they should hang him or carry him back prisoner to Lyons; before they could decide, by good luck somebody arrived who knew his person and he was allowed to proceed. On his arrival at Turin a messenger was dispatched to Paris; the Sardinian Ambassador has presented a memorial from his Court and there the affair rests at present' (*Despatches of Earl Gower,* ed. Oscar Browning, Cambridge, 1885, p. 10).

23. 'Perhaps the most bewitching impure in Europe' (quoted by Horace Bleackley, *Ladies Fair and Frail,* [1925] p. 220, from an unidentified source), 'Madame de St Albin, the prettiest woman in England when she arrives there' (Philip Francis to his wife, from Paris, 7 Sept. 1784, *Francis Letters,* ed. Beata Francis and Eliza Keary, [1901] ii. 354), 'a courtesan whose address in her profession France as well as England had witnessed' before she became Lord Cholmondeley's mistress in 1785 ([Charles Pigott] *The Whig Club,* 1794, p. 139; N&Q 1916, 12th ser. i. 233). She remained his mistress until her marriage in 1791, and bore him two, and possibly three, children (*post* 2 Aug. 1790, 10 April 1791). Gainsborough is said to have painted her portrait, but its whereabouts is not known (N&Q 1916, 12th ser. i. 286–7). She evidently died before 1812, as in a notice of the marriage of her daughter, Harriet Cholmondeley, she is mentioned as 'the late celebrated Madam St Alban' (GM 1812, lxxxii pt i. 188).

24. George James Cholmondeley (1749–

gate, and had all her papers seized and examined. While I was writing this paragraph, Mrs Grenville called to see me; and had just seen a Mrs Hamlyn lately returned from Italy with her husband;[25] between Boulogne and Calais they were stopped *seven times* by vagabonds liberty drunk; and obliged to drink with them; and yesterday I heard of a Mr Prescot being stopped in France and imprisoned for a night—but 'tis for Wednesday that everybody trembles.[26] The son of Madame de Boufflers[27] has written to his mother in a style of taking leave of her, his wife[28] and child,[29] as not knowing if he shall ever see them again—I do not coin these tragedies to frighten you, but they will terrify me, if you still think of setting your foot on French ground!

What say you to that mischievous lunatic Lord Stanhope,[30] who is to celebrate the French jubilee at the Crown and Anchor?[31] I was told

1827), 4th E. of Cholmondeley; cr. (1815) M. of Cholmondeley; chamberlain to the Prince of Wales 1795–1800; Lord Steward of the Household 1812–21. He was the grandson of HW's sister Mary by George, 3d E. of Cholmondeley.

25. James Hamlyn (d. 1811), cr. (7 July 1795) Bt., of Clovelly Court, Devon, and of Edwinsford, Carmarthenshire; M.P. Carmarthenshire 1793–1802; m. (1762) Arabella Williams (d. 1797), dau. of Thomas Williams of Great Russell Street, London.

26. 'The public apprehensions concerning something tragical that is to happen at the approaching confederation . . . take greater consistence; many people have given up all intention of going there, and some are determined to leave Paris. What is most curious is that nobody can assign a reason for this terror, or define in the least degree what is to happen' (extract of a letter from Paris, 4 July, in *London Chronicle* 8–10 July 1790, lxviii. 40).

27. Louis-Édouard (1746–94), Comte de Boufflers, on whose behalf HW wrote to Mann 11 July 1766. In ill health in 1792, he went to Aix-la-Chapelle, but died at Dortmund (P.-E. Schazmann, *La Comtesse de Boufflers*, 1933, pp. 30, 225; DU DEFFAND i. 172 *et passim*).

28. Amélie-Constance Puchot des Alleurs (ca 1750–1825), dau. of Roland Puchot (d. 1755), French ambassador at Constantinople; m. (1768) Louis-Édouard, Comte de

Boufflers, from whom she later separated (DU DEFFAND ii. 58–9 *et passim*).

29. Emmanuel de Boufflers (1785–1858), the last of his line ('Lettres de Gustave III . . . [et] la Comtesse de Boufflers,' *Actes de l'académie nationale . . . de Bordeaux*, 1898, lx. 21–2, 363–6). George Selwyn comments on him in letters of 1789–90; see Hist. MSS Commission, 15th Report, Appendix, Part VI, *Manuscripts of the Earl of Carlisle*, 1897, pp. 677, 693.

30. Charles Stanhope (1753–1816), styled Vct Mahon 1763–86; 3d E. Stanhope, 1786; a man of science, a politician, and a supporter of revolutionary principles.

31. 'Conviviality and harmony highly distinguished itself yesterday [14 July] at the Crown and Anchor Tavern in the Strand, in the celebration of the late glorious Revolution in France, when upwards of 700 gentlemen met upon the occasion, to whom a most elegant dinner was given, with the best of wines, etc. Many loyal and constitutional toasts were drank to the Glory of the Revolution and Prosperity to Old England. The Honourable Earl Stanhope, and the rest of the Stewards [of the Revolution Society], as well as several of the first merchants in the city, attended' (*London Chronicle* 13–15 July 1790, lxviii. 56). Lord Stanhope, or 'Mr Charles Stanhope,' as he was called on this occasion (*St James's Chronicle* 10–13 July 1790), delivered a speech praising the French for hav-

today but have not seen it of an excellent advertisement against him from the oyster women of Billingsgate, professing their *dis*loyalty, and desiring to be associated to his banquet.[32]

I am still confined, and like others who are well, sitting by the fire —in short, one must have fire-summer, if sun-summer is not to be had. Mrs Anderson and Mr Wheeler called on me this morning from Hampton; she looks lean and ill, and goes to Ramsgate: her parents[33] next week to Tunbridge for a month. One would think all the English were ducks, they are forever waddling to the water—but I must stop; I shall not have an inch of paper for tomorrow.

Tuesday.

It is past twelve and no post yet, and ours goes away at one.[34] Lady Valetort[35] was brought to bed of a dead daughter yesterday but Lady Mount Edgcumbe is more likely to die of the miscarriage than she— Here is your letter—I do not like your resolution not being shaken— I will say no more, but that I have not invented one of the circumstances I have stated in this or my last. I am grieved that Miss Agnes does not advance. About me you may be quite easy; my lameness is no bigger than a limp. I only do not go out because I dread a relapse; and as I have company *quantum sufficit* in a morning, and can write to you all the evening, I do not mind voluntary confinement. It rains again this minute cold rain. I am sorry your coast is as bad.

I have nothing to add to my letter but a new edition or correction of an old proverb that I made this morning on Lady Cecilia's and everybody's jaunts to watering places—Home is never home, though ever so comely[36]—Mr Udney[37] is just come in, the post is just going out—I must finish abruptly—if my letters ever do finish—

ing gained civil and religious liberty. Sheridan proposed a resolution of congratulations on the establishment of liberty in France; it was sent to the National Assembly, there read 21 July, circulated in French, and answered by the Assembly (Ghita Stanhope and G. P. Gooch, *Life of Charles third Earl Stanhope*, 1914, pp. 93–5). HW noted in 'Mem. 1783–91,' *sub* 14 July 1790: 'Lord Stanhope, Price and Sawbridge celebrated the French jubilee at the Crown and Anchor, Horne [Tooke] . . . there and was hissed; and Sheridan. Much riot and drunkenness.'

32. The advertisement has not been found.

33. Gen. James and Lady Cecilia Johnston.

34. Cf. HW to Pinkerton 14 Aug. 1788: 'The new regulation of the post proves very inconvenient to this little district; for it arrives and departs again in half an hour.'

35. Lady Sophia Hobart (1768–1806), 3d dau. of the 2d E. of Buckinghamshire; m. (21 Feb. 1789) Hon. Richard Edgcumbe, styled Vct Valletort 31 Aug. 1789—4 Feb. 1795, 2d E. of Mount Edgcumbe, 1795.

36. 'Home is home, though it be never so homely' (John Clarke, *Parœmiologia Anglo-Latina*, 1639, p. 101, cited in Bartlett, *Familiar Quotations*, 1937).

37. HW's neighbour at Teddington,

To Mary Berry, Saturday 17 July 1790

Address: To Miss Berry to be left at the Post House at Lymington, Hants.
Postmark: 20 JY 90.

Strawberry Hill, July 17, Saturday, 1790.

I HAVE received yours of the 14th and since you seem so determined on your journey, I shall say little more on the subject,
though if my arguments have had no weight, yours, I assure you, are
as far from convincing me. That Miss Crawford[1] or Mrs Lockart[2]
may have met with no disturbances on their routes is probably true,
but proves nothing as to safety; nor, when there is so much danger,
does it become a jot wiser to run the contrary risk. That our papers

Robert Fullarton Udny (1722–1802), West India merchant of London and later (1792) of Udny Castle, Aberdeenshire; F.R.S., 1785; well known for his collection of pictures, chiefly Italian; friend and patron of Edward Edwards (sometime employed by HW) and Richard Cosway, the latter of whom painted his portrait and designed a memorial for him (William Temple, *Thanage of Fermartyn*, Aberdeen, 1894, pp. 433–4; *The Genealogist*, 1878, ii. 89–90; Burke, *Landed Gentry*, 1879, ii. 1644; *Scots Magazine*, 1802, lxiv. 182–3; Frederick B. Daniell, *Catalogue . . . of the Engraved Works of Richard Cosway*, 1890, pp. 37, 48; Edward Edwards, *Anecdotes of Painters*, 1808, pp. iv–vi; William Hogarth, *Anecdotes*, 1833, p. 409; Daniel Lysons, *Environs of London*, 1792–6, iii. 505). Cosway's portrait, engraved by W. N. Gardiner, is reproduced in *The Home Counties Magazine*, 1899, i. 273. 'He was a man of general information, great liberality, and a very hospitable disposition; indeed, he was one of the old breed of true English gentlemen, which seems to be nearly exhausted and lost amidst the frivo-lous vanity and impertinence of the present race of our countrymen' (GM 1802, lxxii pt i. 182). Previous editors of HW and Mary Berry, and Mary Berry herself (see *post* 6 Sept. 1795, n. 6) have confused him with his younger brother, John Udny (1727–1800), sometime British consul at Venice and at Leghorn. His collections were sold in four sales 1802–4 (Lugt, op. cit.).

1. Probably Sarah Craufurd (1751–96), dau. of Patrick Craufurd of Auchinames; half-sister of HW's friend, John ('Fish') Craufurd, and of James Craufurd, Governor of Bermuda; died unmarried at Bermuda, Oct. 1796. 'Her good understanding was much enlarged by travel. Her friendship was ardent, and truly sincere; and her heart and purse were ever open to the solicitations of distress' (GM 1796, lxvi pt ii. 967; *Times* 22 Nov. 1796; Burke, *Landed Gentry*, 1879, i. 383; George Crawford, *General Description of the Shire of Renfrew*, ed. George Robertson, Paisley, 1818, p. 368).

2. Not identified.

are very untrue, is certain; but nothing upon earth is less true than that they have exaggerated the barbarities in France—they have not specified an hundredth part of them! They have not mentioned a third part of the châteaux that have been burnt. Have they said a syllable of the murder of poor Monsieur Dolan, or of five nuns massacred there, or of a young man just going to be married to a pretty young woman with whom he was in love, and whom they hanged before her window? Will Miss Crawford deny these facts? Or Mrs Lockart deny the disturbances in Tuscany, of which I do know the government received an account? I have heard that they are pacified[3]—so were the disturbances in Hungary said to be—but they have broken out again.[4]

You need not have the most trifling apprehension of what I said I could not write:[5] it is merely a project for suspending your journey, till you see a little farther, and that you shall know when I see you.

It is said that an account has come in forty-eight hours that everything of St Bartelemi's jubilee passed tranquilly the first day[6]—and I did suppose that the fears of the *États* would make them take all manner of precautions—but my notion all along has been that the great danger of confusion will be when the deputies, double-poisoned by the levellers, shall return into their several provinces. The Duke of Orleans after much fluctuation did go to Paris,[7] and made a speech

3. 'The last letters from Florence advise that the tumults in that city begin to subside, none but the lowest classes of the people being engaged in them. On the first alarm, the English families, and travellers of distinction, were preparing to leave the place; but . . . a deputation from the magistracy waited on Lord Hervey, the British envoy, to assure his Excellency of the perfect safety of the lives and security of the property of the English. They also waited on Lady Hervey to request her influence with the English ladies not to depart the city, and to quiet their fears' (*London Chronicle* 15–17 July 1790, lxviii. 58; *St James's Chronicle* 15–17 July 1790). See also *ante* 3 July 1790.

4. From Vienna, 23 June, came the report that 'the Diet of Hungary is at this moment nearly in the same situation as the States General of France were the latter end of May last year. The two chambers cannot agree on any point' (*St James's Chronicle* 13–15 July 1790).

5. Probably in his missing letter to Agnes Berry, ca 7 July 1790, or possibly in that of ca 28 June 1790, to Mary Berry.

6. 'Last night [Friday 16 July] a courier arrived at the hotel of his Excellency the French Ambassador in Portman Square, who left Paris at five o'clock on Wednesday evening, after the principal bustle of the day was over. He announces . . . that everything had been conducted on that day with great good order, and that the city of Paris was in profound tranquillity at the time of his departure' (*London Chronicle* 15–17 July 1790, lxviii. 64).

7. His fluctuation is reflected in the newspaper reports. He arrived in Paris

to the *États,* as you will see in our papers; but it is said to have been ill received[8]—This is all I know *des parties d'outre-mer.* We seem to be very preparatory for war with Spain—but I still have no faith in its taking place.

Lord Camelford has at last heard of his son's safety[9]—and there ends all my knowledge.

My gout did not last so long as a common cold. I was at Hampton on Friday and at Richmond last night making visits, but found nobody at home; it was the first tolerable evening, and everybody had flown out. Today it has been warmer, but as moist as if a sirocco.

either on Saturday evening (*London Chonicle* 15–17 July 1790, lxviii. 62; Evarts Seelye Scudder, *Prince of the Blood,* 1937, p. 209) or on Sunday, 11 July, at 4 A.M. (*London Chronicle* 15–17 July 1790, lxviii. 58; *St James's Chronicle,* same date).

8. On Sunday morning, 11 July, the Duc d'Orléans went to the National Assembly, spoke briefly, and 'took the oath prescribed to all members of that body' (*London Chronicle* 15–17 July 1790, lxviii. 58; *St James's Chronicle,* same date). The complete silence which met him when he rose to speak was followed by applause variously described as 'considerable' (*St James's Chronicle,* loc. cit.), 'the loudest applause of the majority' (*London Chronicle,* same date, lxviii. 62).

9. Thomas Pitt (1775–1804), 2d Bn Camelford, 1793; died from the effects of a bullet wound received in a duel. Entering the navy against his father's wishes (*Times* 28 April 1790), he sailed in 1789 in the *Guardian,* commanded by Lt Edward Riou, and laden with stores for Botany Bay. When the vessel was almost wrecked near

the Cape of Good Hope, Riou gave permission to the crew to take to the boats. Some ninety members, including Pitt, stayed aboard and finally brought the ship into Table Bay, although the Admiralty for a time considered the *Guardian* lost (GM 1790, lx pt i. 367, 465–70; *Times* 28 April 1790; Sir Bernard Burke, *Romance of the Aristocracy,* 1855, ii. 351). Letters from Riou received 'in the course of the late week' (*St James's Chronicle* 10–13 July 1790) may have brought news of Pitt's safety, but the *London Chronicle* as late as 24–27 July 1790 (lxviii. 96) reports: 'We are happy to be able to inform Lord Camelford . . . and all others who had sons or relations on board the Guardian, that by the unremitting attention of Lieutenent Riou, he did not lose one man. . . . This intelligence comes to us by a letter dated the first of March, brought by a Dutch ship.' See also ibid. 29–31 July 1790, lxviii. 111; *St James's Chronicle* 7–10 Aug. 1790. Young Pitt returned to England in Sept. 1790 (Burke, loc. cit.).

Thus, you see, Lymington is not more eventless. The two male Edgcumbes[10] and Mr Williams[11] were with me this morning, and the two Lysonses[12] dined with me, and Gen. Conway breakfasted with me on Thursday morning on his way from town, so if there were a wherewithal of news, I might have learnt some.

Tomorrow I go to London, on Tuesday to Mr Barrett's in Kent, and on Friday I shall be here again.

My week of confined evenings has been employed in writing notes to Mr Pennant's *London*.[13] Ever since the appearance of *Les Rues de Paris*[14] I had been collecting notices for such a work,[15] though probably now should not have executed it. When Mr Pennant had something of such an idea the winter before last, I told him such hints as I recollected[16]—but as he is more impetuous than digestive, I had not looked out my memorandums, and he has made such a bungling use of those I gave him (for instance, in calling the Duchess of Tircon-

10. George Edgcumbe, 1st E. of Mount Edgcumbe, and his only son, Richard Edgcumbe (1764–1839), 2d E. of Mount Edgcumbe, styled Vct Valletort 1789–95. The son was much interested in music; he was the author of *Musical Reminiscences of an Old Amateur; chiefly respecting the Italian Opera in England for fifty years, from 1773 to 1823* (printed for private circulation, 1823; 2d edn, published anonymously, 1827, 3d edn, with his authorship acknowledged, 1828; 4th edn, with additions, 1834). He was also an amateur actor, and the author as well as the speaker of a prologue to an amateur performance at SH in November 1800 (MBJ ii. 113–14). For HW's estimate of him, see *Royal and Noble Authors, Works* i. 461–2.

11. George James ('Gilly') Williams (ca 1719–1805), intimate friend of HW, Selwyn, and Lord Mount Edgcumbe; best known for his letters to Selwyn (MONTAGU i. 186 *et passim*).

12. Daniel Lysons and his younger brother, Samuel Lysons (1763–1819), also an antiquary and a correspondent of HW.

13. Thomas Pennant (1726–98), traveller and naturalist, friend of Gilbert White, occasional correspondent of HW and William Cole, was the author of several tours. For HW's opinion of him, see COLE i. 328–30

et passim. Pennant's *Of London* was advertised 'this day is published' in *The Times* 22 April 1790; *Additions and Corrections* to it (54 pp.) appeared in the following year. HW's copies of both works, bound in one volume, with 'a number of interesting manuscript additions by Lord Orford,' were sold SH vii. 42 (Lond. 919) to the Earl of Buckinghamshire.

14. Germain-François Poullain de Saint-Foix (1698–1776) was the author of *Essais historiques sur Paris,* first published in Paris, 5 vols, 1754–7. The first part contains an historical account of the streets of Paris. See COLE i. 134, 137–8.

15. HW devoted one section of a MS 'Book of Materials,' which he began in Sept. 1759, to 'Anecdotes of the Streets of London and other places,' and in another, which he began in 1771, to 'The Streets of London.' Both books, formerly in the Waller Collection, are now in the Folger Library.

16. Pennant gives HW as his authority for statements on pp. 99, 103, 104, 129, 157, 336, and quotes *Anecdotes of Painting* seven times. In *Additions and Corrections to the First Edition of Mr Pennant's Account of London,* 1791, Pennant mentions HW at p. 12, in his account of Theodore, King of Corsica.

nel[17] *the white milliner* instead of *the white widow*)[18] that I am glad I furnished him with no more.[19]

What can I say more? Nothing tonight, but that both Philip and I have looked and inquired and can find nothing here that even calls itself a ready-furnished house. I am persuaded, though Miss Cambridge did not tell you so, that she had inquired and knows there is not one.

This being such a *chip in paper*,[20] I will carry it with me to town tomorrow, and even keep it back till after Monday evening, when I may possibly be able to satisfy your curiosity about the *quiet peaceable French*[21] and their modest jubilee, in honour of their destroying tyranny, and restoring liberty to everybody of hanging whom they please without trial.

Monday 19th.

I came to town yesterday, and at the door my maid told me that two persons had called to inquire, who had heard that I was dangerously ill, and even supposed dead—to be sure at my age that would be no miracle; but as upon my honour I have seen myself every day, and know nothing of any illness I have had but a fillip of gout, I cannot believe there is any truth in those reports.

17. Frances Jennings (ca 1649–1731), sister of Sarah, Ds of Marlborough; m. (1) (?1666) Sir George Hamilton, Count Hamilton in France; m. (2) (?1681) Richard Talbot (ca 1625–91), cr. (1685) E. and (1689) D. of Tyrconnell (GEC; Philip W. Sergeant, *Little Jennings and Fighting Dick Talbot*, 1913, i. 6, 201, 280). Her portrait, a copy by John Milbourn from the original at Lord Spencer's, hung in the Great North Bedchamber at SH (*Works* ii. 495–6; HW to Conway 16 Sept. 1777), and was sold SH xx. 106 to H. Rodd, for £8.8.o.

18. 'Above stairs [at the New Exchange] sat, in the character of a milliner, the reduced Duchess of Tyrconnel, wife to Richard Talbot, Lord Deputy of Ireland under James II. . . . A female, suspected to have been his duchess, after his death, supported herself for a few days . . . by the little trade of the place: had delicacy enough to wish not to be detected: she sat in a white mask, and a white dress, and was known by the name of the White Milliner' (*Of London*, pp. 134–5). Pennant does not give HW as his authority for this note. HW mentions the Duchess of Tyrconnell in his 'Book of

Materials,' 1786, but does not give this story. According to Sergeant (op. cit. ii. 582), 'The story which Horace Walpole tells of the "White Widow" . . . is not accepted as genuine,' but in a note on the same page he adds, 'It may be noted that the story is not referred to the year 1708 and that therefore it might belong to 1692 —in which case it might be true, for the Duchess was in London in 1692.'

19. George Selwyn wrote to Lady Carlisle 12 Aug. 1790 that 'such an absurd superficial pretender to learning [as Pennant] I never met with, and after all of what learning! Then he tries to copy Mr Walpole's style in his Book of Antient Authors [*Royal and Noble Authors*]: *le tout est pitoyable*' (Hist. MSS Comm., Report XV, Appendix VI, *Manuscripts of the Earl of Carlisle*, 1897, pp. 683–4).

20. A variation of '*chip in porridge (pottage, broth)*: an addition which does neither good nor harm, a thing of no moment' (OED).

21. Possibly an echo of a passage in Mary Berry's missing letter to which this is a reply.

I supped at my sister's[22] last night with several Churchills, Miss Carter,[23] and Mr Fawkener clerk of the Council,[24] and even he had only heard that the Wednesday you wot of, passed at Paris without disturbance. If I hear more of it this evening, you shall know. I did hear a deal about Lord Barrymore[25] and theatres he is building;[26] and of Lord Salisbury's[27] licence to O'Reilly[28] for operas at the Pantheon, but caring nothing about those matters, I did not listen.

22. Lady Mary Churchill's, in Lower Grosvenor Street, now 60 Grosvenor Street. At her death in 1730, Mrs Oldfield left the house to her son Charles Churchill, who occupied it until his death in 1812.

23. Mary Carter (d. 1812), dau. of Thomas Carter of Robertstown and Rathnally, co. Meath, sometime secretary of state for Ireland; friend and correspondent of HW, Edward Jerningham, and Lady Mount Edgcumbe; donor of 'an ancient knife with a curious handle of gold' at SH ('Des. of SH,' Works ii. 512) and of two mineral specimens sent from Venice (Mary Carter to HW 3 June 1794); 'that worthy singular woman' (Miss M. D. Harland to Jerningham 6 Jan. 1783, Edward Jerningham and His Friends, ed. Lewis Bettany, 1919, pp. 157–8). See also ibid. 159, 215, 217, 219; Burke, Landed Gentry, 1894, i. 299; Edward Gibbon, Private Letters, ed. Rowland E. Prothero, 1896, ii. 135; GM 1812, lxxxii pt i. 499; Early Married Life of Maria Josepha Lady Stanley, ed. Jane H. Adeane, 1899, p. 40. She appears as 'Mrs Mary Carter, Hill Street,' in HW's MS list of people to whom he bequeathed 'Des. of SH,' 1784, and as 'Miss Carter, 7, Hill Street Berkeley Square,' in Directory to the Nobility, Gentry . . . for 1793.

24. Charles Churchill's nephew, William Augustus Fawkener (1747–1811), 1st son of Sir Everard Fawkener; clerk extraordinary (1763–78) and clerk in ordinary (1778–1811) to the Privy Council; envoy to Portugal 1786–7, and to Russia, 1791. His eldest daughter, Mary, married (1812) Horatio,

Lord Walpole, later 3d Earl of Orford of the 3d creation (Richard A. Austen-Leigh, Eton College Register 1753–1790, Eton, 1921; British Diplomatic Representatives 1689–1789, ed. D. B. Horn, 1932, p. 101; British Diplomatic Representatives 1789–1852, ed. S. T. Bindoff et al., 1934, p. 109; Sylvester Douglas, Lord Glenbervie, Journals, ed. Walter Sichel, 1910, p. 196; idem, Diaries, ed. Francis Bickley, 1928, passim; DU DEFFAND iii. 429, 432, 435; Royal Kalendar 1763–1811; Trial between William Fawkener . . . and the Honourable John Townshend, 1786).

25. Richard Barry (1769–93), 7th E. of Barrymore. Less than a month later HW saw him 'perform a buffoon-dance and act Scaramouch in a pantomime at Richmond' (HW to Lord Strafford 12 Aug. 1790).

26. See following letter.

27. James Cecil (1748–1823), styled Vct Cranborne until 1780; 7th E. of Salisbury, 1780; cr. (1789) M. of Salisbury; Lord Chamberlain of the Household 1783–1804. HW considered him 'a stately simpleton' ('Mem. 1783–91,' sub 24 Dec. 1783).

28. Robert Bray O'Reilly, a proprietor of the Opera House which burned down in 1789 (ante 23 June 1789; St James's Chronicle 10–12 Aug. 1790). He received the licence through the interest of the Duke of Bedford (Edward Wedlake Brayley, Historical and Descriptive Accounts of The Theatres of London, 1826, p. 29). His rival, William Taylor, in A Concise Statement (post 4 Feb. 1791) gives an unfavourable view of his abilities and character.

Tonight. I have seen Madame de Vilgagnon-Walpole[29] and Madame de la Villebague[30] this evening and all they have heard yet is, that the Wednesday passed quietly, except that one cannon burst and killed five or six persons[31]—but lives go for nothing upon good occasions. The King tramped on foot on the left hand of his superior the president of the Assembly;[32] the Queen was so lucky as to be worse treated, and was not forced to be present![33]—There, I think Miss Crawford cannot send you a more peaceable or a more inviting account!—Oh! yes, had you been at Lyons[34] lately you might have been obliged to receive most condescending civilities from two of the greatest personages in France. Lady Rivers[35] has written to my sister that she was at Lyons when two Amazons[36] arrived there, deputed by their legislative body *Mesdames les Poissardes* to invite the *late* Comtesse d'Artois[37] to return to Paris; and those two embassadresses

---

29. Jeanne-Marguerite Batailhe de Montval m. (1) (1755) —— Durand, Marquis de Villegagnon; m. (2) (1787) HW's cousin, Hon. Thomas Walpole. HW had met her in Paris and had entertained her at SH (DU DEFFAND ii. 336 *et passim*).

30. Not identified.

31. 'The bursting of a cannon, owing to the unskilfulness of the novices to whom it was entrusted, was fatal to three or four men; and but for this only accident, a commemoration so confidently predicted to be the scene of massacre and revolution, would have been bloodless' (*St James's Chronicle* 17–20 July 1790). See also *London Chronicle* 17–20 July 1790, lxviii. 71.

32. Charles-François Bonnay (1750–1825), ci-devant Marquis de Bonnay, twice elected President of the National Assembly for the usual term of two weeks: 12 April 1790 and 3 July 1790. Accused of being cognizant of the King's flight to Varennes, he cleared himself, but emigrated to England in 1791 and did not return to France until 1814 (NBG; *La Grande encyclopédie;* DU DEFFAND *passim; Moniteur* 13 avril 1790, 5 juillet 1790).

33. She was present; see following letter.

34. Then in a tumult: 'Despotism and aristocracy are no more, but licentiousness prevails in their room' (*London Chronicle* 24–27 July 1790, lxviii. 92; ibid. 29–31 July 1790, lxviii. 111). See *post* 29 July, 2 Aug. 1790.

35. Penelope Atkins (ca 1727–95), dau. of Sir Henry Atkins, 4th Bt; m. (1746) George Pitt (1721–1803), sometime M.P., cr. (1776) Bn Rivers of Stratfield Saye and (1802) Bn Rivers of Sudley Castle. One of the beauties mentioned in HW's 'The Beauties,' 1746, she lived much of her life abroad, and died at Milan; cf. *London Chronicle* 26–28 Feb. 1795, lxxvii. 208.

36. 'A great many women dressed as *Amazons* are to attend the Fête at Paris on the 14th. Among them, it is said, there will be 200 French women who are to form themselves into a regular body, habited as Amazons' (*Times*, 12 July 1790).

37. Marie-Thérèse (1756–1805) of Savoy, m. (1773) Charles-Philippe, Comte d'Artois, later Charles X of France. 'Much beloved' in Paris (*Despatches from Paris 1784–90*, ed. Oscar Browning, ii [1910]. 247), she did not leave the city until Sept. 1789, about two months after her husband (*Cor-*

lodged in the same hotel. Lady R. was told she ought to wait on them—not she indeed—Oh! yes, you had much better—and so she found she had. They received her very graciously, and said, '*Nous nous reverrons.*'—How could I imagine that it is not charming travelling through France! I go into Kent tomorrow; how you will envy me if I meet a detachment of *poissardes* on the road to Chevening[38] to create Earl Stanhope no peer! Good night!

To Mary Berry, Friday 23 July 1790

Address: To Miss Berry to be left at the Post House at Lymington, Hants.
Postmark: ISLEWORTH 26 JY 90.

Strawberry Hill, Friday night, July 23, 1790.[1]

I ARRIVED at Lee on the day[2] and hour I had promised Mr Barret; returned to town on the day and hour I had promised myself,[3] and was back here as punctually in my promise to Strawberry.[4] Nothing in this was extraordinary, as I have always had the felicity of knowing my own mind—but the marvel was, that I, who have not been farther than Park Place these four years, and am moreover four years older and have had half a dozen more fits of gout, was not at all fatigued by an hundred and twenty miles in three days, was new-dressed by seven yesterday evening, went to Madame Walpole's,[5] and then supped at Lady M. Churchill's.[6] In short I am so proud of all these feats of activity, that if you two should elope, I will say like portly Hal the moment he had beheaded Anne Boleyn,

> Cock's bones! now again I stand
> The jolliest bachelor i' th' land;[7]

and I will marry two more wives the next day—so, at your peril be it!

respondance intime du Comte de Vaudreuil et du Comte d'Artois, ed. Léonce Pingaud, 1889, i. 5), and joined him at Turin. The two 'Amazons' were passing through Lyons on their way to Turin.

38. Lord Stanhope's seat, Chevening Park, near Sevenoaks, in Kent.

———

1. 'No. 17' (B).
2. Tuesday, 20 July; see preceding letter.
3. Thursday, 22 July; see ibid.
4. On Friday, the date of this letter.
5. 'Madame de Villegagnon, a French

lady married to Mr Thomas Walpole, a younger son of the first Lord Walpole of Woolterton' (B).

6. 'A daughter of Sir Robert Walpole by Miss Skerret, the lady he afterwards married. When Sir Robert was created Earl of Orford, this daughter had the King's letter to rank as an earl's daughter. She married Charles Churchill, Esq., himself a natural son of the Gen. Churchill of Marlbro's wars, by Mrs Oldfield, the celebrated actress' (B).

7. In his copy of Archibald Robertson,

I found Mr Barrett's house complete, and the most perfect thing ever formed! Such taste, every inch so well finished, and the drawing room and eating room so magnificent! I think if Strawberry were not its parent, it would be jealous. My journey too delighted me: such a face of plenty and beauty; the corn, the hay harvest, the cherry orchards, the hop grounds, all in their different ages so promising or so fulfilling! All the farms and hedges so tight and neat, and such rows of houses tacking themselves on to every town, that every five miles were an answer to Dr Price[8] and Lord Stanhope[9]—and on t'other side what an answer is coming from France!—but I must keep to a little regularity—

The day of the jubilee was a deluge, and like Noah's flood and the *États*, almost swept away everything; it rained fourteen hours, and not a dry thread[10] but on the Queen (who *was* there) and had an awning for her and a few ladies, behind the King.[11] The rest you

Topographical Survey of the Great Road from London to Bath, 1792, now BM, HW wrote on a leaf inserted opposite i. 29: 'Richmond or New Park was made or rather, I suppose, enlarged by Charles I, as on a small mount . . . on the western ridge near the lodge belonging to the Countess of Pembroke by a grant of George III, tradition says Henry VIII waited for a signal from the Tower of London to notify to him the moment the execution of Anne Boleyn should be completed, and that he uttered that brutal and sensual sentence,

"Cock's bones! now again I stand
The jolliest bachelor in the land." '

In Prior's 'The Turtle and the Sparrow,' one of HW's favourite poems (*post* 16 Oct. 1790), occurs the following passage, ll. 269–72:

'And as Old Harry whilome said,
Reflecting on Anne Bullen dead,
Cocksbones, I now again do stand
The jolly'st Batchelor i' th' land.'

8. Richard Price (1723–1791), D.D. (Marischal College, Aberdeen, 1767), LL.D. (Yale, 1783), moralist, economist, and defender of the American and French Revolutions. If HW has a particular passage in mind, he probably refers to Price's *Discourse on the Love of Our Country, Delivered on Nov. 4, 1789*, particularly the paragraph near the end, beginning 'It is too evident that the state of this country is such as renders it an object of concern and anxiety' (3d edn, 1790, pp. 46 ff.). HW's copy of the third edition is now wsl.

9. Now in the possession of wsl are the following pamphlets, formerly HW's: *A Letter from Earl Stanhope to The Rt. Hon. Edmund Burke containing a Short Answer to his Late Speech on the French Revolution*, 1790, and *A Letter to Earl Stanhope on the Subject of the Test, as Objected to in a Pamphlet Recommended by His Lordship*, Oxford, 1789. (The pamphlet was *The Right of the Protestant Dissenters to a Complete Toleration Asserted*.) The last of these has many marginalia by HW.

10. 'The day [14 July] was extremely unfavourable; it rained almost the whole time, but not one person was induced from that circumstance to quit his seat' (*London Chronicle* 17–20 July 1790, lxviii. 71). See also *St James's Chronicle* 17–20 July 1790.

11. 'The President of the National Assembly [sat] on his [Louis XVI's] right, on a seat of equal magnificence. It had been destined for the Queen, by those who had directed the ceremonial, but the National Assembly having determined that the Royal Family should appear only as spectators, it was appointed for the chief of the Legislative Power' (*St James's Chronicle* 17–20 July, 1790).

know—but now list! When Philip d'Orléans waited on the still-King,[12] M. Gouvion[13] (second under La Fayette) jostled him and said, 'If you do not resent this, you are a scoundrel'—*ce n'est pas tout*—five and twenty of the *Garde Nationale* have bound themselves to fight the aforesaid Philip, provided that like a bowl[14] he can tip down Gouvion and the first four and twenty[15]—I left London on tiptoe for the event —and Mr Lenox, I suppose, is not one of the least impatient.[16]

The twenty-seventh is to be the octave to the fourteenth,[17] and is expected to produce fearful events.[18] On that day La Fayette's commission is to be renewed, or a successor appointed[19]—but all this is nothing to an event that has happened, and the detail of which *I saw* last night in a letter to Madame Walpole from her sister[20] at Paris, and which Mr Fawkener had heard, though not quite so circumstantially.

On the thirteenth arrived at Paris fifteen hundred Bretons on foot, their commander alone mounted. They marched to the *pont tournant*[21] of the Tuilleries;[22] the *Garde Nationale* would have stayed them and have obliged the commander to dismount—*point du tout*. They advanced into the garden under the windows of the King, who ap-

12. Presumably HW refers to the interview between the Duc d'Orléans and Louis XVI, 11 July (*St James's Chronicle* 15–17 July 1790). On 14 July Louis XVI was crowned 'Emperor,' and on that day the Duc d'Orléans was present only in his capacity as a member of the National Assembly (ibid. 17–20 July 1790).

13. Jean-Baptiste Gouvion (1747–92), served under La Fayette in America; second (under La Fayette) in command of the French National Guard, 1789; killed in battle (Jean-François-Eugène Robinet *et al., Dictionnaire . . . de la révolution,* [1899] ii. 87; NBG).

14. That is, a bowling-ball.

15. No further reference to the jostling has been found.

16. As a principal in two duels, Lennox would be interested in the outcome of such an affair. See *ante* 9 July 1789.

17. The celebration began 14 and ended 20 July.

18. Nothing unusual occurred.

19. Although no mention of the renewal of this commission has been found, La Fayette remained in command of the National Guard until his resignation in 1791 (see *post* 4 May 1791), but his popularity was on the decline: the day of the federation, 14 July 1790, is usually considered the high point of his career.

20. Mme Blondel, 'a person much admired and esteemed, from the united good qualities both of her head and heart' (B, quoted in DU DEFFAND iv. 443, n. 4). She was possibly the wife of Louis-Augustin Blondel (ibid. n. 5, *et passim*).

21. 'Du côté de la place Louis XV [now Place de la Concorde], les hautes terrasses et un pont tournant jeté sur un fossé rendaient inaccessible le jardin des Tuileries' (G. Lenôtre [L. L. T. Gosselin], *Paris révolutionnaire,* 1902, p. 53).

22. See ibid. 52–61 for an account of the Tuileries as it was 6 Oct. 1789 when the royal family came there to reside.

peared in the balcony and *gracieused* them. They demanded admission to him and were admitted, when the commandant bending one knee, laid his sword at the King's feet, and said, '*Sire, je suis chargé par la nation bretonne de venir jurer amour et fidélité à votre Majesté, et je verserai la dernière goutte de mon sang pour vous, pour la Reine et pour Monseigneur le Dauphin.*' The King embraced him. The whole troop then went to a little garden parted off for the Dauphin[23] on the terrace of the Tuilleries, where he was gathering flowers. The pretty boy gave a flower as long as they lasted to every Breton, and then gathered lilac leaves, and for fear *they* should not last, tore them in two, and gave half a leaf apiece to the rest[24]—and what, you will cry, were their Majesties the *États* doing all this time —Oh! I suppose, they had more important business on their hands, and were consulting metaphysically where they should deposit that old rag the Oriflamme,[25] for they are exceedingly attentive to making laws for types and symbols, and probably are as much afraid of the Bretons, as they are of myladies the *poissardes*—but I do not add a tittle to my text—and thus leave these chapters in the middle.

Our papers say the Margrave of Anspach is dead suddenly[26]—so Lady Craven is widow, though still wife.[27]

23. Charles (1785–95), 2d but 1st surviving son of Louis XVI; titular King of France as Louis XVII, 1793. Mary Berry refers to his death 'by the slow and cruel means of ill-usage, and every species of moral and physical neglect' (*Comparative View of Social Life in England and France,* 1844, i. 323).

24. A brief account of this incident is given in an 'Extract of a letter from Paris,' *London Chronicle* 17–20 July 1790, lxviii. 71: 'No less than 500 [sic] Bretons came in a body, encamping on the road the whole way till they came to Paris, where their chief waited on the king, and laid his sword at his Majesty's feet.'

25. Presented to the army by the city of Paris, carried in the procession 14 July between two marshals at the head of the army and navy deputations, and placed, during the ceremony at the Champ-de-Mars, on the Autel de la Patrie facing the King's throne (*Moniteur* 16 juillet 1790). It was not discussed in the National Assembly 13 July (see *Moniteur* 14, 16 juillet 1790), but on 15 July, after considerable discussion as to its significance as a symbol, the Assem-

bly decided that it should be hung in the roof of the hall of the National Assembly (*London Chronicle* 22–24 July 1790, lxviii. 86).

26. He lived until 1806. Karl Alexander (1736–1806), Margrave of Brandenburg-Anspach; m. (1) Friederike Karoline (d. 1791), Princess of Sachsen-Coburg-Saalfeld; m. (2) (1791) Lady Craven (see n. 27). He abdicated his principality in favour of the King of Prussia, settled in England at Brandenburg House, Hammersmith (GEC, *sub* Craven), and died at his seat at Benham near Newbury, Berks. 'He chose rather to live like a private gentleman in England than to rule as an absolute prince in Germany. . . . His goodness of heart and extreme affability endeared him to all ranks of people who knew him' (GM 1806, lxxvi pt i. 91). The false report of his death appears under 'Foreign Intelligence, Berlin, July 6,' in the *London Chronicle* 20–22 July 1790, lxviii. 79, and in the *St James's Chronicle* 22–24 July 1790. Another notice appears in ibid. 29–31 July 1790.

27. HW's friend and correspondent, Elizabeth Berkeley (1750–1828), dau. of

I went to carry my niece Sophia Walpole home last night from her mother's,[28] and found little Burlington Street[29] blocked up by coaches. Lord Barrymore, his sister Lady Caroline,[30] and Mrs Goodall the actress,[31] were performing *The Beaux' Stratagem*[32] in Squib's[33] auction room which his Lordship has converted into a theatre.[34] I do not

Augustus, 4th E. of Berkeley; m. (1) (1767) William Craven (1738–27 Sept. 1791), later (1769) 6th Bn Craven. They separated in 1780 and at the time of this letter she had become the mistress of the Margrave of Anspach, who married her 13 Oct. 1791.

28. Lady Mary Churchill's.

29. Parallel with Savile Row, in which the theatrical performance was taking place.

30. Lady Caroline Barry (b. 1768), m. (1788), under 'romantic' circumstances, Louis Pierre Francis Malcolm Drummond, Comte de Melfort (John Lodge and Mervyn Archdall, *Peerage of Ireland*, 1789, i. 313; GM 1788, lviii pt ii. 750; *Scots Peerage* vi. 69; Lady Clementina Davies, *Recollections of Society in France and England*, 1872, i. 19–25). A query about her death in N&Q 1858, 2d ser. v. 393, brought no satisfactory reply.

31. Charlotte Stanton (ca 1766–1830), dau. of a provincial theatrical manager; m. (1787) Thomas Goodall, later 'Admiral of Haiti,' by whom she was divorced in 1813; first appeared at Drury Lane in 1788. She also acted at Lord Barrymore's theatre at Wargrave, Berks (John Robert Robinson, *The Last Earls of Barrymore*, 1893, pp. 67, 164).

32. By George Farquhar (1678–1707).

33. Probably 'James Squibb, Savile Row, auctioneer,' who is listed among the bankrupts in GM 1784, liv pt ii. 959, and whose wife died in 1788 (GM 1788, lviii pt ii. 661). He was probably assisted by (? his son) George Squibb (ca 1764–1831), 'the celebrated auctioneer' who died in Savile Row,

and whose 'Great Room' was in Savile Row (GM 1831, ci pt ii. 569; *Autobiography . . . of Mrs Piozzi*, ed. A. Hayward, 2d edn, 1861, ii. 332, 337; N&Q 1940, clxxviii. 261). In 1790 the room was evidently used for a puppet theatre as well as for amateur performances; see following note.

34. 'The Fantoccini Theatre in Saville Row has been enlarged and decorated by Lord Barrymore; and on Thursday evening [22 July] his Lordship and several gentlemen amateurs treated the fashionable world with an exhibition of *The Beaux' Stratagem* and *The Citizen*—Scrub and Young Philpot by Lord Barrymore—the female characters by Mrs Rivers, Miss Richards, and others from the Richmond stage. A grotesque *pas russe* was performed by his Lordship and Delpini, to the great diversion of the audience. The performance of the theatrical pieces was very pleasing—refreshments were distributed with great profusion to the whole assembly, which consisted of persons of the first rank and brilliancy, among whom was his Royal Highness the Prince of Wales. The whole was concluded with a select supper party at *two* in the morning' (*St James's Chronicle* 22–24 July 1790; in the *London Chronicle* 22–24 July 1790, lxviii. 82, it is incorrectly said that the performance was at Lord Barrymore's 'house in Saville Row'). Scrub was probably Lord Barrymore's best and best-known role; see BM, *Satiric Prints*, vi. 841, No. 7957; 855–6, No. 7993; BM *Catalogue of Engraved British Portraits*, ed. Freeman O'Donoghue and Henry M. Hake, 1908–25.

know the rest of the company, nor are you probably curious. Having now emptied my pouch of news, I will come to your letter of the 20th which I have received.

I thank you for saying at least that you will take time to consider before you finally determine on your journey. I do not promise myself much from that consideration, for if you *can* still hesitate, it must be by the *coup de baguette* of some guardian angel that the face of Europe can be tranquillized in two months. The position of France indeed may be much worse; but the talisman which I conclude you possess, and that is to convey you invulnerable or invisible through that nation of barbarians, must have as much virtue as it had a fortnight ago—and as I have no amulet that can lull asleep my fears for you, I am not at all comforted nor quieted by the composing draught you have sent me. Those alarms have set *me* on considering too, and unless you have reasons that are unknown to me, those you did give me, appear by no means adequate to so strange a fancy as that of leaving your country again, when it is and appears to everybody else, the only country in Europe at present that one would wish to be in. I fear my dread of letting my self-love preponderate over my attachment to dear you and dear Agnes made me too rashly forbear to contend against your scheme. I heartily repent of my acquiescence, which was as full of self-love as opposition would have been. In the cooler moments I have had since, it appears to me a wild uncomfortable plan, that will not produce one of the purposes you seemed to propose by it, and therefore I ascribe it to a volatile roving humour, or to some motive of which I am ignorant, and into which I have no right to inquire.

Any amendment in your sister that you announce is always the most grateful part of your letters, agreeable as they are to me. Dull they cannot be when one is so interested as I am. It is for your sake not my own that I wish you better amused. Of whom, were all the world at Lymington, could you talk, that would engage my attention so much, as what you tell me about yourselves? Good night. Don't forget to tell me when I am to change my direction.

To Mary Berry, Thursday 29 July 1790

Address: To Miss Berry to be left at the Post House at Lymington, Hants.
Postmark: 30 JY 90.

Strawberry Hill, Thursday, July 29, 1790.

IF you give yourself an air and pretend to write dull letters, which I defy you to do when they are to pass through the medium of my eyes, I will lay you a wager that this shall beat you hollow,[1] and even please Mr Cumberland,[2] who told me it was pity Mr Gray's letters had been printed;[3] and consequently I suppose poor gentleman! he thinks private letters ought to be as insipid as his own comedies.[4] One comfort is, that if I have nothing to say, I trust it will be the last that you will receive till I see you, and therefore if it is as dull as the last scene in any comedy, no matter.

Yours of the 26th that I have just received, tells me you will be in town by Thursday at farthest—so will I certainly, and call on you in the evening.[5] I have most seriously been house-hunting for you. I saw bills on two doors in Montpellier Row—but neither are furnished[6]—and yesterday to a larger at Teddington, but it was not only stark naked, but tumbling down. You shall come to me, and then we will see what can be done.

I do hope you will be staggered about a longer journey for some time. But two days ago I saw a new paragraph of Tuscan disturbances.[7] Every paper talks of horrid ones at Lyons[8]—but I will say no more now, as you promise to be guided by farther accounts.

1. The first appearance of this phrase in OED is 1786, Peter Pindar.

2. Richard Cumberland (1732–1811), the dramatist, nephew of HW's friend and correspondent, Richard Bentley.

3. In William Mason's *The Poems of Mr Gray. To Which are prefixed Memoirs of his Life and Writings,* first published at York, 1775. HW wrote to Mason 27 Nov. 1775, 'Mr Cumberland, the maker of plays, told me lately, it *was pity Gray's letters were printed; they had disappointed him much*'; and again, 30 Jan. 1780, 'Cumberland, of all men living . . . the worst judge [of literary excellence] . . . told me it was pity Gray's letters were printed, as they disgraced him.' HW wrote that Gray's 'letters were the best I ever saw, and had more novelty and wit' (*Gray's Corr.* iii. 1287).

4. HW's letters contain frequent and usually derogatory remarks on Cumberland's plays.

5. He apparently did so; see following letter.

6. Nevertheless the Berrys lived in an unidentified house in Montpelier Row for three weeks in August or in August–September (MBJ i. 194). For an account of Montpelier Row, see R. S. Cobbett, *Memorials of Twickenham,* 1872, pp. 375–7.

7. See *ante* 10, 17 July 1790.

8. 'The tumults in the great city of Lyons . . . are extremely alarming. All its barriers have been broken down, and all kinds of merchandise, subject to duty, have been introduced, to the great injury of the revenue. The Commissioners cannot discharge their duty but at the hazard of

I have learnt nothing fresher from Paris—only that all the letters talk of repeated insults to the Duke of Orleans, and it is thought he will return hither.[9] Nor of the Bretons, *non plus*.

The Duchesse de Biron[10] and the Boufflerses[11] are to dine here on Saturday, and the Edgcumbes.[12] The Duchess returns to Paris next week—but as she must leave her duchy behind,[13] why should not Lord Abercorn desire the King to seize it as a wreck and give it to Lady Cecil Hamilton?[14]

The Argyles are returned,[15] the Duchess, I hear, looking very ill. They have got a foolish notion at Richmond that Lord Blandford[16] is to marry Miss Gunning; an idea so improbable, that even the luck of the Gunnings[17] cannot make one believe it.

You are in the right to look better, and I would advise Agnes to do so too as fast as possible, for to tell you the truth I feel myself growing inconstant—I have seen Mrs Udney[18]—Oh! she is charming, looks

their lives. . . . The National Assembly are sedulously engaged in adopting measures for the restoration of good order' (*London Chronicle* 24–27 July 1790 lxviii. 92; the same report, with minor changes, in *St James's Chronicle* 24–27 July 1790). See also following letter.

9. He remained in Paris.

10. Amélie de Boufflers (1751–94), dau. of Charles-Joseph (d. 1751), Duc de Boufflers; m. (1766) Armand-Louis de Gontaut, Comte de Biron, later Duc de Lauzun and Duc de Biron. She was guillotined (DU DEFFAND i. 24 *et passim*).

11. Mme de Boufflers and her daughter-in-law, Comtesse de Boufflers.

12. Lord and Lady Mount Edgcumbe, and probably their son and daughter-in-law, Lord and Lady Valletort.

13. Because of the recent abolition of titles in France.

14. John James Hamilton (1756–1818), 9th E. and later (15 Oct. 1790) M. of Abercorn, although married, was reputedly on intimate terms with his first cousin, Cecil Hamilton (1770–1819), 8th and next to youngest daughter of his uncle, the Hon. and Rev. George Hamilton, Canon of Windsor. By Royal Warrant dated 27 Oct. 1789 she was raised to the precedency of an earl's daughter, an honour denied to her sisters, and gained through Lord Abercorn's influence with Pitt. She became Lord Abercorn's wife (second) 4 March 1792, was

separated from him in 1798, and was divorced by Act of Parliament in April 1799. She later (23 May 1799) married Capt. Joseph Copley, later 3d Bt.

15. 'On Sunday evening [25 July] their Graces the Duke and Duchess of Argyll arrived at their house in Argyll Street from Italy' (*London Chronicle* 27–29 July 1790, lxviii. 97).

16. George Spencer, afterwards (1817) Spencer-Churchill (1766–1840) styled M. of Blandford until 1817; 4th D. of Marlborough, 1817; m. (15 Sept. 1791) Susan Stewart (1767–1841), 2d dau. of the 7th E. of Galloway. See *post* 11 Sept. 1791.

17. Two of Miss Gunning's aunts, famous beauties, made great marriages. Maria (or Mary) Gunning (1732–60), considered the more beautiful, m. (1752) George William Coventry, 6th E. of Coventry. Elizabeth, for whom Miss Gunning was named, became in succession Duchess of Hamilton and of Argyll (*ante* 6 Aug. 1789).

18. Margaret (or Martha) Jordan (or Jourdan) (b. ca 1752), daughter of Thomas Jordan of Pheasant Lodge, Chislehurst, Kent; m. (17 Oct. 1787) as 2d wife, Robert Udny; sub-governess to Princess Charlotte 1805–13 (GM 1787, lvii pt ii. 1022; GM 1813, lxxxiii pt i. 219; *Royal Kalendar* 1806–13; Dormer Creston [Dorothy Julia Baynes], *The Regent and His Daughter*, Boston, 1932, pp. 103, 109–10, 141–2; Sylvester

so sensible and—unluckily, so modest—but then, as Mr Udney looks as old and decrepit as I do, there may be some hopes.

At night.

Mr Lysons the divine and I have been this evening to see the late Duke of Montagu's[19] at Richmond, where I had not been for many years. Formerly I was much there,[20] but *her* Grace[21] broke with me on what I had said in my *Noble Authors* of her grandfather Marlborough,[22] as if I had been the first to propagate his avarice![23] I softened it in the second edition to please her,[24] but not being the most placable of her soft sex, she never forgave it.[25] The new garden that clambers up the hill is delightful and disposed with admirable taste

Douglas, Bn Glenbervie, *Journals*, ed. Walter Sichel, 1910, pp. 194–5; Burke, *Landed Gentry*, 1879, ii. 1644; William Temple, *Thanage of Fermartyn*, Aberdeen, 1894, pp. 433–4; *The Genealogist*, 1878, ii. 89–90; *post* 2 Aug. 1790). Cosway painted a portrait of her, 'whole length, standing on stone steps leading from a garden [her garden at Teddington]; facing and looking towards the front; bunch of roses in right hand; left hand holding up dress' (Frederick B. Daniell, *Catalogue . . . of the Engraved Works of Richard Cosway*, 1890, p. 37; George C. Williamson, *Richard Cosway*, 1905, p. 62). Mrs Mee painted a miniature of her which in 1865 was in the possession of Sir T. W. Holburne, Bt (*Catalogue of the Special Exhibition of Portrait Miniatures on Loan at the South Kensington Museum, June 1865*, 1865, p. 59). In HW's copy of *Etchings by Amateurs*, vol. ii, sold London 1126 (now WSL), the following note is inserted: 'Ambitious of keeping the best company, these trifling performances beg the honour of admittance into Mr Walpole's collection.' Three etchings by Mrs Udny are inserted after the note.

19. George Brudenell (Montagu after 1749) (1712–23 May 1790), 4th E. of Cardigan, cr. (1766) D. of Montagu; considered by HW in 1776 'one of the weakest and most ignorant men living' (*Last Journals* i. 558).

20. See particularly HW to Conway 6 Oct. 1748.

21. Mary Montagu (ca 1711–75), dau. of

John, 2d D. of Montagu, by Mary Churchill, youngest dau. of 1st D. of Marlborough; m. (1730) George Brudenell, later 4th E. of Cardigan and D. of Montagu.

22. In his account of the Duchess of Marlborough (*Royal and Noble Authors*, 1st edn, 1758, ii. 179–80), HW wrote: 'Had Marlborough himself written his own history from his heart as the partner of his fortunes did, he would probably have dwelt on the diamond sword, which the Emperor gave him, and have scrupulously told us how many carats each diamond weighed. I say not this in detraction from his merits and services; it is from our passions and foibles that Providence calls forth its great purposes. If the Duke could have been content with an hundred thousand pounds he might possibly have stopped at the taking of Leige: As he thirsted for a million, he penetrated to Hockstet' (i.e., Höchstädt [battle of Blenheim]).

23. The pamphleteers of Marlborough's day frequently attacked him for his avarice. Swift, for example, while acknowledging Marlborough's courage and military capacity, attacked him in pamphlets and in the *Examiner*, and wrote in his *Journal to Stella* 31 Dec. 1710: 'He is covetous as Hell, and ambitious as the Prince of it.'

24. HW omitted the passage quoted in n. 22, but restored it in the 1787 edition, incorporated in *Works* i. 490–1.

25. See HW to Lord Hertford 27 March 1764, and MONTAGU ii. 89.

and variety. It is perfectly screened from human eyes, though in the bosom of so populous a village; and you climb till at last, treading the houses under foot, you recover the Thames and all the world at a little distance. I am amazed that it is not more talked of—and I am glad Mrs Udney did not see me in my ascent or descent—I was no very graceful figure as Mr Lysons was dragging me up and down. I will take care to make love on plain ground—and things do go on well, for at my return I found a note from Mrs Udney to invite me to a concert on Sunday, so I must have made some impression, for I never saw her till yesterday morning.

While I write, Mr Lysons has been turning over LeNeve's *Monumenta Anglicana*,[26] and has found that *nine* aldermen of London died in one year—I concluded it must have been in one of the years of the plague—no, it was in 1711. Then it certainly was in 1711 that turtles were first imported.

Adieu! how glad I am to have no more of these empty letters to write! Don't you think it tiresome to write letters at all—pray let us have no more occasion to write any.

PS. Mr Lysons was last Monday at Mrs Piozzi's fête at Streatham.[27] Five and forty persons sat down to dinner. In the evening was a concert, and a little hopping, and a supper.

---

26. John Le Neve (1679–1741), *Monumenta Anglicana*, 5 vols, 1719. HW's copy, with many notes and additions, is now WSL. The names of the aldermen, of which there are only eight, appear iv. 231–4.

27. 'On the side of the small common between Streatham and Tooting, is a villa which belonged to the late Henry Thrale, Esq., and is now the residence of Gabriel Piozzi, Esq., who married his widow. The house, which is pleasant and commodious, has been much improved by Mr Piozzi. In the library is a very valuable set of portraits painted by Sir Joshua Reynolds. . . . The kitchen-gardens belonging to this villa are remarkably spacious, and surrounded by brick walls fourteen feet in height, built for the reception of forcing-frames, and producing a great abundance of fine fruit. Adjoining the house is an enclosure of about 100 acres, surrounded with a shrubbery and gravel walk of nearly two miles in circumference' (Lysons, *Environs of London*, 1792–6, i. 482–3). The house, Streatham Park, was pulled down in 1863 (*London and Its Environs*, ed. Findlay Muirhead, 3d edn, 1927, p. 329).

TO MARY BERRY, Monday 2 August 1790

Address: To Miss Mary Berry in Somerset Street, London.
Postmark: ISLEWORTH 4 AU 90.

Strawberry Hill, Monday night, Aug. 2, 1790.

BY yours of Friday which I received yesterday, I find you got one from me on Wednesday, and I hope one on Friday too.

I shall certainly see you in Somerset Street on Thursday evening. I have changed my language, not my wishes; and scarce a morsel of my opinion about your going abroad, though, as I have told you, I did at first acquiesce, because I knew how much my own happiness was at stake, and I would not suffer that to preponderate with me—but, oh, my beloved friend, can I be so interested about you, and not be alarmed? Every day I hear new causes of terror. Lyons is all tumult and violence.[1] The Duke of Argyle, who is just arrived, had his chaise pelted, and the coronet over his arms rubbed out. Miss Cheap,[2] whom I met last night at a concert at Mrs Udney's, is frightened for you, like me and very sorry for your project. She told me she has just received a letter from an English family abroad, whom probably you know, who are longing to come home; but dare not venture—are these vain terrors in me?—and though I did not remonstrate at first, can I love you and be silent now?

---

1. A dispatch from Paris 26 July 1790: 'Nor is Lyons . . . quiet; all the barriers are thrown down, and all subordination destroyed. Some pretend that the inhabitants have declared themselves independent, and have armed themselves in defence of their ancient rights . . . the town is in the greatest disorder, and . . . the number of workmen now unemployed threaten some very terrible consequences' (*London Chronicle* 29–31 July 1790, lxviii. 111). In a letter from Paris 29 July it was reported that 'at Lyons everything was quiet when the last

accounts came away' (ibid. 31 July–3 Aug. 1790, lxviii. 119).

2. Possibly Marianne Cheape (d. 1849), dau. of George (*Scots Peerage* viii. 313) or James (GM 1792, lxii pt ii. 865) or John (GEC, *Baronetage* iv. 333; Burke, *Peerage*, 1928, p. 2197, *sub* Strathmore) Cheape of Sauchie; m. (1) (1792) Sir Alexander Campbell, 4th Bt, of Ardkinglass, Argyllshire; m. (2) (1817) as 3d wife, Thomas Lyon-Bowes (now Bowes-Lyon) 11th E. of Strathmore and Kinghorne.

Though I cannot yet believe it will be, there is certainly much more probability than I thought of another Gunning becoming a duchess. General Conway wrote[3] to me that it is all settled, and that she[4] is to have the same jointure as the Duchess of Marlborough—but *Lady Clackmannan*[5] who has questioned (you may be sure) both the Duke and Lord Lorne,[6] says, the former answered coolly, 'They tell me it is to be,' but the other told her he knew nothing of the matter, and that he had even not seen Lord Blandford. The Duchess of Gloucester says that Mrs Howe,[7] who is apt to be well informed, does not believe it. My incredulity is still better founded, and hangs on the Duchess of Marlborough's wavering weathercockhood, which always rests at forbidding the banns.[8]

My dinner for the Biron and Boufflers went off agreeably. Yesterday I had Mr Thomas Walpole, his French wife, who is most amiable, and his sister[9] and daughters,[10] and that too passed well. The Bretons,[11] who are *party per pale*,[11a] loyal and levellers, have promised the Seigneur de Chilly[12] to burn his château at their return, if they find a

3. His letter to HW is missing.
4. Elizabeth Gunning.
5. Probably Lady Greenwich, cousin of the Duke of Argyll, and a great gossip.
6. George William Campbell (1768–1839), styled M. of Lorn until 1806; 6th D. of Argyll, 1806; m. (1810) Caroline Elizabeth Villiers (d. 1835), divorced wife of 1st M. of Anglesey, and 3d dau. of George Bussey Villiers, 4th E. of Jersey.
7. 'The Honourable Caroline Howe [sister of Richard, Earl Howe] married [1742] John Howe of Branslop [Hanslope], Bucks; died June 1814, in her ninety-third year. She possessed an extraordinary force of mind, clearness of understanding, and remarkable powers of thought and combination. She retained these faculties unimpaired to the great age of eighty-five, by exercising them daily, both in the practice of mathematics and in reading the two dead languages, of which late in life she had made herself mistress. To these acquirements must be added warm and lively feelings joined to a perfect knowledge of the world, and of the society of which she had always been a distinguished member' (B, quoted in MBJ ii. 66). Mary Berry became acquainted with her in 1798 (ibid.). See also GM 1814, lxxxiv pt i. 703; *Victoria*

History of Buckinghamshire, ed. William Page, vol. iv. 1927, p. 354, where she is erroneously called Constance. A friend of Mrs Elizabeth Carter and Mrs Montagu, she is mentioned in *Letters from Mrs Elizabeth Carter to Mrs Montagu*, ed. Montagu Pennington, 1817, iii. 43, 49, 52, 102, 267.
8. According to HW, she had forbidden the marriage of Lord Blandford to Lady Caroline Waldegrave, and the marriage of one of her daughters to Lord Strathaven; see *post* 11 Sept. 1791.
9. He had two unmarried sisters: Hon. Henrietta Louisa (1731–1824), and Hon. Anne (1733–97) (Burke, *Peerage*, 1928, p. 1786, *sub* Orford).
10. Catherine Mary and Elizabeth.
11. For the remainder of this paragraph HW was doubtless indebted to Mme Villegagnon-Walpole.
11a. A heraldic term denoting a shield divided by a vertical line down the centre.
12. As no Seigneur de Chilly has been associated with Brittany, possibly HW refers to Jean-Baptiste du Chilleau (1735–1824), Seigneur du Chilleau, Bishop of Châlons-sur-Saône, 1781; Archbishop of Tours, 1819; Comte du Chilleau, 1822 (Pol Potier de Courcy, *Nobiliaire et Armorial de Bretagne*, 3d edn, Rennes, 1890; Jean-Baptiste-

soupçon of any seigneurial marks remaining. They joined in the jubilee with alacrity, and yet since have quelled a mob who were proceeding to great lengths against *le Capet* for not taking the oath on the altar.[13] The Queen they call nothing but *la Dame Capet,* as in the Fronde Anne of Austria[14] was *Dame Anne.*

It has rained all day. I had ordered my coach to go to Richmond in the evening, but bade it set up again, and preferred having the fires lighted, and writing to you comfortably.

Miss Cheap is certainly your true friend, for she told me that Mrs Udney, whom I took for two and twenty, is eight and thirty. There I found the Abbé[15] singing glees with the Abrahams.[16] He came to Mr Barrett's a day later than he had promised: I insisted that he had been warbling at the Worcester and Gloucester music meeting.[17]

My nephew George Cholmondeley is to be married on Saturday.[18] As Madame de *St Alban* is breeding,[19] I told him I hoped his cousin the

Pierre Jullien de Courcelles, *Histoire généalogique . . . des pairs de France,* 1822–33, vi. 157–8).

13. La Fayette having taken his oath of fidelity to the Nation on the Altar of Liberty (the steps of which were made with stones from the Bastille), the populace expected Louis XVI to take his oath there. 'A general exclamation was heard of "Le roi à l'autel." The Marquis de la Fayette, on hearing this, represented to his Majesty the desire of the people; but the King . . . positively refused to comply, and pronounced the oath in his place in the balcony. This refusal, notwithstanding a cry of "God save the King," gave great dissatisfaction, and the whole assembly broke up without waiting for any order, or observing any regularity' (*London Chronicle* 17–20 July 1790, lxviii. 71). According to another interpretation, La Fayette wished the King *not* to take his oath on the altar (Brand Whitlock, *La Fayette,* 1929, i. 395).

14. (1602–66), dau. of Philip III of Spain and Marguerite of Austria; m. (1615) Louis XIII of France; mother of Louis XIV.

15. Rev. Norton Nicholls.

16. Three Abrams sisters, well-known concert singers. Harriet (1760–ca 1825), soprano, was also a composer of songs, glees, and duets. Theodosia (1766–1849), mezzo-soprano or contralto, m. Joseph Garrow, and died at Braddons, Torquay (GM 1849,

n.s. xxxii. 666). 'The youngest . . . Eliza, was accustomed to join with her sisters in the pieces which were sung at the Ladies' Catch and Glee Concerts. The elder two sang at the commemoration of Handel in Westminster Abbey in 1784, and at the principal London concerts for several years afterwards, when they retired into private life' (William H. Husk, in Sir George Grove, *Dictionary of Music and Musicians,* 3d edn, ed. H. C. Colles, 1927–8; James D. Brown and Stephen S. Stratton, *British Musical Biography,* Birmingham, 1897; Cole ii. 331). References to their singing 1799–1802 are in *The Francis Letters,* ed. Beata Francis and Eliza Keary, [1901] ii. 449, 469, 477, 481, 492.

17. The annual meeting of the three choirs of Gloucester, Worcester, and Hereford was not held at Gloucester until 8–10 Sept. 1790 (*St James's Chronicle* 2–4 Sept. 1790; Daniel Lysons, *History of the Origin and Progress of the Meeting of the Three Choirs,* Gloucester, 1812, pp. 229–31).

18. See *ante* 3 July 1790.

19. 'A few days since Madame St Alban was delivered of a son who it is expected will *not* succeed to its father's title' (*Oracle* 15 Jan. 1791). HW's comment *post* 10 April 1791, which is supported by other evidence, indicates that this child was a daughter.

Earl[20] will not disinherit him for a ready-made heir.[21] I would allow her to be a duchess, but then it should be without changing *her name*.[22] Good night, I am glad I shall say so in person on Thursday.[23]

To Mary Berry, Sunday 10 October 1790

Address: À Mademoiselle Mademoiselle Berry à la poste restante à Lyon, France. *Postmark:* 12 OC 90.

In 'Visitors,' HW noted: 'The Berrys set out Sunday Oct. 10, 1790.'

Mrs Damer wrote to Mary Berry 12 Oct. 1790: 'I received yesterday Mr Walpole's letter for you, which I send to the post with this' (*Berry Papers* 26).

Between the date of HW's letter of 2 Aug. 1790 and this one, the Berrys spent three weeks at Montpelier Row, Twickenham, and were doubtless with HW much of the time. The following newspaper item may refer partly to them: 'The Hon. Horace Walpole has now passed by his *ninetieth* year [he was 73 on 24 Sept. 1790], and has this last month been doing the honours of Strawberry Hill to a select party of intimate friends' (*St James's Chronicle* 16–18 Sept. 1790).

> [Strawberry Hill], Sunday, Oct. 10, 1790.
> The day of your departure.[1]

No. 1.[2]

IS it possible to write to my beloved friends and refrain from speaking of my grief for losing you, though it is but the continuation of what I have felt ever since I was stunned by your intention of going abroad this autumn.[3] Still I will not tire you with it often. In happy days I smiled and called you *my dear wives—now* I can only think on you as *darling children* of whom I am bereaved! As such I have loved and do love you; and charming as you both are, I have had no occasion to remind myself that I am past seventy-three. Your hearts, your understandings, your virtues, and the cruel injustice of

---

20. Of Cholmondeley.

21. His mistress's (Mme de St Alban's) coming child. As Lord Cholmondeley had no brothers and was unmarried, his uncle, Rev. Robert Cholmondeley (1727–1804), was next in succession to the earldom, and after him, his eldest son, George James Cholmondeley.

22. Evidently as the second wife of the Duke of St Albans, whose wife had died in the preceding year (*ante* 30 June, 27 Aug. 1789).

23. In the lower corner of the letter is written in an unknown hand: 'Note to Miss Pitt.'

---

1. 'No. 18' (B).

2. Of the series addressed to the Berrys abroad.

3. HW first learned of the Berrys' intention from John Thomas Batt; see *post* 13 Nov. 1790.

your fate,[4] have interested me in everything that concerns you; and so far from having occasion to blush for any unbecoming weakness, I am proud of my affection for you, and very proud of your condescending to pass so many hours with a very old man, when everybody admires you, and the most insensible allow that your good sense and information (I speak of both) have formed you to converse with the most intelligent of our sex as well as your own; and neither can tax you with airs of pretension or affectation. Your simplicity, and natural ease set off all your other merits—all these graces are lost to me, alas! when I have no time to lose!

Sensible as I am to my loss, it will occupy but part of my thoughts, till I know you safely landed,[5] and arrived safely at Turin.[6] Not till you are there and I learn so, will my anxiety subside and settle into steady selfish sorrow. I looked at every weathercock as I came along the road today, and was happy to see everyone point northeast—may they do so tomorrow![7]

I found here the frame for Wolsey,[8] and tomorrow morning Kirgate will place him in it, and then I shall begin pulling the Little

4. 'This alludes to Miss Berry's father having been disinherited by an uncle to whom he was heir at law, and a large property left to his younger brother' (B, from Wright vi. 369). Robert Ferguson (1690–1781) of Raith, co. Fife, having no issue, disinherited his elder nephew, Robert Berry (who had no male issue, and refused to marry a second time), and made his younger nephew, William Berry (d. 1810), his heir. William Berry, by royal licence dated 12 Jan. 1782, assumed the surname and arms of Ferguson (Burke, *Landed Gentry*, 1900, p. 537, *sub* Ferguson of Raith; GM 1810, lxxx pt ii. 497, where William Berry Ferguson is erroneously called Robert Ferguson; *Scots Magazine*, 1810, lxxii. 879; MBJ ii. 438).

5. At Dieppe. After going from London to Brighthelmstone on Sunday 10 Oct., the Berrys embarked the following day at 6 P.M., and were exactly twenty-four hours in reaching Dieppe (MBJ i. 214).

6. They arrived at Turin 1 Nov. (MBJ i. 228).

7. When the Berrys were to embark for Dieppe. Mary Berry records that they had a fair wind (MBJ i. 214).

8. 'The "Death of Cardinal Wolsey," copied by Miss Agnes Berry in water-colours, of the same size, and with all the strength of the original in oil by Mr William Lock—a sublime composition, in which the expressions are worthy of the greatest masters, as the colouring and chiaroscuro are equal to Rubens' ('Des. of SH,' *Works* ii. 511). The only drawing by Agnes Berry included in the *Description*, it was sold SH xxii. 99 to —— Zimmermann for £2.15.0. William Lock (1767–1847) the younger, who is mentioned later in the correspondence, was 1st son of William Lock of Norbury Park near Mickleham, Surrey; pupil and friend of Henry Fuseli; 'painted several historical and allegorical subjects in a strained and affected style; one, "The Last Moments of Cardinal Wolsey," was engraved in stipple by Charles Knight' (DNB); chosen a member of the Literary Club, 1800, on recommendation of Dr Burney, who considered him a worthy successor to Sir Joshua Reynolds (Frances Burney d'Arblay, *Memoirs of Doctor Burney*, 1832, iii. 297–300). See also Samuel Redgrave, *Dictionary of Artists*, 1878; Sir Joshua Reynolds, *Letters*, ed. Frederick W. Hilles, Cambridge, 1929, p. 174; 'Sonnet, to William Lock, Jun., on his Picture of the Death of Cardinal Wolsey,' in William Parsons, *Travelling Recreations*, 1807, ii. 151–2, and particularly Vittoria Colonna Caetani, Duchessa di Sermoneta, *The Locks*

Parlour to pieces that it may be hung anew to receive him.[9] I have also obeyed Miss Agnes, though with regret, for on trying it I found her Arcadia[10] would fit the place of the picture she condemns,[11] which shall therefore be hung in its room, though the latter should give way to nothing else, nor shall be laid aside, but shall hang where I shall see it almost as often. I long to hear that its dear paintress is well; I thought her not at all so last night.[12] You will tell me the truth, though she in her own case, and in that alone, allows herself mental reservation.

Forgive me for writing nothing tonight but about you two and myself. Of what can I have thought else? I have not spoken to a single person but my own servants since we parted last night. I found a message here from Miss Howe[13] to invite me for this evening—do you think I have not preferred staying at home to write to you, as this must go to London tomorrow morning by the coach to be ready for Tuesday's post? My future letters shall talk of other things, whenever I know anything worth repeating—or perhaps any trifle, for I am determined to forbid myself lamentations that would weary you;[14] and the frequency of my letters will prove there is no forgetfulness— if I live to see you again, you will then judge whether I am changed —but a friendship so rational and so pure as mine is, and so equal for both, is not likely to have any of the fickleness of youth, when it has none of its other ingredients. It was a sweet consolation to the short time that I may have left, to fall into such a society—no wonder then that I am unhappy at that consolation being abridged. I pique myself on no philosophy, but what a long use and knowledge of the world had given me, the philosophy of indifference to most persons and events. I do pique myself on not being ridiculous at this very

of *Norbury,* [1940] *passim.* He had visited SH in 1787 and again in 1788 ('Visitors,' *sub* 20 Sept. 1788).

9. For an account of the contents of the Little Parlour before it received Agnes Berry's water-colour, see 'Des. of SH,' *Works* ii. 418. 'The room is hung with Gothic paper of stone colour in mosaic, on which are wooden prints by Jackson of Venice' (ibid.). The new paper was a 'sober brown' (*post* 16 Oct. 1790).

10. 'A drawing by Miss Agnes Berry' (?B, Wright vi. 370). It is perhaps the coloured drawing 'designed and executed by Miss Agnes Berry, 1788' sold SH xxii. 71.

11. Not identified, but evidently another drawing by Agnes Berry.

12. Evidently at the Berrys' house in North Audley Street; see *post* 22 Oct. 1790, 27 March 1791.

13. 'An unmarried sister of the first Earl Howe, then living at Richmond' (B). Hon. Juliana Howe (ca 1732–1803), sister of Hon. Mrs Howe and of Richard, Earl Howe. She had lived at Richmond for a number of years, and died there (GM 1803, lxxiii pt i. 292; Collins, *Peerage,* 1812, viii. 144; HW to Lady Ossory 7 Oct. 1781). The message is missing.

14. HW's determination frequently failed him.

late period of my life; but when there is not a grain of passion in my affection for you two, and when you both have the good sense not to be displeased at my telling you so (though I hope you would have despised me for the contrary) I am not ashamed to say that your loss is heavy to me, and that I am only reconciled to it by hoping that a winter in Italy and the journeys and sea air will be very beneficial to two constitutions so delicate as yours. Adieu! my dearest friends—it would be tautology to subscribe a name to a letter, every line of which would suit no other man in the world but the writer.

To Mary Berry, Tuesday 12 October 1790

Address: Italy. À Mademoiselle Mademoiselle Berry, Posta Restante, Torino.
Postmark: Not stamped, but marked in ink in several places by post officials; one signature is (?) 'Wishartz,' possibly the name of a carrier.
The letter was posted 16 Oct. ('Visitors').

[Strawberry Hill], Tuesday, Oct. 12, 1790.
No. 2.

YESTERDAY was so serene and the wind so favourable, that I hoped the packet was ready and that you sailed.[1] Today is blowing and more to the south. I wish for a brisk wind to carry you swiftly; yet if I could hold the bag, I should open it so timorously, that Boreas would not be able to squeeze his puffed cheeks through the vent, though I might hear of you sooner. Then I shall long for a line from Rouen,[2] and then from Lyons,[3] and most of all from Turin[4] —Oh! how you have made me long to dip deep into the almanac, and even into that of next year, though it is most prodigal in me to be willing to hurry away a day, who may have so few in bank.

Yesterday morning I had just framed Wolsey and hung him over the chimney of the Little Parlour, when the Duchess of Gloucester came, and could scarce be persuaded it was the work of Agnes—but who else *could* have painted it? Milbourne,[5] who is here drawing

1. They did; see preceding letter.
2. On Wednesday 13 Oct. the Berrys travelled from Dieppe to Rouen, and left Rouen for Paris the following morning (MBJ i. 214–15).
3. Arrived at Lyons 22 Oct., the Berrys left for Chambéry 25 Oct. (MBJ i. 222–3).
4. Which they reached 1 Nov. (MBJ i. 228).

5. John Milbourn (fl. 1773–95), artist and copyist, pupil of Francis Cotes; mentioned in 1795 as 'drawing-master in the New Road, Mary-la-bonne' (GM 1795, lxv pt ii. 880; Basil S. Long, *British Miniaturists*, 1929, pp. 296–7). As early as 1777, he copied for HW a portrait of Frances Jennings, later Duchess of Tyrconnell ('Des. of SH,' *Works* ii. 495–6; HW to Conway 16 Sept.

from some of my pictures for his prints to Shakespeare,[6] cried out at it as the finest piece of water-colours he ever beheld, before he knew whose work it is—This was my employment yesterday—but not the only one—for I had my lawyer[7] with me to prepare for securing Cliveden,[8] if I should not have another almanac; and he is to bring me a proper *clause* on Monday next.

At night.

The wind has been so high since noon that I should have been very uneasy if it were not full south-west, with which I think you could not sail. I have been fully apprehensive about the whole of your journey, but had not foreseen that I should be alarmed about your voyage—now I am impatient for a letter from Dieppe.[9]

I have dined today at Bushy with the Guilfords,[10] where were only the two daughters,[11] Mr Storer[12] and Sir Harry Englefield,[13] who per-

1777). It was sold SH xx. 106. He also copied at least three other portraits for HW; see 'Des. of SH,' *Works* ii. 460, 497, 504. They were sold SH xvii. 37, xx. 62, 111.

6. None of the accounts of Milbourn mentions his prints to Shakespeare.

7. Perhaps Robert Blake (*post* 24 Nov. 1795), or 'James Hall, Poultry,' who drew HW's will in 1793.

8. To Mary and Agnes Berry; the matter was settled 16 Dec. 1790 (*post* that date).

9. On Friday 15 Oct. HW heard of their safe passage to Dieppe (see last two paragraphs of this letter), but he did not receive a letter until 17 Oct. (see following letter).

10. Frederick North (1732–92), styled Lord North 1752–90, who had become 2d E. of Guilford on the death of his father 4 Aug. 1790; and his wife, Anne Speke.

11. That is, the two unmarried daughters (the eldest, Lady Catherine Anne, had married Sylvester Douglas in 1789). Lady Anne North (1764–1832) m. (1798) as 3d wife, John Baker-Holroyd, 1st Bn Sheffield, cr. (1816) E. of Sheffield. She is frequently mentioned in *The Early Married Life of Maria Josepha Lady Stanley*, ed. Jane H. Adeane, 1899. The youngest, Lady Charlotte North (1770–1849) m. (1800) Hon. Lt-Col. John Lindsay, 7th son of 5th E. of Balcarres (Burke, *Peerage*, 1937, p. 660, *sub* Crawford; Collins, *Peerage*, 1812, iv. 484; GM 1849, n.s. xxxii. 664); she became one

of the Berrys' most intimate friends (MBJ iii. 509 *et passim; Berry Papers, passim*). All three sisters were sometime ladies of the Bedchamber to the Princess of Wales, later Queen Caroline. They are frequently mentioned in Sylvester Douglas, Lord Glenbervie, *Journals,* ed. Walter Sichel, 1910, and *Diaries,* ed. Francis Bickley, 1928.

12. Anthony Morris Storer (1746–99), 'long a habitué in the North family, and wishing, but I believe (qu.) never directly having proposed, to marry Lady Anne, then become rich and a miser from having been one of the finest of fine gentlemen, and, though ugly, active, graceful, a famous dancer and skater, a cracked [*sic*] scholar from Eton and the University, contemporary at Eton and of the set of Charles Fox, considered to be a successful friend of many of the more fashionable ladies of that day, the Pylades of Lord Carlisle . . . supercilious to all not of the *ton* or class of superiors, as they were called, to all, men and women, though of no distinction himself by birth, connections, office or any transcendent parts or talents. But, in society, when he chose, he was somewhat above par, and he made himself agreeable by showing his best side to Lord North' (Sylvester Douglas, Lord Glenbervie, *Diaries,* ed. Francis Bickley, 1928, ii. 349). His fine collection of the publications of the SH Press is now in the Eton College Library.

13. Sir Henry Charles Englefield (1752–

formed *en professeur* at the game I thought Turkish, but which sounds Moorish; he calls it, *Bandalore*.[14] I had written a note[15] to Mrs Grenville to inquire its name, but I think this will serve, as you only wanted to be told some name, no matter what, as one does about a new face; who is that? one cares not whether the reply is Thompson or Johnson.

This will be only a journal of scraps, till you are settled somewhere, and I can write regularly. Moreover, it is the only way of filling random letters—unless I were to indulge myself on the theme that for your sakes I will avoid.[16] I am little likely here to learn or do anything worth repeating; yet if you will be content with trifles, my wanting better subjects shall not be an excuse for not writing. It is a common plea with the unwilling; and persons abroad, I know, are often told by their correspondents, who have not the grace of friendship before their eyes, that they did not send them news, concluding they had better information. I may apologize for writing too often, but have too much pleasure in conversing with you in any manner, to lose the opportunity, provided I can hope to give you the least entertainment. Remember however that I ask no punctuality of replies, nay beg you to restrain them. You are young, have much to revisit,[17] many pleasures, I fervently hope, to enjoy; many friends besides to write to, and your healths to reestablish. I certainly have nothing to do that I like half so well as writing to you two. Do but tell me in short notes your stations, your motions and intentions, and particularly how you both do, and I shall be content: I do give you my word I shall. Writing is bad for delicate constitutions: in the day you must sacrifice some sight or amusement, at night you may be

1822), 7th and last Bt, 1780, of White Knights, Sonning, Berks; F.R.S., 1778; F.S.A., 1779; antiquary and astronomer. Elected P.S.A., he was not so confirmed because he was a Roman Catholic.

14. A toy, rather than a game, introduced into England ca 1790. It contained a 'coiled spring [?string], which caused it, when thrown down, to rise again to the hand, by the winding up of the string by which it was held' (OED). Of uncertain origin, the word is perhaps of Indian or East Indian, rather than of Turkish, Moorish, or French derivation. HW's use antedates by thirty-four years the earliest example given in OED, and the passage has apparently es-caped the notice of etymologists; see N&Q 1853, 1st ser., vii. 153; 1856, 2d ser., ii. 350, 416; 1887, 7th ser., iii. 66–7, 230–1, 358. In its twentieth-century adaptation, the toy is known by the less euphonious name of 'yo-yo'; see *The Shorter Oxford English Dictionary* and *Webster's New International Dictionary*, 2d edn, unabridged. For references to the toy as 'bandelure,' see BM, *Satiric Prints* vi. 768, 922.

15. Missing.

16. The difficulties and dangers of their journey.

17. The Berrys had been abroad in 1783–5; see MBJ.

writing too late, or fatiguing yourself when you should repose. Never, I beseech you, let the person who studies your well-being the most, be accessory to causing you the least trouble, disquiet or disorder. This is a positive injunction. Good night.

Wednesday night, 13th.

I received your kind letter from Brighth[elmstone] this morning, and give you a million of thanks for it. It gives me some hopes that you might be landed on Tuesday morning before the wind changed and rose[18]—but it revived a thousand more anxieties. I do not like a vessel smaller than the packet;[19] and the tempestuous wind of yesterday shocks me, lest it should have overtaken you at sea. That good soul Miss Seton[20] walked over from Richmond[21] to communicate her letter to me—how I love her for it! And she had previously called at Cambridge's to consult him, where his son George,[22] who has often crossed to Dieppe, assured her the vessel would put back to England, or put in to Boulogne on change of the wind—It may be so, but I cannot get out of my head the storm of yesterday, every blast of which made me quake and I tremble more now lest you should have been in its power! Oh! when shall I hear you are safe! I have written to Mrs D.[23] and told her your being summoned on board suddenly prevented your writing to her.

As you desire my second letter might be directed to Turin, I have settled with good Miss S. that she shall write this next Friday to Lyons, and that I will defer this till Tuesday for Turin, that you may be sure of a letter either at the one or the other, and know why

18. They did not land until six in the evening (MBJ i. 214).

19. The Berrys made the passage from Brighton to Dieppe in 'the Speedwell sloop of forty tons, Captain Lyn, which we hired, paying eight guineas and a half; the captain put our carriage and baggage aboard' (ibid.).

20. Barbara Cecilia Seton, cousin of the Berrys, known as 'Bab'; only child of George Seton (in the service of the East India Company) by Barbara Seton, youngest of the Berrys' four maternal aunts. HW's letters to her are published in this volume. She m. (1807) Rev. James Bannister, rector of Iddesleigh, Devon, and is said to have been living at Honiton, Devon, in 1838 (GM 1807, lxxvii pt ii. 1231; Robert

Seton, *An Old Family*, New York, 1899, pp. 254–5; George Seton, *History of the Family of Seton*, Edinburgh, 1896, i. 301–2).

21. She was the guest of the Dundases at Richmond Green; see *post* 11 Nov. 1791.

22. Rev. George Owen Cambridge (1756–1841), educated at Oxford (B.A., Queen's, 1778; M.A., Merton, 1781); rector of Elme, Cambs, 1793; Prebendary of Ely, 1795; Archdeacon of Middlesex 1806–40; edited his father's *Works*, 1803 (R. S. Cobbett, *Memorials of Twickenham*, 1872, pp. 52, 95; Joseph Foster, *Alumni Oxonienses . . . 1715–1886*, 1887–8; GM 1841, n.s. xvi. 214; John Le Neve and T. Duffus Hardy, *Fasti Ecclesiæ Anglicanæ*, Oxford, 1854, i. 356, ii. 332).

23. Mrs Damer; the letter is missing.

you do not hear from us both at once. I hope in God you are safe, and that my fears are groundless! All my letters and fears are for both, which I will not repeat any more. As I shall always I find be writing, you will order any letters to be sent after you from Turin, till I know how to direct farther on. When you are settled anywhere, I shall be more composed, and will think of the more insignificant things of the world.

Friday, 15th.

Words cannot tell what I have felt and do now feel! The storm on Tuesday terrified me beyond measure and so I have remained till this minute that Mrs D. has most humanely sent me an express to tell me you are landed[24]—I must send him back with this, and will instantly send to Miss Seton to tell her the happy news, and to Cambridge—I am not composed enough to say anything else—but I will write again on Tuesday—Heaven preserve you all!

I have not got my letter yet, but am easy for the present.

To Mary Berry, Saturday 16 October 1790

Address: Italy. À Mademoiselle Mademoiselle Berry, Posta Restante, Torino.
Postmark: None; several marks made on cover by postal officials, including 'P Pd 1[?] Wishartz.'
The letter was posted 19 Oct. ('Visitors').

Saturday night, Oct. 16, 1790.[1]

No. 3

THE hurry and confusion in which I finished my letter this morning which I had prepared for the post, will have told you better than I can describe the terror I have been under from the storm of Tuesday, and ever since, and the transport of a line from Mrs D. to tell me you are landed—I will not dwell but on one circumstance, but a dreadful one! I saw in yesterday's newspaper that two hoys had been lost off Plymouth on Tuesday night.[2] You, I believe, know how affection's imagination travels on such an occasion! My letter from you I have not yet received, but expect tomorrow

24. Letter missing.

1. 'No. 19' (B).

2. The paragraph has not been found in the four newspapers available for 15 Oct. 1790.

morning, and then will resume the subject of your voyage—now my fears are returning to land.

This will not depart till Tuesday; yet I have chosen to stay at home and write to you, for my thoughts are not resettled enough for anything else. I met G. H.[3] on Wednesday, who was beginning to condole with me on losing you, but the storm was in my head and I cut him short crossly, for as you are no longer my wives but my children, I can talk of you to nobody but those who love you almost as much as I do.

Not having been out of my house these three days, nor scarce seen a soul in it, I am not yet come to my wordly[3a] talk, but hope to be able to entertain you a little soon—arrive but at Turin. I know nothing but two events, not likely to please you. Poor Mr Ogilvie[4] has been near killed at Goodwood by an astonishing indiscretion of his own. He went, yes, and with one of his daughters,[5] and without even a stick, into an enclosure where the Duke[6] keeps an elk. The animal attacked him, threw him down, gored him, bruised him—in short, he is not yet out of danger.[7]

3. George Hardinge.

3a. So in MS.

4. '—— Ogilvie, Esq., who was married to the Duchess Dowager of Leinster, sister to the Duke of Richmond' (B). William Ogilvie (1740–1832), tutor to the sons of James Fitzgerald (1722–73), 1st D. of Leinster, m. (1774) the Duke's widow, Emilia Mary Lennox, by whom he had two daughters (Scots Peerage v. 365; GEC, sub Leinster). Among friends the couple were known as 'the Duke and Duchess of Ogilvie' (A. M. W. Stirling, The Hothams, 1918, ii. 179). See also DU DEFFAND. For numerous references to him, some of his letters, and a caricature of him by his son-in-law, Charles Lock, see Vittoria Colonna Caetani, Duchessa di Sermoneta, The Locks of Norbury, [1940] passim. HW considered him 'a very sensible Scot' ('Mem. 1783–91,' sub 17 Feb. 1784).

5. The younger (see n. 7), Emily Charlotte ('Mimi') Ogilvie (1778–1832), m. (1799) Charles George Beauclerk, only son of Topham Beauclerk and Lady Diana Spencer (Collins, Peerage, 1812, vi. 197; Burke, Peerage, 1928, p. 2016, sub St Albans). On the day of the marriage, 29 April 1799, Lady Diana wrote of her: 'I have seen her twice

and her manner is really delightful and interesting; I don't think her so very handsome; tall and a good figure, and in short a very fine-looking woman' (Mrs Steuart Erskine, Lady Diana Beauclerk, 1903, pp. 270–1). See also the Duchessa di Sermoneta, op. cit. 213–15 et passim.

6. Of Richmond: Charles Lennox (1735–1806), 3d D. of Richmond, 1750; m. (1757) Lady Mary Bruce, Lady Ailesbury's only child by her first marriage; he was a great favourite with HW, who dedicated vol. iv of the Anecdotes to him.

7. In the London Chronicle 19–21 Oct. 1790, lxviii. 392, is the following account: 'Mr Ogilvie, who was unfortunately gored by a stag some days ago at . . . Goodwood, still lies dangerously ill of his wounds. Two of his ribs are beaten in, and his lungs much hurt. . . . Mr Ogilvie's curiosity having led him into the fields . . . to view an American stag, which is remarkably fierce, was accompanied . . . by his younger daughter. He had no sooner crossed the pales which surround the spot where the animal is kept, than he was . . . attacked, and . . . was wounded by the beast in about fifty places, and had it not been for the loud and continued shrieks of his

Boyd[8] is made governor of Gibraltar, and somebody I know not whom, is appointed lieutenant-governor[9] in the place of your friend Ohara[10]—I know not how or why, but shall be sorry if he is mortified, and you consequently.

I believe I have one or two nephews in *war*[11] going with the Guards to the West Indies,[12] and therefore one or two nieces that are mourning brides—but I do not inquire, for I should be a poor comforter just now. The proclamation is out for the Parliament meeting the 25th of next month;[13] but the definitive porter from Spain,[14] that is

daughter, he would have been killed on the spot.' A similar account appears in *St James's Chronicle* 19–21 Oct. 1790, and in ibid. 23–26 Oct. and 4–6 Nov. 1790 Ogilvie's recovery is mentioned. Mrs Damer and George Selwyn also refer to the accident: see A. M. W. Stirling, *The Hothams*, 1918, ii. 245–6; Hist. MSS Commission, 15th Report, Appendix, Part VI, *Manuscripts of the Earl of Carlisle*, 1897, p. 692.

8. Sir Robert Boyd (1710–94), K.B., 1785; Col. of the 39th Regiment of Foot, 1766; Lt-Gen., 1777; Gen., 1793; Lt-Gov. (1768–90) and Gov. (13 Oct. 1790–4) of Gibraltar (*Morning Herald* 18 Oct. 1790; *London Chronicle* 14–16 Oct. 1790, lxviii. 370; William A. Shaw, *Knights of England*, 1906, i. 173; see also DNB). Rumours concerning his appointment to the governorship were prevalent as early as July; see *The London Chronicle* 13–15, 15–17, 22–24 July 1790, lxviii. 55, 63, 85; *St James's Chronicle* 22–24, 24–27 July 1790.

9. Sir Henry Calder (ca 1740–92), 4th Bt, 1774, of Park House near Maidstone, Kent; Col., 1778; Maj.-Gen., 1782; Col. of the 30th Regiment of Foot; Lt-Gov. of Gibraltar from 13 Oct. 1790 until his death at Bath 3 Feb. 1792 (*London Chronicle* 14–16 Oct. 1790, lxviii. 370; *Morning Herald* 18 Oct. 1790).

10. Maj.-Gen. Charles O'Hara (ca 1740–1802), natural son of James, 2d Bn Tyrawley; entered the army, 1752; distinguished himself in America, where he was taken prisoner; Maj.-Gen., 1781; Lt-Gen., 1793; Gen., 1798. He was Commandant at Gibraltar 1787–91 (E. R. Kenyon, *Gibraltar*, [1938] p. 67), and rumours prevailed that he would succeed Sir Robert Boyd as Lieutenant-Governor (*London Chronicle* 13–15 July 1790, lxviii. 55; *St James's Chronicle*

14–16 Oct. 1790), but not until April 1792, two months after the death of Sir Henry Calder, was he appointed to that position (*Annual Register*, 1792, xxxiv pt ii. 56). He was Governor of Gibraltar 1795–1802. Mary Berry met him in Italy in 1784 (MBJ i. 103), and in 1795–6 was engaged to him for 'the six happiest months of my long and insignificant existence' (*Berry Papers* 194). For the letters of O'Hara, Mary Berry, Mrs Damer, and others during that period, see ibid. 134–95.

11. At least two of HW's grandnieces had husbands in the army at this time: Anna Maria Keppel, dau. of Hon. Frederick Keppel by Laura Walpole, m. (1790) William Stapleton, Captain in the 2d Foot; and Laura Keppel, her sister, m. (1784) Hon. George Fitzroy, 2d Bn Southampton, 1797. The following newspaper paragraph is of interest in connection with HW's pun here: 'Lord Orford does not often make puns; but the designs, drawings, etc., with which our young ladies are kind enough frequently to disfigure the wainscots of their Papa's rooms, he calls them *Miss-doings*' (*Times* 17 Oct. 1795).

12. Where rioting and the dissemination of 'levelling principles' were causing considerable unrest; see GM 1790, lx pt ii. 657–8, 758, 948, 1044. Preparations were still being made, too, for the possible war with Spain: 'All the recruits belonging to the regiments either in the East or West Indies are under orders to join their respective regiments' (*Morning Herald* 13 Oct. 1790). See also following letter.

13. The proclamation, dated 13 Oct., appears in *The London Chronicle* 12–14 Oct. 1790, lxviii. 368, and in *The St James's Chronicle* 14–16 Oct. 1790.

14. That is, the King's Messenger who

to open or shut Janus's gates, is not expected back till the 27th of this. That is all I can tell Mr Berry.

Sunday noon.

Here is your letter from Dieppe as I expected, and strange it is, that as much as I abhor sea-sickness myself, I am very hard-hearted about yours[15]—to have been only less sick than usual, when I would have compounded for your both rivalling the cascades of St Cloud, if I could have been certain that you would soon be as dusty as those of Versailles[16]—Oh! don't talk of it—but what harlequin of a Triton whisked your vessel about so as to escape the tempest, though you were twenty-four hours at sea—nay, are not you silent about it lest you should give me a posthumous panic? Thank God you are all safe! I will say no more of the storm, though I shall not forget it nor recover soon of *that* sea-sickness.

I think it probable that good Miss Seton[17] may take a walk hither after church, as October is dressed out in all its diamonds; I have my coach ready to convey her back if she does—if not, I will call on her this evening; we must drink the health of your sea-sickness.

I have seen nothing of the Hamptonians;[18] I could not bear to go to them, while my mind was so agitated—consequently I know nothing of the person[19] who was to come to town yesterday to be married on the 20th[20]—but I do know that his aunt[21] at the foot of yonder hill had heard nothing of it four days ago, nor believes a word of it—nor has her brother[22] been near town these two months.

Mrs D. dines here tomorrow,[23] and will probably carry this to town with her for Tuesday's post—but I may add a few words.

was expected to bring news of the final success or failure of the negotiations with Spain; see *post* 8 Nov. 1790.

15. 'I went to bed the instant we got aboard, and never moved hand or foot till I got into the boat to be landed at Dieppe' (mbj i. 214).

16. The fountains at St Cloud usually played when those at Versailles were not playing. HW may also be contrasting the low, marshy situation of St Cloud with the higher, drier location of Versailles.

17. 'A cousin of Miss Berry's, then on a visit in the neighbourhood of Strawberry Hill' (B).

18. Lady Cecilia Johnston and Mrs Anderson.

19. The Marquess of Blandford.

20. To Elizabeth Gunning.

21. Lady Diana Beauclerk.

22. The Duke of Marlborough.

23. Mrs Damer wrote to Mary Berry 11 Oct. 1790, from London: 'I shall go to see Mr Walpole the moment I am able, which, from what Fordyce [her physician] says today, may, I hope, be in a few days' (*Berry Papers* 25).

Sunday night.

If I could continue to predict as well as I have done today, I would turn prophet, and I know what I would foretell. Miss S. did come to me, and we had an hour and half of comfortable conversation, and nobody interrupted us, nor would any mortal have been welcome— you may guess the topics—the storm was not forgot. She saw Wolsey over his chimney in a comely frame of black and gold, and tomorrow the paper-man comes to new-hang the room in sober brown suiting the occasion. As she was going she desired me to read to her Prior's *Turtle and Sparrow,* and his *Apollo and Daphne,* with which you were so delighted, and which though scarce known, are two of his wittiest and genteelest poems. There should be new way-posts on our common roads to some of our best poets, since Dr Johnson from want of taste and ear and from mean party-malice defaced the old indexes as the mob do milestones.

I have heard at Richmond this evening that at Ealing[24] the match is talked of as indubitable; yet yesterday morning the old grandam in Pall Mall[25] disavowed it, and laid the invention on L. M. C.[26]— from all this you will not much expect to hear the ceremony is performed. Lord Stopford marries the D. of Buccleugh's eldest daughter;[27] the Duchess[28] gives her £20,000, the Duke £10,000, and they settle fifteen more.

Monday evening.

I have nothing to add, but what I am sure would not be new, and therefore as Mrs D. is returning and will carry this to town, I will conclude.

24. Ealing Grove, the Duke of Argyll's seat.

25. Lord Blandford's grandmother, the Duchess of Bedford: Gertrude Leveson-Gower (ca 1719–94), dau. of 1st E. Gower; m. (1737) as 2d wife, John Russell, 4th D. of Bedford. She had a reputation as a matchmaker (*Harcourt Papers* vi. 294).

26. Lady Mary Coke, HW's friend and correspondent: Lady Mary Campbell (1727–1811), youngest dau. of John, 2d D. of Argyll, and sister of Lady Greenwich;

m. (1747) Edward, Viscount Coke (Burke, *Peerage,* 1928, p. 133, *sub* Argyll).

27. James George Stopford (1765–1835), styled Vct Stopford 1770–1810; 3d E. of Courtown, 1810; m. (29 Jan. 1791) his second cousin, Lady Mary Scott (1769–1823), dau. of Henry Scott (1746–1812), 3d D. of Buccleuch.

28. Of Buccleuch: Elizabeth Montagu (1743–1827), only dau. of George, 1st D. of Montagu. She had married the D. of Buccleuch in 1767.

To Mary Berry, Friday 22 October 1790

Address: Italy. À Mademoiselle Mademoiselle Berry à Torino. Posta restante.
Postmark: None; several marks by postal officials, including 'P Pd 1 Wishartz.'
Posted 25 Oct. ('Visitors').

[Strawberry Hill], Oct. 22, 1790.

No. 4.

THOUGH Mrs D.[1] and Mrs B.[2] recommended your going through Paris, I should have had a new alarm, could I have known you would be reduced to take that route[3]—but you had left it, before I had any apprehension of it, and I hope are actually at Lyons, or beyond it.[4] Still I shall not feel comfortably till I hear from Turin—and what an age that will be!

I was in town yesterday, passed the evening with Mrs D., where were Mrs B. and the *Charming Man;*[5] I did not see another crea-

<hr />

1. Damer.
2. Mrs Buller: Mary Coxe (ca 1744–1812), 2d dau. and coheir of John Hippisley Coxe of Ston Easton, Somerset; sister of Lady Basset (*post* 10 Aug. 1791); m. (1770) as 2d wife, James Buller (1740–72) of Downes, Devonshire (Burke, *Landed Gentry*, 1937, pp. 278, 1119, *sub* Buller of Downes and Hippisley of Ston Easton). In 1793 she lived at '44, Upper Brook Street' (*Directory to the Nobility, Gentry . . . for 1793*), and she died in Upper Grosvenor Street (GM 1812, lxxxii pt i. 605). Mrs Damer wrote to Mary Berry 7 July 1791 that HW 'was in very good spirits here [Mrs Damer's] yesterday evening, and had his dear Mrs Buller, the only person, I think, that he thoroughly likes talking to in your absence' (*Berry Papers* 48). See also ibid., *passim.* HW had known her at least since 1784 (*Autobiography of Mrs Piozzi*, ed. A. Hayward, 2d edn, 1861, i. 223; HW to Duc de Nivernais 6 Jan. 1785). Fanny Burney, who met her about 1782, described her as 'tall and elegant in her person, genteel and ugly in her face, and abrupt and singular in her manners . . . very clever, sprightly, and witty, and much in vogue . . . a Greek scholar, a celebrated traveller in search of foreign customs and persons, and every way original in her knowledge and her enterprising way of life. And she has had the maternal heroism—which with me is her

first quality—of being the guide of her young son in making the grand tour' (Frances Burney d'Arblay, *Memoirs of Doctor Burney*, 1832, ii. 291–2; see also ibid. 293–5).
3. At Rouen 13 Oct. 1790 'we found ourselves obliged to alter our intended course; for our bankers . . . could not give us £5 in money instead of the £60 which we wanted—as much as we pleased in assignats of 800 florins each, but money of any sort was not to be had at Rouen; so that instead of going from St Germains to Versailles, and avoiding Paris, we were obliged to go there in search of money—that one thing needful, above all on a journey' (MBJ i. 215). Cf. the following passage from *The St James's Chronicle* 30 Oct.–2 Nov. 1790: 'At Rouen, one of the first commercial towns in France, the current coin of the kingdom is so scarce that letters of credit from the first houses of London cannot produce a single louis d'or. Many English travellers who expected to be supplied there with money to proceed to Italy, have been under the necessity of taking the circuitous route of Paris, in order to get the *sine qua non* of all expeditions.'
4. The Berrys arrived at Lyons 22 Oct., the date of this letter (MBJ i. 222), and at Turin 1 Nov. (MBJ i. 228).
5. Mrs Damer wrote to Mary Berry 30 Oct. 1790: 'Jerningham told me that the

ANNE SEYMOUR DAMER, BY RICHARD COSWAY

ture, and returned hither today—but I shall go again on Thursday to take leave of Mrs D. who sets out on Saturday.[6] She writes to you tonight,[7] for which reason I agreed I would not till Tuesday—and indeed I have already said all I have to say, or at least all I will say. Three days may furnish something. The Johnstones have been at Nuneham and are actually at Park Place, or I might have heard more of *Marchioness to be or not to be*,[8] for those I saw in town knew not a tittle more of the matter, yet the Ides of March, i.e. the 20th of October, are come and gone!—consequently faith *minifies*,[9] instead of increasing; and unless Lord Abercorn insists upon the King's declaring that she was born a Marchioness,[10] I doubt whether she ever will be one.

My dates hitherto have been of the 12th to Lyons, of 16th, 19th, and this, to Turin.[11] Whither I am to direct next, I shall not know till you tell me.

Sunday 24th after dinner.

I should be tired of talking of the silly Miss and her match, and of inquiring about them, if you had not charged me to send you the progress of a history that at the eve of your departure revived so strangely,[12] without having had a beginning. In its present stage it is a war of duchesses. The bride's aunt firmly asserts it is to be; the bridegroom's grandmother positively denies it—and she ought to know as first inventress. In the meantime no *sposo* appears, nor his

night Mr W. was here (he set Mrs B. and him down), when he got into the coach he could not contain himself. There was nothing melancholy he did not say. He was quite in an agony. I have not written to him for fear that, seeing a letter come from me, he should be disappointed in finding that I had no news from France' (MBJ i. 247–8).

6. For Lisbon, for her health: 'She was not ill, but only not quite well, the harsh winters here generally affect her, and in point of climate I believe that [Lisbon] is among the first' (Henry Seymour Conway to Sir William Hamilton 28 Nov. 1790, in Percy Noble, *Anne Seymour Damer*, 1908, p. 119). She sailed from Falmouth ca 8 Nov. (*post* 13 Nov. 1790).

7. The letter apparently has not survived.

8. Elizabeth Gunning.

9. A play on the maiden name of Miss Gunning's mother, Susannah Minifie, author of sentimental novels; see *post* 22 Jan. 1791.

10. An allusion to the title procured by Lord Abercorn for his cousin Cecil Hamilton; see *ante* 29 July 1790.

11. HW refers to the date of posting; for the dates he gives, read *10th . . . 12th, 16th*.

12. At the Berrys', when Miss Gunning announced that she was to be married to Lord Blandford 20 Oct. 1790; see *post* 27 March 1791.

parents, M—— House wanting repainting—in short, everybody but the ducal aunt suspects *the* letter[13] was fictitious somewhence or other.

I have called twice on Miss Seton at Richmond and made her very happy by your safe arrival at Paris.[14] I went afterwards to Lady Betty Mackinsy, where the Comtesse Emilie[15] played admirably on the harp! The Penns[16] were there and delighted to hear of you. Lady Dillon[17] told me she heard Lady Goodere[18] say that I have been mighty obliging and offered to buy the furniture if she and her knight[19] would stay in my house—I am rejoiced at having been so civil, without having said or intended any such thing. I *have* agreed to buy the furniture[20]—but I do not believe it is for the *Gooderes*— though it may be for the *good year.* I wish I was as sure that the one is true, as I am certain that the other is false!

I can tell Mr B. nothing about war or peace.[21] We have a fleet mighty enough to take, ay, and bring home Peru and Mexico and deposit them in a *West India warehouse, vis-à-vis* that in Leadenhall Street.[22] Though we should come by them a little more honestly than

13. A letter purporting to be from Lord Blandford to Miss Gunning, to set the wedding day; see *post* 13 Nov., 17 Dec. 1790, 27 March 1791.

14. 15 Oct. 1790 (MBJ i. 215).

15. De Boufflers.

16. Lady Juliana and her daughter Sophia Margaret.

17. Charlotte Lee (1720–94), 1st dau. of George Henry, 2d E. of Lichfield; m. (1744) Henry Dillon (d. 1787), 11th Vct Dillon of Costello-Gallen (GEC; Collins, *Peerage,* 1768, iii. 436).

18. —— Pitts m. (25 Sept. 1770) Sir Robert Goodere, Kt (GM 1770, xl. 486).

19. Sir Robert Goodere (ca 1720–1800), Kt, 1762; lieutenant of the Band of Gentlemen Pensioners 1762–72; water bailiff of the Thames above Staines, 1760, 1762 (GM 1760, xxx. 395; GM 1762, xxxii. 553; GM 1800, lxx pt ii. 700; William A. Shaw, *Knights of England,* 1906, ii. 291; *Court and City Reg-*

ister 1762–72). The Gooderes were HW's tenants at Cliveden or Little SH from 1785 (the death of Mrs Clive) until 25 Dec. 1790 (*SH Accounts* 176–7). When Sir Robert died, they were living in his house in Margaret Street, Cavendish Square (GM 1800, lxx pt ii. 700).

20. Formerly Mrs Clive's; during their occupancy of Cliveden, the Gooderes evidently hired the furniture from Miss Pope, Mrs Clive's friend and presumably her legatee. HW bought the furniture for £192 (HW to Miss Jane Pope 30 Dec. 1790; *SH Accounts* 18, 177), for Mary and Agnes Berry.

21. With Spain.

22. East India House, built in 1726, stood 'on the south side of Leadenhall Street, and a little to the west of Lime Street . . . with warehouses in the back part toward Lime Street' (*London and Its Environs Described,* 1761, ii. 262–4).

we did by the diamonds of Bengal,[23] I shall not be sorry if we make peace and condescend to leave the new world where it was.

Mr Burke's pamphlet is at last literally advertised for the first of November.[24]

Monday 25.

The Little Parlour is new hung, and Wolsey has been installed this morning, and proclaimed president of all the *waterworks* in the world,[25] with shouts of *Viva Santa Agnese!*—with these festivities I must conclude for this post—disposed as I am to be always writing to you two, be sure matter, *outward* matter only is wanting. I send you heaps of trifles, lest I should omit anything you might like to know, especially as I know not when you will see an English newspaper. You are not to answer any of those trumpery articles—let me write, it amuses me—but remember, you are gone for your healths, and are not to be sitting against the edge of a table—adieu! adieu!

PS. I have just permitted four foreigners to see my house, though past the season,[26] because all their names end in *i*'s, and I must propitiate Italians, when you are, as I hope, on Hesperian ground.

To Mary Berry, Sunday 31 October 1790

Address: À Mademoiselle Mademoiselle Berry à la poste restante à Florence, Italie. *Postmark:* Illegible. Endorsed: 'Post pd 1s.'
Posted 2 Nov. ('Visitors').

23. The East India Company made settlements in Bengal in the first half of the seventeenth century, fought during the next century to protect its interests, and in 1765 procured treaties by which Bengal and other provinces came under British administration. The British thus gained 'the diamonds of Bengal' by right of conquest. If Peru and Mexico, both Spanish colonies, were taken, there would be the defence that the British were retaliating for Spanish action at Nootka Sound; see *ante* 2 July 1790, n. 14.

24. 'On the 1st of November will be pub-

lished, in octavo, price five shillings, sewed, *Reflections on the Revolution in France, and on the Proceedings in certain Societies in London Relative to that Event. In a Letter intended to have been sent to a Gentleman in Paris,* by the Right Honourable Edmund Burke. Printed for J. Dodsley in Pall Mall' (*St James's Chronicle* 21–23 Oct. 1790). It was advertised 'This day was published,' in ibid. 30 Oct.–2 Nov. 1790.

25. Presumably 'The Death of Cardinal Wolsey' contained several weeping figures.

26. SH was shown to visitors by appointment 1 May–30 Sept.

Strawberry, Sunday, Oct. 31, 1790.[1]

No. 5.

PERHAPS I am unreasonably impatient, and expect letters before they can come. I expected a letter from Lyons three days ago, though Mrs Damer[2] told me I should not have one till tomorrow: I have got one today—but alas! from Pougues[3] only, 11½ posts short of Lyons![4] Oh! may Mrs Damer prove in the right tomorrow—well! I must be happy for the past, and that you had such delightful weather, and but one little accident to your carriage.[5] We have had equal summer till Wednesday last, when it blew a hurricane—I said to it, 'Blow, blow, thou winter wind,[6] I don't mind you now.'—But I have not forgotten Tuesday 12th.—And now I hope it will be as calm, as it is today, on Wednesday next, when Mrs Damer is to sail.[7] I was in town on Thursday and Friday, and so were her parents[8] to take our leaves, as we did on Friday night, supping all at Richmond House.[9] She set out yesterday morning, and I returned hither.[10]

1. 'No. 20' (B).

2. Expanded throughout this paragraph by Mary Berry from HW's 'D.'

3. Leaving Paris Sunday 17 Oct., the Berrys arrived at Pougues, 150 miles distant and approximately midway between Paris and Lyons, on Tuesday 19 Oct.: 'Lay at Pougues; tolerable inn, civil people' (MBJ i. 221).

4. According to *The Gentleman's Guide through France*, 10th edn, 1788, the post road from Paris to Lyons *via* Moulins was '56½ posts. English miles 297. Time about 48 hours' (p. 152). From Paris to Pougues was 27½ posts, and from Pougues to Lyons was 29, not 11½ posts (ibid. 152–4).

5. 'Sunday, 17th [Oct. 1790] . . . At Chailly, a post and a half from Fontainebleau, we observed that the bed of the carriage was broken. After some delay, continued our route, and arrived at Fontainebleau . . . Monday, 18th.—The *charron* at Fontainebleau, as usual, not getting his work done as soon as he promised, we could not leave Fontainebleau till twelve o'clock' (MBJ i. 220–1).

6. *As You Like It* II. vii. 174.

7. From Falmouth, for Lisbon; she did not sail until ca 8 Nov.; see *post* 13 Nov. 1790.

8. Hon. Henry Seymour Conway and Lady Ailesbury.

9. Expanded by Mary Berry from HW's 'Rd House.'

10. Mrs Damer wrote to Mary Berry on Thursday 28 Oct. 1790: 'Mr W. comes today. I know how melancholy he will be, for we have no letters from you yet, and I fear that I shall leave London without hearing again' (MBJ i. 247, misdated 30 Oct.). From Hertford Bridge, 30 Oct. 1790, she wrote: 'I left Mr W., I really think, in health well; but he receives no degree of comfort as to his fears, nor will, till he hears and receives letters from another country. The interest and tenderness he shows makes me feel infinitely more sensibly giving him any additional pain, and depriving him of the satisfaction he may, heaven knows! indulge with me of saying all he thinks' (MBJ i. 248).

I am glad you had the amusement of seeing the National Assembly:[11] did Mr B. find it quite so august as he intended it should
be? Burke's pamphlet[12] is to appear tomorrow, and Calonne has published a thumping one of 440 pages.[13] I have but begun it, for there
is such a quantity of calculations, and one is forced to bait so often to
boil milliards[14] of livres down to a rob[15] of pounds sterling, that my
head is only filled with figures instead of arguments, and I understand arithmetic less than logic.

Our war still hangs by a hair, they say, and that this approaching
week must terminate its fluctuations. Brabant, I am told, is to be
pacified by negotiations at The Hague[16]—though I talk like a newspaper, I do not assume their airs, nor give my intelligence of any sort
for authentic, unless when the *Gazette*[17] endorses the articles. Thus
Lord Louvain is made Earl of Beverley,[18] and Lord, Earl of, Digby;[19]

11. The Berrys visited the National Assembly for about two hours 16 Oct.: 'While
we were present, there were seldom fewer
than three or four [deputies] speaking at
once—often many more—with such a noise
that it was impossible anything could be
heard; the President in vain ringing a great
bell, which stands by him on the table, by
way of enforcing silence or drowning other
noises, and the criers in vain demanding
it. . . . Their appearance is not more gentlemanlike than their manner of debating—
such a set of shabby, ill-dressed, strange-
looking people I hardly ever saw together.
Our House of Commons is not half so bad.'
For this and much more, see MBJ i. 217–19.

12. *Reflections on the Revolution in
France.*

13. *De l'État de la France, présent & à
venir . . . à* Londres, de l'imprimerie de
T. Spilsbury & fils, octobre 1790. It is mentioned in *The Times* 28 Oct. 1790 as having
'just come from the press.' Other editions
with slightly different titles appeared in the
same year, but this is the only one of 440
pages. In reality it contains (in addition to
an introduction, pp. i–xvi) 464 pages, for
sixteen pages, numbered 81 *bis*–96 *bis*, are
inserted after p. 96, and eight pages, numbered 119 *bis*–126 *bis*, follow p. 126. Burke
considered it 'not only an eloquent, but an
able and instructive performance' (*Reflec-*

tions on the Revolution in France, in his
Writings and Speeches, New York, 1901, iii.
479).

14. A thousand millions; the earliest
quotation in OED is dated 1793.

15. This passage is quoted in OED to illus-
trate use of 'rob,' a word of Arabic or Persian origin, defined as 'the juice of a fruit,
reduced by boiling to the consistency of a
syrup and preserved with sugar; a conserve
of fruit.'

16. This proved untrue. The Brabançon
revolt of 1789 against Austrian domination,
at first successful, led to internal dissension, and in December 1790 Austrian troops
brought the country for a short time under
complete subjection. See also *post* 8 Nov.,
20 Dec. 1790.

17. *The London Gazette,* 'published by
authority.'

18. Algernon Percy (1750–1830), 2d son
of 1st D. of Northumberland, succeeded his
father in 1786 as 2d Bn Lovaine, and was
created (2 Nov. 1790) E. of Beverley. His
new title and that of Lord Digby are announced in *The London Gazette* 26–30
Oct. 1790 under the dateline, 'Whitehall,
October 30.'

19. Henry Digby (1731–93), 7th Bn Digby
of Geashill, cr. (1765) Bn Digby of Sher-
borne, and (1 Nov. 1790) E. Digby.

but in no *Gazette,* though still in the Songs of Sion,[20] do I find that Miss G. is a marchioness. It is not that I suppose you care who gains a step in the *aristocracy,* but I tell you those trifles to keep you *au courant,* and that at your return you may not make only a baronial curtsy, when it should be lower by two rows of ermine to some new-hatched countess. This [is] all the news market furnishes.

Your description of the National Assembly and of the Champ de Mars[21] were both admirable; but the altar of boards and canvas seems a type of their perishable constitution, as their air-balloons were before.[22] French visions are generally full of vapour, and terminate accordingly.

I have been at Mrs Grenville's[23] this evening, who had a small party for the Duchess of Gloucester; there were many inquiries after my wives.

You license me to direct this to Bologna,[24] but I prefer Florence, for you will not lose more time by its waiting for you, than by its being sent after you; and I always think that the less complicated the manœuvres of the post, the safer.[25]

20. An allusion to Sion or Syon Hill, a seat of the Duke of Marlborough; see following note, and *ante* 3 July 1790.

21. After dinner on Oct. 16, the Berrys, accompanied by a friend, 'went to the Champ de Mars, now called Le Champ de la Confédération. . . . I should indeed have been sorry not to have seen what I think more truly in good taste and in great style of anything I ever saw in France. The sort of covered pavilion, under which [on 14 July 1790] sat the King, the *États,* etc., etc., groups so well with the higher edifice of the École Militaire, which it joins by a covered passage; the enclosure is so large and so well *encadré* by the trees round it, and the altar in the middle, though only composed of canvas and boards, is in such perfect good taste, that it puts one in mind of N. Poussin's fine ideal landscapes of Greece. We saw it all by the finest moonlight that ever was, which perhaps was not without its effect upon the whole scene' (MBJ i. 219).

22. HW's skeptical attitude toward balloons is clearly illustrated in J. E. Hodgson, *The History of Aeronautics in Great Britain,* 1924, pp. 199–203, where several quotations from HW's earlier letters are given. See also *post* 31 March 1791, 10 Oct. 1793.

23. 'Margaret Banks, widow of the Hon. Henry Grenville, who died in 1784. Their only daughter was married in 1781 to Viscount Mahon, afterwards Earl Stanhope' (?B, Wright vi. 372). Mrs Grenville lived at Hampton Court Green (*ante* 1 Nov. 1788).

24. 'Friday, 12th [Nov. 1790] . . . Arrived at Bologna before 3 P.M.' (MBJ i. 244). They left the following day (ibid. 245).

25. In her journal, Mary Berry does not mention disappointment at not receiving mail at Bologna, but on arrival at Florence two days later, 14 Nov., she notes: 'Found ourselves again disappointed in our hopes of receiving letters, and were very melancholy' (MBJ i. 245).

You say nothing of your healths—how are Miss Agnes's teeth? Don't omit such essential articles.

Miss Seton has called here again today, and was delighted to see your letter which I had just received. She does not leave Richmond[26] till Tuesday, and is to write to me for news of you, if she is long without hearing from one or other of you. I proposed this to her, not only for her satisfaction, but that you may not be worn out by writing. For this reason I make my letters shorter, to set you the example, though I promise not to omit a tittle that I can think you would like to know; and in that light nothing will seem too insignificant to tell you. Even articles that would scarce do for home consumption, acquire a value, I know by coming from home. Besides, Lord Hervey[27] I think is not at present at Florence,[28] and you may not get a newspaper. Those wretched tattlers, that one so justly despises on their own dunghill, are welcome abroad in hopes of finding a barley-corn or two that are eatable.

I shall go to Park Place next Saturday 6th—*you* know why I postponed my visit so long.[29] I announce it to you now, because I shall probably not write on the following Tuesday, but wait till Friday 12th when I shall be returned hither, for I do not love letters taking so many hops before they get into the high post road.

PS. Monday. No letter from Lyons—it may be in B[erkeley] Sq[uare] and I may get it tomorrow—but it will be after this is gone by the coach to my servant in town. If I do get it, it will not damp my impatience for one from Turin, nor that extinguish the same eagerness for one from Florence.—In short, I shall not be *perfectly indifferent* till I know you [are] settled somewhere.

26. For Caversham Hill near Reading, Berks: see *post*, HW to Barbara Cecilia Seton 13 Nov. 1790.

27. John Augustus Hervey (1757–96), 2d but 1st surviving son of Frederick Augustus, 4th E. of Bristol, whom he predeceased; styled Bn Hervey; captain R.N., 1780; envoy extraordinary 1787–91 and envoy extraordinary and minister plenipotentiary 1791–4, to Tuscany (*British Diplomatic Representatives*, ed. S. T. Bindoff *et al.*, 1934, p. 171).

28. He was there; see following letter.

29. He waited until the Berrys had started on their journey.

To Mary Berry, Monday 8 November 1790

Address: À Mademoiselle Mademoiselle Berry à la poste restante à Florence, Italie. *Postmark:* FIRENZE 48.
Posted 11 Nov. ('Visitors').

Park Place, Nov. 8, 1790.[1]

No. 6.

NO letter since Pougues![2]—I think you can guess how uneasy I am! It is not the fault of the wind which has blown from every quarter. Today I cannot hear, for no post comes in on Mondays.[3] What can have occasioned my receiving no letter from Lyons, when on the 18th of last month you were within twelve posts of it?[4] I am now sorry I came hither, lest by my change of place a letter may have shuttle-cocked about, and not have known where to find me—and yet I left orders with Kirgate to send it after me if one came to Str[awberry] on Saturday. I return thither tomorrow, but not till after the post is come in here—I am writing to you now (while the company[5] are walked out) to divert my impatience, which however is but a bad recipe, and not exactly the way to put you out of my head.

The first and great piece of news is the pacification with Spain. The courier arrived on Thursday morning with a most acquiescent answer to our ultimatum[6]—what that was, I don't know—nor much care—Peace contents me; and for my part I shall not haggle about the terms; I have a good general digestion, and it is not a small matter that will lie at my stomach, when I have no hand in dressing the ingredients.

The pacification of Brabant is likely to be volume the second. The Emperor[7] and their Majesties of Great Britain and Prussia[8] and his

1. 'No. 21' (B).
2. 31 Oct.; see preceding letter.
3. No post left London on Sunday; the post that left London on Monday arrived at Henley-on-Thames, one mile west of Park Place, at 1 A.M. Tuesday (*Cary's New and Correct English Atlas,* 1793, ad fin.).
4. At Pougues.
5. See p. 132.
6. 'Whitehall, Nov. 4. This morning Mr Dressins, one of his Majesty's messengers in ordinary, arrived at the office of . . . the Duke of Leeds . . . with dispatches from the Right Hon. Alleyne Fitzherbert . . . dated the 24th of October last, containing an account that a convention, for terminating the differences which had arisen with . . . [the Spanish] Court, had been agreed upon . . . and that the convention was to be signed . . . on the 27th of the same month' (*London Gazette Extraordinary* 4 Nov. 1790, quoted in *St James's Chronicle* 4–6 Nov. 1790).
7. Leopold II.
8. Frederick William II (1744–97), K. of Prussia 1786–97.

Serene Highness the Republic of Holland[9] have sent a card to his Turbulent Lowness of Brabant[10] that they allow him but three weeks to submit to his old sovereign,[11] on promise of a general pardon—or the choice of threescore thousand men ready to march without a pardon.[12]

The third volume, expected, but not yet in the press, is a counter-revolution in France—of that I know nothing but rumour—yet it certainly is not the most incredible event that rumour ever foretold. In this country the stock of the National Assembly is fallen down to bankruptcy. Their only renegade-aristocrat Earl Stanhope has (with Lord W. Russel[13]) scratched his name out of the Revolution Club.[14] But the fatal blow has been at last given by Mr *Burke*.[15] His pam-

9. Willem V (1748–1806), Prince of Orange and Hereditary Stadtholder of the United Netherlands, who in 1795 was forced by the French conquest of his country to seek refuge in England; see *post* 18–26 Aug. 1795. He abdicated his throne in 1802.

10. Leopold II himself was nominally the Duke of Brabant, but on 24 Oct. 1789 the Breda Committee (ringleaders of the opposition to the Emperor) 'issued a decree that the Emperor Joseph [II] was no longer Duke of Brabant' (Demetrius C. Boulger, *History of Belgium*, 1902–9, i. 408). HW's 'Turbulent Lowness' therefore refers to the people of Brabant, not their leader.

11. Leopold II.

12. 'Negotiations between Prussia, Holland, and Great Britain . . . resulted in the conclusion of an arrangement (27th July 1790) for the prompt restoration of the Low Countries to Austria, subject to the conditions that "the ancient constitution should be preserved, that a full amnesty and perfect wiping out of all that had happened during the trouble should be accorded, and that the whole arrangement should be made with the guarantee of the three powers named" ' (ibid., i. 412). HW's 'card' refers to Leopold's reaffirmation of the above conditions and the issuance of an ultimatum that expired 21 Nov.: but, as the inhabitants of Brabant refused to capitulate, the Austrian army invaded Brabant, and conquered it early in December (ibid. 413; *St James's Chronicle* 18–20, 27–30 Nov. 1790).

13. Lord William Russell (1767–1840), 3d and posthumous son of Francis, M. of Tavistock (eldest son of 4th D. of Bedford) (*Old Westminsters;* GM 1840, n.s. xiv. 86, 204–5).

14. Lord Stanhope wrote to the secretary of the Revolution Society, 12 Aug. 1790: 'I have received from you a printed paper containing resolutions said to have been passed at the General Meeting of the Revolution Society on July 20, by which it appears that members may be rendered responsible for resolutions of other members, though they may possibly not approve thereof. This appears to me so extremely improper that I judged it right to take my name yesterday out of the list of members. Having taken this step, I think it proper to inform you, as their Secretary, of my reasons. I cannot, however, help expressing at the same time the very great esteem I shall always have for many worthy members of that Society' (Ghita Stanhope and G. P. Gooch, *The Life of Charles third Earl Stanhope*, 1914, p. 97). 'The resignation was due to no change in his political convictions, and was followed by no slackening in his activity' (ibid. 98). In *The St James's Chronicle* 2–4 Nov. 1790 it was said that 'Lord Stanhope, convinced by the powerful argument and brilliant language of Burke, has, it is reported, seceded from the Society against which the shafts of that orator's eloquence have been so pointedly levelled.'

15. See *post* p. 135.

phlet[16] came out this day sennight, and is far superior to what was expected even by his warmest admirers. I have read it twice, and though of 350 pages,[17] I wish I could repeat every page by heart. It is sublime, profound and gay. The wit and satire are equally brilliant, and the whole is wise, though in some points he goes too far—yet in general there is far less want of judgment than could be expected from *him*. If it could be translated, which from the wit and metaphors and allusions is almost impossible, I should think it would be a classic book in all countries, except in *present* France—To their tribunes it speaks daggers, though, unlike them, it uses none. Seven *thousand* copies have been taken off by the booksellers already—and a new edition is preparing. I hope you will see it soon. There ends my gazette.

There is nobody here at present but Mrs Hervey,[18] Mrs E. Hervey[19] and Mrs Cotton[20]—but what did I find on Saturday?—Why the Prince

16. *Reflections on the Revolution in France.* 'Mr Burke ordered Dodsley to send me his book, though I have not seen him three times in three years. Good breeding obliged me to thank him' (HW to Lady Ossory 9 Dec. 1790). HW's letter of thanks is missing.

17. That is, 356, plus four pages of introduction.

18. Expanded by Mary Berry from HW's 'H.' Elizabeth March (b. between 1748 and 1756, d. ?1820), only child of Francis March by Maria, dau. of Hon. George Hamilton, son of 6th E. of Abercorn; half-sister of William Beckford, author of *Vathek* (their mother m., 1st, 24 Aug. 1747, Francis March, and 2d, 8 June 1756, William Beckford, alderman of London); m. (1774) Col. William Thomas Hervey, son of Hon. Thomas Hervey, 3d son of John, 1st E. of Bristol; author of at least four novels, some of which were satirized by her half-brother (Burke, *Peerage*, 1928, p. 55, *sub* Abercorn, and p. 352, *sub* Bristol; *Register Book of Marriages . . . of St George, Hanover Square . . . Vol. I—1725 to 1787,* ed. John

H. Chapman, 1886, pp. 38, 240; N&Q 1927, cliii. 350; HW to Lady Ossory 26 Dec. 1789). For her correspondence and relations with William Beckford, see Lewis Melville, *Life and Letters of William Beckford of Fonthill,* 1910, *passim;* Guy Chapman, *Beckford,* [1937], *passim.*

19. Expanded by Mary Berry from HW's 'H.' Elizabeth Hervey (b. 1730, d. after 1800), only child of Hon. William Hervey, Capt. R. N., 4th son of John, 1st E. of Bristol; cousin by marriage of 'Mrs Hervey,' mentioned above; died unmarried (Collins, *Peerage,* 1812, iv. 153; Burke, *Peerage,* 1937, p. 371, *sub* Bristol). Boswell, in connection with her literary assemblies and Johnson's fondness for her, refers to her as 'Miss E. Hervey' (*Johnson* iii. 436n, where she is confused with Lady Emily Hervey).

20. Possibly Philadelphia Rowley (ca 1763–1855), 1st dau. of Admiral Sir Joshua Rowley, 1st Bt; m. (27 Feb. 1788) Charles Cotton, Capt. R. N., later (1795) Sir Charles, 5th Bt, and (1808) Admiral (GEC; GM 1788, lviii pt i. 178).

of Furstemberg,[21] his son,[22] and son's governor![23]—I was ready to turn about and go back—but they really proved not at all unpleasant. The embassador has not the least German stiffness or hauteur, is extremely civil, and so domestic a man, that he talked comfortably of his wife[24] and eight children,[25] and of his fondness for them. He understands English, though he does not speak it. The son, a good-humoured lad of fifteen, seems well informed; the governor, a middle-aged officer, speaks English so perfectly, that even by his accent I should not have discovered him for a foreigner. They stayed all night, and went to Oxford next morning before I rose.[26]

Today is very fine, and the wind has been favourable these two days for Mrs Damer.

I am out of humour with Miss Foldson;[27] though paid for, she has

21. Joachim Egon (1749–1828), Landgraf of Furstenberg, of the Austrian branch (*Almanach de Gotha*, 1790–1829; Constantin Wurzbach, *Biographisches Lexikon des Kaiserthums Oesterreich*, Wien, 1856–90, v. 17; Peter Joseph Burke, *Royal Register . . . for 1831*, p. 78). He was in England as Leopold II's ambassador-extraordinary to notify George III of Leopold's 'election to be King of the Romans, and his subsequent coronation as Emperor of Germany.'

22. Friedrich Carl Johann Nepomuc Egon (1774–1856), succeeded his father 1828 as Landgraf of Furstenberg; became privy counsellor and master of the ceremonies of the Austrian Court (*Almanach de Gotha*, 1790–1857; Wurzbach, op. cit., v. 16; Burke, loc. cit.).

23. Not identified.

24. Whom he had married in 1772: Sophia Theresa (1751–1835), dau. of Philipp Carl, Count of Oettingen-Wallerstein (*Almanach de Gotha*, 1790–1836; Burke, loc. cit.).

25. For their names see *Almanach de Gotha*, 1800–65; Christian Friedrich Jacobi, *Europaisches genealogisches Handbuch auf das Jahr 1800*, Leipzig, 1800, p. 418.

26. 'The Landgrave of Furstenberg and his son are now on a tour through the kingdom, previous to their return shortly to the Continent' (*St James's Chronicle* 9–11 Nov. 1790). They left for the Continent 2 Dec. (ibid. 30 Nov.–2 Dec. 1790), and were in Paris 14 Dec. (ibid. 18–21 Dec. 1790).

27. Anne Foldsone (b. ca 1770–5, d. 1851), miniaturist, better known by her married name; dau. of John Foldsone, artist and copyist; pupil and protégé of Romney; later patronized by the Prince of Wales; m. (1793) Joseph Mee of Mount Anna, Armagh (Basil S. Long, *British Miniaturists*, 1929, pp. 291–2; *Register of Marriages of St Mary le Bone, Middlesex, 1792–1796*, ed. W. Bruce Bannerman, 1923, p. 32). Before their departure, Mary and Agnes Berry sat to her for their miniature portraits for HW, but he had not received them from her by 11

not yet sent me your pictures; and has twice broken her promise of finishing them.

I have taken a great liberty which I hope Mr B. will forgive, though a breach of trust. Having only a coach myself, and Saturday being very wet, and being afraid of a bad hired chaise, I did allow myself to use his hither—I will do so no more.

I reserve the rest of my paper for, I hope, an answer—O! I do hope so!

Strawberry, 9th, at night.

This morning before I left Park Place I had the relief and joy of receiving your letter of Oct. 24 from Lyons—It would have been still more welcome if dated from Turin; but as you have met with no impediments so far, I trust you got out of France as well as through it. I do hope too that Miss *Agnes* is better, as you say; but when one is very anxious about a person, credulity does not take long strides in proportion. I am not surprised at your finding *voiturins* or anybody or anything dearer:[28] where all credit and all control are swept away, every man will be a tyrant in proportion to his necessities and his strength. Societies were invented to temperate force—but it seems, force was liberty—and much good may [it] do the French with being delivered from everything but violence!—which I believe they will soon taste pro and con—For the impositions on *you* there is a remedy at Charing Cross.[29]

I have received all your five letters; I *have sent three to Turin of 16,* 19, 25 of Oct. and one of Nov. 2 to Florence.[30]

Today's paper says the ratification of the peace with Spain is arrived;[31] the stocks are extremely pleased with it.[32]

Sept. 1791. They were sold SH xxii. 60 to Lord Waldegrave for £4.14.6. That of Mary Berry was engraved by H. Adlard as the frontispiece to MBJ, vol. ii.

28. 'Sunday, 24th [Oct. 1790, at Lyons]— it rained all day. Spoke to two or three different voituriers, all so unreasonable in their demands, asking us nearly the double of what we had formerly paid' (MBJ i. 223).

29. HW had given the Berrys permission to draw on his banker in Charing Cross if they needed money; see *post* 19 March 1791.

30. HW's dates refer to the day of posting each letter; see *ante* 12, 16, 22, 31 Oct. 1790.

31. The Convention between Spain and Great Britain, signed at the Escurial 28 Oct. 1790, reached the office of the Duke of Leeds on Sunday, 7 Nov. 1790. For the text of the agreement, see GM 1790, lx pt ii. 1046, or *St James's Chronicle* 6–9 Nov. 1790.

32. On 4 Nov. a report was read at the Stock Exchange that the Convention with Spain was soon to be signed; 'the stocks

I thought in one of my last that Lord Hervey was in England, but it is only my Lady,[33] as his cousins[34] told me yesterday at P. P.

You make me smile by desiring me to continue my affection—have I so much time left for inconstancy? For threescore years and ten I have not been very fickle in my friendships—in all those years I never found such a pair as you and your sister; should I meet with a superior pair—but then they must not be deficient in any one of the qualities which I found in you two—why perhaps I may change—but with that double mortgage on my affections, I do not think you are in much danger of losing them. You shall have timely notice if a second couple drops out of the clouds and falls in my way.

Nov. 11th.

I had a letter from Mrs Damer at Falmouth: She suffered much by cold and fatigue, and probably sailed on Saturday evening last, and may be at Lisbon by this time, as you, I trust, are in Italy.[35]

Mr Burke's pamphlet has quite turned Dr Price's head; he got upon a table at their club,[36] toasted to our Parl[iament] becoming a National Assembly,[37] and to admitting no more peers of their assembly[38]—having lost the only one[39] they had—They themselves are very like the French *États!*[40] Two more members got on the table (their pulpit) and broke it down—so be it!

rose, at one jump, three per cent' (*St James's Chronicle* 2–4 Nov. 1790). Five-percent annuities quoted 2 Nov. at 111, rose on 4 Nov. to 116, and by 11 Nov. had reached 118¼; other stocks rose in proportion. See *St James's Chronicle* 30 Oct.–2 Nov. to 9–11 Nov. 1790.

33. Elizabeth Drummond (d. 1818), dau. of Colin Drummond of Megginch Castle, co. Perth, and of Quebec; m. (1779) at Quebec, John Augustus Hervey, styled Bn Hervey.

34. Elizabeth Hervey, his first cousin, and Mrs William Thomas Hervey, his first cousin by marriage.

35. On 11 Nov. the Berrys travelled from Reggio to Modena; see MBJ i. 243–4.

36. The Revolution Society.

37. For Dr Price's explanation of his toast to 'the Parliament of Britain—may it

become a National Assembly,' see his *Discourse on the Love of Our Country, Delivered on Nov. 4, 1789,* 4th edn, 1790, Appendix, pp. 42–4.

38. 'The Revolution Society met to dine at the London Tavern on Thursday last [4 Nov.,] in spite of Mr Burke's pamphlet; but should the secession of next year prove equal to that of the present, they will in all probability fix on a much smaller room— and a place of less public notoriety. Mr (no longer Dr) Price was called to the chair, and some curious motions and toasts were produced in consequence of the galling remarks of the celebrated orator' (*St James's Chronicle* 4–6 Nov. 1790).

39. Lord Stanhope.

40. Probably a reference to Mary Berry's description of the noise and bustle in the National Assembly; see *ante* 31 Oct. 1790.

The Marquisate is just where it was—to be and not to be—Duchess Argyll is said to be worse. Della Crusca[41] has published a poem called *The Laurel of Liberty*,[42] which like the *Enragés*[43] has confounded and overturned all ideas—there are *gossamery tears* and *silky oceans*—the first time to be sure that anybody ever *cried cobwebs*, or that the *sea* was made of *paduasoy*.[44] There is besides a violent tirade against a considerable personage,[45] who it is supposed the author was jealous of as too much favoured a few years ago by a certain Countess.[46] You may guess why I am not more explicit—for the same reason I beg you not to mention it at all: it would be exceedingly improper.

As the Parl[iament] will meet in a fortnight and the town be plumper, my letters may grow more amusing, though, unless the weather grows worse, I shall not contribute my leanness to its *embonpoint*.[47] Adieu!

41. Robert Merry (1755–98), who signed himself 'Della Crusca' in a series of verses contributed to *The World*, 1787–9. A member of the Della Cruscan Academy, he was at Florence 1784–7, where he contributed flowery verses to miscellanies published by the English there.

42. HW read Mrs Hervey's copy at Park Place; see his letter to Jerningham 10 Nov. 1790.

43. Or 'Blancs,' the extreme democrats or left wing of the National Assembly (Ludovic Lalanne, *Dictionnaire historique de la France*, 1872). 'The violent democrats, who have the reputation of being so much republican in principle, that they do not admit any political necessity for having even the name of a king, are called the *enragés*' (Arthur Young, *Travels in France*, sub 10 Jan. 1790; cf. *idem*, *Voyages en France*, ed. Henri Sée, 1931, i. 465, n. 2).

44. It appears from *The Gazetteer and New Daily Advertiser* 3 Feb. 1791 that Merry's phrases attracted general attention. Under the heading, 'New phrases, alliterative and otherwise, by Della Crusca,' the following are listed: 'Radiant rivers, majestic mountains, summer seas, blissful blessings, dauntless days, sable showers, lettered lightnings, moody monarchs, mingling murders, horrid heads . . . Lawny vales,

gleamy meteors, streamy warblings, paly shrouds, pearly panoplies, lightless crowds, tissued rays, gauzy zephyrs, filmy rains, and gossamery tears.'

45. Leopold II, Grand Duke of Tuscany 1765–90, and Holy Roman Emperor 1790–2.

46. The Countess Cowper: Hannah Anne Gore (ca 1758–1826), dau. of Charles Gore of Horkestowe, Lincs; m. (1775) George Nassau Clavering-Cowper, 3d E. Cowper. According to Sir Nathaniel William Wraxall, she was 'distinguished by his [Leopold's] attachment, and the exertion of his interest with Joseph II, his brother, procured her husband, Earl Cowper, to be created soon afterwards [31 Jan. 1778] a Prince of the German [Holy Roman] Empire' (*Memoirs*, ed. Henry B. Wheatley, 1884, i. 195). Mrs Piozzi's note on this passage is: 'She was beautiful when no longer a court favourite, in 1786. Her attachment was then to Mr Merry, the highly accomplished poet, known afterwards by name of Della Crusca' (*Autobiography*, ed. A. Hayward, 2d edn, 1861, ii. 93, quoted in Wraxall, loc. cit. See also the *Autobiography*, ii. 198, and DNB, *sub* Merry, Robert.

47. HW remained at SH, except for occasional visits to London on business, until 14 Jan. 1791 (*post* 15 Jan. 1791).

To Barbara Cecilia Seton, Saturday
13 November 1790

Address: To Miss Seton at Caversham Hill near Reading, Berks.
Postmark: [I]SLEWOR[TH] 13 NO 90.

Miss Seton was doubtless visiting the Lovedays. John Loveday (1711–89) of Caversham married (1756), as his third wife, Penelope Forrest (d. 1801), dau. of Arthur Forrest of Jamaica, and cousin of Miss Seton's (and the Berrys') grandmother, by whom he had four children. Mary Berry wrote in her 'Notes of Early Life': 'In 1774 my grandmother [Mrs John Seton] took us to visit at Mr Loveday's at Caversham near Reading, an old Tory country gentleman who had married a cousin of hers, and had two [*sic*] daughters much about our age: with them we formed an intimacy which lasted till their death thirty or forty years afterwards. The intimacy gave me occasion to learn in several visits to them afterwards, and when I was able to observe it, the character of Tory country gentlemen of those days, or rather of days before, and the sample I saw was certainly a rare and most respectable one' (MBJ i. 8–9). The estate at Caversham descended to Loveday's son by his first marriage, John Loveday (1742–1809), who sold it (DNB, *sub* Loveday, John), but presumably the elder Loveday's widow and children were living there in 1790, and possibly until Mrs Loveday's death in 1801.

Strawberry Hill, Nov. 13, 1790.

Dear Madam,

I RECEIVED a letter last night from Chamberry, where our dear friends were safely arrived.[1] They were a little troubled in the last village in France,[2] and had their trunks ransacked with some insolence; but that was all. Thank God! they are out of that distracted country! You probably have heard from them too; but I would not risk your not knowing it as soon as I could inform you of it—and now we have nothing to apprehend. I am with great regard, Madam,

Your most obedient humble servant,

Hor. Walpole

1. The Berrys arrived at Chambéry 26 and left 28 Oct. 1790 (MBJ i. 224–5).
2. Bourgoin, near which Rousseau lived 1768–70 and wrote his *Confessions;* see following letter. Chambéry was not occupied by the French until 1792.

To Mary Berry, Saturday 13 November 1790

Address: À Mademoiselle Mademoiselle Berry à la poste restante à Florence, Italie. *Postmark:* FIR[ENZE.] Endorsed: 'Pd 1s.'
Posted 16 Nov. ('Visitors').

Strawberry Hill, Nov. 13, 1790.[1]

No. 7.

OH! yes, yes, Chamberry is more welcome than Turin, though I thought nothing could make me so happy as a letter from the latter—but Chamberry is nearer, and has made me easy sooner. What a melancholy forlorn object did I think that antique capital of a dismal duchy formerly! It looked like a wife who had been deserted by her husband for many years and kept at his old mansion in Westmorland,[2] while he was living with an actress in London—now I am surprised the King of Sardinia[3] does not return to that delightful spot, which appears to me like the palace of the sun diffusing light and warmth even to the northern islands—with what anxiety did I read your letter while you were in the hands of the savages at Burgoin![4] I

1. 'No. 22' (B).
2. 'Westmorland' suggests that HW had in mind Lord Lonsdale, whose estate was there, and who was separated from his wife.
3. Victor Amadeus III (1726–96), King of Sardinia and Duke of Savoy 1773–96; forced to relinquish Savoy to France, 1796. The Berrys saw him returning from the hunt 3 Nov. 1790, 'a very gentlemanlike old man, easy and dignified in his manner' (MBJ i. 238).
4. 'Monday, 25th [Oct. 1790] . . . Slept at Bourgoin, a poor little town. Tuesday, 26th.—The postilion, in leaving Bourgoin, stopped us at a *corps de garde nationale,* where our *passeport* was demanded, which was one from the French Ambassador in London, which had been signed by the Mayor at Lyons. Our carriage was immediately surrounded by a number of people without uniforms or anything else to distinguish them, who, whilst they were examining our *passeport* and asking eagerly if we were French people, told us they

must search our trunks "pas pour la contrebande, mais pour des papiers." This wise demand, an officer of the regular troops told us, there was no avoiding; when he went into the guardroom with us he told us he saw all the folly, and wished he could prevent what they were doing, but did not dare, for fear they should fall upon him, or complain he did not do his duty. Two or three of them immediately mounted upon the back of the carriage and began rummaging over everything in the large trunk behind, where, certainly, if we had been *conspirators,* it would have been mighty likely we should put our *papers!* One of them—a saucy lad who called himself a corporal, and was foremost in turning everything *dessus dessous*—when I asked him if he was content, replied in the most impertinent manner, "Non, je ne suis pas content, et ne parlez pas tant vous, cela ne vous fera aucun bien." Another of them, observing something sticking out of our courier's pocket, came behind him and took

figured them with scalping knives and setting up a war-whoop!—but you are all safe—and I shall not have another panic till you are returning, which I hope will not be through European Abyssinia, that land of hyenas! Pray, burn all my letters;[5] I trembled when they were ransacking your trunks, lest they should meet with any of them; for though I was very cautious while you were in France, I was afraid that my eagerness to learn your arrival at Turin, might be misinterpreted, though meaning nothing but impatience to know you out of France, into which I hope you will never set your feet more, but return home through Swisserland and Flanders, which I conclude will be resettled shortly. At any rate, I insist on your burning this, that you may not forget it and have it in your trunk. I was the more alarmed, as I have lately heard[6] that Lord Bruce[7] and Mr Lock,[8] whom Miss Agnes has rivalled, riding out in Languedoc, escorted by two national guards, and the former spitting, the wind carried the

---

them out; they happened to be bills of the hotel at Lyons, which I hope relieved the fears of the *patriot*. Upon the officers coming out again, and telling them that our *passeport* was a perfectly good one, that they saw, or rather *heard,* we were English, and that having searched our trunk they need not look farther, we were allowed to proceed; the officer having put upon our *passeport* "vu et fouillé," which he said would prevent our being searched again at the Pont de Beauvoisin. I really began to dread being searched at every village. No such thing, however, happened; and at the Pont, our *passeport* was only shown to the commandant, and no further trouble given us about *papers;* our trunks and imperial were just opened at the douane' (MBJ i. 223–4).

5. They burned none of them.

6. Probably from Dr Charles Burney (1726–1814), whom HW had invited to SH for 10 or 11 Nov. to discuss matters relating

to the will of Jacob Colomb, Fanny Burney's deceased manservant; see HW to Fanny Burney 3 Nov. 1790. The Burneys were intimate friends of the William Locks, parents of the Mr Lock mentioned later in the sentence.

7. 'The present Marquis of Ailesbury' (B). Charles Brudenell-Bruce (1773–1856), styled Lord Bruce; 2d E. of Ailesbury, 1814; cr. (1821) M. of Ailesbury. He was much abroad in the 1790's: he was married at Florence in 1793, and was presented at Court in 1795 'on his arrival from France' (*London Chronicle* 1–3 Dec. 1795, lxxviii. 536).

8. He went abroad in the autumn of 1789, and did not return to England until about a year and a half later. 'We know nothing of William Lock's travels except an incident recorded by Horace Walpole' in this letter (Vittoria Colonna Caetani, Duchessa di Sermoneta, *The Locks of Norbury,* [1940] pp. 45, 49).

spittle on one of those heroes, on which they seized our countrymen and imprisoned them all night in a sentry-box, for imprisonment is the characteristic of liberty, and when all men are equal, accidents are punished, as only crimes used to be; which makes it delicious to live in a state of nature! I am so relieved by your letter, that I do not believe I shall be uneasy about *you* again this—month—about Miss Agnes, yes, unless I hear she is as well as if every day was a Chamberry day—by the way, you affront my dear city, by calling it *a dirty place*[9]—so far from that, it is smug, beautiful, *sublimibus alta columnis*,[10] and deserves to be the metropolis of Europe. You must have been charmed at the Comédie[11]—I was, though not there, and prefer Mlle (what is her name?)[12] to the Sainval.[13] In short, I am so content, that I shall not inquire any more about the foreign post,[14] nor care whether you write to me or not—at least, pray don't plague me with long letters the moment you arrive anywhere fatigued and cold— seriously, I do beg you not to write long letters—let me chatter to you as much as I will. My mind is at peace, which it has not been at all since the first moment you talked of passing through France, and I was

9. 'I walked all over the town of Chambéry with my father, over the shoes in mud' (MBJ i. 225).

10. 'Regia Solis erat sublimibus alta columnis' (Ovid, *Met.* ii. 1).

11. 'In the evening, walked through the mud to the theatre; it would have held Drury Lane within it. There was a large box in the middle for the court, but so empty a theatre I think I never saw: there might be about thirty people in the pit, not near a dozen in the boxes, including ourselves, and yet we had *Les deux nièces* and *L'Amant bourru*, very tolerably acted; and a very tolerable orchestra, composed, I fancy, of the band of the regiment. In the next box to us sat a French *cordon-bleu*, and another gentleman, with whom I had some conversation. I found he was an officer in the French Garde du Corps, and had escaped from Paris after the memorable days of October last. He said he had been at Chambéry ever since, and that it was wonderful the number of French scattered all over Savoy and Piedmont' (MBJ i. 225).

12. Mary Berry does not mention the name in MBJ.

13. At Lyons 23 Oct. 1790 the Berrys went 'in the evening to the play, where Mlle St Val happens to be acting for a few nights. She pleased me much, though in an uninteresting character in Crébillon's *Rhadamiste et Zénobie*. She has a charming tone of voice, speaks well, without either ranting or affectation; her figure and face not remarkable—*ni en bien, ni en mal*' (MBJ i. 222–3). There were two sisters known as Mlles St Val *aînée* and *cadette*, whose real names were Marie-Pauline Alziary de Roquefort (1743–1830) and Marie-Blanche Alziary de Roquefort (1752–1836); both were *tragédiennes* and both had acted earlier in their careers at Lyon (Pierre Grosclaude, *La Vie intellectuelle à Lyon*, 1933, pp. 239, 250). The elder, banished from the Paris stage 1779–89 after her quarrel with Mme Vestris, was very popular in the provinces; the younger seems to have acted with more general acclaim and in 1790 was a favourite at Paris. The identity of the actress the Berrys saw therefore remains uncertain. For their portraits and accounts of their lives, see Jules Belleudy, *La Grande querelle de trois tragédiennes provençales*, Marseille, 1933; *Annales dramatiques, ou dictionnaire général des théâtres*, 1808–12, viii. 231–2.

14. That is, its arrival in London.

not the happiest man in the world from the day Mr Batt told me of your intention of going abroad. After both, came the storm the day you sailed! Chamberry has made amends for a good deal—and I will pass a few—oh! I fear more than a *few* months contentedly—but then there is to come a journey back—not through France, I hope—the sea to cross, which I shall not leave out of my reckoning a second time! All may be forgotten, if I see you next autumn at Clivden, at *your own* Clivden, alias, little Chamberry.

I know nothing, nothing at all; but I go to town tomorrow for two days, and may pick up something—but I could not help indulging my joy by writing this against Tuesday's post, though I wrote but yesterday—for the future I will not be so intemperate. I have sent a line from Chamberry to Miss Seton,[15] and shall dispatch another by the first packet to Lisbon,[16] for I am not so very particular; others can be anxious about you as well as I.

Berkeley Square—for now you are clear of the Abyssinians,[17] no place is afraid of signing its own name—Tuesday 15th.

I might as well be in a country village; you will not be a tittle the wiser for my being in London, which is still a solitude. I have not heard a syllable of news: I supped at Miss Farren's[18] last night. There were only Lord Derby[19] and Lady Milner;[20] the latter produced a letter from her sister-in-law Mrs Sturt,[21] where Lord Blandford is and

15. That is, the preceding letter.
16. To Mrs Damer; missing.
17. The French.
18. 'Afterwards Countess of Derby' (B). She lived in Green Street, Grosvenor Square (*London Chronicle* 29 Nov.—1 Dec. 1796, lxxx. 526).
19. Edward Smith-Stanley (1752–1834), 12th E. of Derby, m. (1774) Elizabeth Hamilton (1753–97), dau. of James, 6th D. of Hamilton, by Elizabeth Gunning (later Duchess of Argyll). When she was involved in an intrigue with the Duke of Dorset in 1778, Lord Derby refused to divorce her, but after her death 14 March 1797 he married, 1 May 1797, Miss Farren, to whom he had been attached for several years. At John Philip Kemble's 24 Dec. 1789, Boswell found 'Lord Derby . . . very pleasant. The attachment between him and Miss Farren was, I really thought, as fine a thing as I had ever seen: truly virtuous admiration

on his part, respect on hers' (*Boswell Papers* xviii. 13).
20. '—— Sturt, married to Sir William Milner of Nunappleton in Yorkshire' (B). Diana Sturt (d. 1805), 1st dau. of Humphrey Sturt, of More Crichel, Dorset, m. (1776) Sir William Mordaunt Milner, 3d Bt, of Nun Appleton Hall, Yorks. Miss Farren had been her guest in Yorkshire in Aug. 1789; see *ante* 4 Sept. 1789, n. 13.
21. Mary Woodcock, daughter of the Rev. Edward Woodcock, vicar of Watford, Herts, and rector of the united parishes of St Michael, Wood Street, and St Mary Steyning, in London; m. (1781) Lady Milner's eldest brother, Humphrey Ashley Sturt, whose father, because of this marriage, settled his unentailed estates on his second son. On the death of his father in 1786, Humphrey Ashley Sturt inherited the estate at Horton, Dorset, where Lord Blandford, presumably, was visiting him;

has been these three months; she says he has heard of his pretended letter, laughs at it, and protests it is not his, nor is there the least foundation for it.

Mrs Damer did not sail so soon as she expected; at least the wind was contrary both on the Saturday and Sunday;[22] but it has been favourable since, and I hope she is at Chamberry—pho! I mean, Lisbon.

If I learn nothing before tomorrow morning, when I shall return to Strawberry, I shall let this amble to Florence without a word more. Adieu!

To Mary Berry, Thursday 18 November 1790

Address: À Mademoiselle Mademoiselle Berry à la poste restante à Florence, Italie. Par Paris. [Forwarded: 'à Pisa.']
Postmark: 19 NO 90. ANGLETERRE. FIRENZE.
Posted 19 Nov. ('Visitors').

Str[awberry Hill], Thursday, Nov. 18, 1790.[1]
No. 8.

ON Tuesday morning after my letter was gone to the post, I received yours of the 2nd (as I have all the rest) from Turin[2]—and it gave me very little of the joy I had so much meditated to receive from a letter thence—and why did not it! because I had got one on Saturday, which anticipated and augmented all the satisfaction I had allotted for Turin. You will find my Tuesday's letter, if ever you receive it, intoxicated with Chamberry, for which and all your kind punctuality I give you a million of thanks—but how cruel to find that you found none of my letters at Turin![3] There ought to have

sold the estate in 1793, and later was of Barking Hall, Suffolk (Burke, *Peerage*, 1928, *sub* Alington; John Hutchins, *History . . . of Dorset*, 1861–70, iii. 148–9; GM 1792, lxii pt i. 580).

22. 6 and 7 Nov.; she probably sailed from Falmouth 8 Nov. and arrived at Lisbon after a passage of seven days (Percy Noble, *Anne Seymour Damer*, 1908, p. 119).

———

1. 'No. 23' (B).
2. The Berrys arrived there 1 Nov. (MBJ i. 228).
3. After having difficulty in finding lodg-

ings at Turin, the Berrys 'had the much greater annoyance of being disappointed of the letters we expected, and for which we sent in vain to the post and to the banker's. I cannot describe, and I am sure I do not wish anybody to experience, the regret and discomfort we felt. We had desired everybody to direct to us at Turin, and expected a large bundle of letters, but having foolishly forgotten to desire our friends to put *par Paris* on the address, they had all gone round by Germany, and we had arrived before them. This the banker told us the next morning, and comforted us as to the safety

been two at least, of Oct. 16 and 19th.[4]—I have since directed two[5] thither, of the 25th[6] and two to Florence of Nov. 2nd and 11th[7] besides Tuesday's of the 16th[8]—but alas! from ignorance there was *par Paris* on none of them, and the Lord knows at how many little German courts they may have been baiting!—I shall put *par Paris* on this, but beg you will tell me as soon as you can which route is the shortest and the safest, that is, by which you are most likely to receive them. You do me justice in concluding there has been no negligence of mine in the case; indeed I have been ashamed of the multiplicity of my letters, when I had scarce anything to tell you but my own anxiety to hear of your being quietly settled at Florence, out of the reach of all commotions—and how could I but dread your being molested by some accident in the present state of France, and how could your healths mend in bad inns, and till you can repose somewhere? Repose you will have at Florence, but I shall fear the winter for you there: I suffered more by cold there[9] than by any place in my life, and never came home at night without a pain in my breast, which I never felt elsewhere, yet then I was very young and in perfect health[10] —if either of you suffer there in any shape, I hope you will retire to Pisa.[11]

My inquietude, that presented so many alarms to me before you set out, has I find and am grieved for it, not been quite in the wrong —Some inconveniencies I am persuaded you have sunk—yet the difficulty of landing at Dieppe and the ransack of your poor harmless trunks at Burgoin, and the wretched lodgings with which you were forced to take up at Turin,[12] count deeply with me—and I had much

of our letters, but still we must wait for them a cruel time' (MBJ i. 229).

4. *Ante* 12, 16 Oct. 1790.

5. HW first wrote 'one,' which is correct; cf. 'Visitors.'

6. *Ante* 22 Oct. 1790.

7. *Ante* 31 Oct., 8 Nov. 1790.

8. *Ante* 13 Nov. 1790.

9. In 1740–1.

10. Writing to West from Siena 22 March 1740, HW says: 'In Italy they seem to have found out how hot their climate is, but not how cold; for there are scarce any chimneys, and most of the apartments painted in fresco; so that one has the additional horror of freezing with imaginary marble.'

11. The Berrys arrived in Florence 14

Nov., and left for Pisa 11 Dec. 1790 (MBJ i. 245, 255; see also *post* 2 Jan. 1791).

12. 'When we got to Turin [1 Nov.], we went first to the Auberge Royale, which was quite full; then to the Armes d'Angleterre, the next best hotel. Here they showed us two rooms only, very bad accommodation for which they asked ten livres a day. Thought we should do better at La Bonne Femme, and found all full there, and returned to the Armes d'Angleterre, but were stopped from driving into the court: a gentleman had in the meantime taken the rooms. We were now at a loss what to do. I knew of no other hotels in Turin; the people mentioned an Hôtel de Provence, a vile place which my father went to look at, and which luckily was quite full. In the

rather have lost all credit as a prophet, since I could not prevent your journey. May it answer for your healths! I doubt it will not in any other respect,[13] as you have already found by the *voiturins*—in point of pleasure—is it possible to divest myself so radically of all self-love, as to wish you may find Italy as agreeable as you did formerly? In all other lights I do most fervently hope there will be no drawbacks on your plan. Should you be disappointed any way, you know what a warm heart is open to receive you back, and so will *your own* Cliveden be too.

I am glad you met the Bishop of Arras,[14] and am much pleased that he remembers me. I saw him very frequently at my dear old friend's,[15] and liked him the best of all the Frenchmen I ever knew.[16] He is extremely sensible, easy, lively, and void of prejudices. Should he fall in your way again, I beg you will tell him how sincere a regard I have for him. He lived in the strictest union with his brother the Archbishop of Tours,[17] whom I was much less acquainted with, nor know if he be living.

I have heard nothing since my Tuesday's letter. As I still hope its predecessors will reach you, I will not repeat the trifling scraps of news I have sent you in them. In fact this is only a trial whether *par Paris* is a better passport than a direction without it; but I am grievously sorry to find difficulty of correspondence superadded to the vexation of losing you. Writing to you was grown my chief occupation—I wish Europe and its broils were in the East Indies, if they embarrass us quiet folks who have nothing to do with their squabbles.

meantime the voiturier and a civil coffee-house man proposed our going to the Dogana Vecchia, an auberge I had never even heard of; thither we went, and found room enough, but not a bit better accommodated than we should have been in one of the smallest towns in Italy—common brick floors, doors and windows that would not shut, dishes full of oil and garlic, etc.' (MBJ i. 228–9).

13. That is, for economy; the Berrys had found the cost of travel almost twice as much as it had been five years earlier (MBJ i. 223, 225).

14. Louis-François-Marc-Hilaire de Conzié (1732–1804), Bishop of Saint-Omer 1766–9, and of Arras 1769–90; see DU DEFFAND *passim*. Forced to flee to England in 1792, he busied himself until his death (in England) with various counter-revolutionary schemes.

15. Mme du Deffand's.

16. HW may be carried away by the enthusiasm of the moment; he thought very highly of the Duc de Nivernais as well.

17. Joachim-François-Mamert de Conzié (1736–95), Bp of Saint-Omer 1769–74, Abp of Tours 1774–90 (DU DEFFAND *passim*).

The Duchess of Gloucester, who called on me yesterday, charged me to give her compliments to you both.

Miss Foldson has not yet sent me your pictures: I was in town on Monday and sent to reproach her with having twice broken her promise: her mother[18] told my servant that Miss was at Windsor drawing the Queen and Princesses[19]—That is not the work of a moment—I am glad *all* the Princes are not on the spot.[20] The Charming Man passed Tuesday here and part of yesterday, and I carried him back to Lady Mount Edgcumbe—today he goes to Park Place and thence to Nuneham. Old Brutus[21] was at the point of death the night before last; I have not heard of her since.

I think of continuing here till the weather grows very bad,[22] which it has not been at all yet, though not equal to what I am rejoiced you have found. I have no Somerset or Audley Street[23] to receive me; Mrs Damer is gone too; the Conways remain at Park Place till after Christmas: it is entirely out of fashion for women to grow old and stay at home in an evening—They invite you indeed now and then, but do not expect to see you till midnight, which is rather too late to

18. Elizabeth ——, m. John Foldsone, painter, at whose death ca 1783–4 she was left with a considerable family. She was living 23 April 1793, on which date she gave her consent to the marriage of her daughter, Amelia, a minor (*Registers of Marriages of St Mary le Bone, Middlesex, 1792–1796*, ed. W. Bruce Bannerman, 1923, p. 31).

19. Queen Charlotte had six daughters. 'The royal collection of miniatures at Windsor Castle comprises one of Queen Charlotte which is believed on stylistic grounds to be by Mrs Mee, though it is unsigned. It is No. 143. There is also one of Princess Sophia . . . and one of Princess Charlotte (the Regent's daughter), but this latter would be of later date than 1790. Possibly at one time there was a complete set of miniatures of Queen Charlotte and her daughters by Mrs Mee; but whether this was so or not (and I know of no evidence that it was) these are all that remain' (information supplied by Mr Owen F. Morshead, 5 June 1940).

20. There were seven of them: 1) the Prince of Wales, later George IV; 2) Frederick Augustus, D. of York and Albany; 3) William Henry, D. of Clarence, later William IV; 4) Edward Augustus (1767–1820), cr. D. of Kent, 1799; father of Queen Victoria; 5) Ernest Augustus (1771–1851), cr. D. of Cumberland, 1799; K. of Hanover and D. of Brunswick-Luneburg, 1837; 6) Augustus Frederick (1773–1843), cr. D. of Sussex, 1801; 7) Adolphus Frederick (1774–1850), cr. D. of Cambridge, 1801. Only the first three were in England: Prince Edward was at Gibraltar, and the three youngest were at the University of Göttingen (DNB; *St James's Chronicle* 7–9 Dec. 1790; *London Chronicle* 13–16 Nov. 1790, lxviii. 474).

21. Mrs Katherine French.

22. Except for occasional visits to London, HW remained at SH until 14 Jan. 1791 (*post* 15 Jan. 1791).

23. The Berrys formerly lived in Somerset Street, and at this time had a house in North Audley Street.

begin the day, unless one was born but twenty years ago. I do not
condemn any fashions, which the young ought to set, for the old certainly ought not; but an oak that has been going on in its old way
for an hundred years, cannot shoot into a Maypole in three years,
because it is the mode to plant Lombardy poplars.[24] What I should
have suffered, if *your* letters like mine had wandered through Germany! I, you was sure had written, and was in no danger. Dr Price,
who had whetted his ancient talons last year to no purpose,[25] has had
them all drawn by Burke,[26] and the Revolution Club is as much exploded as the Cock Lane Ghost:[27] but you, in order to pass a quiet
winter in Italy, *would* pass through a fiery furnace. Fortunately you
have not been singed, and the letter from Chamberry has composed
all my panics, but has by no means convinced me that I was not perfectly in the right to endeavour to keep you at home. One does not
put one's hand in the fire to burn off a hangnail; and though health
is delightful, neither of you were out of order enough to make a rash
experiment. I would not be so absurd as to revert to old arguments,
that happily proved no prophecies, if my great anxiety about you did
not wish in time to persuade you to return through Swisserland and
Flanders, if the latter is pacified and France is not, of which I see no
likelihood. Pray forgive me, if parts of my letters are sometimes tiresome—but can I appear only and always cheerful, when you two are
absent, and have another long journey to make, ay, and the sea to
cross again? My fears cannot go to sleep like a *paroli* at faro till there
is a new deal,[28] in which even then I should not be sure of winning—

24. According to Mary Berry, 'the first
poplar pine (or, as they have since been
called, Lombardy poplar) planted in England is that at Park Place, on the bank
of the river near the great arch. It was a
cutting brought from Turin by the late
Lord Rochford in his carriage, and planted
by General Conway's own hand' (note on
HW to Conway 25 Dec. 1770, in HW's
Works v. 142).

25. In his *Discourse on the Love of Our
Country, Delivered on Nov. 4, 1789;* see
ante 23 July 1790, n. 8.

26. In his *Reflections on the Revolution
in France.*

27. Elizabeth Parsons (1749–1807), daughter of the deputy parish clerk of St Sepul-
chre's, London, made the noises supposed
to proceed from the ghost; the hoax was detected in 1762. See Montagu ii. 6–7; HW to
Mann 29 Jan., 25 Feb., and 22 March 1762.

28. Paroli: 'In faro and similar card
games, the leaving of the money staked and
the money won as a further stake; the stak-
ing of double the sum before staked' (OED).
After making a paroli, which the player did
by turning up a corner of a card, apparently he had no further part in the hand
(Montagu ii. 50).

If I see you again, I will think I have gained another *milleleva* as I literally once did,[29] with this exception—that I was vehemently against risking a doit at the game of travelling. Adieu!

To MARY and AGNES BERRY, Friday 26 November 1790

Address: À Mademoiselle Mademoiselle Berry à la poste restante à Florence, Italie. ['Par Paris' heavily scored through, evidently not by HW; see first paragraph of this letter. Forwarded: 'Pisa.'] Endorsed: 'Pd 1s.'
Postmark: FIRENZE.
Unexplained memorandum on cover in HW's hand: 14

$$2\frac{1}{2}$$
$$2$$

$$18\frac{1}{2}$$

Posted 29 Nov. ('Visitors').

Strawberry Hill, Friday night, Nov. 27 [26], 1790.[1]

No. 9.

I AM waiting for a letter from[2] Florence, not with perfect patience, though I could barely have one, even if you did arrive as you intended on the 12th[3]—but twenty temptations might have occurred to detain you in that land of eye- and ear-sight. My chief eagerness is to learn that you have received at least some of my letters. I wish too to know, though I cannot yet, whether you would have me direct *par Paris,* or as I did before. In this state of uncertainty I did not prepare this to depart this morning; nor, though the Parliament met yesterday, have I a syllable of news for you, as there will be no debate till all the members have been sworn, which takes two or three days.[4] Moreover I am still here; the weather though very rainy is quite

29. 'I truly and seriously this winter won and was paid a *milleleva* at faro; literally received a thousand and twenty-three sixpences for one' (HW to Mann 14 July 1748). See also HW to Bentley 27 March 1755.

———

1. 'No. 24' (B).

2. MS reads 'for.'
3. They arrived at Florence 14 Nov. (MBJ i. 245).
4. The only business transacted on the opening day, 25 Nov., was the re-election of Henry Addington (cr. Vct Sidmouth, 1805) as Speaker of the House of Commons. See GM 1790, lx pt ii. 1048.

warm, and I have much more agreeable society at Richmond with small companies and better hours, than in town, and shall have till after Christmas, unless great cold drives me thither. Lady Di,[5] Selwyn,[6] the Penns,[7] the Onslows,[8] Douglases,[9] Mackinsys, Keenes,[10] Lady Mt Edgcumbe all stay, and some of them meet every evening. The Boufflerses[11] too are constantly invited, and the Comtesse Emilie sometimes carries her harp, on which they say she plays better than Orpheus; but as I never heard him on earth, nor *chez* Proserpine, I do not pretend to decide. Lord Fitzwilliam has been here too, but was in the utmost danger of being lost on Saturday night in a violent storm between Calais and Dover, as the captain confessed to him when they were landed—do you think I did not ache at the recollection of a certain Tuesday when you were sailing to Dieppe!

5. Lady Diana Beauclerk, who had recently moved from Little Marble Hill, Twickenham, to Devonshire Cottage, Richmond, her residence until her death. Devonshire Cottage, now pulled down, 'stood on the site of the Wilderness Club; it overlooked Petersham meadow and had a beautiful view of the river' (Mrs Steuart Erskine, *Lady Diana Beauclerk*, 1903, p. 191).

6. He remained at Richmond until a few days before Christmas (*Gazetteer and New Daily Advertiser* 27 Jan. 1791).

7. Lady Juliana and her daughter Sophia Margaret.

8. George Onslow (1731–1814), 4th Bn Onslow, cr. (1801) E. Onslow; comptroller of the Household 1777–9; treasurer of the Household 1779–80; a lord of the Bedchamber 1780–1814; m. (1753) Henrietta Shelley (1730–1809), dau. of Sir John Shelley, 4th Bt.

9. Archibald James Edward Douglas (formerly Stewart) (1748–1827), cr. (8 July 1790) Bn Douglas of Douglas; younger son of Sir John Stewart, 3d Bt, by Lady Jane Douglas, dau. of James Douglas, 2d M. of Douglas; the successful claimant in the famous 'Douglas cause,' 1762–9; m. (1783) as 2d wife, Lady Frances Scott (1750–1817), sister of Henry Scott, 3d D. of Buccleuch. For mention of Lady Douglas's unpublished literary works, see *Letters of Lady Louisa Stuart to Miss Louisa Clinton*, 2d ser., ed. Hon.

James A. Home, Edinburgh, 1903, pp. 199–200.

10. Whitshed Keene (ca 1732–1822), born in Ireland; in the army until 1768 (Capt., 5th Reg. of Foot, Ireland, 1759; Maj. 1762–8); M.P. for fifty years: Wareham 1768–74; Ludgershall 1774, Montgomery 1774–1818; appointed a commissioner for trade and plantations, 1774; surveyor-general of works, 1779; a commissioner of the Admiralty, 1783. He m. (1771) Hon. Elizabeth Legge (ca 1732–1801), youngest dau. of George, Vct Lewisham (eldest son of 1st E. of Dartmouth, whom he predeceased). Daniel Lysons mentions Keene's 'elegant villa' at Richmond (*Environs of London*, 1792–6, i. 444), and Anthony Morris Storer comments on the 'alterations and improvements' he was making in his 'most delightful villa at Richmond' in 1786 (*Journal and Correspondence of William Lord Auckland*, ed. Robert John Eden, 3d Bn Auckland, 1861–2, i. 385; GM 1822, xcii pt i. 278; GM 1801, lxxi pt ii. 1157; DU DEFFAND *passim*; GM 1771, xli. 377; *Army Lists*; Sylvester Douglas, Bn Glenbervie, *Diaries*, ed. Francis Bickley, 1928, i. 6–7 *et passim*; Lysons, *Supplement to the . . . Environs of London*, 1811, p. 71; 'Mem. 1783–91,' *sub* March 1784).

11. Madame de Boufflers and Comtesse Amélie de Boufflers.

Mr Cambridge[12] sent me notice yesterday that he and his daughter[13] have let your house very favourably for *five*[14] months—will you forgive me when I own I was glad it was for no longer? His Parnassian vein is opened again—it is full moon.[15]

Sunday 28. Particularly to Miss *Agnes*.

Though I write to both at once, and reckon your letters to come equally from both, yet I delight in seeing your hand with a pen as well as with a pencil, and you express yourself as well with the one as with the other. Your part in that which I have been so happy as to receive this moment,[16] has singularly obliged me, by your having saved me the terror of knowing you had a torrent to cross after heavy rain.[17] No cat is so afraid of water for herself, as I am grown to be for you. That panic which will last for many months, adds to my fervent desire of your returning early in the autumn, that you may have neither fresh water nor the *silky* ocean[18] to cross in winter. Precious as our insular situation is, I am ready to wish with the Frenchman that you could somehow or other get to it by land, '*Oui, c'est une île toujours, je le sais bien; mais par exemple en allant d'alentour, n'y aurait-il pas moyen d'y arriver par terre?*' I was delighted too to hear yesterday from Mr C. from your sister's letter, that *you* have recovered your healthy looks—pray bring them back with you. Your house is let for *six* months, and at seven guineas a week. This and the rest is to both, and in answer.

Correggio never pleased me in proportion to his fame; his grace touches upon grimace: the mouth of the beautiful angel at Parma curls up almost into a half-moon[19]—still I prefer Correggio to the

---

12. Expanded by Mary Berry from HW's 'C.'

13. Charlotte.

14. HW says 'six' in the following paragraph.

15. A sarcastic reference to the quality of Cambridge's verse.

16. Written from Bologna; see following paragraph and following letter.

17. Because of heavy rain on the night of 8 Nov., the Berrys were unable to go from Parma to Modena on the following day: 'We resolved, however, to get to Reggio. The rain still pouring, crossed upon a brick bridge a river which divides the states of Parma from Modena; it entirely filled its wide channel, and was rushing like a torrent, every ditch was a considerable stream, and many of the fields overflowed' (MBJ i. 242–3). On 11 Nov. they 'left Reggio for Modena. We passed the Secchia in a good boat . . . the boatman said no creature had passed it the day before' (MBJ i. 243). On the following day, between Modena and Bologna, 'we passed the Panaro in a boat; it is a deep, narrow, rapid river, the banks steep, and consequently there is a great difficulty in getting in and out of the boat' (MBJ i. 244).

18. An allusion to Robert Merry's descriptions; see *ante* 8 Nov. 1790.

19. '*Curled smiles* . . . is very intelligible to anyone who has seen an angel of Correggio, whose mouth is generally curled

lourd want of grace in Guercino,[20] who is to me a German edition of Guido.[21] I am sorry the bookseller[22] would not let you have an *Otranto*.[23] Edwards[24] told me above two months ago that he every day expected the whole impression; and he has never mentioned it waiting for my corrections.[25] I will make Kirgate write to him,[26] for I have told you that I am still here: we have had much rain but no flood, and yesterday and today, have exhibited Florentine skies.

From town I know nothing, but that on Friday after the King's speech[27] Earl Stanhope made a most frantic speech on the National Assembly and against Calonne's book,[28] which he wanted to have

into a crescent, and in truth I think strains grace into almost a grimace' (HW to Lady Ossory 4 Sept. 1781). Under date of 8 Nov. 1790, at Parma, Mary Berry writes: 'Correggio does not delight me more than formerly; his boasted grace is to me affectation —has no simplicity, no dignity about it, and never touches me' (MBJ i. 242). See also *Ædes Walpolianæ, Works* ii. 232; HW to Mann 8 Oct. 1741, 15 Dec. 1743, 18 Nov. 1771.

20. See also *post* 9 Oct. 1791. Mary Berry did not share HW's dislike of Guercino, although she believed that some of his pictures were too dark; see MBJ i. 45, 72, 99, 104, 116. At Bologna 12 Nov. 1790 Guercino's 'Abraham and Hagar' delighted her 'if possible, more than ever' (MBJ i. 244).

21. 'In Guido were the grace and delicacy of Correggio, and colouring as natural as Titian's' (*Ædes Walpolianæ, Works* ii. 235). For Mary Berry's generally enthusiastic remarks on Guido, see MBJ i. 65, 69, 71, 97, 99, 104, 114, 116.

22. The printer, Giambattista Bodoni (1740–1813).

23. At Parma 8 Nov. 1790, 'at the printing-office they go on very slowly, but their work is excellent: they had just finished an impression of three hundred copies of the *Castle of Otranto* for Edwards the book-

seller in London, and five copies upon vellum. With the director (Bodoni), who seems to be a clever man and fond of his art, I had a good deal of conversation in a bookseller's shop' (MBJ i. 242). For a description of this, the 6th edn of the *Castle of Otranto*, 'Parma. Printed by Bodoni, for J. Edwards, bookseller of London. MDCCXCI,' see H. C. Brooks, *Compendiosa bibliografia di edizioni Bodoniane*, Firenze, 1927, p. 79, where it is said there were six copies on vellum.

24. James Edwards (1757–1816), bookseller, bibliographer, and bibliophile, who probably had met Bodoni when in Italy in 1788 to examine the Pinelli library; see DNB. His shop was in Pall Mall.

25. See *post* 20 Dec. 1790.

26. The letter is missing. HW did not get his copies for nearly a year; see Edwards to HW 21 Oct. 1791, bound into HW's copy of the Bodoni *Otranto*, now WSL.

27. For the text of the speech, see GM 1790, lx pt ii. 1048–9. It dealt with the recent agreement with Spain, the state of Europe and British colonial possessions, and the budget.

28. *De l'État de la France* . . . (cf. *ante* 31 Oct. 1790).

MARY BERRY'S BOOK-PLATE

taken up for high treason. He was every minute interrupted by loud bursts of laughter, which was all the answer he received or deserved.[29] His suffragan Price has published a short sneaking equivocal answer to Burke,[30] in which he pretends his triumph over the King of France alluded to July not to October, though his sermon was preached in November.[31] *Credat*—but not Judæus Apella, as Mr Burke so wittily says of the assignats.[32] Mr Grenville, the Secretary of State, is made a peer,[33] they say to assist the Chancellor[34] in the House of Lords; yet

29. According to Stanhope's biographers, this is 'an exaggerated version' of the speech and its reception (Ghita Stanhope and G. P. Gooch, *Life of Charles third Earl Stanhope*, 1914, p. 99). In HW's 'Mem. 1783–91' under 26 Nov. is this entry: 'Lord Stanhope's frantic speech in the Lords in favour of French Revolution and against Calonne's book—laughed at by all.' *The St James's Chronicle* 25–27 Nov. 1790 reported that 'Earl Stanhope . . . rose to congratulate their Lordships on the prospect [of peace] . . . he observed that if we were in the enjoyment of peace, it was owing to the French Revolution; that event had reconciled the people of France to those of England.' He then recommended an alliance between France and England, and mentioned Calonne's book as 'containing a gross *libel on our King*': Calonne 'had pathetically recommended the promotion of a civil war in France to effect a counter-revolution, and had asserted that those who promoted it would be protected by *every sovereign in Europe*. This assertion . . . included the King of Great Britain, and was, he believed to his soul, a foul calumny, a gross and unwarrantable libel. . . . His Lordship said it behoved his Majesty's ministers to prevent its evil operation by publicly denying the infamous assertion.'

30. Price replied to Burke in the fourth edition of his *Discourse on the Love of Our Country, Delivered on Nov. 4, 1789*, which was advertised 'This day was published' under 24 Nov. in *The St James's Chronicle* 23–25 Nov. 1790.

31. Toward the close of his sermon Price remarked: 'What an eventful period is this! I am thankful that I have lived to it. . . . I have lived to see thirty millions of people, indignant and resolute, spurning at slavery, and demanding liberty with an irresistible voice; their king led in triumph, and an arbitrary monarch surrendering himself to his subjects' (op. cit. 49). In the Preface, p. vii, he explains: 'I hope I shall be credited when . . . I assure the public that the events to which I referred in these words were not those of the 6th of October, but those only of the 14th of July and the subsequent days.' This last passage was quoted in *The St James's Chronicle* 23–25 Nov. 1790.

32. Burke refers to the French legislators who 'made a sort of swaggering declaration . . . that there is no difference in value between metallic money and their assignats . . . *Credat* who will—certainly not *Judæus Apella*' (*Reflections*, 1790, p. 346). Burke here reverses and gives a fiscal interpretation to the much-discussed passage in Horace: '*Credat Judæus Apella, non ego*' (*Sat.* I. v. 100–1).

33. William Wyndham Grenville (1759–1834), younger brother of George, 1st M. of Buckingham; cr. (25 Nov. 1790) Bn Grenville of Wotton-under-Bernewood; home secretary 1789–91; foreign secretary 1791–1801; prime minister 1806–7.

34. Edward Thurlow (1731–1806), cr. (1778) Bn Thurlow of Ashfield and (1792) of Thurlow; lord high chancellor 1778–92 (except for April–Dec. 1783).

the papers pretend the Chancellor is out of humour and will resign
—the first may be true, the latter probably not.

Richmond, my metropolis, flourishes exceedingly. The D. of Clarence[35] arrived at his palace there last night between eleven and twelve
as I came from Lady Douglas. His eldest brother and Mrs Fitzherbert dine there today with the D. of Queensbury as his Grace, who
called here this morning, told me,[36] on the very spot where lived
Charles I[37] and where are the portraits of his principal courtiers from
Cornbury.[38] Q. has taken to that palace[39] at last, and has frequently
company and music there in an evening. I intend to go.

The very old uncle of the Abbé Nichols is dead,[40] and as he tells
me, has left well to his mother[41] and him, and he is come to live there

35. Who had just returned from Portsmouth: he left London 20 Nov. and arrived at Portsmouth the following day
(*London Chronicle* 20–23 Nov. 1790, lxviii.
498, 504).

36. 'Yesterday the three Royal brothers,
with a large company of their friends, dined
with his Grace the Duke of Queensberry at
his country residence near Richmond' (*St
James's Chronicle* 27–30 Nov. 1790).

37. Richmond Palace, completed early
in the sixteenth century for Henry VII, was
a favourite residence of Charles I. After the
greater part of the building was demolished early in the eighteenth century, the
second Earl of Cholmondeley was granted
(1708) part of the land on lease. Cholmondeley House, begun by him and completed
by the third Earl, HW's brother-in-law, was
purchased by the Duke of Queensberry in
1780, and was thereafter known as Queensberry House until its demolition in 1828
(N&Q 1939, clxxvii. 390–1; E. Beresford
Chancellor, *History and Antiquities of
Richmond*, Richmond, 1894, pp. 161–5;
F. C. Hodgson, *Thames-Side in the Past*,
1913, pp. 331, 344–5).

38. In 1751 Henry Hyde, Bn Hyde of
Hindon (styled Vct Cornbury until 1750)
was forced to sell the estate of Cornbury,
Oxon, to Charles Spencer, 3d D. of Marl-

borough. The collection of pictures, formed
by the first Earl of Clarendon, was allowed
to remain at Cornbury until 1763, when, on
the termination of a lawsuit, the collection
was divided. Half went to Catherine Hyde,
the famous Duchess of Queensberry, who
removed her share to Amesbury, Wilts.
About 1786 the 4th D. of Queensberry removed the pictures to Richmond, and on
his death in 1810 they were removed to
Bothwell (Vernon J. Watney, *Cornbury and
the Forest of Wychwood*, 1910, p. 191). For
a list of the pictures in 1751, before their
division, see ibid. 235–44. HW had seen
them at Cornbury and at Richmond; see
Montagu i. 5; HW to Mann 1 Sept. 1750;
to Bentley Sept. 1753; to Lady Ossory 1
Dec. 1786.

39. Queensberry House. For George Selwyn's references to the Duke's new partiality for Richmond in Oct.–Nov. 1790, see
Hist. MSS Commission, 15th Report, Appendix, Part VI, *Manuscripts of the Earl
of Carlisle*, 1897, pp. 692–4.

40. William Turner, Nicholls' maternal
great-uncle, died at Richmond 11 Nov.
1790, aged 92 (GM 1790, lx pt ii. 1057).

41. Jane Floyer, dau. of Lt-Col. Charles
Floyer of Richmond, m. (1741) Norton
Nicholls, by whom she had an only son, the
'Abbé,' who was deeply attached to her.

with her, and I shall hear him sing, I conclude, at the Duke's concerts.

The Gunning match remains, I believe, *in statu quo non*. My coachman does air your chaise: have you received my letter which tells you how much liberty *I* took in airing it?[42]

Two mails have arrived at Falmouth this week from Lisbon,[43] and yet I have not yet heard of Mrs. D.'s arrival there, but I conclude her father has.

Monday 29th.

I am going to dine at Hampton with Lady Cecilia and am to attend her in the evening to Lady Mary Duncan's[44] Monday, whom I never happened to visit before, though we have been so long inhabitants of the same planet. I hope not to pass so many evenings out of my own parish this time twelvemonth! Old Brutus is still alive, but almost insensible.

I suppose none of my Florentine acquaintance are still upon earth. The handsomest woman there of my days was a Madame Grifoni,[45] *my* fair Geraldine;[46] she would now be a Methusalemmess, and much

42. *Ante* 8 Nov. 1790.

43. One mail arrived in London on 22 Nov. and another (which was brought from Lisbon to Falmouth in nine days) on 26 Nov. (*St James's Chronicle* 20–23, 25–27 Nov. 1790).

44. Lady Mary Tufton (1723–1806), 1st dau. of 7th E. of Thanet; m. (1763) William Duncan, M.D., cr. (1764) Bt, of Marybone, Middlesex; friend and patron of Pacchierotti and Dr Burney, to the latter of whom she left her collection of music and a legacy of £600; 'one of the most singular females of her day . . . she had a manly courage, a manly stamp, and a manly hard-featured face: but her heart was as invariably generous and good, as her manners were original and grotesque' (Frances Burney d'Arblay, *Memoirs of Doctor Burney*, 1832, ii. 119–20; iii. 37, 341, 345–7). She had a summer villa at Hampton (ibid. iii. 259). Her musical assemblies were almost as famous as the philosophical gatherings of Sir Joseph Banks. For an account of an assembly at her house in London, 21 Feb. 1790, see *The Early Married Life of Maria Josepha Lady Stanley*, ed. Jane H. Adeane, 1899, p. 95.

45. Elisabetta Capponi (1714–80), 1st dau. of Roberto Domenico Capponi of Florence; m. (1732) Pietro Grifoni (Pompeo Litta, *Famiglie celebri italiane*, Milano e Torino, [1819–85] *sub* Capponi di Firenze, tav. XXI). There is indirect evidence in Mann's letters to HW that she was HW's mistress. After his Italian journey in 1739–41, HW started a correspondence (missing) with her, which he soon dropped, as it became embarrassing and tiresome; see HW–Mann Correspondence. In reply to this paragraph, Mary Berry sent HW some 'memoirs of the Grifonis'; see *post* 15 Jan. 1791.

46. An allusion to 'the fair Geraldine,' the subject of poems by Henry Howard (ca

more like a frightful picture I have of her by a one-eyed German painter.[47] I lived then with Sir Horace Mann[48] in Casa Mannetti in Via de' Santi Apostoli by the Ponte di Trinità.[49] Pray worship the works of Masaccio,[50] if any remain, though I think the best have been burnt in a church:[51] Raphael himself borrowed from him. Fra Bartolomeo[52] too is one of my standards for great ideas;[53] and Benvenuto Cellini's Perseus[54] a rival of the antique, though Mrs D. will not allow it. Over against the Perseus is a beautiful small front of a house with only three windows designed by Raphael,[55] and another, I think, near the Porta San Gallo, and I believe called Casa Panciatici or Pandolfini.[56]

1517–47), styled Earl of Surrey. She, like Signora Grifoni, was named Elizabeth and was (according to legend) descended from an old Florentine family: Lady Elizabeth Fitzgerald (ca 1528–90), dau. of Gerald, 9th E. of Kildare; m. (1) (1543) Sir Anthony Browne, K.B.; m. (2) (ca 1552) Edward Fiennes de Clinton, 9th Bn Clinton, cr. (1572) E. of Lincoln.

47. In HW's bedchamber at SH was a portrait of 'La Signora Elisabetta Capponi Grifoni, a Florentine beauty; by Ferd. Richter, 1741' (Works ii. 452, but not recorded in the SH Sale Catalogue). HW wrote to Mann 3 Aug. 1774 that Richter 'drew Madame Grifoni like a surly Margravine.'

48. (Ca 1706–86), cr. (1755) Bt; HW's correspondent for more than forty years.

49. The Casa Mannetti (now Bonfiglio), a fifteenth-century building, in Via S. Spirito 29, on the corner of the Via Maffia, opposite the Palazzo Lanfredini. Mann's mention of a feast 'at my neighbour Rinuccini's' (Mann to HW 17 Sept. 1741, N.S.) accurately determines the location of the Casa Mannetti. The Palazzo Rinuccini, Via S. Spirito 31, is next to the Casa Mannetti, on the left-hand corner of the Via Maffia (see Walther Limburger, Die Gebäude von Florenz, Leipzig, 1910, pp. 95, 148). HW's reference to the 'Casa Mannetti in Via de' Santi Apostoli by the Ponte di Trinità' is a slip for 'Via S. Spirito,' since in a note on HW to Mann 2 Oct. 1746, O.S., HW says: 'Mr Mann hired a large palace of

the Mannetti family at Florence in Via di Santo Spirito.' Both the Via SS. Apostoli (now Chiasso Borgherini, a small street between the Piazza del Limbo and the Arno, on the right bank of the river) and the Via S. Spirito are near the Ponte S. Trinità, but on opposite banks of the river. Part of the time he was in Florence HW lived in the Palazzo Manelli, Via de' Bardi 40; see HW to West 4 Dec. 1740, N.S.

50. Tommaso Guidi (1401–ca 1428), known as Masaccio. His best known and most influential work, six paintings in fresco, is in the Brancacci Chapel in the Carmine at Florence.

51. S. Andrea: Mann mentions the fire and the destruction of Masaccio's works in his letter to HW 22 Feb. 1771.

52. Fra Bartolommeo di Pagholo (1475–1517), friend of Raphael; the best collection of his works is in the Pitti Palace, Florence.

53. But see in this connection, HW to Mann 28 Dec. 1771, 12 March 1773.

54. Cellini's bronze group of 'Perseus holding the Head of Medusa,' now in the Loggia dei Lanzi at Florence.

55. No building of this description is mentioned in Enrico di Geymüller, Raffaello . . . come architetto, Milano, 1884.

56. The Palazzo Pandolfini, ca 1520, was executed by San Gallo from a design by Raphael, and is now No. 74 Via San Gallo. The Palazzo Panciatichi, No. 2 Via Cavour (No. 15 Via de' Ricasoli), was not built until about 1700 (Karl Baedeker, Northern Italy, 1892, p. 400; Limburger, op. cit. 128, 129).

I hope tomorrow or next day to receive your letter from Florence, but am forced to send this to town tonight. If you have not received all my letters, you will not understand some passages in this. You have I trust recovered the fatigues of your journey. Adieu!

To Mary Berry, Friday 10 December 1790

Address: À Mademoiselle Mademoiselle Berry à la poste restante à Florence, Italie. [Forwarded: 'Pisa.'] *Postmark:* Illegible. Endorsed: 'Pd 1s.'

In 'Visitors,' HW notes that this letter, unlike the two preceding ones, was sent '*not* par Paris,' and was posted 11 Dec. Actually, it must have been posted Friday 10 Dec., since Friday was the day the foreign post left London. Furthermore, in his letter to Miss Seton 11 Dec. 1790 he says, 'I did write a short letter yesterday.' See also the last paragraph below, where he mentions Philip's errand.

Strawberry Hill, Thursday at midnight, Dec. 10, 1790.[1]

No. 10.

AFTER receiving yours from Bologna ten days ago,[2] I expected another from Florence in three days, as you promised to write thence on your arrival, but I have none till this minute that on returning from Richmond I find one on my table dated as long ago as the 16th of last month[3]—and what alas! has it told me but your utter disappointment and most natural vexation at the loss—at least, at the want of any one letter, but Mrs D.'s, from England.[4] Oh! how shall I expect you to receive any, if all have miscarried? how shall I direct mine? Till you told me to put *par Paris,* I did direct like Mrs D. yet you have not received them! I know but one consolation to offer to you, and that is, *all* failing, you have no reason to be alarmed particularly for any of your friends; and for a succedaneum to your loss of the thread of domestic occurrences, I will keep a minute journal[5] of all I know and hear, and keep it till I can send it by some secure hand or method. In my present distress for you and myself on this cruel disappointment and uncertainty, I cannot recollect any-

1. Thursday was 9 Dec., but HW dates his letter 10 Dec. because he writes after midnight.

2. Actually on 28 Nov.; see preceding letter.

3. Two days after the Berrys arrived in Florence; 'found ourselves again disappointed in our hopes of receiving letters, and were very melancholy' (MBJ i. 245).

4. Extracts from Mrs Damer's letter of 28–30 Oct. 1790 (MBJ i. 247–8) are quoted in notes *ante* 22, 31 Oct. 1790.

5. No such journal has been discovered, and with the establishment of regular correspondence, HW apparently abandoned this plan.

thing I have said, and I must send this away to town tomorrow in time, or it will not set out before Tuesday, by which time I will try to remember what events have happened, though at this moment, I cannot recall a single one of any consequence. How happy I shall be if by that day I can learn that your letters have at last reached you!

This being but a momentary essay to see if you can get a line from me, and half in despair at the sad cruel prospect of our correspondence being cut off, I will say but few words more, but to assure you I am perfectly well, and will search every method upon earth of conveying letters to you. I have not heard from Mrs D. yet, but conclude her parents have, as I see by the papers two packets have arrived from Lisbon, and the last I conclude since she must have landed there.

That letters to you, two private young Englishwomen going to Italy for health, and connected with nobody ministerial here, and corresponding with nobody but persons involved in no party and writing about nothing political, should be opened in France, and still more wonderful, should continue to be opened there and not forwarded, is quite astonishing![6] I should rather suspect they have gone by Flanders and been lost in the confusions there; but as the Emperor[7] is now in possession again of that country,[8] I hope our terrible interruption will cease.

If you receive this, you may be satisfied that your grandmother has heard of you, as I have received every one of yours. Why yours should come, and ours be stopped or retarded, is inconceivable!

I could write on this subject all night—but as it is so late, and Philip[9] must carry this [to] town by eight tomorrow, I will conclude

---

6. Mrs Damer wrote to Mary Berry from Lisbon 25 Dec. 1790: 'I cannot help thinking of poor dear Mr W., if his mind was tolerably at ease about you, and that he could turn it to any other object. What a fuss he must have been in about his letters! he has always a horror of his letters being seen except by those they are intended for; and though I dare say he took care to put no politics in them, I should not wonder if his imagination presented them to him read aloud in the *Assemblée Nationale*.— Still no packets, and it is an age since I have heard from him, and my last letters from England are of above a month' (MBJ i. 273–4).

7. Leopold II.

8. Extract of a letter from Flanders, 3 Dec. 1790: 'The troubles which have for some time past afflicted these unfortunate provinces are at an end. The respective states have at last returned to their allegiance, and submitted to the Emperor Leopold' (*St James's Chronicle* 9–11 Dec. 1790).

9. Philip Colomb, HW's valet.

for the present, after telling you that I wrote to you, directed to Turin
Oct. 16, 19, 25,[10] and to Florence Nov. 2, 11, 16th,[11] and thither *par
Paris* 19th and 29th.[12] How I do hope you have got some at least!
Adieu! adieu!

To Barbara Cecilia Seton, Saturday 11 December 1790

Address: To Miss Cecilia Seton at Caversham Hill near Reading, Berks.
Postmark: ISLEWORTH 11 DE 90.

Strawberry Hill, Dec. 11, 1790.

INSTEAD of your making apologies to me, dear Madam, for the
length of your letter, it is I who owe a thousand thanks to you for
it. I can never be weary of hearing from you, or about our dear
friends, though so unhappy at their present vexatious disappointment. I had a letter from Mary of the same date;[1] and what adds to
my surprise at their want of all letters from England is, that I have
assuredly received every one of theirs. Why they should be stopped
when going, and not, coming, is quite inconceivable. I did write a
short letter yesterday, though equally uncertain of what will be its
fate. I will wait till the next foreign post comes in, and if then I find
that they are still in the same letterless situation, I will inquire at the
office of the Secretary of State[2] or of Lady Bristol,[3] mother of Lord
Hervey Minister at Florence, or of some foreign minister, whether I
cannot get leave to send one letter at least in one of their packets.

One of their principal miseries is the dread of their grandmother's
not hearing of them, as they cannot know that we do get their letters.
If they do not, how can we make them easy on that head?

Though I dreaded numberless calamities for them, which thank

10. *Ante* 12, 16, 22 Oct. 1790.
11. *Ante* 31 Oct., 8 Nov., to Mary Berry
13 Nov. 1790.
12. *Ante* 18, 26 Nov. 1790.

―――――

1. 16 Nov., from Florence (missing); see
preceding letter.

2. Francis Godolphin Osborne (1751–99),
5th D. of Leeds (styled M. of Carmarthen
1761–89); foreign secretary of state 1783–91.
3. Elizabeth (1733–1800), dau. of Sir
Jermyn Davers, 4th Bt; m. (1752) Frederick
Augustus Hervey, later (1768) Bp of Derry
and (1779) 4th E. of Bristol.

God! did not happen in their journey through France, yet others, to which I did not advert, have unfortunately proved how happy it would have been, could I have succeeded in my most earnest entreaties to dissuade them from their journey during the distractions in France and Flanders. By how very few hours did they escape the storm when sailing to Dieppe! At Burgoin they were rudely treated; the price of voitures they have found doubled; at Turin could scarce get a lodging; met with torrents—and have now not found a single letter at Florence—where and everywhere else I fear the dearness of everything from the swarms of French exiles will be a lasting inconvenience; to which will be added the anxiety they will feel from apprehending that their letters asking advice or assistance may not reach us. This terror, if I do not find removed on the arrival of next post, I will certainly if possible find some method of quieting. Depend upon it, dear Madam, I will sooner dispatch a messenger myself, than leave them in such a dreadful suspense; or will write to Lord Hervey myself to beg him to make them easy.

I cannot wish them during winter to think of returning rather than live in perfect ignorance of all their friends; but since this misfortune has happened, I do trust it will open their eyes on the dangers and inconvenience of living out of their own country. Mr Berry is a healthy man and not an old one, but how frequently has it occurred to me how dreadful would be the situation of two handsome unmarried young women if they found themselves in a foreign country without a protector, and curtailed in their circumstances![4] I dare mention this to you, dear Madam, as I am sure it will not pass your own lips, unless you could artfully a little while hence, when they do receive letters, suggest a hint—They will be more open to persuasion *now,* than when they were setting out, and fond of their scheme. Believe me it is not for my own sake that I desire this—but as I am so very old, believe me it will be kind to them and to me too, to observe to them that while I exist, I can be of use to them—but not afterwards.[5]

I saw with grief before they went, and now perceive by the melan-

4. On inheriting his uncle's estate in 1781, William Berry settled on his brother Robert an annuity of £1000, but made no provisions for Mary and Agnes Berry after their father's death: they, 'he concluded, would marry, and be thus got rid of' (MBJ i. 10). HW's fears were realized almost twenty-seven years later, for Robert Berry died at Genoa 19 May 1817 (GM 1817, lxxxvii pt i. 570).

5. HW was of use to them then: he left them the life use of Little SH and £2000 apiece.

choly reflections in Agnes's letter to you, how much chagrin and disappointment had driven them to take this imprudent journey, and therefore I do but feel the more for them, and attribute all to the true causes, their vile great-uncle,[7] and almost as unjust uncle[8]—pardon me if I speak so hardly of your relations, Madam!

I cannot at present say more—I find by my watch I have written till our post is going out[9]—and I should be sorry not to answer yours immediately—I must not therefore add a word more at present—You are persuaded, I trust, how sincerely I am, dear Madam,

Your most obliged and obedient humble servant,

HOR. WALPOLE

To Mary Berry, Thursday 16 December 1790

Address: À Mademoiselle Mademoiselle Berry à la poste restante à Florence, Italie. [Forwarded: 'Pisa.'] *Postmark:* FIRENZE. Posted 17 Dec. ('Visitors').

Berkeley Square, Dec. 16, 1790.

No. 11.

I AM still infinitely distressed about your receiving no letters from England, and still ignorant whether you have yet received any. Your last was from Florence of the 16th of last month, and you promised to write again immediately; but the strong westerly winds (which on Sunday night blew a tempest, and broke off a considerable branch of my beautiful ivied walnut tree at Strawberry) have prevented (and I hope nothing else has) our receiving any letters from the Continent. My best consolation has been from Miss Penn, who tells me her brother,[1] now at Florence, was some time without letters, but then did receive them—may this have been your case! You may ask him. I desired her to write to him to acquaint you, that Miss Seton and I have received all your letters regularly—consequently your grandmother has *not* been alarmed.

7. Robert Ferguson of Raith; see *ante* 10 Oct. 1790.
8. William Berry Ferguson; see ibid.
9. The post left Twickenham at 1 P.M.; see *ante* 10 July 1790.

———

1. John Penn (1760–1834), 4th but 1st surviving son of Thomas and Lady Juliana Penn; author of poems, plays, and critical pamphlets; travelled abroad ca 1780–3, 1790–1; lived in Pennsylvania 1783–8; erected at Stoke Park a cenotaph to Gray, 1799; founder of the Outinian Society, ca 1817 (DNB; Howard M. Jenkins, *Family of William Penn*, Philadelphia, 1899, pp. 154–65).

In this suspense I only write, that if our letters do find passage to you, you may have no interval; though till I hear they do, I cannot write comfortably. Should any French have stopped them, surely they must have discovered by this time that they might as well have a curiosity about letters to Abyssinia!—but how unpleasant that you cannot, not only hear the common chit-chat of your own country, but receive no account of your own private affairs. You perhaps do not yet know that your house is let for six months at seven guineas a week. I called on Mr Cambridge on Sunday evening: his son George, as well as I, have sent you notice of it, and the latter too of what I did not know, that he has sold Mr Berry's horse. If you have received our letters, these will be unnecessary repetitions; but I want so much to give such satisfactory information, that I shall not spare *redits,* till I am sure you are informed.

In mine of last week I was so confounded at your disappointment that I forgot to give you, as you desired, the direction to Mrs D. It is *Aux soins de Messieurs Mellish et de Visme[2] à Lisbon.* I have heard from her thence;[3] she had a passage but of seven days.

I came to town yesterday purely on your account and return to-morrow. Cliveden was this morning secured to you and your sister in form.

Poor Lady Herries has lost the use of her limbs and is at Bath in a melancholy way.[4] I called on Mrs Buller last night and unluckily found seven persons[5] who had dined with her—so you may imagine my visit was short.

Lord Bute[6] has had a fall from his own cliff of 28 feet, sprained his ankle and broke the little bone of it, but though 77 is recovering.[7]

2. A well-known firm of merchants, originally Purry, Mellish and De Visme; in 1760 the firm hired the house of the Marquis of Pombal in the Rua Formosa (Julio de Castilho, *Lisboa Antiga,* 2d edn, Lisboa, 1902–4, iii. 212; Marcus Cheke, *Dictator of Portugal,* [1938] p. 158).

3. Letter missing.

4. Although HW mentions her partial recovery *post* 26 Feb. 1791, Mrs Carter wrote to Mrs Montagu 21 Sept. 1795: 'I had a letter lately from Lady Herries, who has most unexpectedly recovered the power of walking, which her physician ascribes to the use of viper broth. Her general health remains as it was, and she has received no

benefit from the baths of Valdagno' (*Letters from Mrs Elizabeth Carter to Mrs Montagu,* ed. Montagu Pennington, 1817, iii. 346–7).

5. Not identified.

6. John Stuart (1713–92), 3d E. of Bute, 1723; prime minister 1762–3; HW's occasional correspondent.

7. 'Lord Bute has been most miraculously saved from a very alarming accident. As he was walking a few days since on the cliff near his house at Christchurch, he went rather too near the brink of it, when the earth gave way, and he fell headlong down a precipice of 40 feet, with no other injury to himself but breaking a small bone

The Opposition seem very temperate and tame and the Court's majorities are great. The three Garters[8] were given away yesterday to the Duke of Saxe-Gotha,[9] the Duke of Leeds and Lord Chatham.[10] All this perhaps you will learn earlier from our newspapers. Of private news I do not know a tittle—but I would try once more to acquaint you with your own affairs by the common post. If none of these succeed, I will try some other channel, for I cannot bear your living ignorant of all that concerns you. I will write round by Russia, and beg the Empress[11] to make it a condition of peace, that the Grand Signor[12] shall send a zebecque to Leghorn with my letters. Adieu! for the present.

PS. I am sorry I was so much in the right, when I endeavoured to dissuade your journey, from the various inconveniencies I foresaw, though I own loss of letters was not one of the number.

To Mary and Agnes Berry, Friday 17 December 1790

Address: To Miss Mary and Miss Agnes Berry at Florence or Pisa.
Postmark: None; the letter, as HW notes in 'Visitors,' was enclosed 'in Lord Hervey's packet,' and was sent 21 Dec. See also below, and *post* 20 Dec. 1790.

Strawberry, Friday night, Dec. 17, [1790].

No. 12.

MY letters set out on the back of one another—I wish I could know that any one of them, but that at Lyons,[1] had reached you! I sent off the eleventh from London this morning—but here is a

about the ankle. The fright which such an accident must occasion to a man of his Lordship's advanced years, being near 80, is much to be dreaded, though we are happy to learn that at present there is no immediate danger. This is the second time within these few years that the ground about Lord Bute's house has fallen in' (*St James's Chronicle* 7–9 Dec. 1790).

8. Vacant by the recent deaths of the Dukes of Cumberland, Montagu, and Leeds.

9. Ernst II (1745–1804), Duke of Saxe-Gotha and Altenburg, 1772; first cousin to George III; mathematician, astronomer, and an enlightened ruler.

10. John Pitt (1756–1835), 2d E. of Chatham; elder brother of William Pitt the younger; first lord of the Admiralty 1788–94; lord privy seal 1794–6; lord president of the Council 1796–1801.

11. Catherine II (1729–96), the Great, Empress of Russia 1762–96.

12. Selim III (1761–1808), Sultan of Turkey 1789–1807; deposed and murdered. With his throne he inherited a war with Russia which, after Turkish reverses, was ended by the peace of Jassy, 1792.

1. *Ante* 10 Oct. 1790.

new and great distress! Last week I received your first from Florence, with an account of your shocking disappointment in finding no letters from England there or at Turin, though all yours have come regularly to me and Miss Seton and I conclude to others, so you may be satisfied that your grandmother has been under no alarm about you. Your Florentine letter promised another in which I trusted I should learn that your letters had followed you, as Mr Penn's have done him—but alas! if you have sent such a letter, I shall probably never receive it, for a French packet from Calais to Dover sunk in the great storm on Tuesday with all the crew, thirty persons, and I suppose the mails too, for the English packet escaped at the same time,[2] and yet I have no letter, which I must have had tonight, for Kirgate followed me by the evening coach. One great consolation he has brought me, a permission to send *this* in Lord Hervey's packet, which sets me to writing with confidence.

In this morning's letter I have told you that in the uncertainty of any of my letters reaching you, I must, till I know they do, use many repetitions. The most material are, that your house in Audley Street is let for six months at seven guineas a week; and Mr G. Cambridge has sold Mr Berry's horse. Cliveden was secured to you both in form yesterday morning.

The Parliament has been moderate, and the Court's majorities considerable. The chief difficulty is whether Hastings's trial is to proceed, and that point is not yet settled.[3] The Duke of Montrose is Master of the Horse;[4] Mr W. Grenville a peer; the Duke of Saxe-

---

2. 'Tuesday night a French packet-boat coming from Calais to Dover sunk with the violence of the storm, by which the captain and every person on board, consisting of near thirty, perished; the sufferers were chiefly French. The English packet, which sailed in company, fortunately got into Dover, and brought the above melancholy information' (*St James's Chronicle* 14–16 Dec. 1790). The French packet did not sink; see *post* 20 Dec. 1790.

3. Burke introduced in the House of Commons, 30 Nov. and 9 Dec. 1790, the subject of the continuation of Hastings's trial. Some members argued that the intervening dissolution of Parliament put an end to the proceedings. On 17 Dec., the date of this letter, Burke moved that the trial 'is now depending'; after heated debate the motion was carried. Further debate followed 22–23 Dec., and on 14 Feb. 1791 a motion was passed 'that a message be sent to the Lords, informing them that the Commons are ready to proceed on the trial of Warren Hastings, Esq.' Debate in the House of Lords followed, and the trial did not proceed until 23 May 1791. For a full account of the debates, see *History of the Trial of Warren Hastings*, 1796, Part IV, pp. 1–61.

4. James Graham (1755–1836), styled M. of Graham until 1790; 3d D. of Montrose, 23 Sept. 1790; Master of the Horse 1790–5, 1807–21; Lord Chamberlain 1821–7, 1828–

Gotha, the Duke of Leeds and Lord Chatham have got the three vacant Garters. This kind of articles, that are in all newspapers, I shall not send you, if I learn that you see the papers.

Poor Lady Herries has lost the use of her limbs, and is very ill at Bath.

Mrs Damer had a passage of only seven days; her direction is *Aux soins de Messieurs Mellish et de Visme à Lisbon.* The famous letter[5] and another to the same purport, of which we were told the night before you set out, is discovered to be a forgery, but the writer not found out, yet supposed to be the very person[6] who repeated it to us —but do not write this back to England, nor mention it where you are, I beg.

Mrs Siddons[7] is playing again to crowded houses.[8]

For my own history, I am still resident here. We have had several beautiful days, a vast deal of rain and high winds, but scarce any cold. Richmond is still full, and will be so till after Christmas. The Duke of Clarence is there and every night at Mrs Bouverie's,[9] Lady Di's, at home or at the Duke of Queensberry's,[10] with suppers that

---

30. He was appointed Master of the Horse 17 Nov. (*London Chronicle* 16–18, 18–20 Nov. 1790, lxviii. 488, 494).

5. Purporting to be from Lord Blandford to Miss Gunning, to set the wedding day; see *ante* 22 Oct., 13 Nov. 1790, and *post* 27 March 1791.

6. Miss Gunning.

7. Sarah Kemble (1755–1831), m. (1773) William Siddons.

8. Partly because of ill health and partly because of difficulty in getting her salary from the management, Mrs Siddons did not act at Drury Lane in the season of 1789–90. After an absence of almost two years, she returned 7 Dec. 1790 as Isabella in Thomas Southerne's (and David Garrick's) *Isabella or the Fatal Marriage.* On 7 Dec. 'the house was crowded in every part before six o'clock, in the boxes every place was taken, even back rows up two pair of stairs. On Mrs Siddons coming forward, the applause was so tumultuous as to shake the walls of Old Drury, nor did the audience cease clapping and shouting for near five minutes' (*London Chronicle* 7–9 Dec. 1790, lxviii. 554).

9. Henrietta or Harriet Fawkener (ca 1750–1825), sister of William Augustus Fawkener (*ante* 17 July 1790); m. (1) (1764) Hon. Edward Bouverie; m. (2) (1811) Lord Robert Spencer. Sir Joshua Reynolds painted her with her sister Mrs Crewe (Burke, *Peerage*, 1928, p. 1911, *sub* Radnor; Collins, *Peerage*, 1812, v. 36; DNB, *sub* Fawkener, Sir Everard). Philip (later Sir Philip) Francis considered her in 1791 'one of the most accomplished women in England' (*Francis Letters*, ed. Beata Francis and Eliza Keary, [1901] ii. 391), and Lady Louisa Stuart testifies to her beauty (*Notes on Jesse's Selwyn*, ed. W. S. Lewis, New York, 1928, p. 42).

10. George Selwyn wrote to Lady Carlisle in Nov. 1790: 'The Duke's [D. of Queensberry's] passion for Richmond does not as yet abate; and I am afraid that H.R.H. the D[uke] of Clarence will rather keep it alive. . . . He supped at the D[uke's] the night before last. *Il tient des propos trop indécentes*—thinks that sort of discourse will give him the reputation of wit. It may, on the forecastle deck, but our Richmond ladies do not relish it' (Hist. MSS Comm., 15th Report, Appendix, Part VI, *Manuscripts of the Earl of Carlisle*, 1897, p. 694).

finish at twelve. I have been at three—but I do not think seventy-three just suited to twenty-five,[11] and therefore have excused myself from as many—and believe I shall settle in town before New Year's Day,[12] though the hours in London even of old folks, are not half so reasonable as those of this young prince, who never drinks or games, and is extremely good humoured and well bred.[13]

If I have anything more to tell you before Sunday morning when this must go to town for Tuesday's post, I will add it; but still trusting that you may at last have received my former letters, I have been very brief on what I have mentioned in them. One thing I must repeat with emphasis; I implore you not to return through France, especially as Flanders is now resettled. I as earnestly beseech you to be in England by the end of September. I never shall forget the storm which you so narrowly escaped going to Dieppe, and this last Tuesday has been still more tremendous. Torrents in Italy too!—for France, the horrors increase. The son of a friend of mine called on me yesterday; he is of Cambridge, and told me that two lords of his acquaintance had the curiosity to go to France this summer; and he was on the point of going with them, but was prevented. At Lyons they were seized for spies and had the rope about their necks, but a man of letters coming by, they explained themselves to him in Latin, which they had not been able to do sufficiently in French, and he saved them. I know how well you speak Latin and French too; but as *the benefit of clergy*[14] is so lately taken away in that country, I beg you will never set your foot in it.—But seriously and most seriously, spare me more alarms! I shall have no tranquillity till you are safe in England again—I know I have no right to ask you to sacrifice your own satisfactions to mine; but mine are not the sole; yourselves have been suffering for what you thought your grandmother must have felt on your accounts. The present state of France, and surely it is not mending, has already caused you many inconveniencies. At Rouen

11. The Duke of Clarence's age. During this time he paid a visit to SH which was celebrated by HW's verses, 'The Press at Strawberry Hill to his Royal Highness William Duke of Clarence, 1790' (*Works* iv. 406–7; Hazen, *SH Bibliography* 234–5).

12. He did not settle in London until 14 Jan. 1791 (*post* 15 Jan. 1791).

13. 'The Duke of Clarence is so popular among, and so happy with his Richmond neighbours, that he talks of passing a great part of the winter with them' (*St. James's Chronicle* 21–23 Dec. 1790). But see Selwyn's opinion, n. 10.

14. A play on the legal significance of the phrase and on the civil constitution of the French clergy, decreed by the National Assembly 27 Nov. 1790, and sanctioned by Louis XVI a month later (*London Chronicle* 1–4 Jan. 1791, lxix. 14).

you could get nothing but paper[15]—it is ten times worse now. What if you should not be able to proceed from want of assistance from bankers! Who could come and relieve you!—nay, should we be sure of getting your letters? Oh! ponder these things, and listen to me at least for your return!—I will not look back, but I must look forward, while I am on earth to study your happiness and security. That cannot be long—but should I fail before your return, who will be equally active for your service? You have been so kind as to tell me I am your true friend: should I be so, if I did not labour to prevent dangers for you, and did not warn you of them! I write so freely and warmly, as sure of your receiving this, though not certain I shall have leave to make use of the same conveyance often. Cultivate Lord Hervey; he may perhaps allow you to receive Miss Seton's and my letters in his packets—but keep that a secret. I could write all night—but surely you must see that my fears are neither ill-founded nor selfish. Good night! may Heaven preserve you!

Saturday night.

I have nothing to add, but that I am persuaded the mail is lost, for I have no letter, and have written to Miss Seton[16] to acquaint her with my suspicion that she may tranquillize your grandmother—This is a vile sheet of paper and sucks up the ink, and I have not time to transcribe it.

Poor Lady Douglas (Lady Frances Scott) was brought to bed ten days ago,[17] is most dangerously ill, and this morning's message said the fever no better.

I fear a particular passage to Miss Agnes[18] in answer to her kind scrap must have been amongst the letters whose fate is still unknown to me—but all mine are equally to both, as Cliveden is: and for fear of mistakes or your removal,[19] I make the address of this double.

---

15. Paper money: assignats; see *ante* 22 Oct. 1790, n. 3.

16. See following letter.

17. Of her second daughter, Hon. Frances Elizabeth Douglas (9 Dec. 1790–1854), m. (1826) William Moray Stirling of Abercairny and Ardoch, Perthshire (William Fraser, *The Douglas Book*, Edinburgh, 1885, ii. 535).

18. *Ante* 26 Nov. 1790.

19. The Berrys left Florence for Pisa 11 Dec. 1790 (MBJ i. 255).

To Barbara Cecilia Seton, Friday 17 December 1790

Address: To Miss Cecilia Seton at Caversham Hill near Reading, Berks.
Postmark: ISLEWORTH 18 DE 90.

Strawberry Hill, Friday night, Dec. 17, [1790.]

My dear Madam,

HERE is new distress, with which I must acquaint you to prevent you from various alarms. I have waited anxiously for a second letter from Florence, but in vain! Our letters I fear are lost. Today's papers say a French packet from Dover to Calais sunk in the storm on Tuesday with every soul on board, thirty persons! and I conclude the mails too, for as the English packet escaped at the same time[1] and has brought me no letter, I can expect none by that post, as I had a servant[2] in town, who did not leave London today till four o'clock— So we may be a fortnight or three weeks before we can guess whether any of our letters have reached Florence, and it may be mere guess if they had already told us so by the lost mail. Oh! that unfortunate journey!

I have got leave by a friend[3] in the Secretary's Office[4] to send a letter in Lord Hervey's next packet, and have been writing accordingly all the evening, repeating everything material that I could recollect to have said in my former letters—indeed my hand is so weary that I can scarce write this, but I fear interruptions tomorrow, and would make sure of these moments.

A thousand new anxieties arise every day. I now dread from the irregularity of the posts and these losses by sea, lest at any time they should draw for money and their draughts not arrive! I am ten thousand times more afraid of their returning through France, and of their being at sea in tempestuous weather. I would not suggest these apprehensions to *you* but that I wish you to drop them now and then as from yourself, and sometimes perhaps from their grandmother. I really cannot write more now, and am, dear Madam,

Your most sincere humble servant,

H. Walpole

1. See preceding letter; the French packet boat was not lost (*post* 21 Dec. 1790).
2. Thomas Kirgate; see preceding letter. The denomination of Kirgate as a servant is noteworthy, as showing the position of a secretary and 'domestic printer.' Kirgate is mentioned in HW's will as 'my printer' and received £100, the same sum left to 'my house maid' and 'my housekeeper.'
3. Not identified.
4. Office of the Duke of Leeds, foreign secretary.

To Mary Berry, Monday 20 December 1790

Address: À Mademoiselle Mademoiselle Berry à la poste restante à Florence, Italie. [Forwarded: 'Pisa.'] *Postmark:* Illegible. Endorsed: 'Pd 1s.'
After his entry of letter No. 12 (*ante* 17 Dec. 1790), HW notes in 'Visitors' that he sent 'another the same day [i.e., 21 Dec.] by post, not numero'd.'

Strawberry Hill, Dec. 20, 1790, very late at night.[1]

THIS being a duplicate or rather a codicil to one that goes away tomorrow from the Secretary's[2] office in Lord Hervey's packet I do not put any *numero* to it, and as it must go hence tomorrow very early by the coach, I write a few lines just to contradict what I have said about lost letters in the letter you will receive from our minister.[3] The French packet that was said to be lost on Tuesday last, and which did hang out signals of distress was saved,[4] but did not bring any letters—but three Flemish mails that were due, are arrived,[5] and did bring letters, and to my inexpressible joy, *two* from you of the 22nd and 29th of last month, telling me that you have received as far as No. 4 and 5, of mine—I am ashamed to say that with this there are *eight* more arrived or on the road. Yours received tonight are 10 and 11. I conclude Miss Seton will receive one or two from one of you tomorrow at farthest, as I am sorry to say she has one from me this morning I suppose, lamenting the loss of the French packet. Thank all the stars in Herschell's telescope[6] or beyond its reach, that our correspondence is out of the reach of France and all its ravages!

I truly have been in such distress and confusion about your finding no letters at Florence, that I have scarce thought or talked of anything else, but contrivances to remedy that disaster. Your two letters have made me quite easy, and I shall fall into our natural commerce again.

Your letters, though I still maintain longer than I wish you to write, contain everything I like to know except the last article, but the uppermost in my thoughts, your drinking whey from having

1. 'No. 25' (B).
2. Duke of Leeds, foreign secretary.
3. Lord Hervey.
4. 'The report of a packet being lost with the Flanders mail on board is without the slightest foundation' (*London Chronicle* 18–21 Dec. 1790, lxviii. 594).
5. 'This day [18 Dec. 1790] arrived three mails from Flanders, and one from France' (ibid. 16–18 Dec. 1790, lxviii. 592).

6. William Herschel (1738–1822), cr. Knight of the Royal Hanoverian Guelphic Order, 1816, whose discoveries and improvements in the past fifteen years had revolutionized astronomy, had recently (Aug.–Sept. 1789) discovered, with the aid of a forty-foot mirror, the sixth and seventh satellites of Saturn.

been overheated by your journey. I hope your next will be as minute on that article, and as satisfactory as your account of Miss *Agnes,* which doubles the pleasure the arrival of these letters have[7] given me, and of which I despaired. Should any feverishness remain, I beg you to have recourse to five grains of James's powder.[8] I rejoice that Mr Berry continues so well.

After a deluge of letters for some days, I have not left myself a tittle to tell you—nay, doubting whether any would reach you, but hoping that some at least would, I have repeated three or four times every tittle I wanted you to know.

Thank you a million of times for all your details about yourselves. When even the apprehension of any danger disquiets me so much, judge whether I do not interest myself in every particular of your pleasures and amusements! Florence was my delight as it is yours— but—I don't know how—I wish you did not like it quite so much!— and after the gallery—how will any silver-penny of a gallery look?[9] Indeed for your Boboli,[10] which I thought horrible even fifty years ago, before *shepherds* had seen the Star of Taste in the *west,* and glad tidings were proclaimed to their flocks,[11] I do think there is not an acre on the banks of the Thames that should vail the bonnet[11a] to it.

Of Mr Burke's book[12] if I have not yet told you my opinion, I do now, that it is one of the finest compositions in print. There is reason, logic, wit, truth, eloquence, and enthusiasm in the brightest colours. That it has given a mortal stab to sedition I believe and hope, because the fury of the Brabanters,[13] whom however as having been aggrieved, I pitied[14] and distinguish totally from the savage

---

7. So in MS.

8. A fever powder, composed chiefly of antimony and phosphate of lime, prepared by Dr Robert James (1705–76). It was a favourite remedy with HW. See Cole i. 337; du Deffand i. 110.

9. Specifically, the Gallery at SH.

10. The Royal Boboli Gardens at the Palazzo Pitti in Florence.

11. A reference to HW's belief in the superiority of English gardening. In his 'Essay on Modern Gardening' he proclaimed the glad tidings: 'We have given the true model of gardening to the world; let other countries mimic or corrupt our taste; but let it reign here on its verdant throne, original by its elegant simplicity, and proud of no other art than that of softening na-

ture's harshnesses and copying her graceful touch' (*Works* ii. 542).

11a. I.e., submit or yield. The last illustration of this phrase (followed by 'to') in OED is 1675.

12. *Reflections on the Revolution in France.*

13. In opposing Leopold II and refusing to submit to him at the expiration of his ultimatum, 21 Nov. 1790.

14. 'Feeling as every man must for the fanaticism of the people of Brabant, every friend to man must hope that the ratifying powers will not suffer the Emperor to take advantage of their blind devotion to their leaders' (*London Chronicle* 4–7 Dec. 1790, lxviii. 550).

Gauls; and the unmitigated and execrable injustices of the latter, have made almost any state preferable to such anarchy and desolation, that increases every day.

Admiring thus as I do, I am very far from subscribing to the extent of almost all Mr Burke's principles. The work I have no doubt will hereafter be applied to support very high[15] doctrines—and to you I will say, that I think it an *Apocrypha,* that in many a council of bishops will be added to the *Old* Testament. Still such an Almanzor[16] was wanting at this crisis—and his foes show how deeply they are wounded by their abusive pamphlets.[17] Their Amazonian allies, headed by Kate Macaulay[18] and the virago Barbaud,[19] whom Mr Burke

15. That is, high church.

16. The hero of Dryden's *Conquest of Granada, or Almanzor and Almahide,* 1670.

17. Between 1 Nov., when Burke's *Reflections* were published, and 20 Dec., the date of this letter, at least eight (and probably ten or more) pamphlets in reply to Burke were published. In the following list the newspaper references indicate the earliest appearance of an advertisement, 'This day was published': 1. [John Scott-Waring], *A Letter to the Right Hon. Edmund Burke, in Reply to His* 'Reflections . . .,' 'by a Member of the Revolution Society' (*St James's Chronicle* 11–13 Nov. 1790); 2. *Short Observations on the Right Honourable Edmund Burke's Reflections* (ibid. 13–16 Nov. 1790); 3. Richard Price (see *ante* 26 Nov. 1790, n. 30); 4. *An Address to the National Assembly of France; Containing Strictures on Mr Burke's Reflections on the Revolution in France,* Cambridge (*St James's Chronicle* 25–27 Nov. 1790); 5. Mary Wollstonecraft (later Mrs William Godwin), *A Vindication of the Rights of Men, in a Letter to the Right Honourable Edmund Burke, Occasioned by His Reflections on the Revolution in France* (ibid. 27–30 Nov. 1790); 6. Mrs Macaulay-Graham (see following note); 7. Capel Lofft, *Remarks on the Letter of the Rt Hon. Edmund Burke, Concerning the Revolution in France* . . . (ibid. 7–9 Dec. 1790); Joseph Towers, *Thoughts on the Commencement of a New Parliament. With an Appendix, Containing Remarks on the Letter of the Right Hon. Edmund Burke, on the Revolution in France* (*St James's Chronicle* 16–18 Dec. 1790). Numbers 2 and 4 are known to the editors from the advertisements only.

Two other pamphlets, for which no advertisements have been found, are dated 1790: George Rous, *Thoughts on Government, Occasioned by Mr Burke's Reflections. In a Letter to a Friend* (BM Cat.), and Robert Woolsey, *Reflections upon Reflections . . . in Two Letters to the Right Hon. Edmund Burke in Answer to His Pamphlet,* dated at end, 'Dec. 1790.'

18. Catharine Sawbridge (1731–91), m. (1) (1760) George Macaulay, M.D.; m. (2) (1778) William Graham, younger brother of the quack doctor James Graham; HW's occasional correspondent. HW refers to her anonymous pamphlet of 95 pages liberally sprinkled with italics, *Observations on the Reflections of the Right Hon. Edmund Burke on the Revolution in France, in a Letter to the Right Hon., the Earl of Stanhope,* published 30 Nov. 1790 (*London Chronicle* 27–30 Nov. 1790, lxviii. 525). A full page of extracts from the work is in ibid. 4–7 Dec. 1790, lxviii. 545. In addition to disliking her principles, HW would hardly have admired her reference (p. 13) to 'that dreadful *necessity* by which Sir Robert Walpole excused the introducing a settled *system of corruption* into the administration.'

19. Anna Letitia Aikin (1743–1825), m. (1774) Rev. Rochemont Barbauld; poet, editor, and miscellaneous writer. As she apparently did not publish a reply to Burke, HW must refer to her liberal tendencies as shown, for example, in her *Address to the Opposers of the Repeal of the Corporation and Test Acts,* signed 'A Dissenter,' 3 March 1790. See in this connection Grace A. Ellis, *Memoir, Letters . . . of Anna Laetitia Barbauld,* 1874, i. 192–4.

calls our *poissardes,* spit their rage at eighteen pence a head,[20] and will return to Fleet Ditch,[21] more fortunate in being forgotten than their predecessors immortalized in the *Dunciad.*

I must now bid you good night, and night it is to the tune of morning. Adieu all three!

PS. I am glad you did not get a Parmesan *Otranto.* A copy is come so full of faults, that it is not fit to be sold here.[22]

To Barbara Cecilia Seton, Tuesday 21 December 1790

Address: To Miss Cecilia Seton at Caversham Hill near Reading, Berkshire.
Postmark: ISLEWO[RTH] 21 DE 90.
Addressed by Kirgate.

Strawberry Hill, Dec. 21, 1790.

Dear Madam,

I HAVE received your letter and conclude that at the same time you received one from me,[1] and from our friends too. I had the comfort of receiving two from them last night of Nov. 22nd and 29th, and of learning that at last they have got their letters from England, and do receive them regularly through Germany; but I doubt still whether they will receive my three next which went *par Paris.*

I am not quite delighted at their seeming to be so much pleased with Florence a second time, though it is sure that I wish them happy anywhere and everywhere; but I had rather they could find felicity in England.

You will excuse my saying no more now, for though I write this myself, I have a little gout in my left wrist—but I beg you will not mention it to them, for it is going off, and will be gone long before they could hear of it, and I did write to them last night by the common post, and it will go away tonight, to contradict what I had said about the French pacquet, which at last did escape, and which ac-

---

20. Mrs Macaulay's pamphlet sold for 2s. 6d., but Numbers 1, 2, and 4 of the list given in n. 17 sold for 1s. 6d.
21. See Pope, *Dunciad,* ii. 271 ff.
22. HW must refer to proofs or to an ad- vance copy, for the book was not published until Oct. 1791; see Edwards to HW 21 Oct. 1791.

1. *Ante* 17 Dec. 1790.

count I had given in the letter that goes today in Lord Hervey's packet.

Adieu! my dear Madam,

Yours most sincerely,

Hor. Walpole

To Robert Berry, Wednesday 22 December 1790

Address: À Monsieur Monsieur Robert Berry à la poste restante à Florence, Italie. [Forwarded: 'Pisa.'] *Postmark:* FIRENZE. Endorsed: 'Pd 1s.'

Endorsed on cover by Robert Berry: 'Letter from Mr Walpole 8 December 1790,' apparently a double mistake for '8 January 1791'; the letter would have reached Pisa about that date. This letter is not recorded in 'Visitors.'

Strawberry Hill, Dec. [22], 1790.[1]

Dear Sir,

IF your letter did not give me so much pleasure from many particulars, I should be vexed at your thinking it necessary to thank me for an affection, by which I am certainly by far the greatest gainer. At my great age, and decrepit as I am, what could happen so fortunate to me in the dregs of life, as to meet with you and your daughters, and them very pretty young women universally admired, and still more for their virtues, sweet tempers, knowledge and such funds of good sense, as makes them company for the most sensible of both sexes as you constantly have seen—was not this an acquisition to value as I do, when you allowed me to enjoy so much of your society?—Indeed I sometimes reproach myself and say 'Did not I engross too much of their time, and may not my blind self-love have contributed to deprive me of that blessing?' Yes, I know I was unreasonable—and may never be so happy again! Can I at past 73 depend on a great life? —I am not so vainly sanguine. Nay, can I be so unjust as to wish to shorten their stay in a country to which they are so partial? Yet human nature, though worn out, cannot, with all its reason, philosophy, and what is much stronger in me, friendship, put itself so entirely out of the question, as to eradicate every hope that they may

1. MS reads 'Dec. 23, 1790,' but HW also gives the same date to the second part, which he wrote on the following day, the day of the storm, 23 Dec. In the first part he mentions the death of the Duchess of Argyll 'the day before yesterday': she died 20 Dec.

have a wish to return home; though you alarm me, sir, when you speak hypothetically of being in England by the annual period of your setting out[2]—should there be any *if*[3] in the case, I doubt there will be no *if* for me—Forgive my returning your favour by this melancholy strain; I am too weak to command myself, and the best advice I can give to your daughters, is to gratify their own, and so reasonable inclinations and ascribe my grief to what I should think myself and would allow to be dotage, if there were one spark of ridiculous love in my affection for your daughters, and which is equal for both. I am most happy in the accounts you and they give of their health and looks.

On reading what I have been writing, I perceive I had omitted half my words. In fact your letter arrived at nine tonight, and affected me so much, that I began to answer it the instant I had read it, and have written in great precipitation—I will now turn to subjects less interesting, as indeed to me almost all other subjects are. I will only first say, that I know your daughters have friendships in Swisserland that may detain them;[4] but on that point I most assuredly prefer your safeties to the whole mass of my personalities, and implore again and again that you will cross to Flanders, and avoid total France.

The Duchess of Argyle died the day before yesterday: she had kept her bed for some days.

Poor Lady Douglas has been twice thought out of danger, but is relapsed and in extreme danger. This would make another gap in my society: she is very sensible and amiable.

Thursday, 23rd.

My head was so confused last night, and I have made so many interlineations, that I can scarce read it myself—if you cannot, you will have no loss.

When I went to bed, the wind was very high, yet I got to sleep. At half an hour after four I was waked by such volleys of thunder, lightning, hail, and then a torrent of rain, as I believe was never known in this temperate clime two days before Christmas.[5] I thought my

---

2. See first paragraph of following letter.

3. MS reads 'be an any *if.*'

4. This reference is unexplained. The Berrys returned through Switzerland in 1791, but Mary Berry records no visits to friends; see MBJ i. 358–60.

5. 'The storm on Thursday morning last is thought to be the greatest, during its continuance, of any that has happened in England since 1703' (*London Chronicle* 25–28 Dec. 1790, lxviii. 618). Conway mentions the violence of the storm, in his letter to HW 23 Dec. 1790.

little castle would be crushed under the bombardment. The lightning darted down the chimney, through the crevices of the shutters
and the linen curtains of my bed: Some of my servants and others of
the village got [out] of their beds—yet I find no mischief done here,
nor yet, anywhere else[6]—and with this *no* accident I must supply part
of my letter for want of more important news. The debates in Parliament on the Spanish Peace[7] and the new taxes[8] have produced some
long days,[9] but less heat than ever,[10] and hitherto most decided majorities. About Hastings's trial[11] they are more puzzled than angry.

I propose settling in town the beginning of next week,[12] and after
the holidays shall probably be less sterile.

Give me leave to finish with an observation, that for three, not
new, travellers, you seem not to choose the most judicious months
for your journeys: the coldest and the hottest cannot both be the
most suitable. You went to Florence in November, and propose setting out for Swisserland towards the middle of June—surely May
would be preferable!

Adieu! dear Sir. I shall always be happy to hear from you, if without thanks. Your daughters seem to write too much for their delicate
breasts—why not take it by turns?

Yours most cordially

H. W.

To Mary Berry, Sunday 2 January 1791

Address: À Mademoiselle Mademoiselle Berry à la poste restante à Florence,
Italie. [Forwarded: 'Pisa.'] *Postmark:* Illegible. Endorsed: 'Pd 1s.'
Posted 3 Jan. ('Visitors').
The address and the middle section dated 'Sunday evening' are in Kirgate's
hand.

6. For a summary of the considerable
damage done by the storm, see GM 1790, lx
pt ii. 1143–4.

7. And particularly the armament budget
arising from the preparations preceding
the peace; see, for example, the *St James's
Chronicle* 16–18 Dec. 1790.

8. For a discussion of the new taxes on
sugar, malt, spirits, game licences, and as-
sessed taxes, see ibid. 16–18 Dec. to 21–23
Dec. 1790.

9. In the ten days preceding HW's letter
the House of Commons adjourned as follows: 13 Dec., 10:30 P.M.; 14 Dec., 2 A.M.;

15 Dec., 9 P.M.; 16 Dec., 10 P.M.; 17 Dec.,
2:30 A.M.; 20 Dec., 8 P.M.; 21 Dec., 8 P.M.;
22 Dec., 2:30 A.M. (ibid. 11–14 Dec. to 21–23
Dec. 1790).

10. The debate on the armament budget,
for example, was 'tedious and desultory'
(ibid. 16–18 Dec. 1790).

11. Which had been discussed 22 Dec.,
and was further debated on the day HW
wrote this part of his letter (ibid. 21–23,
23–25 Dec. 1790).

12. HW was forced to change his plan
because of an attack of gout and rheumatism; see following letter.

Strawberry Hill, Jan. 2, 1791.

No. 13.

I DOUBT the letter I wrote lask week[1] to Mr B. was both confused and illegible—for the latter, no matter. The truth is, I had got the gout in my left hand; and whenever a fit comes, I suppose it may be my last; and the consequence of that idea was, the thought that I might never see you more! I had just been delighting myself with having settled Clivden—then came Mr B.'s letter, which after relating your plan, and mentioning your intention of being at home by the period of your setting out, talked of a visit in Swisserland, which I dreaded would detain you, and then said, '*all subject to correction and alteration*'—Those words went to my heart, as if threatening prolongation of your term, though perhaps meaning only the intervening time—in short, I quite despaired!

I have had the gout in my hand for above a fortnight now; it mends very slowly indeed—but I have been much worse with the rheumatism, which joined it, and still possesses that whole arm and shoulder. I have been quite immovable, but by two servants; and this is the first day I have been able to attempt writing to you. I have not had much pain but in being put to bed and in being taken up. I have no fever, my appetite quite perfect, and my sleep so excellent, that I do little else but sleep. The exact state of my case is, that I do not recover so fast as I used to do, which is not at all surprising at my age; nor perhaps so soon as I should in town; but I dread a relapse; and besides as my greatest danger always lies in the weakness of my breast, I am safer here, where I see nobody, and cannot be made to talk. I have written all this in my lap without stopping; so you may be sure I am not very bad—I could not have done as much yesterday, but I certainly am better today than I have been at all—now I will rest.

Sunday evening.

Having written enough with my own hand to convince you that I am not very ill, I will, for ease, let Kirgate continue. I received yours, No. 12, of December the 6th two days ago, a long time coming! However, if this is as slow, you will be pretty sure that I am well when you receive it.

1. The preceding letter.

I am glad you are going to Pisa,[2] Florence is too cold for you. You divert me with the account of the Charming's brother[3] being a democrat: upon my word, the transition from an English Catholic non-juror to a French leveller, is Pindaric enough.[4] Still it does not look well for the National Assembly when their proselytes fly the country, as well as those they persecute.[5] That synod has lately ordered £500,000 sterling to be issued to the famished in the provinces:[6] they asked for *bread,* and they have given them *paper.* They might as well have sent the useless clergy,

And helpt to bury those they helpt to starve.[7]

The Duchess of Biron is returned to London, where, with her spirit, I am sure she is better than at Paris: she was at the play there, and a song applicable to the Queen being encored as a compliment, and the Duchess applauding with her fan on the box, a shower of apples flew at her, and with them a penknife that hardly missed her.[8] She took it away with her, and the next morning sent it to La Fa-

2. They had been in Pisa since 11 Dec. 1790 (MBJ i. 255). Robert Berry wrote to Bertie Greatheed from Florence 7 Dec. 1790: 'Here, at first, we thought of establishing ourselves for good, but the mildness of the climate of Pisa, and my daughters not choosing to form any liaison with some of our countrywomen who happen to be here at present, nor to give offence by shunning their company, made us resolve to spend the three winter months there, and to return to Florence in March' (MBJ i. 246).

3. Charles Jerningham.

4. Elsewhere HW refers to the suddenness of Pindar's transitions (to Dalrymple 3 Feb. 1760) and to his 'eccentric flights' (to Pinkerton 14 Aug. 1788).

5. 'At the Revolution he [Charles Jerningham] was stripped of the whole of his property placed in that kingdom, and [was] compelled to return to England. At the peace of Amiens, in 1802, he returned to France, to recover his property if possible; but all his efforts were vain, and on the breaking out of war, in 1803, he was detained prisoner with the rest of his countrymen till the King's restoration' (John Kirk, *Biographies of English Catholics in the Eighteenth Century,* ed. John Hungerford Pollen and Edwin Burton, 1909, p. 139).

6. See the *Moniteur* 5 décembre 1790; the amount was about 125,000 livres.

7. 'He help'd to bury whom he help'd to starve' (Pope, 'Epistle to Dr Arbuthnot,' l. 248).

8. The following account appears in a letter from Paris, 21 Dec. 1790: 'The playhouses here are now without sentinels; sentinels who formerly gave laws to the theatres, and from whose bayonets there was no appeal. The opera of *Iphigenia* has caused some bustle within these few days; the *aristocrates* repeatedly applauded the chorus of "Chantons, célébrons notre Reine," which was resented by the pit; the unpopular gentry of the boxes threw apples among the sticklers for liberty, which insolence had like to have cost them dear; already preparations were making to scale the boxes, and deal destruction among the party; but by the happy intervention of some officers, who called in the guard, the offenders were taken up, and the fury of the pit was appeased; the same piece has been represented since, without any disturbance' (*St James's Chronicle* 23–25 Dec. 1790). Mrs Montagu, in a letter to her sister 7 Jan. 1791, refers to the incident (*Mrs Montagu,* ed. Reginald Blunt, [1923] ii. 255).

yette, and desired he would lay it on the Altar of Liberty—and then came away.

I have little or no English news for you. Lady Douglas, after so many struggles, will live. It is declared that Mrs Child is going to marry Lord Ducie;[9] as they are both fifty, nobody can have any objection, if they have not themselves. She gives him ten thousand pounds; they are to live on her twenty thousand pounds a year from the shop,[10] and she reserves in her own power £70,000 that she has saved; my Lord laying up his own estate for his two sons.[11]

Monday 3rd.

I choose to finish with my own hand, that you may not think me worse: indeed I am better; but the amendment is very slow. I have no actual pain at all, nor any more gout coming; but the swelling of my left hand remains, and the elbow and shoulder are still lame. This is the whole truth.

Lady Mt Edgcumbe and Madame de la Villebague have been here from Richmond this morning, and says Mrs Siddons has suffered so much by her late exertions[12] that she has relapsed,[13] and they think must quit the stage. They told me nothing else, and so I will conclude. My next week's letter will I trust be more satisfactory. Adieu!

9. Sarah Jodrell (1741–93), dau. of Gilbert Jodrell of Ankerwycke; m. (1) (1763) the banker, Robert Child (ca 1740–82) of Osterley Park, Middlesex; m. (2) (18 Jan. 1791) as 2d wife, Francis Reynolds-Moreton (1739–1808), 3d Bn Ducie of Tortworth, 1785 (GEC; GM 1763, xxxiii. 517; GM 1782, lii. 406).

10. That is, the bank of Child and Co., 1 Fleet Street (John Trusler, *London Adviser and Guide*, 1786, p. 182; F. G. Hilton Price, *Handbook of London Bankers*, 1876, pp. 25–36). In *post* 23 Nov. 1793, HW sets the income at £25,000.

11. Thomas Reynolds-Moreton (1776–1840), 4th Bn Ducie, 1808: cr (1837) E. of Ducie; and Hon. Augustus John Francis Reynolds-Moreton (1777–1854), Lt 1st Dragoons, 1794; Lt and Capt. 1st Foot Guards, 1796; Lt-Col., 1805; retired, 1810 (Collins, *Peerage*, 1812, vii. 414; Burke, *Peerage*, 1928, p. 786, *sub* Ducie; GM 1854, n.s. xlii.

207; *Army Lists*). According to a newspaper report, Mrs Child settled £10,000 on each of them.

12. Following performances on 7 and 14 Dec. 1790 (*ante* 17 Dec. 1790), Mrs Siddons acted in *Isabella* 21 Dec. 1790 (*St James's Chronicle* 18–21 Dec. 1790), apparently her only performances before the date of this letter.

13. 'Mrs Siddons, we learn with much regret, has relapsed into her former ailment—nothing like the disorder so falsely insinuated; but one of extreme danger; for which we believe the faculty are less assistant than any other—a cancer' (*St James's Chronicle* 4–6 Jan. 1791). But in ibid. 11–13 Jan. 1791, it is reported that her 'health was yesterday considerably better, and there are hopes that she will again be enabled to return to the stage,' and a week later she was 'in a fair way of recovery' (*London Chronicle* 20–22 Jan. 1791, lxix. 80).

To Mary Berry, Sunday 9 January 1791

Address: À Mademoiselle Mademoiselle Berry à Pisa, Italie.
Posted 11 Jan. ('Visitors').
The address and part of the letter are in Kirgate's hand; see below.

Strawberry Hill, Sunday, Jan. 9, 1791.

No. 14.

I AM unfortunate, for when I want most to satisfy you by writing with my own hand, I am least able to do so comfortably, for the rheumatism is got into my right elbow too, and nothing can be more awkward, than my writing at all. You may be assured now, that though my disorder began with a little gout, it is a decided rheumatism, which I think much worse, as it is not so sure of quitting its hold. My best prospect is being carried to town,[1] but I do not think I could yet bear a carriage. All I have done yet is to walk with a little help from the Red Bedchamber[2] to the Blue Room—that is, down three steps; and that journey contains my daily and whole history.[3]

Now I have satisfied you that my handwriting is alive, it shall act by proxy; but it will not be like a king that says a few words, and then tells the assembly that his chancellor will deliver the rest; now it happens, that Chancellor Kirgate has nothing to deliver, for he nor his Majesty know a word of news.

I am glad you are pleased with your lodgings at Pisa, and think you shall like the company. It is a novelty to me that you have put up some learned men there; Mr Pinkerton,[4] who is of no great authority with you, has often talked to me of the mighty science and learning of the Italians. They may live at Pisa for what I know; Mr Parsons[5] was out of luck, to live so long at Florence, and be forced to go to search for the wise men in Germany[6]—I shall rest at present, and finish this tomorrow evening.

1. See following letter.
2. Which HW usually used during attacks of gout; see *ante* 18 Sept. 1789.
3. The two following paragraphs are in Kirgate's hand.
4. John Pinkerton (1758–1826), antiquary and historian; HW's correspondent.
5. William Parsons (fl. 1785–1807), dilettante writer of verses, who with Bertie Greatheed, Robert Merry, and Mrs Piozzi contributed to *The Florence Miscellany*,

1785. Mary Berry refers to him *post* 28 Sept. 1794 as 'that high priest of ennui.'
6. After living for several years in Italy, chiefly at Florence, Parsons visited Weimar in 1790, as appears from his 'Sonnet, on Leaving Weimar, in Saxony, in the Year 1790,' in which he eulogizes Goethe, Schiller, and Wieland. See *Travelling Recreations*, 1807, ii. 95–6; see also 'Briefe der Frau Sophie v. Schardt an v. Seckendorff,' *Goethe-Jahrbuch*, 1904, xxv. 79, and Hein-

Monday 10th.

I try to write a little myself, and you see I can, but it shall be only to tell you my exact case, in which I have not deceived you. It is most clearly rheumatism, all over my left hand, arm and shoulder, which I do not find mend at all, and for the last two nights the right elbow has been bad too, though not near so helpless as the other. I rise every day and sit in the Blue Room till eleven at night; but the weather is most unfortunate for me, either tempests, or rains—the meadows quite overflowed. I will undoubtedly be carried to town the moment it is possible.

I hope I shall be able to give you a better account next week; and that shows my confidence that you will be wishing for a better account, I mean, all three. Adieu, all three!

To Mary Berry, Saturday 15 January 1791

Address: À Mademoiselle Mademoiselle Berry à Pisa, Italia. [Written between the lines of the address, and marked through: 'Monsr (word illegible) Officiale della Posta.']
Posted 18 Jan. ('Visitors').
Address and entire letter in Kirgate's hand.

Berkeley Square, Jan. 15, 1791.

No. 15.

IF I had not promised to write again this post I should have been disinclined to it, for I cannot give you a better account of myself. The first amendment I perceived was on Tuesday morning last, and I really thought the worst over, but after dinner the gout came into my right hand, and has taken possession of that whole arm too, while the left hand and arm is so very little better that I have scarce any use from either. In this most uncomfortable state I did determine to come to town, and here I actually arrived yesterday: I bore the journey very well, and had a better night after it than I had had for some time; so that probably the warmth of London has contributed a little already, and may in time do more—You see I do not make the case better than it is. Danger there is none, but the case of the sufferer is not much mitigated by that consideration.

rich Düntzer, *'Zwei Bekehrte.' Zacharias Werner und Sophie von Schardt,* Leipzig, 1873, p. 353. The last two references are kindly supplied by Prof. Carl F. Schreiber, Yale University.

Sunday[1] the 16th.

Though I have had a good night, my journal does not yet improve, not one of my limbs mends, and I have the additional dread of the gout coming into one of my knees. In this deplorable state you may imagine I scarce see anybody, nor can have anything almost to talk of but my suffering, helpless self. It is vexatious to give you such an account, but I am sure you had rather receive this true than a fictitious one; besides, you may reasonably conclude that by the time you receive this letter there may be some considerable amendment in me.

Yesterday I received your No. 14, of the 22nd of last month, with an account of your Pisan life and acquaintance; just what I wanted to know, yet you call it a dull detail: think, then, what I send you in return, the journal of a sick room! Thank you for the memoirs of the Grifonis, and for Miss Agnes's horse[2]—Now I will bate a little.

Sunday evening.

I do think I begin to use a finger or two of my left hand, which is a great event in this room, as I admit no others. The Edgcumbes and Johnstones, and a few more have called here this morning, but I could not see them. Lady Mary and Mr Churchill are almost the only persons I do receive, and Jerningham I have seen once. The town, they say, is quite empty, but probably will be fuller by Tuesday, for the Queen's birthday.[3] I shall leave a little of my paper for my progress tomorrow, if I make any: in any case, this bulletin is long enough already.

Monday the 17th.

I am reduced to make bonfires for negatives; the gout is not come into my knee, and I must rejoice that I have no other matter of triumph, as I have not recovered one joint in either arm or hand; so I will finish this letter, as I shall have certainly nothing better to tell you by this post. Adieu.

1. Kirgate first wrote 'Monday.'
2. Both the Berrys were riding for their health; see following letter.
3. For a description of the 'very numer-ous and splendid Court,' and of the ball which followed, see *St James's Chronicle* 18–20 Jan. 1791, and *London Chronicle* 18–20 Jan. 1791, lxix. 66–8.

Tuesday morning the 18th.

I just add one line before this goes to the post, to say that I have had another very good night, and yet, alas! I do not find any amendment; what time may do I do not know.

To Mary Berry, Saturday 22 January 1791

Address: À Mademoiselle Mademoiselle Berry.
Posted 25 Jan. ('Visitors').
Address and entire letter in Kirgate's hand.

Berkeley Square, Sat., Jan. 22, 1791.[1]

No. 16.

I HAVE been most unwillingly forced to send you such bad accounts of myself by my two last letters, but as I could not conceal all, it was best to tell you the whole truth. Though I do not know that there was any real danger, I could not be so blind to my own age and weakness, as not to think that with so much gout and fever the conclusion might very probably be fatal, and therefore it was better you should be prepared for what might happen. The danger appears to be entirely over; there seems to be no more gout to come; I have no fever, have a very good appetite, and sleep well. Mr Watson,[2] who is all tenderness and attention, is persuaded today that I shall recover the use of my left hand, of which I despaired much more than of the right, as having been seized three weeks earlier. Emaciated, and altered, I am incredibly, as you would find were you ever to see me again—But this illness has dispelled all visions! And as I have so little prospect of passing another happy autumn, I must wean myself from whatever would embitter my remaining time by disappointments.

Your No. 15 came two days ago, and gives me the pleasure of knowing that you both are the better for riding, which I hope you will continue. I am glad too, that you are pleased with your Duchess of

1. 'No. 26' (B).

2. 'His surgeon' (?B, Wright vi. 384). Henry Watson (d. 1793), of Rathbone Place; sometime warden of the Corporation of Surgeons and member of the Court of Examiners; surgeon to the Middlesex Hospital, and later to the Westminster Infirmary; F.R.S., 1767 (GM 1793, lxiii pt ii. 1054; GM 1794, lxiv pt ii. 1017; *London Chronicle* 31 Oct.–2 Nov. 1793, lxxiv. 427; *Record of the Royal Society of London,* 3d edn, 1912, p. 354). He gave to HW 'a splendid carving in ivory of Venus and Cupid, finely drawn and executed, but in the Flemish style,' sold SH xvi. 115.

Fleury[3] and your Latin professor;[4] but I own, except your climate and the six hundred camels,[5] you seem to me to have met with no treasure which you might not have found here without going twenty miles; and even the camels, according to Soame Jennings's[6] spelling, were to be had from Carrick and other places.[7]

I doubt you apply Tully *De Amicitia* too favourably[8]—at least, I fear, there is no paragraph that countenances seventy-three and twenty-seven.

I wonder you have not heard oftener from Lisbon.[9] She[10] seems perfectly well, and to have settled her return, which is to be through Spain: after the 20th of February our letters are to be directed to Madrid.[11] She is in great distress, and I heartily pity her, about Fidèle,[12] which seems dying.

3. Anne-Françoise-Aimée de Franquetot de Coigny (1769–1820), only child of the Comte de Coigny (*post* 12 Feb. 1791); a famous beauty, generous with her favours; m. (1) (1784) André-Hercule-Marie-Louis de Rosset de Rocozel de Pérignan, Marquis, later (1788) Duc, de Fleury; divorced May 1793; m. (2) (1795) Claude-Philibert-Hippolyte de Mouret, Comte de Montrond; was divorced from him in 1802, and was known thereafter as Mme Aimée de Coigny (Woelmont de Brumagne vii. 788–90; L.-J. Arrigon, *La Jeune captive,* 1921, p. 227 *et passim*). In Oct. 1790 she joined her father at Pisa, and her husband, who had remained at Nice, followed her there in December; they went to Rome in the spring of 1791 (Arrigon, op. cit. 121–2). When HW met her in 1792, he described her as 'much the prettiest Frenchwoman I ever beheld. Though little, and more than nut-brown, she is perfect of her size, with very fine eyes and nose, and a most beautiful mouth and teeth, and natural colour. She is but two and twenty, very lively, and very sensible' (HW to Lady Ossory 8 Oct. 1792). See also *post* 15 Oct. 1793.

4. Not identified.

5. 'Camels were, and are still, bred at San Rossore near Pisa. They were introduced into Tuscany in 1622 by the Grand Duke Ferdinand II' (T). HW exaggerates: in 1789 there were only 196 camels (Montgomery Carmichael, *In Tuscany,* 1901, pp. 175–7).

6. Soame Jenyns (1704–87), poetaster; M.P. 1742–80; see COLE i. 202 *et passim.* In the 1780's, according to Fanny Burney, HW, Richard Owen Cambridge, and Soame Jenyns 'were commonly, then, denominated the old wits' (Frances Burney d'Arblay, *Memoirs of Doctor Burney,* 1832, ii. 268; see also ibid. 287–99).

7. A pun on Campbells. HW wrote to Lady Ossory 23 July 1775: 'I tell you an excellent story and quote my author, Lord North. Mr Cambridge, with all his propensity to credit new-imported marvels, was struck with hearing Mr Bruce affirm having sent some camels to Abyssinia, and suspended his faith till the fact could be examined. He galloped to Soame Jenyns, and begged to have the registers of exportation in the Board of Trade searched. After some days, Jenyns wrote to tell him that he had scrutinized all the records relating to Philadelphia, Carolina, Virginia, etc., etc., and did indeed find a prodigious number of the species in question had gone to all those provinces, but that they did not spell their names like the *camels* he wotted of.'

8. In the absence of Mary Berry's letter, the reference is unexplained.

9. Extracts of Mrs Damer's letters to Mary Berry from Lisbon 21 Nov. and 2, 8, and 25 Dec. 1790 are printed in MBJ i. 270–4.

10. 'Mrs Damer' (B).

11. She arrived at Madrid 30 March 1791 (Percy Noble, *Anne Seymour Damer,* 1908, p. 128).

12. 'Mrs Damer's dog; it died at Lisbon' (?B, MBJ i. 280).

Monday the 24th.

I think I shall give you pleasure, by telling you that I am very sure now of recovering from the present fit. It has almost always happened to me, in my considerable fits of the gout, to have one critical night that celebrates its departure: at the end of two different fits I each time slept eleven hours: Morpheus is not quite so young, nor so generous now, but with the interruption of a few minutes, he presented me with eight hours last night, and thence I shall date my recovery.

I shall now begin to let in a little company, and as the Parliament will meet in a week,[13] my letters will probably not be so dull as they have been, nor shall I have occasion, nor be obliged to talk so much of myself, of which I am sure others must be tired, when I am so much tired myself.

Tuesday the 25th.

I have had another good night, and clearly do mend. I even hope that in a fortnight I shall be able to write a few lines with my own hand, which makes me less solicitous to lengthen my letters now, especially in this interval of Parliament when nothing happens.

Old Mrs French[14] is dead, at last; and I am on the point of losing, or have lost, my oldest acquaintance and friend, George Selwyn, who was yesterday at the extremity.[15] These misfortunes, though they can be so but for a short time, are very sensible to the old; but him I really loved, not only for his infinite wit, but for a thousand good qualities.

Lady Cecilia Johnstone was here yesterday; I said much for you, and she as much to you. The Gunnings[16] are still playing the fool, and perhaps somebody with them, but I cannot tell you the particulars now. Adieu.

13. On 29 Dec. 1790, the House of Lords adjourned to 31 Jan. 1791, and the House of Commons to 2 Feb. 1791 (*St James's Chronicle* 28–30 Dec. 1790).

14. 'An Irish lady who, during the latter part of her life, had a country house at Hampton Court' (B, MBJ i. 281; cf. Wright vi. 385).

15. Selwyn died at 2:30 P.M. 25 Jan. 1791

at his house in Cleveland Row, St James's (*St James's Chronicle* 25–27 Jan. 1791; John Heneage Jesse, *George Selwyn and His Contemporaries*, 1882, i. 30).

16. Elizabeth Gunning and her mother: Susannah Minifie (ca 1740–1800), sentimental novelist, m. (1768) John Gunning (cf. following letter).

To Mary Berry, Saturday 29 January 1791

Address: À Mademoiselle Mademoiselle Berry.
Posted 1 Feb. ('Visitors').
Address and part of letter in Kirgate's hand; see below.

[Berkeley Square], Saturday, Jan. 29, 1791.[1]

No. 17.

VOICI *de ma propre écriture!* the best proof that I am recovering, though not rapidly, which is not the march of my time of life. For these last six days I have mended more than I expected. My left hand, the first seized, is the most dilatory, and of which I have least hopes. The rheumatism, that I thought so clear and predominant, is so entirely gone, that I now rather think it was hussar gout attacking in flying squadrons the outposts—no matter which: very ill I was, and you might see what I thought of myself—nor can I stand many such victories. My countenance was so totally altered, that I could not trace it myself. Its outlines have returned to their posts, though with deep gaps. This is a true picture and too long an one of self—and too hideous for a bracelet—apropos your sweet Miss Foldsone I believe is painting portraits of *all* our princesses,[2] to be sent to all the princes upon earth, for though I have sent her several written duns,[3] she has not deigned even to answer one in writing—I don't know whether Mrs Buller is not appointed Royal Academician too, for though I desired *the Charming,*[4] who was to dine with her that day, to tell her above a week ago that I should be glad to see her, she has not taken the least notice of it. Mr Batt ditto, who was at Cambridge's when I was at the worst and knew so, has not once inquired after me in town or country—so you see you have carried off your friends from me as well as yourselves—and it is not *them* I regret—or rather in fact I outlive all my friends! Poor Selwyn is gone to my sorrow, and no wonder Ucalegon feels it![5] He has left about thirty thou-

1. 'No. 27' (B).
2. See *ante* 18 Nov. 1790.
3. Missing.
4. Jerningham.
5. 'Iam proximus ardet/Ucalegon' (*Æneid* ii. 311–12). Cambridge wrote to Mary Berry

29 Jan. 1791: 'That I have not writ sooner is owing to my having had nothing interesting to tell you unless I had alarmed you with my fears for Walpole who was I feared dangerously attacked at once by the rheumatism and gout. But now he and I have

sand pounds to Mlle Fagnani,[6] twenty of which, if she has no children, to go to those of Lord Carlisle;[7] the Duke of Queensberry, residuary legatee.[8]

Old French has died as foolishly as she lived[9] and left £6,000 to you don't know whom, but to be raised out of her judicious collection of trumpery pictures, etc.[10]

Pray delight in the following story; Caroline Vernon,[11] *fille d'hon-*

buried George Selwyn. The newspapers have lately often put us three together; and this very day (Jan. 29) there is this paragraph: Mr Walpole preserves his spirits in the midst of all his infirmities. Owen Camb[ridge] puns and sets infirmities at defiance, and George Selwyn has cut his last joke' (Richard D. Altick, *Richard Owen Cambridge*, Philadelphia, 1941, p. 71).

6. Maria Emily Fagnani (1771–1856), legally the dau. of the Marchese Fagnani, although 'there seems little doubt that her father was the Duke of Queensberry.' She was Selwyn's adopted daughter, the 'Mie Mie' of his letters. She m. (1798) Francis Charles Seymour-Conway, styled E. of Yarmouth, later (1822) 3d M. of Hertford, the 'Marquis of Steyne' of Thackeray's *Vanity Fair*. According to GEC, Selwyn's legacy was 'more than £30,000.'

7. A somewhat different account of the provision in Selwyn's will is given in John Heneage Jesse, *George Selwyn and His Contemporaries*, 1882, i. 30: 'By his will he bequeathed to Maria Fagnani . . . £10,000, four per cent annuities, together with the sum of £23,000, to be paid either on her coming of age or on her marriage; but in the event of her dying previously to either of those events, to be paid to the children of Lord Carlisle.' In 1791 at least six children of Lord Carlisle were living. See Burke, *Peerage*, 1928, pp. 457–8, *sub* Carlisle; Collins, *Peerage*, 1812, iii. 509, 801; John Debrett, *Peerage*, 1806, i. 115.

8. 'With the exception of Ludgershall, which estate, agreeably with the provisions

of his father's will, descended to the Townshend family' (Jesse, loc. cit.).

9. HW doubtless has in mind her difficulties with her husband (HW to Mann 6 Jan. 1743; Montagu i. 113), as well as her collecting of mediocre art objects.

10. By will dated 23 May 1786, with four codicils, offered for probate 29 Jan. 1791, and proved 7 Feb. 1791, Mrs French, after mentioning the disposition of her life interest in an estate in Norfolk, directed her executors to sell her household goods and chattels and her pictures. She gave legacies of 1000 guineas each to the following: her nephews, 1) Richard Lloyd of Bylaugh, Norfolk, and 2) the Rev. Henry Lloyd, also of Norfolk; 3) Mrs Stella Clementina Freeman, spinster, of Charles Street, Cavendish Square, and 4) her sister Mrs Mary Freeman (following the death of Mary Freeman, Mrs French directed in the second codicil that Stella Clementina Freeman receive 2000 guineas); 5) her first servant, William Spencer, and 6) his wife, Mary Spencer, also in her service. The two last-named also received Mrs French's 'animals,' and Mrs Spencer received her wearing apparel and personal effects.

11. Hon. Caroline Vernon (1751–1829), 4th dau. of Henry Vernon of Hilton Park, Staffs, by Lady Henrietta Wentworth (sister of HW's friend and correspondent, Lord Strafford); maid of honour to Queen Charlotte from ca 1769 to the Queen's death in 1818 (Burke, *Landed Gentry*, 1900, p. 1623; *Royal Kalendar* 1769–1818).

neur, lost t'other night £200 at faro, and bade Martindale[12] mark it up: he said he had rather have a draft on her banker—oh! willingly; and she gave him one. Next morning he hurried to Drummond's,[13] lest all her money should be drawn out. 'Sir,' said the clerk, 'would you receive the contents immediately?'—assuredly—'Why, sir, have you read the note?' Martindale took it, it was, 'Pay to the bearer 200 blows well applied.' The nymph tells the story herself—and yet I think the clerk had the more humour of the two.

The Gunninghiad[14] draws to a conclusion. The General[15] a few weeks ago, to prove the equality of his daughter to any match, literally put into the newspapers that he himself is the thirty-second descendant in a line from Charlemagne[16]—*oui, vraiment*—yet he had better have, like Prior's Madam,

> To cut things short, gone up to Adam—[17]

However, this Carlovingian hero does now allow that *the letters* are forgeries, and rather suspects the novelist his lady for the authoress—and if she is, probably Miss Charlemagne is not quite innocent of the plot, though she still maintains that her mother-in-law elect[18] did give

12. Henry Martindale, sometime keeper of a public gaming table; fined £200 on 11 March 1797 for keeping the faro table at Lady Buckinghamshire's; refused a licence in 1799 for a new club of which the Prince of Wales was to be a patron ([W. B. Boulton], *History of White's,* [1892] i. 136–7; *Annual Register,* 1797, xxxix pt ii. 14; [Alexander Dyce], *Recollections of the Table-Talk of Samuel Rogers,* 3d edn, 1856, pp. 193–4; *Journal and Correspondence of William Lord Auckland,* ed. Robert John Eden, 3d Bn Auckland, 1861–2, i. 461).

13. The bank of Robert, Henry, Andrew and John Drummond and Co., Charing Cross (*Supplement to the British Directory of Trade, Commerce, and Manufacture,* 1792, p. [1]). It was also HW's bank; see *post* 19 March 1791, n. 15.

14. 'Meaning the strange, imagined history of a marriage supposed to have been likely to take place between Miss Gunning and the Marquis of Blandford' (?B, Wright vi. 387).

15. John Gunning (ca 1741–97), father of Elizabeth Gunning and only brother of the famous Gunning sisters; attended Westminster school ca 1751–4; entered the army,

1757, and through the influence of his brother-in-law, the Duke of Argyll, became colonel, 1781, colonel of the 65th Foot, 1788, and major-general, 1787 (*Old Westminsters* and *Supp.;* Horace Bleackley, *The Story of a Beautiful Duchess,* 1908, pp. 32, 312; DNB, *sub* Gunning, Susannah). Dissolute and licentious, he seems nevertheless to have played a more admirable part in the Gunning affair than did his wife and daughter, although his actions are placed in the worst light in *An Apology for the Life of Major-General G———,* 1792, and in other pamphlets and prints of the day. For some years previous to 1791 he had been HW's neighbour at Twickenham (Edward Ironside, *History and Antiquities of Twickenham,* 1797, p. 107).

16. The paragraph has not been found.

17. 'And lest I should be wearied, madam,
> To cut things short, came down to Adam.'
> *(Alma* ii. 373–4.)

HW also misquotes the passage in his letter to Mason 23 March 1774.

18. The Duchess of Marlborough. The

her much encouragement; which, considering her Grace's conduct about her children, is not the most incredible part of this strange story.—I have written this at twice, and will now rest—

Sunday evening.

I wish that complaining of people for abandoning me were an infallible recipe for bringing them *back!*—but, I doubt it will not do in acute cases. Today, a few hours after writing the latter part of this, appeared Mr Batt—He asked many pardons, and I easily forgave him, for the mortification was not begun. He asked much after you both. I had a crowd of visits besides; but they all come past two o'clock, and sweep one another away before any can take root: my evenings are solitary enough, for I ask nobody to come; nor indeed does anybody's evening begin, till I am going to bed. I have outlived daylight, as well as my cotemporaries—What have I not survived? the Jesuits, and the monarchy of France—and both without a struggle! Semiramis[19] seems to intend to add Constantinople to the mass of revolutions[20]—but is not her permanence almost as wonderful as the contrary explosions! I wish—I wish we may not be actually flippancying ourselves into an embroil with that Ursa Major of the North Pole.[21] What a vixen little island are we, if we fight with the Aurora Borealis and Tippoo Saib[22] at the end of Asia at the same time!—You, damsels, will be like the end of the conundrum,[23]

You've seen the man, who saw these wondrous sights.[24]

phrase anticipates Katisha by ninety-odd years.

19. Catherine II of Russia, frequently called 'Semiramis,' or 'Semiramis of the North.'

20. Russia and Turkey were at war. HW evidently believed Catherine was responsible for fomenting the disturbances at Constantinople, mentioned in a letter from Vienna 15 Dec. 1790: 'According to letters from Constantinople, the people of that capital, we know not by what means, have been informed of the French Revolution. They are no longer satisfied with their present government: they assemble in crowds, talk loud, and make comparisons which are necessarily to the disadvantage of absolute despotism' (*London Chronicle* 6–8 Jan. 1791, lxix. 26). An account of the

'present state of the war' appears in ibid. 8–11 Jan. 1791, lxix. 35.

21. British mediation between Russia and Turkey is mentioned in the *London Chronicle* 4–6 Jan. 1791, lxix. 23; and Catherine II was reported to be 'proceeding in her design of rivalling us with her navy' (ibid. 27–29 Jan. 1791, lxix. 98).

22. Tippoo Sahib (1753–99), Sultan of Mysore 1782–99. By his attacks on the territory of the Raja of Travancore, he provoked British invasion in 1789, and after Cornwallis's victory at Seringapatam in 1792, he was forced to give up half his dominions. For the state of the war at this time, see *London Chronicle* 20–22 Jan. 1791, lxix. 73.

23. MS reads 'the end of the of the conundrum.'

24. HW is alluding to the well-known

Monday[25] evening.

I cannot finish this with my own hand, for the gout has returned a little into my right[26] arm and wrist, and I am not quite so well as I was yesterday, but I had said my say, and have little to add. The town talk of a marriage between the Duchess of Rutland[27] and Lord Paget,[28] which is all I know of it.[29] The Duchess of Gordon,[30] t'other night, coming out of an assembly, said to Dundas,[31] 'Mr Dundas, you are used to speak in public, will you call my servant?'

Here I receive your long letter of the 7th, 9th, and 10th which it is impossible for me to answer now: there is one part to which I wish to reply, but must defer till next post,[32] by which time I hope to have recovered my own pen. You ask about the House of Argyll;[33] you know I have no connexion with them, nor any curiosity about them. Their relations and mine[34] have been in town but four days, so I know little from them: Mrs Grenville, today, told me the Duke proposes

'Ambiguous Lines' which appear to be non-sensical until properly punctuated. The version given by Carolyn Wells in *The Book of Humorous Verse* (New York [1920], p. 804) runs in part as follows:

'I saw a peacock with a fiery tail
I saw a blazing comet pour down hail
I saw a cloud . . .
          . . . in flames of living fire
I saw a house as high as the moon and
    higher
I saw the glorious sun at deep midnight
I saw the man who saw this wondrous
    sight.'

25. The remainder of the letter is in Kirgate's hand.

26. MS reads 'my my right.'

27. Mary Isabella Somerset (1756–1831), 5th dau. of 4th D. of Beaufort; m. (1776) Charles Manners (1754–87), M. of Granby, later (1779) 4th D. of Rutland. She did not remarry. A famous beauty, she was in politics and fashion a rival of the Duchess of Devonshire.

28. Henry William Paget (1768–1854), styled Lord Paget 1768–1812; 2d E. of Uxbridge, n.c., 1812; cr. (1815) M. of Anglesey; noted cavalryman; distinguished himself at the Battle of Waterloo; field marshal, 1846; m. (1) (25 July 1795) Caroline Elizabeth Villiers (1774–1835), 3d dau. of 4th E. of Jersey; divorced 1810; m. (2) (1810) his mis-

tress, Charlotte Cadogan (1781–1853), divorced wife of Sir Henry Wellesley (later Bn Cowley), and dau. of Charles Sloane Cadogan, 1st E. Cadogan, by HW's niece, Mary Churchill.

29. The possibility of the marriage is mentioned in *The Gazetteer and New Daily Advertiser* 31 Jan., 4, 5, 7, 16, 18, 19, 24, 28 Feb., and 2, 4 March 1791; but in *The Oracle* 9 April it is said that 'the report . . . totally subsides in the fashionable world.' See also *post* 10 April 1791.

30. Jane Maxwell (1748–1812), 2d dau. of Sir William Maxwell, 3d Bt; a celebrated beauty, hostess, wit, and matchmaker; m. (1767) Alexander Gordon (1743–1827), 4th D. of Gordon. Her portrait by Reynolds (1785) is well known.

31. Henry Dundas (1742–1811), cr. (1802) Vct Melville; M.P.; home secretary 1791–4; impeached, but acquitted, on charges of misusing public money, 1806. In Farington's diary for 8 May 1808 it is said that he 'speaks such broad Scotch that he can hardly be understood' (quoted in GEC). According to HW, the Duchess of Gordon's sister, Lady Wallace, was Dundas' mistress ('Mem. 1783–91,' *sub* April, May 1787).

32. See opening section of following letter.

33. Expanded by Mary Berry from HW's 'A.'

34. The Conways.

to continue the same life he used to lead with a cribbage-table and his family.[35] Everybody admires the youngest daughter's[36] person and understanding, but laments her want of education and control. Adieu. I will begin to write again myself as soon as I can.

To Mary Berry, Friday 4 February 1791

Address: À Mademoiselle Mademoiselle Berry.

Addressed by Kirgate; posted 8 Feb. HW noted its subject, 'on not return-[ing],' in 'Visitors.'

Berkeley Square, Friday, Feb. 4, 1791.[1]

No. 18.

LAST post I sent you as cheerful a letter as I could, to convince you that I was recovering. This will be less gay[2]—not because I have had a little return in both arms, but because I have much more pain in my mind than in my limbs.

I see and thank you for all the kindness of your intention, but as it has the contrary effect from what you expect, I am forced for my own peace to beseech you not to continue a manœuvre that only tanta-lizes and wounds me. In your last you put together many friendly words to give me hopes of your return—but can I be so blind as not to see that they are vague words—did you mean to return in autumn, would you not say so? would the most artful arrangement of words be so kind as those few simple ones? In fact, I have for some time seen how little you mean it, and for your sakes I cease to desire it. The pleasure you expressed at seeing Florence again, which, forgive me for saying, is the joy of sight merely, for can a little Italian town and wretched Italian company, and travelling English lads and gov-ernors, be comparable to the choice of the best company of so vast a capital as London, unless you have taken an aversion to England?

---

35. Which consisted of four children: Lord Lorn; Lord John Douglas Edward Henry Campbell (1777–1847), 7th D. of Ar-gyll, 1839; Lady Augusta Clavering; and Lady Charlotte Susan Maria Campbell (see following note; Burke, *Peerage*, 1928, p. 133, *sub* Argyll).

36. Lady Charlotte Susan Maria Camp-bell (1775–1861), m. (1) (1796) Col. John Campbell (d. 1809); m. (2) (1818) Rev. Ed-ward John Bury (d. 1832). A famous beauty, as was her mother, she became a popular novelist and diarist.

---

1. 'No. 28' (B).

2. It is probably the most plaintive letter of the correspondence. HW himself refers to it (*post* 19 March 1791) as 'criminal,' 'complaining,' and 'unjust.'

and your renewed transports at a less and still more insipid town Pisa—these plainly told me your thoughts, which vague words cannot efface—you then dropped, that you could let your London house till next Christmas, and then talked of a visit to Swisserland—and since all this, Mrs Damer[3] has warned me not to expect you till *next spring* —I shall not, nor do I expect *that next* spring—I have little expected this next! My dearest Madam, I allow all my folly and unreasonableness and give them up and abandon them totally. I have most impertinently and absurdly tried *for my own sake merely,* to exact from two young ladies above forty years younger than myself a promise of sacrificing their rooted inclinations to my whims and satisfaction— but my eyes are opened, my reason is returned, I condemn myself— and I now make you but one request, which is, that though I am convinced it would be with the most friendly and good-natured meaning possible, I do implore you not to try to help me to delude myself any more. You never knew half the shock it gave me when I learned from Mr Batt what you had concealed from me, your *fixed* resolution of going abroad last October—and though I did in vain deprecate it, your coming to Twickenham in September, which I know and from my inmost soul believe was from mere compassion and kindness to me—yet it did aggravate my parting with you—I would not repeat all this—but to prevail with you, while I do live, and while you do condescend to have any friendship for me, never to let me deceive myself. I have no right to inquire into your plans, views or designs, and never will question you more about them. I shall deserve to be deluded if I do—but what you do please to say to me, I beg may be frank—I am in every light too weak to stand disappointment—now—I cannot be disappointed. You have a *firmness* that nothing shakes—and therefore it would be unjust to betray your good nature into any degree of insincerity. You do nothing that is not reasonable and right, and I am conscious that you bore a thousand times more from my self-love and vanity than any other two persons but yourselves would have supported with patience so long. Be assured that what I say, I think, feel and mean: derange none of your plans for me. I now wish you to take no one step, but what is conformable to your views, interests and satisfaction. It would hurt me now to interfere with them. I reproach myself with having so ungenerously tried to lay you under any difficulties, and I approve your resolution

3. In a letter now missing.

in adhering steadily to your point. Two posts ago I hinted that I was weaning myself from the anxiety of an attachment to two persons that must have been so uneasy to them, and has ended so sorrowfully to myself[4]—but that anxiety I restrict solely to the desire of your return: my friendship, had I years to live, could not alter or be shaken; and there is no kind of proof or instance of it, that I will not give you both while I have breath.

I have vented what I had at my heart and feel relieved. Do not take ill a word I have said. Be assured I can love you as much as ever I did and do, though I am no longer so unjust as to prefer my own satisfaction to yours. Here I drop the subject—before Tuesday perhaps I shall be able to talk on some other.

Monday 7th.

Though the Parliament is met,[5] and the town, they say, full, I have not heard a tittle of news of any sort, and yet my prison is a coffee-house in a morning, though I have been far from well this whole week. Yesterday and Saturday the gout was so painful in my right shoulder, that I could not stoop or turn round. Today it is in my left elbow, and I doubt, coming into my right foot—in short, it seems to be going its circle over again. I am not very sorry—sufferings reconcile one to parting with one's self. Poor Lady Herries has lost the use of her legs and arms and feet, and cannot walk alone.

One of our numerous tempests threw down Mrs Damer's chimney last week and it fell through her workshop, but fortunately touched none of her own works, and only broke two or three insignificant casts. I suppose you know she returns through Spain.[6]

This minute I have heard that Lord Lothian's[7] daughter Lady Mary St John,[8] and daughter-in-law of Lady Di Beauclerc, died yesterday, having been delivered of a fine boy but the day before.[9]

4. See opening paragraph of *ante* 22 Jan. 1791.

5. The House of Lords on 31 Jan., and the House of Commons 2 Feb. (*St James's Chronicle* 29 Jan.—1 Feb., 1–3 Feb. 1791).

6. HW mentioned it *ante* 22 Jan. 1791.

7. William John Ker (1737–1815), 5th M. of Lothian, 1775.

8. His third daughter, Lady Mary Ker (1767–6 Feb. 1791), m. (1788) at Lady Diana Beauclerk's, Twickenham, Major (later, 1814, General) Hon. Frederick St John (1765–1844), 2d son of 2d Vct Bolingbroke,

by Lady Diana Spencer (afterwards Beauclerk). Lady Mary St John died 'at her house in Park Lane.' Her husband remarried in 1793 and 1821 (Burke, *Peerage*, 1928, pp. 304–5, *sub* Bolingbroke; GM 1788, lviii pt ii. 1124; GM 1791, lxi pt i. 188; *Letters from Mrs Elizabeth Carter to Mrs Montagu*, ed. Montagu Pennington, 1817, iii. 281; *Middlesex Parish Registers*, vol. iii, ed. W. P. W. Phillimore and Thomas Gurney, 1911, p. 88).

9. Robert William St John (5 Feb. 1791–1851), later consul-general at Algiers

If you are curious to know the chief topic of conversation, it is the rival opera houses,[10] neither of which are opened yet, both saying the other is falling down.[11] Taylor[12] has published a pamphlet[13] that does not prove that the Marquis[14] is the most upright Chamberlain that ever dropped from the skies, nor the skies are quite true blue[15]—Adieu! if no postscript tomorrow.—None!

(Burke, *Peerage*, loc. cit., where the date of his death is incorrect; Joseph Foster, *Alumni Oxonienses . . . 1715–1886*, 1887–8; GM 1851, n.s. xxxvi. 99). In his youth he was left much in the care of Lady Diana Beauclerk (Mrs Steuart Erskine, *Lady Diana Beauclerk*, 1903, p. 233).

10. The Pantheon, newly licensed for opera (*ante* 17 July 1790), and the Opera House (King's Theatre, Haymarket), newly rebuilt (*ante* 23 June 1789). During January the Prince of Wales and others attempted to adjust the differences between the two houses, but after more than three weeks of negotiations, the Pantheon (which held the licence and had nothing to lose) refused the overtures of the Haymarket. See *The London Chronicle* 1–4 Jan. to 22–25 Jan. 1791, lxix. 16, 31, 63, 72, 86. Both companies then went into rehearsal (ibid. 27–29 Jan. 1791, 5–8 Feb. 1791, lxix. 102, 136). The rivalry produced a satirical print, 'High Committee, or, Operatical Contest,' which shows Taylor and O'Reilly, the rival managers, as pugilists (BM, *Satiric Prints* vi. 864–5, No. 8010; see also ibid. 862–3, Nos 8007–8).

11. Following an accident 15 Jan. 1791 at the new Opera House, when a flight of unfinished steps gave way, 'by which 15 men [workmen at the theatre] and a boy were much hurt, nine of whom had bones broken, and one is since dead' (*London Chronicle* 15–18 Jan. 1791, lxix. 58), the parish officers in the interests of public safety ordered a survey of the two theatres (ibid. 22–25 Jan. 1791, lxix. 86).

12. William Taylor (ca 1753–1825), who had been a principal proprietor of the Opera House (King's Theatre, Haymarket) since 1781, and who managed it for many years; M.P. Leominster 1797–1802 (GM 1825, xcv pt i. 476). According to Joseph Farington (*Diary*, ed. James Greig, 1922–8, i. 210), he was 'a Scotchman [who] came to London —was a clerk in Mayner House; lent Sheridan £1000—got connected with opera—and into Parliament at recommendation of

Prince of Wales—Duke of Norfolk who brought him in now [10 July 1797] sorry— 2 members were not easily found to present him to the Speaker.' For numerous comments on his pecuniary and operatic difficulties, and his love of practical jokes, see John Ebers, *Seven Years of the King's Theatre*, 1828, pp. 2–30, 241–2 *et passim*. For the last several years of his life he was a prisoner of the King's Bench for debt.

13. *A Concise Statement of Transactions and Circumstances respecting the King's Theatre, in the Haymarket*. By Mr Taylor, the Proprietor. *Together with the Official Correspondence upon the same Subject, between the Rt Hon. the Lord Chamberlain, and Earl Cholmondeley, &c.*, 1791, dated on p. 1, 'January, 1791,' and consisting of 46 pages. Four of the letters in the pamphlet were printed in *The Gazetteer and New Daily Advertiser* 8 Feb. 1791. HW noted in 'Mem. 1783–91' *sub* Jan. 1791: 'Taylor's pamphlet against Lord Salisbury for not licensing the Opera House in the Haymarket published.'

14. 'Of Salisbury' (?B, Wright vi. 392).

15. After the Opera House was burned down in 1789, Taylor and his associates soon made plans to rebuild it. Lord Cholmondeley and other noblemen who had tentative plans for building a new theatre, withdrew, in favour of the old proprietors; but another group, of which O'Reilly (*ante* 17 July 1790) was the nominal head, had plans drawn up for a new building. When the latter plan was dropped, the Lord Chamberlain gave O'Reilly a licence for opera performances at the Pantheon. Taylor hints (p. 45) that this discrimination against the rights of the proprietors of the Opera House was due to 'noble persons, whose countenance, I have been given to understand, he [O'Reilly] has obtained.' (Chief among these 'noble persons' was the Duke of Bedford.) Taylor points out (pp. 38–9) that the licensing of the Opera House under the previous Lord Chamberlain had

To Mary Berry, Saturday 12 February 1791

Address: À Mademoiselle Mademoiselle Berry.
Posted 15 Feb. ('Visitors').

Berkeley Square, Feb. 12, 1791.[1]

No. 19.

I HAVE received your *two* letters of Jan. 17 and 24th with an account of your objects and plans, and the latter are very much what I expected, as before you receive this, you will have seen by my last No. 18. Indeed you most kindly offer to break so far into your plan, as to return at the beginning of next winter; but as that would, as you say, not only be a sacrifice, but risk your healths, can anything upon earth be more impossible than for me to accept or consent to such a sacrifice? Were I even in love with one of you, could I agree to it? and being only a most zealous friend, do you think I will hear of it? Should I be a friend at all, if I wished you, for my sake, to travel in winter over mountains, or risk the storms at sea, that I have not forgotten when you went away? Can I desire you to derange a reasonable plan of economy, that would put you quite at your ease at your return? Have I any pretensions for expecting, still less for asking such or any sacrifices? Have I interested myself in your affairs only to embarrass them?—The only point on which I can make a shadow of complaint, is your talking of what I did to assist your going, as a reason for your wishing to stay longer abroad—that would be *hard* indeed on *me* and would be punishing me severely for doing you a trifling service!—but when you have other and substantial reasons for not returning before spring twelvemonth, it is useless to talk on the other. I do in the most positive and solemn manner refuse to accept the smallest sacrifice of any part of your plan but the single point that would be so *hard* on me. I will say not a word more on your return, and beg your pardon for having been so selfish as to desire it—my only request now is that we may say no more about it— I am grieved that the great distance we are at, must make me still receive letters about it for some weeks. I shall not forget how very un-

become a matter of form, says (p. 43) that 'the building of the theatre itself is completely finished, on a plan of magnificence and accommodation to challenge comparison with any theatre in Europe,' and applies (p. 45) to the King, through the Lord Chamberlain, for a continuation of his licence.

1. 'No. 29' (B).

reasonable I have been myself, nor shall I try to forget it, lest I should be so silly again; but I earnestly desire to be totally silent on a subject that I have totally abandoned, and which it is not at all improbable I may never have occasion to renew.

Your other letter talks as kindly as possible on my illness, on which I am sure I have not deceived you, though I have talked too much on it, and on which to satisfy you, I will still be particular. A fortnight ago I had every reason to think myself quite recovering, but in my left hand—then my pains returned for a week—they are again gone but in my left wrist, which today is uneasy enough. One comfort however I have, which is conviction that all my pains have been and are gouty not rheumatic, which I dread much more as less likely to leave me. Though I am worse at night, I am perfectly easy the moment I lie down in bed, where I go to sleep directly, and often sleep five, nay, seven hours together without waking, though I sometimes sleep in the day too—and my stomach is as strong as ever—but there lies my whole strength—for no baby is weaker, nor less able to help himself. A lover, especially one of seventy-three, would not give you these details—but though I have been unreasonable, and I suspect, vain; I am not ridiculous—let us pass to better, that is, to any other subjects.

Miss Foldsone is a prodigy of dishonest impertinence—I sent her word a week ago by Kirgate that I was glad she had so much employment, but wished she would recollect that your pictures had been paid for these four months. She was such a fool as to take the compliment seriously and to thank me for it, but verbally, and I have heard no more—so I suppose she thinks me as drunk with *her* honours as she is—I shall undeceive her, by sending for the pictures again and telling her I can get twenty persons to finish them as well as she can —and so they could the likenesses, and I doubt, better. What glories have befallen Mrs Buller I know not—but I have not heard a word more of her!

I knew the Comte de Coigny[2] in the year '66; he was then lively and jovial: I did not then think he would turn out a writer,[3] or even

2. 'Great-uncle of the present Duc de Coigny' (?B, Wright vi. 393). Ange-Augustin-Gabriel de Franquetot (1740–1817), Comte de Coigny (Woelmont de Brumagne vii. 789; DU DEFFAND *passim*). His daughter, the Duchesse de Fleury, had joined him at Pisa in Oct. 1790 (*ante* 22 Jan. 1791); he

was in London in 1792–3 (*post* 4 Dec. 1793; L.-J. Arrigon, *La Jeune captive*, 1921, p. 156).

3. In the absence of Mary Berry's letter, this reference remains unexplained. No work of the Comte de Coigny is listed in the Bibl. Nat. Cat. or the BM Cat.

reader; but he was agreeable. I say nothing on France; you must know as much as I do, and probably sooner. I will only tell you that my opinion is not altered in a tittle; what will happen I do not pretend to guess, but am thoroughly persuaded that the present system, if it can be called so, cannot take root.

The flirts towards anarchy here, have no effect at all—Horne Tooke before Christmas presented a saucy libel to the House of Commons as a petition on his election[4]—The House contemptuously voted it only frivolous and vexatious,[5] and disappointed him of a ray of martyrdom—but his fees, etc., will cost him three or four hundred pounds,[6] which never go into a mob's calculation of the ingredients of martyrdom.

I believe I am rather worse than I know (and yet you need not be alarmed) for some of my relations, who never troubled themselves much about me grow very attentive and send me game and sweetmeats, which rather do me good, for they make me smile—and though this fit may be going, they are sure I cannot grow younger.

Monday morning 14th.

I have a story to tell you much too long to add to this, which I will send next post, unless I have leisure enough today from people that call on me to finish it today (having begun it last night) and in that case I will direct it to Miss Agnes.

Mr Lysons the clergyman has just been here, and told me of a Welsh sportsman[7] (a Jacobite, I suppose) who has very recently had

4. On 9 Dec. 1790 Tooke's petition concerning the Westminster election of that year (*ante* 3 July 1790) was read and discussed in the House of Commons; further discussion was postponed to 4 Feb. 1791. For the text of the petition and a summary of the debate, see *Parliamentary History of England . . . Vol. XXVIII* (8 May 1789– 15 March 1791), 1816, columns 921–30. In 'Mem. 1783–91,' *sub* December 1790, HW recorded: 'Horne Tooke's libel on the House of Commons presented as a petition for Westminster. The lawyers for rejecting it, but Mr Fox and Mr Pitt for receiving it for consideration and censure in February.'

5. On 7 Feb. 1791, following Tooke's appearance before the committee.

6. 'An Act for the further regulation of the trials of controverted elections, or returns of members to serve in Parliament'

(1788: 28 Geo. III, c. 52) provided that in case the parliamentary committee reported a petition 'frivolous or vexatious' (Section XVIII), 'the party or parties, if any, who shall have appeared before the committee in opposition to such petition, shall be entitled to recover, from the person or persons, or any of them, who shall have signed such petition, the full costs and expenses which such party or parties shall have incurred in opposing the same' (Section XIX). Lord Hood did not sue Tooke, but Fox brought suit against him in the Court of King's Bench for £198 2s. 2d. At the trial, which did not begin until 30 April 1792, a verdict in favour of the plaintiff was brought in (Minnie Clare Yarborough, *John Horne Tooke*, New York, 1926, pp. 147–50).

7. Thomas Boycott (1734–98), of Boycott,

his daughter christened, Louisa Victoria Maria Sobieski Foxhunter Moll Boycot.[8] The curate[9] of the minister[10] who baptized her, confirmed the truth of it to Mr L.   When Belgioioso[11] the Austrian minister was here, and thought he could write English, he sent a letter to Miss Kennedy, a woman of the town,[12] that began, 'My Kennedy Polly dear girl.'—Apropos—and not much—pray tell me whether the Cardinal of York calls himself King; and whether James VIII, Charles IV, or what?[13]

Tuesday.

I have finished my narrative[14] and it goes tonight with this. I have been without pain these two days. Adieu!

Hinton, and Rudge Hall in Shropshire (Burke, *Landed Gentry*, 1900, p. 168, *sub* Wight-Boycott).

8. (1778–1849), his 7th and youngest dau.; m. (1807) Walter Smythe of Brambridge, Hants, brother of Mrs Fitzherbert. Her name appears in none of the printed registers of Shropshire, but it is given elsewhere as 'Louisa Victoria' (Burke, *Commoners* iv. 471), 'Louisa Victoria Sobieski' (Burke, *Landed Gentry*, 1900, p. 168, *sub* Wight-Boycott), and 'Louisa Sobieski Foxhunting-Moll' (ibid., 1914, p. 219, and in other editions). In the story of the christening she is sometimes confused with her niece, Harriet Boycott (1805–68), 3d dau. of Thomas Boycott (1771–1856); see John Randall, *Old Sports and Sportsmen*, 1873, pp. 120–1; Staffordshire Parish Registers Society, *Pattingham Parish Register, 1559–1812*, ed. H. R. Thomas, 1934, p. xxvi. She has also been confused with her older sister, Maria, who married the 4th Earl of Guilford (Toynbee xiv. 370).

9. Not identified.

10. Perhaps Michael Pye Stephens, whose name occurs in the Sheinton register 1778–1812 as rector (Joseph Foster, *Alumni Oxonienses . . . 1715–1886*, 1887–8; Shropshire Parish Registers, *Diocese of Lichfield*, vol. ii, 1901, Register of Sheinton, p. 20 *et passim*).

11. Lodovico Carlo Maria (1728–1801), Conte di Barbiano di Belgioioso; Knight of Malta; Austrian minister to Stockholm 1764–70, to London 1770–83; minister plenipotentiary and vice-governor of Austrian Netherlands 1783–7. HW thought him 'a sensible good sort of man' (to Lady Mary Coke 27 Jan. 1771), but his tyranny gained him many enemies (du Deffand iii. 75 *et passim;* Marchese Vittorio Spreti, *Enciclopedia storico-nobiliare italiana*, Milano, 1928–36, *Appendice, Parte I*, 1935, p. 284; *Biographie nationale de Belgique*, Bruxelles, 1866–1938, where the date of his death is erroneously given as 1802; Cornelia Knight, *Autobiography*, 1861, i. 77).

12. Presumably Polly Kennedy of Great Russell Street, Bloomsbury, a famous courtesan who 'reached the height of her fame about 1772' (Horace Bleackley, *Ladies Fair and Frail*, [1925] pp. 153–4, 316–18 *et passim;* N&Q 1908, 10th ser. ix. 97; *Mémoires de J. Casanova de Seingault*, ed. Raoul Vèze, 1924–32, ix. 293–4, 422), but possibly the younger and less famous Polly Kennedy, ' "a fine, tall, genteel girl," who lived in Piercy Street . . . who did not attract attention until two or three years later' (Bleackley, op. cit., p. 154). Both flourished at the time of Belgioioso's stay in London.

13. Henry Benedict Maria Clement Stuart (1725–1807), 2d son of the 'Old Pretender'; styled D. of York; cardinal, 1747, and thenceforth known as Cardinal York or Cardinal of York. On the death of his brother in 1788 he assumed the title of Henry IX.

14. The following letter.

To Agnes Berry, Sunday 13 February 1791

Address: À Mademoiselle Mlle Agnes Berry.

Following the notation that No. 19, the preceding letter, was posted 15 Feb., HW wrote 'and ditto to Miss Agnes on Gunn[ings]' ('Visitors').

Memoranda on cover in pencil in unidentified hand:

'Mlle Maclin'

'Mlle Bouguet.'

In connection with the Gunning affair, see also Frances Gerard, 'General Gunning and his Daughter Gunilda,' in her *Some Celebrated Irish Beauties of the Last Century*, 1895, pp. 100–17. This account, though inaccurate in many details, is useful for its quotation of several of the important documents.

[Berkeley Square], Feb. 13, 1791.[1]

No. 19, 2d part.

THE following narrative, though only the termination of a legend, of which you know the foregoing chapters, is too singular and too long to be added to my letter; and therefore, though you will receive two by the same post, you will not repine—in short,

The Gunninghiad is completed—not by a marriage, like other novels of the Minifies.[2] *Voici* how the denouement happened.

Another supposed love-letter had come from the Marquis[3] within these few weeks, which was so improbable, that it raised more suspicions, and was more closely examined, and thence was discovered to have been both altered and interlined. On this the General[4] sent *all* the letters down to the Marquis, desiring to be certified of their authenticity, or the contrary—I should tell you that all this has happened since the death of his sister,[5] who kept up the high tone, and said *her* brother was not a man to be trifled with. The Marquis immediately distinguished the two kinds, owned the few letters that disclaimed all inclination for Miss Charlemagne;[6] disavowed the rest. Thence fell the General's wrath on his consort, of which I have told you.[7]

1. 'No. 30' (B).

2. 'The name of the family of Mrs Gunning' (?B, Wright vi. 394). Before her marriage, Mrs Gunning and her sister Margaret Minifie wrote in collaboration *The Histories of Lady Frances S—— and Lady Caroline S——*, 4 vols, 1763 (*Marriage, Baptismal, and Burial Registers of the Collegiate Church of St Peter, Westminster*, ed.

Joseph Lemuel Chester, 1876, p. 464; DNB, *sub* Gunning, Susannah).

3. Of Blandford.

4. General Gunning.

5. The Duchess of Argyll, who died 20 Dec. 1790.

6. Miss Gunning: an allusion to General Gunning's claim of descent from Charlemagne (*ante* 29 Jan. 1791).

7. No reference to the General's wrath

However, the General and his ducal brother-in-law[8] thought it expedient that Miss Charly's character should be cleared as far as possible, she still maintaining the prodigious encouragement she had received from the parents of her intended *sposo*. She was ordered to draw up a narrative,[9] which should be laid before the D[uke] of M[arlborough][10] and if allowed by him, to be shown for her vindication. She obeyed, and her former assertions did not suffer by the new statement—but one singular circumstance was added—she confessed —ingenuous maid!—that though she had not been able to resist so dazzling an offer, her heart was still her cousin's, the other Marquis.[11]

Well! this narrative, after being laid before a confidential junto[12] at Argyll House,[13] was sent to Blenheim[14] by the General by his own groom.[15]

Judge of the astonishment of the junto when Carloman,[16] almost as soon as was possible, laid before them a short letter from the Prince of Mindleheim,[17] declaring how delighted he and his princess had been at their son's having made choice of so *beautiful* and *amiable* a virgin for his bride; how greatly they had encouraged the match, and how chagrined they were, that from the lightness and inconstancy of

appears in HW's extant letters to the Berrys. The General, however, had ordered Mrs Gunning to leave his house; see *A Letter from Mrs Gunning, addressed to His Grace the Duke of Argyll*, 2d edn, 1791, p. 8.

8. The Duke of Argyll.

9. It is not printed in Mrs Gunning's *Letter*.

10. Expanded to 'Marlbro' by Mary Berry from HW's 'M.'

11. Of Lorn.

12. It appears from Mrs Gunning's *Letter* 115, and Capt. Essex Bowen's affidavit in his *A Statement of Facts, in Answer to Mrs Gunning's Letter*, 1791, p. 45, that the junto consisted of General Gunning; the Duke of Argyll; his brother and brother-in-law: Lord Frederick Campbell (*post* 27 March 1791) and General Conway; and Andrew Stuart (d. 1801), lawyer and friend of the family. There is no doubt that HW received his account from Conway.

13. Expanded by Mary Berry from HW's 'A.' Town house of the Duke of Argyll, in Argyll Street, on the site of the present No. 7 Argyll Street (Regent Street).

14. Expanded by Mary Berry from HW's 'Bl.'

15. William Pearce (b. ca 1741), who had come from Ireland with General Gunning in May 1790 (Mrs Gunning, *Letter* 25), and whose affidavit concerning his part in the affair is printed in Capt. Essex Bowen's *A Statement of Facts, in Answer to Mrs Gunning's Letter*, 1791, pp. 47–55. According to his account, he was given Miss Gunning's narrative and a letter from General Gunning to the Duke of Marlborough on the morning of 3 Feb. and was ordered to go to Blenheim; he returned 4 Feb. with the supposed reply, which was dated 3 Feb. on the cover (ibid. 2–5). Mrs Gunning gives the dates as 2–3 Feb., and does not mention Miss Gunning's narrative (*Letter* 24–37).

16. The groom: another allusion to General Gunning's descent from Charlemagne.

17. The Duke of Marlborough, whose great-grandfather, the first Duke, received (18 Nov. 1705) from the Emperor Joseph I, in gratitude for the Duke's services to the Empire, the principality of Mindleheim in Swabia. The letter said to have been written by him to General Gunning 3 Feb. 1791 is printed in Bowen, op. cit. 5–7.

his temper the proposed alliance was quite at an end. This wonderful acquittal of the damsel the groom deposed he had received *in half an hour* after his arrival at Blenheim and he gave the most natural and unembarrassed account of all the stages he had made going and coming.

You may still suspect, and so did some of the Council, that every tittle of this report and of the letter, were not gospel—though I own I thought the epistle not irreconcilable to other parts of the conduct of their Graces about their children—still I defy you to guess a thousandth part of the marvellous explanation of the mystery.

The first circumstance that struck was, that the Duke in his own son's name had forgotten the *d* in the middle—That was possible in the hurry of doing justice—Next, the wax was black, and nobody could discover for whom such illustrious personages were in mourning[18]—Well, that was no proof one way or other—Unluckily, somebody suggested that Lord Henry Sp[encer][19] was in town, though to return the next day to Holland[20]—A messenger was sent to him, though very late at night,[21] to beg he would repair to Argyll House; he did, the letter was shown to him; he laughed and said it had not the least resemblance to his father's hand. This was negative detection enough —but now comes the most positive and wonderful unravelling!

The next day the General received a letter from a gentleman,[22]

18. Cf. Bowen, op. cit. 8: 'What first induced a suspicion that this letter of the 3d of February was a forgery was that the word *Blandford* was spelt *Blanford;* that the wax with which it was sealed was black, though the letter was wrote on gilt paper; and the envelope was a different hand to the letter itself.'

19. Lord Henry John Spencer (1770–95), 2d son of the D. of Marlborough; secretary to Lord Auckland, ambassador at The Hague 1790–93; a diplomat of great promise, recommended by his mother 'to Pitt as the hope of her family' (entry dated 21 Feb. 1790, diary of John Thomas Stanley, later 7th Bt and 1st Bn Stanley of Alderley, *Early Married Life of Maria Josepha Lady Stanley*, ed. Jane H. Adeane, 1899, p. 95). For his detection of the forgery, 8 Feb., see Bowen, op. cit. 8, 29–30.

20. He had been in England since ca 21 Dec. 1790 (*London Chronicle* 21–23 Dec. 1790, lxviii. 601), part of the time at Blenheim; apparently he left London as HW intimates, 8 Feb. (*Gazetteer and New Daily Advertiser*, 10 Jan., 9 Feb. 1791; *Oracle* 10 Feb. 1791).

21. 'Tuesday the 8th of February, in the forenoon of which day General Gunning had seen Lord Henry Spencer' (Bowen, op. cit. 8).

22. Capt. Essex Bowen (see PS.), Lt, 1781, Captain on half-pay in Waller's Corps 1783–97, Capt. 82d Foot 1797–1800, and Lt-Col. in the army 1798–1800. He m. (1787), against the wishes of the bride's parents, General Gunning's first cousin once removed, Lizetta (or Lisetta) Margaret Kirwan Lyster (b. ca 1747–52, d. 1832), dau. of Christopher Kirwan of Ash Park, co. Ros-

confessing that his wife, a friend of Miss Charly, had lately[23] received from her a copy of a most satisfactory testimonial from the D[uke] of M[arlborough] in her favour (though, note, the narrative was not then gone to Blenheim) and begging the gentlewoman's husband would transcribe it and send it to her, as she wished to send a copy to a friend in the country. The husband had done so, but had had the precaution to write at top *copy*, and before the signature had written *signed* M., both which words Miss had erased,[24] and then delivered the gentleman's identic transcript to the groom to be brought back as from Bl[enheim]—which the *steady* groom on being examined anew, confessed, and that being bribed <by Miss Gunning>[25] he had gone but one post,[26] and invented the rest.

You will now pity the poor General, who has been a dupe from the beginning and sheds floods of tears—nay, has actually turned his daughter out of doors,[27] as she is banished from A[rgyll] House too; and Lady Charlotte[28] to her honour speaks of her with the utmost indignation. In fact, there never was a more extraordinary tissue of effrontery, folly, and imposture.

It is a strange, but not a miraculous part of this strange story, that Gunnilda is actually harboured by and lodges with the old Duchess in Pall Mall,[29] the grandmother of whom she has miscarried, and who was the first that was big with her.[30]

common, by Jane Lyster (Kirwan assumed his wife's name), and grand-daughter of William Lyster of Athleague, co. Roscommon, by Margaret Gunning, dau. of Bryan Gunning (*Army Lists;* Mrs Gunning, *Letter* 11, 15–18, 82; Henry Lyttleton Lyster Denny, *Memorials of an Ancient House,* Edinburgh, 1913, pp. 104–5).

23. On Tuesday 1 Feb. 1791 (Bowen, op. cit. 10–13).

24. See Bowen, op. cit. 22, 43–5.

25. Passage obliterated in MS. The suggested reading is not clear, but it is supported by the PS., where HW evidently wishes to correct a suggestion he had made, and which is made nowhere else in the letter. See also the groom's affidavit, cited above, in which all responsibility is placed on Miss Gunning.

26. To General Gunning's house at Twickenham (Bowen, op. cit. 50).

27. On 9 Feb. 1791 (Mrs. Gunning, *Letter* 96–112).

28. Expanded by Mary Berry from HW's 'Ch.': Lady Charlotte Campbell, Miss Gunning's first cousin.

29. The Dowager Duchess of Bedford. The Gunnings did not go to her house, but to one provided by her for them (see last paragraph of following letter), 49 Pall Mall: 'a house of her *dearest* and almost *only* friend was made ready for her reception' (ibid. 110, 120). The Duchess of Bedford is eulogized as Miss Gunning's '*most dear and revered patroness*,' etc. (ibid. 70).

30. In his letter *ante* 22 Oct. 1790 HW referred to the Duchess as 'first inventress' of the Blandford-Gunning match.

You may depend on the authenticity of this narrative, and may guess from whom I received all the circumstances day by day[31]—but pray do not quote me for that reason, nor let it out of your hands, nor *transcribe* any part of it. The town knows the story confusedly, and a million of false readings there will be; but though you know it exactly, do not send it back hither. You will perhaps be diverted by the various ways in which it will be related.[32]

> Yours etc.
> Eginhart, Secretary
> to Charlemagne and the
> Princess Gunnilda his daughter.[33]

PS. *Bowen* is the name of the gentleman who gave information of the letter sent to him to be copied, on hearing of the suspected forgeries. The whole *Minifry* are involved in the suspicions, as they defend the damsel, who still confesses nothing; and it is her mother, not she, who is supposed to have tampered with the groom,[34] and is discarded too by her husband.

To Mary Berry, Friday 18 February 1791

Address: À Mademoiselle Mademoiselle Berry.
Posted 22 Feb. ('Visitors').

No. 20.   Berkeley Square, Feb. 18, 1791.[1]

THE history of myself will be short, but sweet: my pains are all gone, and if there is dry weather, I think I shall get out next week; but I am so afraid of a relapse, that I will run no risks—I am content to be at ease: what calls have I abroad?

---

31. That is, from General Conway (n. 12).

32. An account of the affair, headed 'Fashionable Scandal,' is in *The Gazetteer and New Daily Advertiser* 19 Feb. 1791, and further comment and elucidation in ibid. 21–25 Feb. 1791. A more detailed and more accurate account is in *The London Chronicle* 19–22 Feb. 1791, lxix. 180–1.

33. 'This signature is in part taken from

. . . *Memoirs of Europe, towards the Close of the Eighth Century. Written by Eginardus, Secretary and Favourite to Charlemagne; and done into English by the Translator of the New Atlantis'* (T), 2 vols, 1710, by Mrs Mary de la Rivière Manley (1663–1724).

34. But see n. 25.

---

1. 'No. 31' (B).

Our papers say General Ohara is arrived,[2] but as General Conway has not seen him, he concludes him performing quarantine.[3]

Here is a shocking (not a fatal) codicil to Gunnilda's story—but first I should tell you, that two days after the explosion, the Signora Madre took a post chaise and four and drove to Blenheim;[4] but not finding the Duke and Duchess there,[5] she inquired where the Marquis was, and pursued him to Sir H. Dashwood's;[6] finding him there, she began about her poor daughter—but he interrupted her, said there was an end put to all that, and desired to lead her to her chaise, which he insisted on doing, and did.[7] I think this is another symptom of the Minifry being accomplices to the daughter's enterprises—well, after the groom's confession, and after Mr Bowen had been confronted with her and produced to her face her note to his wife,[8] which she resolutely disowned, she desired the Duke of Argyll to let her take an oath on the Bible of her perfect innocence of every circumstance of the whole transaction, which you may be sure he did not permit—n'importe—the next day, taking two of the Duchess of Bedford's servants for witnesses,[9] she went before a justice of peace,[10] swore to her innocence and ignorance throughout, even of the note to Mrs Bowen, and then said to the magistrate, 'Sir, from my youth you may imagine I do not know the solemnity of an oath; but to convince you I do, I know my salvation depends on what I have now

2. Extract of a letter from Portsmouth 13 Feb. 1791: 'Yesterday arrived at the Mother Bank, where she is now performing quarantine, his Majesty's ship *Assistance* [of 50 guns] from Gibraltar and Lisbon; she sailed from the latter place the 31st ult. In this ship came passenger Major-General O'Hara, late commanding officer of Gibraltar' (*London Chronicle* 12–15 Feb. 1791, lxix. 160).

3. As provided by statute 26 Geo. II, c. 6.

4. Mrs Gunning mentions this journey in her *Letter* 113: 'In twenty-four hours I began and completed a journey of a hundred and forty miles, without taking off my clothes for two nights, or any refreshment whatever, but one glass of water and one of wine.' She left at 4 A.M. Thursday 10 Feb., and was back in Pall Mall at 4:30 the following morning (ibid. 112–13); thus according to her account (whether truthfully or for effect does not appear) she began the journey the day after the explosion of 9

Feb., and not, as HW says, two days after it.

5. They were probably at Syon Hill, only a few miles from London: a letter from the Duke of Marlborough to General Gunning is headed 'Sion Hill, Feby 12, 1791' (Essex Bowen, *A Statement of Facts*, 1791, pp. 33–4). They had left Syon Hill for Blenheim the preceding 16 Nov. (*Times* 17 Nov. 1790).

6. Kirtlington Park, about six miles from Blenheim, was the seat of Sir Henry Watkin Dashwood (1745–1828), 3d Bt, 1779; M.P. Woodstock 1784–1820.

7. Mrs. Gunning of course does not mention these details.

8. 1 Feb. 1791: it is printed in Bowen, *A Statement of Facts*, 1791, pp. 11–13; another letter from Miss Gunning to Mrs Bowen 6 Feb. 1791 appears in ibid. 16–17.

9. A mistake HW corrects in the last paragraph of this letter.

10. William Hyde; see last paragraph of this letter, and Mrs Gunning, *Letter* 118.

sworn'[11]—solve all this if you can! is it madness?—does even romance extend its inventions so far? or its dispensations?—it is but a burlesque part of this wonderful tale, that old crazy Bedford exhibits Miss every morning on the Causeway[12] in Hide Park, and declares her protégée some time ago refused the hand of your acquaintance Mr Trevilyan[13]—Except of the contending opera houses,[14] one can hear of nothing but Miss Gunning—but it is now grown so disgusting a story, that I shall be glad to hear and repeat to you no more about it.

The Pantheon has opened,[15] and is small, they say, but pretty and simple;[16] all the rest ill-conducted, and from the singers to the scene-shifters imperfect; the dances long and bad, and the whole performance so dilatory and tedious, that it lasted from eight to half an hour past twelve.[17]

The rival theatre is said to be magnificent and lofty, but doubtful whether it will be suffered to come to life[18]—in short, the contest will

11. According to Mrs Gunning, Miss Gunning wrote the following sentence beneath her statement of innocence: 'As I may perhaps from my time of life be supposed not to understand the nature of the solemn oath I am about to take to attest my innocence of the above charges, I beg to assure the magistrate who shall administer the oath to me and the witnesses present, that I know, on the truth of what I assert depends my character in the world and my everlasting salvation in the world to come' (*Letter* 118).

12. 'A circular drive between Grosvenor Gate and the Serpentine, which was formerly the only drive in Hyde Park' (Toynbee, *Supp.* ii. 184).

13. John Trevelyan (1761–1846), eldest son of Sir John Trevelyan, 4th Bt, whom he succeeded in 1828. He m. (9 Aug. 1791) Maria Wilson, dau. of Sir Thomas Spencer Wilson, 6th Bt (Burke, *Peerage*, 1928, p. 2285, *sub* Trevelyan of Nettlecombe; GM 1791, lxi pt ii. 775).

14. Pantheon and the King's Theatre, Haymarket (Opera House).

15. Subscribers were permitted to attend rehearsals during the week beginning 10 Feb. (*St James's Chronicle* 10–12 Feb. 1791), but the formal opening occurred 17 Feb. with the performance of the 'opera of *Armida*, the music by the late [Antonio Maria Gasparo] Sacchini [1734–86]; with addi-

tions, etc., under the direction of Signor Mazzinghi' (ibid. 17–19 Feb. 1791).

16. Richard Edgcumbe, 3d E. of Mount Edgcumbe, considered the Pantheon after its 'transformation' 'by far the most genteel and comfortable theatre I ever saw, of a moderate size and excellent shape, and admirably adapted both for seeing and hearing. . . . On the whole I never enjoyed the opera so well as at this theatre' (*Musical Reminiscences*, 3d edn, 1828, pp. 66–7).

17. 'The managers of the Pantheon Opera opened their season last Thursday . . . unprepared for public exhibition. It was after eight before the curtain drew up; and it was half-past twelve before it finally descended. The opera, though finely supported by Pacchierotti and Mara, from cross accidents and delays, became insufferably tedious.' A gulf opened prematurely, forcing the devils to scamper back precipitately, and Pacchierotti had his face scorched and his clothes almost set on fire by a devil's torch. 'The concluding dance . . . fatigued all patience, outlived expiring tapers, and half emptied the house long before little Theodore had taken her last step for the dismission of the audience' (*St James's Chronicle* 17–19 Feb. 1791).

18. 'The Lord Chamberlain, on Friday last [11 Feb.], formally signified to the proprietors of the King's Theatre in the Haymarket that "he has granted a licence for

grow politics; *Dieu et mon Droit* supporting the Pantheon,[19] and *Ich Dien* countenancing the Haymarket—it is unlucky that the amplest receptacle is to hold the minority!

20th.

Ohara is come to town—you will love him better than ever; he persuaded the captain of the ship,[20] whom you will love for being persuaded, to stop at Lisbon that he might see Mrs Damer. Ohara has been shockingly treated![21]

The House of Richmond is on the point of receiving a very great blow—Colonel Lenox, who had been dangerously ill,[22] but was better, has relapsed, with all the worst symptoms, and is too weak to be sent to the south, as the physicians recommended.[23] Lady Charlotte[24] is breeding, but that is very precarious; and should it even be a son, how many years e'er that can be a comfortable resource![25]

Is not it strange that London in February and Parliament sitting,

operas to be performed in the Pantheon, and that his Majesty did not think any other Italian theatre necessary" ' (*Gazetteer and New Daily Advertiser* 15 Feb. 1791).

19. 'His Majesty takes a box at the Pantheon Opera House, for which he pays 1000 guineas a year' (*St James's Chronicle* 15–17 Feb. 1791). He and Queen Charlotte first attended the opera at the Pantheon 22 Feb. (*Gazetteer and New Daily Advertiser* 23 Feb. 1791).

20. According to the *Royal Kalendar*, 1791, the captain of the *Assistance* (see n. 2) was Lord Cranstoun: James Cranstoun (1755–96), 8th Bn Cranstoun, 1778; Capt. R.N., 1782 (*Scots Peerage* ii. 600).

21. In not being made Lieutenant-Governor of Gibraltar.

22. As early as 25 Jan. it was reported that 'Colonel Lenox lies dangerously ill of a fever at his house in Privy Gardens, Whitehall. He is attended by Dr Brocklesby' (*St James's Chronicle* 22–25 Jan. 1791).

23. 'The report of Colonel Lennox's relapse arose merely from the journey of Doctor Brocklesby, his physician, to pay him a friendly visit' (*Gazetteer and New Daily Advertiser* 22 Feb. 1791). 'The papers have been rather premature in anticipating the extinction of the Lenox family. Colonel Lenox is nearly recovered, and his lady is said to be in such a way as to have already given birth—to the hopes of a boy' (ibid. 23 Feb. 1791).

24. Corrected by Mary Berry from HW's 'Lady Catherine.' Lady Charlotte Gordon (1768–1842), dau. of Alexander, 4th D. of Gordon; m. (9 Sept. 1789) Charles Lennox, who succeeded as 4th Duke of Richmond in 1806.

25. A son, her second child, was born 3 Aug. 1791 (*post* 8 Aug. 1791): Charles Lennox (after 1836 Gordon-Lennox) (d. 1860), styled E. of March 1806–19; 5th D. of Richmond, 1819.

should furnish no more paragraphs! yet confined at home, and in everybody's way, and consequently my room being a coffee-house from two to four, I probably hear all events worth relating as soon as they are born, and I send you them before they are a week old. Indeed I think the Gunninghiana may last you a month at Pisa, where I suppose the grass grows in the streets as fast as news. When I go out again, I am likely to know less; I go but to few and those the privatest places I can find, which are not the common growth of London—nor but to amuse you, should I inquire after news. What is a juvenile world to me, or its pleasures, interests or squabbles? I scarce know the performers by sight.

21st.

It is very hard! the Gunnings will not let me or the town have done with them. La Madre has advertised a letter to the Duke of Argyll[26]—so he is forced to collect counter-affidavits.[27] The groom[28] has deposed that she promised him £20 a year for his life, and he has given up a letter that she wrote to him.[29] The mother when she went after the Marquis[30] would have persuaded him to get into her chaise, but he would not venture being carried to Gretna Green and married by force. She then wanted him to sign a paper that all was over between him and her daughter—he said, 'Madam, nothing was ever begun'—and refused.

I told you wrong—mother and daughter were not actually in the Duchess of Bedford's house, but in Lord J. Russel's[31] which she lent

26. The advertisement to which HW refers has not been found, but in *The Gazetteer and New Daily Advertiser* 23 Feb. 1791 is the following letter from Mrs Gunning, dated 22 Feb. 1791: 'To the Editor. Sir, Having signified publicly my intention to address a letter to his Grace the Duke of Argyle, it will be doing me a favour if you will be so good to permit me, through the channel of your paper, as one of the best in circulation, to inform his Grace that my letter is now in the press, and will be published with as much expedition as the nature of the business will permit. I am, Sir, Your humble servant, S. Gunning.' Not all of the letter could have been 'in the press,' for Mrs Gunning was writing p. 30 on 22 Feb., and it is dated at the end, 'St James's Street, March 9, 1791.'

27. These were included in Essex Bowen, *A Statement of Facts, in Answer to Mrs Gunning's Letter,* 1791, also frequently quoted in notes to the preceding letter. The affidavits are dated 17, 21, and 24 Feb. 1791.

28. William Pearce, who swore that *Miss* Gunning (not *Mrs* Gunning, as HW's 'she' implies) offered him a pension of £20 a year (Bowen, op. cit. 53–4). His affidavit is dated 21 Feb., the date of this section of HW's letter.

29. Her note, addressed 'For William,' is printed in ibid. 50 n: 'William, you must tell papa, when you give him the Duke's letter, that his Grace sent his compliments, and that he would return the papers when he had done with them.'

30. Of Blandford.

31. Lord John Russell (1766–1839),

to them; nor were her servants witnesses to the oath before Justice
Hide, but Dr Halifax[32] and the apothecary.[33] The Signora and her
Infanta now *for privacy* are retired into St James's Street,[34] next door
Brooks's, whence it is supposed Miss will angle for unmarried marquises—perhaps for Lord Titchfield.[35] It is lost time for people to
write novels, who can compose such a romance as these good folks
have invented. Adieu!

To Mary Berry, Saturday 26 February 1791

Address: À Mademoiselle Mademoiselle Berry à la poste restante à Florence,
Italie. [Forwarded: 'Pisa.'] *Postmark:* <FIRENZE>. Endorsed: 'Pd. 1s.'
Posted 28 Feb. ('Visitors').

Berkeley Square, Feb. 26, 1791.[1]

No. 21.

I HAVE no letter from you to answer, nor anything new that is the
least interesting to tell you. The Duke of Argyll has sent a gentleman[2] with a cartload of affidavits, which the latter read to mother

grandson of the Dowager Duchess of Bedford; succeeded his brother as 6th D. of
Bedford, 1802. His house was then No. 49
Pall Mall (*ante* 13 Feb. 1791, n. 29). As he
and his wife arrived in London from their
country seat 2 Feb. 1791 (*Gazetteer and
New Daily Advertiser* 3 Feb. 1791), the arrangement by which the Gunnings occupied their house remains unexplained. An
item in *The Oracle* 21 April 1791 mentions
that 'Lord John Russell has fixed his spring
residence in St James's Street.'

32. Robert Hallifax (1735–1810), apothecary to the King's household, and apothecary and physician (1788–1810) to the
Prince of Wales; cr. (1783) Doctor of Medicine by the Archbishop of Canterbury (William Munk, *Roll of the Royal College of
Physicians,* 2d edn, 1878, ii. 336; GM 1810,
lxxx pt ii. 390; *Court and City Register*). He
attended Miss Gunning at the request of
the Duchess of Bedford (Mrs Gunning, *Letter* 93). Without naming them, Mrs Gunning mentions him and the apothecary as
'two gentlemen of probity' (ibid. 118–19).

33. 'Mr Y——' (ibid. 93). He is possibly
—— Yatman or Yateman of 7 Percy Street
(*List of the Whole Body of Liverymen of*

London, 1792, p. 155; *Directory to the Nobility, Gentry . . . for 1793,* p. 50).

34. They moved from Pall Mall to St
James's Street 19 Feb. (Mrs Gunning, op.
cit. 120, 129). 'It was probably in [Charles
James] Fox's house that . . . [they] lodged'
(E. Beresford Chancellor, *Memorials of St
James's Street,* New York, 1922, p. 182).
Fox's rooms were on the first floor of the
house next door to Brooks's, 'and immediately above them were apartments occupied
by James Hare—"the Hare with many
friends"' (ibid. 181 n; *Journal and Correspondence of William Lord Auckland,* ed.
Robert John Eden, 3d Bn Auckland,
1861–2, i. 15).

35. William Henry Cavendish Caven-
dish-Scott-Bentinck (1768–1854), styled M.
of Titchfield until 1809; 4th D. of Portland, 1809. He m. (4 Aug. 1795) Henrietta
Scott (d. 1844), dau. of Maj.-Gen. John
Scott, the heiress mentioned by HW *post*
19, 23 Nov. 1793.

1. 'No. 32' (B).
2. Not identified. In Essex Bowen, *A
Statement of Facts,* 1791, p. 35, it is said
that copies of the affidavits 'were sent' to

and daughter, in order to prevent the publication of their libel—but it only enraged the former, who vows she will print all she knows— that is, anything she has heard by their entire intimacy in the family, or, no doubt, what she can invent or misrepresent—what a Medusa!

There has been a fragment of a rehearsal in the Haymarket;[3] but still the Pantheon remains master of the field of battle: the vanquished are preparing manifestoes; but *they* seldom recover the day.

The Duchess of Dorset[4] is brought to bed of a dead child.[5] Madame du Barry[6] is come over to recover her jewels, of which she has been robbed[7]—*not* by the National Assembly, but by four Jews who have been seized here and committed to Newgate.[8] Though the late Lord Barrymore[9] acknowledged her husband to be of his noble blood,[10] will

Mrs Gunning. Mrs Gunning, in *A Letter*, 1791, p. 130, says: 'On the evening of the 23d of February, a person, the *respectability* of whose name and character opened my doors when they were shut to others of a *different* description, did me the honour of calling, and left in my hands copies of six affidavits, sworn to by six of General Gunning's *friends*.' The copies were left with Mrs and Miss Gunning, not read to them, and the same person returned the next day to talk with Mrs Gunning about the publication of her pamphlet (ibid. 130–2).

3. 'The Haymarket Opera had a rehearsal last night [23 Feb.], with much promise of future excellence and support' (*St James's Chronicle* 22–24 Feb. 1791).

4. Arabella Diana Cope (1769–1825), 1st dau. and coheiress of Sir Charles Cope, 2d Bt; m. (1) (4 Jan. 1790) John Frederick Sackville, 3d D. of Dorset; m. (2) (1801) Charles Whitworth, E. Whitworth.

5. 'The Duchess of Dorset was delivered, at six o'clock yesterday morning [25 Feb.], of a still-born female infant, at his Grace's house in Piccadilly' (*St James's Chronicle* 24–26 Feb. 1791).

6. The mistress of Louis XV, Jeanne Bécu (1743–93), m. (1768) Guillaume, Comte du Barry (DU DEFFAND, *passim*).

7. 'Madam du Barré arrived in town on Monday [21 Feb.], with a view of identifying the property of which she was lately robbed' (*St James's Chronicle* 22–24 Feb. 1791). 'The robbery in France of Madame du Barré's jewels is one of the most extraordinary in recollection. They were stolen from her seat called Lucienne, near Marli, in the night of the 10th and 11th ult.

Among the most valuable are: a ring, white brilliant, weight 35 grains; ditto, brilliant, 50 grains; a rose, of 528 brilliants, the centre jewel weighing near 24 grains; buckles, composed of 84 brilliants, weight 77 carats; girandoles, brilliants, value 120,000 livres; a chain, containing 200 pearls; pictures of Louis XIV and XV, richly mounted, etc., etc. The reward offered for them is 2000 louis d'ors' (*St James's Chronicle* 8–10 Feb. 1791). See also *The London Chronicle* 12– 15, 15–17 Feb. 1791, lxix. 155, 164. While in London, she stayed at Grenier's Hotel, Jermyn Street (*Gazetteer and New Daily Advertiser* 26 Feb. 1791).

8. 'Yesterday John Baptiste Levit, Simon Josephs, Jacob Moses, and Moses Abrahams were committed to Newgate by the Right Hon. the Lord Mayor [Boydell], for stealing a large quantity of pearls, diamonds, etc., the property of the Countess du Barré' (*Gazetteer and New Daily Advertiser* 25 Feb. 1791). At the Old Bailey 19 April 1791 'the prosecution against . . . [them] was relinquished' (*Oracle* 20 April 1791). In an action of trover at Guildhall 27 July 1791, when the jewels were finally awarded to Mme du Barry, their names are given as Jean-Baptiste Levette, Joseph Harris, Isaac Moses, and Moses Abrahams (*Oracle* 28 July 1791; *London Chronicle* 26–28 July 1791, lxx. 95–6).

9. Richard Barry (1745–73), 6th E. of Barrymore.

10. HW to Mann 11 May 1769: 'Oh, I forgot to tell you that the Comte du Barri, who has been acknowledged by Lord Barrymore ['As a relation' (HW)], insists on calling himself by that title.' The connection

she own the present Earl for a relation, when she finds him turned strolling player?[11] If she regains her diamonds, perhaps Mrs Hastings may carry her to court.[12]

If you want bigger events, you may send to the Russian army, who will cut you 15,000 throats in a paragraph[13]—or, *en attendant* you may piddle with the havoc made at Chantilly, which has been half demolished by the rights of men;[14] as the poor old Mesdames[15] have been stopped by the rights of the *poissardes;*[16] for, as it is true that extremes meet, the moment despotism was hurled from the throne, it devolved to the mob, whose majesties not being able to write their names, do not issue *lettres de cachet,* but execute their wills with their own hands; for hanging which degrades an executioner, *ne déroge pas* in sovereigns—witness the Czar Peter the Great,[17] Muley Ishmael,[18] and many religious and gracious African monarchs.

After eleven weeks of close confinement, I went out yesterday to take the air, but was soon driven back by rain and sleet, which soon ripened to a tempest of wind and snow, and continued all night; it does not freeze, but blows so hard, that I shall sally out no more, till the weather has recovered its temper—I do not mean that I expect Pisan skies.

between the Barrys and Du Barrys is discussed in N&Q 1859, 2d ser., vii. 273–4, 362, but no definite conclusion is reached.

11. See *ante* 17, 23 July 1790.

12. 'Mrs [Warren] Hastings was supposed, by the party violence of the day, to have received immense bribes in diamonds' (?B, Wright vi. 402). Anna Maria Apollonia von Chapuset (1747–1837), m. (1) (1764) Baron Christof Adam Karl von Imhoff, from whom she was divorced, 1776; m. (2) (1777) as 2d wife, Warren Hastings (K. L. Murray, *Beloved Marian,* [1938], *passim*).

13. An allusion to the siege of Ismail, Nov.–Dec. 1790, in which 38,000 Turks were killed by the Russians. See Byron's *Don Juan,* Cantos vii–viii.

14. 'The populace have broken into the Prince Condé's park at Chantilly, and destroyed all his game. The Prince had been always remarkably tenacious of it, and of course very severe against all transgressors. They have also demolished several of the plantations, out of resentment for the Prince's continuing abroad in opposition

to the late revolution' (*London Chronicle* 19–22 Feb. 1791, lxix. 178).

15. Madame Marie-Adélaïde de Bourbon (1732–1800) and Madame Victoire-Louise-Marie-Thérèse de Bourbon (1733–99), daughters of Louis XV and aunts of Louis XVI. HW met them in Paris in 1765 (DU DEFFAND v. 266 *et passim;* HW to Lady Hervey 3 Oct. 1765; to Chute 3 Oct. 1765; to Conway 6 Oct. 1765).

16. 'The Mesdames Poissardes, to prevent the escape of the French King's aunts, it is said, have brought them from Belle Vue, and escorted them safe to the Thuilleries at Paris' (*St James's Chronicle* 17–19 Feb. 1791). For the opposition of the *poissardes* to their departure, see also the Paris letter 17 Feb. 1791, in ibid. 19–22 Feb. 1791; 24–26 Feb. 1791.

17. Peter I (1672–1725), 'the Great,' Emperor of Russia 1689–1725.

18. Muley Ismail (1646–1727), 'the Bloodthirsty,' Sultan of Morocco 1672–1727. HW mentions that he 'used for a morning's exercise to dispatch a dozen or two of his subjects' (HW to Lady Ossory 10 Sept. 1792; to Governor Pownall 27 Oct. 1783).

It was on Saturday that I began this; it is now Monday, and I have no letter from you, though we have had dozens of east winds. I am sorry to find that it costs above six weeks to say a word at Pisa and have an answer in London. This makes correspondence very uncomfortable—you will be talking to me of Miss Gunning, when perhaps she may be sent to Botany Bay, and be as much forgotten here as *the Monster*.[19] Still she has been a great resource this winter, for though London is apt to produce Wilkeses,[20] and George Gordons,[21] and Mrs Rudds[22] and Horne Tookes and other phenomena wet and dry, the present season has been very unprolific, and we are forced to import French news, as we used to do fashions and *opéras comiques*. The Mesdames are actually set out[23]—I shall be glad to hear they are safe at Turin, for are there no *poissardes* but at Paris? *Natio poissarda est.*

19. Renwick Williams, dancing-master and maker of artificial flowers, who terrorized the women of London by accosting some of them, cutting their garments with a penknife, and occasionally wounding them slightly. He was apprehended, tried at the Old Bailey 8 July 1790, respited, convicted of a misdemeanour, and sentenced 13 Dec. 1790 to imprisonment for six years. See *Annual Register*, 1790, xxxii pt i. 208, 227 *et passim; Times* 15 Dec. 1790; GM 1790, lx pt ii. 660–2, 1143; BM, *Satiric Prints* vi. *passim;* E. Hodgson, *The Trial at Large of Rhynwick Williams* [1790]. In 1792 he published *An Appeal to the Public . . . containing Observations . . . on his Extraordinary and Melancholy Case* (BM Cat.). He was released 14 Dec. 1796 (*London Chronicle* 15–17 Dec. 1796, lxxx. 577).

20. John Wilkes (1727–97), politician.

21. Lord George Gordon (1751–93), the agitator in the No-Popery riots of 1780, who had been imprisoned since 1788 for his libels on the British Government and Marie-Antoinette. He died in Newgate Prison.

22. Margaret Caroline Young (or Youngson) (ca 1745–97) m. (ca 1762) Valentine Rudd, lieutenant in the 62d Regiment of Foot; soon left him; became mistress of Daniel Perreau, 1770; involved with Daniel and Robert Perreau, and tried for forgery, 1775; the Perreaus were hanged, but she was acquitted; later became mistress of James Boswell. The date of her death is usually given as 3 Feb. 1800, but, as Horace

Bleackley pointed out, the reference is to a Mrs William Rudd (N&Q 1907, 10th ser., viii. 361). According to the *True Briton* 4 Feb. 1797, 'the once celebrated Mrs Rudd died a short time since in an obscure apartment near Moorfields.' Although Mrs Rudd was 'often killed by the newspapers,' the year 1797 as the date of her death has at least as much to recommend it as the year 1800; furthermore, the acceptance of 1797 relieves her husband of a gratuitous charge of bigamy (he remarried 8 Oct. 1798). See GM 1800, lxx pt i. 188, 483; GM 1809, lxxix pt i. 581; *Trial of Henry Fauntleroy and Other Famous Trials for Forgery*, ed. Horace Bleackley, [1924] pp. 173–84; *Boswell Papers, passim.*

23. From Paris 21 Feb.: 'On Saturday [19 Feb.], at ten o'clock at night, Mesdames, the King's aunts, left the Castle of Bellevue, and proceeded on their way to Rome; the public mind is much incensed at their departure, as it was the general wish that they should stay' (*St James's Chronicle* 26 Feb.— 1 March 1791). They left with the King's permission, but they were twice stopped, at Moret and Arnay-le-Duc, by the populace, and did not cross the French border into Savoy until 5 March. Forced to flee from Rome in 1799, they went to Naples, Corfu, and finally to Trieste, where they both died. For an account of their journey to Rome, and its effect in France, see H. Babled, 'Le Départ de Mesdames,' *La Révolution française*, 1891, xx. 418–41, xxi. 51–75.

Mr Gibbon[24] writes that he has seen Necker, and found him still devoured by ambition[25]—and I should think by mortification at the foolish figure he has made. Gibbon admires Burke to the skies, and even the religious parts, he says.[26]

I am forced to return to that old story, myself. Though a wet night, I went out yesterday evening, but into a warm private room, and was not the worse for it: I trust I am safe now from a relapse.

Monday evening.

The east winds are making me amends; one of them has brought me twins.[27] I am sorry to find that even Pisa's sky is not quite sovereign, but that you have both been out of order, though thank God! quite recovered both. If a Florentine March is at all like an English one, I hope you will not remove thither till April. Some of its months, I am sure, were sharper than those of our common wear are. Pray be quite easy about me: I am entirely recovered, though if change were bad, we have scarce had one day without every variety of bad weather, with a momentary leaf-gold of sun. I have been out three times, and today have made five and twenty visits, and, was let in at six, and though a little fatigued, am still able you see to finish my letter. You seem to think I palliated my illness: I certainly did not tell you that I thought it doubtful how it would end—yet I told you all the circumstances, and surely did not speak sanguinely.

I wish in No. 20 you had not again named October or November.[28] I have quite given up those months, and am vexed I ever pressed for them, as they would break into your reasonable plans, for which I abandon any foolish ones of my own—but I am a poor philosopher, or rather am like all philosophers, have no presence of mind, and must study my part before I can act it. I have now settled myself not to expect you this year—do not unsettle me—I dread a disappointment, as I do a relapse of the gout—and therefore cut this article

24. Edward Gibbon (1737–94), the historian. No letter from him to HW at this time has been found.

25. See *Private Letters of Edward Gibbon*, ed. Rowland E. Prothero, 1896, ii. 236–7.

26. 'Burke's book is a most admirable medicine against the French disease, which has made too much progress even in this happy country [Switzerland]. I admire his eloquence, I approve his politics, I adore his chivalry, and I can forgive even his superstition. The primitive Church, which I have treated with some freedom, was itself at that time an innovation, and I was attached to the old Pagan establishment' (ibid. 237).

27. Two letters from the Berrys.

28. As the date of their return to England.

short, that I may not indulge vain hopes. My affection for you both
is unalterable—can I give so strong a proof as by supplicating you as
I do earnestly to act as is most prudent for your healths and interests—a long journey in November would be the worst part you could
take, and I beseech you not to think of it—for me you see I take a
great deal of killing—nor is it so easy to die as is imagined.

Thank you, my dearest Miss Agnes, for your postscript—I love to
see your handwriting, and yet do not press for it as you are shy,
though I address myself equally to both, and consult the healths of
both in what I have recommended above. Here is a postscript for
yours; Madame du Barry was to go and swear to her jewels before
the Lord Mayor—Boydell, who is a little better bred than Monsieur
Baillie,[29] made excuses for being obliged to administer the oath *chez
lui,* but begged she would name her hour; and when she did, he
fetched her himself in the state coach,[30] and had a mayoroyal[31] banquet ready for her.[32] She has got most of her jewels again.[33] I want
the King to send her four *Jews* to the National Assembly, and tell
them it is the change or *la monnaie* of Lord George Gordon, the
Israelite.[34]

29. Jean-Sylvain Bailly (1736–93), astronomer; mayor of Paris 16 July 1789—18
Nov. 1791; guillotined (NBG).

30. When the Lord Mayor's new coach
made its first appearance 2 Nov. 1790, it
was described as 'of singular taste and
beauty. The ground of the panels consists
of horizontal stripes in blue and gold, the
collar of S's, which is a part of the City re-
galia, forming a very rich and appropriate
border. The arms of the City, and the Lord
Mayor appear in two distinct shields, properly connected, enriched with official em-
blems, and guarded by the City supporters
beautifully painted. Indeed we never remember to have seen a carriage, in which
the convenience of private use, and the dignity of public station, were so happily associated' (*St James's Chronicle* 2–4 Nov.
1790).

31. Presumably HW's coinage; not in
OED.

32. 'The Countess du Barré, having
identified her property in the stolen jewels,
has received them from the hands of the
Lord Mayor. . . . She was magnificently
entertained, with her suite, by his Lord-

ship at the Mansion House' (*Gazetteer and
New Daily Advertiser* 3 March 1791).

33. 'Madame du Barré has recovered in
value about £40,000 of her jewels—to these
she has sworn, and they have been delivered to her; the rest, having been taken out
of snuff-boxes, buckles, and other toys, she
is not able to swear to, and has therefore
sent for a jeweller from Paris, who has had
them in his possession' (*St James's Chronicle* 1–3 March 1791). After her death the
jewels remaining in England, ordered by
the Lord Chancellor to be sold, brought
'upwards of £30,000' (*London Chronicle*
29–31 Jan., 21–24 Feb. 1795, lxxvii. 107,
186).

34. About 1786 Lord George Gordon was
'corresponding with the Jews (having had
some flirtations with the Quakers), and became a Jew himself, partly in order . . .
to give celebrity to his financial scheme. He
hoped that the Jews would combine to
withhold loans for carrying on wars.' After
being convicted for libel (6, 13 June 1787),
he was at liberty for about six months, during which time he wore a long beard and
adopted Jewish customs. In Newgate from

BOOK-PLATE DESIGNED BY AGNES BERRY FOR MRS. DAMER, 1793

Col. Lenox is much better. The Duchess of Leinster[35] had a letter from Goodwood today which says he rides out.[36] I am glad you do. I said nothing on *the Charming Man's* poem[37]—I fear I said too much to him himself—he said, others liked it, and showed me a note from Mr Burke that was hyperbole itself.[38] I wish him so well, that I am sorry he should be so flattered, when in truth he has no genius; there is no novelty, no plan, and no suite in his poetry, though many of the lines are pretty. Dr Darwin alone can exceed his predecessors.

Let me repeat to both, that distance of place and time can make no alteration in my friendship: It grew from esteem for your characters and understandings and tempers, and became affection from your good-natured attentions to me, where there is so vast a disproportion in our ages. Indeed that complaisance spoiled me, but I have weaned myself of my own self-love, and you shall hear no more of its dictates. Adieu!

PS. I had left myself no room but this to tell you I have seen Pepys but once since I came to town. Now I shall meet him sometimes. Mr Batt always inquires after you. Lady Cecilia is in bed with a cold. I have been at Lady Herries's tonight;[39] she is better and begins to crawl about a little.

1788 until his death, he 'conformed in all respects to the Jewish religion' (DNB). See also the discussion of the satirical prints dealing with his conversion, in BM, *Satiric Prints*, vi. Nos. 7423–5, 8249; 'Mem. 1783–91,' *sub* 10 Dec. 1787, 28 Jan. 1788.

35. That is, the Dowager Duchess: Emilia Mary Lennox (1731–1814), dau. of 2d D. of Richmond; aunt of Colonel Lennox, afterwards (1806) 4th D. of Richmond; m. (1) (1747) James FitzGerald (1722–73), 20th E. of Kildare, cr. (1766) D. of Leinster; m. (2) (1774) William Ogilvie, her children's tutor. At this time she was at her house in Harley Street (*Gazetteer and New Daily Advertiser* 2 Feb. 1791).

36. 'Colonel Lenox is quite recovered . . . at Goodwood House' (*Gazetteer and New Daily Advertiser* 7 March 1791).

37. Edward Jerningham, *The Shakespeare Gallery: a Poem*, 1791; advertised 'This day was published' in *St James's Chronicle* 18–20 Jan. 1791; *Oracle* 19 Jan.

1791. A second edition also appeared in 1791 (BM Cat.).

38. Burke wrote to Jerningham 18 Jan. 1791: 'I owe you my best thanks for the obliging present you have made me of your fine poem on "The Shakespeare Gallery." I have not for a long time seen anything so well finished. You have caught new fire by approaching, in your Perihelion, so near to the sun of our poetical system. How long will the astronomers calculate the time before you can cool? The painters have warmed their imaginations at the same reservoir of heat and light. You reflect new rays on them. Their pictures have never been before placed in a light so advantageous to them' (*Edward Jerningham and His Friends*, ed. Lewis Bettany, 1919, p. 38). The editor notes (ibid. 39) that 'Burke's praise . . . though seemingly enthusiastic, is really very artfully guarded.'

39. Lady Herries lived at 16 St James's Street (*Directory to the Nobility, Gentry . . . for 1793*).

To Mary Berry, Saturday 5 March 1791

Address: À Mademoiselle Mademoiselle Berry à la poste restante à Florence, Italie. [Forwarded: 'Pisa.'] *Postmark:* FIRENZE. Endorsed: 'Pd 1s.' Posted 8 March ('Visitors').

Berkeley Square, March 5, 1791.[1]

No. 22.

ONE may live in a vast capital and know no more of three parts of it than of Carthage. When I was at Florence, I have surprised some Florentines by telling them that London was built like their city (where you often cross the bridges several times in a day,) on each side of the river, and yet that I had never been but on one side, for then I had never been in Southwark. When I was very young and in the height of the opposition to my father, my mother[2] wanted a large parcel of bugles,[2a] for what use I forget. As they were then out of fashion she could get none. At last she was told of a quantity in a little shop in an obscure alley in the City: we drove thither, found a great stock, she bought it and bade the proprietor send it home—he said, 'Whither?'—to Sir Robert Walpole's. He asked coolly 'Who is Sir Robert Walpole?'

This is very like Cambridge who tells you three stories to make you understand a fourth. In short, t'other morning a gentleman[3] made me a visit and asked, if I had heard of the great misfortune that had happened? The Albion mills are burnt down. I asked, where were they?—supposing they were powder mills in the country that had blown up. I had literally never seen or heard of the spacious lofty building at the end of Black-friars Bridge. At first it was supposed maliciously burnt—and it is certain the mob stood and enjoyed the conflagration as of a monopoly—but it had been on fire, and it was thought extinguished. The building had cost an hundred thousand pounds, and the loss in corn and flour is calculated at £140,000 —I do not answer for the truth of the sums, but it is certain that Pal-

---

1. 'No. 33' (B).
2. Catharine Shorter (1682–1737), m. (1700) Robert Walpole, K.G., 1726, and 1st E. of Orford, 1742.
2a. Bugle: 'a tube-shaped glass bead, usually black, used to ornament wearing apparel' (OED).

3. Not identified.
4. New Palace Yard, 'the open space before the north entrance to Westminster Hall' (Henry B. Wheatley, *London Past and Present,* 1891, iii. 6).

ace Yard[4] and part of St James's Park were covered with half-burnt grain.[5]

This accident and my introduction have helped me to a good part of my letter; for you must have observed that even in this overgrown town, the winter has not been productive of events. Scandal I hate, and would not send you what I thought so; but it is not doubted now but two of our finest ladies, sisters, have descended into the *basse cour* of the Alley[6] with Jews and brokers, and waddled out with a large loss of feathers, though not so considerable as was said—yet 23 thousand makes a great gap in pin-money. You will find the initials of both, without going so far as the fifth letter of the alphabet.[7] Good Hannah More is labouring to amend our region,[7a] and has just pub-

---

5. 'Yesterday morning [2 March] about half past six o'clock a fire broke out at the Albion Mills, on the Surrey side of Black-fryars Bridge; which in a short time entirely destroyed the whole of that extensive building, as also several small houses adjoining and opposite the side; together with a very large quantity of corn (we believe not less than 10,000 sacks) ground and unground, to the value of several thousand pounds.

'The manner in which it began cannot be accurately ascertained; but it is imagined to have arisen from the very great friction of the wheels, particularly aggravated by some coarse high-dried wheat. It is said some fire had been discovered the preceding evening, which was supposed to have been extinguished, but which continued smothering the whole night. The inside of the building, consisting of timber, made a tremendous blaze, and the heat was so great that the engines could not for a long time approach to be of any service. The floating engine played, but owing to the tide being down at the time the fire burst out, water could not at first be easily procured. . . .

'Much of the chaff and parched corn was carried a considerable distance by the force of the fire and wind—Scotland Yard, Palace Yard, and the Park were strewed with it.

'It has been suggested that this fire was not entirely accidental; but no reasons appear for any particular suspicion, except the general dislike in the lower class of people, arising from an opinion that the undertaking enhanced the price of corn, and decreased the value of labour. We are

not satisfied how far this was really the case; and it is reported that the proprietors did not find it answer their pecuniary purposes, and that the mills will in consequence not be erected. The populace, of which great numbers were present, seemed by no means to pity the sufferers by the conflagration.

'The reports respecting the loss are various—from 4,000 to 40,000 sacks of flour; and the whole value, buildings and stock, from fifty to one hundred and fifty thousand pounds' (*St James's Chronicle* 1–3 March 1791). The property was insured for £41,000 (ibid.). An account which differs from this only in minor details is in the *London Chronicle* 1–3 March 1791, lxix. 216.

6. Exchange or 'Change Alley, Cornhill, 'so called from its being situated opposite to the Royal Exchange' (*London and its Environs Described*, 1761, ii. 282).

7. The Duchess of Devonshire and her younger sister Lady Duncannon: Henrietta Frances Spencer (1761–1821) m. (1780) Frederick Ponsonby, styled Vct Duncannon, 3d E. of Bessborough, 1793. 'The malevolent report that has been so industriously circulated concerning two ladies of the first distinction (the D——s of D——e and Lady D——n), we are assured, from undoubted authority, is *fabrication all*. Lady D——n, in a letter to a friend, says, "I have not the most faint idea what could give rise to so shocking an insinuation." We are happy to have it in our power to announce the falsehood of it' (*Gazetteer and New Daily Advertiser* 2 March 1791).

7a. *Sic;* 'religion'?

lished a book called, *An Estimate of the Religion of the Fashionable World.*[8] It is prettily written—but her enthusiasm[9] increases; and when she comes to town, I shall tell her, that if she preaches to people of fashion, she will be a bishop *in partibus infidelium.*

Lady Cecilia's[10] disorder has literally terminated in the gout in her foot. I called on her this evening, but as she was in her bedchamber up two pair of stairs,[11] my gout would not let me be so clambera-ceous; and indeed she sent Miss Johnstone[12] down to the coach to me to desire I would not attempt it. I think, if the remedy is not as bad, that the gout may relieve her headaches.

Goodnight! I have two days to wait for a letter that I may answer —stay, I should tell you that I have been at Sir Joseph Banks's liter-ary saturnalia,[13] where was a Parisian watchmaker,[14] who produced the smallest automaton that I suppose was ever created. It was a rich snuffbox, not too large for a woman. On opening the lid, an en-amelled bird started up, sat on the rim, turned round, fluttered its wings, and piped in a delightful tone the notes of different birds, particularly the jug, jug, of the nightingale. It is the prettiest play-thing you ever saw—the price tempting—only five hundred pounds. That economist the P. of W.[15] could not resist it and has bought one of those dickybirds. If the maker finds such customers, he will not end like one of his profession here,[16] who made the serpent in *Or-*

8. Published anonymously, 'By one of the laity,' 22 Feb. 1791 (*Gazetteer and New Daily Advertiser* 17–23 Feb. 1791); a second edition appeared 28 March 1791 (ibid. 9 March 1791; *St James's Chronicle* 26–29 March 1791), and a fifth in 1793 (BM Cat.).

9. 'A vain confidence of divine favour or communication' (Johnson).

10. Lady Cecilia Johnston's.

11. Lady Cecilia lived at 12 South Aud-ley Street (*Directory to the Nobility, Gentry . . . for 1793*).

12. As Mrs Anderson was Lady Cecilia's only daughter to survive infancy, presum-ably 'Miss Johnstone' is General John-ston's sister, Margaret Johnston of Hilton Lodge, co. Haddington, who is mentioned in his will (*The Marriage, Baptismal, and Burial Registers of the Collegiate Church or Abbey of St Peter, Westminster*, ed. Jo-seph Lemuel Chester, 1876, p. 460 n.; GM 1817, lxxxvii pt i. 281).

13. 'Sir Joseph Banks, while president of

the Royal Society [1778–1820], had a weekly evening reception of all persons dis-tinguished in science or the arts' (?B, Wright vi. 408). John Thomas Stanley, later 7th Bt and 1st Bn Stanley of Alderley, wrote to a friend 21 Feb. 1790: 'Every Satur-day evening I spend at Sir Joseph Banks'. His house is constantly open on this day for all his friends. These are chiefly men who are engaged directly or indirectly in the lit-erary world. Three rooms, filled with books, etc., are thrown open. The company assem-bled generally may amount to thirty or more; all scientific foreigners are there. The conversations are interesting, and the man-ners of the landlord most hospitable' (*Early Married Life of Maria Josepha Lady Stan-ley*, ed. Jane H. Adeane, 1899, pp. 93–4).

14. Not identified.

15. The extravagance of the Prince of Wales had already brought him into diffi-culties.

16. Not identified.

pheus and Euridice,[17] and who fell so deeply in love with his own works, that he did nothing afterwards but make serpents of all sorts and sizes till he was ruined and broke.[18]

It is six o'clock of Monday evening the 7th, and no letters from Pisa, but I will not seal this till tomorrow noon in hopes—otherwise I have not a tittle to add—but that Lady Mary Palk is dead in child-bed:[19] I think I have heard you mention her, or I should not, for I did not know her.

The Mesdames[20] are said to be safely out of France, after being stopped three times.[21] There have been great mobs at the Luxembourg[22] and the Thuilleries, and La Fayette is said rather to have acted the royalist.[23] The provinces grow turbulent,[24] but you must hear French news sooner and more authentically than I do. Of the Gunning

17. 'A celebrated opera' (?B, Wright vi. 408). There were twenty or more operatic versions of *Orpheus and Eurydice* or *Orfeo e Euridice*, but HW doubtless refers to Gluck's.

18. See HW to Mason 17 Jan. 1780.

19. Lady Mary Bligh (1768–4 March 1791), 1st dau. of 3d E. of Darnley, m. (1789) Lawrence Palk, M.P., later (1798) 2d Bt of Haldon, Devon (GEC; John Lodge and Mervyn Archdall, *Peerage of Ireland*, 1789, ii. 213). The child, Robert, born 15 Feb., survived her only a few days (William Betham, *Baronetage of England*, 1801–5, iv. 109; GM 1791, lxi pt i. 183).

20. Mesdames Marie-Adélaïde and Victoire-Louise-Marie-Thérèse.

21. They crossed the French border 5 March, after being stopped twice; see preceding letter.

22. The Paris correspondent of *The St James's Chronicle* wrote 24 Feb.: 'Tuesday evening [22 Feb.] was a festival for the mob; it was rumoured that the King's brother, Monsieur, and his consort, were preparing to follow Mesdames out of the kingdom; above ten thousand men, women, and children of every age, but only of *one* condition, proceeded with lighted flambeaux to Monsieur's palace at the Luxembourg; they soon forced admittance, and the amazons of the capital—the fishwomen—at the head of the canaille, harangued the Prince somewhat cavalierly. . . . They concluded, after having cordially embraced him and Madame, with insisting that they should both go to the Louvre under the friendly escort of the loyal people of Paris. . . . Monsieur and Madame were obliged to pass the night at the Louvre; to attempt to return to their usual residence would have been madness.' Lafayette reinforced the guard at the Louvre, but nothing happened (*St James's Chronicle* 3–5 March 1791).

23. On the evening of 24 Feb. 'all the active citizens of Paris, in a very riotous manner, assembled in the Thuilleries and the avenues leading to the Louvre; the primary cause of the tumult was two-fold: the porters of the corn-market thinking . . . themselves aggrieved . . . resolved to apply to the King for redress. . . . The fish-ladies also, ever at the service of the ill-inclined . . . crowded to the Palace to insist on [the return of Mesdames]. . . . The outer gates were . . . shut against the mob, and above 30,000 of the National Guards attended to quiet the King's alarmed mind. . . . Paris that evening wore all the appearance of a besieged town; the mayor [Bailly] and M. de la Fayette were repeatedly threatened with the *lanterne*—the French pill to cure aristocracy. However . . . nothing disastrous took place' (*St James's Chronicle* 5–8 March 1791).

24. 'Languedoc is . . . miserably distracted—a banditti of 6000 men are carrying terror and desolation through that most enchanting part of France. Normandy . . . has caught the flame of sedition. . . . All information from the frontier provinces, chiefly from Alsace, announces war' (ibid.).

not a word since my last: nor of Mrs Buller, though I have called on her, nor of the righteous Miss Foldsone. The Lord Mayor did not fetch Madame du Barry in the city-royal coach, but kept her to dinner. She is gone,[25] but returns in April.

Tuesday morning.

I find your No. 21 on my table, but as it only talks of your life at Pisa, and of the community of apartments, which appears as bad as Buxton or Harrowgate, I have nothing to add but to wonder how anyone can seek such an uncomfortable life a second time.[26] Adieu!

PS. I should not wonder if Italians flock hither, for Carnavali,[27] the exhibitor of the *fantoccini*,[28] has got one of the £20,000's in the lottery—but had unluckily for him sold two-thirds of it.[29]

To Mary Berry, Friday 11 March 1791

Address: À Mademoiselle Mademoiselle Berry à la poste restante à Florence, Italie. [Forwarded: 'Pisa.'] *Postmark:* FIRENZE 13. Endorsed: 'Pd 1s.' Posted 15 March ('Visitors').

Berkeley Square, March 11, 1791.

No. 23.[1]

I USUALLY begin my letters to you on Fridays, but today for a different reason, not because I have anything to say, but like the French lady to her husband, because I have nothing to do.[2] In short,

25. She 'set off on Saturday morning [26 Feb.] with her suite for Dover, on her return to France' (*London Chronicle* 1–3 March 1791, lxix. 209).

26. When the Berrys were in Italy 1783–4, they spent a few days (5–7 June 1784) in Pisa (MBJ i. 123–4).

27. Possibly Pietro Carnivalli, who is said to have set fire to the Opera House which burned down in 1789; he 'died at Bristol about a twelvemonth afterwards' (Edward Wedlake Brayley, *Historical and Descriptive Accounts of the Theatres of London*, 1826, p. 28). Brayley's 'about a twelvemonth' is sufficiently elastic to extend to 1791.

28. The puppet-shows were given at the theatre in Savile Row, the one used by Lord Barrymore for amateur theatricals (*ante* 23 July 1790). 'The beautiful little theatre in Saville Row was opened on Saturday eve-

ning [5 Feb. 1791] with a Fantoccini performance. It was considerably improved while in the possession of Lord Barrymore' (*Gazetteer and New Daily Advertiser* 7 Feb. 1791). 'Lord Barrymore is supposed to have spent near £1500 on the Fantoccini, which is one of the prettiest theatres we ever saw. The puppets are much better managed than in Carnivalle's time' (*Times* 19 March 1791). See also C. F. Pohl, *Mozart und Haydn in London*, Wien, 1867, ii. 161–3.

29. 'One of the £20,000 prizes [two, No. 10,000 and No. 48,476, were drawn 7 March] has fallen to three Italians: Carnevale, and two performers engaged with him last year in the puppet show called the Fantoccini' (*London Chronicle* 5–8 March 1791, lxix. 232).

———

1. 'No. 34' (B).

2. See *ante* 19 July 1789.

I have got a little codicil to my gout. It returned into my ankle on Monday and Tuesday, left it on Wednesday, and yesterday came into my knee—I have no pain, unless I attempt to walk; so have been forced just now to send an excuse to Lady Louisa Macdonald,[3] where I was to have been tonight—and so must amuse myself *en famille*.[4]

The Gunnings continue to supply me with matter. As it is now known that two of the Minifry have been mad,[5] I should conclude the mother and daughter were so, if two persons could lose their senses at the same period, and on the same subject. Well, these two outpensioners of Bedlam have sent a new narrative[6] to the Duke of Marlborough, wherein the infanta maintains to his Grace's face, that she passed three *days* with him and the Duchess this summer at Sion, though it was but three *hours;* and cites a kind speech of his to her, for the truth of which she appeals to Sir John Riddel,[7] who was present and heard it. The Duke, doubting his own eyes or memory, questions Sir John, who equally amazed, says, 'Your Grace knows I had not the honour of being with you at Sion, when Miss Gunning was there.'—All this is a new style of romancing—and though I repeat it, I can scarce believe it while I repeat it.

The letter to the Duke of Argyll is to appear next week.[8] Some-

3. 'Daughter to ——, Earl Gower, and sister to the first Duke of Sutherland' (B). Lady Louisa Leveson-Gower (1749–1827), eldest dau. of 2d E. Gower, cr. (1786) M. of Stafford; sister to George Granville, 2d M. of Stafford, cr. (1833) D. of Sutherland; m. (1777) Archibald Macdonald, eminent lawyer, cr. (1788) Kt, and (1813) Bt (Collins, *Peerage*, 1812, ii. 451; Burke, *Peerage*, 1928, p. 2218, *sub* Sutherland). She lived at 8 Adelphi Terrace (*Directory to the Nobility, Gentry . . . for 1793*). HW's 'excuse' is missing.

4. A newspaper item states on the following day: 'Whoever wishes to see assembled the wits and beauties of the last age, must visit Mrs Cornwallis on a Saturday evening. Nothing is played but ombre, quadrille, and cribbage, nor anybody admitted who has not passed their grand climacteric. Horace Walpole, Lord Bathurst, Lady Mary Macdonald, etc., are constant attendants on this polite but antiquated assembly' (*Gazetteer and New Daily Advertiser* 12 March 1791). In the last paragraph of

this letter, however, HW intimates that he has not been out since the arrival of his 'codicil' of gout. Furthermore, HW rarely mentions Mrs Cornwallis.

5. They have not been identified.

6. It is not mentioned in Mrs Gunning's *Letter* or in Essex Bowen's *A Statement of Facts;* it probably was sent after the first was in the press.

7. Sir John Buchanan Riddell (1768–1819), 9th Bt, 1784, of Riddell, Roxburghshire.

8. According to 'A Card' inserted in the *St James's Chronicle* 8–10 March 1791, 'Mrs Gunning begs leave to convey this information, through the channel of *The St James's Chronicle,* to his Grace the Duke of Argyll, that her letter addressed to his Grace will be published on Thursday the 17th inst.' In the *Gazetteer and New Daily Advertiser* 17 March 1791 appeared an advertisement that the letter would be published 'On Monday next [21 March 1791], at noon. . . . The publication . . . deferred . . . owing to unavoidable delays at the press.'

body has sent a proof of the frontispiece to the Duke, who showed it to Gen. Conway, as Lord Lorn has to Mrs. Anderson. There is a medallion of Gunnilda supported by two—cupids, not marquises, her name, and four verses beneath.[9] The Duchess of Bedford has written to Lord Lorn, begging him to intercede for his cousin, for the sake of his dear mother[10] who doted on her,[11] and which dear mother she, Duchess Gertrude, introduced into the world[12]—If Pisa or Florence produce more diversion than London, you have but to say so.

The Haymarket Theatre opened last night with an opera gratis. It is computed that four thousand persons accepted the favour, and the theatre is allowed to be the most splendid and convenient, let Naples say what it will;[13] the singers very indifferent, the dancers (Vestris[14] and Hilsberg)[15] and the dances, charming.[16]—Still it is probable there

---

9. Evidently the medallion was not used; it is not in the first and second editions of Mrs Gunning's pamphlet in the Yale University Library, and not in WSL's second edition.

10. 'Elizabeth Gunning, first married [in 1752 to] Duke of Hamilton, and then [in 1759] to John Duke of Argyll' (B). The passages in square brackets were added in a different hand, perhaps Lady Theresa Lewis's.

11. 'We hear that a late Duchess was so fully persuaded of her relation being about to be married to a noble Marquis that she gave her particular instructions for her conduct on that event—even on her deathbed' (*Gazetteer and New Daily Advertiser* 28 Feb. 1791).

12. According to tradition, the Gunning sisters were introduced to society at a ball given by the Duchess of Bedford. They first received a forged invitation from a practical joker, but when the fraud was discovered, either a friend or their mother is said to have prevailed on the Duchess to issue a real invitation (Horace Bleackley, *The Story of a Beautiful Duchess*, 1908, pp. 27–8).

13. 'The interior of this theatre, which is the largest in England, has a very magnificent appearance, both from its vast extent and splendid embellishments; its internal dimensions are within a very few feet of the grand theatre at Milan, in Italy' (Edward Wedlake Brayley, *Historical and Descriptive Accounts of the Theatres of London*, 1826, p. 31).

14. Marie-Auguste Vestris-Allard (1760–1842), natural son of Gaetano Apollino Baldassare Vestris, likewise a famous dancer (NBG; *La Grande encyclopédie*). 'Young Vestris arrived in London from Paris on Saturday [22 Jan. 1791]' (*Gazetteer and New Daily Advertiser*, 25 Jan. 1791).

15. Mlle Helisberg (Hilligsberg, Hillisberg), pupil of Vestris *père*, and partner and mistress of the younger Vestris. She is the 'Madame Hilligsberg,' who died 'lately' (?Dec. 1803) 'at her estate near Tours. . . . She possessed in an eminent degree those winning charms of face and manner which captivate by a look, and fascinate by a smile; her style of dancing was chaste and simple, and her execution light and elegant. The symmetry of her form was universally admired; her limbs, delicately round, were exactly proportioned' (GM 1804, lxxiv pt i. 87; Gaston Capon, *Les Vestris*, 1908, pp. 264–8).

16. In the *St James's Chronicle* (10–12 March 1791), which favoured the Haymarket rather than the Pantheon, is the following account: 'On Thursday evening an opera was rehearsed to the largest and the most splendid audience we have seen in London.

'The constitution of the theatre, and the ease with which all the company and all the performers were seen and heard by all, were circumstances of striking effect. . . .

'The brilliant exertions of Vestris and the yet more affecting simplicity and grace of Hillisberg were enthusiastically applauded, in an excellent ballet composed by the elder

will be no more representations, for people cannot get much by giving operas for nothing.

I have got a solution of Miss Foldsone: she has a mother[17] and eight brothers and sisters,[18] who make her work incessantly to maintain them, and who reckon it loss of time to them, if she finishes any pictures that are paid for beforehand—That however is so very uncommon that I should not think the family would be much the richer. I do know that Lord Carlisle paid for the portraits of his children[19] last July and cannot get them from her—at that rate I may see you before your pictures![20]

I have not so clear[21] an exposition of Mrs Buller's[22] behaviour, yet some suspicion. She is grown extremely Germanized—and of whom did I hear extremely intimate in a private party at her house a few nights ago, but one who lives in the street directly behind hers,[23] and whom I should be as sorry to meet there or anywhere, as he could be to meet me. *These* Germans remind me that I saw in today's newspaper, that the wife of the Margrave of Anspach is dead[24]—Courage, Milady Craven! *donnez-nous une nouvelle édition des aventures de Madame la Duchesse de Kingston![25] et dépêchez-vous, car on dit que Milord Craven[26] se meurt. Il serait indigne de vous que d'attendre la main gauche, et un mariage estimé légitime.*

Vestris, and at one o'clock the company departed.'

17. Mrs John Foldsone.

18. Only two of these have been identified: Amelia Foldsone, a minor 23 April 1793, m. (on that date) John Bentley Walton; Frances Anne Foldsone, who was a witness at the marriage of her sister Anne 15 May 1793 (*Registers of Marriages of St Mary le Bone, Middlesex 1792–1796*, ed. W. Bruce Bannerman, 1923, pp. 31–2).

19. Cf. *ante* 29 Jan. 1791.

20. HW had not received them 11 Sept. 1791 (*post*, that date), and the Berrys reached London exactly two months later (MBJ i. 375).

21. MS reads 'so a clear.' The 'a' may have been inserted by Mary Berry.

22. Expanded by Mary Berry from HW's 'B's.'

23. 'He means William Henry, Duke of Gloucester, brother to George III, who had married his niece the Countess Dowager of Waldegrave' (B). Mrs Buller lived at 44

Upper Brook Street, and the Duke of Gloucester at 93 Upper Grosvenor Street (*Directory to the Nobility, Gentry . . . for 1793*).

24. Friederike Karoline (1735–18 Feb. 1791), Princess of Sachsen-Coburg-Saalfeld; m. (1754) Karl Alexander, Margrave of Brandenburg-Anspach (Wilhelm Karl von Isenburg, *Stammtafeln*, Berlin, 1936, i. 66; GM 1791, lxi pt i. 280).

25. Elizabeth Chudleigh (ca 1720–88), m. privately (1744) Augustus John Hervey, 3d E. of Bristol, 1775. In 1769 she obtained a decree from the Consistory Court declaring her a spinster, and married the 2d D. of Kingston. She was tried for bigamy, 15–22 April 1776, before the House of Lords, and was found guilty, but, pleading her privilege as a peeress, escaped sentence. She lived abroad until her death.

26. William Craven (1738–27 Sept. 1791), 6th Bn Craven of Hampstead Marshall.

Lady Beaumont[27] called on me two days ago, and inquired after you kindly. The rest of my letter must depend on one from you, or on the town and the Gunnings. There is published a Grub print not void of humour, called 'The New Art of Gunning';[28] Miss astride a cannon is firing a volley of forged letters at the Castle of Blenheim, and old Gertrude,[29] emaciated and withered, and very like, lifting up her hoop to shelter injured innocence, as she calls her.[30]

Sunday 13th.

Yesterday I had the misfortune of hearing of the death of my oldest remaining friend, Lord Strafford,[31] whom I knew from the time he was twelve years old,[32] and who was invariably kind and obliging to me—This is the heavy tax one pays for living long!—but as it is not a language necessary to be talked to your time of life, I shall keep my moralizing for my own use, and collect for yours only what will amuse you; though as I gather from hearsay, I must often send you false reports: still I take care they should only be on trifles of no consequence. Thus I told you[33] old French had funded her legacies on her collection—but luckily for her legatees she had money enough in the stocks to discharge the £6,000; or her bequests would have fallen woefully short. Three or four years ago she had wanted to sell her pictures to the Czarina[34] for £1,200 a year, estimating her own

27. 'Marg[aret] Willes, the wife of the late Sir George Beaumont' (B). Margaret Willes (ca 1756–1829), dau. of John Willes of Astrop, Northants; m. (1778) Sir George Howland Beaumont, 7th Bt, the painter and patron of art. She became a strong defender of Wordsworth's poetry (GEC; Joseph Farington, *Diary*, ed. James Greig, 1922–8, *passim*). For the acquaintance of the Berrys with the Beaumonts, see MBJ ii. 88, 379, 497. Lady Beaumont lived at 29 Grosvenor Square (E. Beresford Chancellor, *History of the Squares of London*, 1907, pp. 32, 40).

28. 'The Siege of Blenheim—or—The New System of *Gunning* Discoverd [*sic*],' by James Gillray (1757–1815); published 5 March 1791, and reprinted in *Genuine Works of James Gillray*, 1830. For a full description of it, see BM, *Satiric Prints* vi. 848–9, No. 7980.

29. The Dowager Duchess of Bedford.

30. The Duchess of Bedford says to Mrs and Miss Gunning: 'Come under my protection, deary's I'll hide you in Bedfordshire; and find one of my little Granny-boys to play with Missy' (ibid.).

31. 'The last Earl of Strafford of the family of Wentworth' (B). 'The Earl of Strafford died at his seat at Wentworth Castle in Yorkshire on Thursday [10 March 1791] last; he had been indisposed two months, but felt neither pain nor sickness, it being quite a decay of nature' (*St James's Chronicle* 10–12 March 1791).

32. If HW is correct, he refers to 1734. HW first mentions Lord Strafford in his letter to Mann 4 Feb. 1742. In *The Wentworth Papers 1705–1739*, ed. James J. Cartwright, 1883, p. 462, are two letters of Lord Wentworth, written in 1730, referring to 'Master Wallpole,' who may be HW.

33. *Ante* 29 Jan. 1791.

34. Catherine II.

life, she said, but at two years' purchase. Well, her pictures, with the addition of her bronzes, china, etc., were sold by auction yesterday and Friday, and produced but £978; and yet the pictures went for more than they were worth.[35]

Monday 14th.

Your No. 23, which I received this morning at breakfast, whets no reply, being merely carnivalesque—but you are going to more royal festivities at Florence with their Neapolitan and Tuscan majesties and dukedoms. Shall not you call at Charing Cross[36] on that account —let me know in time.

The *Great Turk* at Petersberg[37] has sent us rather a *de haut en bas* answer to our proposal of mediating to hinder her removing to Constantinople; we have frowned at the rate of eighteen men of war—still, keeping up our dignity costs us so dear, that I hope we shall let her go the Black Sea and be d——d!

Mesdames de Biron and Cambis[38] have taken houses on Richmond Green as well as les Boufflers[39] and Madame de Roncherolles,[40] so it

35. The collection was sold by Christie at his Great Room, Pall Mall, 11–12 March 1791 (Frits Lugt, *Répertoire des catalogues de ventes publiques*, 1938, no. 4685). As the following articles are listed among the 'Additions' at SH, presumably HW bought them at the sale: 'Two very large blue jars; from Mrs French's collection; an ewer of ancient fayence; ditto' ('Des. of SH,' *Works* ii. 512).

36. On HW's banker; see *post* 19 March 1791, n. 15.

37. Catherine II.

38. Gabrielle-Françoise-Charlotte d'Alsace-Hénin-Liétard (1729–1809), m. (1755) Jacques-François-Xavier-Régis-Ignace, Vicomte de Cambis, later Comte de Cambis-Orsan; emigrated to England, October 1789; died at Richmond. HW met her at Paris in 1769, and Mary Berry obtained reminiscences of Mme du Deffand from her in 1808 (DU DEFFAND i. 311 *et passim;* MBJ ii. 350; GM 1809, lxxix pt i. 187). She visited SH with the Duchesse de Biron 31 May 1790 ('Visitors').

39. Madame de Boufflers and her daughter-in-law, Comtesse Amélie de Boufflers. Their house was next to Lord Fitzwilliam's (*post* 8 June 1791).

40. Marie-Louise Amelot de Chaillou (b. ca 1734, living 1807); m. (1752) Claude-Sibylle-Thomas-Gaspard-Nicolas-Dorothée de Roncherolles, Chevalier de Pont-Saint-Pierre to 1752, Marquis de Roncherolles, 1752 (Woelmont de Brumagne i. 666; Jean Nicolas, Comte Dufort de Cheverney, *Mémoires*, 1909, ii. 188, 197, 304; *L'Intermédiaire des chercheurs et curieux*, 1913, lxvii. 821). While George Selwyn liked her 'much more than any of the whole set' of French at Richmond, 'Mr Walpole *ne lui donne pas la préférence*. He must have something *de l'esprit de l'Académie*, etc., something of a *caractère marqué. Je ne cherche rien de tout cela; je suis content du naturel, et de trouver une personne raisonnable, honnête, et de bonne conversation*' (Selwyn to Lady Carlisle 7 Sept. 1790, in Hist. MSS Comm., Appendix, Part VI, *Manuscripts of the Earl of Carlisle*, 1897, p. 691). In Aug. 1790 HW saw her at Selwyn's, and invited her to dine at SH (ibid. 684–5). She was also at SH 19 May 1790 ('Visitors'). Dufort de Cheverney (loc. cit.) refers to her lonely life in Paris in 1796 and 1798. See also *Journal and Correspondence of William Lord Auckland*, ed. Robert John Eden, 3d Bn Auckland,

will be a *Petty France*. Such swarms of Franks have left the country, that I wonder the National Assembly, which delights in wasting time on reviving old names, do not call their sovereign King of Gaul instead of King of the French. On the contrary, Mesdames Adélaïde and Victoire, formidable as the latter's name is, will not put the Romans much in mind of their precursor Brennus.[41]

I have cancelled my codicil of gout, and shall issue forth again this evening, and perhaps at the end of the week go to Strawberry for a day or two, as the weather lately has been uncommonly fine. Adieu!

To Mary Berry, Saturday 19 March 1791

Address: À Mademoiselle Mademoiselle Berry à la poste restante à Florence, Italie. [Forwarded: 'Pisa.'] *Postmark:* FIRENZE 14. Endorsed: 'Pd 1.' Posted 22 March ('Visitors').

No. 24.[1]   Strawberry Hill, Saturday, March 19, 1791.

I DID not begin my letter on customary Friday, because I had nothing new to tell or to say. The town lies fallow—not an incident worth repeating as far as I know. Parliament manufactures only bills, not politics: I never understood anything useful; and now that my time and connections are shrunk to so narrow a compass, what business have I with business? As I have mended considerably for the last four days, and as we have had a fortnight of soft warm weather, and a southwest wind today, I have ventured hither for change of air— and to give orders about some repairs at Cliveden—which by the way Mr H. Bunbury[2] two days ago proposed to take off my hands for his

---

1861–2, i. 399, 456, where she is erroneously called 'Madame de Roucherolles.'

41. According to Livy (V. xlviii–xlix *et passim*), Brennus was a leader of the Gauls who invaded Italy 390 B.C., captured Rome (except the Capitol), and exacted ransom of the Roman army. The Mesdames apparently conquered Rome in their way: they lodged with Cardinal de Bernis until his death in 1794, and appeared at his Friday evening *conversazioni* 'very courteous and affable. Madame Adélaïde still retained traces of that beauty which had distinguished her in her youth, and there was great vivacity in her manner, and in the expression of her countenance. Madame

Victoire had also an agreeable face, much good sense, and great sweetness of temper. Their dress, and that of their suite, were old-fashioned, but unostentatious. . . . They were highly respected by the Romans; not only by the higher orders, but by the common people, who had a horror of the French Revolution' (Cornelia Knight, *Autobiography*, 1861, i. 99–100).

---

1. 'No. 35' (B).
2. Henry William Bunbury (1750–1811), amateur artist and caricaturist, held in high esteem by HW, his occasional correspondent.

life—I really do not think I accepted his offer.[3] I shall return to town on Monday, and hope to find a letter to answer—or what will this do? —Apropos, as the town stands stock still, I believe I shall change my post-days from Tuesdays to Fridays—at least when I am as barren as at this moment—however when you do not hear from me by the former, be assured you will wait but four days longer—besides as I shall now be frequently coming hither, I may have more to say at the end of the week than at the beginning.

I met Mrs Buller[4] t'other night at Lady Mt Edgcumbe's,[5] and she lays all her omissions on the *Charming Man,* who mentioned my message[6] so slightly that she did not comprehend it. I huffed[7] her worse for her bad taste in sending for *double Gloster Cheese*[8] in an evening, and vowed I will never enter her doors, if smelling of it.[9] I have a notion her son[10] is of a regiment that eats of it. The Greatheds[11] are in Mrs Damer's house;[12] I hope they will not be there six weeks![13]

B[erkeley] Sq[uare], Monday evening.

I am returned, and find the only letter I dreaded,[14] and the only one I trust that I shall ever not be impatient to receive from you.

3. See Bunbury to HW 16 March 1791, and HW's reply 17 March 1791.

4. Expanded by Mary Berry from HW's 'B.'

5. Then No. 11 Upper Grosvenor Street (*London Calendar,* 1791, p. 21).

6. *Ante* 29 Jan. 1791: 'though I desired the Charming . . . to tell her above a week ago that I should be glad to see her, she has not taken the least notice of it.'

7. Scolded; cf. OED 6.

8. The Duke of Gloucester. To certain of his contemporaries the Duke was known as 'Slice' (i.e., of Gloucester cheese).

9. Mrs Damer wrote to Mary Berry 31 May 1791 that HW was 'quite revived by the sight of Mrs Buller [at Gen. Conway's]. . . . He regrets seeing her so little, but does not like going there since she is grown so fond of *Gloucester cheese,* as he told her yesterday' (*Berry Papers* 37–8).

10. John Francis Buller (ca 1771–1807), Mrs Buller's only child; ensign in the army, 11 Oct. 1789; ensign in 1st (the Duke of Gloucester's) Regiment of Foot Guards 30 Dec. 1789, Lt and Capt. 25 April 1793–6; by royal licence 19 April 1796 assumed the surname of Hippisley Coxe in addition to

that of Buller; died 'at Worcester, of a decline' (GM 1808, lxxviii pt i. 170; Burke, *Landed Gentry,* 1937, pp. 278, 1119, *sub* Buller of Downes and Hippisley of Ston Easton; *Army Lists*). Mrs Damer in 1791 considered him 'queer,' but did not 'quite dislike' him (*Berry Papers* 65).

11. Bertie Greatheed (1759–1826), of Guy's Cliff near Warwick; dramatist and poet; HW's occasional correspondent; m. (ca 1780) Anne ——. Their only child, Bertie Greatheed (ca 1781–1804), became an amateur artist and was highly praised by HW and others (DNB; Richard A. Austen-Leigh, *Eton College Register 1753–1790,* Eton, 1921). Greatheed's letter to Prince Corsini added to the pleasure of the Berrys' stay in Florence (MBJ i. 246–7), and Mary and Agnes Berry were frequently guests at Guy's Cliff (ibid. *passim*).

12. In Sackville Street (*ante* 12 April 1789).

13. That is, HW hopes Mrs Damer will return from Lisbon within six weeks; she did not return until 12 May 1791 (*post* that date).

14. The reply to HW's complaining letter, *ante* 4 Feb. 1791.

Though ten thousand times kinder than I deserve, it wounds my heart, as I find I have hurt two of the persons I love the best upon earth, and whom I am most constantly studying to please and serve. That I soon repented of my murmurs you have seen by my subsequent letters. The truth, as you may have perceived, though no excuse, was, that I had thought myself dying and should never see you more; that I was extremely weak and low, when Mrs D.'s letter arrived and mentioned her supposing I should not see you till spring twelvemonth. That terrible sentence recalled Mr Batt's being the first to assure me of your going abroad, when I had concluded you had laid aside the design. I did sincerely allow that in both instances you had acted from tenderness in concealing your intentions—but as I knew I could better bear the information from yourselves than from others, I thought it unfriendly to let me learn from others what interested me so deeply—yet I do not in the least excuse my conduct —no, I condemn it in every light—and shall never forgive myself if you do not promise me to be guided entirely by your own convenience and inclinations about your return. I am perfectly well again; and just as likely to live one year as half an one. Indulge your pleasure in being abroad while you are there. I am now reasonable enough to enjoy your happiness, as my own—and since you are most kind when I least deserve it, how can I express my gratitude for giving up the scruple that was so distressing to me! Convince me you are in earnest by giving me notice that you will write to Charing Cross[15] while the Neapolitans are at Florence[16]—I will look on that as a clearer proof of your forgiving my criminal letter, than your return before you like it. It is most sure that nothing is more solid or less personal than my friendship for you two—and even my complaining letter, though unjust and unreasonable, proved that the nearer I thought myself to quitting the world, the more my heart was set on my two friends—nay, *they* had occupied the busiest moments of my illness as well as the most fretful ones. Forgive then, my dearest friends, what could proceed from nothing but too impatient affection. You say most truly you did not deserve my complaints: your patience and

15. 'His correspondents, to settle his mind as to the certainty of their return at the time they had promised, had assured him that no financial difficulties should stand in the way; which is what he means by sending to Charing Cross (to Drummond his banker). No such difficulties occurred. The correspondence, therefore, with Charing Cross never took place' (B, Wright vi. 410; MBJ i. 292).

16. A reference to the festivities at Florence, mentioned in the preceding letter.

temper under them make me but the more in the wrong; and to have hurt you, who have known but too much grief, is such a contradiction to the whole turn of my mind ever since I knew you, that I believe my weakness from illness was beyond even what I suspected. It is sure that when I am in my perfect senses, the whole bent of my thoughts is to promote your and your sister's felicity, and you know nothing can give me satisfaction like your allowing me to be of use to you. I speak honestly, notwithstanding my unjust letter, I had rather serve you than see you. Here let me finish this subject—I do not think I shall be faulty to you again.

The mother Gunning has published her letter to the Duke of Argyll[17]—and it disappoints everybody. It is neither romantic, nor entertaining, nor abusive, but on the General,[18] and Mr and Mrs Bowen[19] and the General's groom.[20] On the Bowens it is so immeasurably scurrilous, that I think they must prosecute her.[21] She accuses them and her husband of a conspiracy to betray and ruin his own daughter, without even attempting to assign a motive to them. Of the House of Argyll she says not a word. In short, it is a most dull incoherent rhapsody, that gives no account at all of the story that gave origin to her book, and at which no mortal could guess from it; and the 246 pages[22] contain nothing but invectives on her four supposed enemies,[23] and endless tiresome encomiums on the virtues of her *glorious darling,* and the unspottable innocence of that harmless lambkin[24]—I would

17. It was published at noon 21 March 1791, the day HW is writing (*ante* 11 March 1791, n. 8), and was out of print by four o'clock that afternoon (*Gazetteer and New Daily Advertiser* 22 March 1791).

18. General Gunning, 'the very reverse of an angel' (p. 105), is represented as the leader of the conspiracy, or as the tool of the Bowens.

19. See n. 21.

20. William Pearce, 'wretch' (pp. 25, 37) and 'villain' (p. 111).

21. After a paragraph attacking Bowen for his low birth, dishonour, and cunning, Mrs Gunning proceeds: 'This man of *words,* and this woman of *deeds* . . . about three years ago had united *themselves* and *evil dispositions* by the ties of marriage in *one* bundle of iniquity' (p. 11). Mrs Bowen is called a 'human monster' (p. 54), a 'sycophant' (p. 138), and an 'enraged fury' (ibid.). Throughout the pamphlet both

are represented as false, hypocritical, insidious schemers. In *The St James's Chronicle* 22–24 March 1791 it is said that 'two of the most prominent characters [in Mrs Gunning's *Letter*] have already declared their intention of appealing to the law for their justification,' but apparently no suit resulted.

22. HW doubtless meant to write *146;* the pamphlet actually contains 147 pages of text.

23. General Gunning, Mr and Mrs Bowen, and the groom.

24. HW does not exaggerate. In 'The Naked Truth, or the Sweet Little Angel Turned Out For Lorn,' a satiric print published 25 March 1791, Mrs Gunning is made to say to her daughter: 'Go in, my dear, sweet, lovely, charming, harmless, innocent, innoxious, immaculate, heavenly, blessed, angelic, celestial cherub' (BM, *Satiric Prints* vi. 849–50, No. 7981). Her de-

not even send it to you if I had an opportunity—you would not have patience to go through it—and there I suppose the absurd legend will end—I am heartily tired of it. Adieu!

PS. That ever *I* should give *you two* an uneasy moment! Oh! forgive me—yet I do not deserve pardon in my own eyes—and less in my own heart.

To Mary Berry, Sunday 27 March 1791

Address: À Mademoiselle Mademoiselle Berry à la poste restante à Florence, Italie. [Forwarded: 'Pisa.'] *Postmark:* Illegible. Endorsed: 'Pd 1.' Posted 29 March ('Visitors').

Berkeley Square, Sunday, March 27, 1791.
No. 25.[1]

THOUGH I begin my dispatch today, I think I shall change my post-days, as I hinted, from Tuesdays to Fridays, not only as more commodious for learning news for you; but as I do not receive your letters generally but on Mondays, I have less time to answer. I have an additional reason for delay this week. Mr Pitt[2] has notified that he is to deliver a message from the King tomorrow to the House of Commons on the situation of Europe;[3] and should there be a long debate, I may not gather the particulars till Tuesday morning, and if my levee lasts late, shall not have time to write to you—Oh! now are you all impatience to hear *that* message—I am sorry to say that I fear it is to be a warlike one. The Autocratrix[4] swears, d——n her eyes, she *will* hack her way to Constantinople through the blood of 100,000 more Turks, and that we are very impertinent for sending her a card with a sprig of olive. On the other hand Prussia bounces and huffs and claims our promise of helping him to make peace by helping

scription of Miss Gunning is also burlesqued in ibid., pp. 850–1, Nos. 7982–3.

1. 'No. 36' (B).
2. Hon. William Pitt (1759–1806) the younger, prime minister. For Mary Berry's

account of him, see *A Comparative View of Social Life in England and France*, 1844, i. 343–52.

3. See following letter.
4. Catherine II of Russia.

him to make war; and so in the most charitable and pacific way in the world, we are, they say, to send twenty ships to the Baltic, and half as many to the Black Sea[5]—this, little Britain, commonly called Great Britain, is to dictate to Petersburgh and Bengal, and cover Constantinople under those wings that reach from the North Pole to the farthest East!—I am mighty sorry for it, and hope we shall not prove a jackdaw that pretends to dress itself in the plumes of imperial eagles![6]

If we bounce abroad, we are more forgiving at home: a gentleman who lives at the east end of St James's Park has been sent for by a lady, who has a large house at the west end,[7] and they have kissed and are friends, which he notified by toasting her health in a bumper at a club the other day.[8] I know no circumstances, but am glad of it—I love peace public or private—not so the chieftains of the contending theatres of harmony. Taylor in wondrous respectful terms and full of affliction, has printed in the newspapers an advertisement[9] declaring that the Marquis's honour the Lord Chamberlain[10] did in one season, and that an unprofitable one, send *orders* (you know, that is, tickets of admission without paying) into the Opera House, to the loss of the managers of £400—servants, it is supposed, and Hertfordshire voters—eke and moreover, that it has been sworn in Chancery that his Lordship, not as Lord Ch[amberlain], had stipulated with Gallini[11] and O'Reilly that he, his heirs and assigns should

5. 'The naval force talked of for immediate equipment is 50 sail of the line, 30 for the Baltic and 20 for the Black Sea' (*St James's Chronicle* 29–31 March 1791).

6. A variation on the fable of the jackdaw and the peacock; see Phædrus, *Fab.*, I. iii.

7. 'The Queen and the Prince of Wales' (?B, Wright vi. 412). The Prince lived at Carlton House, and the Queen at Buckingham House.

8. 'The morning papers detail, with peculiar pride, an account of the reconciliation of certain great personages, between whom the world has not heard of any difference; at least of late' (*St James's Chronicle* 31 March–2 April 1791). According to a long account of the 'Royal Reconciliation' in *The Gazetteer and New Daily Advertiser* 4 April 1791, the coolness began in 1788–9 during the discussion of the Regency Bill, but was ended before 1791; the toast is not

mentioned in this account. A slightly different version is in *The Oracle* 2 April 1791. HW mentions the coolness or quarrel in 'Mem. 1783–91,' *sub* March 1789, and the reconciliation *sub* March 1791: 'The Queen sends for Prince, and desires reconciliation —qu[ery], why!—says indifferent whether Pitt or Fox, but whoever will make the King easy. Prince toasts her at Irish Club.'

9. The advertisement, dated 23 March, and covering almost a column of fine print, appears in *The Oracle* 25 March 1791. It is in reply to another advertisement in the same newspaper: 'Opera Facts,' obviously inserted by, or with the permission of, the Lord Chamberlain.

10. 'The Marquis of Salisbury' (?B, Wright vi. 412).

11. Giovanni Andrea Battista Gallini (1728–1805), dancing master, a proprietor and sometime manager of the King's Theatre, Haymarket; said to have lost £400,000

preserve the power of giving those detrimental *orders* in perpetuity. The immunity is a little new: former Chamberlains, it seems, even *durante officio,* have not exercised the privilege—if they had it.[12]

One word more of the Gunnings. Capt. Bowen informed the authoress by the channel of the papers that he shall prosecute her for the libel.[13] She answered by the same conveyance, that she is extremely glad of it[14]—but there is a difficulty—unless the prosecution is criminal, it is thought, that Madam being *femme couverte,* the charge must be made against her husband—and to be sure it would be droll that the General should be attacked for not hindering his wife from writing a libel that is more virulent against him himself than any-

by the burning of the theatre in 1789, and to have advanced £300,000 for the building of the new one. After receiving from the Pope the knighthood of the Golden Spur, he called himself 'Sir John Gallini.'

12. The last paragraph but one of Taylor's advertisement is: 'The most unpleasant part of my answer to the advertisement yet remains, and which nothing but that advertisement could have drawn from me. It says that "no privileges in this plan (the plan for building in Leicester Fields) were reserved to the Lord Chamberlain except such as had been constantly annexed to his office." What privileges may belong to this high office, it is not my business to inquire; but this I know, that the Marquis of Salisbury is the first Lord Chamberlain of the King's Household who ever claimed or exercised the privilege, if any such exists, of giving orders of free admission to this theatre; and I have also the misfortune to know that his Lordship exercised this privilege, in one season only, to an amount approaching to four hundred pounds, at a time too when his Lordship well knew that the receipts of the theatre were greatly inadequate to the expense. But with respect to the tripartite agreement between the noble Marquis, Gallini, and O'Reilly, for building in Leicester Fields, I aver that it has been stated upon oath in the Court of Chancery, that in that agreement there was a special article which secured "to the noble Marquis of Salisbury, his administrators and assigns (not to the Lord Chamberlain and his successors in office), the discretionary privilege of giving orders of free admission into that theatre"' (*Oracle* 25

March 1791). In 'Opera Facts' (ibid. 31 March 1791) Lord Salisbury stated that he was acting as 'a trustee for every future Lord Chamberlain,' and if the new theatre had been built, the proper documents would have been deposited in the Lord Chamberlain's office. Taylor's reply, dated 30 March, is in ibid. 2 April 1791: he there comments on 'this secret intention . . . fastidiously concealed from the Court of Chancery.' HW recorded in 'Mem. 1783–91,' *sub* March 1791: 'Taylor's violent attack on Lord Salisbury for £400 of orders and wanting to entail himself for orders on the Opera House.'

13. The advertisement has not been found.

14. 'A Card to Captain and Mrs Bowen,' dated St James's Street, 23 March 1791, appears in *The Gazetteer and New Daily Advertiser* 24 March 1791: 'Mrs Gunning, through the same public channel by which Captain and Mrs Bowen convey their card to her, returns them her congratulations on their intended course of law; they have also her most hearty wishes that their counsel may make no delay in settling the most speedy and effectual method for their proceeding, it being an event most devoutly wished for by Mrs Gunning. She is rather surprised that Captain and Mrs Bowen should think it necessary to give a reason why they do not answer her letter, or any part of it, the whole of that letter being addressed to the Duke of Argyll, and not to Captain and Mrs Bowen, who are merely spoken of in that letter for their real and uncontrovertible transactions in her family.'

body. Another little circumstance has come out: till the other day he did not know that he had claimed descent from Charlemagne in the newspapers—which therefore is referred to the same manufacture as the other forgeries. The General said, 'It is true, I am well born, but I know no such family in Ireland as the Charlemagnes.'—Lord Ossory[15] has just been here and told me that Gunnilda has written to Lord Blandford in her own name and *hand* begging his pardon (for promising herself marriage in his name) but imputing the first thought to his grandmother,[16] whom she probably inspired to think of it. This letter the Duchess of Marlborough carried to the Duchess of Bedford to open her eyes on her protégée, but with not much success, for what signify eyes, when the rest of the head is gone—She only said, 'You may be easy, for both mother and daughter are gone to France'[17]—no doubt, on finding her Grace's money not so forthcoming as her countenance, and terrified by Capt. Bowen's prosecution—and there I hope will terminate that strange story, for in France there is not a marquis left to marry her. One has heard of nothing else for these seven months! and it requires some ingenuity to keep up the attention of such a capital as London for above half a year together.

I supped on Thursday at Mrs Buller's with the Conways and Mount Edgcumbes, and the next night at Lady Ailesbury's with the same company and Lady Augusta Clavering.[18] You know on the famous night at your house when Gunnilda pretended that her father had received Lord Blandford's appointment of the wedding day,[19] we suspected, when they were gone, that we had seen doubts in Lady Augusta's face, and I desired her uncle Lord Frederic[20] to ask her if we had guessed right, but she protests she had then no suspicion.

15. John Fitzpatrick (1745–1818), 2d E. of Upper Ossory, HW's friend and correspondent; m. (1769) Hon. Anne Liddell, divorced wife of the 3d D. of Grafton.

16. The Dowager Duchess of Bedford.

17. 'Mrs Gunning, it is now said, is retired to the Continent with her daughter, and that the inexplicable letter business is to remain enveloped in the obscurity by which it has hitherto been surrounded' (St James's Chronicle 31 March–2 April 1791). In The Gazetteer and New Daily Advertiser 5 April 1791 is a letter from Mrs Gunning to the editor, 29 March 1791, in which she

says, 'My daughter's and my own health having obliged me to leave town. . . .' A letter from Paris 11 April mentions that 'we just this moment hear that the *literary* Miss Gunning and mother are at Abbeville, in Picardy' (St James' Chronicle 14–16 April 1791; see also The Oracle 19 April 1791).

18. 'Eldest daughter of John Duke of Argyle' (?B, Wright vi. 413).

19. In a letter; see ante 22 Oct. 1790.

20. Lord Frederick Campbell (1729–1816), 4th son of John, 4th D., and brother of John, 5th D. of Argyll; M.P. Glasgow

I have determined to send this away on Tuesday whether I know the details of the temple of Janus[21] tomorrow in time or not, that you may give yourselves airs of importance, if the Tuscan ministers pretend to tell you news of your own country that you do not know. You may say, your *chargé des affaires* sent you word of the King's message—and you may be mysterious about the rest—for mystery in the diplomatic dictionary is construed knowledge, though like a Hebrew word it means the reverse too.[22]

Sunday night.

I have been at White Pussy's[23] this evening: she asked much after you's. I did not think her Lord[24] looked as if *he* would drive Prince Potemkin[25] out of Bulgaria; but we trust that a new Frederic of Prussia and a new William Pitt will. Could they lay Catherine in the Black Sea, as ghosts used to be laid in the Red,[26] the world would be obliged to them.

I have proved in the right in determining to let this depart on Tuesday, for the martial message is only to be delivered tomorrow, and to be taken into consideration the next day; thence I could not send you the result till Friday, when I may possibly write again, and then adhere to that for my post-days.

Burghs 1761–80, Argyllshire 1780–99; lord register for Scotland 1768–1816 (*Scots Peerage* i. 384–5; Burke, *Peerage*, 1937, p. 141, *sub* Argyll). He was HW's executor.

21. Parliament.

22. Cf. *ante* 2 Feb. 1789.

23. 'Elizabeth Cary, wife of Lord Amherst, at this time Commander-in-Chief' (?B, Wright vi. 414); but see following note. Elizabeth Cary (1740–1830), dau. of Lt-Gen. Hon. George Cary, m. (1767) as 2d wife, Sir Jeffrey Amherst, K.B., cr. (1776) Bn Amherst. The explanation of 'White Pussy' has not been found. She lived at 12 St James's Square (*Directory to the Nobility, Gentry . . . for 1793*).

24. Jeffrey Amherst (1717–97), K.B., 1761; cr. (1776) Bn Amherst of Holmesdale and (1788) of Montreal; best known for his military achievements in North America, particularly in Canada; general, 1778; field marshal, 1796; commander-in-chief 1778–82, 1793–5. HW's comments on him varied from the most extravagant praise to the lowest contempt: for his campaign in America, HW thought him 'provident, methodic, conciliating, and cool' (*Mem. Geo. II*, 2d edn, 1847, iii. 285; see also ibid. 285–9); but he later refers to Amherst as 'the most wrong-headed of men' (*Mem. Geo. III* iv. 38), 'a man totally void of parts' who 'had gained the King's favour by the most servile deference, and, between flattery and dulness, he pleased nobody else' (*Last Journals* ii. 221); a 'wretched and incapable' creature with 'immoderate self-interest and obstinacy' (ibid. 308, 221).

25. Prince Grigory Aleksandrovich Potemkin (1739–5 Oct. 1791), a favourite of Catherine II; commander-in-chief of the Russian forces in the war with Turkey from 1787 until his death. He had been in St Petersburg since 11 March (*St James's Chronicle* 12–14 April 1791).

26. For comments on the laying of ghosts in the Red Sea, mentioned by Addison, see W. Carew Hazlitt, *Faiths and Folklore . . . A New Edition of The Popular Antiquities of Great Britain by Brand and Ellis*, 1905, *sub* Ghosts; N&Q 1867, 3d ser., xii. 56–7; GM 1815, lxxxv pt i. 124, 322.

Tuesday morning.

Your most kind and satisfactory No. 24 is come, and gives me infinite joy—yet still I have a thorn left; for how can I be easy, if I think that you return a moment sooner than you would like in complaisance to me?—and then your house in Audley Street will be unlet from the 25th of May, which I thought was hired till Christmas![27] I know not what to say, but still beg you will do what is most convenient and best for yourselves. I will accept no promise that ties you down to anything; so heartily do I repent of my complaining letter. I have neither time nor paper to say more now, except my concern for your cold[28]—but I shall write again on Friday and will then answer your letter fully, for my heart is full of its kindness. Adieu!

To Mary Berry, Thursday 31 March 1791

Address: À Mademoiselle Mademoiselle Berry à la poste restante à Florence, Italie. *Postmark:* <FIREN>ZE. Endorsed: 'Pd 1s.'
Posted 1 April ('Visitors').

Berkeley Square, Thursday, March 31, 1791.

No. 26.[1]

I POSTPONE my farther answer to your last, till I have satisfied Mr Berry's curiosity about the war with Semiramis. The King's martial message[2] was adopted on Tuesday by both Houses—but the measure is exceedingly unpopular, and even some impression was made on the Court-troops.[3] The Ministerialists affect to give out that matters will not ripen to war,[4] as if our blustering would terrify a

27. Mary Berry had mentioned that their London house *could* be let until Christmas, not that it *had* been let (*ante* 4 Feb. 1791).
28. 'I have been far from well lately, consequently far from gay' (Mary Berry to Mrs Damer, ca 10 March 1791, 'Berry-Damer,' i. 45).

1. 'No. 37' (B).
2. Read in the House of Commons by the Speaker 28 March 1791. He urged strengthening the Navy in view of the continuing Russian-Turkish War.
3. In the House of Lords the motion supporting the King's address was carried, 97 to 34; in the House of Commons, 228 to 135; see an account of the debate in *The St James's Chronicle* 29–31 March 1791. See also HW's account of the reception of the message, in 'Mem. 1783–91,' *sub* 29 March 1791.
4. 'The ministerial prints delight very much in boasting of the honours of victory without the danger of war' (*Gazetteer and New Daily Advertiser* 29 March 1791). Fox and Burke, among others, strongly opposed the motion supporting the King's address (*St James's Chronicle* 29–31 March 1791).

woman, in whom fear of no sort seems to predominate. More this deponent knows not.

Now, my dearest friends, I turn to you, and do most cordially implore you both, not to bind yourselves nor to hold yourselves bound to me by any promise about your return. Let it depend entirely on your own inclinations and convenience. I cannot forgive my sickly impatience in writing that peevish letter[5] which vexed you—It has vexed *me* more. Are you to be pleased only by what would please me? What claim have I to any sacrifice? and why should you make me any? or think you that I cannot sacrifice my own wishes to your content? Oh indeed but I can and wish to do so. These are my earnest sentiments, and I could but repeat them in various words were I to continue writing all night.

We have no other positive news since my Tuesday's letter. There is no peace between the opera theatres: the Haymarket rather triumphs. They have opened twice,[6] taking money, in an evasive manner, pretending themselves concerts;[7] the singers are in their own clothes, the dancers dressed, and no recitative—a sort of opera in dishabille. Threats of arrest have been thrown out, but no *coup de main*.[8] Some think the return of the judges from the circuit is awaited —but perhaps the court is sensible of having begun by being in the wrong.

I never mention France, concluding you more *à portée* to know. The hideous barbarity at Douai, where they have fractured a man's skull, and then taken him out of bed and hanged him after he had

5. *Ante* 4 Feb. 1791.

6. 26, 29 March; a third performance took place on the evening of 31 March, the day HW is writing; see *The Oracle* 26–31 March 1791.

7. The advertisement for 29 March begins: 'King's Theatre. The nobility, gentry, and the public at large are respectfully informed that, in compliance with the wishes of many of the principal subscribers and supporters of this undertaking, and it being found that without offence to law, the entertainments of music and dancing will be given.' Part I consisted of serious music, followed by dancing; Part II, of comic music, followed by 'an historical dance, called *Orpheus and Eurydice*' (*Oracle* 29 March 1791).

8. 'On Saturday Mr O'Reilly lodged an information at the Public Office in Bow Street against the exhibitions given that evening at the King's Theatre in the Haymarket; but the Bench of Justices have declined interfering on account of the recognition of that theatre in the Acts of Parliament, which, in the opinion of some of the first lawyers in the kingdom, amounts to a legal authority, at least for the present entertainments given there, if not even for Italian operas themselves; and because the consequences of enforcing a penal statute in a doubtful case, and where so much property is at stake, were of too great and too serious a nature for the justices to encounter, before the opinions of the Courts of Judicature are taken upon the point of law' (*London Chronicle* 29–31 March 1791, lxix. 312).

been trepanned;[9] while the prisons are over-stuffed,[10] after they found but six prisoners in the Bastile, does not convince me yet that they have got a milder government.

How sorry I am that you have lost the satisfaction of being with your friend Mrs Cholmely in town this season. I doubt the two courts will not make you amends.

I feel every week the disagreeableness of the distance between us: each letter is generally three weeks on its passage, and we receive answers to what one must often forget one has said: and cannot under six weeks learn what one is anxious to know. Balloons, had they succeeded, would have prodigiously abridged delays—but *French* discoveries are not, I believe, endowed with duration; when they have broken necks and cut throats, they find the world forced to content itself with old inventions. French levity never takes disappointment into its calculations.

This must be a short letter, for even London, you see, now the *Gunnings* are gone, cannot furnish a whole sheet once a week: however, I had rather leave half my paper blank, than have any campaign-work to fill it with. Europe at present is in a strange ferment, distracted between the demons of republicanism and universal monarchy—at least Prussia and we say that Semiramis aims at the latter—if she does, we at least might wish her removed to Constantinople—she would be farther off. Nay, I am so ignorant, as to imagine, that, if there, she would cultivate and restore Greece, etc., and be a better customer than the Turks. Nor am I disposed to think Prussia a substantial ally: it is a fictitious power that would have shrunk to little again with its creator,[11] had the successor[12] been an inactive prince. Attention, treasures and a most formidable army he has; but if war dissipates his hoards, and diminishes his force, which the squander

---

9. Following a riot at Douai 14 March, in which an officer of the National Guard was hanged, on the 17th 'a M. Nicolom, who, the evening before had been trepanned, was dragged out of his bed and hung on a tree near his own house! The whole of this business is laid to the charge of the priests . . . and the municipal officers are ordered to Orléans to take their trials' (*St James's Chronicle* 24–26 March 1791).

10. Letter from Paris 14 March 1791: 'Friday last [11 March] it was agitated [in the National Assembly] whether they should not remove to Orléans the different prisoners now confined in the Abbey of St Germains, on suspicion of high treason. On this occasion M. de Montlausier said "there were at the present moment 1801 prisoners in the jails of Paris; which number would, on the morrow, receive an increase of eight hundred more" ' (*St James's Chronicle* 17–19 March 1791).

11. Frederick II (1712–86), the Great, King of Prussia.

12. Frederick William II.

of his wealth will weaken too, *adieu! panier, vendanges sont faites*[13]— these are my speculations—I don't know whether they have come into the head of anybody else, nor care whether they deserve it.[14] I write to amuse you and myself, and only reason, because I have nothing better to send you. I am far from fond of dissertationary letters, which present themselves humbly, but hope to rank as essays[15]—I must be in sad want of nonsense, when I talk seriously on general topics; and I hope that, except when you were in a storm, or travelling through the land of anarchy, or when I was in terror of seeing you no more, or not for an age, you will not charge me with any gravity. I have gossiped to anybody's heart's wish; and the deuce is in it, if any letters are worth receiving, that have the fear of wisdom before their eyes. Adieu to *Arno's vale* till next Friday.

To Mary Berry, Sunday 3 April 1791

Address: À Mademoiselle Mademoiselle Berry à la poste restante à Florence, Italie. *Postmark:* FIRENZE 1[3?]. Endorsed: 'Pd 1.'
Posted 5 April; HW noted the subject: 'fall 16 of March' ('Visitors').

Strawberry Hill, Sunday night, April 3, 1791.
No. 27.[1]

O H! what a shocking accident![2] Oh! how I detest your going abroad more than I have done yet in my crossest mood! You escaped the storm on the 10th of October that gave me such an alarm; you passed unhurt through the cannibals of France and their repub-

---

13. Read 'adieu! paniers' (Rabelais, *Gargantua* i. 27).
14. This speculation was not new to HW: he had written of Prussia in 'Mem. 1783–91,' *sub* 18 Dec. 1785, as 'perhaps a temporary [power] . . . as the successor may neither be able nor disposed to follow his uncle's politics.'
15. Cf. *ante* 18 Sept. 1789.

———

1. 'No. 38' (B).
2. 'Miss Berry had fallen down a bank in the neighbourhood of Pisa, and received a severe cut on the nose' (?B, Wright vi. 414). Mary Berry wrote to Mrs Damer a few days after the accident: 'If you should have any doubts as to the identity of my person, and when I fly up to meet you, turn coolly away

from [me], not recognizing a figure with a scar across the nose for the same person who so reluctantly separated herself from you, I must recount, etc. . . . [So in MS.] I remember the time when I should have been cruelly anxious upon this subject. I am now almost *provoked* at my philosophic indifference about it, but the days of my vanity are over (Heaven knows! they have been too little happy to regret); the comforts, satisfactions, and enjoyments of these that remain to me, depending entirely upon the society, friendship, and affection of a very few persons to whom my life will be dedicated, are, I trust, perfectly independent of a spoilt complexion or a scar upon the face' ('Berry-Damer' i. 46).

lic of *larrons* and *poissardes,* who terrified me sufficiently—but I never
expected that you would dash yourself to pieces at Pisa! You say I
love truth and that you have told me the exact truth—but how can
fear believe? You say you slept *part* of the night after your fall—oh!
but the other part! was not you feverish? How can I wait above a
month for answers to an hundred questions I want to ask; and how a
week for another letter? A little comfort I have had even since I received the horrid account—I have met Mrs Lockart at Lady Hesketh's,[3] and she has assured me that there is a very good surgeon at
Pisa—if he is, he must have blooded you directly. I wish you had had
some arquebusade water.[4] How you must have suffered by washing
the wound with vinegar, though rightly!—and what your father and
sister must have felt at seeing you! How could you be well enough to
write the next day? Why did not Miss Agnes for you? but I conclude
she was not recovered enough of *your* fall. When I am satisfied that
you have not hurt yourself more than you own, I will indulge my
concern about the outside of your nose, about which I shall not have
your indifference.[5] I am not in love with you, yet fully in love enough
not to bear any damage done to that perfect nose or to any of all
your beautiful features—then too I shall scold at your thoughtless-
ness—how I hate a party of pleasure! It never turns out well; fools
fall out, and sensible people fall down!—Still I thank you a million
of times for writing yourself—if Miss Agnes had written for you, I
confess I should have been ten times more alarmed than I am—and
yet I am alarmed enough! My sweet Agnes, I feel for you too, though
you have not the misery of being a thousand miles from your
wounded sister, nor are waiting for a second account. The quantity

3. Harriet Cowper (1733–1807), 1st dau.
of Ashley Cowper, clerk of the Parliaments;
cousin and favourite correspondent of the
poet Cowper; m. (1751) Thomas Hesketh
(1728–78) of Rufford, Lancs, cr. (1761) Bt
(GEC; *Register of Marriages of . . . Oxford Chapel, Vere Street . . . 1736–1754,
Part I,* ed. W. Bruce Bannerman, 1917, p.
264). She lived at 28 New Norfolk Street
(*Directory to the Nobility, Gentry . . . for
1793*). At her house HW introduced the
Berrys to Fanny Burney (Constance Hill,
Juniper Hall, 1904, p. 259).

4. Or Harquebusade water: 'a lotion regarded as a specific for gunshot and other
wounds' (OED). As late as 1802 a correspondent of the *Gentleman's Magazine* (lxxii pt i.

217–18) mentions the recipe in [Robert Dos-
sie,] *The Elaboratory Laid Open, or The
Secrets of Modern Chemistry and Phar-
macy Revealed,* 1758, as the best available.
See also N&Q 1929, clvii. 355, 409; R. James,
A Medicinal Dictionary, 1743–5, vol. i *sub*
'aqua sclopetaria . . . commonly call'd Eau
d'Arquebusade.'

5. See n. 2. After meeting Mrs Cholmeley
at the Pantheon 14 May 1791, Mrs Damer
wrote to Mary Berry 16 May 1791: 'She is,
I find, just of the same opinion as Mr W.
and your most humble servant, as to your
face. She said that she could not by any
means feel the sort of philosophy you expressed on the subject' (*Berry Papers* 28).

of blood she lost has, I trust, prevented any fever. I would ask for every tiny circumstance—but alas! I must wait above a month for an answer!

Though I wrote twice last week, it was impossible to let the first post-day slip me on such a terrible accident. I received the account two days sooner than the letters generally arrive, and the day after my last was gone,[6] so I can have nothing to add, nor indeed do I think of anything but the fall at Pisa, of which I went full to Lady Hesketh's last night, and there were so many of your friends, that my sad news seemed like having thrown a bomb into the room—you would have been flattered at the grief it occasioned: there were Mrs Lockart, the Pepyses, Mrs Buller, Lady Herries, George Cambridge, the Abbé Nichols, Mrs Carter[7]—and some who scarce know you, who yet found they would be very unfashionable if they did not join in the concern for you and in your panegyric. Cambridge had received a letter too, but three days earlier in date. Mr Pepys desired me to tell you that he had written to you a folio of news, but you never received it. However, I am sure I have not let you starve, unless you are curious about suits in Chancery.[8]

Not to torment you more with my fears when I hope you are almost recovered, I will answer the rest of your letter. General Ohara I have unluckily not met yet: he is so dispersed[9] and I am so confined in my resorts and so seldom dine from home, that I have not seen him even at General Conway's. When I do, can you imagine that we shall not talk of you two—yes, and your accident I am sure will be the chief topic. As our *fleets* are to dethrone Catherine Petruchia,[10] Ohara will probably not be sent to Siberia. Apropos to Catherine and Petruchio, I supped with their representatives, Kemble and Mrs Siddons, t'other night at Miss Farren's; the Hothams[11] were there

6. HW's letter of 31 March was posted 1 April, the day the foreign post left London, and a day later he received Mary Berry's letter written at Pisa 17 March, the day after her fall; see also the following letter. If her letter was posted the day after it was written, HW received it in the unusually short time of fifteen days. Although he here intimates that the period was usually seventeen or eighteen days, he says in the preceding letter that three weeks were usually required.

7. Elizabeth Carter (1717–1806), the

translator of Epictetus; HW's occasional correspondent.

8. Pepys was a Master in Chancery.

9. An odd use of this word, not illustrated in OED.

10. Catherine II of Russia.

11. 'Sir Charles Hotham Thompson, married to Lady Dorothy Hobart, sister of John second Earl of Buckinghamshire' (?B, Wright vi. 415). Sir Charles Hotham (1729–94), 8th Bt, of Scarborough and South Dalton, Yorks, 1771; assumed name of Thompson on inheriting estates of that family,

too and Mrs Anderson,[12] who treated the players with acting as many characters as ever they did, particularly Gunnilda and Lady Clackmannan.[13] Mrs Siddons is leaner, but looks well: she has played Jane Shore and Desdemona, and is to play in *The Gamester;* all the parts she will act this year.[14] Kemble, they say, shone in *Othello.*[15]

Mrs Damer has been received at Elvas[16] with all military honours and a banquet by order of Mello, formerly embassador here.[17] It was handsome in him, but must have distressed her, who is so void of ostentation and love of show.

1772, but resumed name of Hotham, 1787; m. (1752) Lady Dorothy Hobart (d. 1798) dau. of John, 1st E. of Buckinghamshire, by his first wife. Their only child, Henrietta Gertrude Hotham (1753–1816), for whom HW wrote *The Magpie and Her Brood,* SH, 1764, was doubtless a member of the party. For the intimacy between the Hothams and Miss Farren, see A. M. W. Stirling, *The Hothams,* 1918, ii. 1–262. Earlier in 1791, Sir Charles had spent two months at Bath. While he was there Mrs Damer wrote him: 'Mr Walpole tells me that during his dreadful confinement last winter you constantly went to see him, and he found his greatest comfort and satisfaction in your visits' (ibid. 260).

12. 'A daughter of Lady Cecilia Johnstone's, married to a brother of Charles Anderson Pelham, Lord Garborough [Yarborough]' (?B, Wright vi. 415).

13. 'A nickname which had been given by the writer to a lady of the society' (?B, Wright vi. 415), probably Lady Greenwich; see *ante* 2 Aug. 1790.

14. Mrs Siddons appeared at Drury Lane in Rowe's *Jane Shore* 21 March; in *Othello* 28 March; and for her benefit and what was advertised as her final performance of the season, 4 April, as Mrs Beverley in *The Gamester,* by Edward Moore (1712–57). For advertisements of and comments on the performances, see *The Oracle* 21, 22, 28, 29 March, and 4, 5 April 1791. She appeared as Zara in Congreve's *The Mourning Bride* 14 May 1791, a benefit for the Theatrical Fund (*Oracle* 4, 16 May 1791; *Berry Papers* 27).

15. 'Mr Kemble's Othello is distinguished by passages, whether of terror or the softer emotions, so exquisitely managed that the applause, loud and lasting as it was

last night, was scarcely equal to the reward of a work so masterly and affecting' (*Oracle* 29 March 1791).

16. From Badajoz 1 March 1791 Mrs Damer wrote to Mary Berry: 'Elvas, the last town in Portugal, is in perfect repair, to appearance, and a remarkably pretty town' (MBJ i. 336).

17. Martinho Mello e Castro (1716–95), Portuguese minister to England ca 1754–69; F.R.S., 1757; later minister of marine (DU DEFFAND ii. 329; MONTAGU ii. 278). Mrs Damer wrote to Mary Berry from Herrera 19 March 1791 that her adventure at Elvas gave her 'a more than common horror of being *shown civilities.* Elvas being the frontier town in Portugal, I was told to ask for a letter to the Governor, that my baggage might not be stopped. This happened to be a brother of old Mello's, who was in England many years, and much at my father's house before you were born. Besides giving me a letter, he chose by way of a fine thing to write to the Governor his brother, who chose to order that I should be received with the *honours of war.* Some miles from the town I met a guard of thirty horsemen who escorted me, and I came into the town, drums beating, trumpets sounding, and cannon firing (it is literally true), was dragged to the Governor's house instead of going quietly to my inn, and sat down almost instantaneously to a great dinner with a dozen or fourteen officers; they carried me all over the town, and with the greatest difficulty I got rid of the company in the evening by saying, what was too true, that I was so much fatigued I must go to my bed' (MBJ i. 341). In reply Mary Berry remarks that her 'imagination figures' Mrs Damer 'much more easily [in her study in Sack-

Miss Boyle,[18] who no more than Miss Pulteney[19] has let herself be snapped up by lovers of her fortune, is going to Italy for a year with Lord and Lady Malden.[20]

I return to town tomorrow morning with a faint hope of receiving another letter about your fall; and I will reserve the rest of my paper for anything I may hear before noon on Tuesday. I will not peremptorily fix my days of writing to Tuesdays or Fridays, but write as you mend, or as I find matter; therefore do not suspect gout, if I am not punctual—I am more likely, I think, to be intercalary, than remiss. This morning has been as warm, as if the day had been born at Pisa; and Cliveden, where I have been giving some orders, did not look ugly.

B. Square, Monday after dinner.

Good news, though not just what I want most—Mirabeau is dead[21] —ay, miraculously, for it was of a putrid fever (that began in his

---

ville Street] than receiving the *honours of war* at Elvas, or making speeches to the *corregidor* in Spain' ('Berry-Damer' i. 50).

18. 'Afterwards married to Lord Henry Fitzgerald' (?B, Wright vi. 415). Charlotte Boyle (1769–1831), dau. and heir of Hon. Robert Boyle-Walsingham, m. (4 Aug. 1791) Lord Henry Fitzgerald (*post* 3–8 Aug. 1791). The abeyance of the barony of Ros being terminated in her favour, she became (1806) *suo jure* Baroness Ros or Roos, and by royal license (6 Oct. 1806) took the name of 'De Ros' after her husband's name.

19. 'Afterwards married to Sir James Murray' (?B, Wright vi. 415). Henrietta Laura Pulteney (formerly Johnstone) (1766–1808), only dau. and heir of Sir William Johnstone (later Pulteney), 5th Bt; cr. (1792) Bns and (1803) Cts of Bath; m. (1794) Sir James Murray (afterwards Murray-Pulteney), Bt. Earlier in 1791 the newspapers commented: 'Is it from the reluctance of our unmarried gentlemen to ask *too much,* or the extreme nicety of the lady, that Miss Pulteney, perhaps the richest spinster in Europe, has at present no ostensible suitor?' (*Gazetteer and New Daily Advertiser* 25 Feb. 1791). 'The fortune of Miss Pulteney, though very great, is not, as has been frequently stated, five and twenty thousand pounds a year. The annual income of her estate is at present

four thousand pounds, which, upon the death of her father, will be increased to sixteen, by the addition of the Bath estate' (ibid. 8 March 1791).

20. 'Lord Malden, afterwards Earl of Essex, was a first cousin of Miss Boyle's. This journey did not take place' (?B, Wright vi. 415). George Capel (-Coningsby from 1781) (1757–1839), styled Vct Malden until 1799; 5th E. of Essex, n.c., 1799; m. (1) (1786) Sarah Bazett (ca 1761–1838), dau. of Henry Bazett of St Helena, and widow of Edward Stephenson; m. (2) (1838) after the death of his first wife, from whom he had long been separated, Catherine ('Kitty') Stephens (1794–1882), actress and singer. The first wife was a painter of miniatures on ivory and in enamel (Basil S. Long, *British Miniaturists*, 1929, p. 286). 'Lady Viscountess Malden painted finely in miniature, i.e. copied. She went to Rome in 1791, and improved there greatly, and made some extraordinary copies from the best masters. . . . She returned in 1792' (HW, *Anecdotes of Painting*, vol. v, ed. Frederick W. Hilles and Philip B. Daghlian, New Haven, 1937, p. 239). For references to their travels in Italy, see *The Times* 5 Sept., 13 Oct., 14, 31 Dec. 1791.

21. Honoré-Gabriel Riquetti (1749–2 April 1791), Comte de Mirabeau.

heart). Dr Price is dying also[22]—fortunate omens for those who hope
to die in their beds too. I think alike of such incendiaries whose lessons tend to blood, whether their stilettos have taken place or not.
That Mr Berry with so much good nature and good sense should be
staggered, I do not wonder. Nobody is more devoted to liberty than
I am. It is therefore that I abhor *the National Assembly,* whose outrageous violence has given, I fear, a lasting wound to the cause; for anarchy is despotism in the hands of thousands. A lion attacks but
when hungry or provoked; but who can live in a desert full of hyenas?—nobody but Mr Bruce—and we have only his word for it.[23]
Here is started up another corsair, one Paine from America, who has
published an answer to Mr Burke, that deserves a putrid fever.[24] His
doctrines go to the extremity of levelling, and his style is so coarse,
that you would think he means to degrade the language as much as
the government: here is one of his delicate paragraphs: 'We do not
want a king, or lords of the bedchamber, or lords of the kitchen, or

22. 'Dr Price is in a very declining state
of health, but preserves his usual equa-
nimity of temper' (*Gazetteer and New
Daily Advertiser* 7 March 1791). 'Dr Price
lies dangerously ill at his house in Hack-
ney. His complaint is a strangury' (*London
Chronicle* 26–29 March 1791, lxix. 304).

23. James Bruce (1730–94), author of
*Travels to Discover the Source of the Nile,
in the Years 1768[–73],* 5 vols, 4to, Edinburgh, 1790. Bruce's report of his travels,
while now generally accepted as authentic
in general if not in detail, was viewed by
HW and many of his contemporaries with
considerable skepticism. A typical comment
is that of 'No Gudgeon,' whose letter to the
editor of *The St James's Chronicle* appears
in the issue of 22–24 July 1790: 'Sir, Mr
Bruce has travelled far, and seemed determined to come home laden with a full cargo
of the marvellous, whatever else he might
leave behind him. Munchausen, Sir, was a
great traveller also, but the Abyssinian re-
searcher has beat him hollow, even in his
own line.' He then quotes an account of
fish resembling gudgeons in water so hot
Bruce was surprised they were not boiled.
See also *post* 25 Sept. 1791.

24. Thomas Paine (1737–1809). The first
part of *The Rights of Man,* dedicated to
George Washington, appeared, appropri-
ately, on Washington's birthday, 22 Feb.

1791 (*Gazetteer and New Daily Advertiser*
19 Feb. 1791; *Times* 21 Feb. 1791; *St James's
Chronicle* 19–22 Feb. 1791), but, the publisher becoming frightened, it was suppressed after only a few copies had got
into circulation (*Gazetteer and New Daily
Advertiser* 25 Feb. 1791, where the date of
publication is said to have been Saturday,
when it was Tuesday). Transferred to a
different publisher, it was republished with
a preface, and with only the minutest
changes (Moncure D. Conway, *Life of
Thomas Paine,* 1892, i. 284). The date of
publication is given by Paine's biographers
as 13 March, which was Sunday; the earliest advertisement found in contemporary
newspapers is 16 March (*Times* and *Oracle*
16 March 1791; *London Chronicle* 15–17
March 1791, lxix. 261, *sub* 16 March). A second edition was advertised in *The Times*
19 March 1791, and a third edition had
been published by the time HW wrote this
letter (*London Chronicle* 29–31 March
1791, lxix. 311, *sub* 31 March). In 'Mem.
1783–91,' *sub* March 1791, HW wrote:
'Paine, author of American *Common Sense,*
writes a violent answer to Burke; grows
frightened as it was thought treason—another bookseller ventures to publish it—and
Whig Club thank Paine and hope his doctrines will spread.'

lords of the necessary house.'[25] This rhetoric I suppose was calculated for our *poissardes*.

Monday night.

I am come home early from the Bishop of London's for the chance of finding another letter from one of you—but ah! you did not know my anxiety! March 16th will be a blacker day in my almanac than Oct. 10th.—I hope after nineteen days, without reckoning the time this will be travelling to you, you would at this moment be capable of laughing at my alarm: alas it is no joke to me!

I learnt nothing new for you but that Lord Strathaven was married this morning to Miss Cope[26]—not at Gretna Green, for they have been asked in church.[27] Adieu! You bid me have no more gout this year—pray do you have [no] more falls.

To Mary Berry, Sunday 10 April 1791

Address: À Mademoiselle Mademoiselle Berry à la poste restante à Florence, Italie. *Postmark:* FIRENZE. Endorsed: 'Pd 1s.'
Posted 12 April ('Visitors').

Berkeley Square, April 10, 1791.

No. 28.

IT is Sunday, but no letter come! I did hope for one yesterday, as the preceding Saturday had brought me the miserable news of your fall, and this I flattered myself would make me amends by a favourable account—but Saturday I see is one of the *Dies nefastos carbone notandos*,[1] and a pupil of *March 16th*. If tomorrow brings good

25. 'If I ask a man in America if he wants a king, he retorts, and asks me if I take him for an idiot. . . . It is easy to conceive that a band of interested men, such as placemen, pensioners, lords of the bedchamber, lords of the kitchen, lords of the necessary-house, and the Lord knows what besides, can find as many reasons for monarchy as their salaries, paid at the expense of the country, amount to' (2d edn, pp. 139–40). Although he was the least covetous of placemen, HW might well object to the passage on grounds other than that of style.

26. George Gordon (1761–1853), styled Lord Strathaven until 1794; 5th E. of Aboyne, 1795; 9th M. of Huntly, 1836. He m. (4 April 1791) Catherine Anne Cope (1771–1832), younger dau. and coheir of Sir Charles Cope, 2d Bt.

27. Stepney Church, according to GEC. But *The St James's Chronicle* 2–5 April 1791 and *The London Chronicle* 2–5 April, lxix. 328, report that the marriage took place at St George's, Hanover Square.

1. An allusion to the ancient custom of marking fair days with a white stone or mark, and unlucky days with a black; see Horace, *Opera*, ed. Arthur John Macleane, 1853, p. 80.

news, I will prefer Mondays,[2] though two days later. I have little news for you, though I begin writing today. If anybody asks me for news, I answer, 'Yes, and very bad, Miss Berry has had a terrible fall, and cut her beautiful nose!'

What novelties there are I will dispatch, for if I have not a most prosperous account tomorrow, I shall forget anything I have heard—at present my gazette would lie in a nutshell; and were it not for the oddity of what happened to myself for two days together, my intelligence would be like to the common articles of a newspaper—On Wednesday my nephew Lord Cholmondeley came and acquainted me that he is going to be married to Lady Charlotte Bertie,[3] who had accepted of him—'But,' says he, 'you will be so good as not to mention it yet, for I am now going to the Duchess of Ancaster[4] to ask her consent'—which her Grace did not refuse.

The next day Captain Waldegrave[5] came, and almost in the same words, the parties excepted, notified a match between his sister Lady Elizabeth, and Lord Cardigan,[6] 'But you must not mention it yet, for the Earl is only now gone into the King to ask his leave.'—I did not know I was so proper a Cato to be trusted with love-tales—I doubt George Cholmondeley and his new wife, and the mothers of both[7] are not delighted with the former match; and Brudenel[8] and his mother[9]

2. The day HW usually received letters from the Berrys; see preceding letter.

3. Georgiana Charlotte Bertie (1764–1838), younger dau. of 3d D. of Ancaster, m. (25 April 1791) George James Cholmondeley, 4th E., cr. (1815) M. of Cholmondeley. The engagement was announced in *The Oracle* 9 April 1791.

4. Mary Panton (d. 1793), dau. of Thomas Panton, master of the King's running horses; m. (1750) as 2d wife, Peregrine Bertie, 3d D. of Ancaster; mistress of the robes 1761–93.

5. Hon. William Waldegrave (1753–1825), 2d son of 3d E. Waldegrave; Capt. R.N., 1776; rear admiral, 1794; admiral, 1802; cr. (1800) Bn Radstock.

6. James Brudenell (1725–1811), 5th E. of Cardigan; master of the robes 1760–91; constable of Windsor Castle 1791–1811; m. (28 April 1791) as 2d wife, Lady Elizabeth Waldegrave (1758–1823), lady of the Bedchamber to the Princess Royal 1783–91, and to Queen Charlotte 1793–1807 (GEC; *Annual Register*, 1783, xxvi pt i. 229; *post*

16 Oct. 1791). The date of the marriage is given in contemporary accounts as above (*Oracle* 28, 29 April 1791; *St James's Chronicle* 28–30 April 1791; Collins, *Peerage*, 1812, iii. 499; GM 1791, lxi pt i. 487), but GEC and late editions of Burke give it ten days earlier.

7. George James Cholmondeley's mother was Mary Woffington (ca 1729–1811), sister of the actress Peg Woffington; m. (1746) Rev. Hon. Robert Cholmondeley, HW's nephew (Burke, *Peerage*, 1928, p. 520, *sub* Cholmondeley; DU DEFFAND i. 299 *et passim*). Mrs Cholmondeley's mother was Marcia Morgan (ca 1735–1819), dau. of Mark Anthony (or Marcus) Morgan of Ireland; m. (1753) John Pitt of Encombe and Kingston House, Dorset, sometime M.P. (John Hutchins, *Dorset,* 3d edn, Westminster, 1861–70, iv. 91; Collins, *Peerage,* 1812, vii. 490; GM 1753, xxiii. 51; GM 1819, lxxxix pt i. 282).

8. Robert Brudenell (1769–1837), posthumous son of Hon. Robert Brudenell,

will be terribly disappointed with the latter,[10] after the old Earl had lain fallow so long. I remember when he married his former wife,[11] they both looked so antique, that I said, they may have grandchildren, but they certainly will have no children—now it seems his Lordship means to have a great-grandson.[12] I was to have met the mother Mrs Cholmondeley last Friday at Mrs Buller's, but the latter turned a very small party into a ball, and I desired to be excused, for though I have married two wives at once, when many years older than Lord Cardigan,[13] I did not choose to jig with Master Buller's friends the officers of the Guards.[14]

I can tell Mr Berry nothing more of our Russian war, but that it is most exceedingly unpopular, and that it is supposed Mr Pitt will avoid it if he possibly can. You know I do not love Catherine Petruchia Slayczar, yet I have no opinion of our fleet dethroning her.

An odd adventure has happened. The Primate of Poland[15] has been here, the King's[16] brother. He bought some scientific toys at Merlin's,[17] paid fifteen guineas for them in the shop, and was to pay

brother of the 4th and 5th Earls of Cardigan; 6th E. of Cardigan, 1811.

9. Anne Bishop (or Bishopp) (ca 1729–1803), 1st dau. of Sir Cecil Bishopp, 6th Bt, of Parham, Sussex; m. (1759) Hon. Robert Brudenell: Bedchamber woman to Queen Charlotte 1761–1803 (Collins, *Peerage*, 1812, iii. 498; GM 1803, lxxiii pt ii. 993; *Royal Kalendar*, 1762–1803).

10. Its effect on Brudenell's sister was immediate. When she heard of the engagement at the Queen's Drawing-Room on Thursday 7 April, 'for the first time, the surprise on her receiving the information was so great as to occasion the young lady to faint, and she was obliged to be supported out of the presence' (*Oracle* 9 April 1791).

11. Anne Legge (d. 1786), dau. of George Legge, styled Vct Lewisham; m. (1760) Hon. James Brudenell, cr. (1780) Bn Brudenell, 5th E. of Cardigan, 1790.

12. Both marriages of Lord Cardigan were childless.

13. At the time this letter was written, HW was 73, Lord Cardigan almost 66 (his birthday was 20 April).

14. Mrs Buller's son was an ensign in the First Regiment of Foot Guards (*ante* 19 March 1791).

15. Prince Michael George Poniatowski

(1736–94), 'brother to the King of Poland, Archbishop of Gnesna [Gnesen], Primate of Poland and Lithuania. . . . This truly benevolent prince was in London in the year 1791, and during his residence here was elected a Fellow of the Royal and Antiquarian Societies, and assisted at several of their meetings' (GM 1794, lxiv pt ii. 958). He was elected F.R.S. 31 March 1791, and F.S.A. (Honorary Member) 7 April 1791 (*Record of the Royal Society*, 3d edn, 1912, p. 367; *List of the Members of the Society of Antiquaries of London*, 1798, p. 50). His arrival in London 'in a private character, under the title of Chevalier de St Michael,' is announced in *The St James's Chronicle* 30 Nov.–2 Dec. 1790 and in *The Times* 1 Dec. 1790.

16. Stanislas (or Stanislaus) II (Stanislas Augustus Poniatowski) (1732–98), elected King of Poland, 1764; forced to abdicate, 1795.

17. John Joseph Merlin (1735–1803), 'of Prince's Street, Hanover Square, Rose's engine-maker, and mathematical instrument and watch and clock-maker in general'; 'an ingenious mechanic,' and a man of 'good qualities.' Born at Huy, on the Meuse, he worked six years in Paris, and in 1760 came to England, where he lived for the remainder of his life (GM 1803, lxxiii

as much more. Merlin pretends he knew him only for a foreigner who was going away in two days, and literally had his Holy Highness arrested and carried to a sponging-house; for which the Chancellor[18] has struck the attorney[19] off the list—but hear the second part. The King of Poland had desired the Primate to send him some English books, who for one sent *The Law of Arrests*.[20] The King wrote, 'This is not so useless a book to me, as some might think; for when I was in England,[21] I was arrested.'[22]—Before the letter arrived, the Archbishop himself was in limbo.

Monday.

Last night I was at Mr Pepys's,[23] where was Lady Juliana Penn, who alarmed me exceedingly, for she had received a letter from her son[24] in Italy, when I had had none—but this morning I have received a comfortable one, which I hope is perfectly true—for you must forgive me, if I cannot help fearing your kindness for me softens your accident and its consequences. You did not sleep for some nights, your nerves were shaken, and the friar's balsam[25] was not taken off. I know that from the 25th of March to the 11th of April is above a fortnight—and yet I shall think it above a fortnight to this day seven-night when I hope for a still better account; for though a little easier, I am far from satisfied—and not yet at all arrived at grieving for a mark on your nose, as I shall do till I actually see you, when the joy of your return will drown less considerations. How good you are to reassure me on that subject!—The Abbé[26] has come in, and distracted me with news for which I do not care a straw, nor would have listened to, but that you like my telling you all I hear.—But what are all those marriages to me who am separated from both my wives; or Miss Bingham's[27] no-marriage with Lord Grey,[28] for which Lord

pt i. 485). For an account of him (as 'Merlin von Lüttich'), his shop, and some of his inventions, see Sophie v. la Roche, *Sophie in London, 1786*, 1933, pp. 139–41; N&Q 1942, clxxxii. 280.

18. Lord Thurlow.

19. Not identified.

20. *The Law of Arrests in both Civil and Criminal Cases*, by 'An Attorney-at-law,' 1742.

21. In 1754, when HW was acquainted with him (HW to Chute 14 May 1754; to Mann 13 Aug. 1764; GM 1798, lxviii pt i. 257).

22. No reference to his arrest has been found.

23. In Wimpole Street (*A Later Pepys*, ed. Alice C. C. Gaussen, 1904, i. 15 *et passim*).

24. John Penn.

25. 'Tincture of benzoin compound used as an application for ulcers and wounds' (OED, where the earliest use cited is 1844).

26. Rev. Norton Nicholls.

27. Hon. (from 1795, Lady) Anne Bingham (d. 1840), dau. of Charles, Bn Lucan, cr. (1795) E. of Lucan; died unmarried (Burke, *Peerage*, 1928, p. 1509, *sub* Lucan).

Stamford[29] has forbid the banns; or the Marquis of Worcester's[30] with Lord Stafford's[31] daughter Lady M.M. or N.N. Leveson,[32] which is declared; or the Duchess of Rutland's with Lord Paget, forbidden too by his father,[33] yet to be or not to be—something. Madame du Barry is again come,[34] and Lady St Asaph[35] died yesterday of a second miscarriage, leaving four young children, a most fond husband, and the families on both sides much afflicted. So much for the Abbé's *Morning Herald,* and I return to your nose and your nerves—how could you write so much, when they are not well—and to be thinking of my gout, and recommending care of myself—I am perfectly recovered of everything but your fall.

I had a letter two days ago from Mrs Damer then at Grenada:[36] she had suffered from the snow on the mountains.[37] Her parents have been in town these two months, and very well. I supped there[38] last

28. George Harry Grey (1765–1845), styled Lord Grey 1768–1819, 6th E. of Stamford, 1819; m. (1797) Henrietta Charlotte Elizabeth Wemyss-Charteris (1773–1838), dau. of Francis, styled Lord Elcho.

29. Lord Grey's father, George Harry Grey (1737–1819), 5th E. of Stamford, 1768, cr. (1796) E. of Warrington.

30. Henry Charles Somerset (1766–1835), styled M. of Worcester until 1803; 6th D. of Beaufort, 1803.

31. Granville Leveson-Gower (1721–1803), 2d E. Gower, 1754; cr. (1786) M. of Stafford.

32. Lady Charlotte Sophia Leveson-Gower (1771–1854), Lord Stafford's dau. by his 3d wife, Susanna Stewart, dau. of Alexander, 6th E. of Galloway; m. (16 May 1791) the Marquess of Worcester. *The Oracle* 15 April 1791 reports the match is 'confidently talked of.' HW's 'M.M. or N.N.' ('Somebody or other') is, of course, a reference to the catechism.

33. Henry Bayly (1744–1812), on succeeding his cousin as 10th Bn Paget, 1769, assumed surname of Paget alone; cr. (1784) E. of Uxbridge.

34. 'The Countess du Barry arrived in London early yesterday morning [8 April]. She left Paris on Monday morning last [4 April] at an early hour, and embarked from Calais on Wednesday. Her passage was a very difficult and dangerous one, for she did not land at Dover till twelve o'clock at night. The Countess is returned to attend

the Sessions; and in the hope of recovering her diamonds which cost her near 2,000,000 of livres' (*St James's Chronicle* 7–9 April 1791).

35. Sophia Thynne (1763–9 April 1791), 3d dau. of 1st M. of Bath, m. (1784) George Ashburnham (1760–1830), styled Vct St Asaph until 1812, 3d E. of Ashburnham, 1812. Their four children, all of whom died unmarried, were: (1) George Ashburnham (1785–1813), styled Vct St Asaph, 1812; (2) Elizabeth Sophia Ashburnham (1786–1879); (3) Sophia Ashburnham (1788–1807); (4) John Ashburnham (1789–1810), an ensign in the Coldstream Regiment of Foot Guards, drowned on his return from Portugal (Collins, *Peerage,* 1812, iv. 262; Edmund Lodge, *Peerage of the British Empire,* 1838, p. 31; Burke, *Peerage,* 1880, p. 53).

36. Mrs Damer's letter to HW is missing, but part of one from her to Mary Berry from Granada 19 March 1791 is printed in MBJ i. 338–40.

37. 'I find a great difference of climate between this place [Granada] and Seville, a sharpness in the air to which I am always sensible, and this must be the case, for the town is almost close to that immense chain of mountains, the Sierra Nevada, the tops of which are always covered with snow' (MBJ i. 340).

38. At General Conway's house: 4 Little Warwick Street (*Directory to the Nobility, Gentry . . . for 1793*).

night with the Duchess of Richmond[39] and Mrs *Pompoustown* Hervey.[40]

Your acquaintance Mrs Horace Churchill,[41] one of my seventy and I don't know how many nephews and nieces, has just presented me with one more of the first gender:[42] Madame de St Alban gave me two of the other[43]—but perhaps might as justly have bestowed them on somebody not so rich in nepotism.

I must have an attestation under the hand of Agnes *aux joues de rose* that you have no fever left, that your nerves are rebraced, and I will bear an oath from any rival, that your nose is as perfect as ever.

Your letter of this morning is an answer to mine of Feb. 28 to Florence—how vexatious such a distant correspondence! If I today say, how do you do? it will be one or two and forty days before you answer, very well thank you!

39. Mary Bruce (1740–96), youngest dau. of Charles Bruce, 3d E. of Ailesbury, and only child by his 3d wife, Caroline Campbell (later, 1747, married to Henry Seymour Conway); half-sister of Mrs Damer; m. (1757) Charles Lennox, 3d D. of Richmond (GEC; GM 1740, x. 203). HW always spoke of her with affection and praise, and after her death he wrote to Lady Ossory 13 Nov. 1796: 'I had loved the Duchess of Richmond most affectionately from the moment I first knew her, when she was but five years old; her sweet temper and unalterable good nature had made her retain a friendship for and confidence in me that was more steady than I ever found in any other person to whom I have been the most attached.'

40. Presumably Mrs William Thomas Hervey.

41. Harriot Ann Modigliani [?Modigham] (d. 1840), m. (20 Oct. 1783) at Old Windsor, Horace Churchill, HW's nephew, then captain of the First Regiment of Foot Guards, later (1811) major-general; died at Genoa (GM 1783, liii. 893; GM 1840, n.s. xiii. 111; cf. GM 1802, lxxii pt i. 586).

42. Chatham Horace Churchill (9 April 1791–1843), entered the army, 1806; Lt-Col., 1815; Lt-Col. of the 31st Regiment of Foot, serving in Bengal, 1832; Col., 1837; quartermaster-general, East Indies, 1837; C.B., 1838; major-general (local rank in the East Indies) at the time of his death. Wounded in action at the battle of Maharajpoor 29 Dec. 1843, he died during that night, following the amputation of one of his legs (GM 1791, lxi pt i. 379; *Army Lists;* GM 1838, n.s. x. 318; *Colburn's United Service Magazine,* 1844, pt i. 320, 621).

43. Only one has been identified: Henrietta Cholmondeley (d. 1815), who m. at Gretna Green 1 Jan. 1812 (and again at Malpas, Cheshire 28 Jan. 1812) John George Lambton; cr. (1828) Bn Durham and (1833) E. of Durham. It is not clear whether she was the younger daughter, born early in 1791 (*ante* 2 Aug. 1790), or the elder. According to a newspaper item which mentions the departure of Mme St Alban for Brussels ('accompanied by Colonel Keppel'), 'Lord C. very handsomely settled £600 on the infant daughter of Madame St Alban' (*Oracle* 21 April 1791).

Monday night.

I am just come from Lady Herries, who with Mrs Hunter[44] charged me to tell you how glad they are to hear you are better of your fall. I said you had just desired me to thank all who are so kind as to inquire after you: I wish I could answer their inquiries oftener!

You will, I trust, be at Florence when you receive this, but it will be May before I know so, which is sad, as it will be a better proof than all you can say, that your face is recovered. I shall apply what was said to one of the sable Finches,[45] 'Sir, if you was to swear till you are white in the face, etc.'—that is, I must have collateral proofs, for my fears are stronger than my faith. Adieu! may heaven preserve you both! and may I have no more days to stigmatize in my almanac!

To Mary Berry, Friday 15 April 1791

Address: À Mademoiselle Mademoiselle Berry à la poste restante à Florence, Italie. *Postmark:* FIRENZE 1[8?].
Posted 19 April ('Visitors').

Berkeley Square, Friday night, April 15, 1791.
No. 29.[1]

MY preface will be short, for I have nothing to tell, and a great deal that I am waiting most impatiently to hear, all which however may be couched in these two phrases, 'I am quite recovered of my fall, and my nose will not be the worse for it'—for with all my pretences, I cannot help having that *nose* a little upon my spirits, though if it were flat, I should love it as much as ever for the sake of the head and heart that belong to it—poor lovely nose! I don't know what business you had to carry it to the mouth of the Arno and throw it down a precipice. I go to Strawberry tomorrow in this jubilee spring that comes but once in fifty years, and shall return on Monday trusting to be met by a letter from Pisa with a prosperous account of all I wot of.

I have seen Ohara, with his face as ruddy and black, and his teeth

44. Anne Home (1742–1821), eldest dau. of Robert Home, surgeon; m. (1771) John Hunter, the famous surgeon; poetess, well known for her literary parties at her house in Leicester Square.

45. In the 'New Ode' by Sir Charles Han-

bury Williams which HW quotes in his letter to Mann 11 Sept. 1742 occurs a reference to 'the black funereal Finches.' See also Montagu i. 82, n. 19.

1. 'No. 39' (B).

as white as ever, and as fond of you two, and as grieved for your fall as anybody—but I. He has got a better regiment.[2]

Strawberry, Sunday night past eleven.

You chose your time ill for going abroad this year; England never saw such a spring since it was fifteen years old. The warmth, blossoms and verdure are unparalleled. I am just come from Richmond, having first called on Lady Di,[3] who is designing and painting pictures for prints to Dryden's *Fables*.[4] Oh! she has done two most beautiful; one of Emily walking in the garden, and Palamon seeing her from the tower; the other, a noble free composition, of Theseus parting the rivals,[5] when fighting in the wood—They are not, as you may well imagine, at all like the pictures in the Shakespear Gallery—no, *they* are worthy of Dryden.[6]

I then went and played at *loto* with the French colony in Petty France,[7] and tomorrow I am to have a most favourable account from Pisa, am I not?

I can tell you nothing at all certain of our war with Russia—if one believes the weather-glass of the stocks, it will be peace; they had fallen to 71, and are risen again, and soberly, to 79.[8] Fawkener, Clerk of the Council, sets out today or tomorrow[9] for Berlin, probably, I

2. O'Hara, who had been colonel of the 22d Regiment of Foot since 18 April 1782, became colonel of the 74th Regiment of Foot 1 April 1791, succeeding Sir Archibald Campbell, K.B., who died the preceding day (*Army Lists; Old Westminsters;* GM 1791, lxi pt i. 383).

3. At Devonshire Cottage, Richmond.

4. The illustrations appeared in *The Fables of John Dryden, Ornamented with Engravings* [by Francesco Bartolozzi and others] *from the Pencil of the Right Hon. Lady Diana Beauclerc*, 1797. Of the seven fables in this edition, HW refers to the illustrations for the first, 'Palamon and Arcite; or, The Knight's Tale,' from Chaucer.

5. Palamon and Arcite, rivals in their love for Emily.

6. Whereas those in the Shakespeare Gallery were not, HW thought, worthy of Shakespeare; see HW to Dalrymple 21 Sept. 1790. A few days after the date of this letter, HW and Lady Diana were mentioned in *The Oracle:* 'Lady Di Beauclerk, in this age of refined taste, is busy in the improve-

ment of the pallet. Her Ladyship is distinguishable by a rapid masterly style, which is visible in her charming suite of drawings from Horace Walpole's play. Horace Walpole's *Mysterious Mother* was composed for Mrs Pritchard's benefit. Mature consideration, however, convinced the elegant author, that the *horror* would be much too powerful for an audience to bear' (25 April 1791). Neither of the drawings mentioned by HW appears in Dryden's *Fables*, 1797. Lady Di's drawings which are in it show that HW, as usual, is partial to his friends' talents.

7. HW was evidently at Mme de Boufflers's; see next page.

8. According to the tables given in GM 1791, lxi pt i. 288, 392, the three-per-cent consols, to which HW evidently refers, at no time in the first four months of 1791 fell to 71; the lowest price there quoted is 75¾ on 26–28 March, with a gradual rise to a high of 79¾ on 15 April.

9. But see following letter.

hope, with an excuse[10]—In the present case I had much rather our ministers were bullies than heroes—no mortal likes the war. The court majority lost thirteen of its former number at the beginning of the week, which put the opposition into spirits; but pursuing their motions on Friday, twelve of the thirteen were recovered.

Lord Onslow told me just now at Madame de Boufflers's that Lady Salisbury was brought to bed of a son and heir[11] last night two hours after she came from the opera;[12] and that Madame du Barry dined yesterday with the Prince of Wales at the Duke of Queensberry's at Richmond. Thus you have all my news, such as it is; and I flatter myself no English at Pisa or Florence can boast of better intelligence than you—but for you, should I care about Madame du Barry or my Lady Salisbury, or which of them lies in or lies out?

Berkeley Square, Monday 18th.

Oh! what a dear letter have I found! and from both at once! and with such a delightful bulletin of the nose's wound, which I trust is all the remainder of the fall. I have but one doubt, and that is from the delay of going to Florence, which I hope is to be placed only to the article of unbecoming.

I should not be pleased with the idleness of the pencil, were it not owing to the chapter of health, which I prefer to everything, high as I hold 'The Death of Wolsey.'[13] The moment I enter Strawberry, I hasten into the Little Parlour, which I have new-hung for his reception, with Lady Di's gipsies,[14] and Mrs Damer's dogs.[15] I defy your favourite Italy to produce three such monuments of female genius.

10. 'Ministers have resolved to send Mr Fawkener . . . to the Court of Berlin, and afterwards to the Court of Petersburgh, with a special commission' (St James's Chronicle 16–19 April 1791). He received his credentials and instructions 26 April as 'envoy extraordinary and minister plenipotentiary on a special mission' to Russia, to act with Sir Charles Whitworth in negotiating a peace between Russia and Turkey (British Diplomatic Representatives 1789–1852, ed. S. T. Bindoff et al., 1934, p. 109). For the success of his mission, see post 26 July 1791, n. 33.

11. James Brownlow William Cecil (Gascoyne-Cecil after 1821) (17 April 1791–1868), styled Vct Cranborne until 1823; 8th E. and 2d M. of Salisbury, 1823.

12. The opera performed at the Pantheon 16 April was Idalide, by Giuseppe Sarti (1729–1802) (Times 16 April 1791).

13. Agnes Berry's copy of Lock's picture.

14. 'A very pleasing drawing, gipsies telling a country girl her fortune at the entrance of a wood, designed and executed by Lady Diana Beauclerc, and considered her chef d'œuvre' (SH Sale Catalogue, xxii. 101). It was sold to 'Cain of Richmond,' for £6.10.0. The original water-colour is now in the Victoria and Albert Museum, South Kensington, and is reproduced in Mrs Steuart Erskine, Lady Diana Beauclerk, 1903, facing p. 208; see also ibid. 100, where it is erroneously said the water-colour was painted in 1792.

15. 'Two sleeping dogs ['a rough dog and

You order me to be particular about my own health: I have nothing to say about it, but that it is as good as before my last fit. Can I expect or desire more at my age? My ambition is to pass a summer with you two established at Cliveden—I shall not reject more if they come—but one must not be presumptuous at seventy-three; and though my eyes, ears, teeth and motion have still lasted to make life comfortable, I do not know that I should be enchanted if surviving any of them; and having no desire to become a philosopher, I had rather be naturally cheerful than affectedly so; for patience I take to be only a resolution of holding one's tongue and not complaining of what one feels—for does one feel or think the less for not owning it?

Though London increases every day, and that Mr Herschell has just discovered a new square or circus somewhere by the new road in the Via Lactea where the cows used to be fed,[16] I believe you will think the town cannot hold all its inhabitants, so prodigiously the population is augmented.[17] I have twice been going to stop my coach in Piccadilly (and the same has happened to Lady Ailesbury) thinking there was a mob, and it was only nymphs and swains sauntering or trudging. T'other morning, i.e. at two o'clock, I went to see Mrs Garrick and Miss H. More at the Adelphi, and was stopped five times before I reached Northumberland House,[17a] for the tides of coaches, chariots, curricles, phaetons, etc., are endless. Indeed the town is so extended, that the breed of chairs is almost lost, for Hercules and Atlas could not carry anybody from one end of this enormous capital to the other. How magnified would be the error of the young woman at St Helena who some years ago said to a captain of an Indiaman, 'I suppose London is very empty, when the India ships come out.'[18] Don't make me excuses then for short letters, nor trouble yourself a moment to lengthen them. You compare little towns to quiet times

a smooth one' ('Visitors')], the original model in terra cotta . . . which she afterwards [1784] executed in marble for the Duke of Richmond' ('Des. of SH,' *Works* ii. 418). Described as 'very spirited in effect under a glass case,' they were sold SH xvi. 116 to the Earl of Derby for £32.0.6. See also HW to Lord Strafford 7 Sept. 1784; to Mann 7 May 1785.

16. Presumably HW refers to Herschel's paper, read before the Royal Society 10 Feb. 1791, 'On Nebulous Stars, properly so called' (*Philosophical Transactions,* lxxxi. 71–88); it presents a new theory of the evo-

lution of stars in the 'telescopic Milky Way': nebulous matter becomes nebulæ, and nebulæ become stars.

17. 'London was perhaps never so full as at the present' (*St James's Chronicle* 10–12 March 1791).

17a. I.e., between Berkeley Square and Charing Cross.

18. 'A woman at St Helena said, "I suppose London is quite a desert when the English fleet is sailed"' (among HW's 'Anecdotes written in 1767,' DU DEFFAND v. 364). Another version is given in HW to Mann 31 Dec. 1780.

which do not feed history, and most justly. If the vagaries of London can be comprised once a week in three or four pages of small quarto paper, and not always that, how should little Pisa, except when a certain nose is at stake, furnish an equal export? When Pisa was at war with the rival republic of Milan, Machiavel was put to it to describe a battle, the slaughter in which amounted to one man slain, and he was trampled to death, by being thrown down and battered in his husk of complete armour,[19] as I remember reading above fifty years ago at Florence.

Eleven at night.

Oh! mercy! I am just come from Mrs Buller's, having left a very pleasant set at Lady Herries's,[20] and for such a collection! eight or ten women and girls, not one of whom I knew by sight, a German count, as stiff and upright as the inflexible Dowager of Beaufort, a fat dean and his wife, he speaking Cornish, and of having dined to-day at Lambeth, four young officers, friends of the boy Buller[21] who played with one of them at tric-trac, while the others made with the Misses a still more noisy commerce, and not a creature but Mrs Cholmondeley who went away immediately, and her son[22] who was speechless with the headache, that I was the least acquainted with; and to add to my sufferings, the Count would talk to me of *les beaux arts,* of which he knows no more than an oyster—at last came in Mrs Blair,[23] whom I know as little; but she asked so kindly after you two, and was so anxious about your fall and your return, that I grew quite fond of her, and beg you would love her for my sake, as I do for yours. Good night—I have this moment received a card[24] from the Duchess Dowager of Ancaster to summon me for tomorrow at three

19. On 29 June 1440, at Anghiari, a Milanese force was routed by a Florentine (not Pisan) force. 'Ed in tanta rotta ed in sì lunga zuffa, che durò dalle XX alle XXIV ore, non vi morì altri che un uomo; il quale, non di ferite o d'altro virtuoso colpo, ma caduto da cavallo e calpesto spirò' (Machiavelli, *Istorie fiorentine*, V. xxxiii). For comment on Machiavelli's gross understatement, see ibid., ed. Averardo Pippi, Torino, [1924] p. 291 n.

20. 'The wife of the banker in St James's Street' (?B, Wright vi. 419).

21. 'Mrs Buller's only child' (?B, Wright vi. 419).

22. George James Cholmondeley.

23. Perhaps Magdalene Fordyce (d. 1817), dau. of John Fordyce of Ayton, co. Berwick, m. (1789) William Blair of Blair, Ayrshire, sometime colonel of the Ayrshire Regiment of Fencible Cavalry (Burke, *Landed Gentry*, 1851, i. 104; GM 1789, lix pt i. 371; *Directory to the Nobility, Gentry . . . for 1793*).

24. Missing.

o'clock—I suppose to sign Lord Cholmondeley's marriage articles with her daughter.[25] The wedding is to be this day sevennight—save me, my old stars! from wedding-dinners! but I trust they are not of this age. I should sooner expect Hymen to jump out of a curricle and walk into the Duchess's dressing-room in boots and a dirty shirt.

To Mary Berry, Saturday 23 April 1791

Address: À Mademoiselle Mademoiselle Berry à la poste restante à Florence, Italie. *Postmark:* FIRENZE 19. Endorsed: 'Pd 1s.'
Posted 26 April ('Visitors').

Strawberry Hill, April 23, 1791.

No. 30.[1]

TODAY, when the town is staring at the sudden resignation of the Duke of Leeds,[2] asking the reason, and gaping to know who will succeed him,[3] I am come hither with an indifference that might pass for philosophy, as the true cause is not known, which it seldom is. Don't tell Europe, but I really am come to look at the repairs of Cliveden, and how they go on; not without an eye to the lilacs and the apple-blossoms; for even *self* can find a corner to wriggle into, though friendship may fit out the vessel. Mr Berry may perhaps wish I had more political curiosity; but as I must return to town on Monday for Lord Cholmondeley's wedding, I may hear before the departure of the post, if the seals are given: for the Duke's reasons, should they be assigned, shall one be certain? His intention was not even whispered till Wednesday evening. The news from India, so long expected, are not *couleur de rose,* but *de sang:* a detachment has been defeated by Tippoo Saib,[4] and Lord Cornwallis[5] is gone to take the

25. 'Lady Charlotte Bertie' (?B, Wright vi. 420).

———

1. 'No. 40' (B).
2. Foreign secretary of state from 1783, he resigned 20 April 1791, and delivered up the seals the following day (*Oracle* 21 April 1791; *St James's Chronicle* 19–21 April 1791). For his account of the events leading to his resignation, see *Political Memoranda of Francis Fifth Duke of Leeds,* ed. Oscar Browning, 1884, pp. 148–73. Criticism of his negotiations with Russia, and his ill health, appear to have been the chief causes of his resignation.

3. Lord Grenville, home secretary 1789–91, received the seals of office as foreign secretary 1 May (*Oracle* 5 May 1791), and held the office until 1801.
4. But see below. The *Princess Amelia,* which sailed from Bengal 31 Nov. 1790 and arrived off the Isle of Wight 19 April 1791, brought news (which reached London 20 April) of an engagement 13–14 Sept. 1790 between Tippoo Saib and General Medows' army under the command of Colonel Floyd. For a full account, see *The St James's Chronicle* 19–21 April 1791.
5. Charles Cornwallis (1738–1805), E.

command of the army himself[6]—will the East be more propitious to him than the West?

The abolition of the slave trade has been rejected by the House of Commons,[7] though Mr Pitt and Mr Fox[8] united earnestly to carry it; but commerce chinked its purse, and that sound is generally prevalent with the majority; and humanity's tears, and eloquence's figures and arguments had no more effect than on those patrons of liberty, the National Assembly in France, who while they proclaim *the rights of men,* did not choose to admit the sable moiety of mankind to a participation of those benefits.[9]

Capt. Bowen has published a little pamphlet of affidavits,[10] which prove that Gunnilda attempted to bribe her father's groom to perjure himself, but he begged to be excused.[11] Nothing more appears against the mother, but that Miss pretended her mama had an aversion to Lord Lorn (an aversion to a Marquis!) and that she did not dare to acquaint so tender a parent with her lasting passion for him.[12] Still I am persuaded that both the mother and the aunt[13] were in the plot, whatever it was.

I saw Lady Cecilia last night, and made all your speeches and received their value in return for you.

Cornwallis, 1762; cr. (1792) M. Cornwallis; served under General Howe in the war with America; governor general of Bengal, and commander-in-chief in the East Indies 1786–93.

6. On hearing of the battle, Lord Cornwallis prepared 'to go to the coast, with a re-enforcement of 3000 men, and was expected to sail in about twenty days' (*St James's Chronicle* 19–21 April 1791).

7. On 19 April 1791, by a vote of 163 to 88; for a full account of the debate, see *The St James's Chronicle* 19–21 April 1791. HW's account of earlier phases of the bill occurs in 'Mem. 1783–91,' *sub* 13 June 1788.

8. Hon. Charles James Fox (1749–1806).

9. In 1790 a delegation of French colonial mulattoes came to France to demand from the National Assembly 'that the articles of the Declaration of the Rights of Man be applied to the colonies,' but 'a committee reported on March 8, 1790, that the local needs and problems of the colonies were definitely not provided for nor covered by the constitution of France itself' (Edward Derbyshire Seeber, *Anti-Slavery Opinion*

in France during the Second Half of the Eighteenth Century, Baltimore, 1937, p. 170). Less than a month after the date of HW's letter, however, on 15 May 1791, 'a resolution was passed by the *Assemblée* granting citizenship rights and seats in colonial assemblies to colored residents born of free parents' (ibid. 171).

10. *A Statement of Facts, in Answer to Mrs Gunning's Letter,* published 19 April 1791 (*St James's Chronicle* 16–19, 19–21 April 1791). Two days later, because of derogatory remarks about him in *The Morning Post,* he was involved in a fracas with the editor; see *The Oracle* 25 April 1791.

11. See Bowen, op. cit. 53–4, and cf. *ante* 18 Feb. 1791.

12. Miss Gunning to Mrs Bowen, 1 Feb. 1791: 'If I could present Lord Lorne to you, he would be an apology for everything I have done. Neither papa or I have courage to tell mama this, for she detests the person dearest to me on earth' (Bowen, op. cit. 12).

13. Margaret Minifie.

Good Hannah More is killing herself by a new fit of benevolence about a young girl with a great fortune, who has been taken from school at Bristol to Gretna Green, and cannot be discovered, nor the apothecary who stole her.[14] Mrs Garrick, who suspects as I do, that Miss Europa is not very angry with Mr Jupiter, had very warm words a few nights ago at the Bishop of London's with Lady Beaumont; but I diverted the quarrel by starting the stale story of the Gunning. You know Lady B.'s eagerness[15]—she is ready to hang the apothecary with her own hands, and he certainly is criminal enough. Poor Hannah lives with attorneys and Sir Sampson Wright,[16] and I have seen her but once since she came to town.[17] Her ungrateful pro-

14. **Clementina Clerke** (b. 1776), dau. of James Clerke by Isabella Ogilvie, and niece of George Ogilvie (d. 23 Jan. 1791) of Langley Park, Langley, who left his Jamaica estates (said to be worth £6000 per annum) to her; student at the school of the Misses Mills (one of whom was destined to become the mother of Thomas Babington Macaulay), formerly the school of Hannah More and her sister; eloped 19 March 1791 with Richard Vining Perry, surgeon and apothecary at Bristol, who married her at Gretna Green, and later at London in the presence of the girl's mother. The elder Miss Mills attempted to forestall the elopement, and, failing that, followed the Perrys to London and later to Flanders. On 4 April a reward of £1000 was offered for the return of Miss Clerke (already Mrs Perry) to Bow Street, London, or to the school at Bristol. On his return to Bristol, Perry spent some time in prison (his wife and daughter with him) before his trial 14 April 1794 at Bristol for 'forcible abduction.' Mrs Perry, allowed to testify after considerable opposition from the prosecution, declared that she went away of her own free will; she had never talked with him, although they had exchanged two notes. Perry was acquitted. For Hannah More's own account of her part in the affair, see William Roberts, *Memoirs of the Life and Correspondence of Mrs Hannah More*, 1834, ii. 335–7, where her letter of 23 April (the same date as HW's letter) to Mrs Kennicott is erroneously inserted among the letters for 1792. See also *The Trial of Richard Vining Perry, Esq. for*

Forcible Abduction, Bristol, [1794]; *Scots Magazine*, 1791, liii. 100; BM, *Satiric Prints* vi. nos 7990–2; *London Chronicle* 22–24, 26–29 March 1791, lxix. 284, 301; *Oracle* 22 March 1791; GM 1794, lxiv pt ii. 1051.

15. For references to Lady Beaumont's 'violent manner' and 'whims and fanciful notions,' see Joseph Farington, *Diary*, ed. James Greig, 1922–8, v. 3, 94.

16. (d. 1793), Kt, 1782; magistrate of the Bow Street Public Office; J.P. for Middlesex, Essex, and Surrey. He 'began life humbly' as apprentice to a grocer, rose because of his 'integrity and ability,' became clerk and (in 1780) successor to Sir John Fielding (GM 1793, lxiii pt i. 377–8; R. Leslie-Melville, *The Life and Work of Sir John Fielding*, n.d., pp. 126, 205, 273; William Shaw, *The Knights of England*, 1906, ii. 297). Hannah More comments in her letter to Mrs Kennicott: 'My time has been literally passed with thief-takers, officers of justice, and such pretty kind of people' (Roberts, loc. cit.).

17. According to Hannah More's letter written on the same day as HW's (Roberts, loc. cit.), 'I have made no visits, but snatched a hasty dinner in Cavendish Square [the Bishop of Salisbury's], or at London House [the Bishop of London's], in my dishabille, and away again, and this only two days ago.' It would appear, then, that Miss More was at the Bishop of London's on the same night that HW was, but she probably left early, before the 'warm words.'

tégée the milkwoman[18] has published her tragedy[19] and dedicated it
to a patron as worthy as herself, the Earl-Bishop of Derry![20]

Monday, in the Square.

I have found a letter from you as I expected, but there was three
pages before I found a word of your nose! You give a good account
of it—yet as you have again deferred your journey to Florence,
though but for a day or two, I do not quite trust to your deposition.
Produce your nose to kings and emperors, or I shall not be satisfied.
I know you are not eager for puppet shows; yet your being at a *fête*
would convince me more than the attestation of a surgeon.

You kindly desire me not to go to Strawberry for fear of relapse—
but this is the case of[20a] so distant a correspondence. I have been there
four or five times without the smallest inconvenience: besides it has
been summer all winter. You desire me too to continue to write
punctually—I do not seem to be in danger of relaxing—at least not
before I am settled in the country; and then indeed I may want matter—but the town goes so late out of itself, that I dare to say it will furnish me with something or other for these two months; and then in
two months more I trust you will be on the road—and then—why
then in two months more—I hope I shall have no occasion to write to
you! Six months of your absence are nearly gone, and I am trying as
much as I can to anticipate the other six!

18. Mrs Ann Yearsley (1756–1806), known
as 'Lactilla' or 'the Bristol Milkwoman';
wife of John Yearsley, a labourer of Clif-
ton, near Bristol; befriended by Hannah
More, who was instrumental in getting a
very distinguished list of subscribers (including HW) to her poems, published in
1784. A second edition appeared in 1785.
Lactilla quarrelled with Hannah More
about the disposal of the profits; received
the money and started a lending library,
with little success; died in retirement, possibly insane (DNB; Robert Southey, *Lives of
Uneducated Poets*, 1836, p. 134). See also
the HW-More correspondence.

19. *Earl Goodwin, an Historical Play,*
previously (Nov. 1789) performed at Bath
and at Bristol, was published 20 April
(*Oracle* 20 April 1791).

20. Frederick Augustus Hervey (1730–
1803), Bp of Derry, 1768; 4th E. of Bristol,
1779. For HW's derogatory comments on
him, see 'Mem. 1783–91,' *sub* 11 Feb. 1784.
Michael Lort wrote to Thomas Percy, Bp
of Dromore, 31 Oct. 1785: 'The Bishop of
Derry is now at Bath, and has given fifty
pounds to the Bristol poetical milkwoman
since she has quarrelled with some of her
first patrons and protectors, and has threatened to write the Life and Adventures of
Hannah More, who first drew her from obscurity' (John Nichols, *Illustrations of the
Literary History of the Eighteenth Century,*
1817–58, vii. 474). Mrs Yearsley dedicated to
the Earl-Bishop her second and third publications, *Poems on Various Subjects,* 1787,
and *A Poem on the Inhumanity of the
Slave Trade,* 1788. In the 1787 volume the
last poem is an 'Effusion' addressed to him,
and it appears from ibid. 61–6 that he
stood sponsor for her son Frederick, who
died an infant.

20a. I.e., 'the way it is with,' etc.

At night.

Well, our wedding is over, very properly, though with little ceremony, for the men were in frocks and white waistcoats, most of the
women in white, and no diamonds but on the Duke's wife;[21] and
nothing of ancient fashion, but two bride-maids: the endowing purse
I believe has been left off, ever since broad pieces were called in and
melted down. We were but eighteen persons in all, chiefly near relations of each side, and of each side a friend or two; of the first sort,
the Greatheds.[22] Sir Peter Burrel[23] gave away the bride: the poor
Duchess-mother wept excessively; she is now left quite alone, her
two daughters[24] married, and her other children dead[25]—she herself I
fear in a very dangerous way. She goes directly to Spa, where the
new-married are to meet her.[26] We all separated in an hour and half.
The Elliot girl[27] was there, and is pretty—she rolls in the numerous

21. Mary Anne Layard (1743–1804), dau.
of Maj. Peter Layard of Sutton Friars, Canterbury, m. (1769) as 2d wife, Brownlow
Bertie (1729–1809), 5th D. of Ancaster, the
bride's uncle. The ceremony was performed
at the Dowager Duchess of Ancaster's house
in Berkeley Square (*Oracle* 27 April 1791).

22. Bertie Greatheed was a first cousin of
the bride, whose father was his mother's
brother.

23. Brother-in-law of the bride: Sir Peter
Burrell (1754–1820), 2d Bt of West Grinstead Park, Sussex; cr. (1796) Bn Gwydir of
Gwydir, co. Carnarvon; m. (1779) Lady
Priscilla Barbara Elizabeth Bertie (1761–
1828), declared (1780) *suo jure* Bns Willoughby of Eresby. After the ceremony,
Lord and Lady Cholmondeley went to his
seat at Beckenham, Kent (*Oracle* 27 April
1791).

24. Lady Willoughby (see preceding
note) and Lady Cholmondeley.

25. Four were dead: (1) Lady Mary
Catherine (1754–67); (2) Peregrine Thomas
(1755–8), styled M. of Lindsey; (3) Robert
(1756–79), 4th D. of Ancaster, 1778; (4) a
son, who died an infant, 1759 (Collins,
Peerage, 1779, ii. 21–2; GEC).

26. 'The Duchess of Ancaster is determined upon a considerable stay upon the
Continent. Her health makes the measure
indispensable' (*Oracle* 26 April 1791). Her
house in Berkeley Square, her furniture
and pictures, were sold at auction 16 May
1791 (*Oracle* 3 May 1791). Lord and Lady

Cholmondeley sailed from Dover for France
on Friday, 29 April (*Oracle* 4, 5 May 1791).
At the King's birthday 4 June 1791 'the
Duchess Dowager of Ancaster went to the
Drawing Room in her chair. Her Grace
looked infinitely amended in her health;
yet, we learn, her purpose is to visit the
Continent' (*Oracle* 6 June 1791). She had
an audience of leave of the King and Queen
16 June 1791, and set off the following day
for France, planning to accompany the
Cholmondeleys to Italy (*Times* 17 June
1791). She was detained at Dover, however,
because of the disturbances following the
flight of Louis XVI (ibid. 28 June 1791).

27. 'A natural daughter of Lord Cholmondeley' (?B, Wright vi. 422). Georgina
(or Georgiana) Augusta Frederica Seymour
Elliott (1782–1813), dau. of Grace Dalrymple Elliott, divorced wife of John Elliott who was knighted, 1776, and cr. Bt,
1778. Her father was probably one of the
following: the Prince of Wales, Charles
Wyndham, or Lord Cholmondeley. She was
christened at St Marylebone 30 July 1782
as 'the daughter of his Royal Highness
George Prince of Wales,' but her paternity
is doubtful. Lord Cholmondeley took her
into his family, and she was married (1808)
from his house at Chester as 'Hon. Miss
Seymour' to Lord Charles Bentinck, 3d son
of the 3d D. of Portland (DNB, *sub* Elliott,
Grace Dalrymple; Horace Bleackley, *Ladies
Fair and Frail*, [1925] pp. 218–19; *A Portion
of the Journal Kept by Thomas Raikes*,

list of my nephews and nieces. Mrs Horace Churchill has just given me one of the former,[28] and Mrs George Cholmondeley is bringing another of one sort or other,[29] and could not be at the wedding tonight, no more than his father[30] and mother, who to my surprise were not invited.

I am now told that our Indian skirmish was a victory, and that Tippoo Saib and all his cavalry and elephants ran away; but sure I am that the first impression made on and by those who spread the news, was not triumphant;—nor can I enjoy success, if it was success, in that country, which we have so abominably usurped and plundered.

You must wait for a new Secretary of State till next post[31]—the Duke of Leeds is said to have resigned from bad health.

The Ducs de Richelieu[32] and de Pienne,[33] and Madame de St Priest[34] are arrived here. Mr Fawkener does not go to Berlin till Wednesday[35]—still the stocks do not believe in the war.

Esq. from 1831 to 1847, 1856–7, iii. 83; GM 1808, lxxviii pt ii. 850; GM 1813, lxxxiii pt ii. 700).

28. Chatham Horace Churchill.

29. The child was stillborn (*post* 26 May 1791).

30. Rev. Hon. Robert Cholmondeley (1727–1804), HW's nephew and Lord Cholmondeley's uncle (Burke, *Peerage*, 1928, p. 520, *sub* Cholmondeley).

31. HW forgot to mention Lord Grenville's appointment in his later letters, but see n. 3.

32. Armand - Emmanuel - Sophie - Septimanie Vignerot du Plessis-Richelieu (1766–1822), Comte de Chinon to 1788; Duc de Fronsac, 1788; Duc de Richelieu on the death of his father 4 Feb. 1791. As a military leader, he served with distinction in Austria, Russia, and France, and as a statesman he served as minister of foreign affairs and president of the Council (Jean-Baptiste-Pierre Jullien de Courcelles, *Histoire généalogique . . . des pairs de France*, 1822–33, viii. 347–53; *La Grande encyclopédie*).

33. Louis-Marie-Céleste d'Aumont de Rochebaron (1762–1831), Marquis d'Aumont to 1780; Duc de Piennes, 1780; styled Duc d'Aumont, 1799, on the death of his uncle, although his father, who preferred to retain his title of Duc de Villequier (see following letter), succeeded to the title; Duc d'Aumont and Duc de Villequier on

death of his father, 1814, but retained former title; 'premier gentilhomme de la Chambre du Roi,' 1785. 'Le Duc de Piennes fut du nombre des seigneurs qui, le 28 février 1791, se rallièrent auprès de Louis XVI, et il fut blessé de deux coups de baïonnette au château des Tuileries. Émigré au mois d'avril de cette année, il a constamment combattu pour la restauration du trône' (Jullien de Courcelles, op. cit. vi. 'Pairs de France,' 16**–18; Woelmont de Brumagne i. 30–7). He remained in London until 25 June 1791, when, on hearing of the news of Louis XVI's escape, he set off for Ostend and Brussels; the news of the King's capture met him at Dover, but he continued his journey 'to join the Royal Princes and the army at Mentz' (*Times* 28 June 1791). According to *The St James's Chronicle* 9–12 July 1791, he returned to London 10 July 1791, and he was still there in September (*Oracle* 19 Sept. 1791).

34. Constance-Guillelmine de Ludolf (1752–1807), m. (1774) at Constantinople, François-Emmanuel Guignard, Comte de Saint-Priest, who resigned his ministerial post in Paris 'le 26 janvier 1791, et alla chercher le repos et la liberté sur la terre étrangère. Passé en Angleterre avec sa famille, M. de Saint-Priest se rendit de là en Suède' (Jullien de Courcelles, op. cit. vii. 115; *La Grande encyclopédie; Biographie universelle*, 1811–28, xl. 74, 86).

35. According to *The Oracle* 25 April

I have exhausted my gazette—and this being both Easter and New-market[36] week, I may possibly have nothing to tell you by tomorrow sennight's post, and may wait till Friday sennight, of which I give you notice, lest you should think I have had a fall and hurt my nose, which I know gives one's friends a dreadful alarm. Good night!

PS. I never saw such a blotted letter; I don't know how you will read it. I am so earnest when writing to you two, that I omit half the words, and write too small, but I will try to mend.

To Mary Berry, Wednesday 4 May 1791

Address: À Mademoiselle Mademoiselle Berry à la poste restante à Florence, Italie. *Postmark:* FIRENZE 20. Endorsed: 'Pd 1s.'
Posted 6 May ('Visitors').

Berkeley Square, May 4, 1791.

No. 31.[1]

THOUGH I have changed my post-days to Fridays, as better market-days for news, the first-fruits do not answer—indeed on Tuesday I should not have had a paragraph to send you; and now my articles will rather be talkables than events, for I know not one that has happened, except the change of weather, January having succeeded to April—but what signifies how the weather was, when you hear it three weeks afterwards?

Nothing more is known of the Russian war, or the new Secretary of State,[2] nor why the last[3] resigned. The Duke of York is gone to Berlin,[4] and the press continues alert—That looks all martial—but the stocks are philosophic and keep their temper. The Prince of

---

1791 he was expected to leave on Tuesday, 26 April, which was the day he received credentials and instructions (*ante* 15 April 1791), and in the same newspaper 29 April 1791 it is said that he 'set out on Tuesday.'

36. 23 April—2 May (James Weatherby, *Racing Calendar . . . 1791,* 1792, pp. 2–10).

---

1. 'No. 41' (B).
2. Lord Grenville; he received the seals as foreign secretary 1 May (*Oracle* 5 May 1791).
3. The Duke of Leeds.

4. His mission was marital, not martial. He left London 1 May in connection with his approaching marriage (29 Sept. 1791) to Princess Frederica Charlotte Ulrica Catherina (1767–1820), eldest daughter of Frederick William II of Prussia. The marriage agreement had been signed 26 Jan. 1791 at Berlin by representatives of the British and Prussian governments (GEC; *Oracle* 3 May 1791; *Annual Register,* 1827, lxix pt ii. 438–9; GM 1791, lxi pt i. 484). See also *post* 26 July, 10 Aug. 1791.

Wales is much out of order, spits blood, and fainted away after his levee on Monday.[5]

General Conway has had a great escape; he was reviewing his Blues[6] on Friday, previous to their being reviewed yesterday by the King.[7] The ground was so slippery, for we have had much rain, that his horse fell down and rolled over him, and he only had his arm and leg much bruised; yet so much bruised, that yesterday he was forced to write to the King to excuse his appearance, and last night he was lamer than I am.

Mrs Damer has written that we may expect her by the tenth. I shall allow two or three days for disappointments.[8]

Here is arrived the pinchbeck Queen Dowager of England, alias the Countess of Albany.[9] I have not much royal curiosity left, yet I have to see her, and it will be satisfied, for as she is great-niece to Lady Ailesbury, and cousin of the Duchess of Richmond,[10] they must visit her, and they will make some assembly or private party for her. At present they say she is going to see Mrs Swinburn in Yorkshire,[11] who it seems is the friend of all sorts of queens.[12]

5. 'Prince of Wales very ill, spit blood, and fainted away after his levee on the second' ('Mem. 1783–91,' *sub* May 1791). 'I understand the Prince of Wales is very far from well. He is supposed to have ulcers on his lungs, like the late Duke of Cumberland, and was actually blooded four times last week. His physicians have ordered him to live upon French beans and barley-water. He, however, dined on Friday with three hundred officers and, as I am informed, made great havoc of sundry savoury meats and much champagne, claret, and burgundy' (J. B. Burges to his sister, 2 May 1791, in *Selections from the Letters and Correspondence of Sir James Bland Burges*, ed. James Hutton, 1885, pp. 170–1).

6. The Royal Regiment of Horse Guards, of which Conway had been colonel since 24 Oct. 1770 (*Army Lists*).

7. 'Yesterday morning at nine o'clock the King got into his post-chaise at the Queen's House, Buckingham Gate, and, attended by Lord Dover, with a party of the Light Horse, proceeded to Blackheath, where his Majesty reviewed General Conway's regiment of Horse Guards Blue; after which he returned to Buckingham House' (*Oracle* 4 May 1791).

8. She arrived 12 May (see following letter).

9. 'Louisa de Stolberg, married to Charles Edward Stuart, the grandson of James II, since the year 1745 known by the title of Comte d'Albany' (B). Luise Maximiliane (1752–1824), 1st dau. of Gustav Adolf, Prince of Stolberg-Gedern, by Élisabeth-Philippine-Claudine (see following note); m. (1772) 'the Young Pretender,' Charles Edward Stuart (1720–88), titular Earl of Albany.

10. The 3d E. of Ailesbury (Lady Ailesbury's first husband) and the Countess of Albany's grandmother were half-brother and -sister; their father was Thomas Bruce (1656–1741), 2d E. of Ailesbury. He m. as 2d wife Charlotte-Jacqueline (ca 1680–1710), Comtesse d'Esneux; their only dau., Marie-Thérèse-Charlotte (1704–36), m. as 1st wife (1722), Maximilian Emmanuel (1695–1763), Prince of Hornes; the 2d dau. of this marriage was Élisabeth-Philippine-Claudine (1733–1826), mother of the Countess of Albany (cf. DU DEFFAND iii. 218).

11. Henry Swinburne's seat, Hamsterley in Durham, not Yorkshire (John Baker, *Diary*, ed. Philip C. Yorke, [1931] pp. 28, 33).

12. In addition to the Countess of Al-

We have received besides a packet of French dukes; the late *Gentilshommes de la Chambre,* Richelieu, Villequier[13] and Duras;[14] the last narrowly escaped with his life at the late violence about the King's journey to St Cloud;[15] the first is returned to Paris at the King's own request. The National Assembly have added new persecution to the fugitives—or to their embassadors, forbidding these to receive those—but are the former obliged to remain embassadors?[16]

You will have heard that La Fayette has resumed his command;[17] which I think an ambitious weakness, and a second tome to Necker's return. A general, who has lost command and authority over his troops, will not recover it for long by imposing an oath on them.[18]

bany, whom the Swinburnes had met in Paris ca 1786 and had entertained with Alfieri, Mrs Swinburne knew or had known intimately the Empress Maria Theresa (1717–80) and her two daughters, Marie Antoinette and Marie Caroline (1752–1814), Queen Consort of Ferdinand IV, King of the Two Sicilies. After her return from France in 1789, she was also summoned to Court to give an account of events in that country to Queen Charlotte. See Baker, op. cit. 29–37, 460, and the references there cited.

13. Father of the Duc de Piennes (see preceding letter): Louis-Alexandre-Céleste d'Aumont (1736–1814), styled Duc de Villequier from 1759 until his death, although he succeeded his brother as Duc d'Aumont in 1799: 'premier gentilhomme de la chambre du roi,' 1762. 'Il était auprès de la personne de Louis XVI, lors de l'insurrection populaire du 28 février 1791, et il favorisa l'évasion de ce prince par son appartement.' He resided chiefly in the Low Countries until the Restoration (Jean-Baptiste-Pierre Jullien de Courcelles, *Histoire généalogique . . . des pairs de France,* 1822–33, vi. 'Pairs de France,' 16*–16**; Woelmont de Brumagne i. 26–30). It appears from *The St James's Chronicle* 9–12 July 1791, that he went to Brussels in June when he heard of Louis XVI's escape, but returned to London 10 July.

14. Emmanuel-Céleste-Augustin de Durfort (1741–1800), Comte, Marquis, and finally, in 1789, Duc de Duras, 'premier gentilhomme de la chambre du roi, par la mort de son père, le 6 septembre 1789' (Courcelles, op. cit. vi. 292, 294–5). He died in London (GM 1800, lxx pt ii. 701).

15. On Monday, 18 April, Louis XVI planned to go to St-Cloud, but the populace 'tumultuously assailed' the Tuileries and shouted, 'Il ne faut pas qu'il part.' When Lafayette threatened that the mayor would proclaim martial law, the soldiers threatened to lay down their arms, and some attacked the King's postilions. The King remained at the Tuileries. See *The St James's Chronicle* 23–26 April 1791; Saul K. Padover, *The Life and Death of Louis XVI,* 1939, pp. 212–16.

16. The minister of foreign affairs, in the King's name, sent a letter of instructions 23 April 1791 to all French ambassadors and ministers abroad. Dealing chiefly with the King's acceptance of the French constitution, it referred also to the émigrés: 'le roi vous charge . . . de déjouer leurs intrigues et leurs projets.' For the complete text, see the *Moniteur* 25 avril 1791 and (in translation) *The St James's Chronicle* 28–30 April 1791.

17. On 21 April, three days after the insubordination of the soldiers, Lafayette resigned his post as commander-in-chief of the National Guard, but resumed his command the following Sunday or Monday, 24 or 25 April (*St James's Chronicle* 26–28, 28–30 April, 3–5 May 1791; *Oracle* 4 May 1791). See also A. Bardoux, *La Jeunesse de La Fayette,* 1892, pp. 315–18.

18. 'Les soixante bataillons de la garde nationale prirent successivement la résolution suivante: "Que tout soldat-citoyen jure sur son honneur et signe d'obéir à la loi; que ceux qui s'y refuseront soient exclus de la garde nationale; que le vœu de cette armée ainsi régénérée soit porté à M. de La Fayette, et il se fera un devoir de re-

The Parisian mob are mounted to the highest note of the gamut of riot, and whoever plays to them in that key, will make them caper away from their commander, or lead them against him.

I am sorry to say that we have discordant people amongst us, who are trying to strike up the same tune here. One Paine, an American, has published the most seditious pamphlet[19] ever seen but in open rebellion: thousands of copies of it have been dispersed[20]—and the Revolution Clubs threaten farther hostilities. We have gained the happiest constitution upon earth by many storms; I trust we shall not lose it by one! nor change it for anarchy, which always ends in despotism, which I am persuaded will be the consequence of the intemperate proceedings in France, and in the end will be fatal to liberty in general; as mankind will dread buying even reformation too dear.

Apropos (an odd apropos, but you will see its descent) the Countess Stanhope[21] t'other night inquired in the kindest[22] and [most] interested manner after you both; so did Hannah More last night at *White Pussy's*.[23]

Friday noon, 6th.

I must finish my letter, though my cargo is so small; regular stage-coaches, you know, set out, whether full or not: I have not sent you so short a gazette yet.

prendre le commandement; que, quelques individus qui ont si indignement outragé la famille royale, soient punis et chassés de la garde nationale"' (Bardoux, op. cit. 317–18).

19. *The Rights of Man*, Part I.

20. The fifth edition was advertised 'This day is published' in *The Oracle* 4 May 1791, but HW probably thought 25,000 copies had been distributed free since Easter Monday ('Mem. 1783–91,' *sub* April 1791). According to an advertisement in *The Oracle* 15 April 1791, an edition of that number, printed for 'a Society of Gentlemen of the Revolution and Constitution Societies,' was to be ready for distribution on Easter Monday: 7,000 for London; 10,000 for England, Scotland, and Wales; and 8,000 for Ireland. In ibid. 26 April 1791, this advertisement is mentioned as 'that species of wit called humbug.' That it was false also appears from Paine's letter to

George Washington 2 July 1791, to the effect that of the 16,000 copies printed, over 11,000 had been sold (DNB, *sub* Paine).

21. 'Louisa Grenville, the mother of the present Earl Stanhope' (B). Louisa Grenville (1758–1829), dau. of Hon. Henry Grenville by Margaret Eleanor Banks (*ante* 1 Nov. 1788); m. (1781) as 2d wife, Charles Stanhope (1753–1816), styled Vct Mahon 1763–86, 3d E. Stanhope, 1786. HW's 'apropos' of course refers to Lord Stanhope's strong revolutionary sympathies. He was reported in Paris at this time (letter from Paris 25 April, in *The St James's Chronicle* 28–30 April 1791).

22. HW wrote 'kindest manner,' then struck through the latter word.

23. 'Elizabeth Cary, wife of Lord Amherst' (note added in MS under notes of Miss Berry, perhaps by Lady Theresa Lewis).

I hope tomorrow or Monday to hear that your nose has exhibited itself *openly* at Florence; and as certain cheeks[24] have got natural roses, will not the pencil resume its practice? The Prince of Wales is better, and in a way to recover by an eruption.[25] Adieu! all three!

To Mary Berry, Thursday 12 May 1791

Address: À Mademoiselle Mademoiselle Berry à la poste restante à Florence, Italie. *Postmark:* FIRENZE 21. Endorsed: 'Pd 1s.'
Posted 13 May ('Visitors').

Berkeley Square, May 12, 1791.

No. 32.[1]

A LETTER from Florence (that of April 20th) does satisfy me about your dear nose—till I can see it with my own eyes: but I will own to you now, that my alarm at first went much farther: I dreaded lest so violent a fall upon rubbish might not have hurt your head, though all your letters since have proved how totally that escaped any damage—yet your great kindness in writing to me yourself so immediately did not tranquillize me, and only proved your good nature—then, I had no high opinion of Italian surgeons—but I will not detail my departed fears—nor need I prove my attachment to you two—If you were really my wives, I could not be more generally applied to for accounts of you; of which I am proud—I should be ashamed, if at my age it were a ridiculous attachment—but don't be sorry for having been circumstantial: my fears did not spring thence, nor did I suspect your not having told the whole—no, but I apprehended the accident might be worse than you knew yourself. Poor Hugh Conway,[2] though his life has long been safe, still suffers at

24. Agnes Berry's.

25. 'His Royal Highness the Prince of Wales was much better yesterday [5 May] than the preceding day, but was, by order of his physicians, prevented from seeing company' (*St James's Chronicle* 5–7 May 1791).

---

1. 'No. 42' (B).

2. 'Lord Hugh Seymour Conway, brother [son] of the then Marquis [Earl] of Hertford' (?B, Wright vi. 424). Hon. Hugh Seymour Conway (1759–1801), 5th son of 1st

E. (cr. 1793, 1st M.) of Hertford; resumed name of Seymour, 1794, and was known thereafter as Lord Hugh Seymour; Capt. R.N., 1779; rear-admiral of the Blue, 1795; of the White, 1797; vice-admiral of the Blue, 1799; M.P. Newport 1784–6, Tregony 1788–90, Wendover 1790–6, and Portsmouth 1796–1801; a lord of the Admiralty 1795–8; died of yellow fever in Jamaica; 'much beloved in the navy, and admired for his gallant spirit' (Collins, *Peerage*, 1812, ii. 565–6); 'one of the most amiable men in England, and of a character

times from his dreadful blow,[3] and has not yet been able to come to town;[4] nor would Lord Chatham's humanity put his ship[5] into commission,[6] which made him so unhappy, that poor Horatia,[7] doting on him as she does, wrote to beg he might be employed; preferring her own misery in parting with him to what she saw him suffer—amiable conduct! but happily her suit did not prevail.

I am not at all surprised at the private interviews between L.[8] and C.[9] I am persuaded that the first must and will take more part than he has yet seemed to do,[10] and so will others too[11]—but as speculations are but guesses, I will say no more on the subject now—nor on your

the most universally esteemed' (HW to Thomas Walpole, Jr., 8 April 1786). See also DNB; *Annual Register*, 1795, xxxvii pt ii. 57; ibid., 1797, p. 62; ibid., 1799, p. 48.

3. In 1790, 'Capt. Conway was appointed to the *Canada* of 74 guns at Portsmouth, and he went down to Spithead to train her crew. Unfortunately, the leadsman in throwing the lead, let it strike the backstay and it came in on the quarter deck, striking Capt. Conway violently on the head. He seemed none the worse for the blow at the moment, and reassured the seaman who came to express his concern. He went ashore, and on the 14th of September went on board again when a salute was fired from every ship on Lord Howe's hoisting his flag. At the first gun, Capt. Conway fell senseless, and it was found that he was suffering from severe concussion of the brain as the result of the blow on his head. . . . He felt the bad effects at times for the rest of his life' (Violet Biddulph, *The Three Ladies Waldegrave* [1938], p. 205). *The Oracle* 31 Jan. 1791 reported him 'so far recovered . . . as to be able to bear gentle exercise, and even to ride some miles on horseback.' He dined at SH late in July 1791 (*post* 26 July 1791), and was reported by *The Oracle* 5 Aug. 1791 to be 'perfectly recovered.' He was not able to go to sea again until early in 1793, when he commanded the *Leviathan*.

4. The 'effect of the unhappy accident' is mentioned in *The St James's Chronicle* 25–27 Jan. 1791: 'In consequence of the violent concussion . . . he cannot bear the faintest ray of light, and any noise distracts him. . . . His senses are not at all affected. . . . Time will perfectly restore him.' He had

been under the care of surgeons at Chichester, but at the time HW is writing, Conway probably was at his small estate, Berry near Hambledon, Hants (Biddulph, op. cit. 205–6; HW to Lady Louisa Lennox 29 Sept., 5 Oct., [10 Nov.] 1790).

5. The *Canada*; see n. 3.

6. Lord Chatham was first lord of the Admiralty.

7. 'Lady Horatia Waldegrave, his wife' (?B, Wright vi. 424). Lady Anna Horatia Waldegrave (1762–1801), dau. of James, 2d E. Waldegrave, by HW's niece, Maria Walpole, m. (1786) Hon. Hugh Seymour Conway. Her husband survived her three months without learning of her death. For an account of the couple, see Biddulph, op. cit. 39, 177–9, 203–44.

8. The Emperor Leopold II, Marie Antoinette's brother, who was in Florence for the festivities connected with the inauguration of his second son, Ferdinand III, as Grand Duke of Tuscany. The royal party made their public entry into Florence 9 April 1791 (GM 1791, lxi pt i. 483).

9. The MS apparently is as above, although there is a possibility that HW intended the letter for 'E,' a letter which is sometimes similar to his 'C.' No 'C' has been identified; but if he wrote 'E' he probably refers to Lord Elgin; see *post* 26 May 1791.

10. As Leopold II died less than a year later, 1 March 1792, he did comparatively little, aside from signing the Declaration of Pillnitz 27 Aug. 1791, to aid the French monarchy. As early as 4 Feb. 1791 he wrote: 'We are too weak to do anything for France now' (Saul K. Padover, *The Life and Death of Louis XVI*, 1939, p. 211).

11. Presumably the English.

English and Irish travellers, none of whom I know—I have one general wish that you may be amused while you stay by the natives of any nation: and I thank you a thousand times for confirming your intention of returning by the beginning of November, which I should not desire *coolly*, but from the earnest wish of putting you in possession of Cliveden while I live, which everybody would approve, at least not wonder at (Mr Batt, to whom I communicated my intention, does extremely) and the rest would follow of course, as I had done the same for Mrs Clive.[12]

I smiled at your making excuses for your double letter—do you think I would not give twelve pence to hear more of you and your proceedings, than a single sheet would contain?[13]

The Prince[14] is recovered; that is all the domestic news, except a most memorable debate last Friday in the House of Commons. Mr Fox had most imprudently thrown out a panegyric on the French Revolution.[15] His most considerable friends were much hurt, and protested to him against such sentiments. Burke went much farther, and vowed to attack those opinions. Great pains were taken to prevent such altercation, and the P[rince] of W[ales] is said to have written a dissuasive letter to Burke—but he was immovable—and on Friday, on the Quebec Bill[16] he broke out, and sounded a trumpet against the plot, which he denounced as carrying on here. Prodigious clamour and interruption arose from Mr Fox's friends; but he, though still applauding the French, burst into tears, and lamentations on the loss of Burke's friendship, and endeavoured to make atonement; but in vain, though Burke wept too—in short, it was the most affecting scene possible, and undoubtedly *an unique* one, for both the commanders were in earnest and *sincere*.[17] Yesterday a second act was

12. Catherine ('Kitty') Raftor (1711–85), m. (1732) George Clive; actress. HW gave her Little Strawberry Hill ('Cliveden') for her life; she lived there from about 1755 to her death (*SH Accounts* 30, 136–7, *et passim*).

13. The postage between London and any part of Italy was twelvepence for a single-sheet letter, to be paid by the recipient; two and three sheets were double and treble that amount (*Universal British Directory*, 1791–8, i. 37).

14. Of Wales.

15. In the course of the debate 15 April 1791 on the armament against Russia, Fox

mentioned that he 'admired the new constitution of France, considered altogether, as the most stupendous and glorious edifice of liberty which had been erected on the foundation of human integrity in any time or country' (*Parliamentary History of England*, xxix, 1817, 249; the words are variously reported).

16. The Quebec Government Bill, a bill for the government of Canada; see ibid. xxix. 359–430.

17. For Mary Berry's comments on Burke and Fox, and for notice of this incident, see her *A Comparative View of Social Life in England and France*, 1844, i. 352–7. The in-

expected—but mutual friends prevailed that the contest should not be renewed—nay, on the same bill Mr Fox made a profession of his faith, and declared he would venture his life in support of the *present* constitution by King, Lords and Commons—in short, I never knew a *wiser* dissertation, if the newspapers deliver it justly, and I think all the writers in England cannot give more profound sense to Mr Fox than he possesses. I know no more particulars, having seen nobody this morning yet.

I will deliver your message to Mr P.[18] Do you know he is not a little infected with (I mean no harm) the French dis-order?[19] Mrs Buller says, 'Did you ever know P. start anything of his own?' I will not tell her or him, what you say of his letter.—But what shall I tell you else? We have expected Mrs Damer[20] from last night, and perhaps she may arrive before this sets out tomorrow.

You know my infinity of nephews and nieces—I am always at a wedding or christening. Two nights ago I was godfather with Lord Chatham and Princess Sophia of Gloucester[21] (represented by Miss Dee)[22] to Horace Churchill's[23] newborn son: It is christened *Chatham Horace*,[24] but is to be called by the latter—it could not, while young,

cident is treated fully in all the lives of Burke and Fox. See also Wright vi. 425–6; *Parliamentary History of England*, loc. cit.

18. Pepys.

19. For a clear statement of Pepys' sympathy with the French Revolution, see his letter to Hannah More 28 Sept. 1791 (*A Later Pepys*, ed. Alice C. C. Gaussen, 1904, ii. 280–3), in which he says, in part: 'I know that I may venture to congratulate you upon the happy settlement (for the present at least) of the French constitution, by which 25 millions of our fellow creatures are restored to the rights of human nature, and which I consider as one of the most wonderful and most important events in the history of mankind' (ibid. 281).

20. Expanded by Mary Berry from HW's 'D.'

21. HW's grand-niece, and first cousin once removed of Horace Churchill: Princess Sophia Matilda (1773–1844), only surviving dau. of the Duke and Duchess of Gloucester.

22. Leonora Dee, sister of Deborah Charlotte Dee who married Commodore George Johnstone (1730–87) and later Charles Ed-

mund Nugent (see *post* 4 Dec. 1793); lived chiefly in Portugal until she accompanied Mrs Johnstone to England in 1782; governess to Princess Sophia of Gloucester, 1787, and was still living with her as companion or lady of the Bedchamber, 1818. A series of letters by and concerning her in 1787 is in *The Harcourt Papers*, ed. Edward William Harcourt, n.d., vi. 313–33. See also Biddulph, op. cit. 199, 201, 295; Sylvester Douglas, Baron Glenbervie, *Diaries*, ed. Francis Bickley, 1928, ii. 297–8; MBJ ii. 489; *Letters from Mrs Elizabeth Carter to Mrs Montagu*, 1817, iii. 283, 290; *Register Book of Marriages . . . Parish of St George, Hanover Square . . . Middlesex*, ed. John H. Chapman, 1888, ii. 44.

23. Horace Churchill (d. 1817), HW's nephew, son of Charles and Lady Mary Churchill; captain in the army, 1779; Capt. First Regiment of Foot Guards, 1782; Capt. First Horse Grenadier Guards, 1787; Maj., 1794; Lt-Col., 1798; Col., 1808; Maj.-Gen., 1811 (John Philippart, *Royal Military Calendar*, 1815, ii. 2; GM 1817, lxxxvii pt ii. 472).

24. He was born 9 April in Margaret

be called *Chat, Chat!*[25] Though all archdukes wear the virgin's name first (with fifty others) nobody says, 'Come hither, Moll'—at least no mortal ever did, but the late Landgrave of Hesse,[26] who had learnt that vulgarism[27] and used it about his wife Princess Mary,[28] when he spoke of her to her sisters Amalie[29] and Caroline,[30] who did not guess whom he meant.

Friday morning 13th.

Last night we were at Lady Fred. Campbell's,[31] the usual cribbage party: Conways, Mount Edgcumbes, Johnstones—at past ten Mrs Damer was announced! Her parents ran down into the hall and I scrambled down some of the stairs[32]—She looks vastly well, was in great spirits, and not at all fatigued though she came from Dover,[33] had been *twelve* hours at sea from Calais, and had rested but four days at Paris[34] from Madrid—We supped and stayed till one o'clock,

Street, Cavendish Square (GM 1791, lxi pt i. 379), where the christening probably took place.

25. Doubtless a reference to the third Duke of Devonshire's practice of calling his daughters by nicknames, such as 'Cat, cat' (Montagu i. 58–9), which HW probably had told to the Berrys when retailing to them 'the old stories' he mentions at the beginning of his *Reminiscences . . . for the Amusement of Miss Mary and Miss Agnes Berry.*

26. Friedrich II (1720–85), Landgrave of Hesse-Cassel, 1760: 'a brutal German, obstinate, of no genius,' who long treated his wife, 'the mildest and gentlest of her race, with great inhumanity' (HW, *Mem. Geo. II* i. 405).

27. 'Moll,' not only a familiar diminutive for 'Mary,' but 'a prostitute' (OED).

28. (1723–72) of England, 4th dau. of George II; m. (1740) Prince Friedrich Wilhelm, Hereditary Prince of Hesse-Cassel, later (1760) Landgrave; 'of the softest, mildest temper in the world' (HW to Mann 12 Aug. 1746); 'a most gentle and amiable being' (ibid. 3 Feb. 1772).

29. Princess Amelia Sophia Eleonora (1711–86), 2d dau. of George II; HW's intimate acquaintance.

30. Princess Caroline Elizabeth (1713–58), 3d dau. of George II.

31. Mary Meredith (ca 1738–1807), sister of Sir William Meredith, 3d Bt; m. (1)

(1752) Laurence Shirley (1720–60), 4th E. Ferrers, who was hanged for the murder of his steward, and from whom she was separated by Act of Parliament, 1758; m. (2) (1769) Lord Frederick Campbell (GEC, *sub* Ferrers; *Scots Peerage* i. 384–5). The town house of the Campbells was in Arlington Street (*Royal Kalendar*, 1791, p. 57).

32. Mrs Damer describes her arrival in her letter to Mary Berry 13 May 1791: 'I got to town between ten and eleven, stayed at my father's, where I had been figuring to myself that I should find them either at home, or expected to supper. Perhaps dear Mr Walpole alone, sitting by the fire, as I often have [found him], waiting their arrival. I drove up to the door . . . "Nobody at home!" . . . Away I drove to Arlington Street . . . A loud knock . . . brought Lady Frederick down stairs; in an instant out I flew, my mother and father followed her, and at the top I saw Mr Walpole. He seemed and is as well as ever; *I* perceive no difference, not thinner, less lively, or less all that you left him, or all that you can wish,—so at least he appeared to me last night. If I see any reason to change my opinions I will tell you with sincerity' (MBJ i. 349–50).

33. 'I was in a state when no fatigue is felt' (ibid.).

34. For Mrs Damer's account of her stay in Paris, see ibid. 346–9.

and I shall go to her as soon as I am dressed. Madrid and the Escurial she owns have gained her a proselyte to painting which her statuarism had totally engrossed[35]—in her, no wonder. Of Titian she had no idea (nor have I a just one, though great faith) as at Venice all his works are now coal-black—but Rubens she says amazed her, and that in Spain he has even grace. Her father yesterday morning from pain remaining still in his shoulder from his fall, had it examined by Dr Hunter[36] and a little bone of the collar was found to be broken, and he must wear his arm for some days in a sling.

Miss Boyle I heard last night has consented to marry Lord Henry Fitzgerald.[37] I think they have both chosen well—but I have chosen better—adieu! *care spose!*

To Mary Berry, Thursday 19 May 1791

Address: À Mademoiselle Mademoiselle Berry à la poste restante à Florence, Italie. *Postmark:* FIR[ENZE] 22. Endorsed: 'Pd 1s.'
Posted 20 May ('Visitors').

Berkeley Square, Thursday, May 19, 1791.

No. 33.[1]

YOUR letter of the 29th for which you are so good as to make excuses on not sending it to the post in time, did arrive but two days later than usual, and as it is now two months from *the 16th of*

---

35. Mrs Damer wrote to Mary Berry 16 April 1791 that she saw 'at the Escurial some divine pictures' (MBJ i. 342). Joseph Farington recorded 5 June 1796, when Mrs Damer and the Berrys were his guests at the exhibition of the Royal Academy: 'The observations of Mrs Damer did not seem to me to prove that she has any exact knowledge of painting, whatever she may have of sculpture; and she did not make intelligent remarks on the latter. I think her manner and particularly her voice very affected and unpleasing' (*Diary*, ed. James Greig, 1922–8, i. 150).

36. John Hunter (1728–93), anatomist and surgeon.

37. (1761–1829), 4th son of the 1st D. of Leinster; succeeded to the estate of Strangford, co. Down; M.P. (Ireland) Kildare bor-

ough 1783–90, city of Dublin 1790–7, and (United Kingdom) co. Kildare 1807–14; retired and was succeeded 23 March 1814 by his nephew Lord William Fitzgerald (*Dublin Evening Post* 22, 24 March 1814); died at Boyle Farm, Thames Ditton, Surrey, and was buried at St John's, Paddington (GEC, *sub* Ros; Marquis of Kildare, *The Earls of Kildare and Their Ancestors,* 4th edn, 1864, pp. 300–1; GM 1829, xcix pt ii. 174). Some of his letters and many addressed to him are printed in Thomas Moore, *The Life and Death of Lord Edward Fitzgerald,* 1831. Hoppner's portrait of him is reproduced in Ida A. Taylor, *Life of Lord Edward Fitzgerald,* 1904, p. 325. For his marriage, see *post* 3 Aug. 1791.

---

1. 'No. 43' (B).

March and I have had so many certificates of the prosperous state of your pretty nose, I attributed the delay to the elements, and took no panic—but how kindly punctual you are, when you charge yourself with an irregularity of two days! and when your letters are so charmingly long and interest me so much in all you do!—but make no more excuses—I reproach myself with occasioning so much waste of your time, that you might employ every hour, for it is impossible to see all that the Medicis had collected or encouraged in the loveliest little city and in such beautiful environs—nor had I forgotten the Cascines,² the only spot containing English verdure.

Mrs Damer is as well, if not better than she has been a great while; her looks surprise everybody, to which, as she is tanned, her Spanish complexion contributes. She and I called the night before last on your friend Mrs Cholmeley, and they are to make me a visit tomorrow morning by their own appointment.³ At Dover Mrs Damer heard the Gunnings are there⁴—here they are forgotten.

You are learning perspective to take views; I am glad; can one have too many resources in one's self? Internal armour is more necessary to your sex than weapons to ours. You have neither professions nor politics nor ways of getting money like men, in any of which, whether successful or not, they are employed. Scandal and cards you will both always hate and despise as much as you do now; and though I shall not flatter Mary so much as to suppose she will ever equal the extraordinary talent of Agnes in painting, yet as Mary like the scrip-

2. The Cascine, 'the favourite promenade of the Florentines . . . were formerly occupied by farm-lands belonging to the Medici and later to the city, and in the 18th cent[ury] were converted into a public garden' (L. V. Bertarelli, *Northern Italy*, ed. Findlay Muirhead, 1924, p. 380).

3. Mrs Damer saw Mrs Cholmeley at the opera 14 May: 'She inquired after Mr W[alpole] and said that you had desired her to go and see him, but that she had not *courage*. I took upon me to do the honours of him, and said how glad I was sure he would be, that *I* would bring him to wait upon her, if she would allow me. If this was too free and impertinent, you must answer for it. My F[ather] and Mother came home with me, where we found G[eneral] O'Hara and him. He was, as you may suppose, pleased with what I told him, and we

agreed to go together to wait upon your friend' (Mrs Damer to Mary Berry 16 May 1791, *Berry Papers* 28). On Friday, 20 May, she continued her letter: 'I shall not send this till Tuesday, as I know that Mr W[alpole] writes today. Of public events he will give you an account and of Mrs Cholmeley's visit to him this morning, to which this will afterwards be a key your quickness will not want. I had received a note from her saying that she wished I would carry her to him at my time. I chose the soonest' (ibid. 31).

4. 'Mrs Gunning, her sister, and her daughter are returned to England from the Continent. They arrived on Monday [9 May] (from Calais) at Dover, where they yet continue' (*St James's Chronicle* 12–14 May 1791). See also ibid. 14–17 May 1791.

tural Martha is occupied in many things, she is quite in the right to add the pencil to her other amusements.[5]

I knew the Duchesse de Brissac[6] a little and but little in 1766; she was lively and seemed sensible, and had an excellent character. Poor M. de Nivernois![7] to be deprived of that only remaining child too![8]— but how many French one pities and how many more one abhors! How dearly will even liberty be bought (if it shall prove to be obtained, which I neither think it *is* or will be) by every kind of injustice and violation of consciences! how little conscience can they have, who leave to others no option but between perjury and starving!

Mrs Beckford[9] I did not know; *Mrs* Hare[10] I do: she is daughter of

5. See illustration. This sketch, signed 'Pisa 1791' by Mary Berry indicates that the lessons in perspective were not yet mastered. It is the first sketch in an oblong, octavo sketchbook (now wsl), on the cover of which Mary Berry has inscribed 'M.B. 1790. Pisa.' The book has only one other sketch dated 'Pisa 1791,' but it has several much better ones of Goodwood and Bognor, dated by Mary Berry July and August 1796. See *post* i. 325.

6. Adélaïde-Diane-Hortense-Délie Mancini de Nevers (1742–1808), dau. of the Duc de Nivernais (see following note); m. (1760) Louis-Hercule-Timoléon de Cossé, Duc de Cossé, later (1784) Duc de Brissac. She had been in Italy since 1787, gravely ill, but she survived her father ten years (Lucien Perey [Clara Adèle Luce Herpin], *Un Petit-neveu de Mazarin*, 1899, p. 572, *et passim; idem*, *La Fin du XVIIIᵉ siècle*, 1891, p. 19, *et passim*; Émile Blampignon, *Le Duc de Nivernais*, n.d., p. 375, *et passim*). HW wrote to Lady Hervey 3 Oct. 1765: 'I meet the Duchesse de Cossé this evening at Madame Geoffrin's. She is pretty, with a great resemblance to her father; lively and good-humoured, not genteel.' She is mentioned about ten times in du Deffand, chiefly in HW's 'Paris Journals.'

7. Louis-Jules-Barbon Mancini-Mazarini (1716–98), Duc de Nivernais, HW's friend and occasional correspondent. HW had known him since 1763 (du Deffand i. 174–5, *et passim*). See also the works cited in the preceding note.

8. His only son, Jules-Frédéric, Comte de

Nevers, was born in 1745 and died in 1753; and another daughter, Hélène-Julie-Rosalie (1740–80), m. (1753) Louis-Marie Fouquet de Belle-Isle, Duc de Gisors, who died in 1758 of wounds received in battle. The Duc de Nivernais also lived through the massacre of his other son-in-law, the Duc de Brissac, in 1792 (Jean-Baptiste-Pierre Jullien de Courcelles, *Histoire généalogique . . . des pairs de France*, 1822–33, vol. v, art. 'Mancini-Mazarini,' pp. 3–4).

9. Louisa Pitt (ca 1756–30 April 1791), 2d dau. of George Pitt, cr., 1776, Bn Rivers; m. (1773) Peter Beckford, sometime M.P., writer on hunting and travel; died at Florence after an illness of several years, and was buried at Leghorn. For an account of her affair with her husband's cousin, William Beckford (the author of *Vathek*), a reproduction of her portrait by Sir Joshua Reynolds, and some of her letters, see A. Henry Higginson, *Peter Beckford*, 1937.

10. Georgiana Shipley (ca 1756–1806), 4th dau. of Jonathan Shipley (see following note); m. (1783) Francis Hare-Naylor (1753–1815) of Hurstmonceaux, Sussex. With an annuity of £200 from the Duchess of Devonshire, Mrs Hare-Naylor's cousin, and the small income of Mr Hare-Naylor, the couple soon after their marriage retired to the Continent. Presumably the Berrys met them in Italy, where they chiefly lived until 1797. See dnb, *sub* Hare-Naylor, Francis; Augustus J. C. Hare, *Memorials of a Quiet Life*, 1873–6, i. 92–154 (verses by Mrs Hare-Naylor on pp. 94–5, 98–9, 151–3), iii. 45, 59 (portraits of her); James Madison

DRAWING BY MARY BERRY, DATED 'PISA 1791'

the late Bishop of St Asaph, Shipley.[11] She is extremely good-natured, has a wild kind of romantic parts and I have seen prettyish verses of hers. She married very indiscreetly, for though her swain[12] was heir to a large estate, it was encumbered, to which load he added before he attained it, nor do I know that it is yet attained. He was said to have wit, and from his namesake,[13] who has so very much, was in his county called *the Leveret*.[14] If these are not the folk you wot of, no matter—if they are, keep my tale to yourselves, for whose use only I utter it. The Prince de Chimay[15] I do not know.

After answering the articles of yours, I shall add what I can of new. After several weeks spent in search of precedents for trials ceasing or not on a dissolution of Parliament,[16] the peers on Monday sat till three in the morning on the report, when the Chancellor[17] and Lord Hawkesbury[18] fought for the cessation, but were beaten by a large majority,[19] which showed that Mr Pitt has more weight (at

Stifler, *'My Dear Girl': The Correspondence of Benjamin Franklin with Polly Stevenson, Georgiana and Catherine Shipley,* New York, [1927] pp. 213, 243–4, *et passim* (portraits of Mrs Hare-Naylor facing pp. 226, 278).

11. Jonathan Shipley (1714–88), Bp of Llandaff, 1769 (for five months) and of St Asaph 1769–88; friend of Benjamin Franklin, Burke, and Reynolds; opponent of George III's American policy.

12. Francis Hare-Naylor.

13. James Hare (1747–1804), intimate friend of Charles James Fox. The Duchess of Gordon described him and his associates as 'the Hare and many friends' (DNB; R. A. Austen-Leigh, *Eton College Register 1753–1790,* Eton, 1921).

14. Cf. Sylvester Douglas, Baron Glenbervie, *Diaries,* ed. Francis Bickley, 1928, ii. 34.

15. Philippe-Gabriel-Maurice-Joseph d' Alsace-Hénin-Liétard (1736–1804), Prince de Chimay. In spite of HW's statement that he did not know the Prince, it appears that they supped together at the Duke of Richmond's in Paris 21 Nov. 1765 and that he visited HW in 1776 (DU DEFFAND iv. 366, v. 273–4).

16. This was apropos of the trial of Warren Hastings. A committee to examine

precedents in the case was appointed in the House of Lords 17 Feb. 1791; on 19 April the report was ordered to be printed; it was briefly considered 4 May; but on Monday 16 May the report of 311 folio pages was fully debated (*History of the Trial of Warren Hastings,* 1796, pt iv, pp. 41–61).

17. Lord Thurlow.

18. Charles Jenkinson (b. 1727 or 1729, d. 1808), cr. (1786) Bn Hawkesbury and (1796) E. of Liverpool; president of the Board of Trade 1786–1804.

19. There were three motions before the House of Lords: (1) 'that a message be sent to the Commons to inform them that the Lords were ready to proceed in the trial of Warren Hastings, Esq.'; (2) Lord Hawkesbury's, that the report be referred to a committee of the House on Privileges; (3) that the judges be summoned to give their opinions upon the question, whether the recognizances of Hastings were or were not in force. The third was defeated by a vote of 70 to 20; the second by 66 to 18; and the original motion was carried without a division (*St James's Chronicle* 14–17 May 1791; *History of the Trial of Warren Hastings,* 1796, pt iv, pp. 46–61). The trial was set for Monday, 23 May, and the session was adjourned at 3:30 A.M.

present) in that House too, than—the diamonds of Bengal. Lord Hawksbury protested.[20] The trial recommences on Monday next, and has already cost the public fourteen thousand pounds—the accused, I suppose, much more.

The Countess of Albany is not only in England, in London, but at this very moment I believe in the palace of St James[21]—not restored by as rapid a revolution as the French, but as was observed last night at supper at Lady Mt Edgcumbe's by that topsy-turvy-hood that characterizes the present age—Within these two months the Pope has been burnt at Paris,[22] Madame du Barry, mistress of Louis Quinze, has dined with the Lord Mayor of London,[23] and the Pretender's[24] widow is presented to the Queen of Great Britain! She is to be introduced by her great-grandfather's niece, the young Countess of Ailesbury.[25] That curiosity should bring her hither, I do not quite wonder—less, that she abhorred her husband; but methinks it is not very well bred to his family, nor very sensible; but a new way of *passing eldest*.[26] Apropos, I hear there is a medal struck at Rome of her brother-in-law as Henry IX,[27] which as one of their papal majesties

20. On Tuesday, 17 May, Lord Hawkesbury entered a formal protest against the vote of the preceding evening (*Oracle* 20 May 1791).

21. The Queen's Drawing Room began at half past two and ended at five o'clock (*Oracle* 20 May 1791).

22. 'Between the hours of ten and eleven last Tuesday [3 May] the Mufti of Rome, Pius VI, vulgarly called the Pope, was burnt in effigy at the Palais-Royal, and his ashes scattered before the wind. . . . The effigy was about eight feet high; on a label before was the word "Fanaticism," and behind the words "Civil War"' (letter from Paris 5 May, in *St James's Chronicle* 7–10 May 1791).

23. John Boydell.

24. Charles Edward Louis Philip Casimir Stuart (1720–88), 'the Young Pretender.'

25. Anne Rawdon (1753–1813), 3d dau. of 1st E. of Moira, m. (1788) as 2d wife, Thomas Bruce, 1st E. of Ailesbury, n.c. 'The Countess of Stalbourg [see below] was introduced by the Countess of Ailesbury' (*Oracle* 20 May 1791).

26. A phrase used in loo, brag, and other card games. After the deal in loo, 'he that is eldest hand [the player to left of dealer] hath the priviledg of passing by the benefit thereof, that is, he hath the advantage of hearing what every one will say, and at last may play or not play according as he finds his game good or bad. If the eldest saith he passeth, the rest may chuse whether they will play or no' (Charles Cotton, *The Compleat Gamester*, 1674, in *Games and Gamesters of the Restoration*, introduction by Cyril Hughes Hartmann, [1930] p. 69). It was a favourite phrase with HW. See also *Hoyle's Games Improved*, New York, 1829, pp. 152–73; OED, *sub* pass; Richard Seymour, *The Compleat Gamester*, 6th edn, 1739, pp. 210–12.

27. Cardinal York had two medals struck in 1788: one bears on the obverse 'Henricus Nonus Magnae Britanniae Rex' and on the reverse 'Non voluntate hominum sed Dei Gratia'; the other is inscribed 'Hen. IX. Mag. Brit. Fr. et Hib. Rex: Fid. Def. Card. Ep. Tusc.' and on the reverse 'Non desideriis hominum sed voluntate Dei An. MDCCLXXXVIII.' (DNB). The latter, as well as another dated 1766, showing him as the Cardinal Duke of York, is illustrated

was so abominably mean as to deny the royal title to their brother, though for Rome he had lost a crown, *I did* not know they allow *his* brother to assume.[28] I should be much obliged to you if you could get me one of those medals in copper; ay, and one of his brother, if there was one with the royal title: I have the father's[29] and mother's, and all the popes in copper,[30] but *my* Pope Benedict XIV[31] is the last, and therefore I should be glad of *one* of each of his successors, if you can procure and bring them with little trouble. I should not be sorry to have *one* of the present Gr[eat] Duke[32] and his father; but they should be in copper, not only for my suite, but they are sharper than in silver.

Thursday night.

Well! I have had an exact account of the interview of the two Queens[33] from one who stood close to them.[34] The Dowager was announced as Princess of Stolberg; she was well dressed, and not at all embarrassed. The King talked to her a good deal, but about her passage, the sea and general topics: the Queen in the same way, but less. Then she stood between the Dukes of Gloucester and Clarence, and had a good deal of conversation with the former, who perhaps may have met her in Italy. Not a word between her and the Princesses,[35] nor did I hear of the Prince, but he was there and probably spoke to her. The Queen looked at her earnestly. To add to the singularity

in Alice Shield, *Henry Stuart Cardinal of York and His Times,* 1908, facing p. 187; see also ibid. 264, where the arrangement of the words on the reverse of the first differs from that given above. One of these as 'Henry IX' was in the SH sale x. 37, together with others relating to the Pretender's family.

28. Cardinal York's assumption of the royal title was without papal sanction, as is shown by Pope Pius VI's letter to him, 1 Feb. 1788, quoted in Shield, p. 265.

29. James Francis Edward Stuart (1688–1766), Chevalier de St George; 'the Old Pretender'; son of James II; m. (1719) Mary Clementina (d. 1735), dau. of Prince James Lewis Sobieski.

30. For HW's description of some of these medals, see 'Des. of SH,' *Works* ii. 449–51. In the SH sale x. 103 was 'a collection of 475 copper and 11 silver [medals], of the Popes and Cardinals, by the Ham-

arani's and other celebrated artists, all in a fine state of preservation.'

31. A reference to HW's partiality for Pope Benedict: see Cole ii. 78–9; du Deffand i. 114–15; HW to Mann 20 June 1757.

32. Ferdinand III (1769–1824), Grand Duke of Tuscany 1790–9, 1814–24; 2d son of Leopold II, Emperor of Germany 1790–2.

33. Queen Charlotte and the Countess of Albany.

34. HW's informant is not known, but among those present at the Drawing Room were Lady Mount Edgcumbe, Lord Valletort, 'Mrs Damer,' and 'Mrs Anderson.' Mrs Damer, however, does not mention the Drawing Room in her letters to Mary Berry (*Berry Papers, passim*).

35. The three elder princesses: the Princess Royal, Augusta Sophia, and Elizabeth (*Oracle* 20 May 1791).

of the day, it is the Queen's birthday—another odd accident; at the opera at the Pantheon Madame D'Albany was carried into the King's box and sat there. It is not of a piece with her going to court, that she seals with the royal arms.[36] I have been told tonight that you will not be able to get me a medal of the Royal Cardinal, as very few were struck, and only for presents—so pray give yourself but little trouble about it.

Boswell has at last published[37] his long-promised life of Dr Johnson in two volumes in quarto.[38] I will give you an account of it when I have gone through it—I have already perceived that in writing the history of Hudibras, Ralpho has not forgot himself,—nor will others I believe forget *him*.

Friday one o'clock.

Your two friends[39] have been here, and amongst other things I think we mentioned you two. Good morrow!

To Mary Berry, Thursday 26 May 1791

Address: À Mademoiselle Mademoiselle Berry à la poste restante à Florence, Italie. *Postmark:* FIRENZE [22?]. Endorsed: 'Pd 1s.'
Posted 27 May ('Visitors').

Berkeley Square, May 26, 1791.

No. 34.[1]

I AM rich in letters from you: I received that by Lord Elgin's[2] courier first, as you expected, and its elder the next day. You tell me mine entertain you; *tant mieux;* it is my wish, but my wonder, for I live so very little in the world, that I do not know the present generation by

---

36. 'The Countess invariably used the royal arms on her seal, generally impaled with those of Stolberg-Gedern, as may be seen on several of her letters in the British Museum' (Herbert M. Vaughan, *The Last Stuart Queen*, 1910, p. 165 n).

37. On Monday, 16 May (*St James's Chronicle* 12–14 May 1791).

38. HW's copy (sold SH v. 31), with a few notes, is now in the Victoria and Albert Museum, South Kensington, in the Dyce Collection, No. 1274.

39. 'Mrs Damer and Mrs Cholmeley' (B). See also n. 3.

1. 'No. 44' (B).

2. Thomas Bruce (1766–1841), 7th E. of Elgin, 1771; on special mission to the Emperor Leopold II (at Vienna and in Italy) 1790–1; minister at Brussels 1792–5; at Berlin 1795–9; ambassador at Constantinople 1799–1803; best known as the collector of the 'Elgin Marbles,' removed from Athens to London 1803–12. After the Emperor came to Florence in the spring of 1791, Lord Elgin conferred with him (10, 11 May) concerning a proposed alliance with England, prior to the peace negotiations of England and Prussia with Russia. Lord El-

sight, for though I pass them in the streets, the hats with valances, the folds above the chin of the ladies, and the dirty shirts and shaggy hair of the young men,[3] who have *levelled nobility* almost as much as the *mobility* in France have, have confounded all individuality. Besides, if I did go to public places and assemblies, which my going to roost earlier prevents, the bats and owls do not begin to fly abroad till far in the night, when they begin to see and be seen. However, one of the empresses of fashion, the Duchess of Gordon, uses fifteen or sixteen hours of her four and twenty. I heard her journal of last Monday—She first went to Handel's music in the Abbey;[4] she then clambered over the benches and went to Hastings's trial in the Hall[5]—after dinner to the play,[6] then to Lady Lucan's assembly;[7] after that to Ranelagh,[8] and returned to Mrs Hobart's faro table;[9] gave a ball herself[10] in the eve-

gin doubtless sent his vague but 'voluminous' reports (and Miss Berry's letter) by courier as soon as possible after the interviews, and his dispatches reached Lord Grenville about 23 or 24 May (*Joseph II, Leopold II, und Kaunitz. Ihr Briefwechsel*, ed. Adolf Beer, Wien, 1873, p. 404, *et passim;* Historical Manuscripts Commission, Fourteenth Report, Appendix, pt V: *The Manuscripts of J. B. Fortescue, Esq.* ii [1894]. 79, *et passim*). See also *ante* 12 May 1791.

3. For illustrations of these fashions, see *The Town and Country Magazine*, 1790, xxii. facing pp. 99, 483, 531, 579; 1791, xxiii. facing pp. 147, 435, 531.

4. It was the first day of the Handel Commemoration of 1791, which was held in Westminster Abbey by royal command and under the direction of the Royal Society of Musicians. The program is given in *The Oracle* for 23 May.

5. Westminster Hall. This was the first day of the trial in 1791 (9 June 1790 had closed the proceedings for the previous year): 'the peeresses' gallery, notwithstanding the contiguous attraction of the Abbey, was crowded, and scarcely ever with a more delightful assemblage of beauty' (*Oracle* 24 May 1791).

6. The only 'play' she could have seen was a performance by the *fantoccini* (see *ante* 5 March 1791, n. 28) of *Les Petites affiches* and two other pieces (*Times* 23 May 1791).

7. 'Lady Lucan's card party last night were too full of the wonders of the Abbey to play with unremitted attention—*whist* there might be—but it was not *hush*' (*Oracle* 24 May 1791).

8. It opened for the season on 25 April, and was open on Mondays, Wednesdays, and Fridays throughout the season (*Oracle* 21 April 1791).

9. Albinia Bertie (ca 1738–1816), 1st dau. and coheir of Lord Vere Bertie (son of Robert, 1st D. of Ancaster); m. (1757) Hon. George Hobart, 3d E. of Buckinghamshire, 1793. She was notorious for her obesity, her campaigning at the polls, her activity in amateur theatricals, and her faro table at her house in St James's Square. Anthony Morris Storer wrote to Lord Auckland 1 Feb. 1791: 'Faro goes on as briskly as ever: those who have not fortune enough of their own to live on have recourse to this profitable game in order to raise contributions on their friends. The ladies are all embarked in banks, Mrs Strutt [Sturt], Lady Archer, Mrs Hobart, Lady Elizabeth Luttrell, are avowed bankers; others, I suppose, are secretly concerned' (*Journal and Correspondence of William [Eden], Lord Auckland,* ed. Robert John Eden, 3d Baron Auckland, 1861–2, ii. 384). For satiric references to her in connection with faro, see also BM, *Satiric Prints* vi. 895–7, 957–8, Nos 8073, 8075, 8166–7.

10. At her house, 6 St James's Square, which she occupied until 1796 (*Directory to*

ning of that morning into which she must have got a good way, and set out for Scotland the next day.[11] Hercules could not have achieved a quarter of her labours in the same space of time. What will the Great Duke[12] think of our Amazons, if he has letters opened, as the Emperor[13] was wont? One of our Camillas[14]—but in a freer style, I hear he saw (I fancy just before your arrival)[15] and he must have wondered at the familiarity of the dame and the nincompoophood of her Prince.[16] Sir William Hamilton[17] is arrived—his nymph of the attitudes was too prudish to visit the rambling peeress.

Mrs Cholmeley was so very good as to call on me again yesterday;[18] Mr French[19] was with me, and fell in love with her understanding, and probably with her face too—but with that he did not trust me. He says we shall have Dr Darwin's stupendous poem[20] in a fortnight, of which

the Nobility, Gentry . . . for 1793; Sun 13 Jan. 1796).

11. That is, Wednesday, 25 May; but she again attended Hastings's trial on that day before her departure (Oracle 26 May 1791). 'Her Grace . . . arrived some days ago at Gordon Castle; and has . . . resumed her wonted hospitalities' (ibid. 13 June 1791).

12. Ferdinand III, Grand Duke of Tuscany.

13. His father, Leopold II, who had been Grand Duke 1765–90.

14. Lady Craven.

15. At Florence.

16. The Margrave of Anspach.

17. Expanded by Mary Berry from HW's 'W.H.' Sir William Hamilton (1730–1803), K.B., 1772; diplomatist and archæologist; plenipotentiary at Naples 1764–1800; HW's occasional correspondent. 'Sir William Hamilton is arrived in town from Naples, where he has resided near 30 years. He is come home on leave of absence' (St James's Chronicle 24–26 May 1791). His 'nymph of the attitudes' was his mistress (since 1786), Emma Hart, born Amy or Emily Lyon (ca 1761 or 1765–1815), whom he married 6 Sept. 1791, and who later became Lord Nelson's mistress. She had a European reputation for her 'attitudes' or tableaux-vivants representing characters from antiquity, the characters of the plays of Racine, etc. See Friedrich Rehberg, Drawings Faithfully Copied from Nature at Naples and with Permission Dedicated to the Right Honour-

able Sir William Hamilton, [1794], where there are twelve plates of her attitudes; Walter Sichel, Emma Lady Hamilton, 1905.

18. After calling on HW, she called on Mrs Damer, who reported to Mary Berry 31 May 1791: 'I must . . . remark a comical peculiarity in him [HW]. Though perfectly communicative with regard to your letters, as in everything that concerns him most nearly, always reading me parts of them, sometimes giving them to me to read, I can scarcely make him attend to those you send me. Mrs Cholmeley the morning she was here, had been with him with a letter from you which she had, I fancy, very lately received, and was struck with the same idea. She said that he "despised her intelligence, and with all the insolence of a lover boasted of three letters which he had himself received." I am sometimes diverted with this, and shall (I hope) one day laugh at him about it with you. Some times I do not half like it; when occupied with one subject, he talks to me with his life and quickness, of another' (Berry Papers 33, 37).

19. Richard French of Derby, HW's occasional correspondent, and friend of Dr Erasmus Darwin.

20. The Botanic Garden. Part I. Containing The Economy of Vegetation . . ., 1791. In four cantos, the poem has a total of 2428 lines. See post 17 Aug. 1791. The second part of the poem had appeared in 1789.

you saw parts.[21] George Cholmondeley's wife after a dreadful labour is delivered of a dead child.[22]

The rest of my letter must be literary, for we have no news. Boswell's book[23] is gossiping, but having numbers of proper names,[24] would be more readable, at least by me, were it reduced from two volumes to one—but there are woeful *longueurs,* both about his hero, and himself, the *fidus Achates,* about whom one has not the smallest curiosity; but I wrong the original Achates; one is satisfied with his fidelity in kee[p]-ing his master's secrets and weaknesses, which modern led-captains betray for their patron's glory, and to hurt their own enemies, which Boswell has done shamefully, particularly against Mrs Piozzi[25] and Mrs Montagu,[26] and Bishop Percy.[27] Dr Blagdon[28] says justly, that it is a new kind of libel, by which you may abuse anybody, by saying, some dead person said so and so of somebody alive—Often indeed Johnson made the most brutal speeches to living persons, for though he was good-natured at bottom, he was very ill-natured at top. He loved to dispute to show his superiority. If his opponents were weak, he told them they were fools; if they vanquished him, he was scurrilous—to nobody more than to Boswell himself who was contemptible for flattering him so grossly, and for enduring the coarse things he was continually vomiting on Boswell's own country, Scotland. I expected amongst the excom-

21. Quoted in French's letter to HW 14 Feb. 1790; from this letter it appears that HW before that date had seen parts of the poem and had offered suggestions for its improvement.

22. Under 'Births' in *The Oracle* 2 June 1791 is listed: 'A few days ago, the lady of George James Cholmondeley, Esq., of a son.'

23. *Life of Johnson.* In connection with this passage, see also 'On Dr Johnson's Biographers,' *post* ii. 258. For HW's copy see *ante* 19 May 1791, n. 38.

24. These comments are intended as praise of the *Life.* See HW to Mann 13 Dec. 1759: 'I have often said it of myself, and it is true, that nothing that has not a proper name of a man or a woman to it, affixes any idea upon my mind.'

25. Boswell mentions her 'extreme inaccuracy' and her indifference to truth; see *Life of Johnson* i. 416 n, iii. 226, 228, 243, 404, *et passim.*

26. Elizabeth Robinson (1720–1800),

elder dau. of Matthew Robinson of West Layton, Yorks; m. (1742) Edward Montagu; the famous Bluestocking; author of *An Essay on the Writings and Genius of Shakespear,* 1769. In *Life of Johnson* ii. 88–9, iii. 244, *et passim,* she is presented as a mere pretender to learning. See also du Deffand, *passim.*

27. Thomas Percy (1729–1811), Bp of Dromore, 1782; editor of the *Reliques;* HW's occasional correspondent. In the heat of argument, Johnson referred to Percy's 'narrow mind,' but was willing to acknowledge his merit; see *Life of Johnson* iii. 272, 277–8, *et passim.*

28. Charles Blagden (1748–1820), M.D. Edinburgh, 1768; Kt, 1792; F.R.S., 1772, and secretary 1784–97; medical officer in the army till 1814; intimate friend of Sir Joseph Banks (dnb; William A. Shaw, *The Knights of England,* 1906, ii. 301; *Record of the Royal Society,* 3d edn, 1912, p. 208; Sylvester Douglas, Bn Glenbervie, *Diaries,* ed. Francis Bickley, 1928, ii. 186, *et passim*).

municated to find myself, but am very gently treated. I never would be in the least acquainted with Johnson, or as Boswell calls it, had not a just value for him, which the biographer imputes to my resentment for the Doctor's putting bad arguments (purposely out of Jacobitism) into the speeches which he wrote fifty years ago for my father in the *Gentleman's Magazine,* which I did not read then, or ever knew Johnson wrote till Johnson died, nor have looked at since.[29] Johnson's blind Toryism and known brutality kept me aloof, nor did I ever exchange a syllable with him; nay, I do not think I ever was in a room with him six times in my days. The first time I think was at the Royal Academy.[30] Sir Joshua[31] said, 'Let me present Dr Goldsmith to you'; he did. 'Now I will present Dr Johnson to you.'—'No,' said I, 'Sir Joshua, for Dr Goldsmith, pass—but you shall *not* present Dr Johnson to me.'

Some time after, Boswell came to me, said Dr J. was writing the lives of the poets, and wished I would give him anecdotes of Mr Gray. I said very coldly, I had given what I knew to Mr Mason.[32] B. hummed and hawed and then dropped, 'I suppose you know Dr J. does not admire Mr Gray'—Putting as much contempt as I could into my look and tone, I said, 'Dr Johnson don't!—humph!'—and with that monosyllable ended our interview[33]—After the Doctor's death, Burke, Sir Joshua Reynolds and Boswell sent an ambling circular letter to me begging subscriptions for a monument for him—the two last, I think impertinently, as they could not but know my opinion, and could not suppose I would contribute to a monument for one who had endeavoured, poor soul! to degrade my friend's superlative poetry—I would not deign to write an answer, but sent down word by my footman, as I would have done to parish officers with a brief, that I would not sub-

29. 'Mr Walpole . . . never was one of the true admirers of that great man. We may suppose a prejudice conceived . . . that when he made the speeches in Parliament for the *Gentleman's Magazine,* "he always took care to put Sir Robert Walpole in the wrong, and to say everything he could against the electorate of Hanover" ' (Boswell, *Johnson* iv. 314; see also ibid. notes 3, 5; i. 504).

30. The meeting with Goldsmith must have occurred between 1769 and 1773; but no record of it has been found.

31. Reynolds.

32. William Mason (1725–97), who published *The Poems of Mr. Gray. To which are prefixed Memoirs of his Life and Writings,* York, 1775 (Cole i. 353, *et passim*).

33. 'Lord Holland . . . said that whenever he [Boswell] came into a company where Horace Walpole was, Walpole would throw back his head, purse up his mouth very significantly, and not speak a word while Boswell remained' (Charles R. Leslie, *Autobiographical Recollections,* 1860, i. 155). Boswell recorded 25 April 1788: 'I found Mr Horace Walpole at home, just the same as ever: genteel, fastidious, priggish. . . . *Hory's* constitutional tranquillity, or affectation of it, and the *tout ensemble* of his connections and history, etc., etc., pleased me' (*Boswell Papers,* xvii. 102). Other interviews with Boswell are mentioned in HW to Gray 18 Feb. 1768, and to Mason 22 May 1781.

scribe.[34] In the two new volumes,[35] Johnson says—and very probably did, or is made to say, that Gray's poetry is *dull*, and that he was a *dull* man![36] The same oracle dislikes Prior, Swift and Fielding. If an elephant could write a book, perhaps one that had read a great deal would say that an Arabian horse is a very clumsy ungraceful animal— pass to a better chapter—

Burke has published another pamphlet against the French Revolution,[37] in which he attacks it still more grievously. The beginning is very good, but it is not equal, nor quite so injudicious as parts of its predecessor;[38] is far less brilliant, as well as much shorter;[39] but were it ever so long, his mind overflows with such a torrent of images, that he cannot be tedious. His invective against Rousseau is admirable, just and new.[40] Voltaire he passes almost contemptuously.[41] I wish he had dissected Mirabeau too:[42] and I grieve that he has omitted the violation of the consciences of the clergy;[43] nor stigmatized those universal plunderers, the National Assembly, who gorge themselves with eighteen *livres* a day,[44] which to many of them would three years ago have been astonishing opulence.

When you return, I shall lend you three volumes in quarto of another work with which you will be delighted. They are state letters in the reigns of Henry VIII, Mary, Elizabeth and James, being the correspondence of the Talbot and Howard families, given by a Duke of Norfolk[45] to the Herald's Office, where they have lain for a century neglected, buried under dust and unknown, till discovered by a Mr

34. 'A monument for him in Westminster Abbey was resolved upon soon after his death, and was supported by a most respectable contribution; but the Dean and Chapter of St Paul's having come to a resolution of admitting monuments there upon a liberal and magnificent plan, that Cathedral was afterwards fixed on, as the place in which a cenotaph should be erected to his memory' (Boswell, *Johnson* iv. 423). See also James Prior, *Life of . . . Edmund Burke*, 5th edn, 1854, p. 240.

35. That is, in Boswell's *Life*.

36. On Tuesday, 28 March 1775, Boswell and Johnson dined at the Thrales': 'He [Johnson] attacked Gray, calling him "a dull fellow" . . . "dull in company, dull in his closet, dull everywhere. He was dull in a new way, and that made people think him GREAT. He was a mechanical poet"' (ibid. ii. 327).

37. *A Letter from Mr Burke, to a Member of the National Assembly; in Answer to* some Objections to His Book on French Affairs, dated 19 Jan. 1791, published earlier in the year in France, and in London 21 May (*Times* 12, 20 May 1791).

38. *Reflections on the Revolution in France.*

39. It has 74 pages; the *Reflections* 360.

40. See pp. 31–42, *passim*.

41. Burke mentions Voltaire only once (p. 33).

42. Mirabeau is mentioned twice (pp. 16–17, 46).

43. While Burke does not mention the conscience of the clergy, he mentions the low and uneducated ecclesiastics who were made bishops (pp. 17–19); some of them, of course, replaced the nonjurors.

44. Cf. *ante* 10 July 1790, n. 15.

45. Henry Howard (1628–84), cr. (1672) E. of Norwich and Earl Marshal of England; 6th D. of Norfolk, 1677. The papers presented by him to the Herald's Office are called, in Lodge's publication, the 'Talbot

Lodge, a genealogist, who to gratify his passion procured to be made a Pursuivant.[46] Oh! how curious they are! Henry seizes an alderman[47] who refused to contribute to a benevolence,[48] sends him to the army on the borders, orders him to be exposed in the front line, and if that does not do, to be treated with the utmost rigour of military discipline.[49] His daughter Bess is not less a Tudor. The mean unworthy treatment of the Queen of Scots is striking;[50] and you will find how Elizabeth's jealousy of her crown and her avarice were at war, and how the more ignoble passion predominated. But the most amusing passage is one in a private letter, as it paints the awe of children for their parents a *little* differently from modern habitudes. Mr Talbot second son of the Earl of Shrewsbury,[51] was a member of the House of Commons and was married. He writes to the Earl his father, and tells him that a young woman of a very good character has been recommended to him for chambermaid to his wife, and if his Lordship does not disapprove of it, he will hire her.[52] There are many letters of news that are very entertaining too—but it is nine o'clock and I must go to Lady Cecilia's.

Friday.

The Conways, Mrs Damer, the Farrens,[53] and Lord Mt Edgcumbe

Papers' to distinguish them from the 'Howard Papers' which were still in the possession of the Dukes of Norfolk.

46. Edmund Lodge (1756–1839), Bluemantle Pursuivant-at-Arms, 1782; F.S.A., 1787; Lancaster Herald, 1793; Norroy, 1822, and Clarenceux, 1838; K.H., 1832. HW refers to his *Illustrations of British History, Biography and Manners in the Reigns of Henry VIII, Edward VI, Mary, Elizabeth, and James I, exhibited in a Series of Original Papers, selected from the Manuscripts of the . . . Families of Howard, Talbot, and Cecil,* not published until 27 May, the day after HW wrote the above passage (*St James's Chronicle* 14–17 May 1791; *Oracle* 25 May 1791). HW had heard of the work at least six weeks before its publication, possibly from George Nicol, for whom it was printed, and possibly from Lodge himself; see HW to Lord Buchan 7 April 1791; to Lodge 19 June 1795. HW's copy (MS Cat. C.3) was sold SH i. 166. A second edition appeared in 1791, and another, called the second edition on the title-page, in 1838.

47. Richard Rede (or Reed) (d. 1550), salter; Alderman of Farringdon Without 13 March 1544–30 March 1546; auditor 1538–40 (Alfred B. Beaven, *Aldermen of the City of London,* 1908–13, i. 156, ii. 31).

48. MS reads 'to a a benevolence.'

49. See edn 1838, i. 98–100.

50. See vols i and ii, *passim,* particularly (edn 1838) i. 458–64, 481–9, 504–7, 546–7; ii. 54–5, 224–8.

51. Gilbert Talbot (1552–1616), 2d but 1st surviving son of George (ca 1528–90), 6th E. of Shrewsbury; styled Lord Talbot 1582–90; 7th E. of Shrewsbury, 1590; m. (1568) Mary Cavendish (d. 1632), sister of William, 1st E. of Devonshire.

52. See edn 1838, ii. 21–2.

53. Elizabeth Farren, later Countess of Derby, and her mother: Margaret Wright (d. 1803), dau. of a publican or brewer of Water Lane, Liverpool, m. George Farren or Farran, surgeon and apothecary at Cork. For a time she acted in the provinces (DNB, *sub* Farren, Elizabeth; GEC, *sub* Derby; *Register Book of Marriages . . . of St George, Hanover Square, Vol. II—*

supped at the Johnstones. Lord Mount Edgcumbe said excellently, that *Mlle D'Éon is her own widow*.[54]

I wish I had seen you both in your court-*plis* at your presentation —but that is only one wish amongst a thousand.

East winds and blights have succeeded our April spring, as you guessed, but though I have been at Strawberry every week, I have caught no cold, I kindly thank you. Adieu!

To Mary Berry, Thursday 2 June 1791

Address: À Mademoiselle Mademoiselle Berry à la poste restante à Florence, Italie. Endorsed: 'Pd 1s.'
Posted 3 June ('Visitors'). On the cover in Mary Berry's hand: 'obliege.'

Berkeley Square, June 2, 1791.

No. 35.[1]

TO the tune of *The Cow with the Crumpledy Horn* etc.[2]

This is the note that nobody wrote;
This is the groom that carried the note that nobody wrote;
This is Ma'am Gunning who was so very cunning to examine the groom that carried the note that nobody wrote.

This is Ma'am Bowen to whom it was owing, that Miss Minify Gunning was so very cunning to examine the groom that carried the note that nobody wrote.

These are the Marquises shy of the horn, who caused the maiden all-for-*Lorn,* to become on a sudden so tatter'd and torn, that Miss Minify Gunning was so very cunning to examine the groom etc.

These are the two Dukes whose sharp rebukes made the two Marquises shy of the horn, and caused the maiden all-for-Lorn etc.

This is the General somewhat too bold, whose head was so hot, though his heart was so cold, who proclaim'd himself single before it was meet, and his wife and his daughter turn'd into the street, to please the two Dukes, whose sharp rebukes etc. etc. etc.[3]

1788 to 1809, ed. John H. Chapman, 1888, p. 163; GM 1803, lxxiii pt i. 602).
54. Cf. *post* ii. 266.

1. 'No. 45' (B).
2. I.e., 'The House that Jack Built.'

3. A somewhat different version of the parody appears in a letter of Joseph Cooper Walker (HW's occasional correspondent) to Thomas Percy, Bp of Dromore, 21 Aug. 1791; according to Walker, the lines, attributed 'to the widow of the late Col. St

This is not at all new; I have heard it once or twice imperfectly, but could not get a copy till now, and I think it will divert you for a moment, though the heroines are as much forgotten as Boadicia;[4] nor have I heard of them since their arrival at Dover.

Well! I have seen Madam D'Albany, who has not a ray of royalty about her. She has good eyes and teeth; but I think can have had no more beauty than remains, except youth. She is civil and easy, but German and ordinary.[5] Lady Ailesbury made a small assemblage for her on Monday, and my curiosity is satisfied.[6] Mr Conway and Lady A[ilesbury], Lord and Lady Frederic Campbell, and Mrs E. Hervey and Mrs Hervey[7] breakfasted with me that morning at Strawberry, at the desire of the latter, who had never been there, and whose commendations were so promiscuous, that I saw she did not at all understand the style of the place. The day was north-easterly and cold and wanting rain, and I was not sorry to return to town. I hope in five months to like staying there much better.[8]

George . . . are now handing about here [Dublin], and [are] much admired' (John Nichols, *Illustrations of the Literary History of the Eighteenth Century, 1817–58*, vii. 716). Still another version was used as the text for a satirical print, 'This is the House that Jack Built,' published 2 Jan. 1792 (BM, *Satiric Prints* vi. 955–6, No. 8163); see also 'The For *Lorn* Maiden,' *The Scots Magazine*, 1791, liii. 505.

4. Less than a month earlier, 5 May, a catchpenny pamphlet on the affair had been published: *The Case of Miss Gunning, Impartially Stated and Discussed: in a Letter from a Barrister, Addressed to the Marquis of Blandford*, dated at the end, 'Lincoln's Inn, May 3, 1791.' See *The Oracle* 5 May 1791. The pamphlet is composed of extracts from Mrs Gunning's *Letter* and Bowen's *Statement of Facts*, plus a few dull remarks by the author.

5. 'She must, no doubt, have been very pretty in early youth. She had fine eyes and teeth, but her figure was not graceful. There was nothing of the ideal beauty about her which one would have imagined as the object of Alfieri's dreams of bliss; but she must have been very much admired, for all the travellers, as I have been told, used to call her the Queen of Hearts. . . . She wrote plain, sensible letters, and was not devoid of intelligence' (Cornelia Knight,

Autobiography, 1861, ii. 253–4). Miss Knight's account refers to the period, ca 1784.

6. Mrs Damer wrote to Mary Berry, Sunday 29 May 1791: 'I shall leave a corner to tell you how Mr W[alpole] looks, as this will only go on Tuesday, and I am to see him tomorrow, after his return from Strawberry, and to carry him to my mother's, who has a party for the Comtesse d'Albanie. She is very pleasant, perfectly easy, and not just in the common style. I have seen her several times since I came. She was very civil to me (the last time I was at Paris, I mean, not now), which, *de mon mieux*, I always wish to return.' On Tuesday morning, 31 May, she added: 'I went with my letter [from Mary Berry], to B[erkeley] Square, meaning to go up and sit a little with him, read him some of my letter, but down he came in one [of] his grand fusses, before I was farther than the bottom of the staircase, determined to get to my Mother's before what he called the crowd came' (*Berry Papers* 36–7).

7. 'Elizabeth Beckford [Elizabeth March], a niece [stepdaughter] of Alderman Beckford, married to ——' (B). See *ante* 8 Nov. 1790.

8. When Mrs Damer went to Berkeley Square on Monday night (see n. 6), HW 'was rather tired of a breakfast which he

I have had no letter from you since Monday sennight, but as I had three almost at once,[9] and as Mrs Damer received one two days ago,[10] I am in no fright about you;[11] and indeed I do not like your sitting and writing so much, which is bad for you. All the difference now is, that I have nothing to answer; and having nothing to tell, this will be very brief.

Mrs Damer, who returned in such Spanish health, has already caught an English north-eastern cold, with pains in all her limbs and a little fever, and yesterday was not above two hours out of bed.[12] Her father came to me from her before dinner, and left her better, and I shall go to her presently; and this not departing till tomorrow, I hope to give you a still more favourable account. These two days may boldly assume the name of June without the courtesy of England. Such weather makes me wish myself at Strawberry, whither I shall betake myself on Saturday for three days; but shall not be able to settle yet—Next week I must go to Doctors' Commons—don't be alarmed—I have not heard a syllable against either of you[13]—but a poor old gentlewoman in the country[14] has made me her executor

gave . . . to my Uncle [Lord Frederick Campbell] and Mrs Hervey (at which he would not have me), Miss [Hervey], my Mother, etc., etc., but only in mind, and that seemed quite revived by the sight of Mrs Buller, whom he saw in Warwick Street [Lady Ailesbury's], and whom we set home afterwards' (*Berry Papers* 37).

9. Cf. preceding letter, n. 18.

10. It was written from Florence, 17 May 1791, and Mrs Damer received it 30 May (*Berry Papers* 36). Cf. n. 6.

11. On Tuesday, 24 May, Mrs Damer called on HW and wrote the same day to Mary Berry: 'He looked well, but seemed discomposed at having heard the night before from Miss Cambridge that she had had a letter from your sister in which she said that she was well, but that she did not think you so.' Three days later she wrote: 'Mr W[alpole] seems less uneasy about what he heard from Mr [?Miss] Cambridge than I expected. He depends on your youth; and the certainty he feels of your return, with the flattering prospect of enjoying your society, makes it not easy to put him out of spirits; that I, for the pleasure of indulging my own melancholy ideas, do not try, you will believe' (*Berry Papers* 32–3).

12. Mrs Damer wrote to Mary Berry 31 May: 'Everybody tells me that I am well, that I look so, and so forth, but today I am more than ever convinced that they *may* mistake. I have a sad cold, and feel a weight and languor that makes me thoroughly uncomfortable, not that I believe it is anything serious, but I have sat up too late, and the weather has been *truly English*—causes sufficient, *you* well know. I am now determined to obey your *cura ut valeas* as far as lays in my power. . . . I think that I am better' (*Berry Papers* 38–9).

13. The consistory court, where divorce cases were tried, sat in Doctors' Commons.

14. This was 'Mrs Day,' mentioned by Mrs Damer in her letter to Mary Berry 7 July 1791: 'I called upon him [HW] this morning and found him rather fidgety, and uncomfortable, but then he was expecting *sa chère soeur*, and the affair of Mrs Day, which you know, is on his mind' (*Berry Papers* 48). 'Mrs Day' was Carey Daye of Chichester, mother of Elizabeth Hunter Daye and Rachel Davison Daye, to whom jointly HW left £3500 in his will. The family connection which HW mentions was through Catherine Daye (d. 1775), HW's half-sister; but the exact nature of

and trustee for her two daughters—and they need not alarm you neither—though somehow or other there was a connection between the
families, which it is not proper to explain by the post, and I must repair into the City to prove the will—some trouble I shall have, for
there are disagreeable circumstances attending both daughters who
are not of the *compos*-ite order—well! one must do the best one can,
and make the best of everything. It is a chequered world, and surely
I have no reason to complain of my lot in it!—a truly hard fate is that
of two of the most amiable young women in the world,[15] punished
without a fault, and before they were capable of having a fault, not
for the fault, but for the virtues of their father!—but Justice is not
only blind, as she ought to be. when sitting on the bench in her scar-
let robe and furs, but when she is at home *en famille!*

Friday noon, 3rd.

I sat with Mrs D. an hour last night and found her much mended.
She was quite alive, and her hand not near so hot as the preceding
evening. Today the message is, 'Much better'—and if she proved so,
she told me she would ask your friend Mrs Cholmeley to meet me
there this evening—My lawyer[16] is just come about my executorship,
and I must finish abruptly—Adieu!

PS. Hastings made his defence yesterday, but the trial is put off till
next session,[17] as the Parliament is to be prorogued next week[18]—
nothing decided about the Russian war,[19] nor a Secretary of State yet,
but Dundas, it is said, is to be the man.[20]

the connection is not clear. In his will HW
refers to the sisters as 'next of kin' to Catherine Daye. They were probably her nieces;
but it is possible that they were her half-
sisters, for it is stated in HW's father's will
that Catherine's mother was Carey Daye.
Charles Churchill was joint trustee with
HW for the Daye sisters (*post* 4 July 1791).

15. Mary and Agnes Berry.

16. Probably Robert Blake of Essex
Street, the Strand; see *post* 24 Nov. 1795.

17. For Hastings's defence, see *The History of the Trial of Warren Hastings*, 1796,
pt iv. 80–104. The trial was deferred to the
first Tuesday of the next session of Parliament (ibid. 104).

18. On Friday, 10 June, it was prorogued
to 16 Aug. 1791 (*Oracle* 11 June 1791), but
was further prorogued to 31 Jan. 1792.

19. In his message proroguing Parliament, 10 June, George III said: 'I am not
yet enabled to inform you of the result of
the steps which I have taken with a view to
the re-establishment of peace between Russia and the Porte: it is my earnest wish that
this important object may be effectuated in
such a manner as may contribute to the
preservation and maintenance of the general tranquillity of Europe' (*Oracle* 11 June
1791).

20. He was; see following letter.

To Mary Berry, Wednesday 8 June 1791

Address: À Mademoiselle Mademoiselle Berry à la poste restante à Florence, Italie. Endorsed: 'Pd 1s.'
Posted 10 June ('Visitors').

Berkeley Square, June 8, 1791.

No. 36.[1]

YOUR No. 34 that was interrupted, and of which the last date was of May 24th, I received on the 6th, and if I could find a fault, it would be in the length, for I do not approve of your writing so much in such hot weather, for, be it known to you, ladies, that from the first of the month, June is not more June at Florence.[2] My hay is crumbling away, and I have ordered it to be cut, as a sure way of bringing rain.

I have a selfish reason too for remonstrating against long letters; I feel the season advancing, when mine will be piteous short, for what can I tell you from Twickenham in the next three or four months? Scandal from Richmond and Hampton Court, or robberies at my own door? The latter indeed are blown already. I went to Strawberry on Saturday, to avoid the birthday crowd and squibs and crackers: at six I drove to Lord Strafford's, where his goods are to be sold by auction,[3] his sister, Lady Anne[4] intending to pull down the house and rebuild it. I returned a quarter before seven, and in the interim between my Gothic gate[5] and Ashe's nursery[6] a gentleman and gentlewoman in a one-horse chair and in the broad face of the sun had

1. 'No. 46' (B).
2. That is, the weather in England in June was as warm as that of Florence in June.
3. 'By Mr Christie, on the premises, on Friday next, and following day [10–11 June], at eleven o'clock, all the neat household furniture, china, linen, pictures, prints, library of books, ale, table beer, pheasants, pea-fowls, poultry, ten pair of capital orange trees, greenhouse plants, and other effects, late the property of the Earl of Strafford, deceased, at his late villa, at Twickenham, Middlesex. To be viewed on Wednesday [8 June]; catalogues may be then had on the premises' (*Oracle* 6 June 1791).
4. 'Lady Anne Wentworth, married to the Right Honourable Thomas [i.e., William] Conolly' (?B, Wright vi. 437).
5. On the western boundary of the pleasure grounds at SH, midway between SH and the southwestern corner of the grounds; it opened (theoretically) upon the road from SH to Hampton Court. Ash's house and nursery joined the pleasure grounds of SH on the south. See 'Genesis of SH' 85, fig. 34; *SH Accounts*, ad fin.: 'A Plan of Strawberry Hill . . . in 1797'; COLE i. 178 (where the gate was placed erroneously on the southeast boundary), *et passim.*
6. 'John Ash, nursery and seedsman, Twickenham, Middlesex,' whose card was printed by Kirgate at SH. Thomas Ashe, presumably his father, had served Pope and HW; see *SH Accounts* 45, *et passim.*

been robbed by a single highwayman *sans* mask.[7] Ashe's mother and sister stood and saw it, but having no notion of a robbery at such an hour, in the high road, and before their men had left work, concluded it was an acquaintance of the robbées.[8] I suppose Lady Cecilia will not descend from her bedchamber to the drawing room without a life-guard man. She quits her house at Hampton this autumn, her term ending then, and the proprietor asking £7,000 for it, though valued by Christie but at £1,500.

The Duke of Bedford[9] eclipsed the whole birthday[10] by his clothes,[11] equipage and servants; six of the latter walked on the sides of the coach to keep off the crowd—or to tempt it, for their liveries were worth an argosy.[12] The Prince was gorgeous too.[13] The latter is to give Madame d'Albany a dinner—she has been introduced to Mrs

7. Only one newspaper item that might refer to this incident has been found: 'Saturday night [4 June] Mr Dean of Twickenham was stopped on Hounslow Heath by a single highwayman, who robbed him of his gold watch, with which he got clear off' (*St James's Chronicle* 4–7 June 1791).

8. For another highway robbery near SH, 26 Aug. 1791, when two ladies and a gentleman were robbed of a watch by two footpads, see *The Oracle* 31 Aug. 1791. See also ibid. 30 Sept. 1791.

9. Francis Russell (1765–1802), 5th D. of Bedford; HW's occasional correspondent; the 'noble lord' addressed in Burke's *A Letter to a Noble Lord*, 1796.

10. The King's Birthday, 4 June.

11. 'The dress of his Grace . . . cost no less a sum than £500. The coat and breeches were of a brown striped silk, shot with green; the ground of the waistcoat white. The embroidery composed of silver, blue foil, and stones, forming the most beautiful wreaths of flowers. All the seams were covered with an embroidery, the same as the border and the ground of the suit, with single brilliants and silver spangles' (*St James's Chronicle* 4–7 June 1791).

12. His carriage 'was so superb as totally to dim and eclipse everything else in the carriage way.' It was 'a vis-à-vis, the most superb and splendid carriage that has been seen at St James's for many years, the body

cream colour, with the arms richly emblazoned, the mouldings and carriage richly carved and gilt; braces of red Morocco leather, the hammer-cloth, covered with a profusion of large gold tassels; the liveries were in the same costly style; the servants' hats, with broad gold lace and white feathers, are said to have cost twelve guineas each' (*Oracle* 6 June 1791). According to *The St James's Chronicle*, loc. cit., the carriage cost £1600 and the hammercloth 400 guineas; 'his attendants were superbly habited in liveries of the finest cloth, the seams covered with rich gold lace; the waistcoats were also laced in a very costly manner. Each livery stood the Duke in £70 exclusive of the hats.'

13. 'The Prince of Wales [wore] a bottle-green and claret-coloured striped silk coat and breeches, and silver tissue waistcoat, very richly embroidered in silver and stones, and coloured silks in curious devices and bouquets of flowers. The coat and waistcoat embroidered down the seams, and spangled all over the body. The coat cuffs the same as the waistcoat. The breeches were likewise covered with spangles. Diamond buttons to the coat, waistcoat, and breeches, which with his brilliant diamond epaulette, and sword, made the whole dress form a most magnificent appearance' (*St James's Chronicle* 4–7 June 1791).

Fitzherbert. You know I used to call Mrs Cosway's concerts,[14] Charon's boat—now methinks London is so. I am glad Mrs Cosway[15] is with you; she is pleasing,—but surely it is odd to drop a child[16] and her husband and country all in a breath!

I am glad you have had the comfort of Miss Craufurd,[17] and are *disfranchised* of the exiles. We have several, I am told, here, but I strictly confine myself to those I knew formerly at Paris,[18] and who all are quartered on Richmond Green. I went to them on Sunday evening, but found them gone to Lord Fitzwilliam's, the next house to Madame de Boufflers, to hear his organ, whither I followed them, and returned with them. The Comtesse Emilie played on her harp, then we all united at lotto; I went home at twelve unrobbed, and Lord Fitzwilliam, who asked much after you both, was to set out the next morning for Dublin, though intending to stay there but four days, and be back in three weeks.

I am sorry you did not hear all Monsieur de Lally Tolendal's tragedy[19] of which I have had a good account. I like his tribute to his

14. Maria Louisa Catherine Cecilia Hadfield (1759–1838) m. (1781) Richard Cosway (ca 1742–1821), the miniature painter. She attracted considerable attention for her own miniatures, drawings, and etchings, but was also well known for her elaborate concerts and entertainments, which HW occasionally attended. From 1781 to 1784 the Cosways lived at 4 Berkeley Street, Berkeley Square; from 1784 to 1791 at Schomberg House, Pall Mall (George C. Williamson, *Richard Cosway, R.A.*, 1905, *passim*). HW had a drawing, 'the Death of Hector, a grand composition by Maria Cosway,' sold Lond. 1253.

15. Expanded by Mary Berry from HW's 'C.' According to a letter which Mrs Cosway wrote 24 May 1830, she went at this time to Florence with her brother George and Lady Wright, because of ill health resulting from the birth of her daughter two years earlier. Her husband's biographer, George C. Williamson, saw no reason to doubt her statement, although it is known that she later travelled abroad with the singer Marchesi. She remained in Italy for almost three years (Williamson, op. cit. 22, 29–30, 49–50). See also *The Times* 19 May

1791 for 'Lines . . . addressed to Mrs Cosway, now at Florence.'

16. Louisa Paolina Angelica Cosway (1789–96), their only child, named for her godmother, the Countess of Albany; her godfather, General Paoli; and her mother's friend, Angelica Kauffmann. Both her father and mother painted portraits of her (Williamson, op. cit. 14, 22–3, 82, and illustrations facing pp. 22, 24, 72). Cf. *post* 16 Aug. 1796.

17. See *ante* 17 July 1790. Mrs Damer wrote to Mary Berry 31 May 1791: 'I am well acquainted with the Craufords, and remember the lady you mention. It is a very numerous family, everywhere to be met with, and with which one passes much time' (*Berry Papers* 38).

18. HW most frequently mentions Mme and Comtesse Amélie de Boufflers, the Duchesse de Biron, Lally-Tollendal, the Princesse d'Hénin, Mme de Cambis, and Mme de Roncherolles, all of whom lived at one time or another at Richmond. Cf. *ante* 11 March 1791.

19. Trophime-Gérard de Lally-Tollendal (1751–1830), Comte, later Marquis, de Lally-Tollendal; son of Thomas Arthur

father's memory.[20] Of French politics you must be tired—and so am I. Nothing appears to me to promise their chaos duration; consequently I expect more chaos, the sediment of which is commonly despotism. Poland ought to make the French blush[21]—but that they are not apt to do on *any* occasion—let us return to Strawberry. The House of Sebright[22] breakfasted there with me on Monday; the daughter[23] had given me a drawing,[24] and I owed her a civility. After dinner I returned to town, and went to Mrs Damer, whom I found quite recovered and intending to go out the next day; as I conclude she did. She proposed to ask the Pepyses, Mrs Cholmely, and Mrs Buller to

Lally (1702–66), Baron de Tollendal, who was unjustly executed for treason. He emigrated to Switzerland in 1790, but at the date of HW's letter he was in Florence, from which his *Lettre écrite au très honorable Edmund Burke* was dated '20 juin 1791.' His tragedy was *Le Comte de Strafford*, a five-act tragedy in verse, based on the life of Thomas Wentworth (1593–1641), 1st E. of Strafford; it remained in manuscript until 1795, when it was published in French in London (NBG; Bibl. Nat. Cat.); in the same year he published an *Essai sur la vie de T. Wentworth, Comte de Strafford* (ibid.).

20. Learning the identity of his father only the day before his father was executed, Lally-Tollendal dedicated himself to the rehabilitation of his father's memory: in 1779 he published *Mémoires et plaidoyers présentés au Conseil d'État pour la mémoire du général Thomas-Arthur, comte de Lally;* in 1781, *Mémoire du comte de Lally-Tollendal en réponse au dernier libelle de M. Duval d'Éprémenil;* and in 1789, *Mémoire apologétique de Lally-Tollendal* (NBG). HW, who defended his own father on all occasions, would naturally sympathize with Lally-Tollendal's point of view.

21. On 3–5 May 1791 there was a 'state revolution' in the government of Poland, the chief points of which were diametrically opposed to the changes which had been made in France: (1) the Roman Catholic religion became the state religion, but universal toleration was allowed; (2) the ancient rights of the nobility were confirmed; (3) the rights of the third estate were renewed and established; (4) all strangers (foreigners) were to enjoy liberty; (5) the government was divided into three branches: legislative, executive, and judicial; (6) the Diet was to have the legislative power; (7) the King and Council (of six ministers) to have the executive; (8) the throne to be hereditary, and to descend to the House of Saxony. For a full discussion of the revolution, see *The Oracle* 23, 28 May 1791.

22. 'Sir J., Lady, and Miss Sebrights' ('Visitors,' 6 June 1791). Sir John Saunders Sebright (1725–94), 6th Bt of Besford, Worcs, and of Beechwood near Flamstead, Herts; entered the army, 1741; general, 1782; M. P. Bath 1763–74, 1775–80; m. (1766) Sarah Knight (d. 1813), 3d dau. of Edward Knight of Wolverley, Worcs. They had two daughters. Henrietta (1770–1840), m. (1794) Henry ('Cupid') Lascelles, later (1820) 2d E. of Harewood. Apropos of her engagement, Queen Charlotte wrote of her to Lady Harcourt, July 1794, as 'sedate and retired,' lacking in beauty and fortune, but 'she has been well educated . . . [and] I hear is possessed of many talents' (*Harcourt Papers* vi. 44). The younger daughter, Mary Anne (ca 1779–1854), m. (1811) Nicholas Lewis Fenwick of Terrington, Norfolk. For an account of the family, and for portraits of Sir John and Lady Sebright, see *Victoria History of Hertfordshire: Hertfordshire Families,* ed. Duncan Warrand, 1907, pp. 216–17; GM 1855, n.s. xliii. 110; *Old Westminsters;* GM 1814, n.s. vii. 97.

23. Henrietta.

24. Not further identified; sold Lond. 1258, in a 'folio, with leaves containing 50 pencil sketches of portraits, etc.; by Lady Diana Beauclerc, Thomas Walpole, Mrs Damer, Miss Sebright,' etc., to Graves.

meet me on Friday evening, to which I willingly consented. More willingly than I should have applauded your dancing reels in sultry weather, though I have as much faith in your both dancing well, as in everything you both undertake. Thank you for reminding me of falls—in one sense I am more liable to them, than when you left me, for I am sensibly much weaker since my last fit; but that weakness makes me move much slower, and depend more on assistance—in a word, there is no care I do not take of myself; my heart is set on installing you at Clivden, and it will not be my fault if I do not preserve myself till then. If another summer is added, it will be happiness indeed—but I am not presumptuous, and count the days only till November. I am glad you on your parts repose till your journey commences, and go not into sultry crowded lodgings at the Ascension.[25] I was at Venice in summer, and thought airing on stinking ditches pestilential,[26] after enjoying the delicious nights on the Ponte di Trinità at Florence in a linen nightgown and a straw hat with *improvisatori*, and music and the coffee houses open with ices—at least such were the customs fifty years ago!

The Duke of St Albans has cut down all the brave old trees at Hanworth, and consequently reduced his park to what it issued from, Hounslow Heath—nay, he has hired a meadow next to mine for the benefit of embarkation, and there lie all the good old corpses of oaks, ashes and chestnuts, directly before *your* windows, and blocking up one of my views of the river![27]—but so impetuous is the rage for building, that his Grace's timber will, I trust, not annoy us long. There will soon be one street from London to Brentford, ay and from London to every village ten miles round. Lord Camden[28] has just let ground at Kentish Town for building fourteen hundred houses—nor do I wonder—London is I am certain much fuller than ever I saw it. I have twice this spring been going to stop my coach in Piccadilly to inquire what was the matter, thinking there was a mob—not at all; it was only passengers. Nor is there any complaint of depopulation from the country: Bath shoots out into new crescents, circuses, squares

25. 2 June 1791.

26. MS reads 'pestinential.'

27. It appears from 'A Plan of Strawberry Hill . . . in 1797' in *SH Accounts,* ad fin., that the Duke of St Albans must have hired the meadow from Mr Davenport (for whom see *post* 22 Aug., 18 Sept. 1795). It was to the east of the meadow marked 'O' on that plan. HW's view to the southeast would have been blocked.

28. Charles Pratt (1714–94), cr. (1786) E. Camden; HW's occasional correspondent. The property at Kentish Town 'became vested in him in right of his wife' (Daniel Lysons, *Environs of London,* 1792–6, iii. 345).

every year. Birmingham, Manchester, Hull and Liverpool would
serve any king in Europe for a capital, and would make the Empress
of Russia's mouth water. Of the war with Catherine Slayczar I hear
not a breath, and thence conjecture it is dozing into peace.

Mr Dundas has kissed hands[29] for Secretary of State; and Bishop
Barrington[30] of Salisbury is transferred to Durham, which he affected
not to desire,[31] having large estates by his wife[32] in the south—but
from the Triple Mitre downwards it is almost always true what I
said some years ago, that 'nolo episcopari is Latin for, *I lie.'*—Tell it
not in Gath that I say so, for I am to dine tomorrow at the Bishop
of London's[33] at Fulham with Hannah *Bonner,* my *imprimée.*[34] This
morning I went with Lysons the Reverend to see Dulwich College
founded in 1619 by Alleyn[35] a player, which I had never seen in my
many days. We were received by a smart divine[36] *très bien poudré*
and with black satin breeches—but they are giving new wings and red

29. 8 June (*Oracle* 9 June 1791).

30. Hon. Shute Barrington (1734–1826),
6th son of John Shute, 1st Vct Barrington;
Bp of Llandaff, 1769; of Salisbury, 1782;
and of Durham, 1791. His appointment to
'the valuable see of Durham' is mentioned
in *The Oracle* 10 June 1791. The previous
incumbent, Thomas Thurlow, brother to
the Lord Chancellor, had died 27 May
1791.

31. 'Dr Barrington's appointment to the
see of Durham was at the express command of the King, and without the slightest solicitation on the part of his Lordship,
who did not expect the promotion. He was
preparing to set out for his bishopric at
Salisbury when he received a letter from Mr
Pitt, announcing his Majesty's wishes, and
that it afforded him very sincere pleasure
in communicating to him the appointment'
(*St James's Chronicle* 16–18 June 1791). In
1762 the see of Durham was worth £6000 a
year, while Salisbury was worth only £3000
(*Correspondence of King George III,* ed.
Sir John Fortescue, 1927–8, i. 36, 40).

32. Jane Guise (ca 1733–1807), only dau.
of Sir John Guise, 4th Bt, of Elmore, Glos;
m. (1770) as 2d wife, Hon. Shute Barrington. On the death in 1783 of her brother,
Sir William Guise, 5th and last Bt, she inherited the family estates in Gloucester-
shire and (through her mother) at Monge-
well, Oxon. See DNB, *sub* Barrington, Shute;
Burke, *Peerage,* 1937, p. 1132, *sub* Guise;
GEC (*Baronetage* iii. 219 n).

33. Beilby Porteus.

34. Hannah More, whose *Bishop Bonner's Ghost* was printed at SH in 1789.

35. Edward Alleyn (1566–1626). For Lysons's account of him, of Dulwich College
(including two views of it), and of the pictures there, see *The Environs of London,*
1792–6, i. 86–118.

36. Following quotation of this passage,
William Young, in his *History of Dulwich
College,* 1889, i. 465 n, says: 'The smart
divine must have been the Rev. Thomas
Jenyns Smith, preacher 1785–1830.' Thomas
Jenyns Smith (or Smyth) (ca 1759–1830), of
Brasenose College, Oxford; Fellow 1782–
1830; usher (1782–5) and preacher (1785–
1830) at Dulwich College. A short time before his death he was described as having
'not a little of the *petit-maître* in his dress,
language, and habits . . . "all primroses
and violets" . . . "eternal coxcomb"'
(ibid. ii. 377–8, *et passim;* GM 1830, c pt i.
650; Joseph Foster, *Alumni Oxonienses
. . . 1715–1886,* 1887–8). He was Lysons's
contemporary at Oxford.

satin breeches to the good old hostel too, and destroying a gallery with a very rich ceiling, and nothing will remain of ancient but the front, and an hundred mouldy portraits,[37] among apostles,[38] sibyls[39] and kings of England.[40] On Sunday I shall settle at Strawberry; and then woe betide you on post days! I cannot make news without straw.

The Johnstones are going to Bath for the healths of both; so Richmond will be my only staple. Adieu all three!

To Mary Berry, Tuesday 14 June 1791

Address: À Mademoiselle Mademoiselle Berry à la poste restante à Florence, Italie. Endorsed: 'Pd 1s.'
Posted 17 June ('Visitors').

Strawberry Hill, June 14, 1791.

No. 37.[1]

I PITY you! what a dozen or fifteen unentertaining letters are you going to receive! for here I am, unlikely to have anything to tell you worth reading: You had better come back incontinently—but pray do not prophesy any more; you have been the death of our summer, and we are in close mourning for it in coals and ashes. It froze hard

37. In 1791 the picture collection at Dulwich comprised the bequests of the founder (28 pictures in all) and William Cartwright (d. 1687). The second bequest consisted originally of 239 pictures, but only about 80 are now identifiable (*Catalogue of the Pictures in the Gallery of Alleyn's College of God's Gift at Dulwich*, [Dulwich], 1926, pp. iv–vi). See also Young, op. cit. i. 470–82.

38. In his diary under 10 Nov. 1620 Alleyn noted that he bought fourteen heads (Christ, Our Lady, and Twelve Apostles) 'att noble a peec.' After quoting the passage, Lysons observes: 'These are in the audit-room [at the south end of the gallery], and very wretched performances they are' (*Environs* i. 117). They have now dis-

appeared (Young, op. cit. ii. 193; *Catalogue of the Pictures . . . at Dulwich* 258, *et passim*).

39. 'These are, if possible, more destitute of artistic merit than the heads of the Kings and Queens' (*Environs* i. 116).

40. 'These are reproductions by a very inferior craftsman of the conventional portraits. They have no artistic value, but possess some interest from their association with the Founder. He seems to have been in the habit of buying his pictures in the gross' (*Catalogue of the Pictures . . . at Dulwich* 258).

———

1. 'No. 47' (B).

last night: I went out for a moment to look at my haymakers and was starved—the contents of an English June are, hay and ice, orange-flowers and rheumatisms! I am now cowering over the fire.[2] Mrs Hobart had announced a rural breakfast at Sans Souci[3] last Saturday; nothing being so pastoral as a fat grandmother[4] in a row of houses on Ham Common. It rained early in the morning; she dispatched post-boys—for want of cupids and zephyrs, to stop the nymphs and shepherds who tend their flocks in Pall Mall and St James's Street, but half of them missed the couriers and arrived.[5] Mrs Montagu was more splendid yesterday morning and breakfasted seven hundred persons on opening her great room, and the room with the hangings of feathers.[6] The King and Queen had been with her last week[7]—I should

2. 'So great a change of weather seldom happens as has taken place since Monday sennight [6 June]. On that day the glass stood at 75°, and people knew no place too cool to sit in; Sunday and Monday last [12–13 June] the glass was so low as 50, and fires and greatcoats began to appear' (St James's Chronicle 14–16 June 1791).

3. Her villa on Ham Common. HW wrote to Lady Ossory 7 July 1781 that Mrs Hobart, 'having made as many conquests as the King of Prussia, has borrowed the name of that hero's villa for her hut on Ham Common.' See also HW to Lady Ossory 10 Nov. 1782, 27 June 1792.

4. Mrs Hobart had several grandchildren; see Burke, Peerage, 1928, p. 386, sub Buckinghamshire.

5. The breakfast was postponed a week; see following letter.

6. At Montagu House in Portman Square (now No. 22 Portman Square): 'On Monday [13 June 1791] at noon a numerous and splendid company of the nobility, foreign ambassadors, illustrious travellers, and persons of distinction, were assembled by invitation to participate of an elegant breakfast, and to view the apartments.

'Two new rooms deserve the particular notice of the connoisseur: a magnificent drawing-room, designed by Bonomi; the centre piece of the ceiling charmingly painted by Rigaud; the beautiful columns of verde antico executed by Bartoli; the chimney-piece by Westmacott; the carvings and gildings by Nelson and Borgnis. The room is hung with white figured damask; the curtains are of white satin fringed with gold; the chandeliers and large looking-glasses are superb; and the whole is an assemblage of art and magnificence which we have never witnessed in a private room.

'The other apartment particularly noticed is the feather-room: the walls are wholly covered with feathers, artfully sewed together, and forming beautiful festoons of flowers and other fanciful decorations. The most brilliant colours, the produce of all climates, have wonderful effects on a feather ground of a dazzling whiteness.

'This room was designed by Bonomi, but executed by Mrs Montagu herself, assisted only by a few female attendants, instructed for that purpose' (St James's Chronicle 11–14 June 1791). See R. Huchon, Mrs Montagu, 1907, pp. 212–21; Mrs Montagu, ed. Reginald Blunt, [1923], passim. The Oracle 17 Jan. 1791 estimated the complete cost of the house at about £27,000.

7. Queen Charlotte and five of the princesses had been at Montagu House a week earlier, 6 June, but the King was not there. Mrs Montagu wrote to Mrs Carter in that month: 'The honour and the delight I received by her Majesty's and the Princesses' visit, no pen can describe, no paper contain. All that a great mind and benevolent heart can inspire appears in every word the Queen speaks, and every look and gesture can express. The Princesses are beyond all description charming. The joy of the day I have lived on ever since, and the fa-

like to have heard the orations she had prepared on the occasion. I
was neither city mouse nor country mouse. I did dine at Fulham on
Saturday with the Bishop of London; Mrs Boscawen, Mrs Garrick
and Hannah More were there and Dr Beattie,[8] whom I had never
seen: he is quiet, simple and cheerful, and pleased me—There ends
my tale, this instant Tuesday! How shall I fill a couple of pages more
by Friday morning? Oh! ye ladies on the Common, and ye uncommon ladies in London, have pity on a poor gazetteer, and supply me
with eclogues or royal panegyrics! Moreover—or rather moreunder, I
have had no letter from you these ten days, though the east wind has
been as constant as Lord Derby.[9] I say not this in reproach as you are
so kindly punctual, but as it stints me from having a single paragraph
to answer. I do not admire specific responses to every article—but
they are great resources on a dearth.

　　Madame de Boufflers is ill of a fever,[10] and the Duchesse de Biron
goes next week to Swisserland[11]—*mais qu'est que cela vous fait?* I
must eke out this with a few passages that I think will divert you
from the heaviest of all books, Mr Malone's Shakespeare in ten thick
octavos[12] with notes that are an extract of all the opium that is spread
through the works of all the bad playwrights of that age—mercy on
the poor gentleman's patience! Amongst his other indefatigable re-
searches, he has discovered some lists of effects in the custody of the
property-man[13] to the Lord Admiral's[14] company of players in 1598.
Of those effects he has given eight pages[15]—you shall be off for a few

tigue, etc., of the succeeding days have not
subdued my health and spirits' (*Mrs Montagu*, ed. Blunt, ii. 257–8; *St James's
Chronicle* 11–14 June 1791).

　8. James Beattie (1735–1803), Hon.
LL.D., Oxford, 1773; poet and divine.

　9. To Miss Farren.

　10. Mme de Boufflers wrote to Gustavus
III of Sweden 22 June 1791: 'J'ai la fièvre
depuis trois semaines, et pour tout autre
objet je ne serais pas même en état d'écrire;
mais Mme la Duchesse de Biron, qui quitte
l'Angleterre pour aller en Suisse et qui
passe par Aix-la-Chapelle pour éviter la
France, m'offre une occasion à laquelle je
ne puis me refuser' ('Lettres de Gustave III
. . . [et] la Comtesse de Boufflers,' *Actes de
l'académie nationale . . . de Bordeaux*,
1898, lx. 422).

　11. She was in Paris before 10 Sept. 1791

(*Harcourt Papers* viii. 344–5), but was
forced to flee from France and return to
England in July–August 1792 (*Mrs Montagu*, ed. Reginald Blunt, [1923] ii. 285–6).

　12. Published in 1790. HW's copy (MS
Cat. H.2, sold SH iii. 48) in 1938 was in the
possession of Miss Margaret A. M. Macalis-
ter of Cambridge. It has a few MS notes by
HW.

　13. Philip Henslowe (d. 1616), theatrical
manager whose diary and papers are the
source of much information about the
Elizabethan stage.

　14. Charles Howard (ca 1536–1624), cr.
(1554) Bn Howard of Effingham and (1597)
E. of Nottingham; Lord High Admiral
1585–1619. For an account of his company
of actors, see E. K. Chambers, *The Elizabethan Stage*, 1923, ii. 134–92.

　15. Vol. i pt ii. 300–7.

items; viz; 'My Lord Caffe's (Caiaphas) gercken (jerkin) and his hoose (hose): one rocke, one tombe, one Hellemought (Hellmouth), two stepelles, and one chyme of belles: one chaine of dragons, two coffenes, one bulles head, one vylter, one goste's crown, and one frame for the heading in black Jone: one payer of stayers for Fayeton; and bought a robe for to goo invisabell.'[16] The pair of stairs for Phaeton reminds one of Hogarth's strollers dressing in a barn, where Cupid on a ladder is reaching Apollo's stockings that are hanging to dry on the clouds;[17] as the steeples do of a story in *L'Histoire du Théâtre Français:*[18] Jodelet,[19] who not only wrote plays, but invented the decorations, was to exhibit of both before Henry III.[20] One scene was to represent a view of the sea, and Jodelet had bespoken two *rochers*—but not having time to rehearse, what did he behold enter on either side of the stage instead of two *rochers,* but two *clochers!*[21]—Who knows but my Lord Admiral bought *them?*

Thursday, 16, Berkeley Square.

I am come to town for one night, having promised to be at Mrs Buller's this evening with Mrs Damer, and I believe your friend Mrs Chomley,[22] whom I have seen two or three times lately and like

16. The MS of the inventory, which was at Dulwich College when Malone quoted from it, has now been lost (Chambers, op. cit. ii. 165; *Henslowe Papers,* ed. Walter W. Greg, 1907, p. 113). See ibid. 113–23 for comment on some of the above items.

17. In Hogarth's 'Strolling Actresses Dressing in a Barn,' published in 1738, and now generally known as 'Strolling Players,' Cupid is reaching the stockings for Jupiter, not Apollo. See John Nichols and George Steevens, *Genuine Works of William Hogarth,* 1808, i. 102–3, ii. 150–1. HW considered this print, 'for wit and imagination, without any other end . . . the best of all' Hogarth's works (*Anecdotes of Painting, Works* iii. 456). HW's copy, in the 'first state' of the plate, and 'extra fine' was sold Lond. 1312 to Robert Boyne, Esq.

18. No work of this general title has been found to contain the anecdote HW tells. HW's most likely source is Pierre-François Godart de Beauchamps (1689–1761), *Recherches sur les théâtres de France, depuis l'année onze cent soixante-un jusques à présent,* 1735 (Bib. Nat. Cat.), listed in MS Cat. G.3.8, and sold SH iv. 55.

19. HW's mistake for Jodelle: Étienne Jodelle (1532–73), one of the members of the *Pléiade;* poet and dramatist. Jodelet, whose real name was Julien Bedeau (d. 1660), was the most famous comic actor of his day (Henry Carrington Lancaster, *History of French Dramatic Literature in the Seventeenth Century, Part II,* Baltimore, 1932, i. 22–4, *et passim*).

20. HW's mistake for Henri II (1519–59), King of France 1547–59.

21. The entertainment took place at the Hôtel de Ville at Paris 17 Feb. 1558. The *rochers* were to be used in an adaptation of the fable of Orpheus. Jodelle's account is in his *Le Recueil des inscriptions, figures, devises, et masquarades,* 1558 (reprinted in his *Œuvres,* ed. Ch. Marty-Laveaux, 1868–70, i. 231–78; see particularly pp. 259–70).

22. Evidently she was not there; see last paragraph of this letter. She left London on the following Sunday, 19 June (*Berry Papers* 41).

much. Three persons have called on me since I came, but have not contributed a tittle of news to my journal. If I hear nothing tonight, this must depart, empty as it is, tomorrow morning, as I shall to Strawberry—I hope without finding a new mortification, as I did last time. Two companies had been to see my house last week,[23] and one of the parties, as vulgar people always see with the ends of their fingers, had broken off the end of my invaluable eagle's bill,[24] and to conceal their mischief, had pocketed the piece. It is true it had been restored at Rome;[25] and my comfort is, that Mrs Damer can repair the damage[26]—but did the fools know that? It almost provokes me to shut up my house, when obliging begets injury!

Friday noon.

We supped at Mrs Buller's with only the four Edgcumbes[27] and Jerningham; and this moment I receive your 35th to which I have nothing to answer, but that I believe Fox and Burke are not very cordial, though I do not know whether there has been any formal reconciliation or not.[28] The Parliament is prorogued, and we shall hear no more of them, I suppose, for some months;[29] nor have I learnt anything new, and am returning to Strawberry, and must finish.[30]

23. On Monday (6 June) HW entertained the Sebrights at breakfast, and returned to London that evening; on Tuesday, 7 June, came 'Mr Falconet, from Mr Savard,' and on Wednesday 'Mrs Stainforth' ('Visitors'). He settled at SH the following Sunday (see preceding letter).

24. One of the chief glories of SH. See DU DEFFAND i. 405, n. 4.

25. In 1747. See HW to Mann 28 July 1747 and Mann to HW 19 Sept. 1747.

26. See post 4 July 1791.

27. Lord and Lady Mount Edgcumbe, and Lord and Lady Valletort.

28. The reconciliation never took place.

29. Parliament was prorogued on 10 June to 16 Aug. 1791, but it did not meet

again until 31 Jan. 1792 (ante 2 June 1791, n. 18).

30. Mrs Damer wrote to Mary Berry 20 June 1791: 'Mr W[alpole], in spite of the weather, returned to Strawberry on Friday, as he will have told you. I wish that he would have stayed. I should have seen him constantly, but you know these are subjects on which he is fixed, and indeed, I believe that he wishes to be near Cliveden. His spirits, when I last saw him [on Thursday, 16 June, at Mrs Buller's], satisfied me, and on your subject he does not at present want comfort. Your return he looks upon as certain. He is easy as to the consequences of your fall, and all will go well in his mind till your journey begins, which will again rouse his fears' (Berry Papers 41).

To Mary Berry, Thursday 23 June 1791

The entry in 'Visitors' suggests that the letter was posted 23 June, the day it was written, but the last paragraph shows that it was not posted until the following day.

Address: À Mademoiselle Mademoiselle Berry à la poste restante à Florence, Italie. Endorsed: 'Pd 1s.'

Strawberry Hill, June 23, 1791.

No. 38.[1]

WOE is me! I have not an atom of news to send you, but that the second edition of *Mother Hubbard's Tale*[2] was again spoiled on Saturday last by the rain, yet she had an ample assemblage of company from London and the neighbourhood.[3] The late Queen of France Madame du Barry was there; and the late Queen of England Madame d'Albany was not. The former, they say, is as much altered as her kingdom, and does not retain a trace of her former powers. I saw her on her throne in the chapel of Versailles,[4] and though then pleasing in face and person, I thought her *un peu passée.*

What shall I tell you more? that Lord Hawkesbury is added to the Cabinet Council[5]—*que vous importe?* and that Dr Robertson has published a *Disquisition into the Trade of the Ancients with India;*[6]

1. 'No. 48' (B).
2. 'He means a second breakfast at the Hon. Mrs Hobart's on Ham Common' (B).
3. 'The Hon. Mrs Hobart's rural breakfast . . . was numerously attended. Many persons of distinction were present: the garden was formed to represent a French village, in which tables were placed under the trees decorated with flowers, at which the company breakfasted; in the centre under a tree, on a tub, a rustic was placed, who played during the repast on the pipe and tabor.

'The lawn was surrounded with trees, and under them a village bake-house, a fruit-shop, and cook's-shop, from which the company refreshed themselves with wines, cakes, fruit, and the most delicate viands.

'It was nearly six o'clock in the afternoon before the whole of the company retired from this novel and pleasing repast' (*St James's Chronicle* 21–23 June 1791; see also

The London Chronicle 21–23 June 1791, lxix. 600).
4. 17 Sept. 1769; see DU DEFFAND v. 330; MONTAGU ii. 292.
5. A rumour thrice repeated in *The Times* during the preceding eight days. It appears, however, that while Lord Hawkesbury was President of the Board of Trade 1786–1804, he was not a member of the Cabinet during that time (GEC, *sub* Harrowby [1882]).
6. *An Historical Disquisition concerning the Knowledge which the Ancients had of India; and the Progress of Trade with that Country prior to the Discovery of the Passage to it by the Cape of Good Hope,* by William Robertson (1721–93); published 4 June 1791 (*Times* 30 May, 4 June 1791). HW received a copy (sold SH v. 155) from the author, and acknowledged the gift 20 June 1791.

a sensible work—but that will be no news to you till you return. It was a piddling trade in those days; they now and then picked up an elephant's tooth or a nutmeg, or one pearl that served Venus for a pair of pendants, when Antony had toasted Cleopatra in a bumper of its fellow—which shows that a couple was imported[7]—but alack the Romans were so ignorant, that waiters from the *Tres Tabernae*[8] in St Apollo's Street[9] did not carry home sacks of diamonds enough to pave the Capitol—I hate exaggerations, and therefore I do not say, to pave the Appian Way. One author, I think, does say that the wife of Fabius Pictor,[10] whom he sold to a proconsul, did present Livia with an ivory bed inlaid with Indian gold;[11] but as Dr Robertson does not mention it, to be sure he does not believe the fact well authenticated.

It is an anxious moment with the poor French here: a strong notion is spread that the Prince of Condé[12] will soon make some attempt,

7. This passage was suggested by pp. 50–9 of Robertson's book, where he discusses the commerce between the Romans and India.

8. A place on the Appian Way, near Ulubræ and Forum Apii, mentioned in Cicero's letters to Atticus. HW's allusion is especially apt, inasmuch as Mary Berry had recently been reading Cicero's letters and had doubtless mentioned that fact to HW. She wrote to Mrs Damer: 'I am charmed, delighted with Cicero's letters to Atticus, not only with their exquisite Latinity, and the curious information they give one, but with the affectionate expressions and the noble and perfect confidence with which they seem wrote—in his other works one admires and wonders at a superior genius; here *on se retrouve soi-même*, sensible to and suffering under all the various ills of humanity, and seeking relief where indeed it is alone to be found, in the warm, faithful, disinterested bosom of virtuous friendship—We shall, I hope, look over it together in England' ('Berry-Damer' i. 52–3). For Mrs Damer's reply to this passage, 31 May 1791, see *Berry Papers* 38.

9. An allusion to two Indian nabobs who, according to HW, had been 'waiters in a tavern' before they made their fortunes: Sir Thomas Rumbold (1736–1791), 1st Bt (1779), and Sir Francis Sykes (ca 1732–1804), 1st Bt (1781). The allegation has been questioned; see James M. Holzman, *The Nabobs in England*, New York, 1926, pp.

39–40; John Edwin Cussans, *History of Hertfordshire*, 1870–81, ii. 170–1. As Sykes went to India in 1749, and Rumbold in 1752, their careers as waiters could not have been long.

10. An allusion to Baron Christof Adam Karl von Imhoff (d. 1802), a painter and the first husband of Mrs Warren Hastings. It was rumoured that he sold his wife to Hastings, or at least agreed to get a divorce, for some £10,000. See K. L. Murray, *Beloved Marian*, [1938] pp. 28, 41, 47, 239; Sydney C. Grier [Hilda Caroline Gregg], *The Great Proconsul*, 1904, pp. 431, 434; Basil S. Long, *British Miniaturists*, 1929, p. 235. In 'Mem. 1783–91,' *sub* 13 Feb. 1787, HW refers to 'the scandal given by the Queen's reception of Mrs Hastings, notoriously the wife of Imhoff, a German painter, by whom she had children living, and who had sold her to Hastings.'

11. 'This alludes to the stories told at the time of an ivory bed inlaid with gold presented to Queen Charlotte by Mrs Hastings, the wife of the then Governor-General of India' (B). See Murray, op. cit. 147, 160. HW recorded in 'Mem. 1783–91,' *sub* Sept. 1784: 'Report, that Mrs Hastings, besides other immense presents, had brought the Queen an ivory bed inlaid with gold, which was stopped at Custom House, and she was forced to say for whom it was, on which it was released. . . .'

12. Louis-Joseph de Bourbon (1736–1818), Prince de Condé (DU DEFFAND); mili-

and the National Assembly by their pompous blustering seem to dread it.[13] Perhaps the moment is yet too early, till anarchy is got to a greater head—but as to the duration of the present revolution, I no more expect it, than I do the millennium before Christmas. Had the revolutionists had the sense and moderation of our ancestors, or of the present Poles,[14] they might have delivered and blessed their country; but violence, injustice, and savage cruelty, tutored by inexperienced pedantry, produce offspring exactly resembling their parents, or turn their enemies into similar demons. Barbarity will be copied by revenge.

Lord Fitzwilliam has *flown* to Dublin and back: he returned to Richmond on the fourteenth day from his departure, and the next morning set out for France: no courier can do more.

In my last in the description of June for *orange-flowers* pray read *roses:* the east winds have starved all the former; but the latter, having been settled here before the wars of York and Lancaster, are naturalized to the climate, and reck not whether June arrives in summer or winter: they blow by their own old-style almanacs: Madame d'Albany might have found plenty of white ones on her own tenth of June[15]—but on that very day she chose to go to see the King in the House of Lords with the crown on his head proroguing the Parliament! What an odd rencontre! Was it philosophy, or insensibility? I believe it is certain that her husband was in Westminster Hall at the coronation.[16]

The patriarchess of the Methodists, Lady Huntingdon,[17] is dead.

---

tary leader of the *émigrés*. At this time he was at Worms in command of the *émigré* army (*St James's Chronicle* 23–25 June 1791), and was daily expected to march into France to lead a counter-revolution; see ibid. 11–25 June 1791, *passim*.

13. An observation inspired by articles in the newspapers: e.g., *St James's Chronicle* 16–18 and 21–23 June 1791.

14. An allusion to the recent revolution in Poland; see *ante* 8 June 1791, n. 21.

15. 'The birthday [Old Style] of her husband's father, the Old Pretender, James II's son' (B). The emblem of the Stuart kings was the white rose.

16. The only authority for the statement that the Young Pretender was present at the coronation of George III in Westminster Abbey 22 Sept. 1761 is a letter of David

Hume to Sir John Pringle 10 Feb. 1773. At the time HW was writing, the letter had been printed in *The St James's Chronicle* 1–3 May 1788; *The Scots Magazine*, 1788, l. 209–11; *Edinburgh Magazine* 'May 1788, p. 340 f.' (David Hume, *Letters*, ed. J. Y. T. Greig, Oxford, 1932, ii. 484), and perhaps elsewhere. Biographers refer to Hume's letter, but question the truth of the story; see Alex. Charles Ewald, *Life and Times of Prince Charles Stuart*, 3d edn, 1904, pp. 363–4; L. Dumont-Wilden, *Le Prince errant*, 1934, pp. 210–11. There is evidence that the Young Pretender was in London early in 1760 (*Stuart Papers at Windsor*, ed. Alistair and Henrietta Tayler, [1939] pp. 249–50).

17. Selina Shirley (1707–91), dau. of 2d E. Ferrers; m. (1728) Theophilus Hastings

Now she and Whitfield[18] and Wesley[19] are gone, the sect will probably decline: a second crop of apostles seldom acquire the influence of the founders.

Today's paper declares upon its say-so, that Mr Fawkener is at hand with Catherine Slayczar's acquiescence to our terms—but I have not entire faith in a precursor on such an occasion, and from Holland too[20]—it looks more like a courier to the stocks[21]—and yet I am in little expectation of a war, as I believe we are boldly determined to remain at peace. As this must take its passage by the stage-coach early tomorrow morning to be ready for the foreign post, I shall perhaps not know the ultimation,[22] but you probably will before you receive this—and now my pen is quite dry—and you are sure not from laziness, but from the season of the year, which is very anti-correspondent. Adieu!

To Mary Berry, Tuesday 28 June 1791

Address: À Mademoiselle Mademoiselle Berry à la poste restante à Florence, Italie. *Postmark:* FIRENZE 28. Endorsed: 'Pd 1s.'
Posted 1 July ('Visitors').

Strawberry Hill, June 28, 1791.

No. 39.

I AM glad you recovered my strayed letter,[1] because one lost leaves a gap in a correspondence, that one thinks might contain something material, which I do not believe was the case. You was right in concluding I should disapprove of your visiting hospitals. One ought to

(1696–1746), 9th E. of Huntingdon; foundress of 'Lady Huntingdon's Connection,' a sect of Calvinistic Methodists opposed to Wesley. She died 17 June at 5:30 P.M. at her house in Spa Fields (*St James's Chronicle* 16–18 June 1791).

18. George Whitefield (1714–70), the evangelist.

19. John Wesley (1703–2 March 1791).

20. 'Yesterday a courier arrived from Holland. . . .

'According to the information we have received, we can state with great confidence that the messenger from Petersburg with Mr Fawkener's dispatches will bring with him the news of the Empress having ac-

ceded to the requisitions of the Allied Courts, and that a GENERAL PEACE will be instantly concluded. The government messenger was not arrived at 11 o'clock last night, though he has been expected every hour since Sunday last' (*Times* 23 June 1791).

21. 'In consequence of the intelligence given in our paper of yesterday, that a general peace might be expected, stocks rose one-half per cent' (*Times* 24 June 1791).

22. This is the earliest use of the word cited in OED.

———

1. Not identified.

surmount disgust, where it is one's duty, or one can do any good, or perform an act of friendship; but it is a rule with me to avoid any disagreeable object or idea, where I have not the smallest power of redress or remedy. I would not read any of the accounts of the earthquakes in Sicily and Calabria;[2] and when I catch a glimpse of a report of condemned malefactors to the Council,[3] I clap my finger on the paragraph, that I may not know when they are to suffer, and have it run in my head. It is worse to go into hospitals—there is contagion into the bargain. I have heard of a French princess, who had a taste for such sights, and once said, *'Il faut avouer, que j'ai vu aujourd'hui une agonie magnifique.'*[4] Your tender nature is not made for such spectacles; and why attrist it, without doing any service? One needs not recur to the index of the book of creation to hunt for miserable sufferers. What would I give not to have heard the calamities fallen on the heads of the King and Queen of France![5] I know no more yet than of their being betrayed and stopped at Clermont,[6] and ordered back to Paris, with *their children!*[7] What superabundance of woe! To expect insult, ignominy, and prison, perhaps separation, or death, without a ray of comfortable hope for their infants! That their imprisonment and danger should have been grievous, I do not wonder—

2. Feb.–May 1783, when the earthquakes were particularly devastating; see HW to Lady Ossory 16 March 1783, to Lord Strafford 12 Sept. 1783. Other earthquakes occurred there in 1785 and 1789 (GM 1783, liii. 785–7; 1787, lvii pt ii. 601–5; 1789, lix pt i. 265).

3. HW refers to an item such as the following: 'Yesterday the recorder of London made his report to the King in Council of the ten prisoners who received sentence of death at the last September Sessions at the Old Bailey' (*Times* 5 Nov. 1791). The names of the convicted and a description of their crimes usually followed; see, for example, *The London Chronicle* 28–30 July 1796, lxxx. 101.

4. This story has not been traced.

5. 'The first news that was received of the escape of the Royal Family of France was by a messenger dispatched [on 22 June; no one was allowed to leave Paris on the 21st, the day of their flight] by Earl Gower to Lord Grenville, who arrived at the Secretary of State's office on Saturday morning [25 June] early' (*Times* 27 June 1791). For Lord Gower's dispatch, see *The Despatches of Earl Gower*, ed. Oscar Browning, Cambridge, 1885, pp. 96–7. Notice of the flight was given in *The London Gazette* and evening newspapers 25 June 1791, and the morning newspapers 27 June 1791 contained full accounts of the escape and capture.

6. Actually at Varennes, a small village ten miles beyond Clermont. The royal family began their flight about 12:30 A.M., 21 June, and were captured about twenty-four hours later. See Carlyle, *The French Revolution*, Pt II, Bk IV, 'Varennes'; Saul K. Padover, *The Life and Death of Louis XVI*, 1939, pp. 220–7. News of the capture was brought by a government courier to the Secretary of State's office at 3:30 A.M., 26 June 1791 (*St James's Chronicle* 25–28 June 1791; *Oracle* 27 June 1791).

7. The Dauphin, later Louis XVII, titular King of France; and Marie-Thérèse-Charlotte (1778–1851), Madame Royale, who m. (1799) her cousin, Louis-Antoine de Bourbon (1775–1844), Duc d'Angoulême (son of Charles Philippe, Comte d'Artois, later, 1824–30, Charles X, King of France).

but to await dissension amongst their tyrants, and anarchy, was the best chance the King and Queen had in store—but though both will still happen in time I still believe, what advantage either or both will produce to those victims, may be very doubtful. That their flight was ill-advised is plain, from that woefully false step of leaving his recantation behind him, before he was safely out of the country.[8] It was strange that his intention being divulged, he should not have learnt the preparations made to prevent it, and desisted! It is equally strange that he should have escaped, though so watched and guarded![9]

Wednesday 29th.

I received your No. 36 on Monday, to which I have partly been replying; and today I have been so happy as to get No. 37 too, to which I will now answer, as I have heard nothing more yet of the poor French Royalties, who must already have felt a thousand times worse than ever,[9a] after a glimpse of safety, and then expecting everything that brutal barbarity can inflict, and which nobody but French and Dr Price could be so shameless as to enjoy![10]

I am glad you escaped from the hospital without infection; and I will trust to your sweet feelings for your never going again unnecessarily to view 800 persons in pain and misery.

I have told you and can only repeat that I did admire Mrs Chomley much, as I did formerly. It is a very clear, sound, well-informed understanding, as far as I saw; but that was but four or five times at most, and chiefly in company, where there were not many of quite her calibre. She seemed to me rather modestly proper and reserved, but not out of spirits.[11]

I am assured, as you justly guessed, that the pamphlet which Monsieur de Lally showed to you, is by no means Mr Burke's genuine sec-

8. Louis XVI's *Déclaration du roi adressée à tous les français* was to be handed to the National Assembly the day after his escape (Padover, op. cit. 218–19). The National Assembly ordered it to be printed and distributed, and translations of it appeared in London newspapers 27 June 1791 (*Oracle*, that date).

9. The escape was made easier by the leisurely departure of the people who had been present at the King's *coucher;* the royal family were able to escape in disguise —Marie-Antoinette only a few minutes before the guard of five men was posted for the night (Carlyle, *French Revolution*, ed. C. R. L. Fletcher, 1902, ii. 98, n. 1; 99).

9a. This word is blotted and doubtful.

10. An allusion to a passage in Price's *Discourse on the Love of Country;* see ante 26 Nov. 1790, n. 31.

11. Mrs Damer gave a different account of Mrs Cholmeley to Mary Berry 20 June 1791. After mentioning Mrs Cholmeley's departure from London, she continues: 'There is a frankness in her manner with which I was charmed. Neither her spirits nor her health appeared to me what I wish' (*Berry Papers* 41).

ond pamphlet,[12] but a spurious one fabricated at Paris and spread about there, to hurt his credit. This I heard last Friday, five days before I received your letter—so, if M. de Lally answers it, he will be the dupe of his own enemies.[13] Mr B. has advertised a new letter today to the Whigs,[14] but I have not yet seen it.

Your Italian paper is thin, but perfectly good. Cliveden will look beautiful with your narcissuses—I wish you were all there today, for we are again soused into Florentine weather, and have scarce had a teacup of rain, which makes us not look so green as the Cascines, though generally we have fifty thousand acres of such verdure—thus I have answered your chief articles.

Late at night.

I have been at Richmond, where I have seen a letter from good authority.[15] The King and Queen were brought to Paris[16] amidst numerous thousands, and without much insult—but they have been separated, and the Queen has been confined at the Val-de-Grâce,[17]

---

12. *Letter . . . to a Member of the National Assembly.*

13. Apparently HW is mistaken about the spurious French pamphlet: possibly he was not aware or had forgotten that Burke's *Letter . . . to a Member of the National Assembly* was published in French at Paris before the English edition appeared in London. The Bib. Nat. Cat. lists only one French edition: '*Lettre de M. Burke à un membre de l'Assemblée nationale de France.* À l'Assemblée nationale, Artaud, 1791. In-8°, 99 p.' Lally-Tollendal published a *Lettre écrite au très honorable Edmund Burke, membre du Parlement d' Angleterre,* 1791, 50 pp., dated 'Florence, 20 juin 1791,' but with no place of publication on the title-page; another edition, Florence, 1791, 87 pp. He subsequently published a pamphlet of 32 pages, *Postscriptum d'une lettre . . . à M. Burcke [sic],* no place, no date; and a *Seconde lettre . . . à M. Burke,* Londres et Paris, 1792, dated 'Londres, 8 mars 1792' (Bib. Nat. Cat.; BM Cat.).

14. *An Appeal from the New to the Old Whigs, in Consequence of some late Discussions in Parliament, relative to the Reflections on the French Revolution.* Although it was widely advertised in June as 'In a few days will be published,' it was

not published until 3 August (*St James's Chronicle* 16–18, 21–23 June, 2–4, 4–6 Aug. 1791; *Times* 22, 25 June, 4, 6, 12 Aug. 1791; *Oracle* 1, 3 Aug. 1791).

15. Doubtless a letter to one of the French colony at Richmond, but not further identified.

16. 25 June, 'attended by three commissioners deputed by the National Assembly to go and meet them, and about 30,000 people of both sexes, of all ranks and complexions, and some battalions of the National Guards' (*Times* 29, 30 June 1791; Saul K. Padover, *Life and Death of Louis XVI,* 1939, pp. 229–30).

17. Formerly a Benedictine nunnery, in the Rue St-Jacques. Marie Antoinette and Louis XVI were confined in separate apartments in the Tuileries (Padover, op. cit. 230, 233), but an early report was that 'the Queen, on her arrival, was immediately separated from the King. The house in which she is confined was formerly a convent' (*St James's Chronicle* 28–30 June 1791; see also *The Oracle* 30 June 1791). The dispatch of Lord Gower, the English ambassador at Paris, was more cautious: 'It is said that the convent of the Val de Grâce will be destined for the residence of the Queen' (*The Despatches of Earl Gower,* ed. Oscar Browning, Cambridge, 1885, p. 99).

where she was to be examined two days ago, and they talk of bringing her to trial for carrying away the child of the state, whom the Assembly wish to crown under a regent, while the Jacobins are for a republic.[18] I soon after saw a gentleman[19] from town, on whose intelligence I do not always depend. He says, the King lost six unnecessary hours on the road in eating and drinking;[20] and that Messieurs de Choiseul[21] and Damas,[22] who I suppose attended the King, are brought, not only in chains to Paris, but with each a grenadier sitting in his lap the whole way—such unnecessary torture, that it must be the taste of the nation to inflict it, if true.[23]

All this and fifty times more true and false, you will hear long before you receive this—but of what can one talk else? Kate Macaulay was so unlucky as to die a few days ago[24]—but she will gossip over it with Dr Price.

18. Accounts in *The Times* and *The Oracle* 30 June 1791 duplicate most of the information given in the first half of this paragraph.

19. Not identified.

20. A false report: 'It is sufficient for the unfortunate to miscarry in their designs; there is no need of loading them with reproaches. We have already combated the report of the French King's being inebriated on his return to Paris. The account of his journey not having succeeded through his love of eating is equally unfounded. It is well known that it was the discovery of his person put a stop to his journey' (*St James's Chronicle* 2–5 July 1791). Cf. *The Oracle* 30 June 1791; Padover, op. cit. 220–7.

21. Claude-Antoine-Clériadus-Gabriel de Choiseul-Beaupré (1760–1838), Duc de Choiseul, 1785; not to be confused with HW's particular friends, 'grand-papa and grand-maman,' to whom he was distantly related (DU DEFFAND v. 69, *et passim*). With the Marquis de Bouillé and Comte Fersen, he made preparations for the King's escape, was arrested at Varennes with the royal family 21 June 1791, and was imprisoned, first at Verdun, then at Orleans, until the King approved the new constitution. After his release, which is mentioned in *The Times* 29 Sept. 1791, he stayed in France near the King until the latter was imprisoned in the Temple in 1792; he then emigrated with some difficulty (Jean-Baptiste-Pierre Jullien de Courcelles, *Histoire géné-*

alogique . . . *des pairs de France*, 1822–33, vi. 159). For his activities 21 June, see his letter to the National Assembly, in the *Moniteur* 26 juin 1791.

22. Joseph-François-Louis-Charles-César Damas d'Antigny (1758–1829), Comte, later (1825) Duc de Damas, as colonel of the 13th Regiment of Dragoons (*Dragons de Monsieur*), was ordered by the Marquis de Bouillé to expedite the escape of the King. Arrested at Varennes on the night of 21 June 1791, he was closely confined at Verdun, Paris, and Orleans until the King approved the new constitution. He emigrated 15 Oct. 1791 (*Times* 29 Sept. 1791; *La Grande encyclopédie*; de Courcelles, op. cit. vi. 247). See also his letter to the National Assembly in the *Moniteur*, loc. cit.

23. As HW suspected, the account is considerably exaggerated. According to a dispatch from Paris, 27 June, in *The Times* 1 July 1791, 'Marshal Damas, the Duke de Choiseul [and others] . . . have been sent to the prison of Verdun, for having attempted to rescue the Royal Family at Varennes.' In *The Oracle* 30 June 1791, 'by express from Paris,' is the following item: 'Two of the attendants [but not Damas and Choiseul] who assisted in the flight were brought in chains in the same coach with their Majesties—two Hussars sitting at the knees of the attendants, guarding them.'

24. 22 June, at her house at Binfield, in Windsor Forest (*Oracle* 25 June 1791).

Frank North,[25] though abroad,[26] has a musical comedy[27] acting at the Little Haymarket, and coldly received.[28] His friends say the music was ill-chosen, or the singers unequal to it.[29] I had had great expectations, for he certainly has much humour and wit[30]—I have seen excellent verses of his in that style.[31] His brother Frederic[32] was stopped from going to Constantinople by the plague,[33] and is supposed on his road home.

Mrs Damer is to come to me on Friday for two days,[34] and Madame D'Albany at her own desire is to breakfast here on Saturday; and at her desire, Alfieri[35] too. Whatever her feelings are *here,* she must rejoice at having been only titular Queen of France!

Nine months are gone and over—I trust there are but four to come e'er we meet. Do not set a foot amongst the Basillissophagi![36] Mon-

25. Francis North (1761–1817), afterwards (1802) 4th E. of Guilford (he succeeded his brother, George Augustus North, 3d E.); at Eton 1768–76; entered the army, 1777, becoming Lt-Col. in 1794.

26. At Lausanne, Switzerland (*Times* 28 June 1791).

27. *The Kentish Barons, A Play in Three Acts, Interspersed with Songs,* first performed at the Theatre Royal, Haymarket, 25 June 1791. HW's copy of the play is now wsl. HW has marked the passage on p. 3, as a sign of admiration, where Clifford describes his lady's confessing her love for him:

'O such a colour ran thro' all her veins,
    As when Aurora tips the mountain's top
    And blushes day to an admiring world.'

28. On the opening night, according to *The Oracle* (27 June 1791), it was received with 'merited applause in a variety of scenes, though some incidents called down from a faction of idle young men a censure which candour blushed at.' Nevertheless, the play was acted ten times between 25 June and 25 July (see *The Oracle, The Times,* between those dates), and was published 9 July 1791 (*Times,* that date).

29. 'We think the music is no great aid to this piece, and except one air of Mrs Kemble, the symphony of which was exquisite, it might [better] have been away' (*Oracle* 27 June 1791).

30. 'It is far from a good play—but several parts of the dialogue have considerable merit' ([John Genest], *Some Account of the English Stage,* Bath, 1832, vii. 38).

31. Examples of his verses have not been found.

32. Frederick North (1766–1827), brother of the 3d and 4th Earls of Guilford; 5th E. of Guilford, 1817; Eton (1775–82) and Christ Church, Oxford (D.C.L., 1793, 1819); cr. LL.D., Cambridge, 1821; 'He was received into the Greek Church 23 Jan. 1791, and remained a member of it till his death. He was an accomplished linguist, speaking French, German, Russian, and modern Greek' (GEC).

33. The plague at Constantinople, Adrianople, and Cairo was the subject of numerous paragraphs in the newspapers for 1791: 'By a letter from a gentleman at Constantinople, we learn that . . . the plague continues to make the most dreadful havoc . . . not less than 200 people had fallen victims . . . every day for a month immediately antecedent to the date of this letter' (*Times* 5 Sept. 1791).

34. Mrs Damer wrote to Mary Berry 28 June 1791: 'On Friday I am to go to Strawberry for a night or two. I shall after that return here [London], and then go the beginning of next week to P[ark] Place' (*Berry Papers* 47).

35. The poet, Vittorio Alfieri (1749–1803), whose attachment to the Countess of Albany lasted from 1777 until his death. See Herbert M. Vaughan, *The Last Stuart Queen,* 1910, *passim;* 'Visitors,' *sub* 2 July 1791.

36. Literally, 'king-eaters'; apparently HW's coinage: the word is not recorded in OED.

sieur and Madame[37] have done right in retiring;[38] none of the family should stay in Paris, but a paltry Duke of Orleans, with his affected trull Mad. de Sillery[39]—and I should not be sorry if they were pelted out of it with contempt.

Lady Clackmannan was here this morning; puss jumped into her lap; I said, 'Madam do you dislike cats?'—'Oh! no, I like all dumb creatures'—Ay, thought I, and so do I, but I am not the better.

France, it seems, will supply my letters with matter, and I shall not be reduced to village-chat—yet I had rather have no letters to write.[40] Adieu!

To Mary Berry, Monday 4 July 1791

Address: À Mademoiselle Mademoiselle Berry à la poste restante à Florence, Italie. *Postmark:* FIRENZE [?]. Endorsed: 'Pd 1s.'
Posted 8 July ('Visitors').

Strawberry Hill, Monday, July 4, 1791.

No. 40.

MRS DAMER has been here on Friday and Saturday, and returned to town yesterday. She has already repaired the eagle's beak with wax, so that he can again receive company; but as that has not force enough to execute the commands of Jove, nor to crush the fingers of those who presume to touch his sacred person, he will soon have another of marble. Madame d'Albany and her *cicisbeo*[1] breakfasted with us on Saturday, and seemed really delighted—conse-

37. The Comte and Comtesse de Provence. The Comte de Provence, afterwards Louis XVIII, m. (1771) Marie-Joséphine-Louise (1753–1810) of Savoy, dau. of Victor Amadeus III, King of Sardinia.

38. They left Paris about the same time as the King and Queen and, travelling different routes, retired to Brussels. For details of their escape, see the Comte de Provence's own account, *Rélation d'un voyage à Bruxelles et à Coblentz. (1791.)*, 1823; Toni-Henri-Auguste, Vicomte de Reiset, *Joséphine de Savoie, Comtesse de Provence*, 1913, pp. 186–93; *The French Quarterly*, 1929, xi. 201–9.

39. Stéphanie-Félicité Ducrest de Saint-Aubin (1746–1830), m. (1763) Charles-Alexis Brulart, Comte de Genlis, later Marquis de Sillery; dramatist and educational writer; governess to the children of the Duc d'Orléans, and formerly his mistress (her place had been taken by the Comtesse de Buffon; see *ante* 10 July 1790, n. 8). See also DU DEFFAND, *passim*. She came to England in the autumn of 1791; see HW to Lady Ossory 4 Feb. 1792.

40. Mrs Damer wrote to Mary Berry 7 July 1791 that HW 'lives in such a passion about French politics that I think it not good for his health. My being *reasonable* makes it worse, when he talks to me on the subject, as that is direct *opposition*—quite the antipodes' (*Berry Papers* 48).

1. Alfieri.

quently, *'c'est la plus grande reine du monde.'* I really found she has more sense, than I had thought the first time I saw her—but she had like to have undone all, for when I showed her 'The death of Wolsey,' with which Mrs D. is anew enchanted, and told her it was painted by her acquaintance Miss Agnes Berry, she recollected neither of you—but at last it came out that she had called you Miss Barrys—I cannot say, that whitewashed her much in my eyes:[2] how anything approaching to the sound would strike me at any distance of time—which I trust will never, while I exist, exceed four months.[3] Apropos, t'other night I visited at the foot of Richmond Bridge,[4] and found a whole circle of old and young gossips. Miss[5] assured me you are to be back in October, which I do not repeat as if violating my promise of contenting myself with the very commencement of November; but to give an opportunity of saying that Cliveden will be quite ready to receive you in October; and as I conclude the lease of your house in town[6] will not be out then, your best way will be not to stop a moment in London, but to drive directly hither, and stay all three, etc., with me till you can settle yourselves in Cliveden. This will not only be the most convenient to yourselves, but you are sure the most agreeable to me; and thus you will have time to unpack and arrange yourselves, without being broken in upon for some days by visits, nor expected to make them: with all my warmth for those I love, I have a rebuffing coldness, that does not glue people to a chair in my house.

Miss Au-près-du-pont told me Miss A. had written to her of my misery about your nose—I was sorry, as that family is in daily and hourly commerce of tattle with all the world, and all the grimalkins in the parish will conclude I am in love with your nose, which I vow I am not—but if I love you both most affectionately as I do, can either of you wound her nose by a dreadful fall, and I not feel for it?[7] Miss

2. 'Madame d'Albany he [HW] turns up his nose at, and will never forgive for not having immediately known your name and recollected you, though I do believe, and must in justice say, that it was the difference in pronunciation that made her, for an instant, hesitate' (Mrs Damer to Mary Berry, 7 July 1791, *Berry Papers* 48).

3. The Berrys returned in a little over four months.

4. At Richard Owen Cambridge's.

5. Charlotte Cambridge.

6. In North Audley Street.

7. On 9 July 1791 Mrs Damer wrote to Mary Berry: 'He [HW] writes to you, I find, of his *anger* at your sister's having told Miss C[ambridge] that he was *so uneasy* about your fall, and the scar on your face. I meant to tell you, if he had not. It is true that there is scarcely anybody one can say anything to. You would have been diverted to hear him scold—"foolish, gossiping people, I can't imagine what *she* can write to them for"' (*Berry Papers* 49).

Du-pont soon quitted the subject to put such a volume of interroga-
tories to me about Lord Strafford's will,[8] that at last I was forced to
say, 'Madam, indeed I cannot answer all those questions'—on which
she did close her incessant lips—and the ball was resumed by the Signora Madre. Oh! those righteous scorpions, that will not touch a card,
but meddle with everybody's affairs with which they have nothing to
do, and never ask themselves whether what they hear is true or false,
but repeat both as conscientiously as the postman delivers letters without knowing what they contain. Thus every falsehood is propagated,
like seeds that birds drop out of their bills. For truth—I believe she
died a maid, and left no issue.

Thence I will not talk on France, for one is overwhelmed with reports contradicting one another, according to the propensities of the
senders and receivers. Of one thing I am certain, of pitying the
Queen, which was so generally felt here as soon as the reverse of her
escape was known, that I was told that if money could serve her, an
hundred thousand pounds would have been subscribed in a quarter
of an hour at Loyd's Coffee-House.[9] There is a wretch, a quondam
Prince du Sang,[10] who has snapped at this moment for making himself more ridiculously contemptible than ever, by protesting he does
not wish for the regency[11]—which I suppose would as soon be offered
to me. I remember an old French refugee here, a Marquise de Montandre[12] (the Mademoiselle Spanheim of the *Spectator*)[13] who on the

8. According to a paragraph in *The London Chronicle* 19–22 March 1791, lxix. 277, 'The late Earl of Strafford has left property to the amount of £75,000, the bulk of which goes to his sister Lady Ann Connolly, for her life, with remainder to Mr. Byng. Sir George Howard, who had great expectations, has a legacy only of £500; Sir George's grandchildren £3000 each. The Lord Chancellor is left executor. Several informalities in the will have occasioned doubts as to its validity; a circumstance that promises to be productive of an immediate litigation.' See also *The St James's Chronicle* 19–22 March 1791; *The Gazetteer and New Daily Advertiser* 22 March 1791.

9. I.e., Lloyd's, the insurance society.

10. The Duc d'Orléans.

11. In a letter addressed 'à l'auteur du journal intitulé *Assemblée nationale*, etc.,' and dated '26 juin 1791,' the Duc d'Orléans

wrote in part: 'Je dois vous répéter ce que j'ai déclaré publiquement dès le 21 et le 22 de ce mois à plusieurs membres de l'Assemblée nationale, que je suis prêt à servir ma patrie sur terre, sur mer, dans la carrière diplomatique, en un mot dans tous les postes qui n'exigeront que du zèle et un dévouement sans bornes au bien public; mais que, s'il est question de régence, je renonce dans ce moment et pour toujours au droit que la constitution m'y donne' (*Moniteur* 28 juin 1791).

12. Mary Anne (ca 1683–1772), only child of Ezekiel, Baron von Spanheim, sometime Prussian ambassador to England; m. (1710) François de la Rochefoucauld, Marquis de Montandre, a religious refugee who d. 1739 a field-marshal in the English army; see David C. A. Agnew, *Protestant Exiles from France*, 2d edn, 1871, ii. 122–5; MONTAGU i. 163 and the references there cited.

13. In *The Lucubrations of Isaac Bicker-*

strength of her pinchbeck marquisate, pretended to precede our sterling countesses—but being sure of its not being allowed, she thus entered her claim: when at a visit tea was brought in; before the groom of the chambers could offer it to anybody, she called out, 'I would not have any tea'; and then when she had thus saved her dignity, she said to him after others had been served, 'I have betought myself; I tink I will have one cup.'

Berkeley Square, Thursday evening, 7th.

I might as well write of French affairs, as have nothing else to write —apropos, we have had such violent west winds, that I have no letter from you this week—A disagreeable affair, with which I will not tire you long, brought me to town on Tuesday.[14] My disordered ward, whom I mentioned to you,[15] was to come to me on Tuesday from Chichester; I was to bring her to town yesterday, and send her with Kirgate and his daughter[16] today into Kent, where I had found a private lodging for her with excellent people,[17] who had had a poor gentleman, in the same way, with them, and had treated him with the utmost tenderness. She had consented and promised to come, with a worthy lawyer, employed by the D. of Richmond, and his daughter, who had submitted to attend her—but on Monday night she changed her mind and would not stir. I sat till eleven at night expecting her every minute, and starting up at the rattle of every chaise that passed.[18] The same next morning till the post came in, when a letter[19] from the lawyer acquainted me she was so disordered, that he

staff, Esq. [The Tatler], ed. John Nichols, 1786, iv. 72 n, Nichols suggests that the 'Belinda' of Tatler 127 is perhaps Mlle Spanheim: ' "As beautiful as Madam Spanheim," was a proverbial expression. This lady is mentioned as a distinguished beauty, under her real maiden name, in the Spectator, where there will be occasion to speak of her more particularly.' Cf. The Tatler, ed. George A. Aitken, 1898–9, iii. 76 n. Nevertheless, no reference to her in The Spectator has been found.

14. Mrs Damer wrote to Mary Berry 7 July 1791: 'I called upon him [HW] this morning. . . . He has not received your letter, which I am sure you have sent him, but it is no wonder this stormy weather, if the post fails' (Berry Papers 48).

15. Ante 2 June 1791.

16. Eleanor Kirgate m. —— Thomas. Mrs Toynbee (Letters i. p. xvi, n. 1) printed a letter from Mrs Thomas to George P. Harding, the copyist and friend of her father, 11 Dec. 1810, giving permission for the destruction of extracts from HW's letters to Mann, which Kirgate had made without permission. The letter was reprinted by Dr Toynbee in the Journal of the Printing-Office at Strawberry Hill, 1923, p. 49.

17. Not identified.

18. HW had suffered similar apprehension because of his nephew, 'the mad Earl'; see Cole i. 348.

19. Missing.

had called in the apothecary, who declared compulsion must be used. To that I have positively refused my consent, unless to prevent her from destroying herself; and have ordered all the gentlest methods to be used as long as possible, and to offer her to settle herself wherever she likes best—for she is not constantly out of her mind. It is a most unfortunate history, and I find will give one great trouble. I was forced to come to consult Mr Churchill, joint trustee with me.

Last night I supped at Mrs Damer's (who goes to Park Place tomorrow for three weeks)[20] with Madame d'Albany, the D. and Duchess of Richmond, the men Mt Edgcumbes,[21] Mrs Buller, and the Charming Man, and tomorrow return to Strawberry.[22]

The Gunnings are not only resettled in St James's Street as boldly as ever,[23] but constantly with old Bedford, who exults in having regained them[24]—but their place in the town-talk is occupied by Lady Mary Duncan, who on receiving tickets for his benefit from Badini[25] at the Pantheon,[26] where Pacchierotti[27] does *not* sing,[28] she returned them with a most abusive letter, calling him impudent monster and wretched poet.[29] This has given somebody an opportunity of return-

20. As planned, Mrs Damer went to Park Place 8 July; she had returned 31 July, when she spent the day with HW at SH (*Berry Papers* 47–8, 56; *post* 3 Aug. 1791).

21. Lord Mount Edgcumbe and his son, Lord Valletort.

22. Mrs Damer wrote to Mary Berry 7 July 1791 that HW 'was in very good spirits here yesterday evening, and had his dear Mrs Buller, the only person, I think, that he thoroughly likes talking to in your absence' (*Berry Papers* 48). Mrs Damer also saw HW at Mrs Buller's on the evening of the 7th, 'and was better satisfied with him than I was in the morning' (ibid. 49).

23. 'Wednesday [29 June 1791] Mrs Gunning and her daughter arrived in town from France. They have taken up their abode in St James's Street' (*Times* 1 July 1791).

24. 'The Duchess Dowager of Bedford, in her persisting encouragement of Miss Gunning, shows in a forcible point of view the superior friendship of the *old school*' (*Oracle* 3 Aug. 1791).

25. Carlo Francesco Badini (fl. 1767–1808), translator, librettist, poet, and pamphleteer. He evidently lived in Paris

1805–8: his books during that period were published there instead of in London (BM Cat.; Bib. Nat. Cat.).

26. HW has confused the two opera houses: Badini had long been connected with the King's Theatre, Haymarket, where his benefit night was 17 June 1791 (*Times* 15, 17 June 1791).

27. Gaspare Pacchierotti (1744–1821), male soprano, with whom Lady Mary had been infatuated for a number of years. See *Enciclopedia italiana;* BM, *Satiric Prints* v. 650, No. 6125 (but see also vi. 866–7, No. 8012); Frances Burney d'Arblay, *Memoirs of Doctor Burney,* 1832, ii. 119; *idem, Diary and Letters,* ed. Charlotte Barrett and Austin Dobson, 1904–5, *passim;* Richard Edgcumbe, 2d Earl of Mount Edgcumbe, *Musical Reminiscences,* 3d edn, 1828, pp. 12–16, *et passim.*

28. HW is mistaken: Pacchierotti had sung in opera at the Pantheon as recently as 10 and 25 June 1791 (*Oracle* 10, 25 June 1791), and was regularly engaged there (Richard Edgcumbe, 2d Earl of Mount Edgcumbe, op. cit. 66–7).

29. 'Mr Badini having sent a most respectful letter to Lady Mary Duncan, en-

ing an answer (in his name) ten times more scurrilous, and which is cried up as full of humour; but by what has been repeated to me out of it, I only found it exceedingly coarse and indelicate.[30] However, she cannot be pitied, having committed herself by being the aggressor towards such a fellow. Adieu! I have exhausted my small sack of gatherings.

treating the honour of her patronage for his benefit, her Ladyship returned the following curious note:

"Queen Ann Street, West[minster].

"Lady Mary Duncan is not a little surprised at the consummate impudence of Badini, in daring to have the insolence to send tickets to her house, without her having sent him orders for it: had she intended going, this *wo'd* have prevented her; nor *dose* she see any *occassion* to employ so bad a poet as Badini; he can be of no service, except to wipe *of* the dust from the dancers' shoes, when they come off the stage" ' (*Oracle* 30 June 1791). The misspellings and italics are retained; see following note.

30. 'The Retort Courteous' follows immediately after Lady Mary's letter in *The Oracle* 30 June 1791:

'My Lady,

'When I received your *polite note*, I happened to be confined with a fever, and as I had just taken a *drastic purge*, your Ladyship's favour was of peculiar service. If your Ladyship should not understand the meaning of that technical word, you may find an explanation in the pharmacopoeia that *Doctor Nostrum*, your late husband, used to keep in his shop.

'You express a surprise, my Lady, *at my consummate impudence in daring to have the insolence of requesting your patronage for my benefit.* It is true that the asperity of your Ladyship's furrowed countenance and the sternness of your presence might have taught me that in applying to your Ladyship I was soliciting the benevolence of *Tisiphone.* I confess myself culpable of a great inadvertence; but as to the double reproach of insolence and effrontery, I am apt to think that it fosters with much more

propriety on the relict of a Scotch apothecary, who arrogates to herself the pride of a princess, and the prerogative of an empress.

'You are pleased, my lady, to add that I am a *bad poet.* I know that your ladyship constantly wears one of the chief decorations of a learned judge—I mean *your wig,* my Lady; yet as your note shows that you cannot spell, I do not think your Ladyship's judgment can have much weight in the Republic of Letters; especially as old women in general are noted for the infirmity of their mental faculties.

'The office of *cleaning the dancers' shoes,* which your Ladyship has thought proper to honour me with, being rather too dirty, I beg leave to resign the place into your Ladyship's hands. Your *old wigs,* my lady, will afford you an opportunity of following that occupation with credit. I thought your Ladyship had only a partiality for the *Cast-Rats:* but I see that the Gentlemen of the Pump are likewise your favourites. It is the poet alone that excites your Ladyship's aversion. There is no accounting for the whimsies of some beings. I remember, my Lady, I had once an old b——, that was astonishingly fond of vermin, and had a mortal antipathy against nightingales and canary-birds.

'I am,
        Your Ladyship's most obedient
                humble servant,
                Badini, the Bad Poet.'

It is quite possible that Badini himself, who published a lampoon in 1793 under the name of 'Vittorio Nemesini' (BM Cat.), was the author of the letter. *The Times,* which did not print the letters, restrainedly refers to this exchange of letters as 'a kind of Billingsgate correspondence' (2 July 1791).

To Mary Berry, Tuesday 12 July 1791

Address: À Mademoiselle Mademoiselle Berry à la poste restante à Florence, Italie. *Postmark:* FIRENZE 30. Endorsed: 'Pd 1s.'

Address and last paragraph of letter in Kirgate's hand; posted 14 July ('Visitors').

Strawberry Hill, Tuesday night, July 12, 1791.

No. 41.[1]

I HAD had no letter from you for ten days, I suppose from west winds, but did receive one this morning, which had been three weeks on the road—and a charming one it was. Mr Batt, who dined with me yesterday, and stayed till after breakfast today, being here, I read part of it to him, and he was as much delighted as I was with your happy quotation of *incedit regina*.[2] If I could spare so much room, I might fill this paper with all he said of you both, and with all the friendly kind things he begged me to say to both from him. Last night I read to him certain reminiscences,[3] and this morning he slipped from me and walked over to Cliveden—and hopes to see it again much more agreeably. I hope so too and that I shall be with him—now to answer you.

The Duke of Argyll and Lady Charlotte[4] are at Inverary, and he, they say, is very low, and not at all well.[5] Lady Derby[6] is at Rich-

---

1. 'No. 49' (B).
2. Presumably a variation of the passage in Virgil, *Æn.* i. 46–8:

'. . . ego, quæ divum incedo regina, Iovisque
Et soror et coniunx, una cum gente tot annos
Bella gero.'

Mary Berry probably had applied the passage to Catherine II of Russia.

3. *Reminiscences written by Mr Horace Walpole in 1788 for the Amusement of Miss Mary and Miss Agnes Berry,* first printed in *Works* iv. 273–318; edited, 'now first printed in full from the original MS.,' by Paget Toynbee, Oxford, 1924.

4. His youngest child, Lady Charlotte Campbell.

5. He lived until 1806. Mrs Damer wrote to Mary Berry 9 July 1791: 'The Campbells are at Inverary—my uncle what people call *thinking* himself ill, that is, *being* so, for otherwise, I am convinced, it is a subject no one *thinks* about. His spirits are low—cause or consequence of the first' (*Berry Papers* 50).

6. Elizabeth Hamilton (1753–97), Countess of Derby (see *ante* 13 Nov. 1790, n. 20), Lady Charlotte Campbell's half-sister. For about the last ten years of her life she was a confirmed invalid (Horace Bleackley, *The Story of a Beautiful Duchess,* 1908, pp. 305–7). Six weeks before the date of this letter she was particularly ill, for John Philip Kemble, the actor, wrote to Sir Charles Hotham, 31 May 1791: 'Lady Derby it is thought cannot live till tomorrow morning'

mond[7]—I hear, much as usual. Mrs D. is at Park Place for three weeks, has been here as I told you in my last, is perfectly well, and looks better than ever I saw her. Mrs, not E., Hervey, is gone thither today from Hampton, where she has been two or three days with the Johnstones (I did not know of such intimacy).[8] They all and Mrs Anderson were here yesterday morning, and I dined with all but Mrs Hervey at Mrs Garrick's last Saturday. Mr Batt and Clackmannan were there too.

I wish there were not so many fêtes at Florence; they are worse for you both than Italian sultriness; but if you do go to them, I am glad you have more northern weather.

News I have none, but that Calonne arrived in London on Sunday[9] —you may be sure I do not know for what[10]—in a word, I have no more opinion of his judgment, than of his integrity.

(A. M. W. Stirling, *The Hothams*, 1918, ii. 255). John Thomas Stanley, later 7th Bt and 1st Bn Stanley of Alderley, saw her a few years before her death, 'on a sofa, retired from the world at Richmond, and palsied in all her limbs' (*Early Married Life of Maria Josepha Lady Stanley*, ed. Jane H. Adeane, 1899, p. 26). The newspapers of 1791 contain numerous references to her health; see, for example, *The Oracle* 14 May, 3 June 1791.

7. Her house was 'on Barnes Terrace, within three miles of Richmond' (*Oracle* 3 June 1791).

8. Mrs Damer wrote to Mary Berry 16 July 1791: 'Mrs Hervey came here on Thursday [?Tuesday] night and brought an account of Mr W[alpole]'s having the rheumatism and of her having seen him sitting in his nightgown, and confined. He perhaps will not tell you this [but see this letter], but I shall. She says that it is in his shoulder. I feel some degree of satisfaction from his having *seen her*, which he would not, had he been then very bad and out of spirits: but I am far from easy. He will not write to me on this, I know, so that I must wait to hear till I have an answer to my letter to him—a sad uncomfortable system of his, I must think. Mrs H[ervey] has been passing some days at Lady Cecilia's who is grown mighty fond of her, and there she says was Mrs A[nderson], "lying away at such a rate, and abusing everybody, that it

made one's hair stand on end." But your humble servant she said *"was perfection."* That is a *seed sent to P[ark] P[lace]*, but it will not grow. What detestable falsehood! Mrs H[ervey] mentioned her abusing Lady Mount Edgcumbe, in particular, and that she had said such things of her, nothing should make her ever repeat. My mother wanted to *hear* them, but she—Mrs H[ervey] —would not' (*Berry Papers* 53–4).

9. According to *The Times* 12 July 1791, 'On Saturday last Monsieur de Calonne and his brother, the Abbé de Calonne, arrived at their house at Hyde Park Corner, from Brussels.' *The Oracle* 11 July 1791 also gives Saturday. He was in London only a short time, as he was at Schönbornlust, near Coblentz, 1 Aug. 1791 (Christian de Parrel, *Les Papiers de Calonne*, Cavaillon, 1932, pp. 72–7).

10. He was on a mission from the Comte d'Artois and the Comte de Provence, in connection with a possible counter-revolution (ibid.). 'M. de Calonne's journey is the topic of universal conjecture. His stay here is to be short; and the flow of spirits he displays at present seems to indicate that the turn of affairs in France is rather favourable to the royal cause; though, from the irritated state of the populace, Paris we should think would be the last place that accomplished statesman would visit' (*Oracle* 13 July 1791).

Now I must say a syllable about myself—but don't be alarmed! it is not the gout; it is worse, it is the rheumatism, which I have had in my shoulder, ever since it attended the gout last December. It was almost gone till last Sunday, when the Bishop of London preaching a charity sermon in our church,[11] whither I very, very seldom venture to hobble,[12] I would go to hear him, both out of civility, and as I am very intimate with him. The church was crammed, and though it rained, every window was open. However, at night I went[13] to bed and to sleep very well; but at two I waked with such exquisite pain in my rheumatic right shoulder, that I think I scarce ever felt greater torture from the gout. It was so grievous, that I considered whether I should not get out of bed—but the thought that I might kill myself, and consequently not live to Cliveden-tide, checked me—upon my honour this is true—I lay—not still, but writhing about, till about five o'clock the agony threw me into a violent perspiration, which soon allayed my suffering, and I fell asleep. I have had but very moderate pain since—still I could not get on my common clothes, but have been these two days in my nightgown and a waistcoat with open sleeves tied with ribbons. I own I did tremble at night when I was to go to bed—but my pain did not return, and I had my usual comfortable night composed of one whole dose of sleep, and as I can moreover sleep at any time, I have slept both before and after dinner today, and could not be very bad yesterday, as I could read to Mr Batt for two hours and half[14] without reposing, nor worse today, when I have been writing this prolix syllable to you, in my lap indeed, without deputing Kirgate. Though the gout could never subdue my courage, nor make me take any precaution against catching cold, the rheumatism and Cliveden have made a coward of me. I now draw up my coach glasses, button my breast, and put a hat on the back of my head, for I cannot yet bear it to touch my forehead, when I go into the garden[15]—you charged me to be particular, when I am

11. There is no reference to this sermon in the life of Porteus, vol. i of his *Works*, ed. Robert Hodgson, new edn, 1823.

12. John Pinkerton reports that HW once told him: 'I go to church sometimes, in order to induce my servants to go to church. I am no hypocrite. I do not go in order to persuade them to believe what I do not believe myself. A good moral sermon may instruct and benefit them. I only set them an example of listening, not of believing' (*Walpoliana* i. 76).

13. HW repeated 'I went.'

14. From the *Reminiscences;* see first paragraph.

15. This was a considerable change from HW's earlier practice. He wrote to Cole 14 Feb. 1782: 'A hat you know I never wear, my breast I never button, nor wear greatcoats, etc.' (Cole ii. 298).

not well—I think I have been circumstantial enough! If I am in love with your nose and long to see it, quite recovered, take root at Cliveden, at least your Corydon does not forget that he is seventy-four, nor conceals one particle of his rheumatism. His dread of being gone before November does not look as if he thought himself immortal—and yet as a true knight, no Orondates[16] ever suffered more for his mistress, than I did heroically on Sunday night in not getting out of bed.[17]

Thursday evening.

I cannot finish this with my own hand, for yesterday morning I had a good deal of pain, and though I had a very tolerable night, the incorporated society of rheumatism and gout have got down to my elbow and wrist, and I cannot move my arm at all—however, as the pain is locomotive, I trust it will soon go quite away. I will write again on Tuesday, though a hors-d'oeuvre; and I could have wished to write more myself today, for this morning I received another charming letter from you, with a most picturesque description of the Great Duke's inthronization in Pan-Athenion in the Piazza del Gran Duca[18]—there, there are as many long words as Dr Johnson's! and you may roll them out to the bottom of the page, since I cannot give it its usual complement, for though the spirit is willing, the flesh is weak. Adieu!

To Mary Berry, Sunday 17 July 1791

Posted 19 July; opposite the entry in 'Visitors' HW noted that the subject of the letter was 'fever,' but that subject applies to the letter of 20 July 1791.

Address: À Mademoiselle Mademoiselle Berry à la poste restante à Florence, Italie. Endorsed: 'Pd 1s.'

Both address and letter are in Kirgate's hand.

16. Oroondates, the son of a Scythian king, whose love for Statira, widow of Alexander the Great, led him to surmount numerous dangers and difficulties. He appears in the romance *Cassandre,* 10 vols, 1642–5, by Gautier de Costes de la Calprenède (ca 1610–63). HW seems to have had only volumes iii–v, of the English translation (*Cassandra,* tr. Sir Charles Cotterell, 5 vols, 1725); they (MS Cat. B. 8) were sold SH i. 90. See also DU DEFFAND i. 44; iii. 436–7, *et passim.*

17. The remainder of the letter is in Kirgate's hand.

18. 'At Florence, on the 24th of June, his Royal Highness the Great Duke made his public entry into that city, and received the homage of the several deputies sent on the

Strawberry Hill, Sunday night, July 17, 1791.

No. 42.

NEXT to being better I am rather a little glad I am worse, i.e., the gout is come to assert his priority of right to me, and when he has expelled the usurper,[1] I trust he will retire quietly too; in the meanwhile, my case is *party per pale* good and bad: I slept last night from twelve to eight without waking, and at this present *not* writing, seven o'clock, I have had a good deal of pain in my elbow ever since two, though now a little easier; but if I want still more gout I think I can draw upon my right knee, where there seems to be a little in store for me. In good earnest, the rapid shifting of my complaint makes me flatter myself that it will not be permanent.

I have not said a word to you of the apprehensions that had been conceived of some mischief to happen on Thursday last, the second intended celebration of the French Revolution. I thought you might be alarmed, and remain anxious for a fortnight; now I can tell you that it totally miscarried. The Revolution Club wished to hold their jubilee at the Opera House[2] or Ranelagh,[3] both were refused; they

occasion with the usual ceremonies. The senate and magistracy were sworn on the Holy Evangelists, after which the former had the honour to kiss his Royal Highness's hand, and the latter his garment' (GM 1791, lxi pt ii. 962).

———

1. Rheumatism.

2. 'The Revolution Club intending to celebrate the French Revolution in the most ostentatious manner on July 14, tried to hire the Opera House, but Gallini would not let it unless they would insure it from fire. They then tried for Ranelagh, proposing to give out 3000 tickets, but it was refused to them. They curiously *sounded* Mr Fox, whether he would go if invited—but he desired they would not, as he must give an answer they would not like. Colours for them came from France, but were stopped at Custom House as the silk contraband' ('Mem. 1783–91,' *sub* May 1791). In ibid., *sub* July 1791, HW wrote: 'Great preparations by the Revolution Club for celebrating the French 14th, and to do much more. Proposed national cockades, and had flags from France, but most stopped. Some had given money to guards; but that nor Paine's pamphlet had any success, though letters

in the papers for raising their pay and that of day-labourers, *rights* of man. The Opera House and Ranelagh were refused to them —Then they declared they would give *no seditious* toasts, yet still bullied. Reduced to Crown and Anchor. Lord Stanhope withdrew—at last they sent begging letters for attendance. Prisoners expected to be released, and one debtor going to compound his debts, refused on that hope. . . . At last, *under 1000* met, and Mr Merry wrote a very dull ode for them; but the government had taken such just measures and precautions that no disturbance happened, and the day ended contemptibly—but at Birmingham the dissenters stuck up such treasonable papers and drank such outrageous toasts that the mob rose against them, drove them out of the town, demolished meeting houses, burnt some houses of rich dissenters, destroyed *Dr Priestly's* house and pursued him into Worcestershire, but he escaped to London. On 17th guards arrived and all was quiet.'

3. The project for hiring Ranelagh elicited the following paragraph of newspaper wit: 'Dr Pr[iestle]y telling a gentleman that the Revolution Club intended to hire Ranelagh for the celebration of the Rebellion

had intended to have exhibited flags and national cockades sent from France, but those sent thence were stopped at the Custom House; and though some cockades were exhibited in a shop or two, nobody wore one;[4] numbers of Paine's pamphlet[5] were distributed, but equally without success. At last the meeting was fixed at the Crown and Anchor,[6] and circular letters of invitation were sent to all sorts of persons,[7] and at most did not produce a thousand head: Mr Fox was sounded, but declined;[8] then, even their solitary peer, Lord Stanhope, withdrew. Mr Sheridan was persuaded not to go,[9] and they had not one man of consequence but Mr Pigot[10] the Prince's Solicitor, who has not made his court by it. In short, it ended with contempt and ridicule, and without any disturbance,[11] except that at eleven at night some glaziers and tallow-chandlers broke a few windows in the Strand and Cheapside, to force people to put out lights, but all was immediately suppressed by the magistrates.[12]

There has been a much worse tumult at Birmingham, on the same day. The faction had stuck up most treasonable papers with long extracts from Dr Price's sermon,[13] but as soon as the people perceived

in France—the gentleman replied, "I hope the directors of that building will not suffer it to be metamorphosed by *Priestly*-craft into a Pandæmonium"' (*Times* 26 May 1791).

4. After the cockades had been confiscated, the stewards of the society advertised: 'No cockade or other badge of distinction is intended to be worn at the . . . meeting' (*Oracle* 11 July 1791).

5. *The Rights of Man*, Pt I.

6. 'The *Crown and Anchor* is the scene of the intended commemoration of the 14th of July, and every precaution has been used by its conductors, to refute the accusation of their detractors, by making it tranquil and decorous' (*Oracle* 2 June 1791).

7. The meeting was also advertised in the newspapers: 'Every gentleman who wishes to commemorate the said anniversary is requested to make early application to any of the stewards for a ticket, or at the bar of the Crown and Anchor Tavern' (*Oracle* 11 July 1791).

8. 'Mr Fox has declined giving his name as a steward to the commemoration of the 14th July. Mr Sheridan, Mr Erskine, etc., have imitated his example. They are afraid of alarming the opulent aristocracy with

which they are connected' (*Oracle* 30 May 1791).

9. 'Mr Sheridan was not present at the Crown and Anchor on Thursday' (*Oracle* 16 July 1791).

10. Arthur Leary Pigott (1749–1819), Kt, 1806; solicitor general to the Prince of Wales from 1783 to 1792, when he was dismissed; M.P. 1806–19. He was one of the stewards of the dinner given by the Revolutionary Society (*Oracle* 13 July 1791), and was one of the signers of the manifesto or declaration of the 'Friends of the People,' a society organized at the Freemasons' Tavern 11 April 1792 (MS of the manifesto, now WSL).

11. For an account of the meeting, the toasts drunk, etc., see *The Oracle* 15 July 1791.

12. 'The Guards were prudently in readiness, if there had been occasion; but their interposition was happily unnecessary. The constables were all ordered out, and their functions faithfully performed. A few *Panes* were broken in a coffee-house window in the Strand' (*Oracle* 15 July 1791).

13. *Discourse on the Love of Our Country;* see *ante* 23 July 1790, n. 8.

the drift of them they arose with indignation and demolished two or three meeting-houses, and the evening papers of last night said,[14] Dr Priestly's house too, but I was told before dinner that the last is not true.[15]

A remarkable circumstance has happened: som<e>body has found and reprinted a sermon by Dr Price, preached some years ago,[16] in which he displays at length the superior happiness of this country to all others, particularly by the increase of liberty from taking off general warrants,[17] etc.

I am tired, and will say no more now, but will reserve the rest of my paper till tomorrow, when I hope to give you a better account of myself, and as good of the public.

Monday evening.

I have had another excessively good night, and though I had some pain in my elbow after breakfast, 'tis gone, and so is the threat in my knee. Thus, at present, I have nothing to do but to recover as fast as

14. The first news of the riots at Birmingham reached the Secretary of State's office on Saturday, 16 July, at 3:30 A.M., too late for the news to appear in the morning newspapers (*Oracle* 18 July 1791). An afternoon newspaper, *The London Chronicle* 14–16 July 1791, lxx. 56, contained the following account: 'This morning an express arrived at the Secretary of State's Office from Birmingham, with an account that a great number of persons, to the amount of some hundreds, who were in opposition to the Revolutionists, had assembled on Thursday last before the house where the Society dined, and broke all the windows; they then pulled part of the house down, and proceeded to the different meeting-houses, which they laid level with the ground; after which they broke into the house of Dr Priestley, took everything out, burnt his books, drank the wine and other liquors found in his cellars, and when the express came away, were demolishing the house to the foundation. The whole town was in an uproar, and the greatest confusion and riot prevailed. A messenger was dispatched to his Majesty at Windsor with the above particulars.'

15. It was true: Priestley's house, Fairhill, about a mile from Birmingham, was com-

pletely demolished; the Old and New Meeting Houses were ransacked and ignited, as were several houses (*Oracle* 18 July 1791).

16. *Britain's Happiness, and its Full Possession of Civil and Religious Liberty, Briefly Stated and Proved,* 'by the late Rev. Dr Richard Price. With an Introduction by the Editor,' published 11 July 1791 (*St James's Chronicle* 7–9 July 1791; *London Chronicle* 12–14 July 1791, lxx. 48; *Times* 15 July 1791). The editor, who signs himself 'A British Manufacturer,' has not been further identified. The pamphlet of 20 pages consists of an introduction (pp. 3–7) and extracts from Price's sermon (pp. 9–20) which was preached at Newington Green 29 Nov. 1759. The entire sermon had been published in 1759 under the title, *Britain's Happiness and the Proper Improvement of It; Represented in a Sermon Preached at Newington Green, on Nov. 29, 1759; Being the Day Appointed for a General Thanksgiving* (Roland Thomas, *Richard Price,* 1924, p. 173).

17. The extracts from Price's sermon contain no reference to general warrants, but in the introduction the editor mentions, among the improvements and alterations in political advantages in England since 1759, that 'general warrants have been done away' (p. 4).

any tortoise in Christendom. News I have none to send you, nor desire to have, of home manufacture. In France, I believe, they will have enough to do to consume their own, without seeing their fashions adopted, as they used to be, by other countries. Adieu! my good friend.

To Mary Berry, Wednesday 20 July 1791

Address: À Mademoiselle Mademoiselle Berry à la poste restante à Florence, Italie.
Postmark: FIRENZE 31. Endorsed: 'Pd 2s.' Below the address: 'Clemson.'
Posted 22 July ('Visitors'); see also introduction to preceding letter.
The address and letter, except the last paragraph, are in Kirgate's hand.

Strawberry Hill, Wednesday evening, July 20, 1791.

No. 43.

THOUGH a supernumerary letter set out for you from London but yesterday evening, yet I will not lose my ordinary Friday's post, and begin this now for two reasons; first, I am sure you will be glad to hear that I am much better, though an accident that happened to me on Monday might have had ugly consequences. Having had a good deal of fever, I take saline draughts: a fresh parcel came on Sunday night, with a bottle in a separate paper, which I concluded was hartshorn, which I had wanted. They were laid on the window, and next morning I bade James give me one of the draughts: he thinking it one of the former parcel, gave me the separate draught, and I swallowed it directly, but instantly found it was something very different, and sent for the apothecary to know what I had taken; yet before he could arrive, I found upon inquiry, and by the effects, that it was a vomit designed for one of the maids—to be sure, in pain and immovable all down my right side, it was not a pleasant adventure, but it had not the least bad effect, and I dictated the conclusion of my letter to you that very night, though I would not then mention my accident, lest you might suspect me poisoned before this could arrive to convince you of the contrary. I was very well all yesterday, and so I am today, and should have walked about the house but have had company the whole day. Before I arose Gen. Conway came to breakfast with me from London, on his way back to Park Place:[1] then came Lady Charlotte North and Mrs. G. Cholmondeley, from Bushy; Mrs Grenville from Hampton Court, and the Mount Edgecumbes from Richmond, whilst three different companies were seeing the house by a confusion I had made during my pain in giving out three tickets for the same day[2]—all this is a trumpery story, but at least will show you that I am very well now.

My second reason for writing now is, that I received yesterday a most kind letter from your father, for which I give him a thousand thanks; particularly, for the good account he gives me of your nose; and, as he desires, I blend my answer with this to you two: he also hints at what I expected, and do not dislike, that he finds Florence not more delightful than England, and shall not be sorry, for which I again thank him, to set up his staff at Cliveden.

Gen. Conway told me that the latest accounts last night in town from Birmingham were, that all was quieted there on the arrival of the military,[3] but that the populace were gone into Worcestershire, some said in pursuit of Dr Priestly; and that they had threatened Ragley, Lord Beauchamp's seat,[4] in their own county, for his having been for taking off the Test Act[5]—but as the Edgecumbes were here at three o'clock and had heard nothing new, I conclude and hope all is over. Great mischief has been done at Birmingham,[6] and indeed

1. Conway went from Park Place to London on Monday, 18 July (*Berry Papers* 55).

2. 'Mrs Chichester of Richmond, Mr Daniel from Mr Lysons, Monsieur Bouteiller, all 3, by mistake the same day' ('Visitors').

3. In an evening newspaper, *The St James's Chronicle* 16–19 July 1791, the latest advice from Birmingham was: 'By the arrival of the soldiers and the departure of the rioters . . . our minds are at present relieved.'

4. Ragley Hall, near Alcester, in Warwickshire, seat of Francis Ingram-Seymour-Conway (1743–1822), styled Lord Beauchamp 1750–93, and E. of Yarmouth 3 July 1793–4; succeeded his father, 23 June 1794, as 2d M. of Hertford.

5. In 1789 and again in 1790 motions for the repeal of the Test and Corporation Acts (25 Car. II, c. 2; 13 Car. II, St. 2, c. 1) were debated and lost in the House of Commons (*Parliamentary History of England*, vol.

xxviii [1789–1791], 1816, pp. 1–41, 387–452), and they were not repealed until 1828. Lord Beauchamp, who was M.P. for Orford 1768–94, spoke in neither debate. The account in *The Oracle* 22 July 1791 suggests another reason for his unpopularity with the populace: 'Lord Beauchamp received an express from Birmingham, dated the second day of the riots, by which his Lordship was greatly alarmed. . . . It was intimated that some of the rioters, hearing that his Lordship honoured Dr Priestley with his friendship, were resolved to proceed to his estate and to commit the most wanton acts of devastation. Lord and Lady Beauchamp and family remained in a state of the greatest anxiety till intelligence was received that the rioters had ceased their depredations, and that his Lordship's possessions had not suffered the smallest annoyance. Lord Beauchamp's beautiful estate near Birmingham is estimated at £150,000 sterling.'

6. For a list of houses and meeting-houses

the provocations there and in London, and in other places, have been grievous; vast numbers of Paine's pamphlet were distributed both to regiments and ships, but were given up voluntarily to the officers, and even money was tried on the guards, but to no purpose: the most seditious hand-bills were stuck up in London and Birmingham,[7] and Dr Priestly is said to have boasted that at the latter, he could raise 20,000 men—and so indeed he has, but against himself.

As not the least spirit of dissatisfaction has appeared anywhere, I trust the French Revolutionists will not hazard any more attempts: nor is France at all likely to emerge out of its own dreadful calamities, which will now tempt no other nations to imitate them. I enclose the best printed account, I have seen, of the riots at Birmingham from yesterday's paper.[8]

Thursday[9] evening.

The moment I had finished dictating this last night I received yours with the continuation of your fêtes, the conflagration of the ball room at the Cascines, and your first news of the flight of the poor French Majesties, to all which I have left myself no paper to answer— but I have written those three lines with my own hand, which I am vain enough to think will satisfy you more. *Thrice,* Adieu!

TO MARY BERRY, Tuesday 26 July 1791

Address: À Mademoiselle Mademoiselle Berry à la poste restante à Florence, Italie. *Postmark:* FIRENZE. Endorsed: 'Pd 1/.'
Posted 29 July ('Visitors').

burnt down, and of houses gutted, see *The London Chronicle* 21–23 July 1791, lxx. 75. In ibid. 76, the property damage was estimated at £25,000.

7. A copy of the 'seditious handbill which is supposed to have occasioned the riots . . . at Birmingham' is given in *The London Chronicle* 19–21 July 1791, lxx. 71, and also in the King's proclamation in which £100 was offered for the discovery of the person or persons concerned in printing or distributing the handbill (ibid. 28–30

July 1791, lxx. 103). Six copies of the handbill had been left at a tavern in Birmingham a few days before July 14, 'which, having been very generally copied, caused no small fermentation in the minds of the people' (GM 1791, lxi pt ii. 674).

8. Enclosure missing; good accounts of the riots appear in *The Times* and *The Oracle* 19 July 1791, and in *The London Chronicle* 16–19 July 1791.

9. The remainder of the letter is in HW's hand.

Strawberry Hill, July 26, 1791.

No. 44.[1]

TEN months are gone of the longest year that ever was born—a baker's year, for it has thirteen months to the dozen! As our letters are so long interchanging, it is not beginning too early to desire you will think of settling the stages to which I must direct to you in your route—nay, I don't know whether it is not already too late: I am sure it will be, if I am to stay for an answer to this—but I hope you will have thought on it before you receive this.

I am so much recovered as to have been abroad. I cannot say my arm is glib yet; but if I waited for the total departure of the rheumatism, I might stay at home till the national debt is paid. My fair writing is a proof of my lameness: I labour as if I were engraving, and drop no words, as I do in my ordinary hasty scribbling.[2]

Lady Cecilia tells me that her nephew Mr West,[3] who was with you at Pisa, declares he is in love with you both—so I am not singular. You two may like to hear this, though no novelty to you, but it will not satisfy Mr Berry, who will be impatient for news from Birmingham, but there are no more, nor any-whence else. There has not been another riot in any of the three kingdoms. The villain Paine came over for the Crown and Anchor,[4] but finding that his pamphlet[5] had not set a straw on fire, and that the 14th of July was as little in fashion as the ancient Gunpowder Plot, he dined at another tavern with a few quaking conspirators,[6] and probably is returned to Paris[7] where he is engaged in a controversy with the Abbé Sieyès[8] about the plus or minus of rebellion.[9] The rioters in Worcestershire, whom I men-

1. 'No. 50' (B).

2. HW's letters were written rapidly, but not carelessly, and there are few 'dropped' words.

3. 'The Hon. Septimus West, uncle to the present Lord De la Warr. He died the [second] year after' (B). Hon. Septimus Henry West (1765–93), sixth son of Lady Cecilia's brother, John, 2d E. De la Warr (Collins, *Peerage*, 1812, v. 27).

4. That is, for the meeting of the 'Revolution Club' at the Crown and Anchor Tavern 14 July (ante 17 July 1791). Paine arrived at the White Bear, Piccadilly, 13 July (Moncure D. Conway, *Life of Thomas Paine*, 1892, i. 312–14).

5. *The Rights of Man*, Pt I.

6. According to *The Times* 16 July 1791, Robert Merry, Horne Tooke, and Boswell, among others, dined at the Shakespeare Tavern 14 July, and Paine joined them after dinner. If Boswell was really there, he was drawn by curiosity, not sympathy.

7. Paine remained in England for over a year: he arrived at White's Hotel, Paris, 19 Sept. 1792 (Conway, op. cit. i. 351–5).

8. Emmanuel-Joseph Sieyès (1748–1836), Comte, divine and politician; author of *Qu'est-ce que le tiers état*, 1789, a pamphlet which gave him considerable influence in the early part of the French Revolution.

9. A short letter of Sieyès in defence of monarchy, elicited partly by Paine's republican writings (though Paine is not named),

tioned in my last, were not a detachment from Birmingham, but volunteer incendiaries from the capital, who went, *according to the rights of men,* with the mere view of plunder, and threatened gentlemen to burn their houses, if not ransomed. Eleven of these disciples of Paine are in custody;[10] and Mr Merry,[11] Mrs Barbauld, and Miss Helen Williams[12] will probably have subjects for elegies. Deborah[13] and Jael,[14] I believe, were invited to the Crown and Anchor, and had let their nails grow accordingly—but somehow or other no *poissonnières* were there, and the two prophetesses had no opportunity that day of exercising their talents or talons. Their French allies, cock and hen, have a fairer field open, and the Jacobins, I think, will soon drive the National Assembly to be better royalists than ever they were, in self-defence. I know nothing else—but it is early in the week. Yes, Mrs Keppel has let her house at Isleworth[15] to Sheridan for £400 a year—

appeared in the *Moniteur* 6 juillet 1791. Paine's reply, in defence of republicanism, dated '8 juillet 1791' and written at Paris just before his departure for England, appeared in *Le Patriote français* 11 July 1791. In the supplement to the *Moniteur* 16 juillet 1791 Paine's reply was reprinted, together with Sieyès' rejoinder, in which Sieyès declined further controversy. Nevertheless Paine replied to Sieyès in the third chapter of *The Rights of Man,* Pt II, 1792. Cf. Paine, *Writings,* ed. Moncure D. Conway, 1894–6, iii. 9–10; Moncure D. Conway, *Life of Thomas Paine,* 1892, i. 312–14; Albéric Neton, *Sieyès,* 1900, pp. 153–7; Library of Congress Cat. Their differences in theory did not prevent their working together on the French constitution in the autumn of 1792 (Conway, *Life of Thomas Paine,* 1892, i. 362).

10. *The Oracle* 21 July 1791 reported: 'Information received by the latest expresses last night from Birmingham report tranquillity to have been perfectly restored . . . the mobs dispersed, and one dozen of the principal rioters in custody.' At Warwick Assizes 22–23 August 1791 the twelve rioters were tried for demolishing or setting fire to houses and meeting-houses; two were hanged, one pardoned, one respited, and the rest found not guilty. See *The Oracle* 26–27, 29 Aug., 10 Sept. 1791; *The Report*

of the *Trials of the Rioters, at the Assizes held at Warwick,* Birmingham, [1791].

11. He was author of an *Ode for the Fourteenth of July, the Day Consecrated to Freedom; being the Anniversary of the Revolution in France* (BM Cat.), which had been published 14 July and had been recited with music at the Crown and Anchor on that day (*Times* 13, 14 July 1791).

12. Helen Maria Williams (1762–1827), who, at the date of HW's letter, had published poems, novels, and *Letters Written in France in the Summer of 1790,* 1790 (she subsequently, 1792–3, published three additional volumes of *Letters from France*). 'She adopted with enthusiasm the principles and ideas of the revolution, and wrote of it with a fervour that amounted almost to frenzy' (DNB: Sir John Knox Laughton). The celebration in Paris of the first anniversary of the fall of the Bastille she thought 'the most sublime spectacle which, perhaps, was ever represented on the theatre of this earth' (*Letters Written in France in the Summer of 1790,* p. 2).

13. Mrs Barbauld; see HW to Hannah More 29 Sept. 1791.

14. Miss Williams.

15. 'The house by the waterside, which is now [1795] the property of the Hon. Mrs Keppel, and in the occupation of the Earl of Warwick, was built by James Lacey, Esq.,

an immense rate—and yet far from a wise bargain; he has just been forced out of his house in Bruton Street[16] by his landlord,[17] who could get no rent from him—almost the night he came to Isleworth, he gave a ball there,[18] which will not precipitate Mrs K.'s receipts.

Wednesday evening, 27th.

This morning I received yours of the 12th so it was but a fortnight on its journey—I wish all journeys from Florence could be as rapid. I am now beginning my fears about roads, bad inns, accidents and winds at sea; and they will increase from the first of September!

You have indeed surprised me by your account of the strange credulity on poor King Louis's escape *in safety!* In these villages we heard of his flight late in the evening,[19] and the very next morning of his being retaken. Much as he, at least the Queen, has suffered, I am persuaded the adventure has hastened general confusion, and will increase the Royal Party; though perhaps their Majesties, for their personal safeties, had better have awaited the natural progress of anarchy. The enormous deficience of money, and the total insubordination of the army, both apparent and uncontradicted from the reports made to the National Assembly, show what is coming—into what such a chaos will subside, it would be silly to attempt to guess. Perhaps it is not wiser in the exiles to expect to live to see a resettlement in their favour. One thing I have for these two years thought probable to arrive, a division, at least a dismemberment of France. Despotism could no longer govern so unwieldy a machine—a republic would be still less likely to hold it together—If foreign powers should interfere,

patentee of Drury Lane Theatre' (Daniel Lysons, *Environs of London*, 1792–6, iii. 100). According to *The Oracle* 17 Sept. 1791 the house 'is now in the market; the price £10,000. It was bought from the unfortunate Mr Lacy by Sir Edward Walpole, the father of Mrs Keppel.' 'Mrs Sheridan still remains at Isleworth, bending her elegant form under the pressure of indisposition' (*Times* 18 Oct. 1791). 'Mr Sheridan has fixed his winter residence at Knightsbridge, next door to Mr Harris' (*Times* 15 Nov. 1791).

16. Where Sheridan had lived since 1784 (Walter Sichel, *Sheridan*, 1909, i. 536).

17. Not identified.

18. 'Yesterday [7 July] Mr Sheridan gave a splendid entertainment to a large party of his political friends at his house near Isleworth, on the banks of the Thames' (*Oracle* 8 July 1791). On the day after HW wrote the above passage, Sheridan gave 'another fête . . . at Isleworth . . . to a numerous political party, vying in splendour and luxury with the most ostentatious festivals of the opulent!' (*Oracle* 28 July 1791).

19. The evening newspapers of 25 June included the information concerning the escape (see *St James's Chronicle* 23–25 June 1791, where the report is called a 'rumour'), but the morning newspapers of that day did not.

they will take care to pay themselves with what is *à leur bienséance*—and that in reality would be serving France too—So much for my speculations, and they have never varied.

We are so far from intending to new-model our government and dismiss the royal family, annihilate the peerage, cashier the hierarchy, and lay open the land to the first occupier, as Dr Priestly and Tom Paine and the Revolution Club humbly proposed, that we are even encouraging the breed of princes. It is generally believed that the Duke of York is going to marry the Princess of Prussia, the King's daughter by his first wife and his favourite child.[20] I do not affirm it, but many others do.

You will be sorry for Mr Batt: when he left me, he was going to Lord Frederic Campbell's,[21] but was sent for to Oxford, where his only brother,[22] a clergyman, was dying, and is dead, of a putrid fever. He was fifteen years younger than Mr Batt, and much beloved by him; Mrs Garrick came and told me of it in tears. Another person[23] has told me that in point of circumstances it may enrich Mr Batt: they have a very rich old uncle,[24] whose partiality was for the younger.

Thank you for remembering the Cardinal of York's medal; how welcome it will be, for from what hand am I to receive it! There is another dear hand from which I wish I sometimes saw a line! I can and do write to both at once, and think to and of both at once; but methinks letters all from one hand are not the same thing. I shall not think I am as equally dear to both, as they are to me, if I never hear but from one. Mary is constant, but I shall fear Martha is busy about many other things! Mr Berry is so good as to write to me—I say no more.

I wrote this latter part tonight, because I don't know whether I

20. Frederica Charlotte Ulrica Catherina (1767–1820), only child of Frederick William II (1744–97), K. of Prussia, 1786, by his first wife Elizabeth Ulrica (d. 1841) of Brunswick-Wolfenbüttel, from whom he was divorced in 1769. The marriage of the Princess and the Duke of York was performed at Berlin 29 Sept. and again at Buckingham Palace 23 Nov. 1791.

21. At Comb Bank, Sundridge, Kent.

22. Charles William Batt (ca 1761–23 July 1791), educated at Westminster School and Christ Church, Oxford (B.A. 1781, M.A. 1784); chaplain to Lord Malmesbury; author of *A Dissertation on the Message from*

St John the Baptist to Our Saviour, published anonymously, 1788; 2d edn, with additions and with the author's name, 1789 (*Old Westminsters*).

23. Possibly Richard Owen Cambridge: his son George was Charles William Batt's older contemporary at Oxford, and John Thomas Batt was a friend of the Cambridges (cf. *ante* 29 Jan. 1791).

24. William Batt (ca 1714–92), of Nunton and New Hall, Wilts. On his death (13 Dec. 1792) John Thomas Batt succeeded to his property (GM 1792, lxii pt ii. 1157; GM 1831, ci pt i. 274; Joseph Foster, *Alumni Oxonienses . . . 1715–1886*, 1887–8).

shall have time tomorrow: Lord Hertford,[25] Lady Elizabeth,[26] Hugh and Lady Horatia[27] are to dine with me from Lady Lincoln's[28] at Putney, and may stay most part of the evening. I reserve a vacuum for any news they may tell me.

Thursday night late.

I heard nothing at my dinner, but I have since been at Richmond, and heard that Lady Valetort is brought to bed of a daughter,[29] so this time Lady Mount will cry with but one eye[30]—but Lady Di has told me an extraordinary fact. Catherine Slayczar sent for Mr Fawkener and desired he will order for her a bust of Charles Fox, and she will place it between Demosthenes and Cicero (pedantry she learnt from her French authors, and which our schoolboys would be above using), for his eloquence has saved two great nations from a war[31]—by

25. Francis Seymour Conway (1718–94), 1st E. of Hertford, n.c.; cr. (1793) M. of Hertford; HW's first cousin, and correspondent 1763–5.

26. Lady Elizabeth Seymour-Conway (resumed name of Seymour in 1794) (1754–1825), 5th dau. of Lord Hertford (Collins, *Peerage*, 1812, ii. 565; Burke, *Peerage*, 1928, p. 1205, *sub* Hertford).

27. Lord Hertford's fifth son, Capt. Hon. Hugh Seymour-Conway (later, 1793, Lord Hugh Conway, and from 1794, Lord Hugh Seymour), and his wife, *née* Lady Horatia Waldegrave.

28. Frances Seymour-Conway (1751–1820), 4th dau. of Lord Hertford; m. (1775) Henry Fiennes Pelham-Clinton (1750–78), styled E. of Lincoln, son of Henry Fiennes Pelham-Clinton, 2d D. of Newcastle-under-Lyne. She occupied a house called Copt Hall, 'near the waterside' of the Thames at Putney (Daniel Lysons, *Environs of London*, 1792–6, i. 423).

29. Emma Sophia Edgcumbe (28 July 1791–1872), her parents' first surviving child, born in Portugal Street, Hyde Park.

30. MS reads 'cry with but with one eye.' Lady Mount Edgcumbe had wept copiously on the death of her first grandson (*ante* 10 July 1790).

31. A slightly different version of this incident appears in *The Oracle* 11 Aug. 1791. The Empress wrote a note in pencil to one of her secretaries of state: 'Write to Count de Woronzoff [envoy extraordinary and minister plenipotentiary to Great Britain], to procure for me the bust of Charles Fox, in white marble. I wish to place it in my gallery, between those of Demosthenes and Cicero. By his eloquence he has delivered his own country and Russia from a war for which there was no pretext of justice or of reason.' The secretary asked and received permission 'to retrace the letters with ink, that Mr Fox may see the original in your Majesty's handwriting.' Woronzoff is said to have shown the note to Fox.

his opposition to it, *s'entend*[32]—so the peace is no doubt made.[33] She could not have addressed her compliment worse than to Mr Fawkener, sent by Mr Pitt, and therefore so addressed, and who of all men does not love Mr Fox—and Mr Fox, who has no vainglory, will not care a straw for the flattery, and will understand it too. Goodnight.

To MARY and AGNES BERRY, Wednesday 3 August 1791

Address: À Mademoiselle Mademoiselle Berry à la poste restante à Florence, Italie. *Postmark:* FIRENZE 24. Endorsed: 'Pd 1s.'

Posted 5 Aug.; in 'Visitors' HW noted the subject of this and the following letter: 'on fever.'

Strawberry Hill, Aug. 3, 1791.

No. 45.

HOW cruel to know you ill at such a distance! how shocking to must have patience, when one has none! I do hope I shall have another line this week—and yet the wind is westwardly! I do believe St James's blessed powder has cured your fever—but I am persuaded it was no slight one, for the effects would not have weakened you so much, as the powder never has great effect without full cause. Your fêtes and balls and the heat have occasioned your illness—you both left England in search of health, and yet have done as much as you could have performed in London, where at least the cold can tolerate crowds and fatigue. Nor have you been temperate even since your fever—you have aired too long, and why see four or five persons so soon, and sit up with them till eleven? All this kind Agnes has owned, though she says she is perfectly easy about you—can I be so, who may be a week without knowing whether you have had no return? I longed to see Agnes's writing, and she never could have sent it more apropos, since there was occasion for it—you yourself were both kind and unkind to write so much—but burn the French! Why write so much

32. This evidence of Fox's reputation abroad is supported by a passage in HW's 'Mem. 1783–91,' *sub* 11 Feb. 1784: 'Count Kagenec, Austr[ian] Min[ister], told Gen. Conway, Mr Fox had contrib[uted] to peace of Russia and Turkey, and was the greatest man alive; that all the foreign ministers agreed on that, admired his frankness, and held all he said for truth.'

33. Fawkener, who had arrived in St Petersburg 24 May and had presented his credentials 26 June 1791, had (with Sir Charles Whitworth) virtually if not completely finished negotiations for a treaty of peace between Russia and Turkey; he had an audience of leave 31 July 1791, and left St Petersburg shortly afterwards, but his recall, dated 6 Oct. 1791, was not delivered by Whitworth until 14 Nov. 1791. The treaty between Russia and Turkey was signed 9 Jan. 1792 (*British Diplomatic Representatives 1789–1852*, ed. S. T. Bindoff *et al.*, 1934, p. 109).

South
View from $\mathcal{C}^{t}$ of Goodwood 14th Augst 1796

GOODWOOD, BY MARY BERRY

about them? For heaven's sake be more careful; you are both of you delicate and far from strong. You bid me take care of myself—to what purpose do I cocker[1] myself against November, if you two fling away your healths—nay, I will now not look so early as to November—do not, I implore you, set out in great heats. Be certain of being quite recovered before you stir—fatigue and hot bad inns may lay you up where there is no assistance—Oh! I now feel again all the aversion I felt last year to your journey! Travel slowly I beseech you—I had rather wait months for you, than have you run any risk. Surely you will keep very quiet till you begin your journey, and perfectly recruit your strength—dear Mr Berry, exert your authority, and do not suffer them to be giddy and rash, nor plunge into any more diversions.

I cannot write about the French, nor think about them now, though I heard of nothing else all yesterday, for Petty France dined here yesterday, and I went back with them to Richmond. They firmly believe that all Europe in arms will march to Paris by Tuesday sennight, drive the Assembly and the Jacobins into the Red Sea, and borrow our fleet to replace the exiles here in their own hotels *sur le quai*. I forget why they believe all this, nor shall I recollect why till I have another letter from you. I believe too that I have not heard a tittle of news, but that you have had a fever at Florence, and that your bedchamber is very noisy—oh! how quiet you would have been at Cliveden, and that Mr and Mrs Legge[2] have been divinely kind, and lent you one more tranquil—what charming people they must be!

Mrs Damer passed Sunday with me; her leg is not well again;[3] she goes to Goodwood on Friday and thence to the sea.[4]

---

1. I.e., pamper (OED).

2. Heneage Legge (1747–1827), only son of Hon. Heneage Legge; m. (1768) Elizabeth Musgrave (d. 1820), 2d dau. of Sir Philip Musgrave, 6th Bt, of Eden Hall, Cumberland. Mrs Legge accompanied the Berrys from Florence to Bologna (*post* 3 Oct. 1791; Burke, *Peerage*, 1928, p. 687, *sub* Dartmouth; Richard A. Austen-Leigh, *Eton College Register 1753–1790*, Eton, 1921; GM 1820, xc pt i. 284; GM 1827, xcvii pt i. 92; Collins, *Peerage*, 1812, iv. 121; Charles James Fèret, *Fulham Old and New*, 1900, iii. 237).

3. It is not clear whether Mrs Damer injured her leg when she fell from her scaffold in June 1791 (*Berry Papers* 40), or whether the ailment was of long standing. On 7 Aug. 1791 Mrs Damer wrote Mary Berry: 'My leg is better, tho' not quite well' (ibid. 60).

4. Mrs Damer's letter to Mary Berry 15 Aug. 1791 was written from Felpham, Sussex (*Berry Papers* 60), where she remained until 26 Aug., returned to Goodwood 'for some days,' and planned to return to Felpham 'for not long' (ibid. 68).

Thursday noon.

I am not at all more easy, though I have slept since I heard of your fever. Your journey haunts me: you will not be strong enough to undertake it so soon as you intended. You would begin it when the weather is too hot, and finish it when too cold. No, I had rather you did not set out till March—though I might never see you more, it had better be prevented by my exit than by yours. Everything terrifies me for you; though I have little faith in a speedy invasion of France, yet I believe it when you may be to pass through armies and camps. My dear, dear wives, be cautious! no risks by land or sea!—in short, I am unquiet to the greatest degree—I had almost forgot to thank you about the medals—bring me but yourselves safe and in good health, and I care about nothing else—yes, I do, for another letter. I ought, when you desire it and are not well, to try to amuse you; but seriously if I have heard any news, I have forgot it—but I think I have heard nothing, but that Lord Henry Fitzgerald and Miss Boyle are to be married today;[5] and that Miss Ogilvie's[6] match with the rich Irish heir apparent[7] is off; her brother Lord Edward[8] carried her dismission of him, and did not deliver it in dulcet words.[9]

5. They were married by the Bishop of Peterborough 4 Aug. (by special licence) at the house of Miss Boyle in Stratford Place (*The Registers of Marriages of St Mary le Bone, Middlesex, 1783–1792*, ed. W. Bruce Bannerman and R. R. Bruce Bannerman, 1922, p. 151).

6. Cecilia Margaret Ogilvie (1775–1824), 1st dau. of William Ogilvie by Emilia Lennox, dau. of Charles, 2d D. of Richmond, and widow of James Fitzgerald, 1st D. of Leinster; m. (1795) Charles Lock, 2d son of William Lock of Norbury Park, Surrey, and brother of William Lock, the amateur painter (Collins, *Peerage*, 1812, vi. 197; GM 1795, lxv pt ii. 613; Vittoria Colonna Caetani, Duchessa di Sermoneta, *The Locks of Norbury*, [1940], *passim*).

7. George Augustus Chichester (1769–1844), styled Vct Chichester 1769–4 July 1791, and E. of Belfast 4 July 1791–9; 2d M. of Donegall, 1799. He became engaged to Cecilia Ogilvie in Oct. 1790, and the marriage was set for May, but Lord Chichester became indifferent, broke off the engagement, and in June the Duchess of Leinster

announced that the marriage would not take place (Duchessa di Sermoneta, op. cit. 97–9).

8. Lord Edward Fitzgerald (1763–98), Miss Ogilvie's uterine brother; 5th son of James, 1st D. of Leinster; entered the army, 1780; M.P. for Athy 1783–90, and for county Kildare 1790–7; became sympathetic with revolutionary principles and was cashiered from the army, 1792; joined the United Irishmen, 1796; wounded while resisting arrest for high treason 19 May 1798; died of his wounds in Newgate Prison, Dublin, 4 June 1798.

9. 'The Duchess [of Leinster] managed the situation so ably that the whole of London thought it was Cecilia who had broken off her engagement; even Horace Walpole was deceived. He wrote to Miss Berry [the above passage follows]' (Duchessa di Sermoneta, op. cit. 99). The newspapers had also circulated false rumours of a duel between Lord Belfast and Lord Henry Fitzgerald; see *The Times* 11 July 1791; *London Chronicle* 9–12 July 1791, lxx. 36. A letter of Lord Henry Fitzgerald 13 July 1791 de-

If I receive good accounts from Florence, my next letter shall tell you anything I learn—if I persisted in adding to this, I could only specify a million more of apprehensions, and execrations of your journey, from the 10th of October to the 16th of March when you had your fall, and then to your fêtes and fever in July! *St James's* day[10] has been my only holiday in ten months—do not give him a post-vigil that may destroy his festival! Adieu! adieu! what would I not give for another letter this moment!

PS. My dearest Agnes, though you have no fever, yet as you have undergone the same heats and fatigues with Mary, I entreat you to take four or five grains of St James, that if you have any lurking disorder, it may remove it before you set out, and prevent your falling [ill] on the road, which I dread—though I wish your journey to be delayed. If you are quite well, the powder will have no effect at all. I hope you will all three observe a very cool strict regimen before you set out for at least ten days—I have not forgotten Italian inns, and how totally void of comforts and assistance—this fever has frightened me horridly.

To Mary Berry, Monday 8 August 1791

Address: À Mademoiselle Mademoiselle Berry à la poste restante à Florence, Italie. *Postmark:* FIRENZE. Endorsed: 'Pd 1s.'
Posted 9 Aug. ('Visitors') ; cf. introductory note to preceding letter.

Monday night, Aug. 8, 1791.

No. 46.

I HAVE received no second letter about your fever, but Mrs Damer had one on Saturday, which says you go on as well as possible.[1] Perhaps I may have one tomorrow—but this must go away by eight tomorrow morning by the coach to save the foreign post. I have been in

fends Miss Ogilvie and blackens Lord Chichester (*The Paget Brothers, 1790–1840,* ed. Lord Hylton, 1918, p. 6).

10. The day Mary Berry took James's powder for her fever.

———

1. Mrs Damer wrote to Mary Berry Saturday evening, 6 Aug. 1791: 'My *magnifying powers,* however suppressed by the perfect confidence I have in everything you say, I could but feel most anxious and uneasy, as you must be and are sensible yourself, and the altered hand of your last lines did not escape me, which you will find by my let-

twenty minds whether I should write again before my usual Friday, for
I feel I shall only tire you with an anxiety about a fever that I hope will
have been quite gone a fortnight at least before you receive my letter—
yet write I must—I am sure you have been very ill, and now I dread
your setting out too soon before you have perfectly recovered your
strength, as much as I was afraid of your not coming at the time you
had fixed. Your journey now will fill me with additional terrors—and I
was tolerably uneasy about the last! To know you in bad inns, and not
even know where! fearful of not receiving your letters regularly—uncertain whether you will get mine—well—only determine on the most
prudent and safe measures that can be taken, and I shall forget all when
I see you return well, how long soever it be first—I give up, I disclaim, I
protest against all promises, that could make you think of setting out
one instant before you are fit for it—I have been too selfish already—I
have not an atom of self-love when your health is in question.

My poor letters that you say are not so barren as I foretold they
would be in summer, will now I doubt have the additional *désagré-
ment* of being teasing and full of repetitions. Can one attend to or inquire after news, when one's mind is occupied about one family, and
anxious about every step they take? Can one relate with interest what
does not interest one? Will it amuse you to be told daily that I went to
Boyle Farm this morning to visit Lord Henry Fitzgerald and his bride,
and carried in my coach an old Lady *Clifden*[2] (oh! not a *Cliveden*) her

ter. Mr W[alpole] sent me your account by
Tuesday's post, and expressed much uneasiness. He even *deigned* to beg that I
would let him know when I heard again.
This you will believe I should have done.
There was more danger of an *express* than
an omission. I stayed in town today, in
hopes that I might hear from you, and I
have not been disappointed. The post, too,
came just in time for me to write to Mr
W[alpole] without *an express*. A few lines
from you would have satisfied my anxiety,
and I *would* if I *could* regret, this time, that
you sent me a longer letter. It would be
trifling with you to say that the extreme
delicacy of your health ever leaves my mind
at ease, but with the most perfect truth I
can assure you, tho' I might not trouble you
with my anxieties, that in this absence they
would have been to me intolerable, were it

not for the dependence I have on your
word. As for your return, I will not, cannot
say how much for your sake I dread it. I
know, and see all the objections' (*Berry
Papers* 59–60).

2. Lucia Martin (ca 1732–1802), 1st dau.
of Col. John Martin of Dublin; m. (1) (before 1753) Henry Boyle-Walsingham, 2d
son of Henry Boyle who was cr. E. of Shannon in 1756, and uncle to Lady Henry Fitzgerald; m. (2) (1760) James Agar (1734–89),
cr. (1776) Bn and (1781) Vct Clifden of Gow-
ran. She died at Lady Mendip's house at
Twickenham, and was buried in Twickenham Church, where the monument to her
memory is said to give her name as 'Louisa,'
not Lucia (R. S. Cobbett, *Memorials of
Twickenham*, 1872, p. 90; John Lodge and
Mervyn Archdall, *Peerage of Ireland*, 1789,
ii. 365; GEC).

aunt, who is at Mr Ellis's, and told me a whole chronicle, about which I did not care a straw, of the no-match of Miss Ogilvie. Then I went and dined at Mrs Garrick's[3] with Les Boufflers,[4] Madame de Cambis and the Johnstones and Mrs Anderson—and the French being afraid of highwaymen, would not return over the common,[5] and desired me to convoy them through Bushy Park, which I did. They wished me to return with them to Richmond, but I chose to alight here, and write to you, though I had nothing better to send you than this dull day's work.

Mr Lenox has got a son.[6] There is to be a ball at Windsor on Friday for the Prince's birthday, which has not lately been noticed there.[7] Lord Lorn and seven other young men of fashion were invited to it. It seems they now crop their hair short and wear no powder,[8] which not being the etiquette yet, the youths, instead of representing that they are not fit to appear so docked, sent excuses, that they were going out of town, or were unavoidably engaged[9]—a message one would think dic-

3. At Hampton.

4. Madame de Boufflers and Comtesse Amélie de Boufflers.

5. Hounslow Heath: the main road from Hampton to Twickenham or Richmond went through Bushy Park, but there was a shorter road across Hounslow Heath (John Cary, *Cary's New Itinerary,* 1798, column 47; Daniel Lysons, *Environs of London,* 1792–6, ii. frontispiece).

6. Charles Lennox (after 1836 Gordon-Lennox) (3 Aug. 1791–1860), styled E. of March 1806–19; 5th D. of Richmond, 1819.

7. Because of the coolness between the Queen and the Prince of Wales; see *ante* 27 March 1791. For an account of the ball, and the list of guests, see *The Oracle* 13 Aug. 1791.

8. 'The present fashion amongst a certain number of our young nobility, viz., that of

what is called shearing their heads, did not, as has been erroneously stated, originate with his Grace of Hamilton. The first *gentleman* that introduced that becoming fashion, being a Mr Townsend, an officer of Bow Street!' (*Oracle* 25 July 1791). 'Cropping' soon became fashionable, as the descriptions of 'A Noble Crop,' 'A Jack a Dandy Crop,' 'A Thundering Crop,' etc., in *The Times* 27 Sept. 1791 attest. See also *The Times* 14 April 1795.

9. It appears from a list of those who received invitations and sent excuses (*Oracle* 13 Aug. 1791), that eight young men in addition to Lord Lorn declined the invitation: Lord Charles Somerset, Lord Belgrave, Lord Herbert, the Hon. Dudley Ryder, Col. the Hon. Henry Phipps, the Hon. Edmund Phipps, the Hon. John Eliot, and the Hon. Edward Finch.

tated by old Prynne[10] or Tom Paine, and certainly unparalleled in all the books in the Lord Chamberlain's office.

This being the sum total of my gazette's knowledge, I will not trust my pen with the rest of my paper, which you may guess how it would fill, if I gave a loose to it. I will suffer it to ask but one question—shall you not recollect Charing Cross[11] before you set out? It would give me a pleasure that would balance my not seeing you so soon as I expected, and you owe me a particular mark of friendship for the uneasiness your fever has given me. Adieu! adieu!

To MARY BERRY, Wednesday 10 August 1791

Address: À Mademoiselle Mademoiselle Berry à la poste restante à Florence, Italie. *Postmark:* FIRENZE 34. Endorsed: 'Pd 1s.' Posted 11 Aug. ('Visitors').

Strawberry Hill, Aug. 10, 1791.

No. 47

YOUR letter of the 25th of last month, which I received yesterday, assures me that you are completely recovered—nay, better than before your fever. I do my utmost to believe so—but belief is not like faith, one cannot swallow it whole at a gulp without proofs, and alas! I am at too great a distance to receive them! I am persuaded you have been very ill; and by *the better than before,* that your fever was generating. Your good nature induces you to make me as easy as you can; but how can I be easy, when you are so far off, have been very weak, have such a journey to take, and while I am uncertain when I shall see you again—or if ever! I do not recant a word in my two last; I wish you to decide on your return from the state of your health, strength, and inclination. The great blow to me was your going abroad at all, and I interested myself in it much more than I had any right to do. It has been followed by all kind of disquiets, which I will not recapitulate. Your last gives me a new alarm: I had flattered myself with your coming directly to Cliveden—I now see a hitch even in that!—I must be obstinate and foolish indeed, if I nurse any more visions, and attempt to harmonize ages so dissonant as yours and mine, and attempt to make their purposes coincide—yet I declare, though my own happiness has a

10. William Prynne (1600–69), Puritan pamphleteer.

11. That is, HW's banker in Charing Cross.

great share in my plan, its ultimate object is to make you two a little
more comfortable when I shall be out of the question. If you have any
speculations more rational, I relinquish mine with pleasure. One point
I can by no means abandon; set not your feet on French ground; I hear
daily of insults and violence offered to English travelling to or through
that frantic country: a Lady Webster[1] was lately ill-used on the fron-
tiers of Swisserland, and her pockets would have been ransacked, had
not her husband interposed roughly. You cannot have a lower opinion
of that whole nation than I have; the residents are barbarians, the exiles have wanted spirit, and neither have any sense. Impatience I have
none for Lally's book;[2] like Necker, he imagines Europe occupied
about him, or would make it so.[3] Miss Gunning acted fainting t'other
night at the play on Lord Lorn entering the next box[4]—but momentary
meteors have no second benefit.

The Emperor, by rejecting Noailles[5] now, will have acted sillily, if

1. Elizabeth Vassall (ca 1770–1845), dau.
of Richard Vassall of Jamaica, m. (1) (1786)
Sir Godfrey Webster (ca 1748–1800), 4th Bt,
1780, of Battle Abbey, Sussex, from whom
she was divorced by Act of Parliament,
1797; m. (2) (1797) Henry Richard Fox
(after 1800 Vassall Fox), 3d Bn Holland,
against whom Sir Godfrey had obtained
£6000 damages in an action of crim. con.
She became famous as the hostess of Holland House.

2. *Lettre écrite au très honorable Edmund Burke;* see *ante* 28 June 1791.

3. Possibly HW's remark was prompted
by recent advertisements of the publication
'in one large volume, octavo,' of the *Historical Review of the Administration of Mr
Necker,* 'written by himself, translated
from the French' (*St James's Chronicle* 4–6
Aug. 1791).

4. 'Miss Gunning on Saturday night [30

July] appeared in the side boxes at the Hay-
market Theatre, under the protection of
the venerable Duchess of Bedford' (*St
James's Chronicle* 30 July–2 Aug. 1791).
The incident HW describes is noticed in
The Oracle 15 Aug. 1791 in an account of
'Cropt Fashionables.'

5. Emmanuel-Marie-Louis (1743–1822),
Marquis de Noailles, French ambassador to
Holland 1770–6, to England 1776–8, and to
the Court of Vienna 1783–92. Leopold II,
who had been in Italy, returned to Vienna
20 July 1791 and held his first levee four
days later (*St James's Chronicle* 6–9 Aug.
1791). According to a dispatch from Vienna,
25 July, 'Prince Kaunitz yesterday informed
M. de Noailles, in the name of the Emperor, that the Court of Vienna "would
not recognize him as a Minister until the
Most Christian King [Louis XVI] was in
the full and complete possession of regal

he does not do more.[6] Had he refused to receive him at first,[7] very well; it would have been condemning rebellion, and would have called for no more, if he did not choose to make war—but now, when the King is not a whit more a prisoner than he was two years ago, it will be the anger of a tame eagle. Still I think the distresses and calamities of France will present more favourable moments than even the present— though I believe the National Assembly frightened almost—into their senses.

The Duke of York's marriage is certain;[8] the Duke of Clarence told me so himself yesterday. He graciously came hither yesterday,[9] though I had not been to pay my court—indeed I concluded he had forgot me, as at his age was very natural—Not having cropped my hair, I went to-day[10] to thank him—He could not see me, but sent to desire I would call on him tomorrow—I asked the page at what hour it would be proper; he answered, between ten and eleven—mercy on me! to be dressed and at Petersham before eleven! I am not got down to modern hours—but neither am I reverted to those of Queen Elizabeth, nor to those of Louis Douze, who is said to have hastened his death by condescending in complaisance to his young Queen Mary Tudor[11] to dine at so late an

---

power." This step is a prelude to some serious declarations, not from our Court alone, but also from several other states' (ibid.). According to *The Times* 13 Aug. 1791, 'the declaration reported to have been made by Prince de Kaunitz to the French ambassador at Vienna, M. de Noailles, is the weak invention of some ignorant newspaper editor.' At any rate, Noailles remained at Vienna, but asked to be recalled 24 March 1792, as his presence there seemed to him to be useless (NBG). HW had dined with Noailles in London (DU DEFFAND iv. 427), and had entertained him at SH (HW to Lady Ossory 15 June 1777).

6. Leopold's rejection of Noailles (if it occurred) was a prelude to his signing with Frederick William II of Prussia the weak Declaration of Pillnitz 27 Aug. 1791: a declaration that 'it was "in the common interest of all sovereigns of Europe" to give Louis the means to establish a monarchical government in France' (Saul K. Padover,

The Life and Death of Louis XVI, 1939, p. 235).

7. That is, at the beginning of the French Revolution.

8. See *ante* 26 July 1791. 'A courier arrived from London at Berlin on the 29th of July, with the consent of his Britannic Majesty to the marriage of the Duke of York with the Princess Frederica of Prussia' (*Oracle* 10 Aug. 1791).

9. The Duke had visited SH 22 Dec. 1790, on which occasion HW composed and printed verses for him (Hazen, *SH Bibliography* 234–5).

10. To Petersham: the Duke of Clarence had purchased in March 1791 the 'beautiful villa' belonging to Lord Camelford, at a price reported as 12,000 guineas (*St James's Chronicle* 10–12 March, 31 March–2 April 1791; *Oracle* 6 Aug. 1791).

11. Mary (1496–1533), sister of Henry VIII.

hour as eleven in the morning[12]—I at least, before I am so rakish, will wait till the arrival of my own Queen *Mary*.

Mrs Buller a month ago told me she should pass a fortnight here at Twickenham in her sister Lady Basset's[13] house—yonder, you know.[14] Her son was ill, and she came not till last Sunday, and then only for a night with him and Miss Wilkes:[15] they came and drank tea here.[16]

As I wrote to you but three nights ago, I will make no excuse for the brevity of this, which is only to acknowledge yours, and to fall in with my own Friday.[17] If you are really quite well, and set out nearly to the time you intended, I expect that our correspondence will be much deranged. News you will not lose of consequence—September is most inactive but against poor partridges, and in horse races, neither of which have places in my gazettes! Adieu!

To Barbara Cecilia Seton, Monday 15 August 1791

Address: To Miss B. Cecilia Seton at Caversham Hill, Berkshire.
Postmark: ISLEWO[RTH] D 15 AU 91.

12. 'Le bon roy, qui a cause de sa femme avoit changé toute maniere de vivre, car ou il souloit disner a huyt heures convenoit qu'il disnast a midy, ou il se souloit coucher a six heures du soir, souvent se couchoit a minuyt, tomba malade a la fin du moys de decembre, de laquelle maladie tout remede humain ne le peult garantir, qu'il ne rendist son ame a Dieu le premier de janvier ensuyvant, après la mi-nuyct' (Jacques de Mailles, *Histoire du Seigneur de Bayart*, 1927 edn, introd. by O. H. Prior, introduction and p. 236). This account was available to HW in his set of the *Collection universelle des mémoires particuliers relatifs à l'histoire de France*, 65 vols, 1785–9 (HW had 67 vols, which probably included the *Table générale*, 2 vols, 1790–1; sold SH v. 173), and no doubt in other works.

13. Frances Susanna Coxe (d. 1823), 4th dau. and coheir of John Hippisley Coxe of Ston Easton, Somerset; m. (1780) Sir Francis Basset (1757–1835), Bt, cr. (1796) Bn de Dunstanville of Tehidy and (1797) Bn Basset of Stratton (GEC; Burke, *Landed Gentry*, 1937, p. 1119, *sub* Hippisley of Ston Easton).

14. Radnor House or 'Mabland' (as HW called it) was across the road from SH on the north. It takes its name from John Robartes (ca 1686–1757), 4th E. of Radnor, who may have built it. Lord Radnor left it to his steward, John Atherton Hindley, who was forced to sell it at auction 28 June 1779 (HW to Lady Ossory 22 June 1779); it was again sold by auction 6 June 1780 (HW to Lady Ossory 6 June 1780), when Sir Francis Basset purchased it (F. C. Hodgson, *Thames-Side in the Past*, 1913, pp. 214–29; Hilda F. Finberg, 'Radnor House, Twickenham,' in *Burlington Magazine*, 1937, lxxi. 168–9; R. S. Cobbett, *Memorials of Twickenham*, 1872, pp. 293–4).

15. Mary Wilkes (1750–1802), dau. of John Wilkes the politician.

16. Mrs Damer wrote to Mary Berry 27 Sept. 1791: 'I have . . . been much disappointed at her [Mrs Buller's] not passing the summer at Twick[enham], which she intended, and she would have talked *sense* to him and amused him, and, *quod omnia superat*, he *likes* her' (*Berry Papers* 77).

17. His usual day for posting a letter to the Berrys.

Strawberry Hill, Aug. 15, 1791.

Dear Madam,

I AM very glad to give you any satisfaction in my power, though I believe, like me, you will not be well satisfied, till you see your cousins in England again. Miss Mary has had a fever, I doubt a more considerable one than they own. It was cured by some James's powder, that I had made them take with them; but as it weakened her much, the operation must have been great, and that the powder never has, without the illness is considerable. I have had two letters from her since, with some lines from Miss Agnes in the first, assuring me the fever was gone, but that she had fatigued herself by too long an airing, and by sitting up too late afterwards. In the second from herself of July 25th, she protests she is better than before her fever. I wish that may be true, though not improbable, for I am convinced they had done a great deal too much, and the powder may have remedied all. There have been such fêtes, shows, balls, etc., both day and night in the great heats for the Great Duke's accession, that I am surprised both are not ill.

I have written two letters to entreat them not to set out till Mary's strength is perfectly recovered—and even then I shall be very uneasy at so long a journey, with bad inns, and in most where no medical assistance is to be had. They have solemnly promised me not to set a foot in France—and yet I fear their travelling in too hot or too cold weather— In short, my dear Madam, how much the whole journey has hurt me!— and not, you may believe me, on my own account alone! They are delighted with Florence, even a second time—I perceive a repugnance to leave it, and they now talk of not being in England till towards the end of November,[1] which, if not for their healths, will be a cruel disappointment to me! Though I have had a good deal of rheumatism, I have been much employed in making their house here comfortable, and did hope they would take possession of it before the fine weather in October is gone—but it is not very sensible in a very old man to expect that what amuses him, would have the same charms for two young women! As they deserve all my partiality, I cannot repent of it—but I shall have bought a few moments of their company, if I do live to see them again, by fourteen or fifteen months of mortification and apprehension. You, dear Madam, I hope enjoy health, and will pass many agreeable years in their society—I dare not make visions to myself

1. They arrived in London 11 Nov. 1791 (MBJ i. 375).

about seeing you at Cliveden next summer! I have the honour to be with the greatest regard and esteem, dear Madam,

Your most obedient humble servant,

Hor. Walpole

To Mary Berry, Wednesday 17 August 1791

Address: À Mademoiselle Mademoiselle Berry à la poste restante à Florence, Italie. *Postmark:* FIRENZE [?]6. Endorsed: 'Pd 1s.'
Posted 19 Aug. ('Visitors').

Strawberry Hill, Aug. 17, 1791.

No. 48.[1]

NO letter from Florence this post, though I am wishing for one every day! The illness of a friend is bad, but is augmented by distance. Your letters say you are quite recovered, but the farther you are from me, the oftener I want to hear that recovery repeated; and any delay in hearing revives my apprehensions of a return of your fever. I am embarrassed too about your plan. It grows near to the time you proposed beginning your journey.[2] I do not write with any view to hastening that, which I trust will entirely depend on the state of your health and strength—nay; I depend on Mr Berry's not leaving it to your own discretion—but I am impatient to know your intentions—in short, I feel that from this time to your arrival my letters will grow very tiresome. I can think of nothing but your journey, which fills me with fears. I have heard today that Lord and Lady Sheffield,[3] who went to visit Mr Gibbon at Lausanne, met with great trouble and impertinence at almost every post in France.[4] In Swisserland there is a furious spirit of democracy or demonocracy; they made great rejoicings on the

1. 'No. 51' (B).

2. The Berrys left Florence exactly a month later, 17 Sept., on their return journey (MBJ i. 353).

3. 'The father of the present Earl Sheffield' (B). John Holroyd (afterwards, 1768, Baker-Holroyd) (1735–1821), cr. (1781) Bn Sheffield (Irish) of Dunamore and (1783) of Roscommon; cr. (1802) Bn Sheffield (English); and finally (1816) Vct Pevensey and E. of Sheffield (Irish); m. (1767) Abigail Way (d. 1793), dau. of Lewis Way of Richmond, Surrey. He was active in suppressing the Gordon riots and in supporting the Irish union. A friend of Gibbon from 1764, Lord

Sheffield edited Gibbon's *Miscellaneous Works . . . With Memoirs of his Life and Writings, composed by Himself. Illustrated from his Letters,* 2 vols, 1796 (vol. 3, 1815). Lord Sheffield's copy of the first two volumes, interleaved with MS notes and letters, is in the Yale University Library, as are seven packets of MS material (some unpublished) relating to Gibbon, Sheffield, and their contemporaries.

4. The Sheffields left England 28 June, reached Paris 4 July, left Paris 16 July for Lausanne, where they arrived 23 July, and remained in and near Lausanne until 4 Oct. (*Private Letters of Edward Gibbon,* ed.

recapture of the King of France—Oh! why did you leave England in such a turbulent era? When will you sit down on the quiet banks of the Thames!

Wednesday night.

Since I began my letter, I have received yours of the 2nd—two days later than usual, and a most comfortable one it is! My belief and my faith are now of the same religion—I do believe you quite recovered. You in the meantime are talking of my rheumatism—quite an old story —not that it is gone, though the pain is; the lameness in my shoulder remains, and I am writing in my lap—but the complaint is put upon the establishment like old servants that are of no use, fill up the place of those who could do something, and yet still remain in the house.

I know nothing new, public or private, that is worth telling. The stocks are transported with the pacification with Russia,[5] and do not care for what it has cost[6] to bully the Empress to no purpose, and say we can afford it; nor can Paine and Priestly persuade them, that France is much happier than we are by having ruined itself. The poor French here are in hourly expectation of as rapid a counter-revolution, as what happened two years ago. Have you seen the King of Sweden's[7] letter to his minister[8] enjoining him to look dismal, and to take care not to be knocked on the head for so doing?[9] It deserves to be framed with M. de Bouillé's bravado.[10]

Rowland E. Prothero, 1896, ii. 254–61; *The Girlhood of Maria Josepha Holroyd*, ed. Jane H. Adeane, 1896, pp. 35–84). Far from being inconvenienced, Lord Sheffield's daughter wrote, 'We have reason to be quite disappointed that we have met with no adventures on the road' (*The Girlhood of Maria Josepha Holroyd* 42). She mentions no inconvenience on the road from Paris to Lausanne. HW, as usual where the Berrys were concerned, probably magnified the report he had heard.

5. 'At half after five o'clock on Sunday morning [14 Aug.] William Lindsay, Esq., secretary of legation arrived at Lord Grenville's office from Petersburg, with the treaty of peace between this court and the Empress of Russia' (*Oracle* 16 Aug. 1791). The stocks, which had been gradually rising because of the favourable news expected, continued to rise: three per cent consols, which were quoted at 83⅛ on 1 Aug., reached 86⅝ on 13 Aug., 88½ on 16 Aug., and 89¼ on 26 Aug. (GM 1791, lxi pt ii. 784).

6. For armament and preparation.

7. Gustav III (1746–92), K. of Sweden 1771–92.

8. Baron de Staël-Holstein.

9. In a letter dated 'Aix-la-Chapelle, June 27, 1791,' Gustav III admonishes the Baron de Staël-Holstein 'not to treat or enter into conversation with any person who is not employed by the free authorization of his Most Christian Majesty. . . . You will . . . shun every occasion of exposing your person and dignity. The most profound sorrow ought to prevail, and be displayed in your household—the exterior of which ought to be regulated by the laws of police, to which, in every situation, a public minister is bound to conform' (*Times* 15 Aug. 1791).

10. François-Claude-Amour (1739–1800), Marquis de Bouillé, who commanded the French army at Metz, and who made arrangements for the escape of Louis XVI and the royal family. On the day of the capture Bouillé left France, and from Luxem-

Mr Gilpin was here on Saturday, and desired me to say a thousand civil things from him. Lord Derby and the Farrens were to dine here tomorrow, but the Earl has got the gout and the party is put off. Our weather for this week has been worthy of Florence, with large showers, very reputable lightning, and a decent proportion of thunder, and yet the warmth has stood the shock bravely. I wish it may keep up its courage till next Monday, when Lord Robert Spencer is to give a cup for a sailing match at Richmond in honour of the Duke of Clarence's birthday.[11] I beg your pardons, but I don't think Lord Dysart's[12] and Cambridge's meadows[13] on such an occasion will yield the apple to the Cascines.

You say you will write me longer letters when you know I am well: your recovery has quite the contrary effect on me; I could scarce restrain my pen while I had apprehensions about you—now you are well, the goose-quill has not a word to say—one would think it had belonged to a physician![14]

I shall fill my vacuum with some lines that General Conway has sent me, written by I know not whom, on Mrs Hart, Sir W. Hamilton's pantomime mistress—or wife,[15] who acts all the antique statues in an Indian

bourg 26 June 1791 he addressed to the National Assembly a loyal but ranting letter which the President read to the Assembly 30 June. In the letter Bouillé justifies the King's escape as the only way to save France from destruction, takes all responsibility for this plot against 'your infernal constitution,' and adds, 'Against me . . . you may sharpen and direct your poignards; against me you may mix your poisons.' He then warns that if 'one hair' of the King's and Queen's heads is touched, 'there will not in a short time remain one stone upon another in the city of Paris.' The National Assembly countered Bouillé's bravado with laughter (*Times* 6 July 1791; *Moniteur* 1 juillet 1791; Saul K. Padover, *The Life and Death of Louis XVI*, 1939, pp. 216–17, 232; NBG).

11. The Duke was 26 on Sunday, 21 Aug. For the sailing match, see following letter.

12. Lionel Tollemache (1734–99), 5th E. of Dysart, husband of HW's late niece, Charlotte Walpole.

13. 'The meadows on each side of the Thames immediately above Richmond Bridge' (B). For a print of the house and grounds as they appeared in the eighteenth century, see *The Works of R. O. Cambridge*, 1803, p. lxvi and the plate, 'Twickenham Meadows.'

14. Who, after a cure has been effected, has no occasion to write more prescriptions.

15. Sir William Hamilton and Emma Hart were at Bath. Mrs Damer wrote to Mary Berry 18 Aug. 1791: 'I had a letter this very day from Lady E[lizabeth Foster], who tells me that *my friend*, Sir William, is there, with his *belle*. They have seen her, and of course admire her talents, and, *par parenthèse*, I do really believe that he means to marry her. I am not sure that it would not be better. One great folly often swallows up little ones, and he does, by all I hear, make himself completely ridiculous in his present state' (*Berry Papers* 63). Sir William married her 6 Sept.; see *post* 11 Sept. 1791.

shawl. I have not seen her yet, so am no judge, but people are mad about her wonderful expression,[16] which I do not conceive, so few antique statues having any expression at all—nor being designed to have it. The Apollo[17] has the symptoms of dignified anger—the Laocoön and his sons, and Niobe and her family, are all expression, and a few more; but what do the Venuses, Floras, Hercules, and a thousand others tell, but the magic art of the sculptor, and their own graces and proportions?[18]—well! no matter—here are the verses—

Attitudes—a Sketch.
To charm the sense, the taste to guide
Sculpture and painting long had tried:
Both call'd ideal beauty forth;
Both claim'd a disputable worth:
When nature looking down on art,
Made a new claim, and show'd us Hart;
All of Corregio's faultless line;
Of Guido's air and look divine;
All that arose to mental view
When Raphael his best angels drew:
The artist's spell, the poet's thought
By her to beauteous life is brought.
The gazer sees each feature move,
Each grace awake and breathing love;
From parts distinct a matchless whole:
She finds the form, and gives the soul.[19]

16. In her 'attitudes'; see *ante* 26 May 1791.

17. Belvedere.

18. HW's references to these statues are probably in answer to remarks in Mary Berry's letter to him. When she visited the Vatican 22 April 1784, she described in her journal under that date 'the famous Apollo, the Laocoön, Venus and Cupid, the torso of M. Angelo . . . a Hercules holding an infant in his hand, a mutilated figure called Antinous. . . . The countenance of the Apollo most remarkable; it is not so handsome, I think, as the Antinous, but it has an unexampled and inimitable dignity about it which marks a god. The marble, too, is uncommonly happy; it has a fine polish upon it, which seems to suit the elegance of the figure. Altogether it does not astonish at first sight. It must be viewed and reviewed to be enjoyed, like all *chefs-d'œuvre* in art. The Laocoön, even upon consideration, astonishes more than it charms. The expression in the father's face and muscles wonderful: the sons have been observed, with justice, to be little men, not boys; but the delicacy of their limbs is beautiful: the arm of the father, which is above his head, with the serpent round it, was restored by Bernini, and is only plaster; those of the sons are in marble, and badly done' (MBJ i. 111–12).

19. This anonymous poem has not been found in eighteenth-century periodicals.

Altogether it is a pretty little poem enough, though not very poetically expressed—but Dr Darwin has destroyed any admiration for any poetry but his own—do you recollect how he has described some antique statues?[20] That canto is not yet published.[21]

I have been making up some pills of patience to take occasionally when you have begun your journey, and I do not receive your letters regularly, which may happen when you are on the road. I recommend you to St James of Compost-antimony,[22] to whom St Luke was an ignorant quack. Adieu!

To Mary Berry, Tuesday 23 August 1791

Address: À Mademoiselle Mademoiselle Berry à la poste restante à Florence, Italie. *Postmark:* FIRENZE [?]o. Endorsed: 'Pd 1s.'
Posted 25 Aug. ('Visitors').

Berkeley Square, Tuesday, Aug. 23, 1791.

No. 49.[1]

I AM come to town to meet Mr Conway and Lady Ailesbury,[2] and as I have no letter from you yet to answer, I will tell you how agreeably I have passed the last three days, though they might have been im-

20. In *The Botanic Garden. Part I. . . . The Economy of Vegetation*, 1791, ii. 101–8:

'Hence wearied Hercules in marble rears
His languid limbs, and rests a thousand years;
Still, as he leans, shall young Antinous please
With careless grace, and unaffected ease;
Onward with loftier step Apollo spring,
And launch the unerring arrow from the string;
In Beauty's bashful form, the veil unfurl'd,
Ideal Venus win the gazing world.'

It appears from Richard French's letter to HW 14 Feb. 1790 that HW before that date had seen the passage in manuscript (when he had doubtless shown or read it to the Berrys), and had suggested to French some alterations in thought and phraseology, which Darwin adopted. In French's letter the last couplet but one reads:

'Onward with step sublime Apollo spring;
And mark the arrow on unerring wing.'

21. The exact date of publication of 'Part I' has not been found. Some of the prints, however, are dated 1 Dec. 1791.

22. 'He means Dr James's Powder' (B). This was a compound of antimony; hence HW's play upon St James of Compostela.

1. 'No. 52' (B).

2. From them, or perhaps from Jerningham (see below), Mrs Damer heard reports of HW. She wrote to Mary Berry 25 Aug. 1791: 'I wish to be with Mr W[alpole], or within his reach, when you begin your journey, for I am the only one to whom he can, or will, tell his anxieties, and numberless they will be. The French continue "*feeding him*," as Jerningham calls it, and with all sorts of atrocious and unwholesome food. I hear of him now, however, in town and in good spirits, also my parents, who, I believe, intend coming to Goodwood next month' (*Berry Papers* 68).

proved, had you shared them, as I wished, and as I *sometimes* do wish. On Saturday evening I was at the Duke of Queensberry's (at Richmond, *s'entend*) with a small company, and there were Sir W. Hamilton and Mrs. Hart, who on the 3rd of next month previous to their departure is to be Madame l'Envoyée à Naples,[3] the Neapolitan Queen[4] having promised to receive her in that quality[5]—here she cannot be presented, where only such over-virtuous wives as the Duchess of Kingston and Mrs Hastings, who could go with a husband in each hand, are admitted. Why the Margravine of Anspach[6] with the same pretensions, was not, I do not understand—perhaps she did not attempt it—but I forget to retract and make *amende honorable* to Mrs Hart. I had only heard of her attitudes—and those, in dumb show, I have not yet seen— Oh, but she sings admirably, has a very fine strong voice, is an excellent *buffa,* and an astonishing tragedian. She sung Nina[7] in the highest perfection, and there her attitudes were a whole theatre of grace and various expressions.[8]

The next evening I was again at Queensberry House where the

3. The marriage did not take place until 6 Sept.; see *post* 11 Sept. 1791.

4. Marie Caroline.

5. Whether or not the Queen promised it, Lady Hamilton was well received: 'I have the pleasure to inform you we arrived safe at Naples. I have been rece[i]ved with open arms by all the Neapolitans of both sexes, by all the foreigners of every distinction. I have been presented to the Queen of Naples by her own desire. She [h]as shown me all sorts of kind and affectionate attentions. In short, I am the happiest woman in the world' (Lady Hamilton to George Romney, the painter, 20 Dec. 1791, in John Cordy Jeaffreson, *Lady Hamilton and Lord Nelson*, 1888, i. 254; see also ibid. 252–3).

6. Lady Craven, not yet Margravine of Anspach (*post* 3 Oct. 1791), although the Margrave had announced a left-handed marriage to her.

7. Mrs Toynbee suggested 'perhaps Pergolesi's song "Tre giorni son che Nina," ' but it is far more likely that Emma Hart sang some of the songs from a recent opera: *Nina . . . la pazza per amore,* Napoli, 1790, an opera in two acts, composed by Giovanni Paisiello (1741–1816), with libretto by Giambattista Lorenzi, first acted in 1789. It was based on *Nina, ou La folle par amour*

(acted 1786, printed 1788), by Benoît-Joseph Marsollier des Vivetières (1750–1817), with music by Nicolas Dalayrac (1753–1809). See Oscar George T. Sonneck, *Catalogue of Opera Librettos* [in the Library of Congress] *Printed before 1800,* Washington, 1914, *sub* Nina; following note. The plot of *Nina* was known in England, although Paisiello's opera was not performed until 1797; see Allardyce Nicoll, *A History of Late Eighteenth Century Drama 1750–1800,* Cambridge, 1927, pp. 338, 358; [John Genest], *Some Account of the English Stage,* Bath, 1832, vi. 448; *Nina, or the Madness of Love,* [1787], advertisement dated 13 April 1787, and the translation dedicated to the Hon. Mrs Hobart, who is said to be largely responsible 'for the fame it has received in this country.'

8. George Romney, in a letter to William Hayley 8 Aug. 1791, mentions a dinner party a few weeks earlier, when she 'performed, both in the serious and comic, to admiration, both in singing and acting; but her Nina surpasses everything I ever saw, and I believe, as a piece of acting, nothing ever surpassed it. The whole company were in an agony of sorrow. Her acting is simple, grand, terrible, and pathetic' (Jeaffreson, op. cit. i. 243; see also ibid. 246).

Comtesse Emilie de Bouflers played on her harp and the Princesse di Castelcigala, the Neapolitan minister's wife,[9] danced one of her country dances with castanets very prettily with her husband. Madame du Barry was there too, and I had a good deal of frank conversation with her about Monsieur de Choiseul, having been at Paris at the end of his reign and the beginning of hers,[10] and of which I knew so much by my intimacy with the Duchesse de Choiseul.[11]

On Monday was the boat-race. I was in the great room at the Castle[12] with the Duke of Clarence, Lady Di, Lord Robert[13] and the House of Bouverie[14] to see the boats start from the bridge to Thistleworth,[15] and back to a tent erected in Lord Dysart's meadow, just before Lady Di's windows, whither we went to see them arrive, and where we had breakfast. For the second heat I sat in my coach on the bridge—and did not stay for the third.[16] The day had been coined on purpose with my favourite southeast wind. The scene both up the river and down was

9. —— —— (living 1816), m. (ca 1782) Fabrizio Ruffo (1763–1832), Prince di Castelcicala, Neapolitan ambassador to England ca 1790–3, and to France 1815–32 (except for short periods in 1816 and 1820) (NBG; *Enciclopedia italiana;* Vittorio Spreti, *Enciclopedia storico-nobiliare italiana,* Milano, 1928–36, v. 861; GM 1816, lxxxvi pt ii. 187; Thomas Raikes, *Journal,* 1856–7, i. 23–4). Their town house was in Portman Street, but they evidently were living at this time at Richmond, where their first son was born 2 July 1791 (Spreti, loc. cit.; *Royal Kalendar,* 1790–3).

10. HW was in Paris Aug.–Oct. 1769, and again July–Sept. 1771; Mme du Barry was presented at Court in the spring of 1769, and through her influence the Duc de Choiseul was dismissed as secretary of state, and exiled to Chanteloup 24 Dec. 1770. See DU DEFFAND, *passim;* Gaston Maugras, *Le Duc et la duchesse de Choiseul,* 1902; *idem, La Disgrâce du duc et de la duchesse de Choiseul,* 1903.

11. Louise-Honorine Crozat du Châtel (1735–1801), m. (1750) Étienne-François de Choiseul-Stainville, Duc de Choiseul; HW's correspondent, frequently mentioned in DU DEFFAND.

12. Richmond Castle.

13. 'Lord Robert Spencer, brother to Lady Di Beauclerc' (B).

14. 'The family of the Hon. Edward Bouverie, brother to the Earl of Radnor' (B). Hon. Edward Bouverie (1738–1810), M.P. Salisbury 1761–74, Northampton 1790–1810; m. (1764) Henrietta or Harriet Fawkener, by whom he had eight children (three sons and five daughters) who at this time ranged from two to twenty-three years of age (Collins, *Peerage,* 1812, v. 36–7; Burke, *Peerage,* 1928, p. 1911, *sub* Radnor).

15. Isleworth. Cf. Philip Luckombe, *England's Gazetteer,* 1790, *sub* Isleworth and Thistleworth.

16. 'A boat race occupied the whole of the forenoon. The boats started from under the bridge at half past twelve o'clock—rowed round a boat moored at Isleworth Upper Ferry, a little below Mr Sheridan's house—went up the river and round the small island opposite the bottom of Petersham Lane, and in return passed a boat moored near the late Duke of Montagu's house, which was the point for the victor to attain.' The Duke of Clarence, Lord Robert Spencer, Lady Diana Beauclerk, and Mr Bouverie were saluted by 'the mob . . . with three huzzas' (*Oracle* 24 Aug. 1791).

what only Richmond upon earth can exhibit; the crowds in those green velvet meadows and on the shores, the yachts, barges, pleasure and small boats and the windows and gardens lined with spectators, were so delightful, that when I came home from that vivid show, I thought Strawberry looked as dull and solitary as a hermitage.[17] At night there was a ball at the Castle,[18] and illuminations with the Duke's cipher, etc., in coloured lamps, as were the houses of his R. H.'s tradesmen—I went again in the evening to the French ladies on the Green,[19] where was a bonfire; but you may believe, not to the ball.

—Well, but you who have had a fever with fêtes, had rather hear the history of the new *soi-disante* Margravine.[20] She has been in England with her foolish Prince, and not only notified their marriage to the Earl her brother,[21] who did not receive it propitiously, but his Highness informed his Lordship by a letter, that they have an usage in his country of taking a wife with the left hand; that he had espoused his Lordship's sister in that manner, and intends, as soon as she shall be a widow, to marry her with his right hand also.[22] The Earl replied, that he knew she was married to an English peer,[23] a most respectable man, and can know nothing of her marrying any other man—and so they are gone to Lisbon.[24]

17. *The Oracle* 24 Aug. 1791 was equally complimentary to the day: 'The weather was particularly propitious to the sports of the day. Very little wind or sun, and a calm serenity of sky, heightened with additional charms the beautiful and variegated scenery of this delightful spot, so well known and so often celebrated.'

18. 'The nobility and gentry who reside in Richmond and the surrounding villages, in compliment to his Royal Highness, gave at the Castle a ball and supper, at which 102 ladies and gentlemen were present, who did not separate till near three o'clock in the morning' (*Oracle* 24 Aug. 1791).

19. Mme de Boufflers and Comtesse Amélie de Boufflers, Mme de Cambis, and perhaps Mme de Roncherolles, all of whom lived at Richmond, if not on Richmond Green. HW was probably at the house of the first two.

20. 'Elizabeth Berkeley, Lady Craven, afterwards married to the Margrave of Anspach here mentioned' (B). Evidently Mary Berry had asked about or had alluded to Lady Craven in a letter to Mrs Damer as well as in one to HW; see Mrs Damer to Mary Berry 18 Aug. 1791 (*Berry Papers* 64–5).

21. Frederick Augustus Berkeley (1745–1810), 5th E. of Berkeley.

22. General Conway wrote to Sir William Hamilton 9 Sept. 1791: 'You had heard, I believe, before your departure your friend Lady Craven's marriage to the Margrave, announced to Lord Berkeley by the Margrave in form. A left hand marriage, *à leur mode*, with a promise to take her with his right hand, when Lord Craven died. That event has already happen'd, poor Lord C. is dead, very opportunely, as I suppose she thinks, and I conclude she is by this time Margravine *dans les formes*' (Percy Noble, *Park Place, Berkshire*, 1905, p. 128).

23. Lord Craven, 'in a bad state of health,' and his daughters were in Switzerland, at Geneva or Lausanne, at this time (*The Girlhood of Maria Josepha Holroyd*, ed. Jane H. Adeane, 1896, pp. 67, 73, 82, 86).

24. Where they were married 13 Oct. 1791; see *post* 3 Oct. 1791, final note. Their departure for Lisbon is mentioned in *The Oracle* 30 Aug. 1791.

Thursday morning, 25th.

London you may conclude is as deserted as Ferrara, for though I have been here two days, and supped on Tuesday at Miss Farren's and last night at Lord Mt Edgcumbe's, I did not hear of one incident worth repeating. Mrs Buller and Jerningham were of the party last night.

Madame d'Albany is gone.[25] I believe she made application for some *deficit*—I doubt much whether she received even an answer.[26]

I have had no letter from you since my last; and having made so barren a campaign in town, I must send this away as it is—not quite certain that it will find you still at Florence; though I suppose it will, as methinks you would have had the providence to furnish me with new directions before your setting out, that my letters might not be trotting after you and perhaps be lost—If your next does not bring me such direction, I shall conclude you have changed your minds, and are not coming so soon. Adieu!

To Mary Berry, ca Thursday 1 September 1791

This letter, No. 50 in the series, is missing. It was posted 1 Sept. ('Visitors') or 2 Sept. (following letter). Its general tone may be inferred from the first paragraph of the following letter. See also the introductory note to the letter of 25 September 1791.

To Mary Berry, Monday 5 September 1791

Address: À Mademoiselle Mademoiselle Berry à la poste restante à Venise, Italie. Endorsed: 'Pd 1s.' and, opposite the address, '14.'
Posted 6 Sept. ('Visitors'); *post* 20 Oct. 1791.

25. Mrs Damer wrote to Mary Berry 21 Aug. 1791: 'Madame d'Albany went no farther than Birmingham on her way to Scotland, and is now gone suddenly away. I yesterday received this news from herself, in a very kind letter. She desires me to direct to her at Brussels. I do not believe this regards French politics further than her pension may be concerned, for she is one of the very few reasonable on this [the French] subject' (*Berry Papers* 67).
26. 'Whether the Countess did actually appeal for financial aid from the Government [in 1791] is unknown, but it seems unlikely that she ever did so appeal directly, though she probably made several efforts in a quiet way to obtain the good offices of such few persons of influence as showed her any attention. . . . Whatever hopes the Countess may have originally built on this visit (and we truly believe pecuniary help to have been its first consideration), she must have been grievously disappointed, for certainly nothing substantial resulted therefrom' (Herbert M. Vaughan, *The Last Stuart Queen*, 1910, p. 163). But on the death of her brother-in-law, the Cardinal of York, in 1807, George III allowed her a pension of £1600 per annum from the Privy Purse (ibid. 258).

Strawberry Hill, Sept. 5, at night, 1791.

No. 51.

I WRITE on my intermediate post-day,[1] both to overtake you, and to apologize for the lamentations in my last, though I had not even imputed the cause of them to you—that letter perhaps you will not receive:[2] I had been so long without one, and so disappointed at not receiving notice to change my direction, as I had calculated I should, that I feared something had happened. On Friday the 2nd, the morning on which my letter had gone to town, I received yours of the 7th and 9th of August, with the very order for changing my direction, but it was too late to recall mine; and therefore if it does not arrive before you leave Florence, as it scarce will if you set out on the 15th or 16th, you may have left orders behind you, for any letters to be sent after you. I am less surprised at yours being so long as twenty-three or twenty-four days on the road, for I believe it had been opened, the seal being quite flat and scarce any mark of impression left. Another proof of its having been delayed, is, that on Saturday I received a second of the 15th of August, and they certainly ought not to have arrived two days together, but at once.

The last contains a charming letter from my Agnes, and both this and the former contain deserved encomiums on Mr Lock, to which I totally agree. He has as much modesty as genius, which is saying that he is the most modest genius in the world; and his virtues are as uncommon as both. I am overjoyed you have met him: and now I shall be impatient to have him see the copy of his Wolsey, which I am sure will surprise and strike him, as much as the original did us—He little thinks that his new scholar is worthy of being his rival. In your letter of the 9th there was a word which I could not read, or at least not understand; you say Mr Lock coloured a drawing in black lead with a *stump*,[3] or, a *thump,* and advised Miss Agnes to use the same method—either nostrum applied to the *black* lead, I suppose, had the effect of *Prussian* blue, and made the drawing black and blue, which may assist connoisseurs in knowing *hands;* but I own I do not wish to have your sister practise that mode of sketching; nor should like to be told, 'I am sure

---

1. That is, for posting on Tuesday, instead of the usual Friday.

2. Since that letter, No. 50 in the series, is missing, HW is perhaps correct, but see introductory note to *post* 25 Sept. 1791.

3. It is strange that HW did not recognize this familiar artist's implement. See OED, 'stump' sb. 2.

this was done by your wife's *fist.*' It would not be of a piece with her or Mr Lock's indolence. Hers I certainly would not have her conquer at the price of a headache; nor would have you both venture travelling too soon in the great heats. Great as my impatience to see you both, you surely know that my impatience is doubled by my alarms about your journey; and when the storm at your setting out terrified me so much, and the terror lest you should be scalped by the French savages has constantly haunted me, even my own personal tranquillity, were I ever so selfish, would not expose you to the smallest risk.

Lally *s'est ravisé* prudently in suppressing his pamphlet;[4] it would not be popular here, where the demonocratic stock is woefully fallen. The sober Presbytyrants are ashamed of Priestly and his imps; and though they would burn the houses of others,[5] they would not like to venture their own; nor is the distress of France inviting. Barnave[6] and Lameth[7] may have tried to negotiate with the Princes,[8] but having miscarried, if they did attempt it, their being desperate, will produce more violence. I should think they had tried, as I see Lameth has lately been outrageous[9]—yet I am told that when the Chevalier de Coigny[10] presented himself (on that errand) to the Comte de Provence, whom he found in a circle of exiles, and desired a private audience, Monsieur said, '*Tous ces messieurs sont mes amis, et je leur dirais d'abord tout ce que vous me diriez.*'[11]

4. *Lettre écrite au très honorable Edmund Burke.* In the absence of Mary Berry's letter, the reasons for and the nature of the suppression are not known. The work exists in at least two states: 50 pages, without place of publication on the title-page, 1791; 87 pages, Florence, 1791 (Bibl. Nat. Cat.; University of Michigan Library Cat.).

5. An allusion to the recent riots at Birmingham.

6. Antoine-Pierre-Joseph-Marie Barnave (1761–93), a violent revolutionist who had become, since the flight of the royal family, equally strong as a royalist and defender of Louis XVI; guillotined 29 Nov. 1793. For his correspondence with Marie-Antoinette, the authenticity of which has been questioned, see *Marie-Antoinette et Barnave,* ed. Alma Söderhjelm, 1934.

7. Alexandre-Théodore-Victor (1760–1829), Comte de Lameth; youngest of three brothers who played a considerable part in the French Revolution. Like Barnave, he

changed from a violent revolutionist to a moderate royalist.

8. Louis XVI's brothers: the Comte de Provence and the Comte d'Artois.

9. Presumably HW refers to Lameth's position in the National Assembly: on 14 Aug. he presented his belief that the title of 'Prince' should be conferred on no one; and on 24 Aug. he spoke in support of a military guard for the King (*Moniteur* 15, 25 août 1791).

10. Jean-Philippe de Franquetot (1743–ca 1806), Chevalier de Coigny; Chevalier de Saint-Jean de Jérusalem; Maréchal de Camp, 1784; died in exile at Düsseldorf (Woelmont de Brumagne vi. 291; Nicolas Viton de Saint-Allais, *Nobiliaire universel de France,* 1872–5, x. 40).

11. Joseph-Thomas, Comte d'Espinchal, wrote in his *Journal d'émigration* (ed. Ernest d'Hauterive, 1912, p. 252) *sub* 10 Aug. 1791: 'Le Chevalier de Coigny . . . arrive aujourd'hui à Coblentz, chargé, dit-on, de commissions importantes pour les prin-

Madame de Staal[12] is returned to Paris;[13] her husband announced his King's[14] commands of *affiching tristesse: elle s'en est mocquée* and sees everybody. Her father is said to be following her with a new plan of constitution and finance,[15] both which no doubt he can more easily settle now that both are fifty times more difficult, than he could at first[16] when he had all the power of the crown, or the second time[17] when he was the idol of the people—Everybody has seen his incapacity but himself—and his restless vanity and ambition of a name will make his name a proverb of ridicule. He always puts me in mind of the Gunnings. The Duchess of B.[18] is having her house new-painted, and retired to her niece Madame de Kutzleben.[19] The Gunnings went and took her away, and have carried her to their lodging in St James's Street—yet cannot make even the newspapers talk of them.

As this departs on Tuesday, it is not likely I shall have anything to

ces. Il est parti, muni de l'attache de l'Assemblée Nationale, ce qui donne un mauvais vernis à sa mission. Il est médiocrement reçu des princes et mal vu de toute la noblesse, qui le croit porteur de quelque négociation insidieuse pour empêcher d'agir.' *The Oracle* 3 Sept. 1791 reported that the Comte d'Artois 'had wrote to the Prince de Condé, requesting him not to enter into any negotiations with this emissary.' It appears, however, that the suspicions of the *émigrés* were unfounded: the Chevalier de Coigny was a devoted royalist who later became an active agent of the princes in France; see *L'Intermédiaire des chercheurs et curieux*, 1921, lxxxiv. 61–3; Eugène-François-Auguste d'Arnaud, Baron de Vitrolles, *Mémoires*, ed. Eugène Forgues, 1884, i. 30–1.

12. Anne-Louise-Germaine Necker (1766–1817), dau. of Jacques Necker; m. (1786) Eric-Magnus, Baron de Staël-Holstein. Mary Berry's acquaintance with her began in 1784, and lasted until Mme de Staël's death. About 1815 Mme de Staël is reported to have said that she loved Mary Berry 'the best, and thought . . . [her] by *far* the cleverest woman in England' (MBJ iii. 13), but Mary Berry's admiration of her was mixed with criticism and envy; see MBJ, *passim*.

13. After meeting Mme de Staël at Coppet 21 July 1791, Maria Josepha Holroyd,

Lord Sheffield's daughter, commented on her ugliness, but found her 'so lively and entertaining that you would totally forget in five minutes whether she was handsome or ugly. They [the Necker family] seem to be very fond of one another. Madame de Staël is perfectly wild, and must keep up her Papa and Mama's spirits very much. She is soon to leave them, and then Coppet will be a very dull lamentable place' (*The Girlhood of Maria Josepha Holroyd*, ed. Jane H. Adeane, 1896, p. 64).

14. Gustav III's; see *ante* 17 Aug. 1791.

15. This was a false report.

16. 1777–81, when Necker was directeur-général des finances.

17. 1788–90, when he held the same office.

18. Bedford.

19. Dorothy Wrottesley (1747–1822), 4th dau. of Rev. Sir Richard Wrottesley, 7th Bt, of Wrottesley, Staffordshire, by the Duchess of Bedford's sister, Lady Mary Leveson-Gower; m. (1780) Christian, Baron von Kutzleben, envoy extraordinary and minister plenipotentiary from Hesse-Cassel (George Wrottesley, *History of the Family of Wrottesley*, Exeter, 1903 [supplement to *The Genealogist*, n.s., vol. 19], p. 353; GM 1822, xciv pt ii. 477). For several years prior to 1791, she had lived in Little Argyll Street (*Royal Kalendar*, 1785–90, p. 105), but in 1792 her residence was in Warwick Street, Golden Square (ibid., 1792, p. 105).

add on Friday; therefore my next you will probably find at Basle; as you had better wait a few days and find one arrived before you, than wait longer for one to recall, or to be sent after you. I fear we must mutually prepare for disappointments while you are on the road, and I will remember, if I can, to be prepared—but I think impatience about you two is the quality on which seventy-four has had the least effect! I wonder you had not heard of your tenant's[20] retreat, for your housekeeper[21] told Philip ten days ago that your house[22] was ready for you—and so will Cliveden be.

I assure you the provocations given by the Revolutionists were so far from being exaggerated by the newspapers on the Court's side, that much worse was suppressed than has been ever told, nor was any other care taken by the government till the approach of the 14th of July had made every precaution necessary, and had even kept away from the Crown and Anchor every man of any consequence, even of the opposition. All the country newspapers and evening posts had been hired by the faction. Remember, I never warrant my news, unless I speak very positively: I have told you[23] that truth died a virgin, and left no children—and often when she herself is said to be here or there, it is as untrue as that King Arthur is still alive, or St John in the Isle of Patmos. I did I think everything but prove that Perkin Warbeck was the true Duke of York, and had not been murdered in the Tower[24]—but as he was beheaded[25] afterwards as publicly as the Duke of Monmouth,[26] I do not believe he is still living, though Monsieur de Saintfoix[27] chose the latter should have been the *Masque de fer*, but forgot the best argument in defence of that hypothesis, which was, that the *Masque de fer* was to conceal the loss of the Duke's real head. Adieu!

---

20. Not identified.

21. Mrs Richardson; see *post* 15 Oct. 1793.

22. In North Audley Street.

23. *Ante* 4 July 1791.

24. HW refers to his *Historic Doubts on the Life and Reign of King Richard the Third*, 1768, pp. 82–94, 130–2. Later historians have not been convinced by HW's arguments, and it is now generally considered that Perkin Warbeck was an impostor.

25. Perkin Warbeck was hanged, not beheaded.

26. James Scott (1649–85), said to be a natural son of Charles II by Lucy Walters, cr. (1663) D. of Monmouth; convicted of treason; beheaded on Tower Hill 15 July 1685.

27. Germain-François Poullain de Saint-Foix (1698–1776), author of a *Lettre au sujet de l'homme au masque de fer*, Amsterdam [Paris], 1768, in which he concluded that the Duke of Monmouth was the Man in the Iron Mask. Mme du Deffand sent the book to HW at his request; like HW, she considered Saint-Foix's supposition absurd (DU Deffand ii. 114, 116, 135).

To Mary Berry, Sunday 11 September 1791

Address: À Mademoiselle Mademoiselle Berry à la poste restante à Basle en Suisse. Endorsed: 'Pd 1s.'
Posted 12 Sept. ('Visitors'); *post* 20 Oct. 1791.

Strawberry Hill, Sept. 11, 1791.

No. 52.[1]

THOUGH I am delighted to know that of thirteen doleful months but two remain, yet how full of anxiety will they be! You set out in still hot weather, and will taste very cold before you arrive! Accidents, inns, roads, mountains, and the sea are all in my map!—but I hope no slopes to be run down, no fêtes for a new Great Duke.[2] I should dread your meeting armies, if I had much faith in the counter-revolution said to be on the anvil. The French ladies in my *vicinage* (a word of the late Lord Chatham's coin)[3] are all *hen-a-hoop*[4] on the expectation of a grand alliance formed for that purpose, and I believe think they shall be at Paris, before you are in England—but I trust one is more certain than the other. That folly and confusion increase in France every hour I have no doubt, and absurdity and contradictions as rapidly. Their constitution, which they had voted should be immortal and unchangeable, though they deny that anything antecedent to themselves ought to have been so, they are now of opinion must be revised at the commencement of next century; and they are agitating a third constitution, before they have thought of a second, or finished the first! Bravo!—in short, Louis Onze[5] could not have laid deeper foundations for despotism than these levellers, who have rendered the name of liberty odious, the surest way of destroying the dear essence!

I have no news for you but a sudden match patched up for Lord Blandford with a little more art than was employed by the fair Gunnilda. It is with Lady Susan Stewart,[6] Lord Galloway's daughter, con-

---

1. 'No. 53' (B).
2. Ferdinand III, who had recently taken the throne as Grand Duke of Tuscany; cf. *ante* 12 July, 15 Aug. 1791.
3. HW is mistaken in attributing the coinage of *vicinage* to William Pitt (1708–78), 1st E. of Chatham. The earliest usage recorded in OED is ca 1325; in the phrase *in the* (also, *this, our,* etc.) *vicinage* the earliest recorded is 1638. No quotation from Lord Chatham is given in OED.

4. That is, elated, exultant; a nonce-word, the feminine counterpart of *cock-a-hoop.* OED, which includes many of HW's nonce-words, omits this.
5. Louis XI (1423–83), K. of France 1461–83.
6. (1767–1841), 2d dau. of John Stewart (1736–1806), 7th E. of Galloway, by his 2d wife, Anne Dashwood (ca 1743–1830), sister of Sir Henry Watkin Dashwood, 3d Bt; m. (15 Sept. 1791) Lord Blandford, later D. of

trived by and at the house of her relation and Lord Blandford's friend, Sir Henry Dashwood, and it is to be so instantly, that her Grace his mother will scarce have time to forbid the banns.[7] She will perhaps repent her veto to Lady Caroline Waldegrave[8]—and perhaps to Lord Strathaven,[9] for I should suspect that Lady Stafford[10] had suggested the first idea when there might be revenge as well as interest in the concoction—no, such a genius never can lie still!

We have got a codicil to summer that is as delightful as, I believe, the seasons in the Fortunate Islands—it is pity it lasts but to seven in the evening, and then one remains with a black chimney for five hours. I wish the sun was not so fashionable as never to come into the country till autumn, and the shooting season,[11] as if Niobe's children were not hatched and fledged before the first of September. Apropos,[12] Sir William Hamilton has actually married his gallery of statues,[13] and they

---

Marlborough. The approaching marriage was mentioned in *The Times* 7 Sept. and *The Oracle* 8 Sept. 1791 as scheduled to occur on the following Tuesday, 13 Sept.; but it did not take place until 15 Sept. Both newspapers also referred to the Gunning affair: 'This match takes one of Miss Gunning's *Marquisses* out of the market' (*Oracle* 8 Sept. 1791); 'The . . . marriage will make an excellent dénouement to the Gunning novel' (*Times* 14 Sept. 1791).

7. Although the Duchess of Marlborough did not forbid the banns, reports in *The Times* 22, 26 Sept., 28 Oct., and 1, 11 Nov. 1791 indicate that she and the Duke were not altogether pleased at their son's marriage: the newly married couple were not invited to entertainments at Blenheim, and there was some difficulty about the income to be allowed to Lord Blandford. See also *The Oracle* 21 Sept. 1791.

8. (1765–1831), 4th and youngest dau. of John, 3d E. Waldegrave; lady of the Bedchamber to the Princesses 1791–8, and to the Dowager Queen of Würtemberg during her visit to England, 1827 (GM 1831, ci pt i. 367; *Royal Kalendar*, 1791–9). When Fanny Burney met her and her sister Lady Elizabeth in 1786, she found them 'gentle and well bred and . . . amiable' (*Diary and Letters of Madame d'Arblay*, ed. Charlotte Barrett and Austin Dobson, 1904–5, ii. 388, iv. 453, *et passim*). See also *ante* 2 Aug. 1790.

9. Cf. *ante* 2 Aug. 1790, n. 8.

10. Susanna Stewart (ca 1745–1805), sister of Lord Galloway, and aunt of Lady Susan, mentioned above; m. (1768) as his 3d wife, Granville Leveson-Gower, 2d E. Gower, cr. (1786) M. of Stafford. HW's dislike of Lady Stafford was of long standing. Her scheming and her unpleasant attitude to his niece, Lady Waldegrave, at the time of her marriage to the Duke of Gloucester, provoked his comment that she was 'of the most interested and intriguing turn . . . [and] had, even before her marriage, obtained three pensions by different channels. After her marriage her life was a series of jobs and solicitations, and she teased every minister for every little office that fell in his department. She made a thousand dependants and enemies, but no friend' (*Last Journals* i. 223).

11. The season for partridges opened 1 Sept.; for pheasants, 1 Oct. (*Times* 2 Sept., 1 Oct. 1791).

12. 'Apropos' because the mention of Niobe suggests Emma Hart, one of whose favourite 'attitudes' was in the character of Niobe.

13. Sir William Hamilton and his mistress, Emma Hart, were married at St Marylebone Church, 6 Sept. Her name appears on the register as 'Amy Lyons' (*The Registers of Marriages of St Mary le Bone, Middlesex, 1783–1792*, Pt IV, ed. W. Bruce Bannerman and R. R. Bruce Bannerman, 1922, p. 153). In *The Times* 7 Sept. 1791 she is mentioned as 'Miss Harte, a lady who

are set out on their return to Naples.[14] I am sorry I did not see her attitudes, which Lady Di (a tolerable judge!) prefers to anything she ever
saw—still I do not much care; I have *at this moment* a commercial
treaty with Italy, and hope in two months to be a great gainer by the
exchange—and I shall not be so generous as Sir William, and exhibit
my wives in pantomime to the public. 'Tis well I am to have the originals again, for that wicked swindler Miss Foldson has not yet given up
their portraits.

The Johnstones go to Bath next week; the General is not well again;
they are to dine with me on Wednesday, and tomorrow my sister and
Mr Churchill come to me. By telling you these trifles you may judge
how little I have to say. Even the newspapers are forced to live upon the
diary of the King's motions at Weymouth.[15] Oh! I had forgot—Lord
Cornwallis has taken Bangalore by storm,[16] promises Seringapatam,[17]
and Tippoo Saib has sued for peace[18]—diamonds will be as plenty as
potatoes, and gold[19] as common as copper-money in Sweden. I was told
last night that a director of the Bank affirms that two millions five hundred thousand pounds in specie have already been remitted or brought
over hither from France since their revolution. I wish Dr Priestley
would be content with robbing the roost, instead of trying to hatch
chickens here from a hen that lays such eggs, which come to our
markets!

has been much admired for her elegance of
manners and extraordinary abilities. The
celebration of this marriage was with the
unanimous approbation of all Sir William
Hamilton's friends. The ceremony was performed in a very private manner, and tomorrow or Friday Sir William and his new-
married Lady will set off on their return to
Naples.' Cf. GM 1791, lxi pt ii. 872.

14. 'Yesterday Sir William Hamilton and
Lady left town on their return to Naples'
(*Times* 9 Sept. 1791).

15. The King and Queen, accompanied
by the three elder princesses, left Windsor
Lodge at five o'clock in the morning, 3
Sept., and arrived at Weymouth that evening soon after nine (*Times* 3, 5 Sept.
1791). 'Their Majesties' trip to Weymouth
has already excited the public attention.
The town will therefore be amused with
authentic narratives from well-informed
folks placed there on purpose—of every
royal dip and movement—a number of

similes, perfectly new, about Venus and the
sea, are preparing in compliment to the
princesses' (*Times* 5 Sept. 1791).

16. 'The purser of the Hawke arrived at
the India House late last night. She left
Madras the 17th of April, and brings advice of the taking of Bangalore by storm
on the night of the 21st of March . . .'
(*Times* 5 Sept. 1791). Additional information, including a list of the dead, appeared
in *The Times* 6, 7 Sept. 1791.

17. Lord Cornwallis appeared before
Seringapatam in May 1791, but for lack of
transport was forced to fall back; the British successfully besieged the city in Feb.–
March 1792, and again 17 April–4 May
1799. Tippoo Sahib was killed in the second siege. See G. B. Malleson, *Seringapatam; Past and Present*, Madras, 1876, *passim*.

18. A false report.

19. MS reads 'and gold is as common . . .'

I direct this to Basle, as it is better my letters should wait for you, than you for them; and I shall send one more to the same place next Tuesday 27th,[20] by which time I shall hope for a farther direction, and an account of what route you are to take. How I shall rejoice over every stage you make.[21] Adieu! Carissime!

To MARY and AGNES BERRY, Friday 16 September 1791

Address: À Mademoiselle Mademoiselle Berry à la poste restante à Basle en Suisse. Endorsed: 'Pd 1s.'

Posted 20 Sept.; HW noted its subject, 'about journey through France' ('Visitors'); *post* 20 Oct. 1791.

Strawberry Hill, Friday night late, Sept. 16, 1791.

No. 53.[1]

AS I am constantly thinking of you two, I am as constantly writing to you, when I have a vacant quarter of an hour. Yesterday was red-lettered in the almanacs of Strawberry and Cliveden, supposing you set out towards them, as you intended:[2] the sun shone all day, and the moon all night, and all nature for three miles round looked gay. Indeed we have had nine or ten days of such warmth and serenity (here called *heat*) as I scarce remember when the year begins to have grey, or rather, yellow, hairs. All windows have been flung up again and fans ventilated,[3] and it is true that hay-carts have been transporting hay-cocks from a second crop all the morning from Sir Francis Basset's[4] island opposite to my windows.[5] The setting sun and the long autumnal shades enriched the landscape to a Claud Lorrain—guess whether I hoped to see such a scene next year—if I do not, may you!—at least, it will make you talk of me!

The Johnstonehood dined here on Wednesday, and Lady Clack,

---

20. He actually addressed the two following letters to Basle, 16 and 25 Sept.

21. MS reads 'made.'

———

1. 'No. 54' (B).

2. The Berrys left Florence for Bologna on their return journey 17 Sept. (MBJ i. 353).

3. That is, the fan-lights opened.

4. Sir Francis Basset (1757–1835), cr. (1779) Bt, of Tehidy, Cornwall; cr. (1796) Bn de Dunstanville of Tehidy, and (1797) Bn Basset of Stratton.

5. The 'island belonging to Radnor House, then occupied by Sir Francis Basset' (F. C. Hodgson, *Thames-Side in the Past*, 1913, p. 222).

and some Richmondians. The first family depart for Bath tomorrow:[6] the good General is not at all well, and falls away much. The Marchioness of Abercorn is dead,[7] and the Marquis of Blandford literally married, *malgré* the Duchess. The papers of today say Monsieur de la Luzerne is dead,[8] but Madame de Boufflers did not know it last night: I have heard nothing else, nor probably shall learn more in town on Monday whither I shall go for two nights on business. The gorgeous season and poor partridges I hear have emptied London entirely, and yet Drury Lane is removed to the Opera House[9]—do you know that Mrs Jordan is acknowledged to be Mrs Ford,[10] and Miss Brunton to be Mrs Merry,[11] but neither quits the stage. The latter's captain I think

6. *The Morning Chronicle* 29 Oct. 1791 recorded: 'General Johnston is gone from Bath to Hampton in Middlesex.'

7. Catharine Copley (d. 13 Sept. 1791), 1st dau. of Sir Joseph Copley, Bt, of Sprotborough, Yorkshire, by Mary Buller, dau. of John Buller, of Morval, Cornwall; m. (1779) as his 1st wife, John James Hamilton (1756–1818), 9th E., cr. (1790) 1st M., of Abercorn. According to *The Oracle* 24 Aug. 1791 she had 'within these few days been so suddenly indisposed, that the result of four physicians' consultations was the recommendation of a tour to the Continent.'

8. La Luzerne, the French ambassador, had died at 4 P.M., 14 Sept. at Southampton, where he had gone for his health (GM 1791, lxi pt ii. 877; *Times* 16 Sept. 1791). In ill health for some time, he suffered two strokes of palsy after his arrival at Southampton, and was insensible for some hours before his death (*Times* 9 Dec. 1790; *London Chronicle* 11–13 Jan. 1791, lxix. 42; *Times* 3, 7, 13, 16 Sept. 1791). The news of his death reached the secretary of state's office early on the morning of 15 Sept. (*Times* 16 Sept. 1791).

9. The demolition of Drury Lane began 13 July 1791 (*Oracle* 14 July 1791), and the Opera House (King's Theatre, Haymarket) was altered for the reception of the Drury Lane company. After various delays the first performance was given 22 Sept. 1791 (ibid. 19, 22 Sept. 1791).

10. Dorothy Bland (1761–1816), after the birth of her first child, took the name of 'Mrs Jordan,' under which name she became famous as an actress and was highly praised by Hazlitt, Hunt, Lamb, and others.

Her second connection was with Richard (afterwards Sir Richard) Ford, by whom she had four children. From about 1790 to 1811 she was the mistress of the Duke of Clarence, by whom she had ten children, all of whom took the name of Fitzclarence (Clare Jerrold, *The Story of Dorothy Jordan*, 1914, p. 31, *et passim;* N&Q 1942, clxxxii. 279). 'The name of Mrs Jordan is only announced in the newspapers and bills of the day; everywhere else that appellation is *forded* over, and the *Country Girl* [the part in which Mrs Jordan made her London début 18 Oct. 1785, and the role in which Romney painted her] acknowledged and announced as a *lawfully married woman*' (*Times* 15 Sept. 1791). She assumed the name of Ford for a time, but was never married. Cf. *post* 16 Oct. 1791.

11. Ann Brunton (1769–1808), dau. of John Brunton, grocer and actor, and sister of Louisa Brunton who married Lord Craven in 1807; acted at Covent Garden Theatre 1785–92 and at various theatres in the United States 1796–1808; m. (1) (26, 27, or 29 Aug. 1791) Robert Merry; m. (2) (1803) Thomas Wignell, a manager of the Philadelphia theatre; m. (3) (1806) William Warren, comedian (*Dictionary of American Biography*, *sub* Merry, Ann Brunton; GM 1791, lxi pt ii. 872; *St James's Chronicle* 27–30 Aug. 1791; *Oracle* 31 Aug. 1791; *Times* 1 Sept. 1791, 29 Nov. 1796). In DNB her name (*sub* Merry, Robert) is given as Elizabeth Brunton. Rumours of her marriage to Merry were current in the summer of 1791; see, for example, *The Times* 18 June 1791.

might quit his poetic profession, without any loss to the public. My gazettes will have kept you so much *au courant,* that you will be as ready for any conversation at your return, as if you had only been at a watering-place—in short, *à votre intention,* and to make my letters as welcome as I can, I listen to and bring home a thousand things, which otherwise I should not know I heard.

Lord Buchan[12] is screwing out a little ephemeridan fame from instituting a jubilee for Thompson.[13] I fear I shall not make my court to Mr Berry by owning I would not give this last week's fine weather for all the four *Seasons* in blank verse. There is more nature in six lines of the *Allegro* and *Penseroso* than in all the laboured imitations of Milton—what is there in Thompson of original?[14]

Sunday noon.

I this moment receive yours of Aug. 29th in which you justly reprove my jealousies and suspicions of your delaying your return, at the moment you are preparing to make such a sacrifice to me, as I am sensible it is—I do not defend or excuse myself—but alas! is it possible not to have doubts sometimes, when I am not only on the very verge of seventy-five, but, if I have a grain of sense left, must know how very precariously I retain this shattered frame? Nay, my dragging you from the country you prefer, would be inexcusable, were self my only mo-

12. David Steuart Erskine (1742–1829), 11th E. of Buchan; patron of literature, antiquary, and HW's correspondent.

13. James Thomson (1700–48), author of *The Seasons.* The ceremony was held at Ednam, Roxburghshire (Thomson's birthplace) 22 Sept. 1791. A 'cast from the bust of the poet in Westminster Abbey, which had been generously transmitted by Mr Coutts, banker at London, to be crowned with a wreath of bays, was broken in a midnight frolick during the race week on the 16th of September; and the Earl of Buchan contented himself with imposing a wreath of laurel . . . on a copy of [the first edition of] the Seasons' (Lord Buchan, *Essays on the Lives and Writings of Fletcher of Saltoun and the Poet Thomson,* 1792, pp. 242–3). Lord Buchan also delivered a bombastic 'Eulogy' which was later printed in GM 1791, lxi pt ii. 1019–21, 1083–5, and in shorter form in Buchan, op. cit. 251 ff. Burns refused an invitation to attend the

'jubilee,' but sent an 'Address to the Shade of Thomson, on Crowning his Bust with a Wreath of Bays' (ibid. 247–8). For other honours paid by Lord Buchan to the memory of Thomson, see Léon Morel, *James Thomson, sa vie et ses œuvres,* 1895, pp. 185–91. An account of the celebration planned, with a copy of Burns's poem for the occasion, appeared in *The Times* 15 Sept. 1791; the poem also appeared in *The Oracle* 17 Sept. 1791.

14. Dr Johnson's view (*Life of Thomson*) is exactly the opposite: 'As a writer he is entitled to one praise of the highest kind: his mode of thinking, and of expressing his thoughts, is original. His blank verse is no more the blank verse of Milton, or of any other poet, than the rhymes of Prior are the rhymes of Cowley. . . . The reader of the *Seasons* wonders that he never saw before what Thomson shows him, and that he never yet has felt what Thomson impresses.'

tive—no, beloved friends, I am neither in love with either of you, nor, though doting on your society, so personal as to consult my own transitory felicity to your amusement. The scope of all I think and do, is, to make your lives more comfortable when I shall be no more—and if I do suffer the selfish wish of seeing you take possession,[15] to enter into my plan—forgive it! Mr Berry does not as a father, meditate your happiness more than I do, nor has purer affection for you both; nor, though a much younger man, has he less of that weakness that often exposes old men. I am vain of my attachment to two such understandings and hearts; and the cruel injustice of fortune makes me proud of trying to smooth one of her least rugged frowns—but even this theme I must drop, as you have raised a still more cruel fear! You talk uncertainly of your route through France or its borders—and you bid me not be alarmed! Oh! can you conjure down that apprehension! I have scarce a grain of belief in German armies marching against the French[16]—yet what can I advise who know nothing but from the loosest reports—oh! I shall abhor myself, yes abhor myself, if I have drawn you from the security of Florence to the smallest risk, or even inconvenience—my dearest friends, return thither, stay there, stop in Swisserland, do anything but hazard yourselves—I beseech you, I implore you, do not venture through France, for though you come from Italy, and have no connection of any sort on the whole continent, you may meet with incivilities and trouble, which even pretty women that are no politicians, may be exposed to in a country so unsettled as France is at present. If there is truth in my soul, it is, that I would give up all my hopes of seeing you again, rather than have you venture on the least danger of any sort. When a storm could terrify me out of my senses last year, do you think, dearest souls, that I can have any peace till I am sure of your safety?—and to risk it for me! Oh! horrible! I cannot bear the idea!

Berkeley Square, Monday night, 19th.

You have alarmed me so exceedingly by talking of returning through France, against which I thought myself quite secure, or I should not have pressed you to stir, that I have been making all the inquiries I could amongst the foreign ministers at Richmond, and here in town,

15. Of Cliveden. Mrs Damer wrote to Mary Berry 18 Aug. 1791: 'I have been writing to Mr W[alpole], and trying to comfort him. If my security for him about Cliveden can quiet his fears, they will be quieted, for you must see how his heart is set upon that, and I mistake indeed if you are not the last of beings to give false hopes' (*Berry Papers* 62).

16. See following letter.

and I cannot find any belief of the march of armies towards France—nay, the Comte d'Artois is said to be gone to Petersburgh,[17] and he must bring back forces in a balloon, if he can be time enough to interrupt your passage through Flanders. One thing I must premise, if, which I deprecate, you should set foot in France, I beg you to burn and not bring a scrip of paper with you. Mere travelling ladies, as young as you, I know have been stopped, and rifled and detained in France to have their papers examined, and one was rudely treated, because the name of a French lady of her acquaintance was mentioned in a private letter to her, though in no political light. Calais is one of the worst places you can pass, for as they suspect money being remitted through that town to England, the search and delays there are extremely strict and rigorous. The pleasure of seeing you sooner would be bought infinitely too dear by your meeting with any disturbance; as my impatience for your setting out is already severely punished by the fright you have given me! One charge I can wipe off, but it were the least of my faults. I never thought of your settling at Cliveden in November if your house in town is free. All my wish was that you would come for a night to Strawberry and that the next day I might put you in possession of Cliveden—I did not think of engrossing you from all your friends, who must wish to embrace you at your return.

Tuesday.

I am told that on the King's acceptance of the Constitution, there is a general amnesty published, and passports taken off.[18] If this is true, the passage through France for mere foreigners and strangers may be easier and safer—but be assured of all. I would not embarrass your journey unnecessarily—but for heaven's sake be well informed. I advise nothing. I dread everything where your safeties are in question, and I hope Mr Berry is as timorous as I am. My very contradictions prove the anxiety of my mind, or I should not torment those I love so much—but how not love those who sacrifice so much for me, and who I hope forgive all my unreasonable inconsistencies. Adieu! adieu!

17. A false report: the Comte d'Artois had recently visited the Emperor at Vienna, but was at this time at his headquarters in Coblentz; see *Correspondance intime du Comte de Vaudreuil et du Comte d'Artois*, ed. Léonce Pingaud, 1889, ii. 20–48.

18. Following Louis XVI's acceptance of the Constitution 13 Sept. 1791, La Fayette proposed a decree, which was accepted, providing for a general amnesty and for the elimination of restraints on liberty, including the use of passports; see the *Moniteur* 14, 15 septembre 1791; *The Oracle* 19 Sept. 1791.

To Mary Berry, Sunday 25 September 1791

Address: À Mademoiselle Mademoiselle Berry à la poste restante à Basle en Suisse. Endorsed: 'Pd 1s.'

After his entry in 'Visitors,' where HW notes that the letter was posted 27 Sept., HW wrote in pencil, 'all received,' which indicates that Mary Berry had received all his letters, including No. 50 (ca 1 September 1791), now missing. Cf. *post* 20, 27 Oct. 1791.

Strawberry Hill, Sept. 25, 1791.

No. 54.[1]

HOW I love to see my numeros increase! I trust they will not reach 60!—in short, I try every nostrum to make absence seem shorter, and yet with all my conjuration I doubt the next five or six weeks will like the harvest-moon appear of a greater magnitude than all the moons of the year its predecessors. I wish its successor the hunter's moon could seem less in proportion—but, on the contrary! I hate travelling and roads and inns myself; while you are on your way, I shall fancy like Don Quixote that every inn is the castle of some necromancer and every windmill a giant—and these will be my smallest terrors!

Whether this will meet or follow you, I know not. Yours of the 5th of this month arrived yesterday, but could not direct me beyond Basle. I must then remain still in ignorance whether you will take the German or French route. It is now, I think, certain that there will no attempt against France be made this year[2]—still I trust that you will *not* decide till you are assured that you may come through France without trouble or molestation; and I still prefer Germany, though it will protract your absence.

Pray write me nothing but notes on your journey, with, 'we arrived here last night, perfectly well, have caught no colds nor accidents, and set out tomorrow for our next stage.' Adventures I hope you will have none to relate; and you shall not be writing, when you are fatigued, very hot, very cold, or very hungry. This civilly calls itself a prayer, but is a command—and if I open a letter, and see more than three lines, I shall be alarmed, and think some mischief has happened, and then I shall not know what I read, till I read the whole letter over again,

---

1. 'No. 55' (B).
2. Mrs Damer wrote to Mary Berry from SH 23 Sept. 1791: 'The newspapers came full of all that could confirm the ideas I have tried to give him of the present state of things; and even the *violents* here are fallen into despair and dejection, and no longer dream and talk of visionary armies, marchings, plots, and plunders, but seem to give up all for lost' (*Berry Papers* 75).

which has been the case several times since you went, as after the storm, after your fall, after your fever—and I believe oftener—but those are the great epochs in my almanac.

Mrs Damer[2a] came hither from Goodwood last Thursday, stayed all Friday, went to town yesterday, returns hither next Friday, takes Madame de Cambis[3] to Park Place on Saturday, and the next day I shall follow them thither.[4] This is the sum total of my history, and I believe of everybody's else—at least to my knowledge. I have not a paragraph of politics for Mr Berry—nay, I am sure there are none, for my neighbour at the foot of the bridge[5] was here this morning, and had nothing to tell me but that Mr Stevens is just *coming out* with his Shakespear[6]—I said, 'Sir, if he does not *come in,* it is perfectly indifferent to me when he *comes out.*'

I am sorry you was disappointed of going to Valombroso—Milton has made everybody wish *to have seen it;*[7] which is my wish, for though I was thirteen months at Florence (at twice)[8] I never did see it—in fact I was so tired of *seeing* when I was abroad, that I have several of those pieces of repentance on my conscience when they come into my head— and yet I saw too much, for the quantity left such a confusion in my head, that I do not remember a quarter clearly. Pictures, statues and buildings were always so much my passion, that for the time I surfeited myself, especially as one is carried to see a vast deal that is not worth seeing. They who are industrious and correct, and wish to forget nothing, should go to Greece where there is nothing left to be seen, but that ugly pigeon-house the Temple of the Winds,[9] that fly-cage Demos-

2a. Expanded by Mary Berry from HW's 'D.'

3. From Goodwood 28 Aug. 1791 Mrs Damer wrote to Mary Berry: 'We have here only Madame de Cambis, who I think must *ennuyer* herself *un peu* while the rest of the company make out the day. . . . Madame de C[ambis] came yesterday evening. I need not describe her. I am sure she was the only one of us all who had *no* interest in what was going on [chemical lectures and experiments]. . . . She has an unsurmountable crossness. So much *acid* is diffused in her composition that it eternally starts forth and often when one least expects it' (*Berry Papers* 71).

4. For Mrs Damer's account of HW's anxiety about the Berrys, his appearance, etc., see her letter to Mary Berry 23–27

Sept. 1791, in *Berry Papers* 73–8. HW reached Park Place according to his plan, 2 Oct. (see following letter).

5. Richard Owen Cambridge.

6. The first number of the illustrated folio *Dramatic Works of Shakspeare,* rev. by George Steevens (1736–1800), and printed by W. Bulmer for John and Josiah Boydell, G. and W. Nicol; issued originally in 18 parts 1791–1802.

7. That is, to be able to boast about it.

8. HW was at Florence from 17 Dec. 1739 to 21 March 1740 and from 8 July 1740 to ca 24 April 1741.

9. The Tower of the Winds, or Horologium of Andronicus Cyrrhestes, in Athens, 1st cent. B.C., an octagon about 26 feet in diameter and 42 feet in height.

thenes's lanthorn,[10] and one or two fragments of a portico—or a piece of a column crushed into a mud wall—and with such a morsel and many quotations, a true classic antiquary can compose a whole folio and call it Ionian antiquities! Such gentry do better still when they journey to Egypt to visit the Pyramids, which are of a form which one would think nobody could conceive without seeing, though their form is all that is to be seen, for it seems that even prints and measures do not help one to an idea of magnitude—indeed measures do not, for no two travellers have agreed on the measures. In that scientific country too you may guess that such or such a vanished city stood within five or ten miles of such a parcel of sand; and when you have conjectured in vain at what some rude birds or rounds or squares on a piece of an old stone may have signified, you may amuse your readers with an account of the rise of the Nile, some hints at the Mamalukes, and finish your work with doleful tales of the robberies of the wild Arabs.[11] One benefit does arise from travelling; it cures one of liking what is worth seeing, especially if what you have seen is bigger than what you do see. Thus Mr Gilpin having visited all the lakes, could find no beauty in Richmond Hill[12]—if he would look through Mr Herschell's telescope at the profusion of worlds beyond worlds, perhaps he would find out that Mount Atlas is but an ant-hill—and that the *sublime and beautiful* may exist separately.

Monday 26th.

I am alarmed again! I heard at Richmond last night that Lord Binning[13] has a relation[14] just come through France who was searched and

10. A choragic monument to Lysicrates, in Athens, ca 335 B.C.; 'vulgarly called the Lantern of Demosthenes, who is said to have erected it with the object of studying in the seclusion of its interior'—a wholly unsupported tradition (William Smith, *Dictionary of Greek and Roman Biography and Mythology*, 1849, ii. 866).

11. HW refers to James Bruce's *Travels to Discover the Source of the Nile*, 1790; cf. *ante* 3 April 1791.

12. The view from SH, which would include Richmond Hill, Gilpin found 'very unlike indeed the grand and simple views we had seen in the highlands of Scotland,

but more assimilated to the character of a southern county' (*Observations on . . . the Highlands of Scotland . . . 1776*, 1808, ii. 194–5; the first edition appeared in 1789). Cf. HW to Lady Ossory 30 Aug. 1790; William D. Templeman, *William Gilpin*, Urbana, 1939, pp. 266–7. In addition to the above passages, HW may be remembering Gilpin's remarks in conversation.

13. Charles Hamilton (1753–1828), styled Lord Binning until 1795; 8th E. of Haddington, 1795; probably living at Ham at this time.

14. Not identified.

very ill treated, so I revert to your coming through Germany, whence I
am persuaded there will be no movement, all the rodomontades issu-
ing, I believe, from Calonne's brain, which can produce armed Mi-
nervas, but not one Mars.[15] I repeat it, and you may be confident of it,
that I had rather hear you was returned to Florence, than have you expose yourselves to any risk anywhere—and I do now heartily repent my
soliciting your return. I wish I had prevailed as little there, as I did
against your journey!—but you have friends in Swisserland[16]—why not
remain with them for some time? France may grow tranquil on the
King's acceptance[17] and the general amnesty, and as England is at perfect peace with them, and will certainly remain so, they will undoubtedly encourage, not discourage English travellers—well! may you be inspired with what is best for you.—I shall only weary you with my
anxiety.—Adieu!

To Mary Berry, Monday 3 October 1791

Address: À Mademoiselle Mademoiselle Berry à la poste restante à Ausbourg,
   Allemagne. Endorsed: 'Presente Augs[burg] ye 12 8bris 1791. Pd 1s. Davis.'
   Posted 4 Oct. ('Visitors'). Cf. *post* 20 Oct. 1791.

Park Place,[1] Monday, Sept. [Oct.][2] 3, 1791.

No. — I have not my list here and forget which[3]—

I HAD exhausted Basle, was at the end of my map, and did not know
a step of my way farther, when on Saturday I was so happy as to receive two letters at once bidding my pen drive to Ausbourg.[4] Your dates
were of the 11th and 16th of Sept. and you was to leave Florence on the
morrow. I do not wonder at Mrs Legge[5] for liking to accompany you to

15. Presumably a reference to the many
plans, much talk, and little action of the
counter-revolutionists, for whom Calonne
acted as something of a liaison officer.
16. Not identified; the only stop longer
than overnight the Berrys made in Switzerland was at Basle (they arrived on Saturday,
22 Oct., and left on Monday, 24 Oct.), and
Mary Berry mentions no visits to friends
(MBJ i. 359).

17. Of the Constitution.
———
1. HW had arrived the preceding day, 2
Oct. (*Berry Papers* 78).
2. Mary Berry's correction.
3. It is No. 55 of HW's series; Mary
Berry numbered it 'No. 56.'
4. The Berrys were at Augsburg 16–18
Oct. 1791 (MBJ i. 356–7).
5. 'Wife of Heneage Legge, Esq., of ——

Bologna, but though my justice can excuse her, I do not love her a bit the better for detaining you two days,[6] for which I am sure of being out of pocket in November. With more days I shall part with pleasure, if, as you seem to intend, you prefer the road through Germany, provided Brussels is quite tranquil, which the newspapers, which I never believe but *quand il s'agit de vous,* represent as still growling. I hope Mr Berry has no more courage than I have, but will listen, like a hare in its form, to every yelp even of a puppy.

I trust you have received my letter[7] in which I explained that I never thought of your settling at Cliveden in November. When I proposed your landing at Strawberry, it was because I thought your house in Audley Street was let till Christmas,[8] and I remembered your description (for what do I forget that you have told me?) of how uncomfortable you found yourselves at your last arrival from abroad.[9] A house in which you would be as much at home as in your own, would be preferable to an hotel—*mais voilà qui est fini.* I did and certainly do still hope, that when you shall have unpacked yourselves, shall have received and returned some dozen of double kisses from and to all that are delighted to see you again—or are not, you will give a couple of days at Strawberry, that on the morning of the second I may carry you to and install and invest you with Cliveden. To *that day* I own I look with an eagerness of impatience that no words could convey, unless they could paint the pulse of fifteen when it has been promised some untasted joy, for which it had long hoped and been denied, and which seldom answers half the expectation—and there I shall have the advantage if I live to attain it, for my felicity cannot but be complete, if that day arrives!

Here is nobody but Mrs Damer and Madame de Cambis,[10] and I am glad there is not. I shall return home on Wednesday and the end of the week shall hope to receive a direction farther, but scarce, I doubt, shall

---

in Staffordshire [Warwickshire]. She with her husband had been spending all the summer at Florence and in its immediate neighbourhood' (B). In MBJ i. 368 the blank is supplied as 'Aston.' Cf. *ante* 3 Aug. 1791.

6. The Berrys had planned to leave Florence 15 Sept. (*ante* 16 Sept. 1791), but did not leave until 17 Sept. (MBJ i. 353).

7. *Ante* 16 Sept. 1791.

8. HW had forgotten that it was let only until 25 May (*ante* 27 March 1791).

9. In June, 1785 (MBJ i. 149–50, *et passim*).

10. Both of whom conspired to keep unpleasant news from HW (*Berry Papers* 78–83).

know so soon that your final determination on your route is fixed. The company is come in from walking and I should not have time to write more, if I had wherewithal, but the totality of my intelligence is bounded to the death of Lord Craven, who this morning's Reading paper[11] says is dead,[12] of which an express came last night, and it is probably credible, as his house is so near Reading[13]—the moment the courier arrives at Lisbon, I suppose the new Margravine[14] will notify her marriage and accession to the devout Queen of Portugal,[15] who will bless herself that she is made an honest woman—if a heretic can be so.[16] Adieu! adieu!

To Mary Berry, Sunday 9 October 1791

Address: À Mademoiselle Mademoiselle Berry à la poste restante à Ausbourg, Allemagne. Forwarded: 'aux soins de Mr Perregaux, banquier, Paris.'
Postmark: 29. ALLEMAGNE. Endorsed: 'd'Angleterre. [?] 21 [?] 8br. 1791.'
Posted 11 Oct. ('Visitors'). Cf. *post* 20 Oct. 1791.

11. *The Reading Mercury and Oxford Gazette* for 1 Oct.

12. He died 26 Sept. in Lausanne, Switzerland (Musgrave, *Obituary;* Collins, *Peerage,* 1812, v. 459; GM 1791, lxi pt ii. 970–1; *The Girlhood of Maria Josepha Holroyd,* ed. Jane H. Adeane, 1896, p. 86). GEC gives the date 27 Sept.

13. Three of Lord Craven's family seats were in Berkshire within twenty to thirty miles of Reading: Benham Place and Hampstead Marshall, the two closest; and Ashdown Park.

14. 'Elizabeth Berkeley, Lady Craven' (B).

15. Maria (Francisca) I (1734–1816), eld. dau. of José I; Queen of Portugal 1777–1816; m. (1760) her uncle, Pedro III, with whom she ruled jointly until his death in 1786. She 'was a woman of weak intellect, completely subservient to her confessor, . . . who found her greatest happiness in raising vast sums of money and sending them to the Latin convent at Jerusalem. . . . It was observed in 1788 that she was quite unfit to transact any business; and in 1792 . . . Dom John [her son] found it necessary to take the management of affairs into his hands, though he was not declared regent until 1799' (H. Morse Stephens, *Portugal,* 1908, pp. 372–3). See also Fortunato de Almeida, *História de Portugal,* Coimbra, 1922–6, iv. 424–515, esp. p. 486.

16. The marriage took place at Lisbon 13 Oct. 1791. It is reported (erroneously under the date of 30 Oct.) in GM lxi pt ii. 1061: 'At Lisbon, by the Rev. Mr Hill, his Serene Highness the Margrave of Anspach and Bayreuth, to the widow of Lord Craven, and sister of the Earl of Berkeley. The ceremony was performed before a number of respectable witnesses; the ambassadors of Russia, Naples, Holland, Vienna, and all the English gentry that could be collected together. Capt. Dorset officiated as father; and the whole company supped with their Highnesses, after the ceremony, at the Prussian Minister's hotel, where the Margrave had taken up his residence.' For the official record of the ceremony, and the list of about twenty witnesses, see *The Beautiful Lady Craven,* ed. A. M. Broadley and Lewis Melville, 1914, i. p. lxxvi. For the Queen's kindness to Lady Craven, see ibid. ii. 40–1.

Strawberry Hill, Oct. 9, 1791.

No. 56.[1]

IT will be a year tomorrow since you set out. Next morning came the
storm that gave me such a panic for you! In March happened your
fall and the wound on your nose; and in July, *your* fever—for sweet
Agnes I have happily had no separate alarm—yet I have still a month of
apprehensions to come for both! All this mass of vexation and fears is
to be compensated by the transport at your return, and by the complete
satisfaction on your installation at Cliveden—but could I have believed
that when my clock had struck seventy-four, I could pass a year in such
agitations! It may be taken for dotage, and I have for some time expected to be superannuated; but though I task myself severely, I do not
find my intellects impaired—though I may be a bad judge myself—you
may perhaps perceive it by my letters—and don't imagine I am laying a
snare for flattery—no—I am only jealous about myself, that you two
may have created such an attachment, without owing it to my weakness. Nay, I have some colt's limbs left, which I as little suspected as my
anxieties. I went with General Conway on Wednesday morning from
Park Place to visit one of my antediluvian passions—not a Statira or
Roxana—but one pre-existent to myself—one—Windsor Castle; and I
was so delighted and so juvenile, that without attending to anything
but my eyes, I stood full two hours and half, and found that half my
lameness consists in my indolence. Two Berrys, a Gothic chapel and an
historic castle are anodynes to a torpid mind—I now fancy that old age
was invented by the lazy. St George's Chapel that I always worshipped,
though so dark and black that I could see nothing distinctly, is now being cleaned and decorated, a scene of lightness and graces. Mr Conway
was so struck with its Gothic beauties and taste, that he owned the Grecian style would not admit half the variety of its imagination.[2] There is
a new screen prefixed to the choir, so airy and harmonious that I concluded it Wyat's,[3] but it is by a Windsor architect whose name I forget.[4]

1. 'No. 57' (B).

2. Mrs Damer was also favourably im-
pressed; see *Berry Papers* 85.

3. James Wyatt (1746–1813), the architect
who designed the offices at SH, and whose
Gothic architecture HW greatly admired;
see *SH Accounts* 176.

4. Henry Emlyn (1729–1815), to whom
George III confided the 'alterations in St
George's Chapel . . . which were executed

(1787–90) entirely after his designs, and
preserved a due harmony with the original
work' (DNB *sub* Emlyn, Henry). 'The present screen to the choir beneath the organ,
executed in cement from a design by Emlyn, may be cited as one of the best works
of its time' (Robert Richard Tighe and
James Edward Davis, *Annals of Windsor*,
1858, ii. 549).

Jarvis's window over the altar after West[5] is rather too sombre for the Resurrection, though it accords with the tone of the choir; but the Christ is a poor figure scrambling to heaven in a fright, as if in dread of being again buried alive; and not ascending calmly in secure dignity; and there is a Judas below so gigantic, that he seems more likely to burst by his bulk than through guilt.[6] In the midst of all this solemnity, in a small angle over the lower stalls is crammed a small bas-relief in oak with the story of Margaret Nicholson,[7] the King and the coachman, as ridiculously added, and as clumsily executed as if it were a monkish miracle. Some loyal zealot has broken away the blade of the knife, as if the sacred wooden personage would have been in danger still.[8] The Castle itself is smugged up, is better glazed, has got some new stools, clocks, and looking glasses, much embroidery in silk, and a gaudy clumsy throne with a medallion at top of the King's and Queen's heads over their own—an odd kind of tautology whenever they sit there![9] There are several tawdry[10] pictures by West of the history of the Garter,[11] but the figures are too small for that majestic palace—however upon the whole, I was glad to see Windsor a little revived.

I had written thus far, waiting for a letter, and happily receive your two from Bologna together for which I give you a million of thanks, and for the repairs of your coach, which I trust will contribute to your safety;[12] but I will swallow my apprehensions, for I doubt I have tor-

5. Thomas Jervais or Jarvis (d. 1799) and his pupil Forrest painted the east window of the chapel after designs by Benjamin West (1738–1820). 'As . . . the design and Jervais's method of execution were wholly unsuited to the place,' the window was removed in 1863 (DNB sub Jervais; T. Eustace Harwood, *Windsor Old and New*, 1929, p. 95). It 'was transferred to the ambulatory behind the altar, where it can still be seen' (W. H. St John Hope, *Windsor Castle: An Architectural History*, 1913, ii. 427).

6. The figure of Judas appeared in West's painting, 'The Last Supper,' on the altar: 'Those who only affect to be critics pretend that the figure of Judas is too predominant; though real judges esteem the whole a masterly composition' (*The Windsor Guide*, Windsor, 1799, p. 58).

7. (ca 1750–1828), who attempted to assassinate George III, 2 Aug. 1786, as he descended from his carriage at St James's Palace.

8. For a detailed description of the group of carvings, see Hope, op. cit. ii. 439. According to Hope (ii. 436), the group has 'a skill and restraint deserving of all praise.'

9. There is a more appreciative description of the King's Audience Chamber in *The Windsor Guide*, Windsor, 1799, pp. 31–2.

10. HW first wrote 'gaudy.'

11. In the King's Audience Chamber were several pictures by West, among them 'The First Installation of the Order of the Garter, in St George's Chapel'; it is fully described in *The Windsor Guide*, Windsor, 1799, p. 33.

12. On Sunday, 18 Sept., the Berrys' second day out of Florence, the perch of their carriage broke almost in two. Following temporary repairs, the carriage proceeded unladen to Bologna (the Berrys walking to the next post and continuing in two smaller vehicles), where it was repaired. The Berrys left Bologna 26 Sept. (MBJ i. 353–4). In her letters to HW Mary Berry evidently mini-

mented you with them.[13] Yet do not wonder that after a year's absence my affection, instead of waning, is increased! Can I help feeling the infinite obligation I have to you both for quitting Italy that you love, to humour Methusalem?—a Methusalem, that is neither king nor priest, to reward and bless you, and whom you condescend to please, because he wishes to see you once more, though he ought to have sacrificed a momentary glimpse to your far more durable satisfaction. Instead of your generosity, I have teased and I fear wearied you with lamentations and disquiets—and how can I make you amends? What pleasure, what benefit can I procure for you in return? The most disinterested generosity, such as yours is, gratifies noble minds—but how paltry am I to hope that the reflections of your own minds will compensate for all the amusements you give up to

Make Languor smile and smooth the bed of Death![14]

—I may boast of having no foolish weakness for your persons, as I certainly have not—but

The soul's dark cottage batter'd and decay'd
Lets in new selfishness through chinks that Time has made[15]—

and I have been as avaricious of hoarding a few moments of agreeable society, as if I had coveted a few more trumpery guineas in my strong box!—and then I have the assurance to tell you I am not superannuated!—Oh! but I am!

As the repairs of your coach cost so many days, I venture to direct this still to Ausbourg, since I have received no farther direction. Do not hurry or fatigue yourselves—surely I can weather out a fortnight more than you announce—shall your old *cavaliere* at Bologna[16] excel

mized the accident, but gave Mrs Damer full details (*Berry Papers* 81).

13. Mrs Damer wrote to Mary Berry, Thursday, 13 (?) Oct. 1791: 'Our dear friend [HW] may, I think, be called well so far, and *tolerable* as to anxieties. I am convinced that he has much less fear about the German road than the other [through France], I mean in proportion. He does not seem to be alarmed about your carriage, and suspects nothing. I, of course, encourage this good disposition' (ibid. 84–5).

14. Pope, 'Epistle to Dr Arbuthnot,' 411.

15. Edmund Waller (1606–87), 'Of the Last Verses in the Book'; the second line reads 'Lets in new light. . . .' HW's copy of Waller's *Works*, ed. Elijah Fenton, 1729, is now WSL. HW correctly quoted these two lines in his letter to Montagu 24 Oct. 1758 and to Lady Ossory 1 July 1782; and, with variations, to Robert Nares 5 Oct. 1793. See also *post* 6 Dec. 1795.

16. After the arrival of their broken carriage at Bologna, the Berrys 'sent to the Chevalier Poggelini, whom we had seen at Florence, to recommend a coachmaker to us. Came himself, and offered us his serv-

me in complaisance! I have been much diverted by all you tell me
thence[17]—the Bolognese school is my favourite, though I do not like
Guercino, whom I call the German Guido,[18] he is so heavy and dark. I
do not, like your friend,[19] venerate Constantinopolitan paintings,
which are scarce preferable to Indian. The characters of the Italian
comedy were certainly adopted even from the *persons* of its several dis-
tricts and dialects. Pantalon is a Venetian even in his countenance; and
I once saw a gentleman of Bergamo whose face was an exact Harlequin's mask.[20]

I have scarce a penful of news for you; the world is at Weymouth[21] or
Newmarket[22]—*en attendant, voici* the Gunnings again. The old gouty
General has carried off his tailor's wife[23]—or rather, she him—whither,

ices. The man he recommended was out of
town, and did not return till the next day
(Tuesday), and the day after (Wednesday)
being a fête, it could not be touched till
Thursday; he promised, however, to let us
have it on Saturday evening, and, contrary
to my expectations, on Saturday evening it
came, finished, to the inn. We made no bargain beforehand, as our friend the chevalier promised to settle that matter for us.
The man's bill was thirty-two sequins—we
paid twenty-seven; for this country it was
tolerably reasonable' (MBJ i. 354).

17. Cf. Mrs Damer to Mary Berry 10
[erroneously printed 18] Oct. 1791: 'I need
not say that I long to hear the further
event of your accident. I am not so much
rejoiced at your being forced to see and
"resee" the noble pictures at Bologna, but
that I think with anxiety of a delay that
may occasion *forced marches* or a still later
and colder journey' (*Berry Papers* 84).

18. Cf. *ante* 26 Nov. 1790.

19. Perhaps one of the following people
who were with the Berrys at Bologna: Mr
or Mrs Legge or the Chevalier Poggelini or
the 'Mr Gianfigliazzi' who accompanied the
Legges when they called on the Berrys (MBJ
i. 354).

20. *Pantaloon* is from Italian *pantalone*,
' "a kind of mask on the Italian stage, representing the Venetian" (Baretti), of whom
Pantalone was a nickname, supposed to be
derived from the name of *San Pantaleone*
or *Pantalone*, formerly a favourite saint of
the Venetians' (OED). *Harlequin* is possibly
from Old French and (earlier) Teutonic,
but 'the *arlecchino* is said, in Italian dic-

tionaries, to have originally represented the
simple and facetious Bergamese man-servant. Cf. the stage Irishman' (OED).

21. Where the King, Queen, and three
eldest princesses remained until 15 Oct.
(*Oracle* 17 Oct. 1791).

22. The first October meeting was held
at Newmarket 3–8 October (James Weatherby, *Racing Calendar . . . 1791*, 1792, pp.
120–8).

23. Rebecca Howard (ca 1767—ca 1805?),
dau. of Gerard Howard of Hampstead,
Middlesex; m. (1787) James Duberly (1758–
1832), of 33 Soho Square, London, and later
of Gaynes Hall, Hunts (Kt, 1803). Duberly,
a prosperous army-clothier, became acquainted with Gunning in connection with
the clothing of the 65th Regiment of Foot,
of which Gunning became colonel 28 Jan.
1788. The General was frequently Duberly's guest, and borrowed money from him.
The intimacy of Mrs Duberly and Gunning
led to discovery and their appearance in
the 'Tête-à-Tête' series of *The Town and
Country Magazine* (October 1791, xxiii.
435–6, the print dated 1 Nov.) as 'Helen of
Hampstead' and 'The Gallant General.'
Duberly brought suit against Gunning for
crim. con. with Mrs Duberly; the trial,
scheduled for 6 Dec. 1791, was postponed to
22 Feb. 1792, when Duberly was awarded
£5000 damages. A request for a new trial,
on the grounds that the damages were excessive, was denied. Gunning and Mrs Duberly left England before the trial and lived
in France and at Naples, where Gunning
died, leaving nothing to Mrs Duberly, but
£1500 to a child she had by him. Presum-

I know not—probably not far, for the next day the General was arrested for £3,000[24] and carried to a sponging house,[25] whence he sent Cupid with a link to a friend to beg help, and a crutch.[26] This amazing folly is generally believed, perhaps because the folly of that race is amazing— so is their whole story. The two beautiful sisters[27] were going on the stage,[28] when they are at once exalted almost as high as they could be, were Countessed and double-Duchessed—and now the rest of the family have dragged themselves through all the kennels of the newspapers!— it is but a trifling codicil, that t'other day poor old Bedford made Miss Gunning read her daughter Marlborough's letter on Lord Blandford's marriage to a lady that came to visit her. By the time of your arrival I suppose the Margravine Craven will have superseded the Gunnings in the eye of the public.

Adieu! forgive all my pouts—I will be perfectly good-humoured, when I have nothing to vex me!

ably Mrs Duberly died before Duberly remarried in 1805: no record of a divorce has been found (*The Remarkable Trial of General Gunning for Adultery with Mrs Duberly*, 1792, *passim; The English Reports*, 176 vols, 1900–30, clxx. 105, c. 1226–30; GM 1797, lxvii pt ii. 892; *Directory of the Nobility, Gentry . . . 1793*, p. 17; Burke, *Landed Gentry*, 1900, p. 453, *sub* Duberly).

24. According to the anonymous and scandalous (but in outline apparently true) *An Apology for the Life of Major General G——, written by Himself. Containing a full Explanation of the G–nn–g Mystery, and of the Author's Connexion with Mr D–ber–y's Family of Soho-Square*, 1792, the couple, after staying two nights at an inn, removed to 'apartments provided for our reception at Somers Town. . . . On the third morning after our arrival at this place . . . I saw myself surrounded by a gang of bailiffs, and arrested for a hundred and thirty odd pounds, at the suit of Mr D——' (pp. 101–2). In *The Remarkable Trial . . .* (p. 11) Gunning's counsel says he was arrested for 'a small sum while he lodged at Somers Town.' It appears, however, that Gunning actually owed Duberly between two and three thousand pounds, but in effect swindled him out of that sum by revoking a power of attorney and filing a suit in Chancery against Duberly (*An Apology . . .*, p. 104).

25. Where he was confined for 'five or six

weeks' (*The Remarkable Trial . . .*, p. 10). He was about to be transferred to Newgate when two merchants advanced him sufficient money to pay his most pressing debts (*An Apology . . .*, pp. 103–4). *The Oracle* 8 Oct. 1791 commented: 'The *Gunning General*, after neglecting his parental and social duty, has now very properly a guard doing duty over him.' 'The *amorous* General is no longer in durance vile. He has found bail for the debt.—Where could he find bail for his good behaviour?' (ibid. 13 Oct. 1791).

26. In the pamphlets connected with the Gunning and Gunning-Duberly affairs General Gunning is pictured as a hoary, gouty, debilitated old man. See, for example, *The Remarkable Trial . . ., passim*, where his age is given as about sixty, and *An Apology . . .*, pp. 3–4, 87–8. He did suffer considerably from the gout, but he was not more than fifty years old.

27. Gen. Gunning's sisters, Maria and Elizabeth, who became respectively the Countess of Coventry and the Duchess of Hamilton and of Argyll.

28. Cf. *Mem. Geo. III* iii. 130 n; *Last Journals* i. 542; and the comment of Horace Bleackley: 'According to the high priest of small talk [HW], whose account is by no means incredible, they [the Gunning sisters] had thoughts of going on the stage' (*The Story of a Beautiful Duchess*, 1908, pp. 11–12).

To Mary Berry, Sunday 16 October 1791

Address: À Mademoiselle Mademoiselle Berry à la poste restante à Bruxelles.
    Forwarded: 'Chez Mess. Perrigaux, Banquiers, Paris.'
Postmark: 1. Endorsed: 'Pd 1s.'
Posted 18 Oct. ('Visitors'). Cf. *post* 20 Oct. 1791.

Strawberry Hill, Sunday, Oct. 16, 1791.

No. 57.

YOU had said you would write from Padua,[1] if you found a good opportunity; but I have not received a letter thence; I am not much dis[ap]pointed, as I saw I had only a chance; and besides have prepared myself to expect miscarriages, while you are on the road, resting my consolation on the trust of seeing you soon, and knowing that from Venice[2] every mile will bring you nearer. I call a month *soon,* but only with reference to the twelve that are gone. That *month* may be composed of five or six weeks—and my impatience is not apt to treat my almanac with supernumerary days—but I will add a codicil of philosophy to the eagerness I have betrayed, in hopes of effacing some of it, and making a better impression against we meet!

Having no letter, and no direction beyond Ausbourg, this will be an adventurer without credentials, and will take its chance for your finding it at Brussels.[3] Having no other business than merely to welcome you so far, it shall be brief. News I have none, nor will you have missed any by being on the road.

The Dowager Lady Effingham[4] is dead and makes a vacancy in the Queen's bedchamber, which it is supposed will be filled by the younger Lady Ailesbury, Lady Cardigan, or Lady Howe.[5]

1. The Berrys arrived at Padua 27 and left 29 Sept. (MBJ i. 355). See the last paragraph of this letter.

2. Apparently the Berrys were at Venice from 29 Sept. to 6 Oct. (MBJ i. 355).

3. But see address of this letter. The Berrys returned via Paris, not Brussels.

4. Elizabeth Beckford (1725–12 or 13 Oct. 1791), sister of William Beckford, Lord Mayor of London in 1770; m. (1) (1745) Thomas Howard (ca 1714–63), 2d E. of Effingham; m. (2) (1776) Field Marshal Sir George Howard (1718–96), K.B.; lady of the Bedchamber to Queen Charlotte 1761–91 (GEC, where the dates of her service to the

Queen are incorrectly given as 1761–9; *Court and City Register,* 1761–91; GM 1791, lxi pt ii. 974; *Oracle* 17 Oct. 1791).

5. Mary Hartopp (1732–1800), dau. and coheiress of Chiverton Hartopp of Welby, Leicestershire; m. (1758) Hon. Richard Howe, 4th Vct Howe, 1758; cr. (1788) E. Howe. Lady Effingham was succeeded by none of the three ladies HW mentions, but by Viscountess Sydney. Lady Howe was never a lady of the Bedchamber, but two years later Lady Cardigan succeeded the Marchioness of Bath (*London Chronicle* 9–12 Nov. 1793, lxxiv. 460; *Sun* 11 Nov. 1793).

Mrs Jordan, whom Mr Ford[6] had declared his wife and presented her as such to some ladies at Richmond,[7] has resumed her former name,[8] and is said to be much at a *princ*ipal villa at Petersham,[9] which I do not affirm—far be it from me to vouch a quarter of what I hear. If I let my memory listen, it is that I may have some ingredients for my letters, and to which you are apprized not to give too much credit, though, while absent, it is natural to like to hear the breath of the day, which at home you despise, as it commonly deserves.

Berkeley Square, Tuesday 18.

I am come to town suddenly and unexpectedly; my footman John had pawned a silver strainer and spoon, which not being found out till now, as it had been done here, he ran away in the night,[10] and I have [been] forced to come and see if he had done no worse, which I do not find he has—and I want another footman in his room[11]—I received yours from Padua and Venice last night, but with no farther direction. I had begun this, and now cannot finish it, for the post is going out, and by coming so unexpected, I have neither ink nor pen to write with, as you perceive[12]—but I will write again on Friday if I receive any direction.

To Mary Berry, Thursday 20 October 1791

Address: À Mademoiselle Mademoiselle Berry à la poste restante à Bruxelles.
 Forwarded: 'Chez M. Perrigaux à Paris.'
Postmark: 28. Endorsed: 'Pd 1s. Clemson.'
Posted 21 Oct. ('Visitors').

6. Richard Ford (ca 1759–1806), admitted to Lincoln's Inn, 1777; called to the bar, 1782; M.P. East Grinstead 1789–90, Appleby 1790–1; police magistrate at Shadwell 1792–6, and at Bow Street, 1793, where he became chief magistrate, 1800; Kt, 1801 (*Old Westminsters* and *Supplement; London Chronicle* 26–28 Sept. 1793, lxxiv. 307; GM 1806, lxxvi pt i. 484). For allusions to his connection with Mrs Jordan, see also BM, *Satiric Prints* vi. 771–2, 820–2.

7. HW had been at Richmond three nights before, on Thursday, 13 Oct.; see following letter.

8. See *The Oracle* 17 Oct. 1791 for two letters written by Ford to Mrs Jordan 'upon a change of her domestic situation': in one

he mentions her generous allowance to her children by Ford, and in the other gives her permission to visit the children 'whenever she pleases. . . .'

9. The Duke of Clarence's.

10. Of Thursday–Friday, 13–14 Oct.; see following letter.

11. In addition to the 'John' here mentioned, HW had another footman, James Colomb (*ante* 20 July 1791). 'John' was succeeded by John Fitzwater, to whom HW in his will dated 15 May 1793 left £10, and in a codicil dated 27 Dec. 1796 an additional £50.

12. The pen was rough, and the ink watery.

Berkeley Square, Oct. 20, 1791.

No. 58.

I WROTE to you a very bit of a letter, but two days ago in a great hurry from being in fear of being too late for the post from various clashing circumstances. This therefore is but the second part of that letter, or rather an explanation of it. I think I did tell you that I was come to town on a sudden, one of my footmen having pawned a little of my plate and run away—This was very true, and a woeful story, as you will hear—but I had other motives. I have had for some time a very troublesome erysipelas on my left arm, which I had not only neglected, but had scratched so unmercifully, that it had become a very serious affair. Mr Gilchrist my apothecary at Twickenham, is dangerously ill at Tunbridge[1]—and on Monday I had a slight attack of the gout in my foot. Dreading to be laid up there where I had no assistance nor advice (with some other fears which *you* may guess) I determined to come away—and did—which has proved fortunate. Mr Watson, my oracle, attends my arm, and it is so much better, that, though with my foot on a stool the whole evening of yesterday, I passed it at Mrs Damer's, and supped there with Lord and Lady Frederic Campbell, Mrs and Miss Farren, Lord Derby and Miss Jennings,[2] and stayed there till past twelve—and today my foot is quite well, and my arm getting well—but now comes the dreadful part of my story!

As I rose out of bed Philip told me he would not disturb my rest last night, but before I came home, a messenger had arrived from Strawberry to say that at five yesterday in the evening one of my gardener's men[3] had in my wood-walk discovered my poor servant John's body hanged in a tree near the chapel and already putrefied![4]—so he must

---

1. Stirling Gilchrist, surgeon and apothecary of Twickenham since his retirement from the army (he was surgeon of the Third Regiment of Dragoon Guards 1761–5; see *Army Lists*). According to *The Oracle* 21 Dec. 1791, he died 'last week, at Twickenham.' See also *The European Magazine* 1792, xxi. 79, where, under date of 18 Dec. 1791, he is said to have died 'lately'; DNB, *sub* Gilchrist, Octavius Graham.

2. A friend and companion (possibly the privileged housekeeper) of Lady Ailesbury, invited to accompany Lady Ailesbury to SH in 1779, and mentioned by Mrs Damer and Mrs Lybbe Powys as being at Park Place in 1795 (HW to Conway 5 June 1779; *Berry*

Papers 170, 176–7; Percy Noble, *Park Place*, 1905, p. 140; *Intimate Society Letters of the Eighteenth Century*, ed. John Campbell, 9th D. of Argyll, n.d., ii. 655).

3. In his will, dated 15 May 1793, HW leaves £10 to his gardener, Christopher Vickers; and £20 to 'my Gardener's Man,' Thomas Farr.

4. 'A melancholy circumstance happened a few days ago, at Strawberry Hill, the seat of the Hon. H. Walpole: the butler missed a silver bowl, and the foot-boy was charged with it, who denied knowing anything of it; it was soon, however, found that he had pawned it for five shillings:—the butler severely chastised the boy, who (it was

have dispatched himself on the Friday morning[5] on which he disappeared—I had then learnt to my astonishment that he had not even taken away his hat with him, and had dropped down from the library window, a dangerous height![6] All this it seems was occasioned by the housekeeper,[7] as she always does, locking all the doors below as soon as she knows everybody is in bed—and thus he could not get his hat out of the servant's hall[8]—if poor soul! he did look for it—probably not!

This remain of shame and principle goes to my heart!—happily for me, I had not even mentioned to him the discovery that had been made of his pawning my plate, and Philip and Kirgate had urged him in the kindest manner to confess it on Thursday evening, which he then would not—but a few hours afterwards owned it to the coachman, and told him he would go away. I since hear he had contracted other debts, and probably feared all would be found out—and he should be arrested and thrown into prison—by me I am sure he would not, for I had not even thought of discharging him—but should rather have tried by pardoning to reclaim him, for I do not think he was more than eighteen!— nay, on Thursday evening after I knew the story, I had let him go behind my coach to Richmond as he used to do, and had not spoken a harsh word to him.

I beg your pardon for dwelling on this melancholy detail, but you may imagine how much it has affected me. It is fortunate for me I was absent from Strawberry when the body was found. Kirgate is gone thither this evening to meet the coroner tomorrow; the corpse was carried into my chapel in the garden—I shall certainly not return thither before Monday at soonest[9]—My greatest comfort is that I cannot on the

thought) ran away; but, as one of the servants went into the wood a few days after, the boy was found hanging amongst the trees; and the body had hung there so long, that the birds had begun pecking it' (*Times* 26 Oct. 1791). An account which varies only slightly in phraseology appears in *The Oracle* of the same date.

5. 14 Oct.

6. Since the height of the Refectory or Great Parlour, the room on the ground floor immediately beneath the Library, was twelve feet, and since the window in the Library was approximately three feet from the floor, the drop from the Library window was probably not more than fifteen or sixteen feet; see 'Des. of SH,' *Works* ii. 401, 442, and plate facing the latter page.

7. Ann Bransom.

8. The men-servants slept on the top floor of the eastern section, the women on the top floor of the middle section. Before the housekeeper retired to her room, probably the one over the Holbein Chamber, she locked all the outside doors and the doors which led to the middle section on all three floors. John, therefore, could not get into this part, on the ground floor of which was the Servants' Hall. Apparently the housekeeper also locked the doors to all the rooms except the one to the Library, for if the other rooms had been accessible, John would have chosen the windows in them, since they were considerably lower than the windows in the Library.

9. On the advice of his surgeon, HW re-

strictest inquiry find that even an angry word had been used towards the poor young man—I may be blamed for taking his fault so calmly—but I know how my concern would be aggravated if a bitter syllable from me had contributed to his despair![10]

I have written all this, that you may know the exact situation of my mind, and because I conceal nothing from you, and lest from the abrupt conclusion of my last, you should suspect I was ill. I do assure you I have not the smallest sensation of pain anywhere, and my arm will be healed in two or three days, and now does not confine me at home. The impression of the unhappy accident will wear off, as I neither contributed to it, nor could foresee it nor prevent it. I talk of nothing else to you, because, except of you as you see, and of your journey, I have for these five last days been occupied only by that adventure and by my own arm. I write to Brussels still, as I compute that this must arrive there before you; but tomorrow or Saturday I shall hope for another letter; and amidst my distresses I am not insensible to the hope of November having a most happy era in store for me! Adieu Adieu!

PS. As I understand that you do not go to Bale, but have ordered the letters sent thither to meet you at Ausbourg,[11] here are my dates, that you may know whether you receive all. To Venice, Sept. 6; to Basle—12, 20, 27; to Ausbourg, Oct. 4, 11; to Brussels—18, 20.[12]

To Mary Berry, Thursday 27 October 1791

Address: À Mademoiselle Mademoiselle Berry <aux> soins de Monsieur Peregaux, <Ban>quier, Rue du Sentier à Paris.
Postmark: 28 OC 91. E. 5. [An]gleterr[e].
Posted 28 Oct. ('Visitors').
Part of the cover has been torn away.
After the last entry relative to the posting of this letter, HW noted in 'Visitors': 'They [the Berrys] arrived in England Nov. 11, 1791.'

mained at Berkeley Square for more than a week longer: he planned to return to SH 29 Oct.; see following letter.

10. HW probably was particularly sensitive because of the unfair accusations made against him in connection with Chatterton's death.

11. They did go to Basle: arrived 22 Oct.

and left 24 Oct. (MBJ i. 359); and the letters addressed to that place bear no indications that they were forwarded to Augsburg.

12. HW gives the date of posting the letters dated as follows: *ante* 5, 11, 16, 25 Sept.; 3, 9, 16 Oct. 1791; and the present letter.

Berkeley Square, Oct. 27, 1791.

No. 59.[1]

NOBODY could be more astonished than I was last night! Mr C. and Lady A.[2] are in town for a few days, and I was to sup with them after the play at Mrs D.'s, whither I went at nine and found her reading a letter from you, saying that you should be at *Paris* today the 27th[3]—I did not know whether her eyes or my ears had lost their senses! I had had no letter from you after your first from Venice, and according to that was reckoning that you would be at Brussels by the beginning of next week—To think you are so near me today gave me a burst of pleasure—but it was soon checked—I am not sure you are there!— Can I be sure you have arrived there without any *embarras*—Can I be certain that while you stay there, everything will remain as quiet as it has been lately? I have no reason, it is true, to apprehend the contrary— but reason's logic is lost against affection's assertions—and you may guess whether I can be overjoyed at your being in Paris—or anywhere that is not as tranquil as the Fortunate Islands!

My next surprise, though marvellously inferior, is, that though you have received all my letters, even the 54th, you should still ask Mrs D. whether I wish you to land at Strawberry Hill first. I think I have over and over explained that I do *not* wish it—nay, thought it would be very uncomfortable to you, till you had unpacked yourselves, seen some few persons, adjusted your family etc.—nay, if your arrival were known, and that you are not in London, you would be tormented with letters, notes, questions, and after that, be still to rest and settle yourselves. Today I have had the satisfaction of *three* letters at once from you, from Venice, Inspruck, Ausburgh,[4] and in the first of them you say it would be more comfortable to go for the two or three first days to Twickenham. I have told you why I am not of that opinion—nor was, when you misunderstood me—now, unluckily, it would not be very practicable. I have been in town these ten days, being forced to come for a violent inflammation on my arm, for which Mr Watson attends me. It is so much better that he has consented to let me go to Strawberry the day after to-

---

1. 'No. 58' (B).
2. General Conway and Lady Ailesbury.
3. They did not arrive until the following day. Because of a broken axle on their carriage, their arrival at Paris was delayed from about 2 P.M. to 7:30 P.M. 28 Oct. (MBJ

i. 360). They left Paris 7 Nov. and arrived at their house in North Audley Street in the late afternoon or early evening of 11 Nov. (MBJ i. 374–5).
4. For the Berrys' visits at these places, 29 Sept.–18 Oct., see MBJ i. 355–7.

morrow for two or three days, where I have left my family, my bills un-paid etc.—and if I did not settle those things before the moments of ex-pecting you, I should be in a confusion very inconvenient and distress-ing. I shall now finish all my business, return to Mr Watson, and be well and quiet, and fit to receive you, first here in town, and then at Strawberry and have the installation.[5] Be assured that this plan is the safest and best I can form; and as you know how earnest I am to be well at your return, you may be certain I would do nothing to counteract a plan that has been rooted in my head and heart for twelve months. Pray do not reprove me for it; your reproof would not be in time to stop me—and as I trust you will find me quite well, though much older than you would expect in a year, let all my faults and impatience be forgotten, that our meeting again, which I doubted might not happen, may be as cloudless, as to me, I am sure, it will be much greater happi-ness than I thought could fall to the lot of seventy-five!

I reserve all answer to your three last letters till we meet, when we may talk of them and of all you have seen and done—at present nothing occupies me but your actual residence and route home—and your pas-sage from Calais to Dover[6]—we have had tremendous storms lately!—I shall grow very seasick towards the tenth of next month!—Adieu! I hope this will be my last to the Continent[7] and that I shall not even reach to No. 60.

To Barbara Cecilia Seton, Friday 11 November 1791

Address: To Miss Seton at Mr. Dundas's at Richmond Green.

The letter did not go through the post.

'Mr. Dundas' was David Dundas (d. 1826), cr. (1815) Bt, of Richmond, Surrey; serjeant surgeon to the King 1791–1826; evidently related to the Seton and Berry families: he was the third son of Ralph Dundas (d. 1789) of Manour, co. Clack-mannan, a merchant, by Mary Berry, dau. of William Berry of Edinburgh, mer-chant (Burke, *Peerage,* 1860, *sub* Dundas; *Times* 27 Dec. 1791; Robert Seton, *An Old Family,* New York, 1899, p. 240; Sir Robert Douglas, *Baronage of Scotland,* Edinburgh, 1798, p. 179).

5. At Cliveden.

6. The Berrys left Calais about 11 P.M. 9 Nov. and arrived at Dover about 9:30 A.M. the following day; their only difficulty was that they were becalmed for a short time (MBJ i. 375).

7. It was.

[Berkeley Square], Friday one o'clock, [Nov. 11, 1791].

Dear good Miss Seton,

THANK God they are landed![1] Mrs Damer has sent me word, and my next thought is to make you easy and happy as I am myself—I know no more, for I have no letter yet, but expect one—I have not time for more—

Your most obliged humble servant,

H. Walpole

To Barbara Cecilia Seton, Saturday 12 November 1791

Address: To Miss Cecilia Seton at Caversham Hill, Berkshire.
Postmark: A 12 NO [91].

Berkeley Square, Nov. 12, 1791.

Dear Madam,

I HAVE but a moment's time to thank you for your letter, and to tell you—not what you know, as Miss Agnes has acquainted you with their arrival, but that your cousins both look quite well, and that Miss Agnes is quite returned to her good looks, though when I pressed it, she could not affirm she is perfectly well; but the great change from what she was thirteen months and a day ago, makes me hope she will be quite recovered after a little rest. I trust we shall all meet comfortably in a few months at Cliveden.

I am, dear Madam

Your most obedient humble servant,

Hor. Walpole

From Mary Berry, ?Friday 9 December 1791

Printed from Mary Berry's copy of the original letter, which has not survived; see *post* 13 Dec. 1791, n. 2.

The date is queried since HW did not receive this note until Tuesday morn-

1. 'Landed at Dover pier at half-past nine o'clock on Thursday morning [10 Nov.] . . . Left Dover at 3 P.M.; arrived at Canterbury at six. *Friday, 11th.*—Reached North Audley Street in about ten hours' (MBJ i. 375).

ing, 13 Dec. (see *post,* that date), and since both he and the Berrys were in London during the interval. 'Monday night' is the date one would expect. It is possible that Miss Berry set down the wrong night when she made this copy.

[?] Friday night, 12 o'clock [9 December 1791].

I DID not like to show you, nor did I myself feel while with you, *how much* I was hurt by the newspaper.[1] To be long honoured with your friendship and remain unnoticed, I knew was impossible, and laid my account with, but to have it imagined, implied, or even hinted, that the purest friendship that ever actuated human bosoms should have any possible foundation in, or view to, interested motives, and that we, whose *hereditary neglect* of fortune[2] has deprived us of what might, and ought to have been, our own, that we should ever afterwards be supposed to have it in view, or be described in a situation, which must mislead the world both as to our sentiments and our conduct, while our principles they cannot know, and if they could, would not enter into—all this I confess I cannot bear—not even your society can make up to me for it.

Would to God we had remained abroad, where we might still have enjoyed as much of your confidence and friendship as ignorance and impertinence seem likely to allow us here.

Even Cliveden, which sensible as I am to the compliment of settling us near you, I declare I consider as our least obligation to you—if it is always to be foremost in the eyes of the world, and considered as the cause of our affection for, and attentions to you, if our seeking your society is supposed by those ignorant of its value, to be with some view beyond its enjoyment, and our situation represented as one which will aid the belief of this to a mean and interested world—I shall think we have perpetual reason to regret the only circumstance in our lives that could be called fortunate—the only one that I thought happy. Excuse the manner in which I write, and in which I feel. My sentiments on newspaper notice have long been known to you with regard to every one who have not so honourably distinguished themselves as to feel above such feeble but venomed shafts.

Do not plague yourself by answering this. The only consolation I can have is in the knowledge of your sentiments, of which I need no

1. One of the newspapers had printed a paragraph hinting that the Berrys' friendship for HW was not disinterested. The paragraph has not been found.

2. A reference to Robert Berry's disinheritance by his uncle, Robert Ferguson.

conviction. I am relieved by writing, and shall sleep the sounder for having thus unburdened my heart. Good night.

To Mary Berry, ?Sunday 11 December 1791

Address: To Miss Mary Berry.
Written before HW had received the preceding letter.

[Berkeley Square, ?11 December 1791.]

YOU have hurt me excessively! We had passed a most agreeable evening, and then you poisoned all by one cruel word—I see you are too proud to like to be obliged by me, though you see that my greatest, and the only pleasure I have left, is to make you and your sister a little happier if I can—and *now* when it is a little more in my power, you cross me in *trifles* even, that would compensate for the troubles that are fallen on me—I thought my age would allow me to have a friendship that consisted in nothing but distinguishing merit—you allow the vilest of all tribunals, the newspapers, to decide how short a way friendship may go! Where is your good sense in this conduct? and will you punish me, because what you nor mortal being can prevent, a low anonymous scribbler pertly takes a liberty with your name?—I cannot help repeating that you have hurt me!

To Mary Berry, Tuesday 13 December 1791

Address: To Miss Mary Berry.

[Berkeley Square,] Dec. 13, 1791.[1]

My dearest Angel,

I HAD two persons talking law to me and was forced to give an immediate answer, so that I could not even read your note, till I had done—and now I do read it, it breaks my heart![2] If my most pure affection has brought grief and mortification on you, I shall be the most miserable of men—My nephew's death[3] has already brought a load

1. 'No. 59' (B).
2. 'The note was in the following words verbatim . . .' (B). Then follows *ante* 9 Dec. 1791.
3. George Walpole (1730–91), 3d E. of Orford of the 2d creation, on whose death 5 Dec. 1791 HW became 4th E. of Orford.

upon me that I have not strength to bear, as I seriously told General Conway this morning. Vexation and fatigue has brought back the eruption in my arm, and I have been half an hour under Mr Watson's hands since breakfast—my flying gout has fallen into my foot—I shall want but your uneasiness to finish me. You know I scarce wish to live but to carry you to Cliveden!—but I talk of myself, when I should speak to your mind—Is all your felicity to be in the power of a newspaper? Who is not so? Are your virtue and purity and my innocence about you, are our consciences no shield against anonymous folly or envy? Would you only condescend to be my friend if I were a beggar? The Duchess of Gloucester, when she heard my intention about Cliveden, came and commended me much for doing some little justice to injured merit—For your own sake, for poor mine, combat such extravagant delicacy, and do not poison the few days of a life which you and *you* only can sweeten—I am too exhausted to write more—but let your heart and your strong understanding remove such chimeras—how could you say you wish you had not returned!

To Mary Berry, December 1791

Address: To Miss Berry.
Apparently written the day after the Berrys were installed at Cliveden.

[Berkeley Square, December, 1791.]

I AM in the utmost anxiety to know how you do. I dread lest what I meant kindly,[1] should have made you ill. I saw the struggle of both your noble minds in submitting to oblige me—and therefore all the obligation is on my side. You both have made the greatest sacrifice to *me*—I have made none to you—on the contrary, I relieve my own mind, whenever I think I can ward off any future difficulty from you, though not a ten thousandth part of what I would do, were it in my power. All I can say is, that you must know by your own minds how happy you have made mine—and sure you will not regret bestowing happiness on one so attached to you, and attached so reasonably; for where could I have made so just a choice, or found two such friends? What did I not feel for both! *Your* tears, and Agnes's agitation divided between the same nobleness and her misery for your sufferings which is ever awake,

1. I.e., making over Cliveden to Mary and Agnes Berry for their lives.

would attach me more to both, if that were possible. Dearest souls, do not regret obliging one so devoted to you—it is the only sincere satisfaction I have left—and be assured that till today, I have, though I said nothing, had nothing but anxiety since your father's illness,[2] so impatient have I been for what I received but yesterday. Adieu!

2. No other reference to Robert Berry's illness has been found.